JESUS, JOBS, AND JUSTICE

Jesus, Jobs, and Justice

African American Women and Religion

Bettye Collier-Thomas

Alfred A. Knopf · New York 2010

THIS IS A BORZOI BOOK
PUBLISHED BY ALFRED A. KNOPF

Copyright © 2010 by Bettye Collier-Thomas

All rights reserved. Published in the United States by Alfred A. Knopf,
a division of Random House, Inc., New York, and in Canada by
Random House of Canada Limited, Toronto.

www.aaknopf.com

Knopf, Borzoi Books, and the colophon are registered trademarks of
Random House, Inc.

Library of Congress Cataloging-in-Publication Data
Collier-Thomas, Bettye.
Jesus, jobs, and justice : African American women and religion /
Bettye Collier-Thomas—1st ed.
p. cm.
"A Borzoi book"—T.p. verso.
Includes bibliographical references and index.
ISBN 978-1-4000-4420-7 (alk. paper)
1. African American women—Religious life. 2. African American
women—Political activity—History. 3. Christian women—Political
activity—United States—History 4. Christianity and politics—United
States—History. 5. Social movements—United States—History. 6. Social
justice—United States—History. 7. African Americans—Politics and
government. 8. African Americans—Social conditions. 9. United
States—Race relations—Political aspects. 10. United States—Race
relations—Religious aspects. I. Title.
BR563.N4C644 2010
277.3'08208996073—dc22   2009038528

Manufactured in the United States of America
First Edition

For Charles

A WOMAN'S PLACE

You talk about a woman's place,
And ask for her location,
As if her teachings all embrace
But part of the creation.
As educator—read her scroll—
"From sea to sea, from pole to pole"
She teacheth love; she teacheth strife;
She knows the bitterest side of life.
She teacheth patience, joy's refrain—
And lulls to rest the heart of pain.
No difference what a woman teaches
Her influence, her power reaches
Above, below—the seamen love her.
She saves their boat—or tips it over.
There is no place—so sings my linnet.
Without a woman in it, in it.

Susie I. Shorter (1901)

Contents

Illustrations

Prologue

Our Club life is the outgrowth of the encouragement and inspiration which the Church has given to the work of women in the Church and, as a "little leven will leven the whole," so have the small beginnings of organized work among women led to these general movements, both state and national that have brought out so prominently the great possibilities of Christian womanhood. . . .

[T]he leaders in religious thought and effort have become the leaders in nearly every fraternal, business, educational and reform movement which has been inaugurated or prosecuted for the improvement, development or advancement of the race.

Mamie E. Steward (1907)

ORGANIZATION HAS GIVEN HOPE for a better future by revealing to colored women their own executive ability. . . . [T]heir organizations have bound the women together in a common interest so strong that no earthly force can sever it. . . . Organization has taught them the art of self government." Through words and deeds, Sarah Jane Woodson Early boldly asserted her right to speak and act, during a time when women were mostly considered appendages to their husbands. In 1894, when she penned these words, Early was sixty-nine years of age. As an independent thinker and pioneering black feminist involved in the early women's movement, she was widely known and revered as a model to be emulated by other women. Yet Early does not fit into any of the niches defined for either women or African Americans of her time. She was neither poor, enslaved, illiterate, nor southern in her upbringing. As the daughter of free blacks who lived in a small town in Chillicothe, Ohio, Sarah Jane Woodson grew up in a black community that revered both religion and education. Her philosophy was shaped by the issues of the time, in particular the abolitionist and women's rights movement. As a graduate of Oberlin College in 1856, she was among the first black women to obtain a college degree. Her appointment to the Wilberforce University faculty in

1859 distinguished her as the first black woman to serve on the faculty of an American university. In 1865, at the end of the Civil War, she went south to Hillsborough, North Carolina, to teach black girls at a school administered by the Freedmen's Bureau. In 1868, at the age of forty-three, Sarah Jane Woodson married Rev. Jordan W. Early, a pioneering minister in the African Methodist Episcopal Church. Accompanying her husband to his many charges, Sarah Early continued to teach, and became deeply immersed in her duties as a minister's wife. In 1888 she became the first black woman to serve as superintendent of the Colored Division of the Woman's Christian Temperance Union. Her experiences at every level of society, among blacks and whites of all classes, confirmed her belief that the involvement of African American women in social and political reform was critical to racial advancement.

Sarah Early is a prototype of the pioneering black feminists whose lives were shaped in the tumultuous events of the nineteenth century—women who defined what it meant to be a woman and an African American. These women created organizations and launched movements whose impact is still felt. The lives of Sarah Early, Ida B. Wells-Barnett, Rev. Julia Foote, Virginia W. Broughton, Fanny Jackson Coppin, Nannie Helen Burroughs, Rev. Florence Spearing Randolph, Sarah Willie Layten, Frances Ellen Watkins Harper, Mamie E. Steward, Mary McLeod Bethune, and numerous other women who came of age in the nineteenth and twentieth century illustrate how religion informed and shaped the public lives and social activism of African American women and how that in turn has influenced the American experience more broadly.

Jesus, Jobs, and Justice: African American Women and Religion takes a historical approach to the subject of women, religion, and politics, analyzing religious, class, and gender dynamics in the black community and racial dynamics in the larger society. *Jesus, Jobs, and Justice* demonstrates how black women have woven their faith into their daily experiences, and illustrates their centrality to the development of African American religion, politics, and public culture. Moreover, it emphasizes their importance to the struggle for racial and gender freedom. Emboldened by their faith and filled with hope, over time black women created an organizational network that has been indispensable to the fight against racism, sexism, and poverty.

It is fitting that this book is published at the beginning of the twenty-first century, and that it recounts the extraordinary history of black American women's struggle for freedom in all aspects of their lives. By the end of the twentieth century all legal barriers to the full participation of women and people of color in American society had been removed. Though it is impossible to predict what the twenty-first century will bring, one thing is certain: the new era will be about maximizing and maintaining the gains that have been made.

Many of the women and movements in this study either are unknown or have received minimal or no treatment. Numerous studies consider the importance of race, class, and sex to black women's history, but few perceive religion or spirituality as significant factors in the shaping of women's thought and actions, or consider the multiple external historical forces that have impacted the lives of generations of African American women. It is impossible to trace the history of black women and religion without contemplating their encounter with the main currents of U.S. and, indeed, world history as exemplified in their transnational interests.

Religion has served as both a source of black women's oppression and a resource for their struggles for gender equality and social justice. Historically, religion has been *the* central guiding force in the lives of most African Americans. Speaking in 1952 about a conference where "women were considered from every angle" but there was no session on religion or philosophy, Virginia Simmons Nyabonga observed, "It was the conviction of everyone that religion and philosophy are basic threads of all existence and activity." This is the underlying premise I have used to interpret the history of black women and religion. Of central importance to this work are questions of how issues of patriarchy, sexism, and gender inequality relate to the African American community, and how issues of racism impacted not only the black community but also the interracial and women's movements. It is an interdisciplinary history that explores the race, class, gender, and religious experiences of women within the context of U.S., black, and women's history from the unique perspective of African American women.

Being black and female and faced with racism and sexism posed special problems for African American women. Unlike white women, they could not simply choose to fight sexism: for black women the chains of race were equally as binding as the chains of sex. However, through it all, most black women never forgot that whatever their struggle was with white America, the sex issue was equally as important to their survival and advancement as women of color. At the same time, they fully recognized that white America, including most white women, viewed them as black first and women second. Race impacted their fathers and mothers, sons and daughters, husbands and other relatives. As long as racism existed, freedom from sexism would not advance black women's social, economic, or political position in the United States.

Combining black women's experiences and perspectives while simultaneously documenting the history of black American women and their organizations, this study looks in depth at the major dimensions of African American women's lives and brings an understanding of the historical significance of religion in most aspects of black life and culture. Many black women leaders were deeply imbued with religious convictions and saw their work as a way of implementing their Christian faith. Expanding far beyond their religious institutions, they created multiple national organizations such as the National Association of Colored Women, the International Council of Women of the Darker Races, the National League of Colored Republican Women, and the National Council of Negro Women; joined white-led quasi-Christian groups such as the Young Women's Christian Association and the Woman's Christian Temperance Union; cooperated with white women in the interracial movement; and worked in numerous male-led organizations such as the National Association for the Advancement of Colored People, the National Urban League, and the United Negro Improvement Association to advance their race, sex, religious, and social agendas.

The themes and broad outlines of women's struggle are similar for Protestant denominations and some non-Christian religions. However, most black women's organizations engaged in organized activities aimed at achieving racial and gender freedom and advancement. Religious women's organizations were differentiated mostly by their geographical and class differences. From the outset, the organizational structures and issues of most women's missionary societies and conventions were influenced by church law and the social status and political ideology of the organizations' leaders.

Scholarly work on African American women has focused almost exclusively on limited aspects of their club work or, more recently, on their discrete roles in specific religious traditions in the period after the Civil War to 1920. Evelyn Brooks Higginbotham's pioneering study of the women's movement in the National Baptist Convention opened up new vistas for the study of women and religion. However, in the absence of historical studies of African American women in other denominations, Higginbotham's *Righteous Discontent: The Women's Movement in the Black Baptist Church 1880–1920* is often utilized to explain the experiences of all black church women. The tendency of scholars to conflate the history of the Woman's Convention, Auxiliary to the National Baptist Convention, with that of women's organizations in other denominations has created a false and monolithic history of black American women and their institutions. Covering more than two centuries of black and women's history, *Jesus, Jobs, and Justice: African American Women and Religion* serves as a corrective to that notion and illustrates the diversity and richness of African American and women's history.

Founded in 1900, the Woman's Convention was among the last of the national black women's religious organizations to be organized. It was preceded by the African Methodist Episcopal Church's Woman's Parent Mite Missionary Society and Women's Home and Foreign Missionary Society; and the African Methodist Episcopal Zion Church's Woman's Home and Foreign Missionary Society. In *Engendering Church: Women, Power, and the A.M.E. Church*, sociologist Jualynne E. Dodson astutely examines how women acquired and used power within the AME Church in the late nineteenth century. In *God in My Mama's House: The Women's Movement in the CME Church*, Bishop Othal Hawthorne Lakey and Betty Beene Stephens, leaders in the Christian Methodist Episcopal Church (founded as the Colored Methodist Episcopal Church), provide insight into the leadership roles of women in the CME Church. In the recently published *Women in the Church of God in Christ: Making a Sanctified World*, Anthea Butler perceptively discusses the activities of Pentecostal women in COGIC's Women's Department. There are no published full-length histories on black Catholic, Episcopalian, African Methodist Episcopal Zion, and Presbyterian women's organizations.

There is no comprehensive history of black women's organizations and their leadership. There are few comparative studies of black women that explore what it meant to be a club woman and a church woman, and how black women constructed their identities in a manner designed to merge their religious and secular experiences and environments. Utilizing the language of evangelical Christianity to argue for both gender equality in the church and community and racial equality and social change in white-dominated organizations and the American body politic, black women skillfully negotiated the different worlds in which they functioned. Several studies of religion and African American history have provided some insight into the opposition black women faced in their endeavors during certain periods of time. However, few focus on the ongoing internal struggle over the meaning of black masculinity and femininity that is evident after the Civil War, escalates in the late nineteenth and early twentieth century, as women demand religious rights and political suffrage, and continues through the civil rights–black power movement of the late twentieth century into the twenty first century.

Critical analysis of the opposition faced by women in black churches and denominations is limited. Yet the church is the base from which African American women first launched their national crusade against sexism. In the late nineteenth and early twentieth century African American women created missionary societies and women's conventions through which they obtained organizational skills and leadership training, asserted their power within the church and community, and began to speak for themselves and fight for women's rights and racial justice. They also engaged in transnational work in Africa, South America, and the Caribbean, believing that improvement of the status and image of women in Africa was necessary for the general acceptance and advancement of black women in the United States and throughout the diaspora.

The granting of political suffrage to women in the United States did not ignite the self-conscious black masculinity that was evident after World War I; rather, it inflamed it. As numerous black women embraced their newfound freedom and became more politically active and outspoken, black men felt even more threatened. The rise of lay-men's and "brotherhood" religious organizations and attempts of male clergy to further control and constrict women's religious freedom after the ratification of the Nineteenth Amendment in 1920 exemplifies the reaction of many men to the changes occurring in the national political status of women. One cannot fully understand sexism and gender discrimination in the black community without a careful evaluation and understanding of religious institutional praxis and the internal discourse over the meaning of black manhood and womanhood. Historical issues of gender, debates about class, and sexist ideologies advanced by black male leaders were often part of their quest for citizenship rights and racial equality in a white-male-dominated society that valued patriarchy. In the nineteenth and twentieth centuries the church was at the center of this struggle. This is reasonable and logical considering that historically the church has been one of the most powerful institutions in the African American community as well as the forum in which most of the first debates about racial equality, black "manhood rights," and women's roles and rights in the church and society occurred.

Women's status in the religious polity owes much to the changes that have occurred in American society. Between 1830 and 1920 black women became more active in religious and public culture, exercising their agency, and contesting and debating ideas about their abilities and the place of women in the church and in public life. Their political and cultural activism was formalized in a network of secular and religious organizations through which they made substantial financial and material contributions to the black community. Imbued by ideas of freedom, and influenced by the abolitionist, women's rights, and suffrage movements, emancipation, Reconstruction, and the growth of Jim Crow laws and practices, black women became active participants in the public discourse about the role and status of women and African Americans in the United States.

Using the church as an essential base of influence while transcending their religious traditions, in 1896 black women of all persuasions were instrumental in launching the National Association of Colored Women. Between 1896 and 1910 black women organized state federations that included a wide range of local clubs. The NACW was an interdenominational organization through which black women could surmount their religious and class differences, define and implement a central agenda, speak collectively to defend the image of black womanhood, address issues of gender and race, and effect social change relevant to their feminist/womanist and race agendas.

Constructed as an intricate network of local, state, regional, and national black female organizations, by 1900 the NACW was recognized as the leading organization of African American women. As practical feminists, or womanists, black women understood that it would be extremely difficult to achieve their goals without the support of white persons of "goodwill," in particular white women. Carefully assessing their options, they calculated that the YWCA, as a Christian organization with major resources and a focus on working-class women and girls, would benefit their cause. Moreover, black women recognized that the YWCA connected many white social and political entities, elites whose influence could be useful for accessing resources and impacting public policy. The YWCA is an example of how the

NACW's influence was used by black women leaders to leverage power in white organizations.

During the late nineteenth century, black church women joined the Woman's Christian Temperance Union. It was the first national white women's organization to accept black women as members, albeit in mostly separate unions. The WCTU, similar to the YWCA, was a quasi-religious organization, built on Protestant women's activism that emerged between 1830 and 1860. Organized in 1873–74, the WCTU was the largest female-led organization in the United States in the nineteenth century. During the 1890s, embracing issues of women's voting rights, the WCTU was an important factor in advancing women into public life. Although on issues such as lynching and rape the organization appeared to be antithetical to the interests of African Americans, middle-class black women leaders viewed it as an important political and social network through which they could address essential moral and social issues, reach working-class and poor black women, and have a national voice. They perceived the WCTU as an important tool for protecting the home and engaging in racial uplift and interracial work. While it continued to function, the WCTU declined in prominence after 1900. The politicalization of the WCTU, especially the alliance of white WCTU activists with white-supremacist southern politicians, made the group less attractive to many black women leaders. However, temperance and prohibition were important issues in the black community during the early twenti-eth century.

Black religious women and their organizations were the foundation for a significant portion of what has been defined as nonreligious or secular in nature. Most women celebrated as leaders in the WCTU, the NACW, and the YWCA were officers and members of religious associations. Some women were founders and presidents and served on the boards and committees of the national and local branches of the NAACP, the National Urban League, and other black organizations. In the twentieth century black women leaders were determined to cross restrictive racial boundaries and assert themselves. They held positions on local and national interracial boards, including municipal committees, and in race relations and ecumenical organizations such as the Southern Commission on Interracial Cooperation, the Federal Council of the Churches of Christ in America and its Church Women's Committee on Race Relations, and Church Women United.

By the 1930s, black women leaders were able to maximize their power through their leadership positions on diverse national boards and coalition efforts with white women and black men. In effect, they were part of a powerful network of interlocking relationships and directorates whose political and social impact was felt at many levels. In a broad sense, their interlocking network consisted of groups and individuals seeking to advance black Americans' economic, political, and social interests. African American women leaders used all the tools at their disposal—contacts, influence, media, and politics—to achieve their ends. The founding of Church Women United in 1940, a watershed event in women's history, represented a consolidation of religious and secular interests. Though largely overlooked by scholars, CWU, with a network of more than ten million members, aggressively pursued a liberal feminist agenda that included social and political reform related to minorities and women.

As scholars have continued to focus almost exclusively on a select few of the individual histories of black and white organizations and their personnel, they have overlooked the very rich and complex history of organizational networks and the ways in which women functioned in, among, and across black and white, male and female, religious and secular organizations. It was the expansive vision and determination of generations of black women activists that helped to hammer down the walls of segregation and bring change in many areas of American life. It was through the collective efforts of African American church women and their organizations, and the work of individual black women in race-specific, gender-specific, biracial, and interracial associations, that the struggle for the rights of women and blacks was conducted. Women such as Alice Felts, Anna Julia Cooper, Hallie Quinn Brown, Addie Hunton, Florence Spearing Randolph, Emma Merritt, Mary Mason, Lugenia Hope, Mary McCrory, Sarah Pettey, Lethia C. Fleming, Lucy Laney, Nannie Helen Burroughs, S. Willie Layten, Mary McLeod Bethune, Maria Lawton, Rosa Parks, Fannie Lou Hamer, Victoria Gray Adams, Septima Poinsette Clark, Dorothy I. Height, and Claire Collins Harvey formed the core of a movement that spanned more than one hundred years.

Legions of black women who were neither leaders nor members of the "talented tenth" were the rank-and-file organizational workers in cities and towns throughout the nation. Not all of these women would be classified as middle class; a considerable number would be considered working class by today's standard. However, class definitions in the black community have historically never paralleled those of white

Americans. Growing up in the 1950s as a middle-class black American whose early experiences were in both the North and the South, I sometimes encountered the expression "the better class of Negroes." However, I paid little attention to its use until the late 1960s, when it was forcefully brought to my attention by a friend's mother, a woman from Mississippi who was born into the southern mulatto elite and lived a rather privileged life. During the Civil Rights–Black Power Movement I found the term offensive and often critiqued her use of it. In hindsight, I now understand that during the early part of the twentieth century it was commonly used by black elites, particularly middle- and upper-class African Americans, who were viewed as the best representatives of the race—persons who historian Glenda Gilmore suggests "saw themselves as ambassadors to the white power structure." The term also had negative connotations and was sometimes used to separate out African Americans who did not meet the standards of individuals and organizations who used skin color and family background to discriminate within the race.

In rural areas, small towns, and cities throughout the nation, class definitions in the African American community remained rather fluid until the 1970s. Desegregation in housing opened up the opportunity for black professionals to move from traditional black urban communities to middle-class and predominantly white suburban enclaves. As a result of desegregation and new job and housing opportunities, traditionally black communities became less inclusive of different classes. However, in small cities—such as Milledgeville, Georgia, where I spent considerable time during my adolescence—a beautician, a bricklayer, a painter, a practical nurse, and a domestic servant might all be accepted into the middle class; the space between the classes was extremely narrow. In a city where the black professional class consisted of a handful of teachers and ministers, one physician, and several small-business owners, one's class designation was related to a number of variables, including family status and lifestyle as well as membership and offices held in prominent religious, fraternal, and other secular organizations. Thus, in the nineteenth and early twentieth centuries, it was common to find men and women of working-class backgrounds mingling, actively socializing, and holding leadership positions and working in race organizations with persons of the so-called "better" classes—especially at the local level. This pattern was widespread and identifiable in many communities throughout the nation.

After 1890, as evidenced by the organization of elite social clubs, class discrimination was on the rise in major urban areas. Nevertheless, most black Baptist and Methodist churches continued to include mixed congregations comprising the working and middle class. Class tended to be more of a factor in the separate black congregations affiliated with mainstream white-led denominations such as the Presbyterian, Episcopal, and Catholic churches than in the historically black denominations. In the early twentieth century, between 1915 and 1930, the Great Migration accelerated the movement of African Americans from rural to urban areas in the North, South, and West, changing the social and political landscape of the black community. The Great Migration also redistributed the black religious groups, aided the growth of the Baptist Church in the North and Midwest, and encouraged the development of Pentecostal, Holiness, and Spiritual churches, as well as numerous cults and sects, especially in northern and western cities such as Chicago, Philadelphia, Detroit, Boston, New York City, Los Angeles, and San Francisco. New patterns of worship and an expanded base of religious institutions became the norm in urban black America.

Black men and women shared experiences of oppression. However, the impact of slavery on black women was distinctly different. Set apart by their sex, black women were more exposed to sexual violence and misuse of their bodies for breeding and other purposes. Used as sex objects and beasts of burden but determined to survive, many women viewed the Bible as a source of inspiration. It became an instrument of freedom and survival and a tool for development of literacy. Within the confines of slavery black women developed boundless spirituality and adopted the Bible as their guide, and Jesus Christ as their personal savior. Slave owners and southern white church leaders attempted to limit and shape the Christian experiences of the enslaved. Ignoring the white slave master's central text, "Slaves Obey your Masters," over a period of many generations black women and men molded and shaped Christianity into a complex mixture with a critical theological perspective that reinforced their sense of identity, self-worth, and personal dignity, while emphasizing freedom. Participating in diverse forms of slave worship, women played various roles.

At the beginning of the nineteenth century, free black men and women were establishing religious and social reform organizations in cities such as Philadelphia, New York, Baltimore, and Boston. By tracing the leadership and issues within and among these groups, a clearer picture of the origins, ideology, and organizing processes of nineteenth-century reformers emerges. Of particular importance is the role of gender politics in the antebellum free black community, and the ways in which women constructed their identities as slave and free women. It is essentially during this period that African Americans articulated a national social and political agenda and laid the foundation for what became the most powerful institution in the black community—the church.

Focusing on gender interactions, leadership roles, and the strategies women mounted to deal with their subordinate position illustrates how laywomen and preaching women constructed their identities in relationship to men after 1865, and the consequences incurred when they subverted prevailing gender conventions. It reveals the issues and struggles they encountered in the creation of women's missionary societies and conventions, and in their efforts to secure laity and clergy rights and formal leadership positions. Missionary societies and women's conventions represent the apex of female leadership and power in the church. However, women have assumed other roles as well. As exhorters, ministers, musicians, leaders of prayer groups, and clergy wives they have been active participants in the creation and expansion of the power and influence of the church. Not a few women gained status and a degree of power functioning in these and other official and unofficial church roles. Of some importance is how church women parlayed and used their influence to promote the feminist and race causes of their religious and secular associations.

The main focus of church women's societies and conventions was domestic and foreign missionary work, broadly defined. As centers of religious activity, women's religious organizations were significant nonpartisan bases of power. Between 1870 and 1970 they were most important in the execution of grassroots social, educational, health, and political reform movements. Because of the sheer size of their collective membership, the Baptist and Methodist women's organizations formed a powerful national network of leaders and workers whose influence was paramount in bringing about reform, especially at the local level. Church women of all classes and persuasions embraced a commitment to religion and racial uplift by fusing these concepts and making them the most central elements of their activism. Recognizing the need for a church that was actively engaged in helping to meet the needs of its community, women's organizations launched programs aimed at providing basic social services. By 1890 their collective voluntary and organizational services constituted the backbone of black community philanthropy. Launching racial uplift programs on an international scale, denominational missionary boards stressed the need for improving the status of Africans and addressing a white Protestant missionary theology that promoted notions of white supremacy. Believing that Christianity could transform a society, eliminate polygamous practices, and effectuate "civilization" in Africa, black women missionaries placed a high priority on converting and uplifting women and girls.

At the beginning of the twentieth century, black women's missionary organizations were at different stages of development. Eschewing deference to male authority, they never gave up their belief in the equality of the sexes and continuously fought for equal rights in the polity. Women variously strove to either achieve or maintain autonomy over their religious associations, to exercise control over their finances, to gain full lay and clergy rights, and to access leadership positions reserved for men. As missionary societies and conventions grew in size, scope, sophistication, and influence, they were perceived by the male clergy and lay leaders as threatening and a challenge to the central authority of the church. As the century advanced and women gained political suffrage, church women became more active in politics, expended more time on secular reform, and grew more insistent on their religious rights. African American women viewed the ballot in general, and politics in particular, as a means to advance their racial and gender goals. Nannie Burroughs perceived political activism as the essence of Christian mission. The political values and views of black women were often informed by religion, and their vote was determined as much by faith as anything else.

Christian women, in particular Baptists and Methodists, faced new problems within their denominations. They encountered internal strife in their organizations, competition with new women's groups created to address regional and sectional differences, and denominational efforts to either control, weaken, or eliminate their associations. In the face of multiple challenges, black women never lost sight of their overall purpose and goals. They neither gave up nor relinquished their religious, race, and gender commitments, but simply pressed forward and continued to fight for what they believed was right and just.

This story is neither neat nor perfect. Rather, it is a tale of struggle and compromise as well as gain and loss. For some women's associations, the struggle was both internal with their female colleagues and the male leadership and external with white women's missionary organizations, on whom they sometimes depended for financial support to launch and implement their programs. Ideological differences and issues of class, color, and status frequently lurked just beneath the surface and threatened to distract women from their purpose and derail group solidarity. In some groups, most notably the Woman's Convention, Auxiliary to the National Baptist Convention, USA, jealousy, competition for leadership positions, and internal power struggles with other women were prevalent. But the most critical problem these women faced was how to achieve their goals while maintaining solidarity with their black brothers.

Critics, pundits, and outsiders question why black women consistently cling to churches and denominations that continue to willfully exploit and deny their personhood and work. While they admire the noble struggle of black women for equality and justice in their religious institutions, they do not understand why black women refuse to use their power to force change and achieve equality and justice for their sex. Why do many black church women continue to accept second-class citizenship in the institutions they have literally built and sustained? The answer to this question is complex and difficult for many to understand, especially outsiders and whites, who tend to see race and gender as discrete subjects and who often hold blacks to a higher standard than whites. However, for black women, including those who consider themselves to be feminist, this is an issue of wholeness. It goes to the heart of who they are and the importance of family and community in their lives.

Being female is only part of the black woman's identity. In the United States, for almost four hundred years, their race has taken precedence over their sex, and has affected every aspect of their lives. As members of a racial group whose color and historical experience have combined to intensify their experience of oppression, they know the importance of community. Thus, as a practical matter, black women overwhelmingly maintain solidarity with black men in the war against the perpetuation of oppression and institutionalized racism. As long as white America continues to ignore the economic and political concerns of black Americans, black women will of necessity maintain their commitment to race organizations and institutions such as the church. Separation is not an option. For generations the church has served as a bulwark against racism, and it provided spiritual sustenance during the long years of slavery, Jim Crow segregation, and discrimination. What the critics have failed to understand is that historically the church has been more than just *a* community institution. Rather, for many it represents a way of life and has been at the center of black life. It continues to create and connect kinship and friendship networks across generations. For many African Americans, it represents, in bold relief, the history of black people in the United States and their long struggle for freedom, equality, and justice. Simply put, the church fulfills spiritual as well as communal needs in the black community that are not addressed by any other institution in the society.

While black women continue to struggle with their black brothers and strive to bring an end to sexism within their own communities and organizations, they volunteer their time and services, raise funds, and work hard to ensure the success and stability of their churches. At critical periods in their history when they have been on the brink of achieving their goal of equality and justice in the religious polity, they have often capitulated to the male clergy and accepted less than they bargained for. In part, they have accepted incremental changes and made concessions in order to keep their institutions strong and viable.

In a community defined by generations of discrimination and neglect, economic depression and educational deprivation, and fraught with violence from within and without, black women are committed to doing whatever it takes to support their families and institutions. Moreover, black women see black men as an endangered species that continues to be under assault in the larger society. They lament the fact that so many young black men are incarcerated and that there is a scarcity of men to marry. They are critically aware of and scarred by the brutal history of black male emasculation, lynching, and the rape of black women at the hands of white America; the vicious racial stereotyping and denial of the humanity of people of African descent; the demeaning Jim Crow segregation and discrimination; and the continued struggle of people of color for simple justice. This never-ending saga frames black women's experience and helps to explain their ongoing struggle for both racial and gender justice.

After 1920, Pentecostal women's associations were active in mostly urban areas. They administered primarily to their own members' needs and rarely engaged in electoral politics. Little attention has been given to the role of black women in mainstream white-dominated groups such as the Presbyterian, Episcopal, and Catholic denominations. This is in part because the majority of African Americans— at least 90 percent—historically have held membership in black churches, in particular the Methodist and Baptist denominations. It is equally, if not more, difficult to locate the records of black women's organizations and leaders of mainstream religious traditions. Secondary sources for the founding and early development of the Oblate Sisters of Providence, for instance, primarily cover the nineteenth century. It is not easy to find or access data relating to the Sisters of the Holy Family and other black Catholic sisterhoods. And scholarship on black Catholic laywomen and their organizations is scarce. Thus, the organizational work of black Presbyterian, Episcopalian, and Catholic women's organizations and the church-related work of many significant feminist activists has been virtually ignored and viewed as separate and unimportant.

The relationship of religion and politics in the lives of black women is extremely important. Churches have been fundamental to the political work of African American women. Nannie Helen Burroughs defined the importance of the church within the community as "The Negro church means the Negro woman." In other words, the African American church as an institution would not exist without the membership and financial support of black women. Black church women and their organizations were a potent factor in the social and political reform movements of the nineteenth and twentieth centuries. They addressed a broad range of issues, including temperance, education, health, protection of women and children, lynching, suffrage, segregation, and discrimination.

The majority of black women leaders were affiliated with and regularly attended a church. In fact, this was understood to be a requirement for membership in some secular organizations as well as for leadership in community organizations. For example, in 1915, Minnie Wright of Boston outlined the qualifications for clubs wishing to become members of the Northeastern Federation of Colored Women's Clubs, one of four regional affiliates of the National Association of Colored Women. Wright asserted that clubs must be engaged in charitable work and that "all members must be connected with some church." Whether or not this requirement extended to all members of the NACW or was exclusive to the Northeastern Federation is not clear. However, most middle-class black leaders agreed with Judge Robert H. Terrell, who believed that persons who were not religious, or who did not attend a church, were not fit to lead any organization. Until the 1970s, church leadership was an important recommendation for community leadership.

Black religious women's work in the public sphere before and after the ratification of the Nineteenth Amendment was extensive. Of particular concern are the ways in which black church women functioned as political operatives in gender- and race-specific organizations as well as their individual and collective efforts of social and political reform. Though some scholars have suggested that the black community was dominated by conservatism, assimilationism, and an inclination to withdraw "from political and social involvement in their communities," this was not the case. In many northern churches, African Americans were politically active, especially in electoral politics. Though blacks in most southern cities were disfranchised, there are numerous examples of women and men who engaged in protest activities aimed at disfranchisement, lynching, and discrimination in general. During the years leading up to the Civil Rights Movement of the 1950s and '60s, black women throughout the nation, including areas of the South, were active in organizing suffrage associations and participating in various kinds of political activities.

In the North and West, black women not only voted but also sought political office. Laywomen and their organizations were actively involved in politics. Their political influence was sometimes limited by their lack of access to the franchise, but they found ways to implement their reform agendas and influence public policy issues through use of their associational network, including social, church, club, and interracial organizations. Using their religious and secular bases of power, especially the missionary societies, women's conventions, and the NACW, they aggressively pursued, organized, and led electoral operations. After 1920, more black women engaged in politics and ran for political office and in 1924 a cadre of NACW women leaders founded the National League of Colored Republican Women. Women such as Rev. Florence Spearing Randolph, S. Willie Layten, Maria C. Lawton, Mary Church Terrell, Lethia Fleming, and Nannie Burroughs were in the vanguard of those who saw the need for a national political organization through which they could educate and organize black women voters at the local and state levels. They skillfully used politics to address public policy issues relevant to the status of women and African Americans.

Where they lacked access to traditional political means, black women developed other strategies for achieving their goals. Utilizing their religious and social networks, they accessed resources to establish state institutions for delinquent black girls, argued for international peace, and lobbied for legislation to eradicate lynching and other forms of racial intimidation and violence. In addition to the NACW and the YWCA, the Eastern Star and the Daughter Elks—quasi-religious interdenominational organizations—also served as resources for black women's political activism. In writing about the political organizing of church women, I became critically aware of the significant political role played by the Masons and the Elks. The Eastern Star and the Daughter Elks were female auxiliaries to the Masons and the Elks. Numerous women joined these organizations, but neither has received sustained scholarly treatment.

During the first half of the twentieth century African American women played an integral role in organizations and institutions struggling for what was considered radical social change. They engaged in separate institution-building efforts and participated in interracial coalitions that crossed religious and secular boundaries. The interracial and interdenominational movements launched by the Federal Council of the Churches of Christ and Church Women United provided fertile ground for black Christian feminist activists to pursue their goals of social justice and equality. These movements were dependent on networking in and among black and white religious and secular organizations, in particular the astute use of certain modes of public discourse, including public speaking and the broadcast and print media, to mobilize supporters, publicize and disseminate information, and develop strategy.

An analysis of the roots of the interracial movement reveals the struggle of black and white women to "cross the divide" and establish meaningful relationships based on mutual understanding and respect for each other. In the 1920s the FCC's Church Women's Committee on Race Relations was responsible for organizing the first national interracial conference of church women and for setting the agenda for much of the work later accomplished by Church Women United. CWU was an active force in helping to lay the groundwork for the Civil Rights–Black Power Movement of the 1950s and '60s. Founded in 1940, it became the most powerful national and interracial organization of women. Exploring the efforts of CWU's national leadership to foster interracial cooperation and integration illustrates the limits of their strategy. Middle-class white women leaders such as Dorothy Tilly, Lillian Smith, and numerous others worked for decades to break down the barriers of segregation and discrimination in their churches and communities; by steadily chipping away the veneer of southern racism, these women succeeded in undermining and weakening the southern system of segregation and in helping to lay the groundwork for dismantling the legal basis for racial discrimination. However, the majority of white Christians—female and male—found it difficult to fully overcome the racial contexts in which they lived.

Motivated by their deep religious convictions and belief in the moral righteousness of their struggle, black women worked long and hard within their organizations and in the interracial church movement to address basic issues of human rights, and to create strategies to improve the economic, social, and political status of females, blacks, and other minorities. Desegregation and self-determination were cornerstones of their philosophy. For African American women, these concerns were not simply civil rights, but were central to the basic tenets of Christianity and self-identity. Their organizational work focused on issues of civil rights covers at least eight decades, extending from the 1890s to the 1970s. Following the Civil War, African American women engaged in the ongoing debate about black "citizenship rights." While the term "civil rights" was not widely used before the 1940s, black women's organizations were active in campaigns prior to the 1950s to protest lynching, segregation, and discrimination in education, and to lobby for voting, public accommodations, housing, and employment—which they defined as citizenship rights. Some black women's organizations, such as the Baptist-led Women's Political Council in Montgomery, Alabama, developed strategies at the local and national levels to advance the civil rights of African Americans, and played an important role in launching the modern Civil Rights Movement, which began with the 1954 *Brown v. Board of Education* Supreme Court decision and ended with the 1965 passage of the Voting Rights Act by Congress. The main focus of women's organizational work in the South during the latter period was on the implementation of the *Brown* decision and subsequent legislation outlawing segregation and discrimination in voting and public accommodations.

The passage of the Civil Rights Act of 1964 and the Voting Rights Act of 1965 represented the end of legal racial segregation and second-class citizenship for African Americans and other nonwhite minorities in the United States. After 1965, the nation's focus shifted to issues of the student rights, antiwar, women's liberation, and black power movements. During the late 1960s and in the early '70s black women focused on critical economic and social issues that remained unresolved, and gave serious consideration to the relationship of black women to the women's rights movement. They engaged in an extensive self-analysis and evaluation of their status in the church and society. The ongoing discourse and intense scrutiny of sexism in society invaded the religious domain and served as a catalyst for the escalating demands for the male clergy to recognize women's gifts and grant them full equality in the religious polity.

As African American men in mainstream denominations such as the Presbyterian and Episcopalian churches embraced the tenets of black power and the emerging theologies of liberation, they demanded acknowledgment of a black theology and reparations. This resulted in the formation of black and women's caucuses and task forces. In 1981, black women in the Episcopal Church reacted to their marginalization within these groups, and articulated their concerns regarding the lack of consideration given women of color in the women's liberation movement. Determined to be heard and have black women's issues addressed, they defined the "Black Woman's Agenda," the first articulation of a new ideology that became known as womanist theology. This movement was profoundly influenced by the struggles of black women with black theology and white feminism. "Womanism" made its formal debut in 1985 at the annual meeting of the American Academy of Religion and the Society of Biblical Literature. During the last two decades the movement has expanded, and its tenets are now embraced by a diversity of scholars in a variety of fields.

Many of the black and white women and organizations that appear in these pages were well known at one time. Their lives and their work not only fill in the gaps in American and African American, religious, and women's history; they also tell a complex but consistent and more complete story about America, one that includes the vision and faith of the countless women who struggled to break down the barriers and make the United States what it is today.

Jesus, Jobs, and Justice

CHAPTER I

"Soul Hunger"

In Slavery and Freedom

Negro slaves longed to be free. Freedom was the burden of their prayers and songs—of their midnight nursings and daily thinking—Freedom was their one dream and ever increasing hope. God always rewards such soul hunger.

Nannie Helen Burroughs

No honey, can't preach from de Bible—can't read a letter. When I preaches, I has jest one text to preach from an' I always preaches from this one. My text is, When I found Jesus!

Sojourner Truth

I know nothing about what God said to the prophets of old but I do know what He has said to me. And I know that I have a counselor in Him that never fails. When danger comes, He works on my mind and conscience and causes me to walk around the snares set for me by my enemies. What earthly friend could do this? Why the latter would say, "I would have warned you, but I didn't know there was danger ahead." That is why I trust in God, because He sees and knows all things. And because I trust in God, He leads me into all wisdom and shows me the failings of hypocrites and liars.

Ex-slave woman, Franklin, Tennessee

THE ANTEBELLUM PERIOD is best characterized by the African American struggle for freedom. James Curry, a fugitive slave from Person County, North Carolina, testified to the desire of the enslaved to be free. Curry wrote, "From my childhood, the desire for freedom reigned predominant in my breast, and I resolved, If I was ever whipped after I became a man, I would no longer be a slave. . . . But if [my master] asked me if I wanted to be free, I should have answered, 'No, Sir.' Of course, no slave would dare to say, in the presence of a white man, that he wished for freedom, but among themselves, it is

their constant theme. No slaves think they were made to be slaves."
Curry asserted that white slave owners might "keep them ever so ignorant, [but] it is impossible to beat it into them that they were made to
be slaves. I have heard some of the most ignorant . . . say, 'it will not
always be so, God *will* bring them to an account.' "

From the arrival of the first Africans in Jamestown, Virginia, in
1619, to the end of the Civil War, black people struggled individually
and collectively in a myriad of ways to break the chains of bondage.
Whether defined by their status as indentured servants, enslaved people, or free men and women of color, Africans in America were bound
together by their heritage, color, class, and marginal status. Within
their circumscribed world they created an intricate web of relationships and a network of formal and informal institutions. If there was a
central thread that ran through their lives and defined their existence,
it might be described as striped, layered, and multicolored, surrounded
by strong fine strands of fiber tied together by their beliefs and traditions. At the core of their world was a deep spirituality that blended
their African and American heritages and experiences, and that eventually was transformed into a distinctive religion. An important,
although much overlooked, factor in the historical development of
African American religious culture is the black woman. As enslaved
women and free women, they were the glue that held the family and
community together, and a significant part of the foundation for the
development of black religious institutions.

African American religion in slavery, from the first introduction of
Africans in the American colonies in the seventeenth century to the
Civil War, was constantly evolving. Generations of Africans, representative of different African ethnic groups like the Wolof, Serer,
Mandinke, Bambara, Fulani, and Hausa, brought to America religious
traditions and celebrations rooted in Islam and traditional African
beliefs. Though some had experienced Christianity in Africa, most
were introduced to it in America. Over time Christianity was melded
with elements of Islam and traditional African beliefs to form a unique
African-Christian worldview. This worldview was forged within the
crucible of slavery, and reflected the intrinsic values of African Americans, representing "the slaves' deep resentment of their exploitation."
This was a slow process. Since almost half of all African-born slaves
came from areas in West Africa heavily populated by Muslims, it is
likely that Islam flourished among the enslaved for several generations.

It is difficult to assess how widespread Christianity was among the enslaved before emancipation. Slaves who became church members were usually household servants, artisans, and urban dwellers. This did not mean that slaves in rural areas had no knowledge of Christianity, or that they did not attend religious services or were lacking in religious beliefs and practices. The black religious experience was diverse and multifaceted. However, whatever religion or religious ideology enslaved persons adhered to, they embraced freedom as a value that was an expression of their relationship and allegiance to God. In the context of their struggle for freedom and their fight to maintain their humanity, black women and men created an extensive moral value system that included elements of their African heritage and addressed their specific needs as an enslaved people.

African American women and men shared many experiences of oppression and adhered to the central values of freedom and liberation, but the impact of slavery on black women was distinctly different. In some instances enslaved men were used as studs and mated with select women to breed a strong stock of offspring, a future generation of slaves. Women were forced to mate with and sometimes marry enslaved men against their will. Enslaved women, unlike men, were more frequently subject to sexual abuse and, as a result, could become carriers of the seeds of their oppressors. Some women responded by destroying their unborn children; many bore the mulatto children of their masters and loved them as much as those born of consensual union. Through no fault of their own, motherhood was foisted upon them, and, as a result, they drew the anger of their white mistresses, some of whom took their vengeance out on the woman instead of the wanton master. Loathing the sight of mulatto children, who often bore a close resemblance to their own children, white women sometimes physically attacked and maimed enslaved women and their children, and/or demanded their sale.

Over a period of two centuries of pain, suffering, and struggle, slaves fashioned and shaped their beliefs into a religion of their own. Operating in two worlds—the world of the slaveholder and that of the slave community—some blacks were obliged to participate in the public forms of worship and preaching ordained by their white masters. To justify slavery as an institution and to deny slaves their freedom, slaveholders used the Bible to explain the source of their domination, and suggested that slavery was permissible because it was the law of God. Many slave owners used biblical text that encouraged obedience and loyalty and emphasized heaven as a reward for good behavior on earth.

The Bible was used as a means of maintaining social control, as well as an instrument for exercising "moral and spiritual authority over the slave."

Beverly Jones, a former slave in Virginia, recalled, "On Sundays they would let us go to church up at Sassafras Stage, near Bethel. [It was] the first church for niggers in these parts. Wasn' no white church; niggers built it an' they had a nigger preacher. 'Couse they wouldn't let us have no services lessen a white man was present. . . . That was the law at that time. Couldn' no nigger preacher preach lessen a white man was present." Describing how slave owners used the Bible to inculcate the enslaved with notions of their duty toward their masters, Jones asserted, "Niggers had to set an' listen to the white man's sermon, but they didn' want to 'cause they knowed it by heart. Always took his text from Ephesians, the white preacher did, the part what said 'Obey your masters, be [a] good servant.' Can' tell you how many times I done heard that text preached on. They always tell the slaves dat ef he be good, an' worked hard fo' his master, dat he would go to heaven, an' dere he gonna live a life of ease. They ain' never tell him he gonna be free in Heaven. You see, they didn' want slaves to start thinkin' 'bout freedom, even in Heaven."

The "Invisible Institution"

IN THE SLAVE COMMUNITY there was an "invisible institution" hidden from whites, in which black men and women bonded and created a world in which the moral values of respect, cooperation, and compassion were central to group identity and survival. Secret meetings were held in the slave quarters or other locations where enslaved women and men might preach, sing, pray, testify, and dance. These religious communities had their own belief systems and styles of worship. According to the testimony of some slaves, clandestine religious services were held in various places on the plantation—swamps, woods, ravines, and cabins. Open-air meetings were referred to variously as "hush arbors," "bush arbors," and "brush arbors." Della Briscoe, formerly enslaved on a large plantation in Putnam County, Georgia, recalled that because of the irregularity of worship services at her master's church, "brush arbor meetings were common. This arbor was constructed of a brush roof supported by posts and crude joists. The seats were usually made of small saplings nailed to short stumps." In these meetings, out of the sight of their masters, slaves emphasized their belief in a God of justice, a liberating God, who would deliver them out of bondage. "Go down Moses, way down in Egypt's land. Tell old pharaoh to let my people go," "On Jordan's stormy banks I stand and cast a wistful eye," "My God delivered Daniel," and other songs with similar themes reinforced their belief that, like the Israelites, they were God's chosen people, and that he did not condone their enslavement. Interestingly, the spiritual "Go Down Moses" originated at a baptismal service following the Nat Turner revolt.

Away from white supervision, in their private lives, slave parents, mothers in particular, often stressed the value of freedom and emphasized their own self-worth. They taught their children through words and example how to dissemble. Charlotte Brooks, formerly enslaved in Louisiana, affectionately called Aunt Charlotte, observed, "[I]t was death for us poor darkies to talk about freedom." Survival was the watchword, and in order to survive one had to "wear the mask"—that is, learn how to conceal the truth and one's true feelings. "Putting on old massa" became an African American art form in which the slave utilized every resource available to simply survive the unceasing psychological, emotional, and physical abuse, and to communicate the moral value of freedom.

Nannie Helen Burroughs—a leader in the National Baptist Convention's Woman's Convention in the twentieth century, recalled the stories her grandmother Maria related about her experience during her enslavement in Virginia. Maria was what she called "a F.F.V. Slave," a First Family of Virginia slave. According to Burroughs, Maria's self-esteem was remarkable. The slave experience neither diminished Maria's sense of self nor made her feel inferior. She was imbued with her faith in God. Her motto was "Don't look down, look up at God." Speaking about Maria's attitude toward slavery, Burroughs stated that Maria proudly asserted, "Yes, honey, I was IN slavery, but I wasn't no slave. I was just in it, that's all. They never made me hold my head down and there was a whole pa'cel (sic) of Negroes just like me; we just couldn't be broke. We obeyed our masters and mistresses and did our work, but we kept on saying 'deliverance will come.' We ain't no hung-down-head race. We're poor, but proud." Reminiscing after the Civil War, Maria stressed, "I used to hold my head up so high that sometimes they would say, 'Maria, why don't you look down at the ground?' [I answered,] I ain't no ground hog, I am looking up at God because that's what He made me for.' Honey, they slaved my body, but they didn't slave my mind. I was thinking high [of] myself, and someday we colored folks is goin' to live high. Walk together, children, don't get weary. There's a better day a-coming in dis here land."

The desire for freedom was frequently expressed through prayers, the selection and reading of scripture, the singing of songs with freedom themes, and a variety of daily acts of resistance. Most slaves knew that it was dangerous to reveal their feelings about equality, justice, or freedom. However, slaves belonging to masters who allowed them to attend and become members of the Catholic Church sometimes freely expressed themselves in their confessions to the priests. In Louisiana, Aunt Lorendo recalled her devotion to the Catholic Church. Her fealty to the church and its doctrine impelled her to "tell the priest everything I did wicked." She never considered that the priest was part and parcel of the white slavocracy and totally invested in the social order, and that revealing one's desire to be free could be dangerous. What a shock it was for Lorendo to discover that when her cousin "told the priest he wanted to get free, and asked him to pray to God to set him free, . . . the priest was about to have my cousin hung. The priest told my cousin's marster about it, and they was talking strong about hanging my cousin. . . . I tell you, from that day on I could not follow my Catholic religion like I had."

The Bible and Jesus

A KEY SOURCE of inspiration for slaves was the Bible. Acceptance of the Bible as a resource that could be employed as an instrument of freedom and survival was not a given. Among the earliest generations of Africans in America who were introduced to Christianity and the Bible, there was "rejection, suspicion and awe of 'book religion.'" Similar to slavery, acceptance of the Bible and biblical interpretation evolved over time. By the mid-eighteenth century, after considerable exposure to the Bible, African Americans had discovered that it could be used to transform "black religion into a religion of slave experiences."

Reading and interpreting the Bible through their own experiences was of central importance to black men and women. Concerns about being able to access Bible learning also stressed the need for literacy. Literacy was a highly valued social skill among slaves, who believed that with it came power, access to salvation, and insight into the workings of the white world. It became a major resource that undergirded all of their hopes and aspirations for freedom. Choosing biblical texts that resonated with their moral values, enslaved women and men created riveting biblical imagery that bolstered their hopes, sustained their souls, enabled them to endure the horrors of slavery, and helped them to live under the most adverse circumstances. The biblical text Exodus and biblical personalities such as Moses and Dorcas were often chosen because of their relationship to freedom themes and African American moral values.

Survival, like freedom, was a powerful motif in the slave experience. Women like Silvia Dubois used the Bible to interpret survival and freedom within the context of resistance. Silvia had a great sense of her own self-worth and did not get along well with her slave mistress. Later known as the "slave who whipped her mistress and gained her freedom," Silvia was a large woman with unusual strength. She was born in New Jersey in 1768, and grew up among Presbyterians. Freed by her master, Silvia immediately set out on foot with her baby to take a raft to Trenton, en route to Flagstown, where she anticipated finding her mother. Along the way she encountered a white man who demanded the pass that was required of all slaves who traveled without their masters—the general assumption was that all black people were slaves. Refusing to identify herself, Silvia said, "I'm no man's nigger— I belong to God—I belong to no man." Silvia's response represents a fundamental tenet of African American Christianity as construed by slaves who used the Bible to interpret their freedom. Silvia also made clear her rejection of the slave master's constant assertion that God sanctioned slavery. Silvia's God was a just and fair God, not a supporter of bondage.

Some enslaved women and men clung tenaciously to the Bible and found meanings and promises in the scriptures that seemed to speak to their oppression and define their missions. The Bible offered hope in a world where there seemed to be only darkness. Contrary to the arguments advanced by some scholars, blacks were not seeking another world; they sought freedom in this world. Harriet Tubman firmly believed that she was following God's command to set her people free. And, when freedom came, Octavia Albert believed that God's will had triumphed over evil, and that as a survivor of slavery she was responsible for telling the truth about the institution. Albert asserted, "I believe we should not only treasure [knowledge], but should transmit [it] to our children's children. That's what the Lord commanded Israel to do in reference to their deliverance from Egyptian bondage." To expel the hypocrisy surrounding slavery and challenge Americans about the

meaning of Christianity, Albert committed herself to the task of collecting and publishing the personal narratives of former slaves. In her
book, *The House of Bondage or Charlotte Brooks and other Slaves*, Albert
illustrated how slavery had grown and prospered in a Christian nation,
and exposed the nature of the sin the institution had supported and
sustained. Similarly, in the postbellum era, Fanny Jackson Coppin, a
deeply religious former slave, devoted her life to educational social
reform. Coppin, like Albert, saw her work as a way to demonstrate her
Christian faith.

For these women, and others like them, Jesus was their personal
savior. More than any others, black women historically have embraced
Jesus Christ. Enslaved women discovered a Jesus who seemed to speak
directly to them and to their painful and protracted struggle for freedom. They saw in their condition a parallel to the suffering and persecution that Jesus had endured—Jesus was crucified, and many enslaved
Africans were beaten, maimed, and killed. In the depths of their pain
they called upon and fervently worshipped Jesus. They understood
that his earthly name was Jesus, but that he was in reality the embodi-
ment of all three persons in the trinity—God the Father, God the Son,
and God the Holy Ghost. These names were used interchangeably in
prayers and daily speech. However, Jesus was accessible: he had walked
the earth, he had been in the world—but he was not of the world.

Belief in Jesus and his biblical promises engendered in enslaved
women and men a deep and unfathomable faith. As a free woman,
Aunt Charlotte attested to this faith: "Many times I have bowed down
between the [sugar] cane-rows, when the cane was high, so nobody
could see me, and would pray in the time of the [civil] war! I used to
say, 'O, my blessed Lord, be pleased to hear my cry; set me free, O my
Lord, and I will serve you the balance of my days.' I knowed God had
promised to hear his children when they cry, and he heard us way down
here in Egypt." Aunt Charlotte's faith did not end with God's deliverance on the promise of freedom. She recalled a preacher telling her,
"Not a foot of land do I possess, not a cottage in the wilderness."
Instead of venting her anger and frustration at her impoverished condition as a free woman, she said, "Just so it is with me; sometimes I
don't have bread to eat; but I tell you, my soul is always feasting on my
dear Jesus. Nobody knows what it is to taste of Jesus but them that has
been washed by him."

Aunt Charlotte's dedication to the worship of Jesus was mirrored in
the lives of thousands of enslaved and free women. Rev. W. B. Allen, a

former slave in Georgia, recalled verses from a song his mother sang when he was a child, in which she celebrated Jesus as her personal savior. In particular, Allen remembered snatches of verses from two songs. One signified his mother's total acceptance of Jesus—"All I want is Jesus; you may have all the world. Just give me Jesus"—and the other expressed her desire for freedom:

> Our troubles will soon be over,
> I'm going to live with Jesus—after while;
> Praying time will soon be over,
> I'm going home to live with Jesus—after while.

Sojourner Truth, a former slave and one of the best-known women among the antebellum reformers, summed up the feelings and beliefs of most black women. Responding to a question raised by a preacher who wanted to know if the Bible was the source of her preaching, Truth said, "No honey, can't preach from de Bible—can't read a letter." She explained, "When I preaches, I has jest one text to preach from an' I always preaches from this one. My text is, 'When I found Jesus!' " In this sermon, Truth traced the history of her family, explaining how they came from Africa, were enslaved, and were sold over and over again; she finally met Jesus in her struggles for the freedom and dignity of African Americans and women. Despite Truth's protestations, the Bible was an important source for much of her teachings. Like most illiterate persons of the time, she was exposed to Bible reading, sermons, and public discourse laced with references to the Bible and religion. Religion infused every aspect of early-nineteenth-century life and culture and could not easily be avoided.

Why is it, then, that African American women steadfastly clung to the Bible and Jesus? Many slaves had a deep and abiding faith in God. However, the God they spoke about and believed in was not the Christian God of their masters. There was too much contradiction between what their masters and mistresses professed and what they actually did. Enslaved women and men needed a fixed point, both within and outside of themselves. Enslaved women rarely adhered to Christian dogma, and were not converted to God—rather, they converted God to themselves. Drawing on their West African religious traditions, women were "totally receptive to the person of Jesus." Given the African background and their belief in God as a divine mediator, it was not difficult for black women to accept Jesus as their personal savior and assign the deity virtual powers. As slaves, many women felt that Jesus was their last refuge. Their Jesus was a very approachable savior, who offered solace and comfort to all who would embrace him. They placed their faith in Jesus and fervently believed that their prayers would be answered. Their spiritualities, in particular their religious beliefs, and what Toinette Eugene calls their "womanist communities of care," served as therapeutic agents that validated their experiences and feelings. Eugene argues that, given "the miracle of Black women's survival in America, sensitive and systematic exploration of the possibly therapeutic functions of the religious experience and spirituality" of these women is warranted.

During slavery women created "communities of care" in the slave quarters that served as foundations for support of females and their families. In times of need, an enslaved woman could call on her sisters to aid her in many ways. Slave narratives speak of women assisting other women during childbirth and sickness, aiding them in their escapes to freedom, attending them following the vicious beatings and rape by their masters and other men, and providing cover for them during their absence. Enslaved women often attended to each other's psychological needs and provided validation for each other's existence as human beings. In some cases, women formed groups and met in clandestine prayer meetings held at night in the slave quarters. Aunt Charlotte revealed that, on a plantation in Louisiana against her master's wishes, she and seven other women regularly met in her cabin. Reveling in the experience and the psychological release it offered her and the other women, Aunt Charlotte said, "La, me! what a good time we all used to have in my cabin on that plantation!" A few men whom they considered to be a part of their community of care were allowed to attend the gatherings. These clandestine meetings were led by Aunt Jane, an enslaved woman who slipped away from her plantation at night to attend.

Aunt Charlotte befriended Aunt Jane Lee and felt a special kinship to her because she was also from Virginia. As a child in Richmond, Virginia, Charlotte had been part of a close-knit family who regularly attended church and participated in other communal activities. Prevented by their Catholic masters from attending church, the little band held worship services in Aunt Charlotte's cabin. Aunt Jane was a valued member of the community. She could read the Bible and knew many hymns. She was, for all intents and purposes, a preacher to the group. Reading biblical text, praying, and singing hymns that spoke directly to the pain and suffering endured by the women and men, Aunt Jane held the group in rapt attention. Her favorite scripture was Daniel in the lion's den (Daniel 6:1–10). To lower the volume of their singing, dancing, and shouting, and to avoid detection by their master, they whispered and sang in low voices, and placed a large washtub filled with water in the middle of the floor to absorb the sounds. When they sang, they marched around and shook hands.

The prayer meetings and worship services held in Aunt Charlotte's cabin were not unique. In Missouri, Alice Sewell revealed how women slipped away to hold prayer meetings. At the conclusion of their gatherings, these women also shook hands and sang, "Fare you well, my sisters, I am going home." Communal experiences like those held in slave cabins and daily prayer in the fields were major sustaining forces in the lives of women in slavery and freedom. Working together each day, in mostly sex-segregated groups, enslaved women developed their own value system and formed strong bonds with each other. They found numerous ways to cooperate and provide the kind of support needed during times of suffering and grief. As Deborah Gray White notes, "[A]dult female cooperation and interdependence [were facts] of female slave life. The self-reliance and self-sufficiency of slave women, therefore, must not only be viewed in the context of what the individual slave woman did for herself, but what slave women as a group were able to do for one another."

Women's Religious Roles in the Slave Community

WOMEN ASSUMED VARIOUS religious leadership roles in the slave community. Slave testimony suggests that most of the shouting and mourning that occurred during religious services was done by women. Shouting was a vocal testimony to preaching, personal testimony, or an expression of one's own spirit. Shouting was a religious role, in that shouters' participation in a meeting had the effect of transforming the service, moving a congregation, or gathering it to an emotional climax. This was most evident at baptisms and during funerals, where women were the chief mourners. A former slave recalled that the women in his family were well known for their shouts:

> All of my people were great Christians. Shouting, singing, praying and good old heartfelt religion make up the things that filled their lives. My grandmother was named Eve. She was a Chris-

tian from head to foot. It didn't take much to get her started and when she called on God she made heaven ring.

There was Aunt Bellow, a heavy, brown-skinned woman. She was a great shouter. Aunt Charlotte used to cry most all the time when she got happy. Aunt Kate was a tall portly woman and a shouter. It took some good ones to hold her down when she got started. Any time Uncle Link or any other preacher touched along the path she had traveled, she would jump and holler. It took some good ones to hold her. The old ones in them times walked over benches and boxes with their eyes fixed on heaven. God was in the midst of them.

Some women assumed the role of preacher and conducted funeral services and, similar to Aunt Jane, preached. However, most slave preachers were male. Conjure women and prophetesses were valued for their special abilities. Though prophetesses appear to have been rare, conjure women were very much in evidence. Sinda, described as a "self-proclaimed prophetess" on a Georgia plantation, in 1839 predicted that the world would end on a certain day. Sinda's prediction led to a work stoppage that undermined the slave owners' power. Many slaves believed in conjuring. Harriette Benton, an ex-slave born near Flat Shoals, Troup County, Georgia, when asked if she believed in conjure said, "Do I believe in conjur? Lor' chile, Ah thought dat Ah wuz conjured one time. Why my feet dey swoll up so big Ah couldn't walk. . . . Ah have hear'd o' folks puttin' a lil' ole ground puppy down where folks kin step on'em, and dey pisins 'em and dey feet done swoll up." Some slaves were mindful of the separate roles of the conjurer and the root doctor. Reflecting on her experiences, a former slave explained, "I don't believe in conjurers because I have asked God to show me such things—if they existed—and He came to me in person while I was in a trance and he said, 'There ain't no such thing as conjurers.' I believe in root-doctors, because, after all, we must depend upon some form of root or weed to cure the sick."

Conjuring, or what became known in America as Vodou (or Voodoo) practices, emanated out of the slave's West African Vodun religious tradition. Combining medicine and magic, so-called Vodou or root doctors possessed the power to summon good and evil spirits, concoct potions, and create charms, dolls, and other magical implements that could be used for good and evil. Conjure women and men were skilled in the art of the occult, and possessed an extensive knowledge of the medicinal value of herbs. Legendary stories of the power of the conjurer or root doctor abounded among the enslaved and master classes. Conjurers were both feared and respected. Reports of the effects of conjuring, similar to the testimony of Harriette Benton, appear in the autobiographies and personal testimonies of numerous former slaves. Throughout the South, women and men reported incidents that occurred on their plantations and had an impact on them. Constant reference is made to the conjurer's use of the "puppy" to inflict a person with pain, suffering, illness, and sometimes death. These stories also make clear the dual power of the conjurer to both place and remove a spell. Albert J. Raboteau notes, "Slaves believed adversity was due not to blind fate or mere happenstance but to the ill will of someone working through a conjurer. . . . The ultimate source of the conjurer's power was either God or the devil. Being born the seventh son of a seventh son or being born with a caul [or veil] also were seen as sources of power."

Though enslaved men and women testified to the widespread nature of Vodou and conjuring practices, Vodou as an organized cult and a system of magic was centered primarily in New Orleans. The growth of the cult in Louisiana was associated with the emigration of slaves and free blacks from the French-controlled island of Saint-Domingue. In 1791 a slave insurrection led by Toussaint L'Overture, involving thousands of slaves, erupted near Cape François; it lasted fifteen years and spread throughout the colony. Beginning in 1793, a large contingent of refugees from Cape François and Saint-Domingue, including whites and mulattoes and some of their slaves, sought asylum in America. Port cities such as New Orleans, Charleston, and Baltimore attracted their share of the émigrés.

As early as 1716, slaves were being imported from the islands of Martinique, Guadeloupe, and Saint-Domingue. In America, the émigrés actively engaged in their religious beliefs and participated in Vodou rituals, which attracted slaves and free blacks. Vodou practitioners, including priests and priestesses, presided over the cult. Among the most celebrated and powerful of the Vodou priestesses were Danite Dede and the two Marie Laveaus, mother and daughter. These three women exerted an inordinate amount of influence among blacks and whites in New Orleans during the nineteenth century. According to one observer, the first Marie Laveau "was perhaps the

most powerful" African American woman in America during the nineteenth century. Known as the "Vodou Queen of New Orleans,"
Laveau was feared by all—black and white, enslaved and free.

By 1860, Marie Laveau's influence and knowledge was secured in
her daughter, the second Marie Laveau. Among the Laveaus' extensive
followers, there was a belief that the Vodou queens could cure their
ills, cast spells upon their masters, bring them luck, help them snare
future wives and husbands, and influence their lives in numerous ways.
The Laveaus counted among their clients slave mistresses, who sought
their advice on love, as well as prominent politicians, all of whom wore
the good-luck amulets, made of wood and bone. The elder Laveau
understood power and how it could be secured. She developed an intimate knowledge of life in New Orleans and hired spies to secure personal and professional information on the most influential politicians
and leaders in the city. She understood that power resided in having
information and being able to influence the thought and behavior of
important persons. Laveau, like many of the New Orleans vodou
practitioners, was Catholic. She merged Catholic beliefs and rituals
with African culture and religious beliefs to create a unique African
Catholic religion. Following the death of the Laveaus, the Vodou cult
lost some of its influence, but it did not disappear.

Patterns of Worship

PATTERNS OF WORSHIP were not uniform. With the exception of
some individuals owned by Methodist masters, slaves rarely were able
to choose the denomination or church they would attend or affiliate
with. A woman born in Robinson County, Tennessee, whose mother
was sold when she was a baby, was owned by a Methodist preacher
whom she described as "a mighty mean one." As a child growing up
without a mother, she "didn't know anything about the Bible and
God." She asserted, "I was almost grown before I had ever heard the
Bible read and the word of God explained." Excited to learn that she
had a "heavenly Father," the "marster of all," she affiliated with a
Seventh-day Adventist Church. After several years she left, claiming,
"They didn't believe in eating meat, having pictures on the walls, or
wearing any kind of jewelry." She maintained her "faith in God but not
just as they taught it." Though there was no set pattern, many slaves
were obligated to attend the churches designated by their masters.

These included local churches and institutions erected on the plantations. Some masters made provisions for slave worship and hired a minister to preach and instruct their slaves as they desired. One enslaved woman recalled, "They had a white man that would come over every fourth Sunday and preach to us. He would say 'Be Honest, don't steal, and obey your marster and mistress.' That was all the preaching we had down in Mississippi."

Some slave owners required attendance at their churches, where blacks sat in the gallery or in pews set aside for them. A former slave claimed that her master regularly attended church and allowed his slaves to go to church on Sunday, "but that did not keep our white people from beating us through the week." In some instances slaves attended special services arranged for them at their master's church. And some slaves were allowed to hold worship services in their cabins or on the plantation with a preacher of their choosing. After 1830 and the Nat Turner revolt and Denmark Vesey conspiracy, many states passed laws requiring that a white person be present at all meetings of slaves. Some Catholics in Louisiana restricted their slaves from attending any worship services and in some instances forbade them from praying. All of this coexisted with the secret worship services organized by the slaves.

Little is known about the patterns of membership, attendance, and participation of enslaved women in the Presbyterian, Episcopalian, Catholic, or many other churches, but it is possible to discuss and analyze the experiences of enslaved Methodist women in particular and, to a lesser extent, Baptist women. During the late eighteenth and early nineteenth centuries, before the founding of the African Methodist Episcopal and the African Methodist Episcopal Zion denominations, the majority of black Christians were affiliated with the Methodist Episcopal and Baptist churches. Of the roughly four million enslaved persons residing in the South in 1860, more than 300,000 worshipped in white churches before emancipation. African Americans initially joined the Methodist Church in the North and South because of the antislavery position taken by some early Methodist preachers. Methodists contributed significantly to the manumission of slaves, primarily in the upper South. This was undoubtedly an important factor in the decision of slave women to affiliate with the denomination. Women like one slave named Alley were very aware of the church's manumission practices and used them to their advantage. In 1790

Alley ran away from her owner in Maryland. She succeeded in her bid for freedom by telling suspicious whites that she was set free by a Methodist minister who married into a slaveholding family.

In cities like Baltimore, Philadelphia, New York, and Boston enslaved and free blacks affiliated with Methodist churches. In New York City in 1786, the John Street Church, known as the mother church of American Methodism, reported 178 members, twenty-five of whom were black—six men and nineteen women. By 1790 the number of black members had grown to seventy. There were many more African Americans in New York City who were attracted to the Methodist religion but refused to attend segregated services, opting instead to hold private meetings in their homes. In 1795, when Bishop Francis Asbury visited the John Street Church, he found 155 black members in eight classes, only two of whom were male. The black membership appears to have been a mixture of enslaved and free persons. Zilpah Montjoy, a slave in New York City, was a member of the "Methodist society" at John Street Church. Zilpah was diligent in her attendance of Methodist class meetings. Though she did not learn how to read until she was sixty-eight years of age, she took great pleasure in reading the New Testament, especially the scriptures that included Christ's Sermon on the Mount, which she called "the blessed chapter." After 1796, the establishment of separate black Methodist worship groups provided additional choices for enslaved and free blacks. For example, in Baltimore the Sharp Street Methodist Episcopal Church membership rolls included slaves who were permitted to hire their time out in the city, as well as fugitive slaves. Fugitives would not have been tolerated in the Lovely Lane or Strawberry Alley Methodist churches. However, black churches such as Sharp Street were pockets of resistance that sheltered fugitives, providing religious sustenance and protection from slave catchers and others who sought the bounties placed on the heads of runaways.

Of great importance to enslaved and free women was the Methodist Episcopal Church's espousal of sanctification and holiness. The Methodist belief in the supremacy of God and the Holy Spirit and the accessibility of these principles to all persons regardless of race, color, gender, or class were essential elements in the empowerment of African American women, particularly enslaved women and early black women preachers. To experience holiness, a believer had to be converted. Conversion, a central element in Methodist doctrine, required acknowledgment of one's sins, repentance, and an agreement to live a life centered in Christ. Following conversion, one became sanctified. The public conversion experience that occurred in a church or at a camp meeting was sometimes filled with drama and excitement, both for the person being converted and for onlookers. During conversion some individuals became highly emotional. In 1945, Fisk University's Social Science Institute published interviews and autobiographies of African Americans, born during and after slavery, who describe the conversion experience and speak about the radical impact it had on their lives and their self-concept. At least half of the testimony was taken from women, who were converted outside the gaze of spectators, often in their homes, in the woods, or at other isolated places. Regardless of where the conversion occurred, enslaved women experienced a powerful validation of their personhood. Inherent in their personal testimonies is a discovery of power, in the sense that they had gained control over their spiritual destiny—something that masters and mistresses could not take away from them.

The evangelical awakenings of the late eighteenth century impacted the patterns of church membership and brought changes in American religious life. Revivals that occurred along the James River in 1785 were fueled in part by the growth of the Baptist Church in Virginia and the Methodist Church in Maryland and Delaware. The egalitarian spirit of the American Revolution and the growing antislavery sentiment inspired many evangelical preachers to allow blacks to participate in aspects of church governance and discipline. In such an environment, African Americans, especially women, with the hope of freedom, affiliated with the Baptist and Methodist churches in the upper South in unprecedented numbers. As evangelicalism spread throughout the South, African Americans flocked to the white Methodist and Baptist churches. The Methodists were in the vanguard of the movement from 1785 to 1815, but as the Baptists and others who embraced evangelical preaching grew in prominence, they became strong competitors for the allegiance of white and black religionists, especially in the southern states.

There were no set patterns defining black membership and participation in Methodist churches. The most important factor in determining the level and type of participation available to black women in these institutions was the size of the congregation. As members of biracial Methodist congregations in Delaware, Maryland, and

Charleston, South Carolina, enslaved women participated in worship services, class meetings, love feasts, and prayer meetings that provided opportunities for fellowship with other women, enslaved and free. In churches with small memberships, class meetings were segregated by gender but integrated by race and social class. In larger churches with many members, class meetings were segregated by race and gender, with white women assigned to the "women's class" and African American women placed in the "black class."

Cynthia Lynn Lyerly asserts that as black and white women attended the same Methodist churches and participated in rituals such as communion and baptism, some slaveholding whites were moved to manumit their slaves. Baptism of children was especially important because it provided enslaved women the opportunity to demonstrate their humanity and maternal feelings. Slavery did not recognize their maternal rights or respect their feelings for their children. In a system where mothers and fathers and children could be sold at will, there was little concern about the bond between mother and child. Moreover, slaveholders denied that blacks had feelings for their children, or that black women and men were capable of expressing feelings of love. The common view was that they mated like animals. However, Methodists viewed baptism as a parental duty, where parents demonstrated their willingness to raise their children in the faith. Parents, especially mothers, who were separated from their children could not fulfill their Christian responsibilities. Methodism reinforced egalitarian values. However, most white women and men still saw black people as intellectually and physically inferior.

Slave mothers also affiliated with the Methodist Church because of its support for the education of black children. In some cases, ministers would encourage slave owners to teach enslaved children how to read. This would ensure that they would better understand the Bible. Slave mothers petitioned Methodist ministers to aid them in keeping their families together and to intercede to prevent brutal beatings by their masters. In effect these women learned that religion, especially membership in mainstream white denominations, could be a force for liberation. They skillfully used their church affiliations and contact with other women to their advantage. Being able to commune with women of various social classes and experiences, they formed a bond of sisterhood that helped them to redefine who they were and to "shape a gender identity of their own choosing."

Manumission and Black Women

IN THE WAKE of the American Revolution, northern blacks gained their freedom. An upsurge of abolitionist and slave activity aimed at eradicating the institution of slavery illustrated the hypocrisy inherent in the revolutionary rhetoric extolling ideals of freedom and equality for the British colonies, and contributed to the pressure to abolish slavery in the North. The revolutionary spirit of the early national period influenced a number of Methodists to manumit their slaves, and undoubtedly contributed to the growth of a free black population, whose presence was acknowledged in the first federal census of 1790. Throughout the antebellum period, women constituted the bulk of the free black population, which was dominated by light- and dark-skinned mulattoes. Between 1820 and 1860 African American women outnumbered black men in fourteen cities. In 1860, mulattoes and persons of mixed ancestry in the lower South constituted 75.8 percent of the free black population. However, in the upper South they comprised a much smaller percentage, only one-third of the free blacks.

Women were manumitted for any number of reasons, including age, religious altruism, legal agreements, acts of bravery, and so on. However, a primary reason was the intimate relationships formed by slave owners with their slaves. Some women who had served for years as concubines for their masters were set free. Also manumitted were the offspring of these relationships. Miscegenation occurred quite frequently during slavery. It was fairly common practice for white men—including masters, their sons, overseers, and other men—to have sex with any female slave they chose. Some women, particularly beautiful mulattoes, were purchased for the express purpose of serving as concubines.

There were no laws prohibiting the rape of African women, and they were available. W. E. B. Du Bois observed, "The black females, were they the wives or growing girls, were the legitimate prey of the men, and in this system there was one, and only one safeguard, the character of the master of the plantation. Where the master was himself lewd and avaricious the degradation of the women was complete." Commenting on how widespread and insidious this practice was, a former slave, self-described as a "preacher from a 'God fearing' plantation," recalled,

> [M]y master . . . was a good man but he was pretty bad among the women. Married or not married made no difference to him. Whoever he wanted among the slaves he went and got her or had her meet him somewhere out in the bushes. I have known him to go to the shack and make the wom[a]n's husband sit outside while he went in to his wife. . . . I am not accusing him of nothing but these are just things that I saw. He wasn't no worse than none of the rest. They all used their women like they wanted to and there wasn't nobody to say anything about it. Neither the [slave] men nor the women could help themselves. They submitted to it but kept praying to God.

Not all enslaved women submitted willingly to the sexual demands of their masters, overseers, or other white men. Those who resisted were most often brutally beaten, maimed, and sometimes killed. Black husbands who challenged a master were subject to the same treatment, and in some instances were sold. Julia Foote, one of the foremost black preaching women in the nineteenth century, recalled the trials her mother had to endure as a slave in New York. For refusing to submit to the sexual demands of her master, and relating the sexual harassment to her mistress, Foote's mother was tied up and whipped. After the whipping, her master washed her back with strong saltwater.

Free Black Women and Church Leadership

MANY OF THE WOMEN who would later distinguish themselves as secular and religious leaders were descendant from either free black ancestry or persons who were members of the slave elite, who tended to be more skilled and possess at least the rudiments of education, and in some cases were highly educated. These included house servants, seamstresses, skilled artisans, and other slaves who had special skills and were allowed to hire themselves out in the city as long as they met their obligations and remitted a percentage of their earnings to their owners. Those whose roots were in the South were more often than not a part of the mulatto elite, while their northern counterparts included a mixture of women from the mulatto elite as well as relatively unmixed families, whose roots were in the upper South and in the North, where slavery was legally abolished by the 1830s. Among the women leaders after the Civil War whose family heritage included mulatto and/or free black antecedents, or who were set free by law,

Julia Foote, AME Zion preacher who was ordained a deacon on May 13, 1895, was the first black woman to achieve this distinction.

were Frances Ellen Watkins Harper, Mary Ann Shadd Cary, Mary Church Terrell, Josephine St. Pierre Ruffin, Margaret Murray Washington, Fannie Jackson Coppin, Fannie Barrier Williams, Victoria Earle Matthews, Hallie Q. Brown, Sara H. Duncan, Rev. Mary J. Small, Rev. Florence Spearing Randolph, Gertrude Bustill Mossell, Rebecca Cox Jackson, Amanda Berry Smith, Julia Foote, Jarena Lee, Sojourner Truth, Eliza Ann Gardner, and the preacher known simply as Elizabeth.

Free women were essential to the founding and development of the antebellum black community and church. Were it not for their numbers, fund-raising and organizing skills, and sheer dedication to their communities and churches, many male leaders would not have achieved the fame and recognition that they did. In discussing the role of western women in the development of the African Methodist Episcopal Church, Sarah J. Early observed, "In the early days of the Church when its ministers were illiterate and humble, and struggles

with poverty and proscription were long and severe, it required perseverance, patience, fortitude, foresight, and labor, the women were
ready with their time, their talent, their influence and their money, to
dedicate all to the upbuilding of the Church." Early stated that where
there were no church buildings women opened up their homes for
public worship and "gladly received the care-worn and weary traveling
preachers into their families" and provided for their necessities.

Many antebellum leaders were ministers who, as heads of independent institutions, possessed a freedom to speak and act that was not
always available to persons dependent on white employers for their
livelihoods. As heads of churches built and funded largely with the
pennies, nickels, and dimes of day workers, domestics, washerwomen,
hucksters (vendors), and other free black women who held a variety of
menial jobs, many ministers rose to prominence. And, although their
efforts were undergirded by a powerful base derived in large part from
the labors of females, they helped comprise the forces that denied
women religious suffrage, equal participation in the polity, and the
right to preach, and relegated women to minor leadership roles in the
church. James Oliver Horton asserts, "[A]s black institutions were
established in the cities and towns in the North, men dominated their
leadership but women played key roles." In northern and southern
cities with large concentrations of free blacks, this was the pattern
established in the antebellum era.

The Rise of Black Women Preachers

MANY FREE BLACK WOMEN were members of the Methodist Episcopal Church prior to the founding of the African Methodist Episcopal and African Methodist Episcopal Zion denominations. Most of the
pioneer women preachers, several of whom were formerly enslaved,
were associated with the Methodist Episcopal Church. Elizabeth, the
earliest known black female preacher, born a slave in Maryland in 1766
and set free in 1796, descended from a family of devout Methodists.
Jarena Lee, born free in Cape May, New Jersey, in 1783, attended a
Methodist church prior to joining the Mother Bethel AME Church in
Philadelphia in 1809. Julia A. J. Foote, born free in Schenectady, New
York, in 1823, was a member of the Methodist Church and the AME
Church in Albany, New York, before affiliating with the AME Zion
Church in Boston. Amanda Berry Smith, although born a slave in
Maryland in 1837, was free by age five, and as a teenager she joined the

Jarena Lee, born free in Cape May, New Jersey, 1783, was the first woman officially sanctioned to preach in the AME Church.

Methodist Church in Shrewsburg, Pennsylvania. Sojourner Truth, born a slave in 1797 and set free by 1826, affiliated with several Methodist churches, including the John Street Church in New York City.

It is no accident that some of the first black women leaders, lay and ministerial, came primarily out of the Methodist Church in the North. Few southern women, Methodist or Baptist, preached. In the South, the Quakers were the only religious denomination that permitted women to preach. The Methodist Church was among the earliest of the denominations to recognize that slaves had souls and, in some quarters, to voice antislavery sentiments. And the Methodist denomination's support of the holiness doctrine, especially its position on spiritual sanctification, was especially appealing to women, black and white, who understood the validation powers that it conferred on women. The holiness doctrine validated women's right to preach. Women adhering to the doctrine "believed that no man or institution

Amanda Berry Smith, AME evangelist and African missionary.

could sanction their right to preach that this was the sole prerogative of God." Essentially, in spite of church law, black and white women interpreted sanctification as an authorization to preach.

In order to become sanctified, one had to be converted. Like the many enslaved women whose lives were transformed by the experience of being converted, female preachers gained a sense of freedom that they had not previously known. Acting on that freedom had conse-quences, but, they willingly forged a path to a level of spiritual attain-ment that set a precedent for other black women to follow. As part of their journey, and as founders of an African American tradition of women preachers, women such as Jarena Lee, Zilpha Elaw, Julia Foote, and Amanda Berry Smith celebrated their success and elo-quently told their stories in spiritual autobiographies that have served as beacons of hope and guides for all those who have followed in their footsteps.

Conversion is not an experience unique to a particular group of people, race, or religion. Historically speaking, the conversion experi-ence is a fairly common phenomenon. However, it has been more gen-erally associated with African Americans, other people of color, and poor people. One reason for the widespread occurrence of related acts of conversion in the diaspora, societies with large populations of African descent, is the persistence of African religious values, beliefs, and customs that over time have fused with Catholicism, Protes-tantism, and other religions to form African Christianity and other religions that are African inspired. Ecstatic religious celebrations that include speaking in tongues, dancing, and the use of drums, cymbals, tambourines, and other instruments all hark back to West African traditions and have special meanings. The remarkable similarity of stories and practices found among peoples of African descent in the diaspora reinforces the historical connections to Africa.

The conversion testimony of slaves and antebellum women preachers are similar. Regardless of age, gender, or social class, all of them relate going through a "dramatic experience, sudden sickness, blurring of vision, painful pressure of heart followed by a 'death' experience in which one sees hell but is saved by the grace of God, or is shown a 'big glorious city' wherein resides a man who commands her to 'go tell others of your experience.' Finally they are brought to life—or rebirth experience." Although each individual tells her "death and rebirth" story in her own way, there is a common thread connecting all of the testimonies. The rituals, visions, and symbols reflect the culture of the society, particularly Christian principles and doctrines.

The public and private performance that encapsulates the act of being converted for enslaved and some free blacks was ecstatic and reflected the rituals and symbols inherent in West African religious practices. The performance art seen in most slave testimony is largely absent from that of the antebellum women preachers. Perhaps preaching women tempered their behavior because among the male clergy there was jealousy of women who were very knowledgeable about the Bible and appeared to be highly spiritual. Ministers, males of all persuasions, and husbands were sometimes threatened by a woman who assumed the mantle of being holy. Being different and seeking a public career as an itinerant preacher was seen by some as an immodest role for a woman. Some persons linked "spiritually proficient women with sexual license." A woman could have her reputation ruined by spurious rumors suggesting that she was a woman of loose morals. It was also common practice to suggest that women preachers were mentally unstable.

Women were excluded from participation in the religious polity, and hence the formal leadership structure, in all evangelical churches, black, white, and biracial. Historically the structure of dominance in all areas of American life has been white over black and other people of color, and men over women. It is of no consequence in this respect that women have consistently outnumbered men in practically all religious traditions. In addition to being preachers, women served in several ex officio preaching roles, namely as exhorters and evangelists. In the Methodist tradition, male exhorters were religious public speakers, licensed by the Quarterly Conference. Exhortation, an intermediate stage between testimony and preaching, included testifying, holding prayer meetings, speaking informally at class meetings, and, in some instances, substituting for an itinerant minister. Licensed exhorters represented the lowest category in the leadership category. Some female exhorters became evangelists. Evangelists were unordained preachers who preached wherever they could. During the antebellum era women exhorters, evangelists, and preachers were not licensed, and with few exceptions lacked church authority. The first generation of black women preachers functioned as evangelists.

Women preachers were valued for their charismatic leadership, but their claims to religious authority were disputed and denied on biblical and doctrinal grounds. Regardless of the challenges to their religious leadership, women ministers clung tenaciously to their doctrinal claim of spiritual sanctification and thus ordination by God. Though a great deal is known about Jarena Lee, Julia Foote, Zilpha Elaw, and Sojourner Truth, much less is known about southern black women preachers during the antebellum era. There were some northern as well as southern women preachers who were well known at the time. For example, Clarinda—a free black woman, described as a "self-appointed preaching woman from Beaufort, South Carolina," in the early nineteenth century—was widely known for her deep piety and unique preaching skills. Born in 1730, she is said to have "endured years of cruelty and persecution" because she asserted that she had been commissioned by God to preach the gospel. At the age of one hundred, Clarinda continued to hold weekly evangelistic meetings at her home. She died in 1832 at the age of 102.

The rise of antebellum black women preachers and their ministries, although not sanctioned by church authority, are significant for a number of reasons. They were among the first to openly confront the clergy and Christian dogma that excluded women from the ministry and limited their participation in religious ritual. The mere presence of female preachers challenged the notion of women's inherent inferiority. Their sermons and writings attest to women's intellectual capacity. As women who traveled and preached to blacks and whites, their lives and images empowered other women to think, to speak, and to act. The very persona of a female preacher—especially a black woman—who professed to holiness and to speak the word of God, was disconcerting for some and empowering for others. It resonated at all levels of society and posited ways of being and acting for young girls and women to whom her mantle might be passed.

In their solid determination to carve out careers in the ministry, black women opened up new opportunities for females to advance in the church and society. Antebellum women preachers were social activists arguing for the liberation of their people. With few exceptions, women like Elizabeth, Sojourner Truth, and Julia Foote protested against slavery and attested to the equality of women. As Lee, Foote, and Elaw gained notoriety and were widely praised for their spiritual gifts, clergymen seized the opportunity to utilize their talents and employed them for revivals and other events used to attract new members and raise funds. It was in this manner that preaching women joined their sisters in the pew in helping to build powerful black churches, out of which developed the first black leaders in the African American struggle for freedom.

Black and Biracial Churches

BY 1800 THE MAJORITY of black Christians were members of the Methodist Episcopal Church. As a result of the increasing segregation and discrimination within the church, as well as concerns about church rituals and worship practices, black Methodists in Baltimore, Philadelphia, New York City, and several other cities withdrew from the Methodist Church and formed separate worship groups exemplifying their African Christian theological beliefs and worship preferences. In a letter to Bishop Francis Asbury, the Baltimore group indicated their concerns "about building a House and forming a distinct African, yet Methodist church." By 1820, practically all white churches had designated seating and separate entrances for black members, as well as separate seating for males and females. One step ahead of the white religious segregationists, black Methodists decided that total freedom meant creating their own denominations. Though African Americans separated from the Strawberry Alley, St. George Methodist Episcopal, and John Street churches in 1787 and 1797, for several decades they maintained their affiliation with the Methodist Episcopal denomination. The African Methodist Episcopal and African Methodist Episcopal Zion denominations were recognized as independent national entities following their separate incorporations, in 1816 and 1820 respectively. Women played key roles in the establishment of all the early black churches and assumed multiple leadership roles that have not been properly acknowledged. Women lacked formal and titled authority in the church, but they were highly influential from the very beginning. And, given their membership numbers, which usually exceeded those of the men, women possessed a great potential for power.

In Philadelphia, in 1787, among the small band of dissenters who walked out of the St. George Methodist Episcopal Church with Richard Allen and Absalom Jones were Jane Ann Murray, Sarah Dougherty, and a woman known as Mother Duncan. In New York City James Varick, the leader of the John Street Church protest, was joined by a number of free black and enslaved women, including Aurelia Varick, Sarah Thompson, Jane Cook, Jane Pontier, Pemilia Pontier, Susannah Moore, Sarah Moore, Amy Jacobs, Jane Miller, Betsy Miller, Sarah Bias, and Elizabeth Brown. Similar patterns existed among the Baptists. Women were instrumental in the initiation of services and aided in the raising of the funds for financing the building of a black Baptist church in Boston in 1806.

Rev. F. A. Mood, minister to the biracial membership at the Methodist Church of Charleston, South Carolina, in speaking of the black leadership, mentioned Mary Ann Berry, Rachel Wells, and Nanny Coates, three black women who were influential leaders. Wells, an enslaved woman, was the first black member of a Methodist society. Berry was praised by William Capers, a bishop of the Methodist Episcopal Church, South, for the high level of service she gave to the church and to the poor. Capers felt that although she lacked formal authority, because of the importance of the leadership role she assumed, she deserved recognition as a "deaconess."

The office of deaconess was established by the Methodist Episcopal Church after 1888. However, during the antebellum era, women were elected as deaconesses at some all-black churches. In 1827 in Petersburg, Virginia, at the Gillfield Baptist Church, composed mostly of free blacks, women were not only formally elected to the office of deaconess but were also assigned several functions usually reserved for men. Men normally were given responsibility for monitoring and citing the behavior of wayward members, inquiring into the lives and conduct of ex-communicants seeking reinstatement of their membership, and accompanying the candidates to the water during baptismal ceremonies. Sylvia R. Frey and Betty Wood argue that these patterns indicate that "[i]n all-black churches the African tradition of female spiritual leadership apparently persisted." The experiences of women in the Gillfield Baptist Church were unique, and do not represent the general pattern of women's participation in most all-black churches during the nineteenth century. However, each case must be carefully analyzed to determine what authority women who assumed the titles of deaconess, stewardess, and so on. actually had. In some cases, the titles were honorific, in that the roles played by the women were stripped of authority.

Baptists were more successful in attracting African Americans in the South than in the North. This was particularly true of women. Frey and Wood assert, "No other movement in British America contained such a large proportion of women," and "black women represented a clear majority in most evangelical churches—biracial as well as all-black." Around 1800, with the advent of the Second Awakening, the southern black Christian community increased its numbers to such an extent that it was virtually converted to a women's organization. In Virginia and South Carolina, women comprised a majority of black Baptist congregations. In Southern Baptist churches such as the biracial Sandy Creek Baptist and Clarke's Station Baptist churches and the all-black Gillfield Baptist Church, there is credible evidence that suggests that black women used "religion as protection against the social order . . . to resist unwelcome sexual advances made by men in the quarters." Enslaved women also, on occasion, brought charges against slave owners, and they used religion to manipulate and control other aspects of their relationships with their white owners as well.

Women were expected to function in subordinate or supporting roles within the church. In the church polity, men made the policy decisions. Deacons, vestrymen, trustees, and other persons entrusted with the power to legislate any aspect of church life were in most cases men. During the antebellum era and for many years afterward, while some women served as Sunday-school teachers and class leaders of mostly all-female groups, these and the positions of clergy, stewards, and superintendents of Sunday schools were reserved for men. In the structure of the Methodist polity, there were two essential elements: the class meeting, and the love feast. John Wesley, the originator of Methodism, organized the first Methodist class for the purpose of instilling a "deeper sense of grace and a better knowledge on the growth and meaning of [one's] conversion."

Class meetings provided an opportunity for members to express themselves privately, and love feasts were occasions for members to express themselves publicly. Pastors appointed class leaders, who provided oversight for the spiritual and social development of members assigned to their classes. Leaders were responsible for providing the proper orientation and education for the members of their group. Their duties included teaching Methodist doctrine and laws, collecting weekly financial donations that were delivered to a steward, and reporting the progress of each member to the pastor and the official church board. In most black churches not only were the classes all male or all female, but the sexes were seated separately, and sometimes women and men were required to enter and depart the church through separate doors. Internal patterns of gender segregation were not exclusive to black churches. They also existed in white religious institutions.

The most acceptable role for free women was fund-raising. However limited their defined roles were, the church provided an opportunity for women to develop organizational and speaking skills that would eventually undergird the development of powerful female-based church organizations—missionary societies and women's conventions, and eventually secular groups such as the National Association of Colored Women. In spite of all the restrictions and the expectations of so-called "true" women, African American women were not powerless. Their power resided in their numbers and their fund-raising prowess. It was generally recognized that without women

Mother Bethel AME Church, like many churches, had separate entrances for male and female congregants and maintained sex segregated seating in the sanctuary prior to the 1870s.

there would be no black church. However, black women also knew that for the health and survival of the black community it was important that each person play his or her part. Racism and sexism were as much a part of the lives of free women as they were for enslaved women.

From the beginning African Americans believed that it was of the utmost importance for women and men to work as a unit in destroying the racist cancer that affected all areas of American life. Their mission was clear, and they understood that their role was to build a nation of strong women and men who were equal, mentally and physically, to any task. To do that, women organized and undertook the task of raising money to build religious and educational institutions, and to create and support newspapers and a variety of businesses to serve the needs of their communities. In the process of organizing and assuming leadership, free black women developed a greater sense of their capabilities and worth. The social and political activism of women would eventually lead to calls for equal treatment and recognition in the church and community.

The church, as the most important community institution, served as the arbiter of individual and community morality. It imparted values and regulated behavior. Irrespective of social class or prominence within the community, all members were expected to conform to church law. During the antebellum era and for many years afterward in Methodist and Baptist churches, committees were organized to review the charges brought against women and men who failed to meet church standards for manners and morals, and for those who did not abide by the rules governing marriage. Members were regularly summoned to appear before the church for misconduct. Unmarried pregnant women were brought before the church and charged with immoral behavior. Women and men who were reported for "walking promiscuously"—meaning that they were inebriated—were tried for indecent and profane behavior. Members found attending dances were also brought before the church and tried. Depending on the charges and an individual's previous record of indiscretions, the committee recommended either probation or expulsion from the church for failure to adhere to church laws governing behavior. It was considered a mark of dishonor to be tried by the church for any infraction. As a slave in Savannah, Georgia, Patience M. Morse was a member of the Second Baptist Church. Many years after slavery ended, she took great pride in what she considered one of her greatest accomplishments: "never [being] disciplined or reprimanded by her church."

In Virginia, church trials were commonly held in black Baptist churches like Gillfield. Similarly, in Baltimore during the 1830s and '40s, the Sharp Street Methodist Episcopal Church regularly held trials to adjudicate disputes and review and regulate the behavior of its members. The church claimed moral jurisdiction over the lives of all members, enslaved and free. Church trials were officiated by class leaders, who were all male. The Sharp Street Church charged Louis Philips, a slave, with abandoning his wife to marry another woman. Like some urban slaves, Philips was permitted by his master to hire out his time. In Baltimore, Philips was free to come and go as he pleased, form relationships, join organizations, and belong to a church. He claimed that although he had formerly lived with an enslaved woman, he was not married to her. Asserting that the reason he did not marry the woman was that his master opposed it, Philips claimed to be married to a Baltimore woman named Margaret. However, the committee of inquiry found that Margaret was married to another man, and that her husband was alive during the time she lived with Philips. Mrs. Mary Berry, the owner of the house where the Philipses resided, claimed that a man by the name of George "was in the habit of coming and sleeping with Margaret in the absence of her husband." Mr. and Mrs. Wesley Chambers, residents in the house, also testified that George came and slept with Margaret. Wesley Chambers claimed that he saw George and Margaret "in the bed together up stairs in the act." The committee exonerated Louis Philips and found Margaret guilty of adultery. Margaret Philips was then expelled from the church.

Church tribunals tended to deal more harshly with women than with men. Similar patterns of dealing with unmarried enslaved women are found in biracial southern Baptist and Methodist churches. Unmarried enslaved women were more likely to be charged with fornication and promiscuity than their male counterparts. The labeling of unmarried black women in biracial churches as women of loose morals was part of the widespread mythology that described slave women as lewd, wanton, and wily temptresses who were sexually available to any man. The most respected and responsible white person accepted the myth of the oversexed black woman, who was supposedly possessed with an insatiable sexual appetite. In part, the myth was related to the need to justify the sexual abuse of black women and girls, and protect white men—owners, overseers, and others, who often forced enslaved and free women into adulterous relationships and demanded their sexual services. Over time this mythology was accepted, widely disseminated, and liberally used to invalidate the collective claims of black women on any number of issues. It became an important part of white cultural memory that continues into the twenty-first century. For example, it was used in the late nineteenth century to challenge Ida Wells-Barnett's veracity in claiming that the real reason for the widespread and wanton lynching of black men on trumped-up charges of raping white women was to halt the growth of a black middle class.

Benevolent and Reform Activities

THE FOUNDATION FOR African American women's extensive philanthropic work, which blossomed after the Civil War, was created primarily by free women, who utilized their religion and their churches as bases for launching their social and political activism. The church served as a center for most social and political activities, community celebrations, and organizing. It was where one received spiritual sustenance and bonded and networked with others who were concerned about the status of the black community, both free and slave. Out of a sense of Christian duty, fealty to one's God, and loyalty to one's people, African American women and men organized benevolent associations. Community activities frequently described as "benevolence" and "moral reform" illustrated the extent of female activism, most of which was dispensed through religious organizations and their affiliates.

The first organization for AME women, the Dorcas Society, was founded in 1824 by Bishop Richard Allen to care for the ministers involved in establishing AME churches. Allen asked the women to meet at the site of the Annual Conference several days before its opening "to sew and patch and clean the suits of the men who had been out on the field preaching the gospel, establishing churches and teaching the people." The second organization, the Daughters of Conference, was founded in 1827 by Sarah Allen for the purpose of raising money to aid ministers in the field. During the antebellum era, the AME Daughters of Conference functioned primarily as a preacher's aid society that, as one founder recalled, was "commonly called Daughters of Conference." For the most part, as Bishop Benjamin Tucker Tanner explained, the early Daughters of Conference "were only brought into play, in the Church that anticipated the coming of a Conference." In the Methodist Church, the conference served as a legislative and judicial system for developing and administering church law. Elected delegates attended the local, state, district, and national conferences, where

Richard Allen, the first bishop of the African Methodist Episcopal denomination

they deliberated and voted on the church legislation that defined every aspect of church life. Women raised money to send itinerant ministers to conference and to bear the overall conference expenses. Frequently this included outfitting the minister and paying the costs of travel, room and board, and miscellaneous expenses. By 1830, branches of the AME Daughters of Conference were established at most churches. In time, like their black and white Methodist sisters, AME Daughters of Conference and their successor missionary organizations would assume the tasks of fund-raising for institutional development, aiding struggling ministers, and engaging in various philanthropic activities at the local and national levels.

The Female Benevolent Society, commonly known as the "Mother Society," was the first AME Zion women's organization. It was established a few years after the beginning of the nineteenth century for the purpose of aiding members of the church in New York City. The society assisted in the support of the orphaned children of deceased members, administered to the sick, and buried the dead. In 1821, following the incorporation of the AME Zion denomination, the AME Zion United Daughters of Conference, a national organization, was formed to raise funds for erecting churches and helping to defray institutional expenses, to assist the needs of unsalaried ministers, and to support a variety of charitable causes. The AME Zion organization was founded in New York City by Eliza Gardner, Sarah Ennalls, Elizabeth A. Purnell, Sarah J. Eato, Marie Vogalsang, Matilda Busle, and Ellen Stevens, with Mary Roberts as the first president. Roberts was responsible for organizing societies within the bounds of the New York conference.

Many free black women, "sister laborers," only a few years removed from slavery, who had enslaved relatives, felt obligated to lift themselves up and aid their families, churches, and communities in any way possible. Scholars have written about the antebellum period and the importance of the church, benevolent and fraternal associations, African Americans in the abolitionist movement, the role of the black press in the freedom movement, and numerous other early protest movements, but they rarely mention or emphasize that the "sister laborers" were the chief source of church and community philanthropy. For fund-raising and charitable giving purposes, women's groups were often formed as auxiliaries to male benevolent and fraternal associations. Free women also had their own benevolent and fraternal organizations.

The first African American mutual aid and benevolent organizations were founded in the 1780s primarily to address the needs of the free black community. Although they were not enslaved, free blacks were still not treated as the equals of whites. Excluded from all but the most menial jobs, forced to live in almost abject poverty, and viewed as pariahs in a society that extolled whiteness and identified color as the badge of servitude, African Americans realized that survival meant self-help. To that end, free blacks created a multiplicity of associations to address the needs of their communities. Benevolent and fraternal organizations were among the first associations to appear. These organizations included moral reform societies and temperance, literary, charity, protection (to rescue and save black women from prostitution), and self-improvement associations. The goals of these organizations were diverse but inclusive of all of the conditions and issues facing the free community, including the abolition of slavery. Some associations comprised both women and men, but the majority were male, and women generally formed their own groups.

The Free African Union Society of Newport, Rhode Island, founded in 1780, included women and men; however, women were not allowed to vote or hold office. Almost three decades after its founding, women withdrew to form an all-female African Benevolent Society. The society sponsored educational programs and found apprenticeships to ensure that members and their children would develop the skills necessary for acquiring employment as carpenters, barbers, masons, seamstresses, tailors, milliners, cooks, and housekeepers. It also provided assistance to members in dire need. In Philadelphia, the Female Benevolent Society of St. Thomas Episcopal Church was founded in 1792, and the Daughters of Tapsico of the Mother Bethel AME Church was established in 1805.

The Colored Female Religious and Moral Society of Salem, Massachusetts, a mutual aid association consisting of between forty and fifty members, was formed in 1818. Membership was open to any woman who agreed to "conform to the constitution." The society required that members pay fifty-two cents a year in dues, participate in weekly meetings that included reading a chapter in the Bible and engaging in "religious conversation," and submit to the moral discipline of the order. In the nineteenth century, beginning in the 1820s, numerous mutual aid, benevolent, and secret societies were formed in cities and towns for the purpose of self-help. Among the most popular centers for women's organizations were Philadelphia, Baltimore, Boston, and New York. During the 1820s, the Union Female Society of Baltimore, the Philadelphia-based Daughters of Africa, and the Daughters of Rush Society organized for mutual aid. As in sister societies being formed in other areas, membership in these associations was not restricted by class. The Daughters of Africa included roughly two hundred working-class women and organized for mutual aid. Anna B. Bedford, an illiterate woman, founded the Sisters of Wisdom, a mutual aid association that began with six members. Renamed the Love and Charity order, by 1861 the group had several thousand members.

Recognizing that many black children either did not attend school or were frequently absent, in New York City the African Dorcas Society was founded in 1828 for strictly benevolent purposes. The organization collected used clothing, shoes, and hats for destitute children who lacked basic attire for attending school. In 1830 the association clothed seventy-four children. Dorcas societies were organized in Harrisburg, Pennsylvania, and numerous other cities to aid poor children. The Female Lundy Society of Albany, New York, and the

Female Benevolent Firm in Boston were unique in that they were formed for self-improvement and charitable purposes that included antislavery activity. The Lundy Society sheltered, fed, and clothed fugitive slaves making their way north on the Underground Railroad. Named in honor of Benjamin Lundy, noted antislavery editor of the *Genius of Universal Emancipation* newspaper, the Lundy Society required that its members fast and pray for sixteen days a year for their enslaved brothers and sisters. The Female Benevolent Firm was organized to secure shoes and clothing for fugitive slaves, in particular women and children rescued by the Underground Railroad.

By 1830, in most cities with large free black populations women's benevolent groups outnumbered the men's organizations. Many of these associations originated in the church and had titles related to some aspect of their religious beliefs and affiliations. These cooperative organizations provided support for food, clothing, shelter, fuel, medical care, funerals, and widows and orphans. Philadelphia had one hundred societies, two-thirds of which were female, with a total membership of 7,600. In Baltimore there were nine female organizations, out of a total of fifteen in the city, including the Daughters of Jerusalem, the Star in the East Association, and the Female Ebenezer Association.

Although most free blacks were poor, women, constituting the majority, were among the poorest of the poor in cities and towns. In most instances females headed households consisting of several children for whom they were the sole support. With meager incomes earned mostly from their jobs as washerwomen, hucksters, and house servants, they were barely able to make ends meet. Membership in the benevolent and secret societies provided comfort and monetary support during difficult times. In Philadelphia poor women were assessed twelve and a half cents per month, or one dollar quarterly, for the support of organizations such as the Dorcas Society, the United Daughters of Wilberforce, the Sisterly Union, and the African Female Union. Many women held multiple memberships in order to benefit from the different programs offered by these groups.

Women's church and community organizations that were formed for literary, self-improvement, and other purposes also dispensed charity. For example, during the brutal winters of 1859 and 1860, the Ladies' Sewing Circle of the Bethel AME Church in Baltimore provided food, clothing, and firewood for almost two hundred poor persons, and hosted dinners and public programs that drew hundreds of

Sojourner Truth, a woman of deep religious faith, was among the best-known black women in the antislavery and women's rights movements.

people. During the 1830s a female benevolent society was organized in Cincinnati with forty members, who concentrated their efforts on working to alleviate the suffering of the poor.

Literary and self-improvement societies were considered by some to be basic to the progress of African Americans. These organizations invariably focused on education, especially the improvement of one's mental capabilities. Education, or the creation of a literate society, was viewed by women as a religious priority. In the preamble to the Garrison Society, the female organizers stated that they felt a deep sense of accountability to God for the improvement they made in the talents God gave them, and thus were obligated to acquire an education. The society, named for abolitionist editor William Lloyd Garrison, purchased books; held weekly meetings devoted to the study of history, reading, writing, and "conversing upon the sufferings of our enslaved sisters"; and gave their attention to any plan that would aid them.

Church women's benevolent and reform activities included charity, social service, education, antislavery, and women's rights work. Close attention to the charters, constitutions, and statements of organizational goals of black women's associations reveals that they often claimed that their work was related to their Christian beliefs. For example, in 1832, a call for volunteers for the Colored Female Charitable Society in Boston attested to the organization's belief that "to visit the widow and fatherless in their afflictions, is a scriptural injunction that ought to be obeyed." The first women's antislavery society in the United States, the Female Antislavery Society of Salem, Massachusetts, was formed by black women in 1832, a year after the launching of the New England Antislavery Society, its parent organization. Between that date and 1865 numerous women's antislavery organizations were founded. Some societies were all white, others all black, and a few were integrated—or, rather, biracial—the most noted of which was the Philadelphia Antislavery Society, founded in 1838. Some societies were affiliated with churches, such as the Female Wesleyan Antislavery Society of the Methodist Episcopal Church in New York City; others, such as the Female Colored Union Society of Nantucket, Massachusetts, and the Union Antislavery Society of Rochester, were purely secular.

While a great deal of the reform work of African American women was centralized in their organizations, it is also important to consider the activism of individual women whose educational, antislavery, and other reform work grew out of and was sustained by their deep spirituality and Christian faith. Many of these women are well-known historical figures. However, the connection between their religious beliefs and activities and their social activism has not been fully explored. Anna Murray Douglass, the wife of Frederick Douglass and a member of the Methodist Episcopal Church, participated in the female antislavery societies in Boston and Lynn, Massachusetts. Eliza Ann Dixon Day, a founding member of the AME Zion Church in New York City, attended abolitionist meetings and supported their causes. She imbued her son William Howard Day with her religious ideals and a strong sense of responsibility to dedicate his life to the abolition of slavery. Harriet Tubman, inspired by biblical teachings, became the Moses of her people, leading slaves on the Underground Railroad to freedom. As a free person in Auburn, New York, Tubman united with the AME Zion Church. Frances Ellen Watkins Harper's religious beliefs and basic philosophy of life were grounded in the biblical teachings she received as a young girl growing up in the Bethel AME Church in Baltimore. In line with many white female abolitionists, during the 1850s she joined the Lutheran Church. However, Harper maintained a close relationship with the AME Church, which continued to support her by publishing her poetry, short stories, and novellas, and reporting on her reform activities. Sojourner Truth's deep religious faith undergirded her activities in the antislavery and women's rights movements. During her lifetime she was affiliated with several religious traditions, cults, and sects, but she was strongly influenced by the Methodist religious teachings she received during her formative years.

Free Black Women and the Cult of True Womanhood

BLACK WOMEN ABOLITIONISTS were exceptions. However, it was the success of black church women's fund-raising efforts that made possible the building of churches and community institutions, the support of abolitionist clergymen, black radical newspapers, and various causes. Frederick Douglass was one of the few black or white male leaders who did not sanction the notion of women being restricted to a separate sphere. On numerous occasions he asserted that women were the equals of men and should be treated as such. In 1853, Douglass criticized two white newspapers, the *Post* and the *Journal*, for continuous "ridicule and sarcasm at every public demonstration in which women took an active part."

Douglass believed that the performance of domestic responsibilities was no bar to women engaging in any public activity designed to improve the social, political, and economic conditions of women, racial and ethnic minorities, or the poor. When Katy Ferguson, the founder of the Sabbath school movement in America, died Douglass, consistent with his beliefs, praised her as a "true woman," a woman who had courageously given her life in public service to others less fortunate than she. Churches thrived on the labor of free women, many of whom were heads of households eking out a living at the most menial of jobs. Black women, including teachers, were the lowest paid of all groups in the society. At the same time they represented the foundation upon which community philanthropy was built. In spite of these economic realities, many black men—clergymen, editors, abolitionists, and community leaders—criticized black women, who they felt moved outside of their "sphere."

The Victorian notions of "true" womanhood and manhood, positing that females must accept four basic virtues supposedly inherent in women's nature—piety, purity, domesticity, and submissiveness—were embraced and freely extolled by some black men and women. The most essential element that undergirded all female virtues was religious piety or commitment. True womanhood required that young unmarried women be virgins (or remain pure) until marriage. Married women were expected to submit to their husbands and remain dependent. The special domain of "true women," where they were advised to fully exercise their virtues, was the home—their true "sphere." The role of a woman was to be a mother and a wife, to remain subordinate to all men, and to serve in support roles as enablers of men and their organizations, whereas true manhood required a man to be the major breadwinner and head of the household and to engage in public activities. Men were expected to be aggressive, assertive, and decisive, to exhibit power and authority, and to appear strong. True men did not engage in so-called "women's activities."

Though the ideology of true womanhood and manhood was more suited to elite white women and men, it was the standard to which African Americans and poor whites, particularly women, were held. Most black men fell outside of the definition of true manhood, since they often lacked the resources to either support or protect their women. For all intents and purposes true womanhood was meaningless to working black women, both wage earners and professionals, whose income was as necessary as their husbands' to support a household. And, of course, most working black women were not married. For white Americans, no black woman could ever achieve true womanhood. Slavery had sullied the black woman's image; she was perceived as sexually promiscuous and did not fit the image of a woman. Hard labor rendered many black women enslaved and free, physically powerful. Taken as a whole, black women appeared buxom and brawny, capable of doing men's work. In essence, black women were considered unsexed.

For free black elites, a very small but highly visible and vocal part of antebellum black society, it was important that women reclaim their virtue and change their image. Education, religion, chastity, community service, and efficiency in the home were avenues to redemption, for a virtuous woman was an asset to her family and community. However, a virtuous woman must remain modest, stay in the background, never criticize her husband or other men, and not engage in what was considered male activity. Women preachers, abolitionists, and public speakers were viewed as functioning outside of their sphere. If a husband went astray or children did not turn out well, it was the woman's fault. Men could travel and have careers that took them away from home, but women were not expected to do so. In speeches and sermons, most black male leaders and some women asserted the ideology of true womanhood. Though they recognized the social and cultural reality of what it meant to be black in America and that the ideology bore no relationship to the lives of most African Americans they used it as a rhetorical strategy to reinforce moral values and define acceptable gender conventions. Moreover, placing emphasis on the ideology of true womanhood symbolized a public effort on the part of the black middle-class leadership to gain credibility among white secular and religious leaders by aligning the African American community with what were considered American cultural values. For black men it was also a way of expressing their masculinity and support for patriarchy.

At least twenty years before abolitionist Mary Ann Shadd Cary and Frances Harper, Maria W. Stewart broke the mold and openly challenged the notion that women should function in supportive domestic roles and eschew public activities considered more appropriate for male leaders. Born free in Hartford, Connecticut, in 1803, Maria grew up in Boston and attended Rev. Thomas Paul's African Baptist Church. Orphaned at the age of five, Maria was bound out in a minister's family, where she learned the values of piety and virtue but received little educational instruction. At the age of fifteen she left that family and lived independently for almost a decade. During that time, she attended several Sabbath schools, where she immersed herself in the Bible and began to formulate her distinct views about race, slavery, and religion. Her marriage to James Stewart in 1826 and his subsequent death in 1829 changed her life in significant ways. As a result of two unscrupulous white male financial executors, whom her husband had named to administer his will, she was defrauded out of her inheritance.

As a woman who had received only six weeks of formal schooling, Maria Stewart recognized that her plight was related to her lack of education and her essential ignorance. Accepting the challenges of widowhood, Stewart decided that it was her Christian responsibility to inform women about the need to obtain education and economic power. In 1831, prior to launching a public speaking tour (1832–33), she published a small pamphlet, *Religion and the Pure Principles of Morality, the Sure Foundation on Which We Must Build.* In 1832, at the beginning of her public speaking career, Stewart also published *Meditations from the Pen of Mrs. Maria W. Stewart.* Unable to "pen her own thoughts," Stewart dictated every word of this book to a ten-year-old girl, who carefully wrote down Stewart's thoughts. Stewart was the first American woman to deliver a public speech. She delivered four lectures, all of which were published by William Lloyd Garrison in the *Liberator.*

Maria Stewart's commitment to racial and gender equality, particularly her public speaking, challenged contemporary notions of acceptable behavior for women. In the 1830s public speaking was viewed as an activity engaged in by individuals, like male clergy and political leaders, who were acknowledged as authoritative leaders in the community. Ministers condemned public speaking as a form of activism unsuitable for "respectable" women, and one that was in violation of the Pauline doctrine—"Let the women keep silent in the church." Mounting the rostrum in September 1832 to deliver her first public lecture, Stewart spoke to the members of the Afric-American Female Intelligence Society. Titling her message "Daughters of Africa, Awake! Arise! Distinguish yourselves," she relied on the Bible to reinforce her message. The first three speeches were noncontroversial and welcomed by women and men. However, at the fourth, delivered in 1833 at the Boston African Masonic Hall, she was greeted by an audience of black men who jeered and threw rotten tomatoes at her. In the aftermath of this event, Stewart was criticized and ostracized, not just because she had delivered a public speech, but because she had ventured into forbidden territory: she publicly criticized black men for their failure to adhere to "basic Christian principles of thrift, sobriety, and hard work."

Education and the Road to Freedom

DURING THE ANTEBELLUM ERA the prevailing view was that the highest standard of education was a priority for white males but not for women and African Americans. Maria Stewart recognized the fallacy inherent in this belief, and how detrimental it was to African American women and men. All women were considered inferior, and needed to be educated only for those roles they were expected to assume. However, free blacks understood that education was essential to the growth and success of the black community. The question was, who should be educated, and for what purpose? There was general agreement that what was needed was a literate community whose members could successfully compete in the job market and move the race from a state of poverty to a level of prosperity.

Some free blacks believed that education and the acquisition of wealth would solve some of the race problems, and that education and self-improvement would make African Americans more acceptable to white Americans. It was important to educate men and women, but for different purposes. Women needed to be educated to provide their children with the rudiments of learning and to manage their households. However, there was no need to teach women math, science, Latin, and other subjects deemed more suitable for men. Male leaders exhibited some degree of ambivalence in their attitudes toward educating women. On the one hand, they knew from experience that in most cases all members of an African American household needed to work to ensure a basic standard of living. Given the limited job opportunities available to black men, and the low wages they received, it was impossible for many men to support their families. At the same time, there was the sense that their manhood was at stake if they could not live up to the credo of what a man is and ought to be. Unfortunately, some free black men approved of Victorian gender roles and corresponding notions about "true" womanhood and manhood, but they lacked the means to meet the standards for achieving that goal.

Though many black men faced the reality that their women had to work, and that education was important to the development of the family and community, they did not relinquish the goal of being so-called true men. Thus, women could be educated as long as they did not compete for jobs that black men should have. In situations where there was a choice between a man and a woman, the man should be hired. Women could teach, but men should supervise and head up educational institutions. In rare cases, the wife was the more prominent figure. Mary Ann Shadd Cary's marriage and career were unusual by nineteenth-century standards. As the newspaper business manager and editor of the *Provincial Freeman*, she wrote under an assumed name, to avoid criticism for functioning outside of a woman's sphere. As the husband of Mary Ann Shadd, Thomas Cary was rare indeed. By any standards, the Carys' marriage was exceptional. Following her marriage, at the age of thirty-three, Mary Ann Shadd continued to travel and work as a newspaper publisher and emigration activist while her husband stayed at home and tended his barber and bathhouse businesses.

In the African American community, education was dispensed in many places and in various forms. During the late eighteenth and early nineteenth century Sunday schools were designed to teach literacy and moral behavior to children. African Americans' hunger for literacy often related to their interest in reading the Bible. Free black leaders stressed the relationship between literacy and community advancement. The first Sabbath, or Sunday, school was established in 1793 by Katy Ferguson, a former slave in New York who had purchased her freedom. Born in 1774 to an enslaved woman from Virginia who was

Katy Ferguson, a former slave and member of the Presbyterian Church, established the first Sabbath, or Sunday school in New York City, 1793.

taken by ship to New York, Katy Williams was orphaned at the age of four when her mother was sold to another master. Katy remembered that her mother had taught her the scriptures, which she memorized and recited by rote. Katy recalled, "[B]efore they tore me asunder, she kneeled down, laid her hand upon my head, and gave me to God." Of her own volition, at around ten or eleven years of age, Katy chose to attend the Old Scotch Presbyterian Church on Cedar Street in New York City. She took it upon herself to visit the pastor's home and discuss the state of her "soul." During her visit with Rev. Dr. John M. Mason, a liberal and caring minister, she experienced conversion. Soon after, Katy decided to join the church. It appears that she was the first African American to attend and profess an interest in affiliating with the church. Many church members protested having a black person kneel at the communion table, but Rev. Mason descended from his pulpit, walked to the pew where Katy sat, took her by the hand, and led her forward to communion. He preached, "For by one Spirit are we all baptized into one body, whether we be Jews or Gentiles, whether we be bond or free; we have all been made to drink into one Spirit."

Katy was permitted by her master to attend church services, but she was not taught to read or write. However, her baking and catering skills were considered exceptional. A contemporary recalled, "[H]er occupation was the making of excellent cake such as was found in the pantries of the Old Dutch housewives of New York, whose daughters alone were able to compete with her skill." In 1792, at the age of eighteen, with the help of friends, she purchased her freedom. Shortly afterward, she married and became known as Katy Ferguson. Following the death of her husband and two children, she took an interest in the many poor black and white children who lived in her neighborhood. Katy lived at 52 Warren Street, one of the side streets leading to Broadway. Gathering up a number of poor orphans, almost half of whom were white, she opened an integrated Sunday school in her home. She taught the children the scriptures and, where possible, found homes for them. The novelty of a former slave woman, who could neither read nor write, opening a Sunday school, and her success in teaching white and black children how to read and write and placing them in good homes, was widely reported. Although Katy was illiterate, she memorized sections of the Bible and had volunteers teach the children how to read and write. Recognizing the importance of Ferguson's work and the need to expand it, Rev. Mason, at the time serving as pastor of the Murray Street Church, invited her to move the school to the basement of his church. Mason employed assistants to teach secular courses, and Ferguson continued to teach the scriptures. For forty years, she directed the education and social services program at the Murray Street Sabbath School.

Sunday schools were formed in many of the early all-black churches established by Methodists at the beginning of the nineteenth century. These schools were the chief avenues for transmitting knowledge of the Bible and teaching reading and writing. At first there was little difference between the day schools and the Sunday schools. Like the day schools, most Sunday schools taught both adults and children to read and write. For the masses of free blacks, the Sunday school provided the only opportunity for literacy. A few urban churches organized day schools and developed curriculums modeled after those taught in the public schools and private academies. For example, in 1802, Baltimore's first Sabbath school, the African Academy, was opened by black Methodists on Sharp Street. The success of this school encouraged other churches to hold classes, staffed by black teachers and for black students of all ages. In the absence of public schools that admitted African Americans, Baltimore's black churches provided most of the educational opportunities for the city's black population.

The early Sunday schools admitted females, but the teachers were predominantly male. By 1850 there was a noticeable shift in this trend. In 1859, among eleven AME churches in the Baltimore area there were 158 teachers, eighty-two of whom were women. Among the most noted educational institutions in Baltimore was the St. Francis Academy, established by the Oblate Sisters of Providence, the first order of black nuns. Founded in 1829, the Oblate Sisters order was responsible for conducting schools for black girls and providing for orphans. In 1828 in Alexandria, Virginia, there were four Sabbath schools for black children: the African Sabbath School, consisting of eighty-five boys and one hundred girls; and schools operated by the Baptist, Presbyterian, and African Methodist Episcopal churches. Jane Crouch began teaching in Alexandria in 1856 "when the colored people were not allowed to teach." She said, "I was a free woman myself, and I taught the free colored people at night; because I couldn't have taught if it had been found out."

Ladies Aid Societies and the Civil War

By 1860 free black women had created a network of religious and secular organizations to serve the needs of the black community. They were firmly ensconced as the official fund-raisers of the race. Quietly developing leadership and managerial skills, conscientiously improving themselves mentally and physically, and filling the coffers of their organizational treasuries, they created model organizations—bases of power from which they confidently exercised influence within the church and society. The outbreak of the Civil War in April 1861 required fortitude and sacrifice on all sides. Northern and southern women, blacks and whites, were eager to participate in the war effort, albeit for different reasons. Ladies aid societies and sewing circles that had previously served as fund-raising, benevolent, and relief associations, usually connected to a local church, focused their beneficence on the needs of the soldiers. Committees and soldiers aid organizations were formed to raise funds to support the volunteer regiments—to sew uniforms and flags for the soldiers, and to solicit community help in assembling food, clothing, and medical supplies needed by the troops.

Black Civil War volunteers, initially rejected by the Union Army, by 1863 were admitted into the service and organized into "colored" regiments under white leadership. The United States Sanitary Commission, established in 1861, developed a coalition of several thousand northern ladies aid societies for the purpose of organizing relief services for soldiers and their families, including widows of soldiers killed in war. However, the relief work of the commission focused almost exclusively on the needs of white regiments. The African American community, with a long tradition of self-help, organized an extensive network of relief work aimed at aiding black soldiers and their families as well as the hundreds of dislocated slaves. In Philadelphia, women organized the Ladies Sanitary Commission of the St. Thomas Episcopal Church, the only African American women's auxiliary to the United States Sanitary Commission. In February 1865 this organization sponsored a fair at Concert Hall that netted $1,226.75. The Episcopal women sent boxes of clothing and food to soldiers in General Sherman's army, and money and other goods to African American women's organizations in Alexandria, Virginia, affiliated with the Toussaint L'Overture General Hospital, which operated out of a local black church. This hospital apparently housed black soldiers. Camp William Penn in Chelton Hills, Pennsylvania, also operated a hospital that aided sick and injured soldiers. A cadre of African American women volunteers, led by a Mrs. Mears, provided assistance in taking care of the needs of sick soldiers, and organized a Sunday school where they taught black soldiers reading and writing on two nights of the week and on Sundays.

Relief work among African Americans involved more than just assembling materials and supplies for the soldiers in the field and aiding widows and children. The issuance of the Emancipation Proclamation by President Abraham Lincoln in 1863 encouraged many slaves to leave the plantations and seek freedom and protection with the advancing Union Army. Technically, the slaves who flocked to the Union Army camps were fugitives, and for political reasons the federal government designated fugitives as contraband of war. Fugitives flowed into the Union Army camps and into the border-state cities sick, ragged, hungry, and uneducated, presenting a problem of major proportions. The care and disposition of these homeless and starving African Americans spurred the development of relief societies

Group of "contrabands" at Cumberland Landing, Virginia, during the Civil War

throughout the North and West. The Union Army's first encounters and initial military occupation were in the South, along the Atlantic coast. The first response for relief or aid came from New York City, Washington, Philadelphia, Boston, and Baltimore. Between 1862 and 1864, some of the relief work, particularly educational efforts, was organized by white societies, but the National Freedmen's Relief Association of Washington, D.C., was started by African Americans.

Free blacks, constituting almost 500,000 persons in 1860, responded to the war efforts by organizing aid for African Americans and, in some cases, working with white organizations. For the most part, relief organizations were segregated. During the early part of 1862, the District of Columbia Colored Constitutional Relief Association was one of the first black organizations founded for the care of the contraband. The National Freedmen's Relief Association of Washington was established later that year. In 1864, Congress incorporated the National Association for the Relief of Destitute Colored Women and Children. Elizabeth Keckley, formerly a seamstress for Mary Todd Lincoln, was elected president of the Contraband Relief Association and empowered to travel for the purpose of collecting funds for the organization. While black men, particularly ministers, supported and articulated the need for this work, the job of collecting money, assembling materials, and finding housing for the contraband was mostly performed by church women community leaders.

In cities throughout the Northeast and Midwest, women responded to the need to develop relief services for African Americans. In Virginia, the First Female Contraband Aid Society of Alexandria was formed in February 1863. Black religionists recognized the relief efforts as extensions of the traditional fund-raising and service work of church women's societies. Sponsoring festivals, picnics, and bake sales and organizing community collections of materials and supplies, women fulfilled their goal to "furnish aid and comfort to the sick, aged and otherwise infirm among the so-called 'contraband.' " In Chicago, during the same year, the Colored Ladies Freedmen's Aid Society sponsored subscription lectures given by well-known black and white antislavery activists. Monies collected were sent south to alleviate suffering among the destitute. In 1864, in Kentucky, the Louisville Soldiers' Aid Society, numbering more than one hundred persons, organized to provide aid and services for more than one hundred wounded black soldiers in segregated wards at the local hospital. A white nurse, commenting upon their efforts, observed, "[T]he Ladies Colored Soldiers' Aid Society of Louisville was doing them more real good than the general government itself was doing them." The Louisville Soldiers' Aid Society also made presentations of "costly" American flags to different regiments of colored soldiers. Similar work was performed by female organizations in Kansas, Connecticut, Tennessee, Maryland, Ohio, New York, Pennsylvania, and the District of Columbia.

In 1865, at the end of the Civil War, an extensive and established pattern of relief work was organized by African Americans, especially women and their religious associations. The experience of caring and providing for the fugitives and soldiers would be useful as African Americans throughout the country sought ways to socialize and educate former slaves whose sole life experience had been the plantation. The Thirteenth Amendment, ratified in 1865, legally abolished slavery in the United States. As of that date, almost four million slaves were set free. Their needs were phenomenal. As the war came to a close, the South was all but devastated; white and black alike were displaced, in need of food and clothing and without organized civil authority. Many African Americans wandered on foot from village, town, and city in search of family members who had been sold as slaves. In March 1865, the government responded to this chaos by establishing the Bureau of Refugees, Freedmen and Abandoned Lands, known as the Freedmen's Bureau. A great deal of the massive work of relief, education, and community development that occurred was organized by African American churches and supported by a powerful base of black church women who raised the funds to support ministers and bishops, female teachers, and others who went to the South to organize churches, Sabbath schools, and day schools and provide basic services for the former slaves. The Civil War relief effort of women, initiated at the local level and expanded beyond mostly northern local congregations and associations, was key to women's press for roles in the church polity, and important to the postwar expansion of women's activism.

CHAPTER 2

"Taxation Without Representation"

Religious Leadership

Freedom came, and with it came the opportunity for planting the church and sustaining the school, and here the colored woman found room for the work of her hands and the love of her heart. . . . In labors spiritual and temporal she has proved the equal of her brethren. She has bought one-half the bricks in all our churches and offered well nigh one-half the prayers.

Frances Ellen Watkins Harper (1877)

If we consider of whom our Church is composed, we may be a little more charitable. I feel safe in saying that two-thirds of the present church membership are women, and that if the Dollar Money, or "taxation" of the Church as some call it, was collected only from the male members, the Church treasury would be decreased in a year to fully three-fourths of its present income. But as it is, the law accepts men and women both on equal basis, and by so doing implies an equal right to representation in that part of the Church that the Dollar Money supports.

Alice Felts (1886)

They are not ministers, not class leaders, not stewards, not superintendents of Sunday schools—in a word, not anything where religious work is to be done—but everything where money is to be raised to be managed by others.

Theophilus Gould Steward (1890)

WHETHER SLAVE OR FREE, black women and men believed that the Civil War was being fought over slavery, and that victory for the Union forces would mean freedom for all African Americans. For the enslaved, it would be a bittersweet victory filled with poverty and struggle and undergirded by a burning desire for knowledge and a belief that God had answered their prayers. The year 1865 marked the end of the Civil War and the beginning of a new era for

African Americans and for the nation. Roughly four million southern blacks gained their freedom and began life anew in a society determined to harness their labor and keep them in a state of perpetual servitude. However, freedom meant that they had choices and to some extent could determine their own destiny. Among the various groups offering aid and critical support to southern blacks during Reconstruction was the church.

There were more than 480,000 free blacks in the United States in 1860. Largely concentrated in the Northeast, they also lived in towns and cities in the South and Midwest. They had built churches, established schools, launched businesses, published newspapers and other literature, and created a network of literary and charitable organizations to accommodate their needs. Thirty years after emancipation, the black population, estimated at roughly nine to ten million, had more than doubled, and at least 95 percent of that number resided in the South. Thus, the black churches of the South were an important factor in the lives of the majority of African Americans. By the late 1890s more than half of all blacks were Baptist. Second in numbers were the Methodists. Almost a decade later, with an estimated total of 4.5 million African Americans enrolled as church members, and at least three million adherents, organized religion was a factor in the lives of more than two-thirds of the entire black population.

After the war, as black men sought an equal social, political, and economic status with white men, they fully asserted what they called their "manhood rights." Fashioning new identities as citizens meant defining the meaning of manhood and masculinity in relationship to their new status as citizens and systematically attacking the long-standing assaults on black male manhood. Defining the meaning of manhood was not an easy process. The term "manhood" was used as a modifier to specify the model or type rights they sought—those available to adult males as opposed to females. Males enjoyed privileges that were off limits to females: in the United States, patriarchy was accepted as a manhood right, and the basic tenet of patriarchy was the belief in the superiority or dominance of males over females. Men were strong and courageous—and defined as warriors and protectors. A much deeper and perhaps more painful longing permeated black male psyches: a desire to be men in the fullest sense and to be able to protect their wives, daughters, sisters, and mothers from the vicious cycle of physical and sexual abuses that had dominated the lives of generations of enslaved Africans in America. It was a yearning propelled by years of suppressed anger, fears of violence, and, in some instances, a desire for retribution.

The Pennsylvania Equal Rights Association in its 1864 "Declaration of Wrongs and Rights" unequivocally stated the views of most black men regarding their manhood rights.

> As a people, we have been denied the ownership of our bodies, our wives, hopes, children and the products of our own labor, we have been compelled, under pain of death to submit to wrongs deeper and darker than the earth ever witnessed in the case of any other people; we have been forced to silence and inaction, in full presence of the infernal spectacle of our sons groaning under the lash, our daughters ravished, our wives violated and our firesides desolated, while we ourselves have been led to the shambles and there sold like beasts of the field. . . . These are our wrongs—these a portion of what we deem to be our rights as *men*, . . . to realize and attain these rights and their practical recognition is our purpose.

Black men seeking equality with white men sought to reinforce the already established patterns of male dominance that had existed among free blacks in the church, the family, the benevolent and secret society, and the black society at large. The slave community, of necessity, supported communal values and promoted the notion that black men and women were equal partners in the struggle for freedom. For the enslaved it was more an issue of "us against them" than women's rights versus men's rights. It was a matter of *our* rights, and freedom for the race. Yet there was always a clear recognition of the other—the world of white people where a premium was placed on patriarchal definitions of manhood, and womanhood was said to be "exalted."

Throughout American history, women have been ambivalent and have resisted black men's claims of manhood rights and rejected community and church hierarchies structured by gender. They challenged forms of masculinity that privileged men and devalued women, and confronted church laws that molded the very definition of a religious masculinity. Recognition of the destructive nature of white proscription of black masculinity and the limited employment and leadership opportunities available to black men contributed to the partial acquiescence of many black women to intraracial gender discrimination and the acceptance of some of the patriarchal norms and expectations prevalent among whites. However, beginning in the late nineteenth century, a significant number of women asserted their rights as American citizens and members of the internal black body politic and fought for racial and gender equality in all areas of American life and culture. Fighting for their rights as women did not interfere, they insisted, with their belief in the solidarity of the race in the face of white racism. Rather, they developed an internal and external agenda—one predicated on their survival as women, and the other related to their survival as persons of African descent.

Geographical and denominational differences influenced the ways in which black women claimed their rights. This was especially true among the various Baptist and Methodist denominations. Historically, the majority of black Baptists have resided in the South. Comprised mainly of the formerly enslaved, the Baptist Church during its early history appealed mostly to poor and working-class blacks. Whereas in the North the majority of black Baptist churches maintained membership in white associations, in the South black Baptists organized separate associations and state conventions immediately after the war. The founding of the National Baptist Convention in 1895 brought together northern and southern Baptists, and unified most of the disparate associations and conventions under one banner. With the exception of the Colored Methodist Episcopal Church, which was organized in 1870 in the South, independent black Methodist denominations such as the African Methodist Episcopal and African Methodist Episcopal Zion churches were formally organized by free blacks in the early nineteenth century, and concentrated mainly in the North and Midwest. After the war, AME and AME Zion churches spread rapidly in the South, but the Baptist Church continued to serve as the dominant religion for African Americans. Thus, the worldview and concerns of the majority of southern black women, conditioned by the experience of slavery, often differed from those of northern and midwestern women, who had lived lives mostly as free persons.

Because of their experiences and the opportunities available to them as free black men and women, northern and western blacks tended to be better educated. Many had received a rudimentary education in the Sabbath schools and various educational establishments developed by blacks, as well as other public and private institutions of learning. Some few had earned higher degrees. Emancipation brought recently freed slaves and northern blacks together, revealing their cultural differences and educational disparities. Northern black and white missionaries were instrumental in forming freedmen and freedwomen into Methodist, Baptist, and other churches. Some of the missionaries were former fugitives who viewed slave culture, speech, and behavior as "defective." Northern blacks residing in the South often demonstrated their class bias and conflicted with the uneducated former slave preachers in their efforts to assume leadership in the new organizations. Similarly, class conflicts also arose among women in the national Methodist missionary associations and the Baptist conventions.

A relatively small percentage of the black population affiliated with the Congregational, Episcopal, Presbyterian, Roman Catholic, Methodist Protestant, Disciples of Christ, Lutheran, Spiritual, and Holiness religious traditions in the nineteenth century. The dominant groups in the period debates were Methodist and Baptist. This would be the case for well into the twentieth century.

Though the black Methodist denominations collectively constituted the largest group during the early nineteenth century, by 1900 the National Baptist Convention, comprised the largest number of black Christians in the United States. In 1915 the NBC, Inc., split into two denominations: the National Baptist Convention of the United States of America, Inc., and the National Baptist Convention of America (Unincorporated). In 1961 the Progressive National Baptist Convention, Inc., an offshoot of the NBC-USA, was founded. The largest and most prominent black Baptist denomination in the twentieth century was the NBC-USA. In the early twentieth century, Pentecostal and Holiness churches, like the Baptist Church, appealed mostly to poor and working-class blacks. At the end of the twentieth century, the Church of God in Christ had become the foremost black Pentecostal tradition in the United States.

Gender and Postbellum Religious Leadership

W. E. B. Du Bois argued that neither before nor after the Civil War was there "to any extent any real home life for the Negro." He demonstrated how the church literally usurped the place of the home and became the social center of black life and the place where most of the community's interests were concentrated. According to Du Bois, the church was "all but supreme and absolute in the development of the race. It became the great agency in the progress of our people because it was the only institution over which we had control." He claimed that practically all of the business of the black community originated in the church, and that it served as a "public forum" for debating and developing strategy to deal with the social and political issues that confronted African Americans.

Since black women comprised the bulk of the black church population—representing anywhere from 65 to 90 percent of its members—they were a critical force in its development and support, and played a major role in the formation of public opinion. Nannie Burroughs, the corresponding secretary of the Woman's Convention, Auxiliary to the National Baptist Convention, concurred with Du Bois, and asserted the preeminence of black women in black church and community development. In 1915 Burroughs proclaimed, "The Negro Church means the Negro woman. Without her, the race could not properly support five hundred churches in the whole world. Today they have 40,000 churches in the United States. . . . She carries the burdens of the Church, and of the school and bears a great deal more than her economic share in the home."

There was little dispute between black women and men about the importance of the church in the black community, but they disagreed significantly about women's religious rights, and what leadership roles women should assume. The most useful source both for defending and rejecting women's bid for equality in the polity was the Bible. Within its pages, scriptural precedents were found to clarify and validate competing claims. Men and women debated the propriety of women's leadership and authority in churches. Prominent male clergy typically developed interpretations of scripture defining women's inferiority, and these were adopted, adapted, and articulated by rank-and-file ministers. In this manner certain beliefs were acknowledged and widely accepted, and over time they became the dominant ideology. A striking example of this is found in the literal interpretation applied to the use of the term "man" in Genesis 1:27–31. Often referred to as the story of creation, this scripture asserts that Eve was created from Adam's rib.

The creation story and the apostle Paul's admonitions that "Women should be silent in the churches"(1 Cor. 14:34) and "I do not permit a woman to teach or have authority over a man" (1 Tim. 2:12) became the standard biblical references for establishing what role or roles women should play in the church and society. Male clergy often referred to these texts "to assert the inferiority of women and to reinforce traditional role expectations." Among the few leaders to use the biblical story of creation to assert women's superiority, AME Bishop Henry McNeal Turner argued in 1894, "[A]s God made woman after he made man, He improved upon her, and has better material in her make-up." In 1899 AME Zion Bishop James Walker Hood asserted neither woman's inferiority nor superiority. Rather, he argued, the creation story "seems to impress us with the idea that the intention was to set them forth as equals. They [Adam and Eve] are together instructed as to their duty, and together given universal dominion. There is no hint that the woman was at all inferior to the man."

In 1869 Rev. Morris Hamilton, in an address at the Fleet Street AME Church in New York City, spoke about "Woman's Agency in Religion." Hamilton noted that "while men boast of themselves, how seldom do we hear of women." Citing the women of the New Testament, Hamilton spoke of Deborah as a prophetess and Mary as the mother of Christ and claimed that women were with Christ through all his labors on earth. "The last at the cross, the first at the sepulcher! The first missionaries to proclaim the glorious news of the resurrection! What are we taught by these examples? We are taught that God has given woman a work to do." Hamilton credited AME women as "co-workers with the men of God in the cause of humanity" for their support of Richard Allen during the days when he protested racial segregation and discrimination in the Methodist Church. Though he was not among those who argued women's inferiority, Hamilton perceived of women's church work as mainly supportive. Hamilton is an example of how male clergy often used the Bible to assert that women played important roles, while simultaneously reinforcing the Victorian notion that as moral women and mothers they had a duty to serve the church and community as well as their families. The emphasis was on service, not leadership or equality. The assumption was that women served, but men led.

To counteract and challenge sexism and gender discrimination, Protestant women of all classes turned to the Bible to argue for their rights. While the Bible was utilized by most blacks to resist racism, women also espoused its doctrines to convey their discontent with popular conceptions regarding the role and place of women. They challenged notions about their supposed inferiority and weakness, emphasizing the historical role of biblical women and the importance of black women's leadership in charitable philanthropic work for the advancement of the race as a whole. Bible women such as Dorcas, Miriam, Deborah, Ruth, Esther, Mary, and Martha were often cited to demonstrate the varied leadership roles of women and their historical agency in religion. Through the use of biblical precedents, black women of all ages, classes, educational backgrounds, and religious persuasions developed a carefully honed feminist theology that they liberally used in all aspects of their lives.

Ophelia McIntosh, of Savannah, Georgia, in an address before the District Grand Lodge of the Grand United Order of Odd Fellows and the Household of Ruth in 1898, observed that the Odd Fellows zealously proclaimed that the success they enjoyed in their philanthropic endeavors resulted from "the mystic ties of friendship, love and truth" that male members shared. Alerting the men to the importance of the work performed by the Household of Ruth, an auxiliary to the order, McIntosh proclaimed,

> Sisters of Ruth, we are not as some think or conjecture, a second department of this grand order but we are the first link of odd-fellowship, and if we are termed weaker vessels allow me to say without fear of contradiction that the weakest link of any chain is the measure of its strength and hence its strength, and in a like manner the department of Ruth is the measure of and strength of odd-fellowship. Show me the community where there are no mothers, no daughters, no sisters of Ruth, and I'll show you a community where there are no brother Odd-Fellows.

McIntosh explained that the Household of Ruth was founded on the "gem of friendship" as illustrated in the relationship between the biblical character Ruth and her mother-in-law, Naomi (Luke 3). McIntosh demonstrated that, like Ruth, the Household of Ruth's service to the Odd Fellows was prompted by a spirit of ancestral love and understanding—the ties that bound men and women of African descent together. However, she insisted that the Household of Ruth was the power behind the throne, for " 'the hand that rocks the cradle rules the world.' "

The most frequently cited biblical text used by women to argue against racial and gender inequality was "There is neither Jew nor Greek, there is neither bond nor free, there is neither male nor female, for ye are all one in Christ Jesus" (Gal. 3:28). Countering white racism and black sexism, African American women embraced and converted the ideology of true womanhood to serve as a unique and subtle form of resistance. This ideology was skillfully woven into a distinctive argument that was often rendered through the use of biblical text, especially "She Hath Done What She Could," which became the mantra of religious women. By the late 1880s this text was being evoked in many settings and formed part of a broader discourse related to the struggle of women against sexism. However, in the interim period immediately after the Civil War and before the resounding debates over women's ordination, African American women defended black women's virtue and posited their value and worth. They wrote articles and delivered talks on "Female Influence," "The Influence of Woman on the Christian World," and other topics discussing "The Place of Woman" in religion, the church, and society. Though the titles might differ, the essential question was, What did God intend for women to do?

Since the majority of male clergy and other leading figures invariably embraced the cult of true womanhood defining separate spheres of activity for men and women, ministers often discerned women's role in terms of domesticity and spoke mostly about what God *did not* intend for women to do. Church women's responses included an interpretation of women's rights and duties and an argument for women's training and education. Implicit in the discourse was the notion that women's influence, though largely unrecognized, was extensive, pervasive, and powerful. Within the question of rights, women subtly translated a pervasive discourse on female duty and influence into one on women's rights and power. Their arguments did not go unnoticed by male leaders of the time. Rather, black men and women engaged in continuous discourse about male and female roles.

Clergymen agreed with Rev. Morgan Dix, a popular white New York divine, who during the height of the debates about women's ordination in the 1880s suggested that the "question about the place and work of a woman in the world is really a question about her place and work in her home and in society." For him, female domesticity was clearly defined in Genesis 2:21–23 and the story about creation. Thus, the place of a woman was in the home, and the purpose of education was to prepare a woman "for her duties in her home." Rev. Dix's views reinforced the arguments of male clergy who favored the education of women. He asserted that the destiny of the church and its ministry depended "largely upon the intellectual and moral training of females," including "female companions as wives" of ministers. Relying on the Bible, ministers overwhelmingly claimed that women were required by God to play supportive, not leading roles. In their writings and sermons, clergymen often posited that the role of women was chiefly as "helpmeets" to their husbands and not as leaders of men.

AME minister Rev. James H. A. Johnson explained that the destiny of nations and "great men" is dependent on women who are acknowledged as the "power behind the throne." He argued that woman is "endowed with pre-eminent talent as an indoor agent," and "has [the] patience and perseverance" to direct the "thinking, reasoning and speaking of the young," illuminate home life, extend the influence of the church, and improve the condition of the world. Therefore, woman stands as a "striking contrast [to] man, the outdoor agent, [who is] made for sterner work. . . . Being endowed for the admiration of man, [woman] is debarred from those pursuits which are derogatory to her gentleness and grace." Johnson cited Edmonia Lewis, a black female sculptor, as an example of a woman who assumed her proper role as an "indoor agent." He claimed that Lewis, "in her studio, gently chiseling the dead marble block into a living statue bringing forth Cleopatra in superbness from her dusty crypt—is an object worthy of the admiration of kings; but let her, with pick, crowbar and drill, proceed to the quarry, and contend with the towering, massive rock that looks defiantly at a thousand giants, and she would be deplored." Johnson concluded that women's struggles for equality and pursuit of the "male" professions were "efforts on her part to masculinize herself," which would tend to "lessen her modesty and damage her standing as a woman." The argument that a woman could be unsexed if she pressed for equality with men, or pursued the so-called "masculine" professions of law, medicine, and the ministry, was introduced by male leaders in the late nineteenth century and widely used in the early twentieth century as more women became educated, were licensed and ordained, and entered the professions.

Ministers such as Dix and Johnson adhered to the true womanhood concept of what a woman should be and do—an idea alien to the status and condition of most black women, the majority of whom were employed as domestic servants and washerwomen. Though they clearly recognized the economic plight of the majority of African Americans, and the fact that most black women could not aspire to true womanhood, Dix and Johnson's concern was with middle- and upper-class women who were clamoring for equality with men—the "woman who claims admission to every position occupied by man." These were the women who posed a direct threat to the male elite, in that their rise in the professions alerted other women to the possibilities of their advancing and pursuing varied professions and leadership positions, including, male ministers feared, those of clergy and bishop.

Gertrude Bustill Mossell, journalist, author, and feminist who argued
for women's rights in the AME Church

Secular discourse about suffrage and women's rights served as a
context for religious debates. In writing about what he perceived as
"Woman's Exalted Status," Johnson responded to AME women such
as Gertrude Bustill Mossell, the intrepid journalist, and Alice Felts and
Katie Campbell, outspoken religious and secular activists who argued
for women's rights and allied with organizations such as the Woman's
Christian Temperance Union and the National Association of Colored
Women to promote suffrage and equal rights for women. In an 1886
article in the *New York Freeman*, Mossell celebrated women who had
succeeded in entering male-dominated fields. She described Millie
Ringgold of Yogo, Montana, as an African American woman who had
developed "quite a reputation as a prospector, hotelier, and owner of
one of the richest silver mines in the West. She spends most of her time
in the mountains, and handles the pick and shovel with as much vigor
and dexterity as a man. . . . By economy and close attention to business
she has come into possession of some very valuable properties." By
Johnson's definition, Ringgold had entered a "masculine" profession
and in doing so had sullied her reputation as a woman.

Without any compunction or fear of retribution, Alice Felts challenged the views of clergy and bishops. In 1886 she was in the vanguard of those AME women who spoke in defense of black women's
right to equal treatment in the church. The challenges to male clergy's
authority hurled by Felts and other AME women leaders during the

1880s were influenced in part by the strong opposition of male clergy to the organizing of women's missionary societies and the woman's suffrage debates. Though Campbell, as the daughter of a bishop, was also related to the clergy, Felts appears to be the first AME minister's wife to ask for "the full recognition of women." In 1891 Felts confessed, "I have long been an advocate of women's rights in the church." She challenged the position of Jabez Campbell and other clergy who spoke against women's rights and ordination. During the late 1880s, while living in New England, Felts's interest in politics was stimulated by her exposure to the speeches and abolitionist writings of William Lloyd Garrison, Mary Livermore, and other members of the National and American Woman Suffrage Associations. Citing their "sound arguments," Felts stressed that the church called for universal suffrage, "at first to empower woman to work and teach and pray; . . . the state demands it on account of universal liberty for all, both white and black. . . . If the white voters want to overpower the colored by the enfranchise[ment of] women, where will the colored women be but by the side of their brothers to swell the colored vote in proportion?" She assured her AME brothers that, similar to the King's Daughters, "we will stand one unbroken link." Felts concluded that when the woman's suffrage amendment passed, those who could read and write would be counted among the voters, and most black men would be "passed over and counted out . . . for on the other side stands their salvation, for the women are already there."

Alice Felts's suggestion that in a climate of growing disfranchisement black men's illiteracy would prevent them from voting was a subtle reminder to male clergy that more women could read and write than men. Rev. Theophilus Gould Steward, known for his support of women, in particular his defense of black church women's rights and integrity, had made that argument months before Felts's views were known. Steward claimed that most ministers agreed that "the number of women in the church who can and do read and write, is not only greater than the number of men of the same class, but is greater in proportion." But this was not the only reason why women should be treated as equals and assume leadership roles in the church. Steward explained that women were more devoted "to the cause of Christ and to her church." For those who would dare suggest that because of the "masculine ministry" the disproportionate number of women in the church was "in part a matter of man worship," Steward asked church men to consider whether they would make that charge against their mothers, wives, sisters, or daughters. He concluded that the majority "of educated and pious people and consequently persons best prepared to do the work in the church" were women.

If one needed more evidence of their ability to assume leadership, Steward emphasized that the women financed the church. He noted that virtually every person directly supported and cared for by the institution was male. This included a "vast array of ministers." Therefore it was only fair that women should be fully employed in all church departments in salaried positions, and that the wives and daughters of pastors should be excluded from these jobs. As leaders in the AME Church who moved in the same circles, Johnson, Steward, and Felts knew each other very well. (And, Steward was Alice Felts's brother.) They were key participants in the ongoing public debate about women's rights.

Like Theophilus Gould Steward, there were other Methodist clergy who supported women's religious rights. The reverends Reverdy Cassius Ransom and bishops James Walker Hood, Alexander Walters, Charles C. Pettey, and Henry McNeal Turner are examples of late-nineteenth-century AME and AME Zion leaders who fully supported women's equality in the religious polity. There were also some clergymen who supported women's right to serve in every area but that of the ministry, and some argued that females should be given equal rights as long as they used their power for the advancement of men and children and did not compete for those leadership positions traditionally reserved for males. Like Steward, Rev. C. S. Whitted, an AME Zion minister, believed that women were important in the affairs of men and should be given, he said in 1903, "the freedom of their latent powers and talents in the home, the society, and the church." They had the power to "influence, save or destroy" the home, "purify or corrupt" society, and either lift up "or drag down to hell" the nation. Whitted's definition of women's power left women vulnerable and open to criticism and blame if failure occurred in any of the arenas where they possessed the capacity to exert influence. Nevertheless, he distanced himself from those persons who suggested that women were inferior or that they must be controlled. Whitted concluded, "The greatest trouble . . . today is [that] our women are kept down too much by jealous husbands."

As the secular debates about women's rights and suffrage became more prominent and widespread, and black women became more assertive about their rights as the chief supporters of religious and community institutions, some male leaders in the larger denominations, especially the Methodists and Baptists, took steps to mute women's arguments and to restrict and/or marginalize their participation in the church polity. In the case of the AME Church, women were afforded some privileges, but in the nineteenth century the only church to grant suffrage, full clergy rights, and equal rights in the polity to women was the AME Zion denomination.

How and why did AME Zion women, as opposed to AME women, succeed in having church law amended to make possible their advance into the polity in the late nineteenth century? And why were women in the National Baptist Convention more circumspect in their pursuit of religious rights for women? As will be seen, the answers to these questions are related to geographical and structural differences in the denominations and their women's missionary societies and conventions, membership capabilities, and the presence of enlightened and progressive male clergy—especially bishops supportive of women's rights in the polity. Issues of sectionalism and disunity were significant in the growth and development of all of these denominations, but especially so for AME and NBC women and their organizations. Also, the extent to which a denomination's antebellum membership had comprised free blacks as opposed to enslaved persons was important to how women perceived themselves and functioned.

During the 1890s the question of full and formal ordination for women was a concern in Methodist Episcopal, AME, and AME Zion churches, but it did not take precedence over issues of religious suffrage and female laity rights. In the Catholic, Episcopal, Presbyterian, and Methodist Episcopal denominations, African Americans functioned as subordinates bound by the laws governing those institutions. This is not to suggest that separate black congregations in white-led denominations did not exercise free will. However, their rituals and legal structures duplicated those of the mother churches, and they were subject to the dictates of their denominations. Though the data is sparse, there is some evidence that black women in these denominations sought gender equality. But this was only a part of their struggle. The status of black women affiliated with mainstream white denominations was further complicated by the fact that their subordination was on multiple levels. They were subject to "triple jeopardy." For example, as members of a segregated denomination black Episcopal women were involved in the fight for the rights of blacks in the Episcopal Church. As women they were subordinated to black men in their churches. And as black Episcopal women, they were subordinates of subordinates, which meant that they were held to the rules and regulations established by white Episcopal women's organizations that were subordinated to white men in the Episcopal Church.

In 1886 Anna Julia Cooper, a prominent Episcopalian, in a speech delivered before the convocation of colored clergy of the Protestant Episcopal Church, noted that some of the most "representative" male clergy were crossing borders and pastoring Methodist and Baptist churches because of the discrimination they faced as black clergy in a white-led denomination. Cooper concluded that the subordination of black Episcopal women was "closely allied to and probably gr[ew] out of" the denomination's treatment of black men.

In the case of the Catholics, all women were excluded from the priesthood. And, until the twentieth century, African American men were excluded from the priesthood. Though black Catholic churches were usually segregated, in the nineteenth and for a considerable time in the twentieth century, white priests officiated in the majority of black parishes. The establishment of black religious communities such as the Oblate Sisters of Providence (1829), Sisters of the Holy Family (1842), and Franciscan Handmaidens of Mary (1916), depended on the approval of the Catholic Church. Moreover, the operations of these communities were regulated by the church. For many decades, these religious orders were under the direct supervision of a white male director and a chaplain who also served as "the protector and spokesman for the sisters."

Denominational Structures of Power

DENOMINATIONS, LIKE NATIONS, function as corporate bodies, have clearly defined structures, and are governed by laws related to who and what they are and the people whom they serve. Understanding the issues related to women's leadership in the nineteenth- and twentieth-century black religious polity requires some knowledge of organizational structures and the formal positions of authority associated with them. Denominations are either Congregational, Episcopal, or Presbyterian in form. For example, whereas the Baptists conform to the congregational form of governance, the Methodist, Episcopal, and Catholic church polities are episcopal. Presbyterian and Pentecostal churches include elements of both the congregational and presbyterian structures and fall somewhere between the two. Each denomina-

The Oblate Sisters of Providence was founded in Baltimore, Maryland, 1829. It was the first order of African American nuns in the United States.

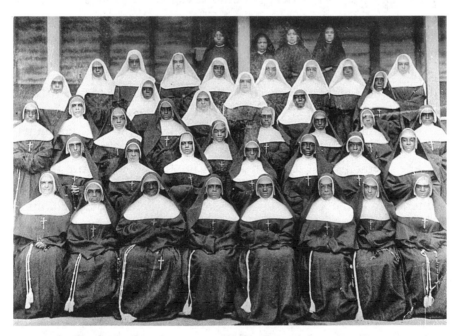

Sisters of the Holy Family religious community, established in New Orleans, 1842, was the second order of African American nuns in the United States.

tion adheres to a basic creed, has an established tradition and rituals, and is governed by a system of laws usually codified in a constitution.

Most religious traditions have three basic structural divisions, namely the clergy, the legislative branch—conference, convention, convocation, synod, or assembly system—and the laity. The organizational arrangements as stated in a constitution define the structural divisions and outline the formal positions of authority. The structures and rituals of most of the black religious institutions and organizations such as the Methodist, Baptist, Presbyterian, and Episcopalian churches are derivative of their parent organizations. However, black Christian church beginnings included survivals of African traditional religions that are traceable to the late seventeenth and early eighteenth centuries.

Black and white Methodists follow the teachings of John Wesley. They believe that God's grace precedes sanctification and enables the sinner to respond to the gospel. Most black Methodists belong to one of four denominations—the predominantly white Methodist Episcopal Church (known as the United Methodist Church after 1968), and the three independent black Methodist denominations, African Methodist Episcopal, African Methodist Episcopal Zion, and Colored Methodist Episcopal (known as Christian Methodist Episcopal Church after 1954). The episcopal form of church government is complex and hierarchical. Of the four legislative bodies, the General Conference is at the top, followed in ascending order by the Annual, District, and Quarterly church conferences. As the chief legislative body, comprising elected representatives from lesser conferences, the General Conference is responsible for erecting laws for the denomination and designating procedures for their implementation.

The Methodist constitution—also called the code or the book of discipline—with amendments, is published annually following the General Conference meeting. The discipline defines the denomination's administrative structure, lists all offices, and states the requirements and procedures for election or appointment of all formal church officers, including clergy. For example, it establishes ordination as the basic prerequisite for entering the ministry. Whereas at the basic level ministers are licensed to preach, ordination is required for five of the six positions in the ministerial hierarchy, which includes, in ascending order, deacon, elder, pastor, presiding elder, and bishop. Though the General Conference has enormous power, it cannot alter basic church law as defined by a denomination in relationship to "the episcopacy, members' privilege of trial and appeal, or general rules of the denomination." It serves as the court of last resort for issues and grievances unresolved by clergy in lower conferences where a presiding elder or bishop officiates. Bishops are elected for life and appointed by the General Conference to oversee conferences in designated geographic areas and oversee implementation of church law. The Council of Bishops (or, in the AME Zion Church, the Board of Bishops) acts as an executive branch. Though the structure of all Methodist denominations is the same, the constitutions vary.

One of the reasons why women in most black Methodist churches were denied ordination and rarely sanctioned for key leadership positions—such as those of traveling and local preachers, exhorters, stewards, trustees of church property, presidents of Epworth League Chapters, class leaders of the circuits, stations, and missions, superintendents of Sunday schools, and secretaries of church conferences—is because these positions conferred membership in the Quarterly Conference. The Quarterly Conference is not a law-making body. It is a judicial body that handles issues related to local churches and circuits. It is responsible for receiving and trying all appeals for church cases that might include any number of charges, hearing complaints, examining church records and registers, and providing oversight of Sunday schools, local preachers, exhorters, and the election of trustees, stewards, and stewardesses. In short, as members of the Quarterly Conference, women would have power over men.

Beginning with several churches in the late eighteenth century, black Baptists have evolved into three denominations. Baptists have a congregational form of government, but, since each church is autonomous, rules and regulations may vary. Every member is theologically, if not in practice, equally qualified to vote and have a voice in the decisions of the church. Anyone who feels called to preach can. Baptists do not have the office of elder; they ordain only clergy and deacons. With minimum education or preparation, one can satisfy the requirements of an ordination council and receive ordination, secure a house or building, rent a room, hang out a shingle, recruit a congregation, officiate at funerals, weddings, and baptisms, and administer the sacraments. As an entity to itself, the local church is in total control of its finances, associations, membership, hiring, and firing. The Bible is the sole source of authority for Baptists in all matters pertaining to faith and morals. Although most Baptist churches affiliate with local, state, and national associations or conventions, unlike the Methodists the

Baptists have no centralized authority. Among most Baptists, there is no hierarchy (although among the Full Gospel Baptists there are bishops). However, control within a church still flows from the top down, and there are entrenched lay power structures that are able to manipulate the leaders, typically with the threat of leaving and taking their money with them. In the black Methodist and Baptist denominations, traditionally male clergy have made the laws and exerted a great deal of power and control within their institutions. Women as members and organizations—Methodist, Presbyterian, Episcopalian, and Pentecostal missionary societies, and Baptist conventions—have had and exerted power by dint of their numbers and their financial capabilities.

Moreover, there has been a strong holiness impulse among not only nineteenth-century black Methodist women preachers in particular, but also Baptist women. Holiness and healing practices were clearly evident in slave religion and recognizable in the free black community, and some African Americans participated in the most prominent holiness and healing organizations and movements of the nineteenth century, particularly the great revivals and camp meetings associated with white religionists. They recognized its significance, especially its power to liberate. Preaching women such as Sojourner Truth, Amanda Berry Smith, Zilpha Elaw, and Julia Foote embraced perfection as a holiness tenet and participated in some organized holiness activities. After the Civil War, as many black Methodists and Baptists adopted mainstream attitudes and behavior, they were less likely to accept what they viewed as the rigid doctrinal beliefs and charismatic behavior associated with holiness groups.

Holiness was very prevalent among rural southern blacks—former slaves deeply invested in patterns of belief and rituals representing an American blend of African and Christian heritage. According to Virginia Broughton, a prominent Baptist leader in Tennessee, the "leading [Baptist] advocates of sanctification in some sections were so radical in their views on this subject [holiness] that a wave of persecution spread far and wide, [and] in some places churches were torn asunder and new churches were formed under the name of Holiness churches." Advocates of Pentecostalism and Holiness began as a small group of Christians in the late nineteenth century. In the twentieth century, beginning with the United Holy Church of America, the Church of Christ (Holiness), USA, the Church of God in Christ, Inc., the Fire Baptized Holiness Church of God of the Americas, and the Pentecostal Assemblies of the World, numerous groups of Pentecostal and Holiness churches were spawned. Strictly defined, Pentecostalism and Holiness are discrete terms. However, in practice, it is difficult to distinguish a church or minister as one or the other. The lines between the two are obscured because of the blending of traditions. Both Pentecostalism and Holiness require conversion and sanctification for salvation. Baptism by the Holy Spirit as evidenced by glossolalia (speaking in tongues) is sought. Some Pentecostal churches require that one speak in tongues for acceptance in the faith; others are more flexible. Holiness devotees emphasize sanctification but are divided (or silent) on the issue of speaking in tongues.

There is diversity in church government among Pentecostal and Holiness groups, but many are congregational. Worship style is spontaneous, informal, and often emotionally charged. The roots of Pentecostalism are in the nineteenth century, but the modern Pentecostal movement's acknowledged origin in the United States is the Azusa Street Revival, which occurred in Los Angeles between 1906 and 1909. The modern Pentecostal movement in the United States is unique in many ways. Beginning in the early twentieth century as a religious movement initiated and led by William J. Seymour, a black Holiness minister, the Azusa Street Revival was interracial and totally independent of the Methodists, Baptists, and other established religions.

Lucy Farrow and Neely Terry were among the pioneering Holiness women preachers at Azusa Street. Seymour's introduction to the idea of the baptism of the Holy Ghost was through Lucy Farrow. Seymour was able to enhance his experience through knowledge of the baptism of the Holy Ghost and the validating phenomenon of speaking in tongues. People of all classes and races came from throughout the nation to hear Seymour preach and experience what was viewed by many as a new awakening. Among the visitors was Charles Harrison Mason, a co-founder of the Church of God in Christ. As a religious phenomenon of the twentieth century, Pentecostalism is now professed by millions of people across the world. Its origins are largely African American. The early movement was interracial and even black led, until whites separated and formed racial churches. Catering largely to the poor, Pentecostalism empowered the oppressed and dispossessed. Pentecostal and Holiness churches in the United States have exercised a high degree of control over the behavior of members. During the first decades of the twentieth century, visiting committees and formal purges reinforced the need to conform to orthodox church principles requiring that one dress plainly and give up "worldliness"—

dancing, attending the theater and other entertainments, imbibing wine and liquor, cursing, and committing adultery.

Historically, the majority of black Protestants have affiliated with Methodist and Baptist denominations. Two types of national black churches emerged in the nineteenth century: the white-controlled churches for African Americans (Catholic, Episcopal, Presbyterian), and the independent black churches. By the late 1920s, the independent churches with 4.5 million Baptists and 1.5 million Methodists were by far the dominant groups. Blacks in white-controlled denominations accounted for fully 600,000 members. Among the white denominations, Episcopal, Presbyterian, and Catholic churches have accounted for the largest percentage of black members.

The Episcopal Church is a branch of the Anglican Church, which originated out of the Catholic Church. The church consists of a union of autonomous dioceses. Each diocese elects a bishop as its religious leader. Each parish elects a rector (also called a priest), who oversees the local congregation. While the denomination accepts the Bible and the historic creeds of the church, members are given great latitude in interpreting Episcopal doctrine. It emphasizes the use of the Book of Common Prayer in worship more than it does the acceptance of particular beliefs. The Eucharist is the most important part of the worship service. There is great diversity in the worship services; some churches are liturgical with a complex ritual, while others are more informal and evangelistic.

Though the names of its governing bodies differ from those of the Methodist Episcopal Church, the organizational structure of the Presbyterian Church is similar. The General Assembly is the national governing body. It comprises an equal number of ministers and ruling elders from each presbytery—geographical divisions that include from three to forty or more churches. The synod, or convention of the bishops and elders within a larger district, includes at least three presbyteries. The General Assembly receives appeals and questions referred from lower judicatories, negotiates controversies over doctrine or discipline, reviews and approves (or censures) the minutes of synods, and creates new synods. It legislates for the denomination, but new regulations must be approved by a majority of the presbyteries (i.e., each presbytery votes on a proposition). Since Presbyterian law leaves the conduct of worship up to the local session, one would expect to find differences in both form and content, running along racial lines. African American Presbyterians trace their origins to the founding of the first African Presbyterian Church of Philadelphia in 1807. Like the Methodist Church, during the antebellum period the Presbyterian Church split into a northern and southern wing over the issue of slavery. More than seven-eighths of its members were in the North and sympathized with the abolitionist movement.

The Historical Context for Women's Religious Leadership

GENDER DISCRIMINATION AND sexism are evident in all denominations. However, women's experiences, and the approaches they have used to assert and gain power, vary according to religious tradition. Geographical, denominational, and class differences influenced women's patterns of thought and action. The experiences, and thus the issues, of southern men and women often differed from those of northern and western blacks. Patterns of slavery, segregation, discrimination, and violence also impacted women's lives. Southern women tended to be more concerned about racial exclusion and discrimination than gender equality.

Women made progress in each denomination at different times, but they faced similar problems. In the late nineteenth century their difficulties included the struggle to found and maintain national organizations, to gain religious suffrage and laity and ordination rights, and to exert some control over the money that they raised. Most of these issues continued to dominate women's struggle for religious leadership in the twentieth century. Women also sought formal leadership positions and vocational opportunities in their denominations as class leaders, Sunday school superintendents, choir directors, parish workers or church secretaries, religious educators, clergy, stewards, and foreign missionaries. The stewardess and deaconess positions were created especially for women, but like alternative models for female lay church workers and clergy in some denominations, most formal leadership roles were reserved for men. However, there were exceptions to the rule. There are token examples of women serving as trustees, class leaders of same-sex and mixed groups, and in other offices.

Among the most controversial of the traditional leadership roles of church women, not legislated by the church, is that of the clergy wives, who were expected to assume multiple roles. Some denominations, such as the Methodists, legislated the leadership of clergy wives, especially the spouses of bishops, who led the national missionary societies and supervised the missionary work in their husbands' episcopal dis-

Mary F. Handy, a founder and president of the AME Woman's Parent Mite Missionary Society, was a suffragist and leading figure in the late-nineteenth- and early-twentieth-century black women's club movement.

tricts. Male clergy often chose to marry women who were educated and endowed with special talents as writers, musicians, and public speakers. These women were viewed as role models for other females. Ministers' wives were expected to be self-sacrificing in their church work, and, with few exceptions, in the nineteenth century the success or failure of a minister in his work was blamed on his wife. In 1886, Mrs. R. A. Hurley, wife of an AME minister, claimed that a pastor's success depended as much on what his wife did not do as on what she did. Hurley asserted that "many of the hardships and sorrows" endured by ministers were directly related to the mistakes they made in "selecting a partner for life."

Clergy wives were expected to subordinate their interests to those of their husbands. During the 1920s and '30s, in articles such as "The Minister's Wife," and "Ministers' Wives," lay women and clergy wives debated the "qualifications" needed to assume the "job," and explored the perceptions of laity on what a minister's wife should be and do. Mary F. Handy, the wife of a bishop and the president of the AME Woman's Parent Mite Missionary Society, held that "many failures in the ministry may be traced to indiscretion in choosing a companion." She stressed that whereas the wives of pioneering ministers "worked in the church, they were not expected to lead off as are the ministers'

wives of today. . . . Unless incapacitated by ill health or environment,"
she should be the leader of women in "all organized church work" and
be an "adviser and consoler" to women and children. Likewise, Nannie
Burroughs argued that men in public life should "take pains" in selecting a wife. Burroughs warned that pastors who failed to follow this rule
might be saddled with "millstones" around their necks.

In some denominations, individual women, with the support of a
congregation, merited informal leadership roles as "church mothers,"
who exercised considerable influence, often exceeding that of the ministers. In 1868 white missionaries found that the "church mothers,
gospel mothers, and old [shepherds], officials," were highly influential
figures, exerting power over both members and ministers. Noting the
continuance of this practice in the late twentieth century, sociologist
Cheryl Townsend Gilkes explains, "In both sacred and secular community settings there are powerful and respected older women addressed
by the title 'Mother.' " The title was extended to women church leaders as well as women who hold important leadership positions in secular organizations. However, the power of the church mother was
mostly local and had little effect on denominational law and practice.

Few male clergy or community leaders wanted women in leadership roles involving supervision over men. It was generally thought
that women should occupy positions that required direct interaction
and supervision of other females. Women leaders and public speakers
were usually applauded and accepted as long as they did not criticize
black men directly, assume a position of authority over men, seek equality, and articulate feminist views. Beginning in the 1870s and extending
throughout the twentieth century, a token number of women were
chosen to occupy positions in the church usually held by men. In the
late 1920s, following secular trends, a few vocations, like that of the
church secretary, were gradually opened to women. The pattern of
employing male stenographers or clerks (secretaries) for institutions
and businesses was prevalent in the nineteenth century. The feminization of clerical work came in the twentieth century.

The male clergy preferred that church women concentrate exclusively on fund-raising. Indeed, women exceeded all expectations in
their ability to raise large sums of money for the building of churches,
support of ministers, and all kinds of charitable causes. As women organized and developed programs and became master philanthropists,
they gained skills and confidence in their ability to lead. Many felt that
their talents were being underutilized and by the 1880s complained

that there was no work for them to do in the church. Others charged that though they provided the bulk of the church's finances, they were not represented in the leadership. In the AME Church Alice Felts was accused of sounding more masculine than feminine for stating that women were represented in the polity only as members who paid dues. However, Felts spoke for many women when she asserted that it was "taxation" without representation. The realization that they were providing most of the material resources and substantial nonmaterial resources in their churches caused women in some denominations to assert and use their power to persuade male clergy and bishops to either reconsider or rescind unfavorable decisions and appointments that were not sanctioned by the leaders of women's organizations.

Women began the twentieth century confident with their growing influence both in religious and secular matters. Concern for the sheer numbers of women patronizing and supporting the church led to the holding of a national conference in Pittsburgh in 1909 of the executive officers of white religious organizations representing the Protestant laity, and the launching of the Men and Religion Forward Movement. Owing to its feminization, the church was said to have "declined in power." To regain what they perceived as lost male power, the organizers avowed to "make the men as important as—if not indeed more important than the women of the church and to outline the work which they may carry forward." In other words, this was an effort to recruit large numbers of men to the church to dilute the growing power of women. Conference organizers made it clear that women would not be "dethroned" from their church work and support, but would remain in the so-called "place of honor and responsibility" they had "earned and gained." Thus, a purpose of the conference was to develop strategies "to supplement [women's] efforts with increased masculine energy." The question was how to restore men to the positions of responsibility and leadership that they had historically occupied in the early Christian church, without taking anything away from women.

Though this was a white Protestant initiative, black clergy and other male leaders took great interest in the Men and Religion Forward Movement. Some of the most prominent leaders in Charleston, South Carolina, joined the campaign and organized a Colored Committee of One Hundred to promote the movement. Lewis G. Jordan, editor of the *Mission Herald*, urged Baptist pastors and leaders to get in touch with the movement. To engage more men in missionary work, in January 1910 National Baptist Convention leaders in Greensboro,

North Carolina, organized the Laymen's Missionary Conference of Pastors and Missionary Committee-Men, held a convention, and formed the Baptist Laymen's Missionary Movement. Similarly, in 1912 the AME General Conference authorized the Laymen's Missionary and Forward Movement and encouraged every pastor to organize a laymen's movement. The NBC-USA and AME denominations proposed denomination-wide programs to engage men in missionary work at every level. Between 1920 and 1950, the AME Laymen's Organization focused on curtailing the power of the bishops and expanding the authority of the mostly male lay leaders. The Baptist Laymen's Missionary Movement attracted very few adherents during the first forty years of its existence, primarily because religious masculinization was already a major factor in the NBC-USA. However, the movement served as a support for the masculinist thrust of the convention driven mostly by Rev. David V. Jemison, an early proponent of a religious masculinity who was determined to defeminize the NBC-USA.

What had happened between 1890 and 1909 to create such consternation among men? Answers to this question lie in the ways women organized among themselves to pursue goals of equality and justice for their sex and race in the religious and secular spheres. Though they were more visible as participants in American life and culture, white women still faced considerable economic, political, and social discrimination. In the face of incredible challenges, black women celebrated their comparatively modest advances. The growing power of women's organizations and the woman's suffrage movement were viewed by most men as a threat to the masculine gender. However, men such as AME Bishop Henry McNeal Turner praised black women's intelligence, loyalty to the race, and success in organizing and accomplishing their goals. Turner acclaimed women as the equals of men, and supported the employment and promotion of qualified women to administrative and leadership positions in the church and society. In 1896 Turner fueled the fires with his statement, "But our women are the only men we have, so let them alone; they are better than our men any way you take them." Many men bristled at being compared with women, and rejected the claims that females were more efficient leaders and fund-raisers than males. Some felt that women as race spokespersons were taking over the reins of race leadership and making males appear weak and ineffective. For example, though Ida Wells-Barnett was praised for her courage in tackling the difficult issue of lynching, she was resented by most male leaders, who felt that she was functioning outside of her sphere and assuming a man's role. The wide-spread rhetoric of black female and male leaders comparing the abilities of black men and women intensified existing gender tension. As a result, black men became more vocal in stressing patriarchal norms.

Male concern for the power women had amassed through their missionary societies and conventions stretched beyond the church to encompass the women's club movement that had advanced far beyond the imagination of most observers. By 1905 black and white women had established a number of important feminist reform organizations, and had launched the women's movement, that would ultimately lead to the freedom of women from most social and political impediments. But it would take at least half a century for women to acquire basic legal rights that men routinely took for granted, to fully advance into the professions and to gain some measure of respect for their intellectual and physical capabilities.

Though black men also suffered legal impediments and confronted race at every turn, for black women the road to equality was even more difficult. In 1890, they were deemed the most inferior of the inferior human beings in America. Stereotyped as ignorant, depraved, and lustful, black women were denied simple courtesies that white women took for granted. As Du Bois emphasized, they "were the legitimate prey of men" and seen as unworthy of any consideration. Words alone cannot capture the dimension of their plight, and yet within two decades they accomplished more than any person could ever have imagined. It would indeed be simplistic to suggest that a single element accounted for their success. What remained constant among the majority of African American Christians was the belief in the supreme power of God to deliver them from adversity. But it was not their faith alone that made the difference; it was also the belief in their own abilities and in the possibilities of the race. Of great importance was the creation of strong women's religious and secular organizations, semi-autonomous spaces offering opportunities for agency, and creative endeavors.

The willingness to persevere, and struggle, against staggering injustice was a sustaining force among black leaders and their followers. Facing even greater obstacles, black women refused to give up. Rather, they creatively developed and pursued strategies related to the reality of their dual existence—as African Americans and as women. This would necessitate that they work with black men and white women to achieve their dual goals. However, the first efforts to organize came in the church as women strove to form missionary societies and conventions. With the exception of the AME and AME Zion associations, most national black church women's organizations were founded after 1900.

The creation in 1896 of the NACW, an organization for the advancement of the black woman's agenda, was a major accomplishment. Founded as an interdenominational organization, the NACW incorporated African American women's religious, racial, and gender concerns, and it was central to most of the achievements of black women for at least fifty years, until the late 1940s. By 1900 NACW leaders had determined that interracial contacts and alliances were necessary for accomplishing their goals. Initial affiliations with quasi-Christian organizations such as the WCTU and the YWCA, and later work with the Federal Council of the Churches of Christ's Church Women's Committee on Race Relations, and Church Women United, were as important to black women as their collaborative work with race-specific male-led organizations such as the National Association for the Advancement of Colored People and the National Urban League.

In spite of the many efforts to restrict women's roles to fundraising, the religious leadership of black women grew, and by the 1920s it was diverse and extensive. The form it took was related to their assumptions, as well as modest modifications in the legal structures of religious traditions. The leadership roles of women in the Catholic, Episcopalian, Presbyterian, Baptist, Methodist, and Pentecostal/Holiness churches were similar, but also different. However, irrespective of denominational affiliation women formed the main support for all churches—for example, in parishes such as St. Elizabeth's Catholic Church in New Orleans the Holy Name Men's organization sponsored many programs, but women performed most of the work. The constantly evolving secular struggles for equal rights and suffrage impacted the way women thought and functioned in the church and larger society. Among Protestants, in particular the Methodist denominations, issues of women preaching, suffrage, female laity rights, and vocational opportunities were the dominant concerns of women in the nineteenth century. However, as the twentieth century unfolded, many events affected the religious and secular status of women, including ratification of the Nineteenth Amendment. Unlike their AME and CME sisters, by 1920 women in the AME Zion and ME churches possessed religious suffrage.

The achievement of political suffrage had a psychological impact on all women and a more direct effect on the standing of women in denominations that discriminated on the basis of sex and denied women voting rights. Irrespective of when they were granted religious suffrage, for women in ME, AME, AME Zion, and CME denominations it was an important milestone. For all women it was incongruous to be granted political suffrage as United States citizens but denied a voice in their churches, institutions they helped to create and in which they formed the major constituency. Religious suffrage meant that women were eligible to vote and participate in their denominational legislative bodies. In most Protestant denominations interest in full and formal ordination would continue to dominate the religious discourse and represent one of the last barriers to women's full equality in the church.

In the majority of denominations, the most important formal leadership roles have been those associated with the clergy. Power has been concentrated mainly in the hands of deacons, elders, and bishops. During the 1880s and '90s, at the peak of the debates over ordaining women, many denominations turned their attention to alternative positions that would provide women recognition in the polity short of ordination. Consideration was given to establishing the offices of stewardess and deaconess. The Protestant Episcopal and the northern Methodist Episcopal Church led in the adaptation of the deaconess model of leadership. In the late 1890s the AME Church sanctioned the pattern established by the MEC and erected the position of deaconess. In the twentieth century the position was accepted by most denominations, including the Baptist, Congregationalist, Presbyterian, and Pentecostal churches, as one way of deflecting attention away from the ordination of women as clergy, while providing women with the title of deaconess. However, a deaconess lacked the formal authority of a deacon.

Historically, a deaconess was a religious woman appointed in the primitive church to do local church work, such as visiting the sick and those in prison, assisting with entertainments, aiding in the provision of support for itinerant preachers, catechizing and instructing new female converts in scripture, and preparing women for baptism and assisting them afterward. The question of whether women should be ministers of religion was not new. It was debated in the third century by early Christian sects, and discussed in Europe for many centuries. The deaconess position emerged out of those early debates. In answering the question about the definition of a deaconess, the AME *Christian Recorder* noted, "A deaconess is not a nun. She remains in the world, but all the while is engaged in church work." The *Vermont Herald* responded, "If this is all, there are from three to ten deaconesses in every church whenever an entertainment is to be given, only they are not called by that name. Sometimes they have been spoken of as the drudgery committee." In other words, though the deaconess position was presented as an alternative to the ordained diaconate position, it was not. Like that of the stewardess, deaconess was a titled position that in practice was related to the varied support roles women were already performing. Church women were pleased to receive recognition in the polity for the work they were already performing, but they understood the difference between the stewardess and deaconess positions and those of the deacon, elder, or bishop. These were separate realities. Women recognized that power resided in the various clergy positions and never gave up the quest for what they considered their right—ordination as deacons and elders.

Antebellum black women preachers were more concerned with the right to preach than with formal ordination. Centered in the urban North, the movement was mostly among Methodist women, persons who grew up in the Methodist tradition but developed ministries in other denominations, or women who converted to Methodism. The first generation of black women preachers (1800–50) were a curious lot whose emergence tended to cause excitement among Christians. Basic acceptance of the ministries of pioneering women such as Jarena Lee, Julia Foote, Zilpha Elaw, and Sophie Murray established a foundation for female ordination and other changes in women's status that occurred in the postbellum era. As the first woman to be licensed to preach in the AME Church, Jarena Lee was instrumental in laying the groundwork for women who desired to preach. The religious activism of Lee and her cohorts helped to secure the right for women to preach. The second generation (1850–1900) included a few pioneers such as Julia Foote and Amanda Berry Smith who served as mentors and role models for young ministerial aspirants like Harriet Baker, Lena Mason, Mary Small, Florence Spearing Randolph, Nora Taylor, and other women born during the 1850s and '60s who sought a new freedom and recognition for women in the church polity. These lesser-known and obscure women became active in religious and secular social reform and led in the struggle in the Methodist Church for ordination. Most Methodist and Baptist denominations accepted women as traveling evangelists until the late twentieth century. AME Zion women basked in their rights and pursued positions as pastors of churches.

The third generation of women preachers that came of age in the twentieth century (1900–50) was a much more diversified group, comprising evangelists, licensed and ordained female clergy, women pastors of churches, and many women who left the Baptist and Methodist churches in search of newfound rights—the right to preach and pastor churches, and the privilege of serving as ecclesiastical leaders of Pentecostal and Holiness church associations. During the early twentieth century women such as Ida Robinson, Rosa Artimus Horn, and Elder Lucy Smith founded numerous Pentecostal and Holiness churches. The growing ranks and influence of black Methodist, Baptist, Pentecostal, and Holiness preachers spurred the organization of the first interdenominational professional organizations of clergy women, and increased involvement of women preachers in the leadership of women's religious and secular organizations.

The Women's Evangelistic Union of America, organized in the late nineteenth century, by 1910 included a number of churches and missions. Under its auspices, women such as Rev. Mary Lark Hill, the founder of the Queen Esther Church in Chicago, became pastors. Rev. Hill, like many women wishing to pursue clerical careers, left traditional Methodist and Baptist churches. As a direct expression of the Women's Evangelistic Union's feminist nature, at the opening of the Queen Esther Church males were not allowed to speak at any of the meetings and services. Rather, female ministers officiated. As a member of the Methodist Episcopal Church, Hill was well known as an evangelist, composer of camp meeting songs, café owner, and "incessant worker for the elevation of the Afro-American race."

The Women's Evangelistic Union was absorbed by the Women's National Evangelistic Missionary Conference, founded in Philadelphia in 1911 by Rev. Alice V. Winston, an AME evangelist. By 1916 organizational branches were active in Virginia, Maryland, Pennsylvania, New York, Michigan, Illinois, Delaware, New Jersey, and Indiana. In 1927, as national president of the association, Winston presided over the sixteenth annual meeting held in New York City and attended by more than one thousand women. Though little is known about the organization, it continued to function throughout the 1940s. The high visibility of the Women's National Evangelistic Conference and the growing numbers of Methodist, Baptist, Pentecostal, and Holiness

Rev. Lena Mason, among the best known AME women evangelists in the late nineteenth and early twentieth centuries, was a pioneer in the field of evangelism.

Rev. Ida B. Robinson withdrew from the United Holy Church of America and in 1924 founded the Mount Sinai Holy Church of America, Inc., in Philadelphia, for which she served as bishop.

women preachers posed a threat to the male clergy. In the late 1940s mixed-gender evangelistic organizations headed by male clergy were established by the AME, AME Zion, Baptist, and Pentecostal churches to harness and control the women's power. Continuing their long quest for equality, AME women clergy established the Commission on Women in Ministry in 1989.

The AME Commission on Women in Ministry is an example of the activism of women in the fourth generation of women preachers (1950–2000). Representing a group of young, educated women, this generation took advantage of the new opportunities made possible because of the ecclesiastical legislative changes of the 1950s and '60s granting full lay and clergy rights to women, and the diminishing numbers of qualified males interested in the ministry. Population shifts from rural to urban areas, the migration of blacks to the North and West, the growth of black institutions of higher learning, and admission of blacks to some northern and midwestern white colleges and universities caused a decline in the numbers of young men entering the ministry in most denominations. Methodist conferences reported that few men appeared for admission to the ministry, and most of those who did were "persons who have reached middle-life and beyond." Not only were men abandoning the ministry for more lucrative positions in the professions, but after 1920 there was also a precipitous decline in the male membership nationally. Men were leaving the church during a period when women's numbers were expanding in the pulpit and the pew.

Religious Leadership Traditions Among Churches

IT WAS COMMON for working-class women to hold leadership roles in the church. In a study of black women's benevolent and social welfare activities in Memphis, Tennessee, after the Civil War, Kathleen C. Berkeley found that the majority—"almost two-thirds"—of the members and leaders of black women's benevolent and social welfare organizations worked as "washerwomen, ironers, and domestic servants." Between 1890 and 1960 black females constituted at least two-thirds of all black churchgoers. Uneducated and mostly limited to employment as servants or in other menial positions, the majority of women filling the pews in most black Baptist, Methodist, Pentecostal, and Holiness churches were poor and working class. This pattern was not isolated to Memphis. Rather, it was repeated in rural and urban areas—cities and towns throughout the nation. Commenting on the chief supporters of AME male clergy, while noting the exclusion of AME women from the polity, in 1904 the editor of the Chicago *Broad Ax* observed that "the women—those who take in washing and hustle early and late in the rear parlors of the wealthy whites furnish most of the money which enables their bishops and preachers to wear rich and expensive long-tailed coats, plug hats, to drink rare old wines, to smoke costly cigars and in every way live on the fat of the land." Similarly, during the 1920s, while serving as the executive director of the black branch of the YWCA in Jersey City, Anna Arnold Hedgeman, a Midwesterner, was impressed by the number of working-class African Americans who attended church on Sunday. She observed, "On the Lord's Day Negro laundry and domestic workers, porters, waiters and janitors became human beings with a recognized soul."

Much has been written about the black middle class and "uplift work." However, there has been little understanding of the fact that most African Americans in the nineteenth and the majority in the twentieth century were working class and poor. Though there were churches, mostly in urban areas, where the membership was predominantly middle class, most of the pews in rural and urban black churches of all sizes were filled with the working class. Working-class women, as leaders and workers in female associations, also engaged in "uplift" activities on behalf of children, the elderly, the disabled and the working poor. In 1901, while arguing for the training of AME women as deaconesses, Bishop Benjamin F. Lee asserted, "The 'masses' with us differs very much in meaning from that of the same word among some other people [white]. With us the 'masses' means about everybody—of 'classes' we have hardly a count. We are all poor; we are all at work; our little children are at home while we are at work."

At the beginning of the twentieth century the majority of Americans were rural. In 1904, 85 percent of African Americans in the South resided on the plantations and farms, and in the country districts where their forebears had lived in slavery for generations. Bishop Lee and other religionists were aware of the pioneering settlement movement work of NACW leaders. Most black settlements were organized by women who promoted social reform in their religious and secular organizations. Some urban and rural reformers embraced the Social Gospel movement, which applied the insights of Christian faith to pressing secular issues of the time. They focused on social problems such as poverty, race, labor, prostitution, and housing conditions.

The movement included many who were anxious to inculcate commonly held religious beliefs and values while dispensing much-needed services and educational training. Rev. Hutchens C. Bishop, the rector at New York's "most fashionable" black parish—St. Phillips Presbyterian Church—observed that most of this work was "extra parochial, . . . that is, under no one church organization, yet it is distinctively religious in its character."

Male clergy such as Bishop and Lee felt that settlement and general uplift work was of the church but not administered by the church. Lee believed that black churches ought to be more directly identified with the work, and that it provided an opportunity to harness the efforts of church women, and perhaps pacify women seeking more formal leadership roles. He envisioned the deaconess engaging in uplift work similar to that advocated by the NACW and other social reform organizations. There was also a concern for the growing settlement work among blacks by white denominations. White women's religious associations with superior resources mounted programs to address the multiple problems confronting poor blacks and white immigrants. Mary Helm, a leader in the Methodist Episcopal Church's Council of Women for Home Missions, observed that plantation or settlement work provided a special opportunity for black women deaconesses or Bible readers "to visit and work in the home, to uplift and guide the women and girls as no man can. She could also hold mothers' meetings, teach sewing schools and Bible classes, and in many respects prove an angel of mercy as well as a teacher of righteousness on many a plantation in the 'back country.' " Helm believed that since black mothers were frequently the "breadwinners" and away from home, "deaconesses and trained nurses might teach moral values, and health care to mothers and girls to keep them from 'the path of sin.' "

Though religious leadership traditions vary among denominations, women encounter similar issues regardless of their affiliations. Irrespective of class and social and economic status, African American females, whether Methodist, Baptist, Presbyterian, Episcopalian, Pentecostal, Holiness, or members of other denominations, face a religious masculinity in their pursuit of roles in the polity. Since denominational structures and constitutions vary widely, and issues of religious leadership resonate in different ways, it is necessary to look at how women asserted and gained their rights and amassed power in each religious tradition, rather than looking at the various gains on one timeline. To understand the specific issues women engaged, and how they advanced in the religious polity, the experiences of Methodist, Baptist, and Pentecostal women will be discussed separately.

African Methodist Episcopal

IN 1890 REV. THEOPHILUS GOULD STEWARD argued that the mutual interests of the church, the kingdom of God, and church women demanded that "competent and pious" women be permitted to assume leadership roles in the church. He regretted that they were "not ministers, not class leaders, not stewards, not superintendents of Sunday schools—in a word, not anything where religious work is to be done—but everything where money is to be raised to be managed by others." Unlike Steward, most men believed that women should occupy certain leadership positions but be restricted from holding others. For example, Rev. Winfield Henri Mixon, of Selma, Alabama, stated that he was willing to consider suffrage but was adamantly against ordination, which he felt was contrary to the teachings of the Bible. However, Mixon did not object to AME women "filing the editorial chairs, or positions of secretaries." Rev. Levi J. Coppin was against licensing, ordaining, and giving regular charges to women, feeling that there was "so much for them to do—missionary work, temperance work, and work of moral reform." Irrespective of the argument, the central concern of AME and most male clergy was that women concentrate their efforts in missionary work and on fundraising for domestic and foreign programs.

AME women were among the first to contend for the right to preach. Antebellum preaching women such as Jarena Lee, Sophie Murray, and Zilpha Elaw opened the door for Harriet Baker, Margaret Wilson, and Sarah Ann Hughes to pursue careers as preachers. As a result of these and other women assuming preaching functions without authorization, the 1884 General Conference approved the licensing of female evangelists, but not the ordination of women to preach, and forbade the appointment of women as pastors. However, Sarah Hughes appears to be the first AME woman to be ordained as a deacon. Hughes's appointment in 1881–82 as the conference evangelist for North Carolina was noncontroversial, as there was little dissension over women functioning as evangelists. Hughes's preaching and evangelistic skills were highly regarded by her peers. At her behest the North Carolina Annual Conference licensed her as a preacher and she became a candidate for a pastorate. Hughes was appointed and served for a short period of time as pastor of the Fayetteville Station, before being assigned to pastor a church in Wilson's Mills, North Carolina.

Prior to 1884 the majority of male clergy were adamantly against women preaching, but there was evidence of support among some male clergy for ordaining women as deacons. At the 1884 General Conference, two of the most prominent and outspoken AME ministers in the nation, James H. A. Johnson and George Washington Bryant, spoke forcefully in support of a resolution that would forbid the assignment of women to separate charges. Johnson argued, "God has circumscribed [woman's] sphere and whenever she goes out of it, injury is done to society." Likewise, Bryant emphasized domesticity, asserting that women should remain at home and take "care of the babies." The resolution passed forbidding women to pastor churches. However, women could be licensed as local preachers under the strict control of the Quarterly Conference. In November 1885, at the North Carolina Annual Conference, Bishop Henry McNeal Turner ordained Sarah Hughes a deacon. The Hughes ordination prompted a spirited debate in the AME Church. In 1887 the North Carolina Annual Conference overturned the Hughes ordination, a move that the 1888 AME General Conference ratified.

AME women continued to seek ordination rights. However, it was not until 1948 that the General Conference passed legislation favoring the ordination of women as local deacons. Local deacons were eligible for temporary ministries in missionary churches, and they were subordinate to male itinerant elders. Full clergy rights were granted to women by the General Conference in 1960. In response to the nineteenth-century demand of women to preach, in 1868 and 1898, respectively, the AME Church established the offices of stewardess and deaconess. The stewardess was a subordinate to the male steward. Women were appointed as stewardesses following a vote of a congregation's stewards and the approval of its pastor. Stressing the importance of the General Conference's approval of a deaconess position, in 1898 Bishop Turner explained that "it is conceded that there are certain kinds of work in the church which the women can do better than the men. A deaconess is a minister of the church called upon to exercise her special gift of teaching, nursing, or whatever else it may be in the service of the church for the purpose of extending the kingdom of the Lord Jesus." Coincidental to the passage of legislation, the Bethel AME Church in Chicago agreed to employ Sarah Slater, a graduate of Moody Bible Institute trained for home and foreign missions and deaconess work, as the church deaconess. Whereas Slater was ordained by the Methodist Episcopal Church for service as a deaconess, the AME Church held that a woman could be consecrated to the office, but not ordained.

In 1901 the AME Church purchased property in Roanoke, Virginia, where it erected a Deaconess Home and Girls' Training School. Bishop Benjamin F. Lee viewed the deaconess home as an institution to train black girls who would be employed to reach the black "masses." Lee asserted that deaconess work would be the "arm of rescue" for the AME Church, and "the heart of sympathy as well. It is not an academy, not a college, not a seminary, not a university, but a serious effort to enlist some of our pious cultured women in the work of inculcating better notions of personal responsibility, of home, of citizenship and religion in others, and themselves . . . while doing a great work among all classes of our people, regardless of denomination, sex or age." As the position was popularized and the numbers of deaconesses swelled, AME women in some states formed associations for the purpose of sharing ideas and assessing the overall quality of their work.

With each gain, AME women became more resolute in their quest for full equality. At the beginning of the twentieth century women argued for religious suffrage and the right to serve as lay delegates. All five hundred of the male delegates at the General Conference of 1904 voted down a resolution in favor of permitting women to serve in this position. In 1924 the General Conference passed legislation granting women, twenty-one years of age and older, suffrage and the right to hold any office in the polity. This meant that AME women were eligible to vote and be elected to the denominational conferences, serve as trustees, stewards, class leaders, Sunday school superintendents, and delegates to the District, Annual, and General conferences. However, the right of religious suffrage did not extend to women at the local level. Until the late twentieth century, that decision continued to rest with individual churches. For example, although women outnumbered men four to one, it was not until 1953 that the female members of the Mother Bethel AME Church in Philadelphia were granted the right to vote on matters pertaining to the local church.

Enacted only four years after, and in part as a reaction to, the ratification of the Nineteenth Amendment, the 1924 legislation was an important milestone, in that it opened the door for women to hold many official and important offices. Among those calling for women to take advantage of the new law was Sadie Tanner Mossell Alexander.

Though still in her twenties, Alexander had gained prominence for her groundbreaking achievements. In 1919, at twenty-one years of age, she was elected as the first national president of the Delta Sigma Theta sorority. In 1921 she became the first African American to earn a PhD in economics—and the second black female to earn a PhD. In 1928 and 1942 she was elected as a delegate to the AME General Conference. Alexander also served as attorney for the First Episcopal District. By 1940 she had gained national notoriety as a civil rights attorney and prominent national black leader. In 1944 Alexander was the first woman to be elected attorney for the AME Council of Bishops. In the late 1970s Willie Roundtree, an attorney and an ordained AME minister, was elected general counsel of the AME denomination.

The 1924 AME legislation also made it possible for women residing in Africa, Haiti, Canada, and other foreign nations, where the denomination had established conferences, to occupy leadership positions. In South Africa, Ntombi Tantsi, wife of the chief of the Zulu tribe, was elected president of the AME's foremost foreign conference, a recognition that eluded American women. But the initial legislation made no provision to grant membership in the General Conference to the presidents of the Woman's Parent Mite Missionary Society and the Women's Home and Foreign Missionary Society. These women were the leaders of organizations that raised the bulk of the funds for the AME domestic and foreign missionary work. *Christian Recorder* readers were reminded that these women certainly deserved to be given this privilege, especially "if army chaplains have a reason to sit in the general conference." It would be eight years before the leaders of these organizations were officially installed as members of the General Conference.

Though men would continue to dominate the polity, women finally had a voice in the denomination's chief legislative body. They would use this newfound right to voice their concerns and lobby for women's advancement in the polity. In 1936 a delegation from Ohio petitioned the body to revise the discipline to permit the ordination of women as deacons and elders. The progressive activities of four high-profile Ohio women, noted evangelists and deaconesses, were presented as evidence of the advantages to be derived by the AME Church from granting women these privileges. As a delegate to the 1936 AME General Conference, Rev. Martha Jayne Keys and her cohorts had the support of prominent ministers and the presiding elder in the Cleveland, Ohio, district, and the AME women's missionary societies, all of whom supported the resolution for a constitutional amendment to the AME discipline. The resolution was defeated, but Keys vowed to reintroduce it at each succeeding General Conference until all restrictions to women attaining full clerical rights were eliminated. Finally, in 1960 the General Conference removed all restrictions to women's advancement in the polity.

During the late 1960s several women ran for offices traditionally held by men. At the 1964 General Conference, Rev. Carrie Hooper became the first female candidate for bishop. Hooper held degrees from New York City College and Drew University and was widely respected for her preaching skills. Originally ordained in the Metropolitan Baptist Church in New York City during the late 1920s, she later affiliated with the AME Church and between 1948 and 1956 was ordained a local deacon, elder, and itinerant elder. She organized and served as pastor of the True Vine AME Church for a number of years. Though Hooper failed in her successive bids for election to the episcopacy in 1964, 1968, 1972, 1976, and 1980, her candidacy represented a major breakthrough in "the long civil rights struggle" of the AME laity and women for equal rights. Indeed, it laid the groundwork for the later election of AME women as general officers and bishops.

AME Zion

IN 1876, THE AME Zion Church was the first Methodist denomination, black or white, to grant women religious suffrage, which meant that they could vote on issues in their local churches and have a voice in the Annual and Quarterly conferences. In 1884,the General Conference revised the church discipline and eliminated the word "male" from its laws. This action technically removed all barriers to women's advancement in the AME Zion Church. At least on paper, women were eligible to serve in any and all positions. This included election as lay delegates to the General Conference, licensing as local preachers, ordination as deacons and elders, and election to the episcopacy as bishops. The elevation of Julia Foote and Mary Small to the diaconate in 1895 distinguished the AME Zion Church as the first black denomination to officially ordain women to the ministry. In 1898, Mary Small was ordained an elder, the first black or white Methodist woman to receive such recognition. Foote was the second woman ordained an elder, in 1899.

The ordination of Julia Foote by James Walker Hood, the senior bishop, at the Seventy-fourth Session of the New York Annual Conference on May 13, 1895, elicited some negative comment, but for the most part it was praised. At eighty-two years of age, Foote had enjoyed a long and successful career as an evangelist. She was widely known among white and black Methodists and revered by many for the power of her preaching and her intellect. Having preached for more than fifty years, Foote was not seen as a threat to the male clergy, and it was not expected that she would be appointed the pastor of a church. Her ordination was more of a "form of recognition than empowerment, because her career was in its twilight. Her primary gain was official denominational recognition of her ministry and admittance to equality with males in the polity." For Foote, it was the culmination of a long struggle in which she had been an active participant.

The ordination of Mary Small as a deacon came days after Foote's elevation. Upon hearing that Bishop Hood had ordained Julia Foote, the clergy attending the Philadelphia and Baltimore Conference (which convened on May 15, 1895, in York, Pennsylvania, at the AME Zion Church, pastored by Rev. John Bryan Small) recommended that Small be elevated to the same position. Bishop Alexander Walters ordained her. Following the ordination of Small as deacon, questions were raised about the propriety of these actions, since the AME Zion Church discipline did not specifically grant women the right to be ordained as deacons or elders. Clergy responsible for the ordinations claimed that "they had power to do this on the grounds that the word 'male' was stricken out of our Discipline." There was an undercurrent of dissatisfaction among AME Zion clergy and members, but for the time being the discussion remained at a subterranean level. The major public debates and raucous dissensions were reserved for the 1898 ordination of Small as elder. Meanwhile, the opportunity for women to advance in the polity now existed.

Foote and Small were part of a small cadre of AME Zion preaching women who were licensed to preach in the decade before Foote became the first female deacon. In that group were women such as A. G. Smith, Mary Elizabeth Taylor, Florence Spearing Randolph, Jane Guinn, Josie C. Mayes, and Lizzie Hill. Guinn and Mayes were widely known and celebrated as preachers in the North and South. Guinn (1899) was the third AME Zion female ordained a deacon. Taylor (ca. 1900) and Randolph (1903) were the third and fourth females ordained as elders. As licensed ministers and deacons, most of these women were active in episcopal districts supervised by Bishop Alexander W.

Rev. Mary Small, ordained by the AME Zion Church as an elder in 1898, was the first woman to be ordained an elder in a black or white Methodist denomination.

Walters, Bishop Charles Calvin Pettey, and Bishop George Wylie Clinton. At the Missouri Annual Conference, in the midst of considerable discussion about whether Lizzie Hill's credentials "entitle[d] her to exercise the function of elder's orders," Walters asserted, "I personally favor the granting of every right of the church to women. I believe that many women are being called to preach because we men do not do our duty better." Thus Walters made clear his support for the ordination of women just eight months before he ordained Small a deacon. However, as a junior bishop he knew that he would be perceived as usurping the power of the senior bishop if he took such action. The support of the clerical members of the Philadelphia and Baltimore Conference, and the ordination of Foote by Hood, made it easier for Walters to ordain Mary Small.

Legislative action alone would not open up the doors for women to serve in judicial bodies or otherwise advance in the polity. For women

Rev. Florence Spearing Randolph was among the first women in the AME Zion denomination to be ordained and to pastor a church. During her long and fruitful lifetime, she was widely known as a leading figure in the NACW, YWCA, temperance and interracial movements.

to access these rights, persistent struggle and consistent demands for recognition would be necessary. Like their AME counterparts, AME Zion women leaders tended to be well educated, politically astute, and pragmatic in their approaches to both gender and race advancement. They understood the need for religious and secular allies, including black men and white women. They also were outspoken in their arguments for women's leadership in the church, particularly as ministers. At the 1896 AME Zion Centennial celebration, Rev. Josie C. Mayes, a highly respected evangelist, stated, "A woman wholly given to the service of the Master has a powerful influence. . . . If the lord gives the women brains under the mistaken idea that they need them, if He endows them with power from on high to preach . . . ; are they to wrap their talents in a napkin?" Unlike Randolph, Foote, Sarah Dudley Pettey, and most of the AME Zion women leaders of her time, Mayes

Sarah Dudley Pettey, as a leader in the AME Zion's Women's Home and Foreign Missionary Society and editor of the *Star of Zion's* "Woman's Column," argued for women's religious and political rights.

did not favor women as suffragists or women in politics. But she argued that women in the church were equal to men.

With a clear perception of their role and place in society, AME Zion women managed to accomplish relatively early what took decades for some of their white and black sisters to achieve. And they did it with the support of the female laity and the wives of male clergy. A staunch supporter of Mary Small's elevation to the episcopacy, Sarah Dudley Pettey was delighted when her husband ordained Small an elder. The *Star of Zion* reported that on the eve of Mary Small's ordination, letters were "continually coming in [from clergy] asking for special preparation for 'my wife,' as she wants to attend the Annual Conference." And, following Small's elevation, when faced with the possibility that the General Conference would declare the ordination illegal, the wives of ministers joined the female laity in their support of Small's ordination. They suggested that as women representing the bulk of the denomination's membership, they had the power to dethrone male ministers. Declaring that the men should "Let Rev. Mrs. Smalls Alone," Carissa Betties said, "[I]t appears to me that men are attending to God's business. If it be of God, men cannot overthrow it. I will say to these men, keep cool, for you know not at what you kick. . . . So I say, Mrs. Small, 'Fear them not, for they that are with you, are more than they that are with them.' Ask God to open the eyes of those men that they may see the horses and chariots of fire that are about thee."

What accounts for the success of AME Zion women, and the failure of AME women, to gain full recognition in the religious polity of the late nineteenth century? Why was the ordination of AME evangelist Sarah Hughes so soundly rejected, and why did she just fade out of the picture? Essentially, it was a confluence of events and persons during the last two decades of the nineteenth century that made possible the AME Zion women's accomplishments. Whereas AME Zion women were less divided and more focused on the achievement of their goals as a unified body of women, AME women were separated into northern and southern camps and competed against each other. In the 1890s the Woman's Home and Foreign Missionary Society's national officers were all wives of bishops; these women were no shrinking violets, but were outspoken in their support of women's equality in the church and society.

The late nineteenth century witnessed the rise of a new, young, and vibrant male and female leadership willing to take risks, go against the old guard, and move the AME Zion Church forward in ways unimaginable to the conservative black male leaders in most denominations. Also, among the AME Zion women were seasoned antebellum radicals and former abolitionists, women's rights activists, and suffragists, such as Eliza Gardner and Julia Foote, who were unwilling to compromise with the old-guard male leaders. These women served as mentors and advisers to a new breed of young, educated, and dedicated women who were born on the eve of the Civil War, had come of age during the turbulent times of the late 1860s and '70s, witnessed the end of Reconstruction and the advance of Jim Crowism, and in the 1890s became advocates of the acclaimed Woman's Era.

Women such as Sarah Dudley Pettey, Marie Clinton, Victoria Richardson, Florence Spearing Randolph, and Mary Small had tasted the first fruits of freedom and became immersed in the women's movement. They understood the power inherent in women's organizations and were willing to fight for their beliefs. The intimate relationships these and other early female preachers and leaders had with the male clergy were of great significance. Unlike her AME Zion counterparts, Sarah Hughes does not appear to have been intimately connected to any of the networks that formed the clergy leadership. Hughes was identified as a mulatto, but nothing is known about her birthplace, her parents, or her husband—whose name is not mentioned in AME

Church records. Hughes began her ministry in the North Carolina AME Annual Conference "as a freelance evangelist." While Hughes was acclaimed as an excellent preacher, she had few loyal supporters among the clergy or female leaders.

The timing of the challenges to traditional AME Zion church authority, and the relationships among and between the key figures, was of the utmost importance to the events that occurred. Of some significance were the kinship and friendship networks that brought together several of the clergy wives most responsible for advancing the women's agenda and arguing the "woman question." Specific reference is made to the bishops most involved in the ordination and promotion of AME Zion women—James Hood, Alexander Walters, Charles Pettey, George Clinton, and John Small. Hood, born free in 1831, was an abolitionist and civil rights activist. Consecrated as a bishop in 1872, he was known for his logic and reasoning, and considered a pacifier. As the senior bishop, Hood was undoubtedly the most revered and respected man in the denomination. In the aftermath of the debates over the legitimacy of Mary Small's ordination, he made clear his support for female elders and served notice that neither the laity nor other clerics were authorized to "tell the Bishops how to discharge the duties of their office."

In 1898 the AME Zion Church had a total of nine bishops, five of whom went on record in support of Mary Small's ordination. Hood, Pettey, Walters, Clinton, and Small all had reasons to support Mary Small. Following his elevation to the episcopacy in 1888, Charles Pettey, a former slave, became one of the most admired and feared bishops in the AME Zion Church. He and his wife, Sarah, cut quite a figure in the denomination. Their intellect, beauty, and style of living were envied by many. Sarah was widely admired by women and respected by many male clergy, but she also drew the ire of numerous men who felt that she was too outspoken and forward in her views. Sarah Dudley Pettey served as treasurer and then secretary of the WHFMS, and originated the feminist "Woman's Column" in the *Star of Zion*. Like most WHFMS officers, clergy women, and leaders of local and state societies, Sarah recognized the missionary society as a key base of operation and power for AME Zion women. Alexander Walters, elected bishop in 1892 at thirty-four years of age, was the second youngest bishop in the history of the AME Zion Church. Walters's respect for women and belief in their equality grew out of his close relationship with his mother, Harriet Mathers Walters, a former slave who challenged the authority of her master and other white men who sought to rein her in. As a young minister, Walters was tutored by Rev. Julia Foote, who shared some of her earlier experiences with him. Walters was extremely fond of Foote and thought of her as a second mother. Bishop Clinton's wife, Marie, was among the founders of the NACW, and influential in organizing the North Carolina Federation of Colored Women, for which she served as president. John Small, like Clinton, was ordained bishop in 1896. Small, a native of Barbados, was considered the most erudite of the AME Zion ministers. He was a staunch supporter of his wife, Mary, and vigorously defended her right to be ordained as a deacon and an elder.

Unlike the AME Church, where the bishops were seriously divided over issues of women's rights, there was a critical mass of support for women's ordination among AME Zion bishops. Thus, the 1900 AME Zion General Conference saw no reason to challenge the actions of the bishops. It was conceded that the AME Zion polity was "in perfect harmony" with their actions, and the recommendation against ordaining women was defeated. Among the most important elements contributing to the success of AME Zion women in obtaining religious rights and full ordination was the church's leadership, its ability to focus intently on organizational goals and build broad constituency support, its relationship to formal authority, and the timing of the demands.

AME Zion women were the first to pastor denominational churches in significant numbers. By 1940 there were at least one hundred female pastors of missions and churches. However, like the women in other denominations, few were elected to lay leadership positions traditionally reserved for men. Though many AME Zion women have been ordained as elders, until 2008 none were elected as bishop. For the most part, women have been restricted to leadership roles in their missionary organizations. These societies enabled women to develop and hone their skills, to amass enormous resources for their domestic and missionary work, and to launch major careers in secular organizations and politics.

Colored Methodist Episcopal

FOLLOWING THE CIVIL WAR, the Colored Methodist Episcopal Church was organized in the South with mainly former slaves affiliated with the Methodist Episcopal Church, South. Ideological differences over slavery had led to a split in the Methodist Episcopal Church in the early 1840s. Whereas the southern wing of the Methodist Church supported slavery, northerners argued for abolition. In 1843 and 1844, the Wesleyan Methodist Church was organized in New York and New England, and in 1844 the Methodist Episcopal Church, South, was formed. As a result of the Civil War, between 1860 and 1866 at least two-thirds of the black members left the MECS. The majority joined the established independent black bodies—the AME and AME Zion denominations—and also the churches organized by the Methodist Episcopal Church in the North. The remaining 35,000 or more black Methodists in the South decided to continue their relationship with the parent church and be set apart as a separate organization. Unlike the conservative MECS, the Methodist Episcopal Church in the North was more liberal on issues regarding slavery and women's rights—"a veritable breeding ground for woman's rights advocates and abolitionists." For many decades the CME Church was considered by other black Methodist denominations to be conservative on issues of race and gender and beholden to southern white Methodists.

During most of its history the CME Church has closely modeled itself after the Methodist Episcopal Church. The CME Church was the sole black denomination to maintain a close relationship with the MECS and was the recipient of philanthropical support for the erection and operation of its schools and churches. Its leaders were wont to criticize or take positions against whites in general or the MECS in particular. As the only one of the three independent black Methodist churches that was not the result of secession, the CME Church was initially the subject of "bitter taunts" and was stigmatized as "Democrats, boot licks, and white folks' niggers." In the late 1860s, as the AME and AME Zion leaders swept into the South, establishing churches and recruiting new members, the CME Church spurned their overtures to separate from the MECS and affiliate with an established black denomination. Having organized in the North more than fifty years before the Civil War, the AME and AME Zion churches possessed able and experienced bishops and preachers and prominent female leaders, many of whom were educated. During Reconstruction, a number of AME and AME Zion men were members of southern state legislatures, and others had served in the Union Army as chaplains or private soldiers. Their names were often associated with reform movements of the nineteenth century. It would take at least twenty-years for the CME Church to gain even a modest foothold and general recognition for its work and worth. The first thirty years of the CME's existence were devoted to establishing the church polity, recruiting new members, and building churches. By 1890 the CME Church had more than 100,000 members. Between 1870 and 1935, the CME Church grew from eight annual conferences, several uneducated preachers, and a small number of members to an organization with thirty-seven annual conferences, more than two thousand pastors, and more than 350,000 members.

Influenced by the secular women's rights and suffrage debates of the late nineteenth century, and concerned about their status in the newly organized denomination, CME women were anxious to organize and to participate in the development of the church. They were denied religious suffrage, ordination, and the right to serve as lay delegates in the church polity. At the local level women were clamoring to serve in some capacity, and male clergy were eager to have them do so, as long as it was in a subordinate untitled role. While other denominations permitted women to function as stewardesses, CME clergy were reluctant to engage them in any capacity, fearful that they would overshadow the accomplishments of men. In 1882 CME bishops and other male delegates broke out in laughter when a resolution to establish the office of stewardess was presented to the General Conference, and the measure was tabled. In 1886 the General Conference was asked to insert a clause in the discipline authorizing the employment of "ladies as stewardess auxiliaries" in the church. The proposal was rejected.

The 1890 General Conference approved the creation of the office of stewardess with the stipulation that they not participate in helping to raise the general fund. Since women were already performing a variety of unacknowledged functions in the church, this simply meant that they would receive some official recognition. Seeing the imprudence of suggesting that women not participate in fund-raising, at the 1894 General Conference CME bishops revised the discipline to ensure that stewardess boards were organized in every congregation. CME bishops were certain that if the church women were "allowed and properly treated," they would help to support the church and increase its finances. In the eight years it had taken to acquire the legislation, CME women had moved beyond the simple request for recognition and begun to press for other rights.

The licensing of women preachers at the local level, the growing numbers of women evangelists, and the use of these women in the Methodist Episcopal, AME, and AME Zion denominations to increase church membership and raise funds caused angst among some CME clergy, who feared that their churches were lagging behind other denominations. Thus, at the 1894 General Conference, resolutions were introduced calling for the licensing of women to preach and do evangelistic work as deaconesses and evangelists. These appeals were denied. The practice of employing female evangelists from rival denominations preceded the introduction of legislation in the CME Church. Though CME women were denied the right to preach, CME male clergy willingly used female evangelists from other denominations to conduct revivals. After all, they were no challenge to CME male authority.

In 1918 the CME Church authorized the licensing of women as local preachers. This action followed the ordination of Ida E. Roberts and Georgia A. Mills at the 1915 Annual Conference, held in Charlotte, North Carolina. Roberts, the wife of a minister, had begun her preaching career in 1890. Although it was not considered legal at the time, Roberts and Mary Mims (1897) of Kentucky were the first women licensed to preach in the CME Church. Occasionally, bishops ignored the law and licensed and sometimes ordained women to preach. The licensing of Roberts and Mims to preach, like the ordination of Sarah Hughes by AME Bishop Henry McNeal Turner, was performed outside of church law. In 1943 Rev. D. B. Whitehead, the pastor of the Williams Temple CME Church in Philadelphia, was the third female known to be ordained in that denomination. In 1948 the CME General Conference approved the licensing of women as local preachers and the ordination of women as local deacons and elders, and in 1966 women were granted full clergy rights. In that year Virgie Amanda Jackson Ghant became the first woman to be ordained an elder in the CME Church.

At the beginning of the twentieth century, the only legitimate constitutional role CME women could claim was that of stewardess. In 1902 serious questions were raised about the treatment of these women. Though they were responsible for assisting the stewards in raising the money for support of the church and paying the salaries of the presiding elder and the minister, they were not permitted to participate in the polity. Legally speaking, stewardesses were officers of local churches, and therefore members of the Quarterly Conference. However, in the eight years after the passage of the original legislation, they were excluded from participation in the Quarterly Conference. This was a bombshell issue that could create problems in the denomination and affect the otherwise successful service of the stewardesses. For more than a decade CME stewardess in local churches had performed beyond all expectations—male clergy and lay leaders were ecstatic about their fund-raising prowess and did not wish to engage in arguments or debates about whether they should have the same rights as male stewards.

Though little is known about the behind-the-scenes discussions, it is likely that the CME bishops decided that it was more feasible to grant women membership and voting privileges in the Quarterly Conference, whose jurisdiction was restricted to local matters, than to allow them a vote in the General Conference. Acceptance of even one female at that level would escalate the debate about admitting women as lay delegates to the General Conference. Thus, the bishops and clergy decided to make stewardesses members of the Quarterly Conference. The 1902 General Conference revised the CME constitution to include stewardesses as voting members. In this manner the male clergy avoided a rancorous debate. Legislation was enacted to admit women as lay delegates to the General Conference in 1926. However, the law specified that only one woman could be elected from each Annual Conference. By severely limiting the number of women lay delegates, the General Conference ensured the continuance of male dominance. Though limited in number, women's participation in the polity had opened up an opportunity for them to champion their causes from the floor, which resulted in the passing of resolutions that would have been ignored.

Baptist

THROUGHOUT AMERICAN HISTORY, the guiding force in the Baptist Church has been its structure and polity. Though there is no theological statement of a faith or doctrinal creed that binds all Baptists, two traditions of polity and practice have been characteristic of Baptist churches. First, among Baptists there has been a consistent emphasis on the authority of the congregation or congregational rule. Second, the sovereignty of the local congregation has been a generally accepted tenet and practice. It is commonly asserted that there is no higher body than the individual church, where every member—male and female—possesses the vote. However, this pattern is more reflective of voting patterns in Baptist churches after 1880. During the colonial and antebellum periods, though women voted in some churches and a few participated in Baptist associations, most were denied suffrage. Independent churches united for certain purposes and formed associations. The latter bodies had no legislative powers; they could only advise. Agreements made by delegates from local churches are binding only on the congregation that adopts or resolves to hold the position.

In late-nineteenth-century churches, though women might still be denied suffrage, many had a "direct voice" and participated in the legislative bodies of the church. At the local level, numerous churches elected males as "delegates" and women as "lady delegates" to the state, regional, and national Baptist associations. For example, in 1895 the members of the First Bryan Baptist Church in Savannah, Georgia, selected Anna Foster, Julia Williams, and Dolly Jackson as the lady delegates to represent their church at the Baptist State Convention. However, given the nature and structure of Baptist churches, there were instances where pastors reserved the right to appoint all delegates and representatives to ecumenical meetings. Unlike First Bryan, the members of the Union Baptist Church in Baltimore had no say in the selection of delegates, since the minister made the appointments. Rev. Harvey Johnson, a powerful and charismatic minister and a secular leader, chose only male delegates and rarely appointed women to any positions of formal leadership during his forty-five years as pastor of Union Baptist.

In all periods, church law and patterns of women's participation in the Baptist polity varied depending on the church, city, state, and region. Some churches established rules for congregational governance in separate constitutions. Some permitted societies within the church to create their own bylaws, while others governed in accordance with a set of constitutions and bylaws that could be amended by a congregational vote. Eligibility for voting might be determined by a constitutionally recognized authority vested in either the full congregation or the pastor. In the absence of detailed studies of local black Baptist churches and associations in different geographic areas, it is difficult to certify an overarching pattern. However, it appears that until the 1870s and '80s women in most southern and many northern Baptist churches rarely participated in discussions of church business or voted on deacons and ministers. Most Baptist churches held monthly church meetings open to members. At these gatherings issues pertaining to the institution and its members were discussed and voted on. In some churches, women lacked voice and vote. In the late nineteenth and early twentieth centuries, in Baptist churches where women had equal votes, they lacked equal status, which frequently meant exclusion from formal leadership positions, like those of minister, deacon, treasurer, sexton, financial secretary, Sunday school superintendent, and church clerk (secretary). Women's participation was limited to teaching Sunday school and working in church missionary societies to raise funds for support of church operations.

The First African Baptist Church of Richmond was the "best-known black church of the post-1840 period." In Richmond during the 1770s, most enslaved blacks affiliated with the white First Baptist Church. As their numbers grew, and exceeded those of the white members, they sought a separate church. By 1838 a plan was devised to permit African Americans to worship and function as a separate unit, in the same building, under the auspices of the First Baptist Church. Known as the First African Baptist Church, the congregation was assigned a white pastor and allowed to choose thirty black deacons, who ran the church with the pastor. However, in the case of disputes, a board of white overseers exercised final jurisdiction.

It was not unusual for women to attend the monthly church meetings and voice their concerns, but they were denied suffrage at the First African and other black Baptist churches in Richmond. Arriving in the city after the Civil War, Boston black minister Peter Randolph was surprised to find that the female members of the Ebenezer Baptist Church were not permitted to vote at the business meetings and that the church maintained sex-segregated seating. Though many churches abandoned this practice and separate entrances to the sanctuary, black Baptist leaders in Richmond were conflicted over the issue of female religious suffrage. Under Randolph's leadership, the Ebenezer Baptist Church granted women religious suffrage on all issues except pastoral appointments. Though women had a voice and could vote, at the beginning of the twentieth century only the male members at Ebenezer were permitted to vote on pastoral appointments.

The First African Baptist Church is an example of an institution dominated by an exceedingly powerful deacon's board whose tentacles reached into the deepest corners of the black community—the board dictated the law and controlled every aspect of the church's business. Following the Civil War, women sought full equality in the polity. Historian Elsa Barkley Brown claims that in 1880, when the women at the First African Baptist Church petitioned for the right to vote in the election of the pastor, they were "reclaiming a lost right." However, between 1841 and 1880 there is no evidence that the female members ever participated in the election of either the pastor or the deacons.

Rev. James H. Holmes was appointed the pastor by the white Baptists who established the church, and he served in this position until his death at the beginning of the twentieth century. Thus, until 1880 the issue of women voting on a minister was moot. Moreover, to clarify the position of women in the polity, the deacon's board had erected a law requiring that "in the church the business must be done by the male members." This meant that women could attend church meetings but were denied a vote in church deliberations. On April 15, 1880, more than two hundred "prominent sisters of the church" submitted a petition to the deacons and male members of the First African Baptist Church requesting that female members of the church be allowed to vote on the reelection or dismissal of Rev. Holmes. The petition was tabled until the June 27, 1880, regular church meeting—or until after the election, at which time it was adopted overwhelmingly by a vote of 413 to 16. In 1901 women church members exercised that right for the first time.

In 1901, in a bitterly contested election for pastor, the First African women played a decisive role in the defeat of Rev. Walter H. Brooks, one of the best known and most distinguished ministers in the nation, and the son-in-law of the then recently deceased Rev. Holmes. Mired in national Baptist politics, the church was divided between those who opposed (separationist) and those who supported cooperation with white Baptists (cooperationist). In the ensuing debate, Brooks and numerous old-line, prominent members were widely characterized by the opposition as being against "factory people or the laboring classes." The First African's membership of 2,500 was predominantly working class and female. By 1900, in numerous black communities, there was a consciousness of the differences between the working class and the elite, often described as the "masses" and the "classes." The working class was poorer and often darker in complexion, and more rooted in traditional African beliefs and practices, including ecstatic church worship. Working-class members were frequently pitted against the more conservative and sedate black middle and upper classes. Prior to the election, male and female canvassers "went door to door telling of the qualities" of Rev. William Thomas Johnson, the cooperationists's candidate. "Clubs were organized and ladies who knew nothing of the machinery at work or the deep laid plans on foot" were told that "Brooks was opposed to the factory people." Women and children (more than eight years of age) fully participated in the election meetings, vociferously voicing their opinions.

As evidence of the class issues at stake, Mrs. Margaret Hewlett, "a plain speaking woman," proclaimed that she did not support Brooks because she heard that, as pastor of the Nineteenth Street Baptist Church in Washington, D.C., "he wouldn't let the sisters give vent to their feelings. He would stop in his sermons and wait for order." Brooks was against the display of uninhibited emotions through shouting and dancing that interrupted the church service. John Mitchell Jr., the editor of the *Richmond Planet* and one of the most respected members of the church and community, like other Brooks supporters was shouted down. As he was told to "shut up" and was ridiculed by the female faction—"Don't he look pretty said one sister in tones of derision"—Mitchell declared that the conduct of "certain females had been disgraceful." Emphasizing the class divide, Mitchell and other noted men and women, including nationally prominent bank executive and NACW leader Maggie Lena Walker, voiced strong concern that the church meetings were dominated by "people without manners . . . who did not know how to respect the ordinary rules of debate." Likewise, "Sister Mildred A. Cross, . . . an interested spectator, denounced the proceedings as the most disgraceful she had ever seen," proclaiming that it was "worse than a minstrel show." Be that as it may, the First African's predominantly working-class female membership flexed its muscles and dictated the outcome of the election.

The mostly female membership, including many former slaves and rural migrants to Richmond, was steeped in traditional forms and styles of worship, elements of which had survived slavery and were transmitted from one generation to the next. Patterns of worship, such as call and response, shouting, and lining out and singing of hymns in common meter, were revered by the "masses" and abhorred by the "classes." Slave spirituals were particular targets of black educators, who attempted to remove them from the repertoires of black college choirs. Like the First African Baptist Church, the various efforts of a primarily urban educated elite leadership to cleanse their institutions of such practices were rebuffed by the mostly working-class congregations. This struggle, evident in a few urban churches after the Civil War, was highly visible at the beginning of the twentieth century. Middle-class African Americans, determined to divest themselves of all vestiges of the slave past, emphasized intellectual development and cultural refinement. There was a particular sensitivity to the emotionally charged religious practices that had been critical to the slave culture and prevalent in most black churches after the war. In some states, such as Virginia, at least two-thirds of all black church members lived in rural districts. Rural churches resisted the "changes and the 'modern ideas' characteristic of the city church" and continued to perpetuate antebellum patterns of worship.

Baptist churches were notorious for their public bickering over the question of selection and dismissal of pastors. In some cases, members of the congregation and ministers and deacons engaged in heated debates that ended in fistfights and razor cuttings. The prevalence of such confrontations, often attributed to the aggressiveness of females, suggests that more women were challenging church authority and exercising their right to critique the behavior of male clergy and have a greater say in the body politic. In 1905 at the Shiloh Baptist Church in Cleveland, Ohio, several women appeared before the deacon's board and charged Rev. Edward Dandridge with "unbecoming conduct." The board sanctioned the charges and withheld the minister's salary. Since the church was divided over the issue, the board's decision was calculated to avoid confrontation. Instead of resigning, the minister continued to serve without pay. In a quarterly business session, attended by more than two hundred persons, the pastor announced that, having received the support of the local white Baptist association, he would continue to lead the church. Irate congregants responded with cries like "We must get rid of him," and "Let's have it out." In the ensuing brawl, a number of persons were slashed with razors. Among those arrested and charged were the minister, two deacons, and one church member. This was just one of many disturbances that occurred at Shiloh during that year. Concern about how such conduct would be perceived by whites led the *Cleveland Gazette* to call for a halt in this type of behavior, suggesting that it did not reflect well on the black community. The minister blamed the debacle on a few "disgruntled" women.

Similar to the women at Shiloh, in 1922 a number of female members of the Florida Avenue Baptist Church in Washington, D.C., challenged the authority of Rev. W. A. Taylor, whom they claimed "ruled with an iron hand, caring nothing for the rights of others." However, at the Florida Avenue Baptist Church there was a split between pew women—the majority of females, and the members of the Ladies Aid Society—a small elite group that supported the pastor. It is likely that there were underlying class issues. In a letter to the public, widely publicized in the black and white press and signed "WOMEN OF FLORIDA AVENUE BAPTIST CHURCH who do not belong to the Ladies Aid," the women announced that they had done their "best to get along with the pastor." They asserted, "No one wants to rule, but taxation without representation did not work in Colonial days and does not set too well now." Clarifying their position, the women stated "emphatically that the Ladies Aid . . . does not represent the entire womanhood of the church, nor does it express their sentiments." Citing numerous examples of how Taylor had ignored and disregarded the congregation's wishes, they revealed the pastor's dictatorial nature. The women's statements were supported by male members of the church who disclosed numerous instances of Taylor's disregard for church procedures, such as refusing to hold regular or special business meetings called for the purpose of electing or dismissing a pastor. One member said, "All business meetings are opened with prayer and closed by the Police. Casualty list to date: one dead and many wounded. The fighting is still going on."

While Baptist women in some late-nineteenth-century churches voted on church matters, the First African, Shiloh, and Florida Avenue Baptist churches are examples of the kind of freedom and power Baptist ministers and deacon boards as representatives of the congregation have possessed, and how in some instances they have been able to arrogate power unto themselves. At the local level the independent autonomy of individual congregations on matters of faith and practice has provided pastors, trustees, and local deacon boards with virtual power to enact whatever legislation they desire and to determine the status of women. Where members of a congregation associate their prestige with a minister's secular status, they tend to acquiesce to his or her wishes in the church. In Baptist churches, what is most important is the tradition of the individual church. Some congregations have been willing to yield authority to the pastor or the minister, or the trustees and deacons. Traditionally, ministers have been the central power brokers in the Baptist church.

Irrespective of time period, pastors such as Rev. Harvey Johnson at Baltimore's Union Baptist, and Adam Clayton Powell Jr. at Harlem's Abyssinian Baptist Church were able to amass a great deal of political power within the church and exert their will. These men—similar to late-twentieth-century religious leaders Martin Luther King, Jr., Ralph David Abernathy, Calvin Butts, Floyd Flake, T. D. Jakes, Joseph Lowery, Eddie Long, and other contemporary figures—were influential in their communities as well as in the nation. Most pastors seek to mold their churches so the authority rests with the clergy. Some, however, have offered a vision for leadership that includes the extension of authority to a trained laity.

Women seeking formal leadership roles and clergy rights in the Baptist denominations have faced an even steeper climb than women in most Protestant churches. Theoretically the Baptist Church's congregational polity supports female ordination, but often the higher authority of holy scripture, as interpreted by male ministers, is invoked. Lacking an overarching ecclesiastical authority to appeal to, Baptist women have been subject to the whims of male clergy in their local churches, the majority of whom have been reluctant to grant women either formal leadership roles or ordination. Women's struggle for ordination in Baptist churches has been extremely difficult. Yet in the twentieth century there were any number of female Baptist evangelists and a few pastors of churches. Female evangelists were active in many states, including Indiana, Pennsylvania, New York, Massachusetts, Virginia, South Carolina, Tennessee, Georgia, South Dakota, and the District of Columbia. The growth of female evangelists in the black Baptist Church was part of the general pattern of development first evidenced in the Methodist denominations in the nineteenth century. Like other male clergy, the pastors of Baptist churches saw a practical value in having women conduct revivals and participate on church programs as singing evangelists. Female evangelists tended to attract larger audiences and raised the visibility of a church. Frequently, this meant an increase in members and larger collections.

At the beginning of the twentieth century evangelists were viewed as a positive influence, but by 1912 male clergy were threatened by the growing power of Baptist lay and clergy women. As Lewis G. Jordan, editor of the Baptist *Mission Herald*, reported, "Our Eastern pastors are far ahead of the Southern pastors on the Woman Preacher question." His concern was not just that women were in the pulpit, but that they were "touring the country as preachers" and were prominent figures at the New England Baptist Convention, preaching "practically every sermon" at the annual meeting. Considering their heightened activism, Jordan speculated that women would soon be pastoring Baptist churches. More ominous concerns were the "methods" or strategies adopted by Baptist women's conventions and missionary societies to achieve their goals. Women were reminded that they were members of Baptist churches pastored by men who could stop their advance from the pew to the pulpit. Fearful of alienating the rank-and-file church women, Jordan assured *Mission Herald* readers of his support for extending opportunities for development to "Godly women," but he concluded that it was "unbaptistic and unbiblical" to have numerous "untrained women neglecting their homes running throughout the country calling themselves preachers."

Neither the rants nor the warnings of editors or male clergy discouraged Baptist women from pursuing formal leadership roles and having a voice in church deliberations. In 1920 at the annual meeting of the National Evangelistic Conference in Boston, in the face of "unfriendly criticism," Rev. Mrs. Devereaux preached a sermon. As a member of the conference, Devereaux was well respected for her evangelistic and philanthropic work among the Baptist and AME churches in Boston and other cities. Like Devereaux, licensed ministers, such as Julia A. Taylor-Birchmore, also held membership in Baptist associations. Taylor-Birchmore belonged to the Allegheny Central Baptist Association. As the numbers of women preachers affiliating and participating in local and state Baptist associations rose, male clergy leaders took drastic actions to impede their advance. In 1934 the Union District Baptist Association in Indiana enacted legislation raising the qualifications for clergy and banning women preachers from Baptist churches. To attract more males, the association considered granting pensions for ministers as well as laymen in leadership positions.

Like many males, there were Baptist women who abhorred the idea of women preaching and serving as pastors but had no problem with female evangelists. Though some were licensed to preach and ordained and a few were pastors of small churches, most female clergy were traveling and singing evangelists. Often female clergy were as qualified as their male counterparts—and sometimes they were better qualified. For example, Alice L. Thompson Waytes, a native of Union County, South Carolina, graduated from Benedict College in the 1890s and completed courses in missionary training at Shaw University (1901) and the Moody Bible Institute (1904), and taught public school for several years prior to her appointment in 1910 as superintendent of Bible school work for the Church Federation Society of New York, a white organization. As "a gospel preacher of no mean ability," Waytes was also an author and writer. Her prominence as a Bible lecturer and preacher led to her appointment as pastor of the Shiloh Baptist Church in West Medford, Massachusetts (1911). Following a short stint at Shiloh, Waytes resigned to pursue a career as a political activist. In the presidential election of 1912 she was a campaign speaker for the Progressive Party, and in 1916 for the Republican Party.

A few women, such as Rena G. Thompson, were ordained. In 1949 Thompson was licensed to preach and ordained by her pastor at the Ebenezer Baptist Church in North Philadelphia. In 1950 she transferred to the Enon Baptist Church, one of the oldest and most influential black churches in Philadelphia. Thompson's request to preach was initially rejected by Rev. William B. Toland. Following Thompson's announcement that she was not interested in pastoring a church, but was content to be an evangelist organizing revivals and preaching in churches throughout the region, Toland reversed his decision. For most of her life, Thompson was confined to "hard domestic work." Though there were Baptist women in Philadelphia licensed to preach many years before Thompson, few were ordained. Even if they favored female preachers, most Baptist ministers and pastors of prominent urban churches such as Enon Baptist would neither ordain nor accept a woman preacher employed as a domestic.

The route to the pulpit in Baptist churches was unpredictable and dependent on many factors, including geographical location, familial, social, and political relations, and church tradition. In 1965, after the death of her husband, Rev. Charles O. Trimm, Trudie Trimm was the first Baptist woman to be unanimously elected by a deacon and trustee board and congregation to pastor a church. The New Testament Church, founded in 1943 by Charles and Trudie Trimm, within two decades was one of the leading Baptist churches in Chicago. As a political activist and leading figure in the Woman's Convention, Trudie Trimm had a successful political career as a precinct captain and a Democratic committeewoman of the predominantly black Second Ward in Chicago. At the time of her ordination there were dissenting ministers, but no hint of the storm of protest that would erupt among local Baptist clergy who did not "want women invading their sacred domain." There was little concern for her qualifications to hold the office—only her gender mattered. Ignoring the objections of several ministers, Rev. E. F. Ledbetter, pastor of the Metropolitan Missionary Baptist Church, agreed to the ordination. Ledbetter knew of the New Testament trustee board's threat to close the church if Trudie Trimm did not become the pastor. In the 1960s, Rev. Trudie Trimm was the first and only female pastor among the 2,700 ministers elected to the National Baptist Convention, USA.

In the 1970s Suzan D. Johnson was the first black woman ordained by the prestigious American Baptist Churches in the USA, and the first woman to be elected president of the ten-thousand-member Hampton University Ministers' Conference (2002), the largest interdenominational conference of black clergy in the United States. This followed Johnson's appointment in 1997, by President William Jefferson Clinton, to the President's Advisory Commission on Race. A graduate of Emerson College in Boston, Teachers College of Columbia University, and Union Theological Seminary, Johnson was well qualified to become the first African American woman called to assume the position as senior pastor of Mariners Temple Baptist Church in the 1980s.

Johnson used her celebrity to open national dialogue about gender and power in churches by speaking and writing in secular venues. Johnson argued that Baptist clergy, in significant numbers, rejected female preachers' ordination not because of gender, but because of the threat to established power. In actuality gender and power are closely linked in all of the women's struggles for entry and advancement in religion and in the professions. As late as 1993, Johnson observed that she knew of only two other black women who had become senior pastors of Baptist churches. It was her feeling that women "will have to create satellite churches as a means of empowerment. . . . If there is no room for us other than in non-pastoral roles, then we have no other choice but to establish our own ministries outside the traditional network." By the mid-1990s there were more ordained black Baptist women, some of whom were pastors of churches, but many local churches and ministerial associations continued to deny ordination to women.

Leadership Roles in Baptist Conventions

THE FIRST KNOWN black Baptist churches were organized by slaves in the South during the late eighteenth century and functioned under the careful oversight of their masters or their representatives. By the early nineteenth century other black churches were formed in cities such as Williamsburg, Richmond, and Petersburg, Virginia, where large numbers of African Americans resided, including a substantial number of free blacks. As required by law, many antebellum southern churches had white pastors. Northern Baptist churches such as the African Baptist Church in Boston, the Abyssinian Baptist Church in New York City, and the First African Baptist Church in Philadelphia were formed by free blacks. Between 1815 and 1880 most black Baptists, through the aegis of the African Baptist Missionary Society, maintained close affiliations with national white Baptist organizations. In 1845, as a result of the white Baptists' split over slavery, the African Baptist Missionary Society joined the Southern Baptist Convention. Other all-black Baptist associations were organized in the North and West, including the Baptist Foreign Mission Convention, the American National Baptist Convention, and the National Baptist Educational Convention. In 1895 these groups merged to form the National Baptist Convention.

In 1900, with a membership of 1,864,000, the National Baptist Convention was the largest black organization in the United States. It was also the major philanthropic agency in black America. For example, in 1899 the NBC contributed near $3 million for education, Sunday school expenses, domestic and foreign mission work, and church expenses. Substantial funds were raised by black Baptist women. Women played a central role in the organization's accomplishments. However, like the women's conventions later associated with the National Baptist Convention of America and the Progressive National Baptist Church, they held no offices on the organization's governing board and operated as a separate convention, auxiliary to the national body. A small number of female delegates attended the meetings of the BFMC, ANBC, and NBEC, a few of whom held token positions. However, Baptist women recognized that these were token positions. Among the educated black Baptist female elite were many outspoken and gender-conscious women who saw no conflict between their commitment to racial justice and feminist self-determination.

The establishment of black women's state conventions grew out of Baptist women's gender consciousness. In their attempts to form missionary societies and state conventions, Baptist women faced male opposition similar to that experienced by women in black Methodist denominations. In Tennessee, white women of the Women's Baptist Home Missionary Society aided black women in organizing Bible bands for daily Bible study and industrial schools throughout the state. Tennessee illustrates the widespread pattern of organizing taking place among black Baptist women in the South after the Civil War. By 1900 a network of local and state women's associations existed. Virginia Broughton, a leader of black Baptist women in Tennessee, noted that ministers and laymen, jealous of the women's growing numbers and the popularity of their work, felt threatened and "rose up in their

churches with all the influence and power of speech they could summon to oppose the woman's work and break it up if possible."

Through daily study, Baptist women developed a deep understanding of the Bible and special skills of analysis, which they exhibited at
church meetings. Moreover, the Bible bands demonstrated that
women, like men, could do theological interpretation, and do it well.
Like their Methodist, Presbyterian, and Episcopalian counterparts,
Baptist women summoned the stories of biblical women and used
evangelical language intricately laced with biblical precedents to create
intellectual and theological justifications for their rights. Similar to
their Methodist counterparts, many Baptist women wanted to establish separate women's societies. As the major Baptist clientele, they
insisted on having an educated and trained ministry and participating
in the selection of ministerial candidates. Similar to the women of
Richmond's First African Baptist Church, Broughton and her cohorts
were requesting a role in the governance of the church.

Pentecostal/Holiness

WOMEN WERE CENTRAL to the founding of Pentecostal/Holiness
denominations and churches. Though the trek from rural to urban and
southern to northern and midwestern towns and cities had begun in
the late nineteenth century, it was accelerated in the early twentieth
century. The event that perhaps had the greatest impact on this mass
movement in the early twentieth century was World War I, which
spurred the Great Migration. During the first four decades of the
twentieth century, 1,634,000 African Americans moved from rural
areas to cities in the South, and to the North and West. Escaping the
plantations and seeking a better life, migrants settled in cities such as
Norfolk, Baltimore, Chicago, Detroit, Philadelphia, Pittsburgh, New
York, Boston, Indianapolis, and Los Angeles. The concentration of a
mostly rural peasantry in these and other cities created new needs and
problems. Organized religion found it difficult to serve this population, which differed from the urbane black population already in the
city. Some churches shunned the poor and unkempt migrants, whom
they perceived as uncouth and threatening to the established black
middle class.

Numerous migrants found the established mainline black
Methodist and Baptist churches too formal and inflexible in their services. The members of these churches often frowned on shouting,

dancing, and hand clapping. Storefront churches, cults, and religious sects literally popped up on every corner. Women concerned about what they perceived as the neglect of holiness in mainline black churches, and interested in pursuing an unfettered ministry, left established Methodist and Baptist churches in search of a new freedom. Hundreds of women joined and founded Pentecostal, Holiness, and Spiritual churches. For example, in 1903 Mother Mary Magdalena Tate established the Latter Day Church of the Foundation of True Holiness and Sanctification. As an advocate of natural healing, Mary Baker Eddy, the founder of the Christian Science movement, attracted numerous black followers, particularly women such as Tate who were interested in the healing arts. Healing was one of many African cultural values that had survived the transatlantic slave trade and the institution of slavery, and it continued to flourish, mainly among blacks concentrated in the rural South.

Given the sheer numbers of Pentecostal/Holiness religious organizations and independent churches, it is impossible to speak about *the* leadership roles of women. Women have occupied a variety of positions and assumed many roles in the diverse institutions. As noted, numerous women founded missions, churches, and a few established denominations in which they served as ministers and bishops, trustees, and chief officers. Women have also served as founders and leaders in denominations where men are the sole leaders. For example, in the Church of God of Prophecy, men conducted the business and women were not permitted to speak at official business meetings. In order to have a voice, women were required to write notes that were given to the men, who could choose to either read or ignore the messages.

Some denominations, such as the United Holy Church of America and the Pentecostal Assemblies of the World, permitted women as pastors but not as bishops. It is for this reason that Mother Susan Gertrude Lightfoot left PAW in 1908 and, following a brief affiliation with the Abyssinia Baptist Church, founded the True Church of God (1910) in New York City, and that Ida Robinson withdrew from the UHCA and founded the Mount Sinai Holy Church of America, Inc., in Philadelphia (1924). Among the best-known women founders and preachers in the twentieth century are Ida Robinson; Rosa Horn, founder of the Pentecostal Faith Church in Harlem (1934); Elder Lucy Smith, founder and pastor of All Nations Pentecostal Church (1928) in Chicago; Johnnie Coleman, of the Christ Universal Temple in Chicago; Barbara King, of the Hillside Internal Truth Center in

Chicago; and Audrey Bronson, founder of the Sanctuary Church in Philadelphia. As founders and pastors, these women were not subject to the dictates of male leaders, but were iconic figures who served as models of success for the emulation of other women interested in developing ministries.

The Church of God in Christ, the largest and most influential black Pentecostal denomination, opposes the ordination of women as clergy. The COGIC *Official Manual* explicitly defines the prohibition against women's ordination as pastor, elder, or bishop while establishing their roles as evangelists and teachers who may "have charge of a church in the absence of the pastor." As in the Baptist and Methodist denominations, women exploit these restrictions and definitions as they continue to contend for the right of the pulpit. And, similar to women in other religious traditions, COGIC women maximized their power in the church by creating a Women's Department that is among the most powerful in any Christian denomination. In 1906 Elizabeth Robinson organized COGIC's Women's Convention (CWC). Comparable in structure to the Baptist Woman's Convention, the CWC was divided into women's state conventions headed by a president and state supervisor and included a state "mother," missionary, and recording secretary for women's work. Beginning with a small group of women concentrated in a few states, the CWC has grown to include eighty state supervisors in the United States and six women's conventions in foreign countries including Haiti, the Bahama Islands, and six stations in Africa and British Honduras. The CWC's annual meetings are held in conjunction with COGIC's Holy Convocation.

Though comparisons can be made between COGIC and the other major black denominations, there are differences. Like Baptist women, some COGIC women have maintained an interest in preaching, but the ordination of women was not a major issue in COGIC during the first half of the twentieth century. Unlike the Baptists, COGIC women have occupied several formal leadership roles such as that of a national treasurer or financial secretary as early as the 1930s. Lillian Brooks Coffey, one of the most important women in COGIC, held that position for a number of years. Though the Baptist Woman's Convention was for many years semi-autonomous and functioned as an auxiliary to NBC-USA, COGIC's Women's Department was never subordinate to male clergy leadership; rather, it was parallel "to and in partnership with the male episcopate of the church. The dual-sexed political structure of the church allowed a place for women's leadership and expertise within the denomination, despite prohibitions of women in pastoral roles." Utilizing this structure, the Women's Department acted as an agent to effectively propagate "the holiness beliefs of the denomination through teaching, discipline, and spiritual direction, to both men and women." The Women's Department, in effect, "embodied, codified and institutionalized the denomination's central doctrine of holiness."

Female Spaces and Formal Leadership

IN 1995, POLITICAL SCIENTIST Linda Faye Williams observed, "Most modern religion has an intimate relationship with patriarchy, and the Black church is no exception.... From the start, Black churches invariably were dominated by men who served as pastors, evangelists and deacons; and as visits to most Black churches reveal every Sunday, the Black church remains a female space dominated by men." Williams is accurate in her assertion that men continue to dominate formal leadership positions in black churches. Throughout the twentieth century women resisted religious masculinity and other forms of patriarchy that have existed throughout African American history. The rise and development of new spaces for religious leadership, especially women's missionary societies, women's conventions, and other female departments in Christian denominations, is extremely significant. It is through these entities that black women exercised self-determination and accomplished their goals in the twentieth century.

CHAPTER 3

"A Woman's Church
Within the Church"

The Woman's Movement in the Church

This is the day of liberalization of women. No longer will they stand for
the dictatorship of man on the mere basis of masculinity.

Kelly Miller (1928)

The women's organizations [are] auxiliaries to the men's and yet they [rep-
resent] the same denomination and they are all supposed to be working for
the same destination. . . . How unnecessary and futile it seems to be an
auxiliary to a Christian church that teaches the Fatherhood of God and the
Brotherhood of man—in its generic sense. Constancy is certainly a jewel!
If Christianity and Democracy are synonymous—where are we tending?

Rebecca Stiles Taylor (1942)

[W]e are concerned and disturbed by the attitude of some of our clergy
toward the missionary cause. Why do they refuse to help build up this
organization [AME Women's Missionary Society] which is one of the
most vital or should be most vital in the church, but seem to seek to tear
down and destroy the spirit of missions among the women?

Queenie L. Carter (1962)

WOMEN'S RELIGIOUS ORGANIZATIONS were originally formed
to raise funds to support the programs of their denominations.
These associations taught women organizational skills, how to work
together, and to value themselves and their abilities. The women's missionary societies and conventions unwittingly laid the groundwork for
a national black feminist awareness. Commenting on this phenomenon in 1897, a member of the Atlanta Prophecy Woman's Club
observed, "We have been taught 'woman.' " But what did this mean,
and how did it manifest itself?

Social activism was fundamental to black women's understanding of their Christian mission. In the 1890s they moved beyond their churches and established the National Association of Colored Women, a secular interdenominational organization. In doing so, they created a powerful feminist vehicle that brought together diverse women of different religious persuasions. The NACW was also another manifestation of Christian women's belief that it was their responsibility to speak for and uplift less fortunate women. They believed that women, like men, were required to address the critical race issues of the times: discrimination, segregation, lynching, suffrage, colonialism, and imperialism. For many black women, a true "race" woman was one who was "deeply interested in every good work designed to benefit her race," and sincerely committed to the advancement of girls and women.

By the late nineteenth century, this feminist consciousness was widespread and recognizable in individuals and institutions. Unlike white women, the feminist efforts of black women did not focus exclusively on issues of sexism. In an assessment of the struggle of African American women for "sex and race emancipation," Gertrude Johnson McDougald explained, "On the whole Negro woman's feminist efforts are directed chiefly toward the realization of the equality of the races, the sex struggle assuming the subordinate place." Black women, out of sheer necessity, fought racism and sexism and developed a practical feminism, or womanism, tailored to their situation and needs. This pattern was seen in the ways in which they operated in their church and community organizations.

At the national level most women's missionary societies organized their domestic programs around issues of gender and race. Their foreign programs focused almost exclusively on the plight of African women and girls. Feminism was broadly defined by Alice Felts, Nannie Burroughs, Rev. Florence Spearing Randolph, Gertrude Johnson McDougald, and other women leaders as organized activity on behalf of women's rights and interests. African American women's interests focused on the well-being of the black community. They understood that as black women in the United States, their status was, first and foremost, based on race. Thus, their feminism did not exclude racial issues. But, they also recognized that in black America women's status was often defined by sex, necessitating an internal struggle for their rights as women.

The masses of Protestant white women, engaged in missionary work, perceived Native Americans, Africans, and other people of color as inferior, ideas reinforced by notions of white supremacy. African American women were critically aware that whites stereotyped black females, describing them as promiscuous and depraved. From their perspective neither white Christian women nor black men could speak for black women or fully address their concerns. They understood that there was a critical need for missionary societies and conventions to provide black female Christian leadership, and a national secular organization—the NACW—to symbolize their work in the public arena.

The commitment of black women toward racial self-help and advancement, as well as their resistance to sexism, contributed to the development of a powerful religious and secular movement. Ironically, the segregation of females into auxiliaries had an unanticipated effect. Women's missionary associations and conventions fostered an independence they had previously not known. Rev. E. P. Murchison, editor of the CME *Christian Index*, observed that as church women's organizations grew strong and gained broad recognition they were perceived as a " 'woman's church within the Church.' " Murchison asserted, "In some denominations . . . the women's missionary society became so strong that there were tendencies to compete with the main church organization, to reject authority of the Church, and act separately on certain matters. This tendency has not been completely absent from all women's missionary societies. It was in reality a revolt against the dominance and discrimination practiced by men in the church." Murchison's statement is accurate. However, most black women's auxiliaries were subject to the dictates of male denominational boards and never "enjoyed complete freedom."

In the AME, AME Zion, and CME denominations the national missionary societies were dominated by the wives of bishops and leading ministers. Unlike the Methodists, the national leadership of Baptist women's conventions comprised mostly middle-class educators, businesswomen, and reformers whose positions were not solely dependent upon their relationship to the male clergy.

The concerns of black Presbyterian, Catholic, and Episcopal women have traditionally focused more on racial practices and the exclusion of black men from governance within their white-led denominations than on religious sexism. Reflecting on the history of Episcopal women, Marjorie Nichols Farmer claimed, "Women's issues are distinctly unimportant" for women at the historic St. Thomas Episcopal Church of Philadelphia. Speaking in the context of the late twentieth century, Farmer was unaware of the historic struggles of black Episcopal women for equality in the religious polity.

Because of their personal relationships with male clergy, especially bishops, the leaders of black Methodist women's organizations did not originally argue for an autonomous status, and they acquiesced to having male supervisors. In the twentieth century this pattern of governance was challenged. Though some of the leaders in the Baptist Woman's Convention were married to clergy, many were not. Also, the WC leadership reflected a more diverse class base, especially at the local level. While women such as Sarah Willie Layten (called S. Willie Layten), president of the Woman's Convention, were raised in families of privilege and were college educated, others, such as Nannie Burroughs (the corresponding secretary), Violet Johnson (a vice president), and Maggie Lena Walker (the first female banker in the United States), came from more humble backgrounds. Like most of the Baptist rank and file, several of the WC leaders came from working-class and poor families. Some had worked as domestic servants or washerwomen, and were sensitive to the plight of the majority of working-class black women and men. For example, Burroughs constantly reminded the Woman's Convention of the need for a diverse leadership, representative of all classes, especially working-class women who "perform menial labor for a living." In 1903, shortly after the formation of the WC, Burroughs argued, "The women who wash for a living have as much right, as much business, to be leaders in our churches, if they are spiritually, morally, [and] intellectually fitted, as the women who are mistresses of their own homes."

Differences in the governing structures of women's organizations critically influenced how they functioned. Methodist Episcopal, Presbyterian, and Episcopal women leaders appear to have maintained a fairly harmonious relationship with the male clergy in their denominations. As members of segregated churches within white denominations, these women were often subject to the sexism of their black brothers and the paternalism of their white sisters. While Baptist women launched broad social and political reform programs and often took independent courses of action, AME, AME Zion, and CME women tended to be more restricted in their operations. Much of the work of these organizations occurred at the local level, and involved evangelizing and dispensing charity to the poor.

The black women's missionary movement was a potent force in grassroots social reform. However, there were sharp differences in the national and international programs of these associations. There was also a power differential, related specifically to an organization's size and reach. For example, during most of the twentieth century, the membership base of the Baptist Woman's Convention was larger than that of any other black Protestant women's group. The WC's large membership and influence at the local level gave it a distinct advantage. The growing power of Pentecostal women, especially the creation and steady growth of the Church of God in Christ's Women's Department and the public activism of several women leaders, helped COGIC achieve a "more mainstream status" by the 1990s. Black churches affiliated with white-led Episcopal and Presbyterian denominations frequently comprised a more middle-class membership than the Baptist and Pentecostal churches. Though fewer black women were affiliated with predominantly white religious denominations, they often exerted considerable influence in secular associations, especially after 1960.

Women's Organizations and Denominational Authority

MALE CHURCH LEADERS recognized the crucial role women played within the churches, but insisted on male leadership and control of all denominational entities. During the antebellum period, whites perpetuated the notion that African Americans were a "feminine race" and weak and submissive. This categorization was widespread during slavery and continued for many years afterward. Male leaders asserted that black men should reclaim their manhood. Given the prominence of the church, this would require the masculinization of every aspect of religious organization, including the missionary process. This would allow male church leaders to take credit for women's work. Women's auxiliaries either reported directly to an all-male denominational mission board or were supervised by a male. The majority of men agreed with Rev. Alexander Crummell when he said, "Men, ministers *must* lead in missions," and did everything in their power to ensure that the image of missionary work was masculine.

In 1893 Gertrude Bustill Mossell was in the vanguard of those who asserted that women should have a say in how denominational funds were spent and receive recognition for their fund-raising activities. Mossell observed, "The usual plan is for the women to do the work and the men largely [get] the credit." For example, in the late nineteenth century some AME pastors protested women reporting money raised by their local Mite Missionary Society to Conference, arguing that only male ministers possessed that right.

Throughout the nineteenth and twentieth centuries male leaders in most denominations were ambivalent about women organizing missionary societies, and concerned about female dominance of home and foreign missionary work. Chief among the reasons for men opposing women's domestic and foreign missionary work was the need to control the collection and distribution of monies raised, and the projection and maintenance of a masculine denominational image. Extensive commentary in speeches, sermons, newspapers, and periodicals is indicative of the prominence of this issue. In addition to these reasons, many ministers opposed the idea of local women's auxiliaries raising money for any purpose outside of their control. In 1904, for example, a Presbyterian synodical secretary observed that the chief difficulty black women faced in trying to establish local women's auxiliaries was "that many . . . colored ministers, unlike their white brethren, are opposed to women's organizations" raising funds for purposes unrelated to "the support of their own churches."

Some pastors were terrified by the idea of women organizing, fearing a loss of power in their churches. For these clergy every suggestion or effort to establish a society was blocked. At the 1924 meeting of the Baptist Woman's Convention the organization's historian recounted the story of the opposition women encountered in trying to organize Baptist women's societies. She recalled that in the 1890s, at a church in Missouri, Mrs. C. R. McDowell was instructed by her pastor to " 'break up the effort' to organize a woman's society." Patterns of opposition to women's organizations, similar to those described by these Presbyterian and Baptist leaders, were widespread among black denominations.

During the 1920s and '30s, Baptist and Methodist men organized laymen's associations. In the NBC-USA the stated goal of the Laymen's Movement was to "harness the full strength of the laymen of the country." In 1925, Rev. David V. Jemison, the president of the Alabama Baptist State Convention and a leader in the Baptist Laymen's Missionary Movement, argued that the "movement will fill a place in our denomination, that cannot be filled by the ministry, nor by the women and girls of our denomination. . . . We are aware of the fact that many of us pastors . . . get the majority of our support from the women and children of our congregations. That may be true, but the fact remains that the men in our churches are the basis of supply. The women and children may give it, but they get it as a rule, from the man." Jemison chose to ignore the fact that most southern black Baptist churches were supported mainly by women, single and married, who worked as washerwomen and domestic servants.

The Baptist Laymen's Missionary Movement, which emphasized the dominance of men in missionary work, was a response to the growing power and assertiveness of black women and their organizations by the 1920s. Though the movement remained in existence through the twentieth century, it attracted relatively few men. However, Jemison's call for religious masculinization gained support among ambitious young clergy who wanted leadership positions in the National Baptist Convention, USA. Similarly, among the Methodists, in particular the AME Church, the laymen's movement emerged during the 1920s as a form of resistance to the growing power of the bishops and women. During the 1930s and '40s AME laymen joined with local clergy to build a national movement that by 1950 had morphed into the "Brotherhood Association" and included the bishops. The Baptist Laymen's Movement and the AME Brotherhood Association exploited the frustration and confusion of men who felt that male leadership of religious organizations was being challenged by females who embraced the ideas inherent in the women's movement.

During the 1940s, in a proposal to "revamp" the AME Church, Bishop Richard R. Wright Jr. made it clear that he was concerned about the growing power of women's missionary societies. He suggested that males be organized into men's service leagues and given social service jobs working with boys around issues such as employment, recreation, and education. Wright claimed that because of the feminization of missionary work, men had lost interest in the church and "drifted into other things. On the other hand, we have 100,000 women organized for missionary work." In the 1950s and '60s, as the black community grappled with the white backlash and violence directed toward the Civil Rights Movement, male leaders in the NBC-USA and AME Church were harsh in their criticism of men for abandoning domestic and foreign mission work and leaving it entirely to denominational women. In speaking of "Men and Missions," Rev. O. M. Locust, a Baptist minister, claimed, "The failure of Christian men to participate in Christian Missions is Spiritual Absence Without Leave, A.W.O.L. . . . . The restriction of Christian missionary activity to women is unchristian and without New Testament precedents." Locust revealed that denominations concurred on the need to sponsor seminars, institutes, and workshops with the intention of "helping our Christian men to rediscover their rightful place in the missionary movement."

Locust's concern, like that of Wright and other male clergy, was for the power and recognition women had gained through their missionary organizations, and how they utilized these and other entities to successfully advance in the church polity and secular society. For many men this represented the fulfillment of the prophecy of their nineteenth-century forefathers, who had opposed the forming of women's missionary societies. Not a few men believed that separate organizations led by women "would give them a sense of power and a desire to 'rule men,' " and that if women were allowed financial control over the monies they collected, men would be emasculated.

By raising funds for domestic and foreign mission programs, women in many denominations developed major political and social capital that they invested in their secular organizations to achieve their racial and gender goals. A detailed examination of Baptist and Methodist women's societies in particular, especially their leadership, organizational structures, and relationship to the polity, reveals how they functioned and what they did. The evolution of these organizations reflects the complexity of black life, especially the gender, class, race, and transnational issues that define much of the history of African Americans after emancipation.

The Baptist Woman's Convention

THE WOMAN'S CONVENTION, Auxiliary to the National Baptist Convention, was founded in Richmond, Virginia, in 1900. Though the word "auxiliary" was included in its title, prior to 1916 it did not function in that capacity. The WC's struggle to have an autonomous status ensued for more than sixty years, ending with Nannie Helen Burroughs's death in 1961. In their respective positions as president and corresponding secretary of the Woman's Convention, S. Willie Layten and Burroughs were the most powerful women in the denomination.

Layten and Burroughs came from different backgrounds and were intense competitors. Though they had a shared understanding about the nature of race, class, and sex discrimination and both embraced the need to counter injustice, they differed in their approaches and willingness to challenge male authority within the NBC. Layten, a very light-complected woman from Philadelphia who married and had a

Members of the Woman's Convention Auxiliary to the National Baptist Convention. Nannie Helen Burroughs is in the foreground with banner, ca. 1905.

child at an early age, was a political activist and feminist who fought assiduously for the rights of blacks and women. As the daughter of Rev. William H. Phillips, she was raised in a middle-class home and was on intimate terms with many of the male leaders in the National Baptist Convention. A graduate of Lemoyne College, she took graduate courses in sociology at Temple University and extension courses in social work at the University of Pennsylvania.

Burroughs was the dark-complected daughter of a domestic worker and a ne'er-do-well preacher. As a child growing up in a working-class community in Washington, D.C., surrounded by domestic servants and washerwomen who were the mainstays of their families, Burroughs developed a special appreciation for wage-earning women and a sincere love and respect for black culture. As a student at the elite Dunbar High School, she became critically aware of the intraracial

Nannie Helen Burroughs, a quintessential feminist, supreme advocate for black civil rights, and preeminent advocate for poor and working-class black women, served for over fifty years as the corresponding secretary and president of the Woman's Convention, Auxiliary to the National Baptist Convention.

color discrimination and class prejudice commonly practiced by some middle- and upper-class blacks. In educational institutions like Dunbar, dark-skinned girls from poor and working-class families were often marginalized, ignored, and shut out of the social activities dominated by elite children. These experiences helped to define and shape Burroughs's social and political views and led her to champion the cause of the poor and working-class black masses.

S. Willie Layten understood sexism and argued for the equality of women in the public sphere, but in the Baptist Convention she often accommodated the wishes of the male clergy. Layten's responses were conditioned by her long-term familial and personal relationships with the Baptist clergy leadership. Her predilection for supporting male efforts to subordinate the Woman's Convention and her stormy relationship with Burroughs caused a permanent division of the women's organization into two factions. Both Burroughs and Layten were strong willed, and each was determined to prevail.

From the beginning Nannie Burroughs was the primary force behind the WC's drive for independence and autonomy. It was no accident that the title of the women's organization included the term "convention," instead of "board." Layten supported Elias Camp Morris, president of the National Baptist Convention, who suggested shortly after the WC's formation that the women relinquish their power and operate as an auxiliary board of the male-dominated NBC. Burroughs disagreed with Layten and Morris, and was determined from the outset that the WC should prevail as an autonomous body. She also refused to have her position as corresponding secretary usurped by Layten, who contrived to undercut her efforts and lessen her influence in the WC.

In 1903 Rev. E. W. D. Isaac, editor of the *National Baptist Union*, closely covered the controversy, making public the much-discussed dispute between Burroughs and Layten over the WC's status. Depicting the WC as engulfed in bitter strife that rendered it impotent and rent by internal divisions, Isaac wrote, "The President of the Women's Convention endorses a certain condition of things, which endorsement the Corresponding Secretary construes as a conspiracy on the one hand and a bold effort on the other, to take away some of the rights which belong to her." According to Isaac, "dissatisfaction and dissension," as well as "heated contests" between Layten and Burroughs for "dual authority," were visible in 1900 at the organization of the WC. Within three years the rancorous and perpetual infighting mushroomed into "deadly combat between official rivals."

In 1915, only fifteen years after the WC's founding, the NBC was torn by bitter internal struggles that split the organization into two separate denominations—the National Baptist Convention of America and the National Baptist Convention of the United States of America, Inc. (NBC-USA). The most immediate concern undergirding the bitter split was the question of ownership of the National Baptist Publishing House, a key component of the black Baptist community. The underlying cause was the question of whether or not black Baptists should continue to rely on northern white Baptists for support of black institutions and publications. A growing concern among some NBC leaders was the issue of ownership of institutions and properties that were created, developed, and controlled by individual NBC members.

Sarah Willie Layten, one of the foremost black Christian feminist activists of the late nineteenth and early twentieth century, was president of the Woman's Convention, Auxiliary to the National Baptist Convention for almost half a century.

Operating under the Educational Board, the publishing business annually reported more than $200,000 in revenues. As the head of the press and the director of the Educational Board, R. H. Boyd exercised great influence. The publishing business and the National Training School for Women and Girls, founded and directed by Nannie Burroughs, developed into major centers of influence. Emphasizing primarily the need to professionalize domestic service, the school aimed to train women as skilled workers capable of working as cooks, laundresses, household workers, missionaries, bookkeepers, stenographers, musicians, and printers. Questions of ownership and NBC efforts to take over and control these institutions created national controversy and internal turmoil as members were torn in their loyalties.

Following the NBC schism, in 1916 the WC was divided into two women's conventions. The more visible of the two groups was the Woman's Convention NBC-USA, headed by Layten and Burroughs.

Students at the National Training School for Women and Girls in Washington, D.C. Founded in 1908, by Nannie Helen Burroughs, the school operated under the auspices of the Woman's Convention, Auxiliary to the National Baptist Convention.

During the early twentieth century the WC's reach and impact on the masses of black Americans was extensive. The organization and its leaders were influential in most of the major social and political movements of the time. At the national level, the voice and leadership of one individual—Nannie Burroughs—stood out. In the decades following the NBC split, the bitter internal struggle between Burroughs and Layten increased as the NBC-USA's male leaders intensified their efforts to gain control of the WC and its finances, and to secure ownership of the National Training School for Women and Girls. NBC-USA's male leaders exhibited little concern for the women's social reform agenda, concentrating more on subduing and, if possible, eliminating Burroughs and muting her national voice.

As a social critic holding white and black America accountable, Burroughs yielded little ground. She was adored by the masses for her fearless honesty and fealty to black people, especially her willingness to champion the issues and causes most important to the poor and working classes. Between 1900 and 1950 Burroughs castigated the middle-class black leadership for its lack of concern for the black masses, and for the perpetuation of intraracial class and color discrimination. Since Burroughs was a columnist for several black newspapers, her views were known and spread to thousands of persons throughout the nation. In "Not Color but Character," Burroughs wrote, "Many Negroes have colorphobia as badly as white folk have Negrophobia. . . . There is no denying it, Negroes have colorphobia. Some Negro men have it. Some Negro women have it. . . . The fairer some Negroes are the better they think themselves, without any thought of an ounce of character to go along with it, and enough good sense to know that color is not a badge of superiority of mind nor soul." Similarly, she told white Americans, "Stop making laws to protect the legal and civil rights of all citizens and when the rights of the Negro are involved, allow white citizens to put themselves above the law and not only deny Negroes their legal rights, but persecute and lynch them. Such acts express vicious race prejudice. Out of such acts and attitudes America can never build a Christian democracy."

As a highly visible and outspoken black social and political activist Burroughs enjoyed the backing of several prominent men in the NBC-USA denomination and numerous national black and white leaders. With a solid base of support among the rank-and-file members of the NBC-USA, comprised mostly of wage-earning women, Burroughs was somewhat insulated from the efforts to remove her from office. However, the opposition was not deterred; they simply devised more ways to isolate and negate her influence in the denomination.

From the outset, there was little interest or support from the male leaders of the National Baptist Convention and S. Willie Layten for Burroughs's proposal to erect a school. The NBC ignored the school during the first decade of its existence, viewing it "with a kind of amused contempt." According to Burroughs, the NBC did not give "one cent" to the school. "Even the Woman's Convention . . . held aloof" and gave "rather parsimoniously to the support of the Training School." Assuming that Burroughs would not be able to accomplish her goal, NBC leaders waited for the fledgling institution to fail. Burroughs invested her own money in the venture. From her perspective the purpose of the woman's movement in the church was to "uplift our sex and improve our home life." She believed that the training school would be a factor in the accomplishment of those goals.

By 1914 NBC leaders could no longer ignore the training school. The sheer value of its property and buildings and the school's ability to attract significant donations brought it to the attention of the NBC board. There were widespread reports of the "intention of the plunderers [NBC executive board]" to take over the National Baptist Publishing House and property in Nashville, and the National Training School, in Washington, D.C. In May 1915, after the NBC split, the newly organized executive board secretly incorporated. Under the new charter, the NBC-USA, Inc., gained exclusive control over the management and properties of the Foreign Mission, the Baptist Young People's Union, and the Woman's Convention. The WC was stripped of all its powers, including the right to elect its own officers and to appoint committee chairs and the trustee board for the school. Moreover, disposition of all contributions and funds raised by the WC and the school would be determined by the NBC-USA's executive board.

WC President S. Willie Layten acceded to the board's wishes; Burroughs did not. The directors of the NBC-USA corporation knew that Burroughs would not willingly succumb to their demands. Subsequently they hatched a plan to discredit her and raise doubts about her honesty, integrity, and ability to operate the school. M. M. Rodgers, a close ally of the NBC-USA board, was appointed auditor and empowered to examine the financial records and assess the properties and institutions held by boards. With no experience as an auditor, Rodgers took a cursory look at the National Training School's records and prepared a financial report with recommendations, suggesting that Burroughs was incompetent and dishonest. The widely publicized report, replete with errors—including nonexistent expenses—indicated that Burroughs had misused funds, paying herself double what she had actually earned. Burroughs and the NBC-USA board of trustees were besieged by letters, telegrams, telephone calls, and news reports, indicating overwhelming national support for Burroughs and the school. In a scathing and detailed response, Burroughs challenged the auditor's assertions and recommendations and stated that in accordance with the new charter the NBC-USA would own and control the National Training School. Confronted with mounting public and denominational support for Burroughs, and embarrassed by the auditor's flawed reports, the NBC-USA board of directors backed down.

Following their defeat, the NBC-USA leaders concentrated on relegating the Woman's Convention to the status of an auxiliary board. The first task was to widen the breach between Layten and Burroughs and create greater divisions among the WC officers. Through innuendo, spurious leaks to the press, and innumerable rebuffs, the NBC-USA executive board relentlessly chipped away at Burroughs's public image and raised doubts about her veracity. Speaking before the entire convention, in 1924 NBC-USA President Lacy Kirk Williams gave notice that the WC "must be both in name and in fact, a subsidiary of the Convention." In 1925, when Burroughs appealed for public support to pay off the school's mounting debts, it was widely reported that the Baptist Convention had contributed more than $73,000 to the school. Fearing that the public would be confused and reluctant to support the school, Burroughs went on the defense, explaining that "the Baptist Convention at its most generous moment never exceeded the sum of $10 in its contribution to the work of the Training School."

In 1928 the NBC-USA demanded that the school's trustees "surrender their charter and turn the school over to the convention to own, manage, and control." Casting doubts on the NBC's ability to manage the school, Burroughs claimed that of the numerous Baptist schools managed by state conventions, many had closed or been "sold by the men of the convention." Burroughs felt that the NBC-USA charter was out of touch with the times, especially as it related to women "in this twentieth century of woman suffrage." Reiterating that the 1915 charter had reduced the heads of boards to "mere hirelings," Burroughs asserted that since there were no women on the NBC-USA's board of directors, the Woman's Convention had "no voice, vote, nor legal status under the charter." For example, Burroughs cited the treatment of Layten, who was rebuffed and not allowed to speak at a convention meeting. According to Burroughs, "Layten came forward and after a whispered consultation, went way back—and sat down. She never said a mumbling word—not a word." Refusing to be subordinated or silenced by the board, Burroughs stated that even if she were removed from office, she would not leave the NBC-USA, nor "be kicked around like a hound dog."

Between 1928 and 1938 the NBC-USA's executive board continued to harass Burroughs and did everything possible to dilute her influence in the Woman's Convention. During the twenty-three years after the National Baptist Convention split, the rancorous dispute between the two had played out in full view of the public. Rumors—"charges and malicious falsehoods"—were "reported, printed, and circulated" about Burroughs and the National Training School. But the bitter recriminations, charges, and countercharges had neither weakened nor lessened the support of many Baptist women and men for Burroughs, and prominent black and white leaders steadfastly stood by her. Burroughs's indomitable will whetted the appetite of her enemies and made them more determined to deal with her. In 1936 the convention established the National Theological Seminary and a woman's training school in Nashville, Tennessee. Following the dictates of the NBC-USA, Layten announced that the WC would provide financial support for the new venture. The convention hoped that the new women's institution would drive Burroughs's school out of existence.

The final showdown between Burroughs and the convention came in 1938. In August 1938, in a last-ditch effort to block white Baptist contributions to the National Training School, representatives of the convention appeared before the Southern Baptist Convention and alleged that the NBC-USA had withdrawn its support from the school. The announcement was made one month before any formal action was taken. Burroughs was ordered to revise the school's charter, place the school under the "province" of the WC, and deed the property to the convention. The NBC-USA devised this strategy to divert attention from the all-male board of directors, and place the onus on Layten and the WC for the denomination's withdrawal of its support. However, Burroughs refused to cooperate, reiterating that since the WC had no power under the new charter, the NBC-USA could close down the school and sell the property. Frustrated over their inability to either take control of the school, drive Burroughs out of office, influence public opinion, or garner the support of the majority of convention members, the board of directors decided to simply shut off all NBC-USA support by ordering all boards, including the Woman's Convention and affiliate churches and organizations, to "withdraw all connections, allegiance and support" from the National Training School. At the NBC-USA's annual meeting in 1938, delegates to the convention were not allowed to either "pass upon the resolution, or even discuss the subject in open meeting."

Over a period of roughly two decades, under the leadership of S. Willie Layten, the Woman's Convention was transformed from a largely independent entity to an auxiliary. As the NBC-USA tightened its control over the WC, the organization's structure was changed. After 1915 the WC constitution was revised to conform with NBC-USA bylaws and resolutions, and by 1942 the WC was being referred to as a subsidiary of the "Parent Body." An annual audit was conducted on the WC's financial records, published minutes, and officers' reports to determine whether there was any "deliberate insubordination on the part of officers of the Woman's Auxiliary to properly constituted authority [the NBC-USA]." The WC committees were either abolished or restructured to conform with the parent body. At the direction of the NBC-USA, Layten appointed "directors" of the national and regional programs and organizational services, formerly coordinated by Burroughs, to work directly with state directors. Burroughs's role as chief spokesperson at the WC regional meetings and leadership training institutes held at the newly organized Baptist Missionary Training School at Nashville was usurped by the male NBC-USA president and the heads of the mission boards. The WC vice president, Jessie Mapp—a Layten crony—supplanted Burroughs as the WC representative at regional and state meetings.

In an effort to further mute Burroughs's voice, the *Worker*, a missionary and educational quarterly founded in 1912 and published under the direction of Burroughs, was replaced by the *Star of Hope* in 1942 as the WC's official organ. To diminish Burroughs's influence in the state and regional WC, more emphasis was placed on the development of Baptist missionary societies. More important, during the early 1940s the WC's financial system was reorganized to assure NBC-USA control of the collection and dissemination of all WC funds. Working through Layten, the NBC-USA succeeded in having the WC accept responsibility for raising funds to pay for the denomination's publishing company, and for the development of the National Baptist Missionary Training School and the American Baptist Theological Seminary in Nashville. At the behest of the NBC-USA, in 1944 the WC agreed to raise $100,000 for the Foreign Mission Board. Prior to the 1940s the bulk of the funds raised by the WC were for home missions. Though it had sponsored several women as foreign missionaries and raised funds for support of mainly mission stations operated by women, the WC's main focus had been home mission work, broadly defined. All challenges to Layten's leadership and questions regarding the constitutionality of the new financial arrangement were dismissed by the NBC-USA president, Dr. David V. Jemison, as insignificant.

Burroughs's election as president of the Woman's Convention in 1948 ended the long reign of S. Willie Layten. Between 1948 and her death in 1961, Burroughs did everything in her power to reclaim the WC's lost authority. She was not amenable to Jemison's assertion that all money raised by the WC should be reported to the parent body and be disbursed as the NBC-USA saw fit. Nor did Burroughs agree that the WC should continue its support for the Nashville Training School and the Missionary Training School, and make donations to the American Baptist Seminary. She argued that the WC should have representation on some of the NBC-USA's policy-making committees. Between 1950 and 1952, Burroughs challenged Jemison's charges that her vision for the operation of the WC was broader than its authority. She blocked all efforts to encroach on her rights as president of the WC. Burroughs concluded that the WC helped the executive board and projects of the NBC-USA, but the organizational boards did not help the women.

In 1961, following Burroughs's death, under the leadership of WC President Mary O. Ross, the National Training School for Girls was turned over to the NBC-USA board. The Woman's Convention was finally converted to a full-fledged auxiliary, closely adhering to the dictates of the all-male executive board. By 1970, as a result of the feminist and women's liberation movements and the changes in women's status in other denominations, Ross and the WC became exceedingly conscious of its subordinate status. In 1972, at the 92nd annual session of the NBC-USA, the WC declared, "Christ was the first liberator of womankind." Stating, "[W]e are living in a time when there is a great need for women to fill high positions—places that have for ages been called masculine positions," the Woman's Convention called for women to be placed in administrative and policy-making positions in the NBC-USA.

At the end of the twentieth century all of the NBC-USA's general offices were held by men. Only one of the fifteen executive board positions was occupied by a woman—the president of the WC. Seven of the fifty-six executive board members were female, owing to their leadership positions in the Woman's Auxiliary, and the Usher's and Nurses' auxiliaries. Thus, at the beginning of the twenty-first century, the progressive programs of the early years had dissipated, and for the most part women remained marginalized in the NBC-USA.

Methodist Women's Organizations

WHILE THE BAPTIST WOMAN'S CONVENTION has been represented as the dominant women's religious organization in black women's religious work, it was not the model for black Methodist women's organizations, nor is its history representative of that of the Methodist or any other black women's organization. While Baptist women were organizing at the local and state levels and the secular club movement was confined to local activities, Methodist women and their leaders had captured the national spotlight during the 1880s and '90s and were organizing and pressing for equal rights for women in the polity and black Americans in general. In 1943 Christine Smith, a veteran club woman and AME church leader, took great pains to explain that in 1893 the AME Woman's Mite Missionary Society held "the first large convention of colored women in America" in Columbus, Ohio, and that "[t]his convention antedates the National Association of Colored Women by a few years." As a witness to the major events defining the early development of the women's club movement, Smith sought to set the record straight.

Collectively, Methodist women account for the second largest contingency of black female religionists. The experiences of Methodist women's organizations are similar yet different from those of Baptist women. In the late nineteenth century, while Baptist women organized at the local and state levels, the AME and AME Zion women formed national missionary societies. The missionary histories and goals of Methodist women's societies diverge in several ways. Though women in most Methodist denominations continuously fought religious subordination, their organizational structures, relationship to the polity, and leadership bases were designed to ensure institutional solidarity and accountability to church authority. Historically, the AME and AME Zion women's organizations have been the largest and perhaps the most influential of all black Methodists. AME, AME Zion, and Baptist women engaged in home and foreign mission work. CME women were limited to home mission work. Black Methodist Episcopal church women, like Episcopalian, Presbyterian, Catholic, and other affiliates of predominantly white denominations, were involved in charity work and performed supportive functions. Black women in white-led denominations were also subordinated to the national denominational women's societies. However, in the early twentieth century, a small number of black women attended the annual meetings of the northern-based Methodist Episcopal women's organization, the Episcopal Women's Missionary Auxiliary, and the National Council of Catholic Women.

Until 1940, and the founding of the Women's Society of Christian Service of the Central Jurisdiction—the first national missionary organization—black women's organized activities within the Methodist

Episcopal Church were devoted to local missionary work in segregated societies. In the late nineteenth century and early twentieth century, black women in the ME and CME denominations maintained a biracial relationship with white Methodist women's organizations, whose influence extended far beyond the boundaries of religion to include the most dominant women's political and social organizations in the United States. For example, by 1890 white Methodist women dominated the leadership of the Woman's Christian Temperance Union. Northern white Methodist women first began home mission work among blacks in the South in the 1870s. During the first half of the twentieth century, a large part of the mission work of southern white Methodist women (MECS) was among African Americans. Confronted with growing racial tensions, these women consciously approached black Methodist women and sought ways to ameliorate racial differences. Between 1920 and the late 1940s, the MECS was at the forefront of the women's interracial movement and invested considerable human and fiscal resources into its ever-expanding program. The MECS attempted to bridge the racial divide by establishing relationships with leading black Methodist women, providing much-needed social services to the black community, and sponsoring religious training institutes and settlement houses.

In some ways, the relationship between the MECS and black women in the CME and ME denominations was beneficial to African Americans; in other ways, it was not. When it came to women's religious rights, the CME Church was by far the most oppressive of all the Methodist churches. Caught in a vise between repudiating black male sexism and white female paternalism, CME women chose to ally with southern white Methodist women who were engaged in a campaign against religious sexism. In acting as they did, CME women pursued a strategy that put pressure on black male clergy and provided leverage and support for their efforts to develop the CME Woman's Connectional Missionary Council. At the same time, the MECS, functioning as patron to a southern African American clientele, impacted the kind of home mission work in which black missionary societies engaged. In underwriting and participating in leadership training institutes and other community activities, white Methodist women were able to exert some influence over the actions of CME women. At the same time, black women were able to gain needed skills and resources.

Working under the direction of male supervisors and adhering to denominational directives, Methodist women raised funds for domestic and foreign missionary programs and support of churches. Methodist women's organizations lacked the level of independence exhibited by the Baptist Woman's Convention, yet they displayed remarkable courage, were outspoken on issues of lay rights and sexism within their organizations, and were active as members and leaders in the major social and political movements of their time. Many women leaders were educated and skilled in the art of negotiation and compromise. When necessary, they used time-worn methods of female influence. Unlike their Baptist sisters, Methodist women consistently fought for equality and advancement in every aspect of the religious polity. They succeeded in having most legal impediments to their advancement removed and, at least on paper, gained full equality with men. By the late twentieth century, though their numbers were small, women in some Methodist denominations were laying claim to church offices formally reserved for males. In the AME Church, by 2005 women occupied several prominent administrative positions, and three female clergy had been elevated to the episcopacy.

With the exception of the CME Church, the constitutions of most Methodist women's missionary societies invariably stipulated that officers would be chosen from the pool of "wives and daughters of bishops and elders, and other influential ladies" in the churches and episcopal districts. What is of interest here is how a leadership so closely allied to the Methodist male clergy was often able to dissociate its familial connections from its organizational allegiances. Yet this is exactly what AME Zion, AME, and CME women such as Sarah Pettey, Mary Handy, Christine Smith, Sarah Tanner, Mattie Coleman, Sarah McAfee, Captola Dent Newbern, Rossie T. Hollis, and numerous clergy wives did. As leaders of the women's missionary societies, these women were outspoken and often led the movements for women's equality in their churches. With few exceptions, the stories of their organizational work and struggles are missing from the denominational histories, which celebrate the leadership and achievements of their spouses and other males. However, between 1870 and 1960, the "woman question," embracing a number of issues related to the legal status and role of women in the church as well as the structure and function of their missionary societies, was consistently debated at the Methodist General Conferences.

At the national level, the AME Zion Woman's Home and Foreign Missionary Society, the CME Woman's Connectional Missionary Council, and the various AME missionary organizations—the

Executive Committee of the Woman's Parent Mite Missionary Society
of the African Methodist Episcopal Church, 1915

Woman's Parent Mite Missionary Society, the Women's Home and
Foreign Missionary Society, and the Women's Missionary Society—
represent the center of women's collective religious power. All of these
groups were subject to the dictates of exclusively male denominational missionary boards. In the nineteenth and twentieth centuries,
the central issue was control. Male clergy held tightly to the reins of
denominational power that extended into women's organizations. A
hegemonic masculinity connected male clergy and laity across denominations, class, time, and region. It needed no explanation, and it simply defined who they were as men and bonded them with men of other
races, nationalities, and ethnicities. As with the Baptist Woman's Convention, for decades Methodist women fought for the right to control
or have a say in how women's organizations were structured and functioned, especially how funds for missionary purposes were raised and
spent.

CME Woman's Connectional Missionary Council

IN SOME WAYS the story of CME women mimics that of AME and
AME Zion women. However, their struggle also differs from that of
other church women. The plight of women in the CME Church is
intricately connected to the history of the denomination—how it was
founded, and the nature of its long-term relationship to the Methodist

Episcopal Church, South, denomination. Unlike women in any other black denomination, CME women sustained a long-term dependence on southern white Methodist Episcopal women for support and resources. In the nineteenth and early twentieth century they faced rejection, ridicule, and male obstinance as they struggled to organize a women's missionary society. CME bishops were anxious to see that CME women were engaged in fund-raising, but these clergymen adamantly opposed organization and female religious rights. During the late nineteenth and early twentieth centuries, when the women's movement in the church was in full swing and black and white women of all persuasions were organizing missionary societies and claiming their religious rights, CME women felt unappreciated and embarrassed by their status.

Formed in 1870 as a Methodist denomination, the CME Church was comprised mostly of illiterate former Methodist slaves who had close relationships to their former masters. As a result, it lacked the sophistication and influence of the AME and AME Zion denominations in the late nineteenth century. Located mostly in rural areas and small southern towns, the CME membership was comprised largely of men and women employed in servile positions. Lacking the education, money, and influence of the AME, AME Zion, and Baptist denominations, and viewed as "white folks' niggers," CME clergy had a greater need—individually and collectively—to prove themselves as men. Thus, during the first fifty years of the church's existence, local pastors were often more invested in their individual prominence than in advancement of the denomination.

At the national level, CME bishops were concerned about developing respect and recognition for the denomination and focused on the masculine image and financial status of the church. While the pattern of CME male dominance was very similar to that of other black denominations, it was far more intense and driven largely by their sense of inferiority to other black Methodists and their relationship to the MECS. The CME Church was beholden to southern white Methodists for the very land and buildings they occupied and for many years received financial support from the MECS. CME bishops curried favor with their parent organization, and competed with the AME and AME Zion denominations.

CME clergy were reluctant to authorize the establishment of a national or local women's missionary society. They feared that funds would be diverted from their individual churches and that women would gain some measure of recognition or influence. In their struggles to organize societies, CME women often faced the deep-seated antagonism of pastors and presiding elders, most of whom did their utmost to thwart their efforts. In the late nineteenth century, CME bishops pressed the General Conference to provide women formal recognition short of religious suffrage and ordination, and bereft of any real power.

In the 1880s, CME women took notice of women in other Methodist denominations, who had organized national missionary societies and were fighting for basic religious rights. Caroline W. Poe, a member of the East Texas Conference, petitioned the General Conference for approval to establish a national women's missionary association. Though the General Conference granted permission for the establishment of a Woman's Missionary Society in each annual conference in 1886, it rejected the idea of a national organization. Pastors and presiding elders were authorized to organize societies in their churches and conferences. The CME male clergy's intention was to exert strict control over every aspect of the society, from organization to operation. Instead of a national organization that would coordinate the activities of women and function as one of the boards under the aegis of the General Conference, the society's operation was restricted to the Annual Conference. There was no central organization, and the Woman's Board appointed by one conference was equal to that of other conferences. This eliminated the need for denominational officers and ensured that no one woman would be recognized as a "national" president.

In 1890 the CME Woman's Missionary Society's constitution and bylaws were amended to include a corresponding secretary—a male member of the Annual Conference, elected by the General Conference. Having a male corresponding secretary as the chief executive obviated the need for a woman to meet with the all-male CME General Missionary Board or appear before the General Conference to report on the society's activities. The Woman's Missionary Society was required to relinquish 25 percent of all monies raised to the General Missionary Board. The remaining funds were restricted to the Annual Conference for the creation and support of mission churches and pastors. In other words, women were made responsible for overall church expansion.

During the late 1880s in Alabama, Tennessee, Texas, Kansas, Missouri, and other areas of CME concentration, Christianna Lloyd, Jennie Lane, Alice Parham, Caroline Poe, and other women undertook the task of organizing their states. Unfortunately, they soon became exasperated by the disinterest of pastors as well as members. In 1887 Lloyd reported that the majority of people in Alabama were poorly informed about the benefits that would accrue from the Woman's Missionary Society, and blamed "preachers, possessing evil hearts, [who] are speaking words to retard the progress," for the inactivity. Rev. F. M. Hamilton, editor of the CME *Christian Index*, acknowledged that there was mounting evidence of male sabotage—specifically, that pastors and elders in only one or two annual conferences had even attempted to organize a missionary society—but blamed the women. Hamilton later admitted that it was useless for the General Conference to make laws that its officers refused to carry out.

'Iypical of black denominational leaders, Hamilton compared the CME Woman's Missionary Society with its white counterpart in the Methodist Episcopal Church, South. He noted that within twelve years the white women had collected $500,000, held property worth $180,000, employed thirty-one missionaries, fifty-seven teachers and assistants, maintained ten boarding schools, thirty-one day schools, and a hospital. He argued that this was "a strong indication" of what CME women could achieve "if they could be sufficiently aroused" and receive encouragement from the male clergy. It was unfair and unrealistic to expect CME women employed mostly as domestic servants, washerwomen, and sharecroppers to meet these expectations.

By 1892 Hamilton had developed a friendship with Mrs. M. E. Thompson of Athens, Alabama, the white secretary of a District Woman's Missionary Society of the Methodist Episcopal Church, South. Relating her experience in missionary work, Thompson stated that the support of pastors was indispensable to women's work. She was against placing the missionary society in the Annual Conference and suggested that women's meetings be held independent of CME conferences. When rank-and-file preachers objected to Thompson's suggestions, to avoid "friction" Hamilton stated that local pastors should decide what was best for their congregations. There was little harmony between the CME male clergy and the women's societies, and strife continued. Of great importance was Hamilton's revelation of discussions with Thompson and the suggestion that there was a relationship brewing between white and black women.

In the early twentieth century, when Lillie B. Morris, the CME missionary for the Shelby District of North Carolina, entered the field, she discovered "that the name of the Woman's Missionary Society had been changed to the P[residing] E[lder's] Missionary Society." This suggests that the presiding elder would support the society only if he received total credit. Blocked from performing her duties as a duly elected officer, Morris decided to suspend her work. This is a telling example of what CME women missionary field-workers encountered in the 1890s and the early decades of the twentieth century as they attempted to organize local societies. Recognizing that the revised constitution of 1890 was little more than a charade presented to them under the guise of progress, CME women continued to press for more control over local organizations.

The minimal gains realized by CME women between 1890 and 1918 were the result of internal pressure brought by CME women, external pressure related to the social and political changes in women's national status, and the involvement of white Methodist women in the affairs of the CME women's society. The MECS considered its activities on behalf of black women as part of its home missionary work, and CME women welcomed the support. CME bishops resented the involvement of the white women, but they felt obligated to accept their presence and activity because of the financial and other supports the CME denomination received from the MECS. At the beginning of the twentieth century, some clergy recognized that it was not just the women's society that was failing in its mission. They argued that the CME General Missionary Department, headed by male clergy, was a "department that is in name only. . . . We have no Missionary Depart-

The CME Connectional Woman's Missionary Society at its organization on September 3–8, 1918, in Nashville, Tennessee

ment." Rev. G. W. Spearman explained that the department raised thousands of dollars that were expended "for [clergy] salaries, traveling expenses and other things of little or no use to the Church." Spearman felt that women were lagging in participation, and CME members were reluctant to donate money because they never saw "anything more than a well-dressed man" for the missionary money they raised, and believed that they were "throwing their money away."

Over a period of at least forty years, the CME women's society underwent a series of constitutional and name changes. The first change occurred in 1918 when the General Conference reluctantly approved legislation for the formation of the Woman's Connectional Missionary Council. With the aid of white Methodist women, CME women leaders fought for a national organization. Helena Cobb and a small cadre of CME women leaders, including Sara J. McAfee and Mamie Dinkins, were instrumental in creating the sentiment that drove the issue for sixteen years. In addition to these women, Rev. Ida E. Roberts fought for a national organization. On the eve of the General Conference, Roberts wrote, "I beg the General Conference to organize a woman's separate missionary society, so we may do a better work, and meet more often, and carry on a more successful work. We want to do more than raise money, we want to make leading women [and] train them to do church work."

In 1918 CME women celebrated their new status. Two of the best known and most outstanding women in the denomination, Dr. Mattie E. Coleman and Helena Cobb, were elected president and vice president of the fledgling Woman's Connectional Missionary Council. These women were known to be outspoken feminists and crusaders for women's political rights. However, the euphoria of obtaining a national status quickly evaporated when the women discovered that all they had was a title, with little or no new authority—the General Conference simply gave them permission to set up a missionary society at the denominational level. The president of the WCMC was not a general officer and had no voice in the polity. The society's constitution and all aspects of its operation were subject to the scrutiny and approval of the College of Bishops. CME women had no significant leadership role, or voice, in how the organization functioned, or in the distribution of the funds they were required to raise. Moreover, they had no budget, and lacked funds for basic expenses such as the purchase of stationery and printing. Also, since the WCMC was designated as a fund-raising group for the denomination, it had no specific function in the local church. Though Coleman stated that "the missionary work of the church was established as an independent institution to be conducted entirely by women," that was not the case. As Lena Jones Rice, president of the Missouri and Illinois annual conference society, explained, "[W]hen the women have tried to put across a project it has been necessary to wait until it could be acted upon by the bishops and ministers, or even if we manage to get our ideas passed on by them for some reason, not known even to the (high ups) themselves, we have been unable to carry out our ideas."

Coleman brought the issue of women's status before the Woman's Connectional Missionary Council in September 1919 at the organization's second meeting. Speaking at length about the changes that had occurred in American women's political status, she noted that World War I illustrated that women were "capable and willing to fill most places held by men" and that women had gained political rights in the church and civil society. In spite of all their gains, Coleman concluded, there was great unrest among women "both in state and church. The whole course for all of this unrest is represented by one sentence and that is: Taxation without representation." Coleman's speech targeted the CME Church and its refusal to grant the WCMC any authority and extend women basic lay rights.

Between 1926 and 1960, CME women realized modest gains in the polity. Perceiving a link between the denomination's image and fiscal viability with CME women's status, in 1926 the College of Bishops recommended that the General Conference enact legislation "to make the Woman's Connectional Missionary Council workable." The recommendation was rejected. The WCMC informed the conference "that what the women desired were laity rights." CME women were granted lay delegate status with the stipulation that only one woman could be elected from each annual conference. In 1930 the first twenty women lay delegates were seated at the General Conference. At that meeting, the WCMC request that women be granted "larger opportunities . . . in the affairs of the church, both locally and generally" was rejected.

Mattie Coleman's presidency ended in 1939 with the election of Rossie Thompson Hollis. During Coleman's twenty-one years as president the WCMC accomplished very little. It managed to raise several thousand dollars a year, most of which was expended for basic operating expenses such as printing and distribution of literature, ministers' aid, and miscellaneous church projects. Their plight is best illustrated

Young Ladies Missionary Society, Israel Colored Methodist Episcopal Church, Washington, D.C., 1944

by the fact that of the thirty-four persons appointed by the General Conference to serve on a WCMC standing committee in 1934, only twelve were women.

The election of Rossie Hollis marked the end of an era. After sixty years, the CME clergy finally recognized that it was because of women's organizations that the AME, AME Zion, and NBC-USA denominations had made substantial progress in their domestic and foreign mission work. Retarding CME women's progress hurt the CME Church and made it appear backward. In 1942 the General Conference acceded to the request of WCMC leaders and granted the society departmental status, made the president a general officer, and levied an assessment of ten cents on the CME membership for support of the council and its programs. The organization was also given an office at the CME Publishing House. By 1965, CME women were no longer embarrassed by their status. They took pride in the fact that the WCMC held memberships in Church Women United, the National

Council of Negro Women, the World Federation of Methodist Women, and the John Milton Society for the Blind. The MECS provided funds for development of leadership training schools to prepare CME women for religious leadership, and paid stipends to the CME and white Methodist women who taught at these schools.

In the 1970s Pauline Grant (1971–79) restructured and streamlined the organization by separating the numerous committees into three divisions, and was instrumental in having the society renamed the Women's Missionary Council (WMC). She believed that the old title, Woman's Connectional Missionary Council, implied that the organization was separate from the CME Church. An easy-going, mild-mannered, down-to-earth, and rather accommodating woman, Grant worked well with the bishops, the male clergy, and the other women. Delegating duties to a wide spectrum of women, across age, class, educational, and geographical lines, she was able to lead the organization into the new era following the civil rights–black power and women's liberation movements. This was extremely important during a period of great political and social change in the life of the church as well as the lives of African Americans.

CME women were far more accommodating to the male-dominated religious hierarchy than women were in any other black denomination. Why did they so overwhelmingly accept patriarchy as the natural order of things in the CME Church? Perhaps it is because for years they lagged behind other church women in the development of a national organization, and were embarrassed by their status. An evaluation of the language of their requests and the manner in which they pursued their rights suggests a level of docility and accommodation out of sync with the twentieth century. It is possible that since for decades the church comprised mostly poor rural black southerners who lived in sparsely populated areas that the pattern established by the bishops and male clergy in the late nineteenth century set the tone for how women would function in the CME Church in the twentieth century. Moreover, CME women sought change, but unlike AME and AME Zion women, they rarely became irate or publicly castigated the male clergy in the way that women in other black churches did. CME women were largely accepting of their subordinate status and willingly let the male clergy define their agenda. Also, while some of their leaders, as individuals, held membership in black feminist organizations such as the NACW and the NCNW, few distinguished themselves at the national level for their social and political activism, either on behalf

Bishop Henry McNeal Turner, editor of the *Christian Recorder* and *Voice of Missions*, was a major supporter of African missions and women's rights. In 1896 he organized the AME Women's Home and Foreign Missionary Society for women in southern states.

of women or the race. CME women leaders and the female membership in general appear to have accepted, and for the most part complied with, the traditional gender roles, and remained in the "subordinate and inferior positions" assigned to them by black males.

AME Woman's Parent Mite Missionary Society

THE WOMAN'S PARENT MITE MISSIONARY SOCIETY was the first national organization established by black American women. Organized in 1874, the WPMMS did not simply spring up. Rather, it was the result of two distinct impulses arising out of the work performed by mostly northern women in the Dorcas Societies and other groups that administered to the poor during the antebellum period. By 1894 missionary societies had been established in each of the AME District conferences and geographical regions. Bishop Henry McNeal Turner organized the Women's Home and Foreign Missionary Society for women in southern states in 1896. Following four decades of intense competition, in 1944 the WPMMS and the WHFMS were united into a single organization, the Women's Missionary Society of the AME Church. Taking full notice of the fund-raising success of white women—namely the Methodist Episcopal, Baptist, and Presby-

terian women's missionary societies—by 1874 AME bishops agreed to
the establishment of a national women's missionary society. To ensure
that this department would function at the direction of the Council of
Bishops, the designated leaders of the Woman's Parent Mite Missionary Society were the wives of bishops and prominent clergy.

As an advocate for foreign mission work, Rev. Benjamin Tucker
Tanner used his influence as editor of the *Christian Recorder* to promote
the AME Church's foreign mission efforts. The denomination had
established a mission in Haiti and initiated a "Missionary Department"
during the antebellum period, but for years it was an organization on
paper only. The AME Church did not have a functioning missionary
department until the Woman's Parent Mite Missionary Society was
formed. Following eight years of promoting the endeavor, on February 19, 1874, Tanner suggested that the bishops' wives "ought to organize a Women's Missionary Society." He admitted that the missionary
department administered by male clergy was a failure.

In his call for women to organize, Tanner referenced Isaiah 23:9–11
as evidence of the biblical warrants supporting his request. Unfortunately, the text also included language suggesting that AME women
were lazy and "careless" and not avidly applying their talents on behalf
of the church. Responding to his critics, Tanner published the offend-
ing text and disavowed making "any charge" against women. However,
he suggested that while other denominations were on the move, the
AME Church was standing still. Tanner urged the bishops' wives to
discuss the matter among themselves, call a meeting, and organize.

The candid public responses to Tanner's overture revealed the different concerns of male and female laity. Mary E. Davis asserted that
women were neither idle nor lazy. She emphasized that in engaging
temperance, women performed extensive home mission work and
were addressing the problems and "blotting out the evil" caused by
"fathers, brothers, husbands, and friends" who indulged in alcohol and
other drugs and were "demoralized." Davis questioned whether
women and their work were appreciated, or would continue to be
despised, with their contributions "ridiculed and trampled under
foot." Likewise, in a not too subtle letter, Mattie V. Holmes of
Augusta, Georgia, spoke of sexism in the church, and about women's
value. She reminded men that they could not achieve their goals without women. Holmes barely hid her sarcasm as she wrote to Tanner "a
few lines to let you know what the women of our church want to do; as
I see you want to know what the women are doing." Holmes informed

Harriet Wayman (top, left), Rachel Ward (top, right), and Sarah Tanner (bottom) were among the clergy wives associated with the founding of the AME Woman's Parent Mite Missionary Society in the late
nineteenth century.

Tanner, "[T]hey are waiting, and have been for some time, for the privilege of doing something. . . . Now my dear brother, allow me to ask, what are the men of our church doing that they don't consider and pray, as you have already done and give the women of Zion, liberty? I will not ask, why don't you men do it? I know your hands are full, and the only chance that we have had before was to pray it out or cry it out, as poor women always do."

Many men, especially the laity, agreed with B. G. Mortimor of Paducah, Kentucky, who praised Tanner's overture to the women. Mortimor argued that the success of the AME Church was dependent on domestic and foreign mission work. He envisioned AME women as the bridge for accomplishing the denomination's mission goals in the United States and abroad. Others, such as Thomas S. Malcom, responded to the much-repeated charge by women that men were not carrying their share of the load in the church. Malcom argued that "if woman was first to sin (Eve in the Garden of Eden) . . . let woman be first in the work of giving the gospel to those who are in moral darkness." In other words, to properly atone for their original sin, women must assume responsibility for the success of the AME missionary program.

In the midst of these debates, on May 8, 1874, the Woman's Parent Mite Missionary Society was temporarily organized by the bishops' wives—Mary Handy, Eliza Payne, Mary Quinn, Harriet Wayman, Mary Campbell, Maria Shorter, Mary L. Brown, and Rachel Ward. In "An Open Letter" to clergy wives, they highlighted their commitment to the "evangelization of the world" and their willingness to cooperate with the denomination's Parent Home and Foreign Missions Board in the support of a Haitian mission. Clergy wives were urged to organize mite missionary societies in their churches, and church women were asked to assist in raising funds to send a missionary to Haiti by September 1874. Tanner exulted in the wives' acceptance, exclaiming that "our missionary coffers will no longer be empty." In August 1874, the Council of Bishops approved the WPMMS "Constitution and Bylaws" and appointed Mary A. Campbell, the wife of Bishop Jabez Campbell, WPMMS president.

The anticipated groundswell of support for the missionary society did not materialize. At best, the response of the male clergy was tepid; at worst, it was destructive. By church law, only male clergy could organize local auxiliary societies, known as the Woman's Mite Missionary Society. While pastors and elders were expected to support the bishops' call for immediate organization, many ministers and some laymen were obstinately opposed to women organizing. Their reasons might vary, but the response was almost uniform. In 1874 very few societies were organized and fund-raising was meager. In addition to the overall fear of women gaining power and competing with men, the bishops and male clergy clashed over the issue of establishing home or foreign missions. The male clergy desired to raise funds to support home missions that would provide financial aid to ministers and churches, whereas the bishops were concerned about the national image of the denomination and favored support for foreign mission work. To develop an organization of workers and ensure local support, some WMMS auxiliaries initially stressed the need to raise funds to support home missionaries as well as a missionary in Haiti. At the same time, members were encouraged to raise funds for foreign missionary work.

The exclusion of southern women from participation in the organizing meetings and the leadership of the WPMMS created tension and divided AME women into northern and southern camps defined by class and experience. The AME Church emerged in the North and experienced its greatest growth among free blacks in major cities before the Civil War. Though there were a few AME churches in the South before 1865, the majority were organized after the Civil War. By 1876 AME membership in the South was double that of the North. At the beginning of the twentieth century only 13 percent of the AME membership resided in the North and West; 80 percent lived in the South.

In 1874, at the organization of the WPMMS, all of the bishops and their wives were northerners. Many clergy wives were born free, highly educated, and active in the early social reform movements. In contrast, the majority of black southerners were poor, uneducated, and rural, including southern ministers and their wives. The leadership of southern churches was also stratified by class. Education, money, and style of living were major factors in the class equation. By 1895 in many southern cities and towns a small but highly visible, educated elite had developed. It comprised teachers, ministers, entrepreneurs, and a smattering of professionals—doctors, dentists, pharmacists, lawyers, undertakers, barbers, and artisans. This group of younger and more ambitious men and women, combined with blacks in the skilled trades, constituted an emerging leadership class. The organization of multiple benevolent and fraternal groups was a further distinguishing factor in class formation. In southern towns several factors combined to force the issue of southern representation in the women's missionary movement, but it took two decades for that to occur. Meanwhile, the WPMMS worked assiduously in the North and South to educate AME women about the purpose of the society and the value of missions, especially foreign mission work.

Most male clergy strongly opposed the organizing of women's missionary societies. Speaking as an insider who understood the episcopal process—especially the power of the male clergy to either empower or destroy a movement—Harriet Wayman acknowledged that Tanner had issued "a grand and noble call" and that women were willing and ready to work. However, in expressing her anxiety, she asked, "What are the gentlemen doing? We have been waiting on them. Will they loan the use of our Churches, will they call the people together and make known the objects of the meeting? If so, we are ready and will do our duty." Wayman's concern was an omen of things to come.

Once established, the WPMMS was expected to produce immediate results. Within three months of its founding, Bishop John Mifflin Brown, president of the Parent Home and Foreign Missions Board, announced to the WPMMS that it was time to send a missionary to Haiti. Bishop Brown's unilateral and premature selection of Rev. J. W. Randolph for the Haitian post lacked the support of the Council of Bishops, the PHFMB, and the WMMS because of a scandal surrounding Randolph's highly publicized behavior—fighting, supposedly to defend himself and save his life. In light of the scandal, local women's mite societies refused to forward funds raised for missions. As the months passed, the WPMMS officers were charged with neglecting their duty. Tanner challenged Mary Campbell's leadership, suggesting that she lacked the skills and energy needed to "rally not only those of her own sex," but also the support of the preachers. Male clergy approved Tanner's rebuke of the WPMMS. In defense of the Mite Missionary Society, Mary Campbell assured the denomination that when the PHFMB chose a "qualified brother—the money will be raised."

In 1876 Rev. Charles W. Mossell, a young graduate of Boston University with impeccable credentials, was selected for the Haitian mission. Mossell's departure for Haiti in 1877 ended the speculation and accusations and validated the WPMMS existence. What was important about this incident is that the women demonstrated their power to block the decisions of bishops and clergy who failed to respond to their concerns. In this instance, the hand that controlled the purse ruled the day! By dint of church law, male clergy held the reins of power and could make decisions affecting the body politic. However, given that at least 80 percent of those decisions required funds for implementation, women were critical to the success of church programs.

Following Mossell's departure for Haiti, Mary Campbell stressed the importance of devising plans to further the foreign mission field and attract more women to missionary work. Admitting that support for the Haitian project had lagged, in late 1878 Campbell resigned as president, and emphasized the immediate need to accumulate funds to support Mossell and his family. Between 1878 and 1895, WPMMS presidents worked assiduously to attract new members and expand the organization. The appointment of Sarah Tanner as WPMMS president suggested a more aggressive approach to organizational development. Her husband, Rev. Benjamin Tucker Tanner, was not yet a bishop, but he was widely known and respected as the editor of the *Christian Recorder*, and had been the "architect" of the WPMMS.

Sarah Tanner, a graduate of Avery Institute, a teacher, and a member of the WPMMS's Board of Managers, was well aware of the difficulties inherent in mounting a successful foreign missionary program. Though Tanner adopted a hands-on approach, she was no more successful than Campbell had been. For more than three decades, Tanner and her successors begged AME pastors to present the cause to their congregations so that "the sisters may be aroused." Tanner reported the missionary successes of the Jesuits, Methodists, and Episcopalians, suggesting that the AME Church was derelict in its duty. Continuing opposition from clergymen and resentment from AME women in the South prevented the WPMMS from the full realization of its purpose. In 1882, frustrated and disappointed with the lagging support, Sarah Tanner resigned. After eight years, the WPMMS acknowledged that there were many churches where there were no societies and others where the societies "apparently ceased to work."

As the presiding prelate over the AME Church's Third Episcopal District, Bishop Daniel A. Payne felt that the women would engage in missionary work if given more leeway in their operations. Thus, on July 3, 1893, he convened a mite missionary convention in Columbus, Ohio, to consider the denomination's foreign mission needs and to "awaken a greater interest in missionary work." Women hailing from cities and towns in Ohio joined women from other midwestern states and the Northeast at the first convention in the United States to be operated entirely by black women. The women were praised for the way they handled the reins of leadership and extolled for the way they exerted power. They established the Central Mite Missionary Society. An onlooker commented, "It was really amusing to see the brothers all huddled together in the corners on both sides of the pulpit, while the woman had full sway, and left no stone unturned. . . . The assertion that 'the hand that rocks the cradle rules the world,' will soon be proven." Little did Payne realize that the convention would not only serve as a model for other AME mite societies, but would also empower women in the Third Episcopal District as well as the WPMMS to seek even more autonomy. In a sense, the women had been "loosed."

While women in the Midwest celebrated their recent success, the WPMMS struggled to raise funds to simply cover the cost of supporting the Haitian mission, and the PHFMB shifted its focus to Africa. Though the WPMMS only limped along, its leaders refused to give up. Continuing struggles with the bishops—their husbands—actually radicalized women such as Sarah Tanner, who experienced an epiphany as they recognized that the problem did not lie solely with the women, but in part was related to the ways in which clergymen oppressed women and abused their own power. For example, in 1894, at the second convention of the Woman's Mite Missionary Society of the Third Episcopal District, held in Cleveland, Ohio, most of the women who spoke criticized the indifference of their pastors to missions. Representing the WPMMS, Sarah Tanner spoke of the women's struggle and urged the bishops to support a pending resolution for the Third District's mite society to be relieved of its status as an auxiliary body. She asked that the women be permitted to coordinate the denomination's missionary work along with the Parent Home and Foreign Missions Board. Bishop Tanner, bolstered by Bishop William B. Derrick, the secretary of missions, was against sharing power with the women and reportedly "waxed warm over the question, and charged it a revolt." Similarly, Susie I. Shorter, the state organizer for the Ohio WMMS, acknowledged that it would be her "Christian duty to let a pastor of my church go hungry and half clad" if he refused to support the women and their mission work. In 1885, the Council of Bishops acknowledged that ministers had misconstrued the law and "crippled the operation of the Mite Society by taking the work out of the hands of the women." The council ruled that clergy, as members of the General Conference, had "nothing whatever to do with the Mite Society" and sanctioned the right of women to organize and operate the group. However, the ruling did not deter those clergy who were determined to prevail at all costs.

AME Women's Home and Foreign Missionary Society

GROWING TENSION BETWEEN the WPMMS and its auxiliary societies reached a peak in 1893. Additionally, women in the South and some parts of the West felt isolated and ignored. In response to these concerns and the need to raise the level of missionary funding, Bishops Turner and Derrick organized the Women's Home and Foreign Missionary Society. The bishops acted unilaterally, without legal sanction of the General Conference. Rev. Lillian F. Thurman of Jackson, Michigan, was employed as lecturer and general organizer of the fledgling organization. Thurman was known in the AME Church as "a wonderful Gospel preacher." As a young, attractive, and dynamic evangelist and the wife of a minister in the Michigan Annual Conference, Thurman had been employed by male pastors to conduct revivals. Though Thurman succeeded in organizing WHFMS auxiliaries in Michigan, Arkansas, Alabama, Georgia, Mississippi, Louisiana, Tennessee, Texas, and Florida, the legitimacy of the WHFMS and her appointment were challenged.

Southern women revered and praised Thurman's work, but believed that one of their own—a woman from the South—should head the WHFMS. In April 1895, the *Christian Recorder* announced under a blazing headline—"Taxation Without Representation"—that "[t]he First National Conference of Colored Women" would be held in Nashville, Tennessee, for the purpose of discussing "questions of interest to colored women and to obtain for them a better recognition in the councils of their church." Rev. Winfield Henri Mixon of Selma, Alabama, a presiding elder and noted figure in Alabama's religious and political circles, placed the call. During the late 1880s Mixon was most prominent among those who opposed women preachers, but he recognized that women constituted the majority in the AME denomination. As a political operative—and labeled by some as the "Acting Bishop of Alabama"—Mixon seized the opportunity to be a power broker in what he envisioned as a women's movement among southern AME women. Sarah J. Early was elected president, and an assortment of other accomplished and well-known women leaders were chosen to be WHFMS officers. The convention met in Nashville in May 1895, effected an organization, and declared that its purpose was to organize AME women "into a Connectional Union." These women, mostly wives of prominent clergymen, were flanked by other leading figures, many of whom were active in the WCTU. The meeting emphasized the need for the General Conference to approve the formation of the WHFMS.

In an effort to unify women and solidify its position as the only legally sanctioned national organization for AME women, the WPMMS convened a national conference in Philadelphia at the Mother Bethel AME Church in November 1895. Southern women criticized the WPMMS for assuming the right to "govern all auxiliary missionary work in the denomination," and disputed its authority to collect and disburse funds raised by the auxiliary societies at the local level. Some women felt that the WPMMS's missionary work was a misnomer. Women such as Jennie Johnson of Louisville, Kentucky, made clear their interest in missionary work and desire for the General Conference to either support the appeal of southern women for a separate organization or approve of the WHFMS as *the* connectional organization for AME women. In May 1896 the General Conference sanctioned the organization of the WHFMS, and Rev. Lillian F. Thurman was appointed its general superintendent.

Following Thurman's resignation in November 1897 to accept a pastoral position in Detroit, Bishop Turner appointed Sara J. Duncan of Selma, Alabama, as general superintendent of the WHFMS. Duncan was representative of the "new" black woman of the 1890s—an educated, confident, outspoken, determined feminist who was part of the small but significant southern black middle-class leadership. She was the daughter of George Hatcher—a former slave, prosperous jeweler, and leading figure at the Brown Chapel AME Church—and the wife of Robert H. Duncan, a grocer, realtor, and owner of a printing business. Duncan's connection to the elite was not limited to the AME Church. Rather, it crossed boundaries and intersected with the leadership of other religious groups. It is for these reasons, and what Bishop Turner perceived as the depth of her Christian faith, that Duncan was chosen as the WHFMS superintendent, a difficult and demanding position fraught with minefields.

Like Nannie Burroughs and other leading figures, Duncan asserted that education, wealth, and morality would solve the problems facing African Americans. For most black leaders these issues were not simply a matter of respectability or the adoption of white values and mores, but, more profoundly, there was a sense that order and stability were needed to advance the race out of poverty and ignorance. The notion that black Americans were simply imitating whites is absurd. Most societies required that individuals "assume responsibility for behavioral self-regulation and self-improvement along moral, educational, and economic lines." Moreover, seeking to advance themselves, many individuals on the lower rungs of American society—white and black—have embraced education, morality, hard work, and personal accountability as values that would help them to achieve their larger upwardly mobile economic goals. As students of history, black leaders such as Burroughs and Duncan were concerned about replicating successful patterns that would aid African Americans in overcoming the heritage of slavery to become full and equal participants in American society. They also felt that if white Americans understood the full meaning of Christianity, they would not allow racial discrimination. Burroughs and others argued, "The American people need help. They need missionaries to go to them and warn them of the awful sin that they are committing by allowing . . . race, . . . to stand in the way of the onward march of religion and civilization."

Like most early-twentieth-century "race women," Duncan believed that historically the African American woman had suffered untold indignities, and "gone through every chasm to which others have seen fit to push her." She emphasized that those who tried to climb the ladder of success were often blocked "from the path of virtue and morality. Yet through it all, we mean to climb and reach the top." Duncan believed that female missionaries were the vehicles for race advancement. She implored AME women to fight against the opposition of male clergy, who impeded their progress. For the most part, Duncan rejected the strict tenets of domesticity and refused to countenance sexism, racism, or classism. Speaking to women throughout the South, Duncan claimed that AME women were "aroused to the sense of their duty" and accepted that there was more for them to do than just the ordinary household duties performed by wives and mothers. Those who could were leaving their homes and engaging in mission work; the women who were compelled to stay at home "are seen to push the cradle with the foot and the pen with the hand." Duncan predicted that mission work was only the first step, but only God knew where women would stop. Duncan found that very few men were willing to support women in missions. In fact, the opposition was often very personal, especially for the clergy wives whose husbands forbade their participation and refused to provide funds for them to attend missionary meetings. Duncan recalled that AME women once "thought it was unladylike to try to go to the front and work for . . . the Kingdom of Christ. . . . [V]ery often [they] met with discouragement" and were told by laymen and ministers, "You must stay in your places."

While women were often opposed by men, Duncan was concerned that some women were drawing class lines in their organizations. She admonished her AME sisters that the exclusion of any class of women from membership was not Christian. Duncan believed that choosing one's associates in secular society was acceptable, but it was not Christian for churches and organizations to shut out, shun, or deny participation to either the poor and disabled or prostitutes and gamblers. Though few were guilty of this type of behavior, Duncan acknowledged that occasionally some members of the missionary societies, stewardesses, and auxiliary boards informed their ministers, "Mrs. So and So is on such and such a board, and I will not work on it."

Duncan made no pretense of soft-pedaling her ideas to either black men or whites in general. Whether speaking to the AME bishops, learned scholars, and national leaders or to the common folk at a rural church, she never failed to bring issues of sex and class discrimination to the fore. In her first major address, she took special pains to highlight sexism in religion, commenting that "heretofore woman has ranked as a collateral rather than an essential factor in the evangelization of the world. Opportunity to make known what she has done is now being presented to her. She is making the most of it in a demonstration so conclusive as to have raised the question, Is woman an important factor in the development of Christian missions? This is being answered . . . that her services in the mission outposts are more effective than man's." At the 1900 General Conference Duncan spoke of her success in evangelizing hundreds of former slaves who worked in "the rice swamp, the cotton fields and river bottoms of the South and West," and organizing societies throughout the Sixth Episcopal District. She claimed that more funds could be raised to support domestic and foreign missionary work if the denomination would pay her travel expenses. With a membership of 8,230, Duncan anticipated that the WHFMS would eventually bring at least $10,000 a year to the church.

The tone of Duncan's inaugural speech and the obvious success of the southern women was alarming to many bishops. In a somewhat surprising move, in 1898 the AME General Conference authorized the incorporation of the Woman's Parent Mite Missionary Society and granted it full control over its funds. The WPMMS was now free to hold an annual women's missionary convention and to receive monies directly from the local WMMS auxiliaries. While this action suggests that the majority of the bishops had capitulated to the demands of the WPMMS, the issue was far more complex. Having failed in their attempt to merge the women's organizations, the bishops simply employed a stopgap measure to certify their support of the WPMMS as *the* legitimate missionary society of the AME Church, as opposed to the WHFMS. In 1911, the AME Parent Board of Missions voted to "recognize" the WMMS and WHFMS as auxiliaries. In effect, the WPMMS lost control over its fund-raising base—the WMMS. As leaders of the WPMMS, the bishops' wives spoke out on many issues; however, they were not as persistent—and, for some observers, not as abrasive as Sara Duncan—in their attacks on the male leadership. Duncan explained the opposition of males in feminist language that was direct and cutting. Her speeches before the General Conference were exercises in history, designed to educate women about their plight. Some bishops perceived Duncan and the southern women as a dangerous threat to the masculine image of the church. It would take almost half a century to effect the merger, but that would not hamper the male clergy's efforts to subordinate both women's organizations.

In spite of its success, the WHFMS failed to quell the voices of those who believed that the WPMMS was the only legitimate AME women's organization and that the WHFMS should be subsumed under its banner. In response to assertions that the organization "doing the real work" was the Woman's Parent Mite Missionary Society, Duncan emphasized that the WHFMS's membership was five times larger than that of the WPMMS and that there was "no dissension" between the two organizations. Acknowledging that the WPMMS was well organized and financially more viable than the WHFMS, Duncan asserted that it was unfair to compare an organization that had been in existence for thirty years with one that was barely seven years old. Moreover, the WHFMS, unlike its counterpart, was dependent on the support of poor working women who earned their "widow's mite" through hard work—"by sweat and tears over the washtub, ironing table, in the school room, in the kitchens, and the cotton fields." Duncan described in stark detail the class differences among the women constituting the two societies. During the three decades of its existence, the WPMMS had included women "of the highest type, the smartest and most intellectual women, . . . the wives, mothers, sisters and daughters of the high dignitaries" of the AME Church. For those waiting for the WHFMS to fail, Duncan assured them that it would not.

Duncan's reign as WHFMS superintendent ended in 1908 with the election of Laura Lemon Turner as the organization's first president. As a writer, lecturer, and outspoken advocate of the WHFMS, Laura Lemon was well known. However, her somewhat controversial marriage to Bishop Turner—a man old enough to be her grandfather—in 1907 heightened her visibility. Laura Lemon was among those who spoke against the proposed merger of the WPMMS and the WHFMS. She exposed the prejudice inherent in denominational organs, such as the *Christian Recorder*, that constantly praised the northern missionary society and gave scant mention to the southern women's activities. Speaking forcefully and with determination, Lemon stated, "We mean to be a power in our territory and thereby give solidity to the forces already at work."

Laura Lemon Turner (1908–15) and her successor Sandy G. Simmons (1915–26) headed the WHFMS during a period when the national focus was on women's suffrage. In the midst of the swirling debates about women's fitness to participate as equals in the American government, these women, as well as Lucy M. Hughes, WHFMS president from 1927 to 1945 and Mary F. Handy, WPMMS president from 1907 to 1931, seized the opportunity to advance AME women's long struggle for religious rights. For at least three decades, leaders of the southern and northern women's missionary societies pressed for religious equality for women. At the 1924 General Conference in Louisville, Kentucky, five hundred women demonstrated for religious suffrage. In response to the protest and to curtail women's independence and decrease the numbers of young female leaders in the missionary societies, male leaders passed a resolution barring women "wearing sleeveless dresses and bobbed hair from holding office in the Church." This action was directed at the WHFMS, especially the numerous young, educated, and outspoken women, representatives of the rising generation of females who adhered to the new feminist ideology of the 1920s. In contrast, the WPMMS comprised older, more established women whose roots were in the nineteenth century.

The year 1924 represented a watershed in AME women's struggle for religious rights. Beginning with the WPMMS, missionary leaders had refused to accept their subordinate status and systematically pressed for equality in the religious polity. In the 1890s the society argued that women's work should be controlled by women, meaning that women should define and execute the work and have full control over the finances. During the first half of the twentieth century, the WPMMS and WHFMS recognized that having a voice and vote in the denomination's legislative bodies was the key to changing women's status. So they joined forces in fighting for women to serve as lay delegates, be ordained, and have access to all denominational rights accorded to men. Through articles and speeches, leaders of the women's societies pressed for an independent missionary department, the election of women to denominational offices, and the appointment of a woman to the male-dominated Parent Home and Foreign Missions Board. In 1924, when the female laity was finally granted the right to vote and to serve as lay delegates at the General Conference, the door to equality was forced ajar. However, the presidents of women's missionary societies and women preachers continued to be denied these rights. In 1928 the presidents of women's missionary societies were admitted to the polity, but female clergy were not. Women preachers, such as Rev. Martha Jayne Keys were well known and intimately involved in the affairs of the WPMMS and WHFMS, and women's missionary societies continued to fight for complete women's suffrage.

As more young women became active in the women's organizations and sought denominational offices, many male clergy felt threatened by women's growing power within the denomination, especially the organized political activism emanating from the two women's societies, most notably the WHFMS. At the same time, the clergy was faced with a revolt of laymen who were demanding equal representation on the episcopal committee that identified and assigned bishops to episcopal districts. During the 1920s and early '30s, the AME's General Conference increasingly became filled with excitement and disorder as male and female delegates joined other religious activists in loudly proclaiming their causes, while candidates for offices negotiated deals behind the scenes.

The struggle of women for equality in the AME polity was an empowering force for the young women and laymen who sought a voice in the shaping of denominational policies. In 1932 the General Conference erupted in an uproar as the women, laymen, and some supporting ministers who were fed up with clergy abuse of power unified against the bishops and ministerial delegates. Female leaders formed a "Common Sense Committee" and circulated an open letter addressed to the bishops and annual conferences urging the elimination of eleven bishops, a drastic reduction in bishops' salaries, and an examination of the denomination's financial records. Similarly, at the 1935 General Conference, young women concerned about the elitism and sexism evident in the administration of the WPMMS asked President Christine Smith to address questions related to the domination of *all* important offices by bishops' wives, the exclusion of young women from office, the exclusive employment of men instead of "competent women" for conducting missionary classes, the continued domination of quadrennial conferences by a few individuals, and other issues regarding convention protocol.

As women became more vocal and forceful in presenting their issues at the General Conference, some men became less respectful in their treatment of female activists. Reflecting on the treatment of women at the 1936 General Conference, Christine Smith stated, "When I think of the scene . . . where a large group of men [forgot] their manhood and howl[ed] down a woman who had the floor and had the right to express her opinion, because her opinion was in opposition to theirs, I grow terribly discouraged. To my thinking it was a sad situation. Not a man stood up to champion the rights of another delegate when that right to speak was taken away by the mob spirit." The General Conference took on the character of a national political convention.

The male clergy, especially the bishops, were concerned about the growing dissatisfaction in the denomination, especially the persistent challenges to their leadership coming from the women and laymen, who gained open support of prominent male clergy in various district conferences, calling for revision of the discipline to provide for women's ordination. The bishops wanted to quell the dissension without giving up much of their authority. Given the gravity of the issues and the publicity accompanying these challenges, in 1936 the General Conference agreed to reduce bishops' salaries and to hire a certified public accountant to audit all financial records. However, the delegates rejected a recommendation for representatives of women's societies to participate with the bishops and the secretary of missions in the formulation of missionary programs. In the midst of this very public debate, perceiving that the time was ripe for election of a woman as secretary of missions, in 1939 WHFMS President Lucy M. Hughes secretly plotted with Claude Barnett, the powerful president of the

Associated Negro Press and editor of the *Chicago Defender*, to develop a strategy for securing the AME secretary of missions position. At the 1940 General Conference, Hughes lost her bid for the office, but not her hunger for power.

During a period exceeding half a century, as the Woman's Parent Mite Missionary Society and the Women's Home and Foreign Missionary Society established numerous missions and service programs, raised funds for home and foreign missions, and provided women with opportunities for leadership on an international scale, they grew in strength. Each of these entities expanded and continued to fulfill its mission. In spite of their successes, it was difficult to overcome the invidious comparisons and internal denominational dissension, and to escape the never-ending pressure of the Council of Bishops and the Parent Home and Foreign Missions Board to merge the societies. The success of the male-dominated Parent Home and Foreign Missions Board was predicated on the fund-raising prowess of women. Thus, the board brokered for full control of the women's organizations.

Between 1900 and 1932, at each successive General Conference a motion was put forth to merge the women's organizations. In 1932, without notice or consultation with either of the women's boards, the Council of Bishops simply ordered the merger of the WPMMS and the WHFMS. While the northern women protested the directive, the southern women accepted it. As astute power brokers, Christine Smith and Lucy Hughes, presidents of the WPMMS and the WHFMS, responded on the basis of their individual experiences and personal needs. Smith, as the wife of a deceased bishop, and as a well-connected NACW political activist, spoke from a position of presumed power and saw no reason why the pioneering and more prominent Woman's Parent Mite Missionary Society should merge with what she considered a lesser group. It mattered not that the southern women were larger in numbers and raised more money than the northern women. Also, Smith was outraged that the bishops had ordered the merger without consulting the women's boards. On the other hand, President Hughes, lacking Smith's connections and national stature, recognized that both she and her organization were perceived as the underdog.

Ambitious and anxious to build a power base for herself, Lucy Hughes undercut Christine Smith by proposing an amendment to merge the bodies and have both executive boards meet with the Council of Bishops to set up the merger. A Merger Commission was established to work out the differences between the WPMMS and the

WHFMS and effect unification. Between 1932 and 1944 a bitter fight ensued, in which the WPMMS contended that as an independent, separately incorporated, volunteer body it was not legally subject to the dictates of the bishops. In point of fact, both societies were by law freestanding corporations. This was an underlying factor in the bishops' order to merge the two societies. The new organization, incorporated by the denomination, would be owned by the AME Church and subject to its dictates. The women's opposition centered around the funds held by each organization and the merger of officers. Unification would reduce the opportunities for women to hold office and give control of all funds to the new organization.

By taking a position supportive of the merger, Lucy Hughes garnered the support of the episcopacy and gained tremendous political capital. Christine Smith, in refusing to yield to the bishops' demands, drew their ire. She was characterized as an "unyielding and uncompromising personality [who] strictly adheres to business principles." To intimidate and influence the clergy and laity, the bishops emphasized that Smith was "the *widow* of a bishop." A common and oft-heard expression within the denomination was, "You had better stick to the bishops' wives whose husbands are living if you want to get anywhere, since the dead bishop can't help you now." In 1944, following a long struggle, the Woman's Parent Mite Missionary Society was defeated in its effort to retain its identity. By a margin of one conference vote, the merger was formalized. At the time of the merger, the two societies constituted 58,000 American women, 22,000 of whom were members of the WPMMS. The Woman's Parent Mite Missionary Society supported missions in West Africa, the West Indies, and British and Dutch Guiana. It also supported schools for boys and girls in Liberia, Sierra Leone, and the African Gold Coast. The Women's Home and Foreign Missionary Society boasted 36,000 members in the United States and twenty thousand African members who raised funds for support of the work on the continent, primarily in South Africa.

AME Women's Missionary Society

THE NAME OF the consolidated organization, Women's Missionary Society of the AME Church, was carefully chosen to reflect its legal status. Having yielded their independent corporate status to become a connectional organization, after 1945 the Women's Missionary Society operated strictly as an auxiliary to the all-male AME Department of Missions. The merger of the WPMMS and the WHFMS was characterized by some as "one of the most significant steps in the annals of the women's movement in the [AME] Church." It eliminated the rivalry between northern and southern women and unified women throughout the denomination. The merger also led to major structural changes in the women's organization, and the elimination of the *Women's Missionary Recorder*, the only AME publication controlled by women. Following the publication's demise, in 1950 the WMS was assigned one page of the *Voice of Missions* for "Women's Missionary News." As editor, A. Beatrice Williams named the page the "Women's Missionary Magazine" and invited ministers and their wives, missionaries, and ordinary members to submit articles less critical of the clergy.

Lucy Hughes was elected as president, and Christine Smith as executive secretary, of the Women's Missionary Society. At Hughes's death in 1945, Anne Heath, WMS's first vice president, became president. The WMS was located in every state of the United States and internationally in Canada, Bermuda, Cuba, the Virgin Islands, the West Indies, Nova Scotia, and Africa. Between 1945 and 1990, Anne Heath (1945–71), Mary Frizzell (1971–74), and Wilhelmenia Lawrence (1974–87) assumed leadership of the WMS and became the architects of a new organization. The merger healed some of the regional tensions, and unified AME women in unexpected ways. As old animosities slowly dissipated and women began to grapple with their changing status, they realized that irrespective of region women were in danger of losing far more than most had anticipated.

The merger coincided with a rising tide of black nationalism, civil rights, and feminist post–World War II activism that was highly visible among African Americans and women. Numerous articles about women's changing status in the church and society appeared in the secular and religious press. While church women were always cognizant of sexism in the church, the changes in American women's political and social status after 1920 profoundly affected the way they perceived their role and place in society. As AME women became more actively engaged in feminist and civil rights activities during the 1940s and '50s, they embraced new ideas about missions and expressed a need to work more closely with ecumenical and secular organizations on "Christian social concerns" designed to shape government decisions on policies affecting education, labor, housing, and segregation.

The 1950s represented a crossroads for women in the church and society. Swirling national and international debates on the question of women's place in the church followed the 1948 formation of a World Council of Churches commission to study the issue. Denominations were challenged to address the concerns of both women and laity. The year 1948 also heralded the emergence of the laymen as a significant factor in the shaping of the AME legislative and administrative programs. At the denomination's 33rd Quadrennial Conference, the laymen were represented by a cadre of prominent lawyers, including Sadie Tanner Alexander. Alexander, the granddaughter of Bishop Benjamin Tucker Tanner, had a long history of civil rights activism and in 1944 became the first woman in the AME Church elected as the attorney for the Council of Bishop's. Her involvement with the laymen's reformation coincided with her appointment to the President's Civil Rights Committee by President Harry S. Truman.

As a member of the AME committee on the revision of the discipline, Alexander played a significant part in the reshaping of church law. She and other AME lawyers formed a coalition with militant and progressive AME ministers to virtually take control of the church and check the power of the bishops. Cognizant of the strength and power of the laymen and their determination to move forward, two bishops joined with them. Though the majority of bishops would later find common ground with the laymen, in the late 1940s they fought the reform movement. Organized laymen succeeded in having the relatives of bishops removed from the powerful Episcopal Committee, which adjudicated cases involving the immorality and misconduct of bishops and controlled the assignment of ministers to episcopal districts. They also garnered delegate support for passage of a resolution to have bishops removed from the districts to which they had been previously assigned by the General Conference.

Recognizing that they were part of a larger debate about clergy malfeasance and the use of power by the bishops, AME women leaders—such as Anne Heath; Pennie Esther Gibbs, supervisor of the WMS's Ninth Episcopal District, in Alabama; A. Beatrice Williams, editor of the *Women's Missionary Magazine*; Wilda Robinson-Smith, editor of the *Christian Recorder*'s Woman's Column; and Alma Polk, the first female elected general officer in the history of the AME Church— were outspoken in their critique of the escalating sexism in the church. Bishops and male clergy were actively engaged in efforts to further marginalize the WMS or subsume its program under the all-male General Missionary Board. Some bishops suggested ousting outspo-

ken women leaders from office. Rev. Jesse L. Glover and Rev. A. Wayman Ward joined forces with the women to thwart what they perceived as a major abuse of power by male clergy.

As a result of constitutional changes legislated in the 1920s,
women—as a separate entity and also as part of the laity—were represented in the polity. With voice and vote, female and mainly male laity,
who accounted for a larger share of the lay delegates, could influence
the outcome of General Conference elections for bishops and general
officers. Alarmed by the growing power of women and the laity in the
1930s, '40s, and '50s, powerful male clergy attempted to control the
legislative process at the local level through the careful selection of
delegates to the General Conference. In 1952, the Rev. Jesse L. Glover
questioned the blatant manipulation of the political process and
argued that the General Conference was not a representative body. He
suggested that some members were elected on the basis of their support of a candidate for general office. Glover insisted, "The laity must
stand firm for freedom. They must work with the minister to keep the
church free [of corruption] at all times."

In 1956, for the first time in its history, the General Conference
adopted a connectional budget. The impetus for this action as well as
other major changes implemented between 1950 and 1970 was the
Brotherhood Movement in the AME Church. Prior to the 1950s, the
Brotherhood was a small and loosely organized group of people who
met periodically to discuss church issues. Between 1952 and 1956,
under the leadership of Rev. H. Ralph Jackson, the organization
became the most potent force in AME politics, especially the General
Conference. As ministers and bishops gravitated to the Brotherhood in
large numbers, its power solidified. Throughout the church there was
a sense of denominational disorder and a recognition of the need for
the church to adjust to the changes taking place in the world. There
were several reasons for the mounting internal problems, including
widespread belief that church politics was interfering with the execution of denominational programs and that some church leaders openly
flaunted church law. For some this created an air of urgency and a
demand for change.

The WMS and the laity agreed that there was a need for change,
but what they envisioned was a restructuring of the church to ensure
greater inclusion and freedom of participation in church affairs by the
membership and closer cooperation among all denominational entities. However, the Brotherhood Movement emphasized accountability

and greater control over church entities. The primary focus of local clergy was how to maximize their control over denominational processes and disrupt the bishops' authority over ministers in the episcopal districts. Adopting the slogan "Reconstruction under God," the Brotherhood advanced the idea of a connectional budget. Until 1956, though the AME Church handled millions of dollars, it did not operate on an overall budget. Rather, each entity raised funds, determined its budget, and spent money at will. The Brotherhood favored centralized control of all programs and funds, and a comprehensive budget that closely tied all denominational fund-raising and expenses to specific program goals. The legislation passed by the 1956 General Conference supporting decentralization of the church, and the election of an AME General Board, represented a major victory for the Brotherhood Movement. Under the new system, the board would draft an annual budget and receive and disburse funds.

Decentralization of the AME denomination gave the local church, specifically the clergy, more power. It meant greater control of the central fund-raising group—women—by local male clergy and church officers. Thus, male laity and clergy gained power, at the expense of women. The local church, regardless of size, grew in importance because it bore the weight of the denomination's program. The General Conference's designation of finance as the measure of success in effect elevated the stature of the local church. Whereas the WMS was accustomed to retaining half of all monies it raised, the new budget required that 75 percent of all funds raised be sent to the national office. The male heads of all denominational entities received salaries of $5,000, and most were given housing and travel stipends. At a salary of only $3,000, the WMS president received less money than her male counterparts and assumed responsibility for her own expenses. Female leaders expressed mixed views about the new budget. In consideration of the many problems faced by the denomination, some felt that a unified national budget would ensure the distribution of funds in a more equitable fashion. Others thought that since women were excluded from the decision-making process, male leaders would be able to tighten their control over women at all levels.

By 1957 there was widespread dissension in the AME Church. The denomination was characterized by disharmony among the members of the Council of Bishops, the Brotherhood, the Laymen's Organization, and the Connectional Council (the AME board of directors) over issues regarding the Women's Missionary Society and the rights of laity. Throughout the late 1950s controversy over the election of additional bishops, redistricting of the church, revision of the flawed 1956 budget, and control of the WMS dominated the meetings of the General Conference. WMS women at every level were dissatisfied. Of critical concern to the WMS was its loss of control over the society's budget.

Loretta C. Spencer, president of the WMS Thirteenth Episcopal District, spoke out about the impact of the new church legislation on AME women. She acknowledged the need for a budget based on needs and Christian objectives, but "not one designed to penalize any groups, individuals and organizations." Spencer questioned why the WMS women who raised money to pay the salaries and expenses of bishops, general officers, and board members were allotted such an insignificant amount of money for their expenses. AME budget limitations made it impossible for WMS representatives to attend the meetings of important national organizations such as Church Women United. Spencer concluded, "We [women] can raise and pay the money, turn it over to be used to pay and operate all departments but our own. The women of the AME Church are losing ground; they are being embarrassed by other communions. By 1960 we will have retrogressed fifty years."

It did not take long for AME women to discover that they had been duped into merging the Woman's Parent Mite Missionary Society and the Women's Home and Foreign Missionary Society, organizations that possessed more autonomy than the Women's Missionary Society. In the pre-1956 budget debates, enlightened clergy, concerned about the advance of the Brotherhood Movement, especially their "fears [that] women can't be 'handled,' " called for the denomination to "UNSHACKLE our WOMEN." In 1955, Rev. A. Wayman Ward argued that women should be granted equal rights with men in all areas of church life. He asserted that there were men as well as women "who can't be handled by gangster methods nor bought with filthy gold and empty promises." Wayman was referring specifically to the Brotherhood's efforts to remove Anne Heath, the WMS president, from office because she could not be "handled." In the late 1950s it became clear to most women that their hands were virtually tied, and that they had lost the power to determine how their organization should function, to initiate programs, or even to convene and run their own meetings.

By 1957, women leaders were scrambling to regain some of their freedom. As their pleas fell on deaf ears and many felt that little could be done to stem the tide, Lorreta Spencer assured them that it was not too late. "Let us not deceive ourselves. Consideration and assistance can be given now. As a last resort, we can stage a righteous sit-down strike. The reins are in our hands. Let us use them, not for political power or a high office, but for the good of the . . . Missionary Society. . . . Yes, this is time for the missionary women to speak up and be respected!"

Spencer meant well, but what she failed to understand was that power yields nothing without a demand. The bishops and male clergy were steeped in politics, understood the nature of power, and would not be swayed simply by women's pleas. Religious masculinity had not disappeared from denominational politics—it was as virulent in the 1950s as it had been a hundred years earlier. As male leaders felt more vulnerable and threatened by the changes in women's overall status in society, there was a sense that they were losing control of the reins of power. For black men, the church was emblematic of masculine control. As Rev. Ward noted, among men the old cliche "Let the women preach, and one of them will want to be a BISHOP" was well known. Though black males were advancing in the professions, the best corporate position for a black man was still the bishopric, and high-paying ministerial positions were more abundant and accessible to black males than jobs in secular society.

By 1959 the triumphant signs of a religious masculinity were everywhere. Many male leaders were profuse in their praise of women for doing "business in a high class way," and performing the majority of church work. They acknowledged that without women's support the church would fail. However, as a rule, most insisted on male domination. In anticipation of the upcoming WMS Quadrennial Conference in June 1959, A. Beatrice Williams and Pennie Esther Gibbs spoke out against the actions of the male clergy. Williams stressed that there was great tension over the issue of the treatment of the WMS and the erosion of women's rights in the church.

As a civil rights activist, a feminist, and the wife of a bishop, Pennie Gibbs was widely known in AME Church politics. She represented a long line of bishops' wives who were outspoken about women's rights. Though their husbands might differ with them, many of these women continued to speak against the gender discrimination in the church and endeavored to change church law and practice. In March 1959 Gibbs assumed the right to speak for AME women; in a widely publicized

Christian Recorder article, Gibbs stated, "We the women of the African Methodist Episcopal Church do hereby take a stand in behalf of the Women's Missionary Society against the position in which we find ourselves in the total picture of the . . . Church." Possessed by an air of militancy, Gibbs argued, "[W]omen have been forced as workers to be relegated to certain positions, which they deem unfair, unjust and unbecoming as laborers in the field of missions. . . . During the last quadrennium the women have been denied the privilege of representing their own organization, the Women's Missionary Society, while upon them rests the heavy responsibility of the Missionary Work, both at home and on the Foreign Fields." Gibbs continued, "No man, be he the head of a home, the head of a country, or the head of a church, is capable of expressing women's views and the women of the Women's Missionary Society feel that they should have expression through a woman as president of the Society and as chairman of the Board." Sadly, Gibbs's words fell mostly on deaf ears.

Rev. J. E. Roberts of Winslow, Arizona, described Pennie Gibbs's plea as "The Bitter Cry" of AME women. Roberts suggested that this was raising questions that the church had "evaded, neglected and ignored. But today they are inevitable questions. Every four years we speak of the tragic waste of the 'fertile intellect' of our fine women, but nobody ever does anything about it." Roberts asked, "What are the roles of our women going to be in the evolving African Methodist Episcopal Church? . . . Even though the 'Bitter Cry' is an old cry . . . today it carries a different tune." Rev. Roberts added his voice to the growing chorus of those who viewed the plight of the WMS within the larger context of sexism in the denomination, and argued that the time had come to ordain women and "give them 'direct leadership' in the total framework and program" of the AME Church.

The bishops closely monitored the Women's Missionary Society after 1956 to ensure that they adhered to the new agenda. Rev. A. Chester Clark, editor of the *Voice of Missions*, was appointed general supervisor of the WMS. Clark directed the WMS's Quadrennial Convention in June 1959, represented the WMS at the meetings of the Board of Missions and the Council of Bishops, revised the WMS's constitution to accommodate the changes desired by the bishops, and was the chief factor in negotiating the WMS's tacit approval of the document. Reporters for the *Voice of Missions* repeated the statements of insiders that "[m]any of the women were hot *and tired and were willing to accept* what had been prepared for them." A major issue was how to devise plans for raising funds outside the budget to cover the WMS's basic expenses. According to the reporters, the ministers were "not anxious for the women to be 'turned loose' " and were fearful of "a wedge being opened to the old pre budget era." Passage of the WMS constitution was subject to its ratification by the 1960 General Conference. While the WMS concentrated on how to retain its rights, the Council of Bishops focused on the "Episcopal Address" for the 1960 General Conference. The address emphasized the recruitment of more male clergy, the expansion and development of missions, the increase of WMS activities, and the adjustment of the AME's overall program to accommodate the changes resulting from post–World War II black migration.

At the 1960 General Conference, the Women's Missionary Society requested permission for its branches to retain annual dues and all monies collected at its annual meeting, for all WMS committees to be permitted to meet, and for the Council of Bishops and the General Mission Board to designate the WMS's foreign missionary projects. With the exception of the last item, their requests were denied. Meanwhile, the Brotherhood Movement reveled in its success in subduing the women and gaining control of the denomination. As the rhetoric grew louder and the debate about the WMS's plight continued, more leaders entered the fray. The recently elected brash president of the Brotherhood, Rev. Sam Davis, was incensed about what he perceived as the immorality of the women's request. He took the offensive by delivering a preemptive strike at the WMS several months before the 1963 Quadrennial Convention, where the restructuring of the WMS would be finalized. Davis argued the need for "men of honor and integrity, *upfront* men [who] will respect the laws they are to administer" by strictly enforcing them. He cited the Women's Missionary Society officers as an example of AME leaders engaged in a "malicious breaking of the law in devious ways, . . . which we cannot condone any longer. They are still taking one-half of the annual conference offering." Davis indicted the so-called law breakers by asserting, "The old 'Missionary Hustlers' are in full swing."

WMS leaders considered Davis's inflammatory statement an unjustified attack on AME women. Several women defended "the womanhood of the church." According to Myrtle Battiste Henry, the expression "Old Missionary Hustlers" originated during the 1962 General Conference when WMS leaders "were pleading for fair legislation." Appalled by the "insult," Henry asked male leaders if they understood that "the woman has left the kitchen and she votes now." She alleged that the "most vicious [male] critics get all their expenses paid, they travel in the fastest jets, live in the most expensive hotels and eat and drink in the most exclusive places; yet when the women complain of injustices . . . and endeavor to lift themselves out of the financial rut in which the dear brethren have pushed them, this crowd of Big Spenders label the women as 'Missionary Hustlers.' " Using the time-worn but truthful argument that no church could exist "if it weren't for the women," Henry reminded clergy that it was because of women that they were fed, clothed, and allowed to function. Henry urged AME women to "rise up and throw off the shackles that hinder us" and "unite and straighten [out] the church . . . and the brethren."

Rank-and-file AME women were outraged over the charge that they were "Missionary Hustlers." As a former member of the WHFMS Executive Board and a dedicated missionary worker, Mrs. P. W. Rogers took umbrage at being referred to as a hustler, and explained that the word had several meanings, including "an obstructor," "a prostitute—a street woman, and one who lives by his wits, averse to making an honest effort to seek legitimate work." She argued, "A Missionary does not stand on street corners, soliciting the attentions and funds of men, as the word 'hustler' indicates," and questioned why Rev. Davis would place AME women missionaries in the same "category" as a prostitute. Suggesting that perhaps Davis had intimate knowledge of prostitutes, Rogers asked whether he was among those who frequented the " 'Preacher's Secret Hide-away' in Harlem, New York, where the 'ministers' of God go to 'let their hair down,' doff their ecclesiastical collars, and revel in the kind of lives they never gave up in the first place. REVEREND, ARE YOU SURE YOU'RE NOT A HABITUATE OF THE 'HIDE-AWAY'?"

Labeling the women as "Foes Within the Church," Rev. Sam Davis stepped out of his role as individual clergyman and assumed his mantle as president and defender of the Brotherhood. Characterizing the women as part of the "scathing denunciations by malignant foes within the church" that "uncover and disclose every [false] form . . . of injustice, and discrimination against the Brotherhood," Davis denounced women leaders such as Anne Heath and Myrtle Henry, and likened them and other so-called female "law breakers" to "Jezebel." Davis assured the WMS that he spoke for many AME men. In July 1963, the WMS's Administrative Committee presented a six-count resolution to the Council of Bishops recounting their century-long history of supporting the AME home and foreign missionary program and articulating their "dissatisfaction and grief over the unmerited epithet hurled at our Missionary women by Rev. Davis." Despite their pleas and protest, the WMS was restructured in 1963.

After 1964 the Women's Missionary Society deflected the discussion away from raising funds as "an end in itself" to utilizing missionary education as a tool to promote mission work. Missionary training and leadership institutes were expanded and used to refocus women's attention on service and less on AME politics. As president of the WMS, Anne Heath continued to plead with the general church to " 'Untie' the hands of the AME Missionary women so they COULD GO TO WORK." Heath recounted that in the past when women were "unhindered and unmolested, they did great financial jobs," and that under the old system they raised more foreign mission money in one year than they had in nine years under the new program. By 1970

Rev. Florence Spearing Randolph (standing, second from left) with AME Zion delegation, at the Third Methodist Ecumenical Conference held September 4–17, 1901, in London, England, as they pose in front of the Memorial to John Wesley, the founder of Methodism

the work of the WMS was largely decentralized. As the organization's power was diminished, so too was the office of the president.

AME Zion

IN THE 1890s AME Zion women were the idols of women in both black and white denominations. All legal barriers to female participation in the polity had been removed, and women possessed all the rights available to the AME Zion male, including religious suffrage, full clergy rights, and equal rights in the polity. Technically, they possessed the right to pursue leadership positions formerly considered off-limits to women. However, it would take more than a century for at least one female to ascend to the highest and most powerful office in the AME Zion Church, the episcopacy, and for a few women to be appointed pastors of the largest and most prestigious churches. In 2007 the AME Zion Woman's Home and Foreign Missionary Society occupied a subordinate status to the denomination's General Mission Board, most general offices were filled by males, and for the most part decision making remained in the hands of the bishops and male clergy. Yet historically more AME Zion women were ordained and pastored churches than women in any other black denomination. They have exercised the right of religious suffrage for over a century and contributed to the denomination's development in innumerable ways. AME Zion women have achieved a measure of equality, but not full justice within the denomination.

AME Zion foreign mission work began in 1856 when the Home and Foreign Mission Board of the New York Conference organized a church in Demerara, South America. In 1876 the denomination established its first African mission in Liberia. As male clergy failed to raise adequate funds to support mission programs in Africa and other foreign stations, it became clear that without the substantial involvement of women the denomination would not be able to mount a successful program. The AME Zion Home and Foreign Mission Board and the Woman's Home and Foreign Missionary Society were organized in 1880. Prior to 1944 and the General Conference's decision to provide funding for development of a domestic program, the AMEZ-WHFMS provided nominal support for home missions. The women's organization operated under the strict control of the all-male General Mission Board, which required that two-thirds of the money raised by the AMEZ-WHFMS be sent to the general treasurer for foreign work.

As Katie P. Hood, president of the AMEZ-WHFMS, explained, "Our effort is for the purpose of raising money to meet the demands upon that Board." The male general secretary directed the women's fund-raising activities.

Given the clearly defined role of the AMEZ-WHFMS and its subordination to the denomination's General Mission Board, it was generally assumed that there would be little opposition from the male clergy. However, that was not the case. As in other Methodist denominations, AME Zion church elders, deacons, and pastors were legally responsible for the forming of missionary societies in their churches. Though the bishops had advanced the effort and orchestrated the passage of legislation by the General Conference, this initiative was not broadly supported by the male leaders at the grassroots level. At the General Conference of 1884, AMEZ-WHFMS officers spoke of the difficulties they encountered in attempting to organize local missionary societies. Of these women, Mary J. Jones, the president, and Mrs. Thompson, the treasurer, were the wives of bishops, and Eliza Gardner, a lay member, was a vice president. Jones and Thompson praised the clergy and spoke in pathetic tones of their fealty to the denomination and willingness to work in cooperation with their brothers. The bishops' wives pleaded with the male leadership to permit them to do missionary work.

Unlike the bishops' wives, Eliza Gardner was unaccustomed to genuflecting before either white people or black men, dissembling, or otherwise ingratiating herself to achieve an objective. Indeed, she spoke forcefully about the treatment of AME Zion women, stating, "I do not think I felt quite so Christian-like as my dear sisters. I come from old Massachusetts, where we have declared that all, not only men, but women too, are created free and equal with certain inalienable rights which men are bound to respect. I am inclined to think that some of my brethren here will regard this as rank heresy. But you will remember that I come from a state where such sentiments prevail." As a veteran abolitionist, a temperance reformer, and a women's rights and suffrage activist, Gardner had devoted more than three decades of her life to fighting racism and sexism. Single, self-supported, educated, and well connected to many white and black leaders of the time, she spoke to the issue of sexism in the church. Gardner declared,

> If I would go back to Boston and tell the people that some of the members of this conference were against the women, it might

have a tendency to prejudice our interests in that city with those upon whom we can rely for assistance. . . . [I]f you will encourage the hearts of the Vice-presidents in your respective districts, you will strengthen our efforts and make us a power. If you commence to talk about the superiority of men, if you persist in telling us that after the fall of man, we were put under your feet and that we are intended to be subject to your will, we cannot help you in New England one bit.

Gardner's comments were loudly applauded at the time, but few male clergy supported her views. Given her prominence among leading black and white reformers, family history of support for the AME Zion Church, and ability to raise large sums of money for the New England Conference, none would counter Gardner's arguments or openly dispute her claims. The lagging support of the women's missionary program and the recognition that without the involvement of females the denomination's mission program would stagnate were factors in the decision of the 1884 General Conference to remove the word "male" from the discipline and open the door for women to advance in the polity. This was the carrot that the male clergy thought would lure women into major fund-raising drives. In part, their actions were motivated by issues of religious masculinity and competition with men in other denominations, in particular the AME and Baptist churches. Granting AME Zion women lay and clergy rights was indeed significant, but there was little change in the attitude of most clergy toward women's role in the local church. Moreover, most pastors preferred that monies be raised and spent at the local level, where their members could witness the effects. Regardless of the reasons for lack of support for women in missions, at least 90 percent of the clergy failed to organize auxiliary missionary societies in their churches.

In 1888 the General Conference adopted a separate constitution for the AMEZ-WHFMS, and in 1900 it granted the society the right to representation at the General Mission Board's meetings, but denied it specific recognition in the General Conference. The denomination also authorized the holding of AMEZ-WHFMS district mass meetings, annual conferences, and quadrennial conventions. During the next sixteen years the AME Zion constitution was amended several times to incorporate the development of local societies, regulate their activities, and channel funds to the AME Zion Annual Conference. The AMEZ-WHFMS offices were expanded to include a president and a vice president for each annual conference district, and a corresponding secretary who served as an agent for the national organization. All of these positions would be appointed by the General Conference.

The changes had little impact on the AMEZ-WHFMS's legal relationship to the General Mission Board. By 1910 bishops' wives were losing their positions to aggressive lay women interested in broadening the leadership. In an effort to slow down the advance of the laity, in 1912 the General Conference ruled that the AMEZ-WHFMS could elect their own officers. Bishops' wives and widows kept their positions as vice presidents and members of the AMEZ-WHFMS's executive board—without a vote.

One example of the kind of supervision bishops could exercise through their wives occurred in 1901. On several occasions James Walker Hood, the senior bishop, used the pages of the *Star of Zion* to answer correspondence addressed to his wife, Katie Hood, the AMEZ-WHFMS president. In response to requests for funds to support mission work, Bishop Hood wrote, "It is true that she is the President of the Woman's Home and Foreign Missionary Society, but the work of that Society is to COLLECT funds. The funds collected are sent to the Treasurer of the Home and Foreign Mission Board." Clarifying the subordinate status of the AMEZ-WHFMS, Bishop Hood emphasized that "the general board disburses the money, and not the Woman's Missionary Society, which some miscall [the] '*Mission Board.*'"

In 1904, in an effort to further clarify the AMEZ-WHFMS's status, Bishop Hood stated that it must "be distinctly understood that it is an auxiliary to the Missionary Department of the AME Zion Church." In response to Hood's assertions, AMEZ-WHFMS leaders, such as the Rev. Florence Spearing Randolph and Eliza Gardner, became more outspoken about the need for the society to control its own affairs. To resolve this issue, the AMEZ-WHFMS agreed to become an auxiliary to the Board of Foreign Missions and raise funds to meet the budget for foreign work, in exchange for the "privilege" of managing its own affairs. Most likely Bishop Hood suggested this strategy to his wife, Katie. Management of the organization simply meant that the AMEZ-WHFMS was free from the dictates of the general secretary of missions, who had defined the society's program and agenda. However, the AMEZ-WHFMS operated under the direction of the Board of Bishops and the AME Zion General Missions Board.

Lay women continued to press for a larger role in the AMEZ-WHFMS. The reign of bishops's wives ended in 1916 with the election of Rev. Florence Spearing Randolph as the AMEZ-WHFMS president. There was no law preventing the election of bishops' wives, but between 1916 and 1970 none served as president. In 1928 the AMEZ-WHFMS was granted the right to hold its own missionary conference, and its constitution was amended to permit the election and appointment of lay women as supervisors of AME Zion episcopal districts. To circumvent the advance of lay women and assure episcopal involvement on the AMEZ-WHFMS's executive board, bishops appointed their wives as missionary supervisors. In 1931 women advocated "radical changes" in the AMEZ-WHFMS's structure, adopting and submitting recommendations to the 1932 General Convention requiring that the management of the women's department be turned over to them and that the AMEZ-WHFMS corresponding secretary be installed as general secretary of the Board of Foreign Missions. In response to these requests, the General Conference revised the AMEZ-WHFMS constitution. The position of corresponding secretary was eliminated and replaced with that of an executive secretary whose responsibilities included fiscal and program management and who reported to the all-male Board of Foreign Missions and Board of Bishops. The beginning salary for the executive secretary was $1,200, a considerable sum in 1935. The new constitution also provided for a paid personal secretary.

Seeking to build upon their gains, in 1944 the AMEZ-WHFMS stirred controversy over the question of purchasing a building that would serve as a headquarters for the society. The Board of Bishops refused to endorse the purchase and ordered the society to abandon the project. The bishops recognized that permitting the AMEZ-WHFMS to establish a headquarters would advance women's power in unacceptable ways. However, they were willing to support purchase of property for the general use of the denomination, but not in the name of the AMEZ-WHFMS. At the behest of the Board of Bishops, the missionary supervisors—bishops' wives—became "full-fledged" voting members of the AMEZ-WHFMS executive board. Having their wives on the AMEZ-WHFMS executive board enabled the bishops to monitor the activities of the women's society, intercede when necessary, and block future initiatives that would advance the power of women in the denomination.

While it may appear that during the first five decades of the

AMEZ-WHFMS's existence women gained some power within the AME Zion denomination, in actuality their relationship to the General Mission Board changed very little. With or without titles, the women's society exercised little control over the distribution of the organization's finances, and the bulk of their national program was devoted to fund-raising. AMEZ-WHFMS leaders pressed for some leeway in the dispensing of funds and monies to help defray the society's expenses for travel and organizing local societies. The AMEZ-WHFMS's request that one-third of their collections should be allowed for travel and other expenses was denied. As the first bishop appointed to oversee the African Conference, Bishop John Bryan Small had discouraged the idea, arguing that "all money collected for missions should be spent on missions alone." The Board of Bishops treated funds collected for missions as part of the general denomination budget to be utilized for whatever purpose they desired.

For years, AMEZ-WHFMS leaders felt that since women were responsible for raising the bulk of the funds for missionary work they should head the denomination's board of missions. In 1892 the AME Zion Church elected its first "missionary secretary." Beginning his work in New England, the secretary incurred the anger of many conference members who were against church entertainment. Though monies were raised, at the end of four years, the secretary had not deposited "one penny" in the missionary treasury. Similarly, the next two secretaries collected monies that never reached the missionary treasury. After eight years of experience with men who at best were derelict in their duties (and possibly criminal in their actions), Bishop Hood saw no need for the position. However, the establishment of an African Conference, the appointment of the first African bishop in 1892, and the expansion of the AME Zion's foreign mission programs in South America, the East Indies, and the Caribbean, emphasized the need for a missionary secretary. In 1900, the AMEZ-WHFMS petitioned the General Conference to eliminate the office, arguing that it hindered their work. The General Conference agreed.

In 1903, when the issue of appointing a missionary secretary was again raised, Bishop Hood questioned the need for the position, suggesting that it could impact the fund-raising efforts of the AMEZ-WHFMS. If the denomination wished to "experiment," he found it "a little remarkable that nobody suggested a woman for this place," especially since women raised most of the money for missions.

From Hood's perspective the most qualified woman for the position was "not a Bishop's wife, widow, mother, or sister," but a lay woman. Considering the constitutional requirements for the position, lay women would be ineligible. At the AME Zion General Conference of 1904 when the office was resurrected, President Katie Hood argued against the election of a male missionary secretary—AMEZ-WHFMS women resented the idea of functioning under the dictates of a male secretary. The discussion was dominated by male clergy who made clear that a man would fill the office. However, AME Zion women did not give up their quest for the office.

During the first two decades of the twentieth century the air was filled with hope and excitement over the possibilities for women in the United States gaining political rights. As AME Zion women engaged the secular debate about the women's suffrage movement, they demanded a share of the denomination's power. In 1924 AMEZ-WHFMS leaders renewed their quest for the election of a female missionary secretary. Buoyed by the ratification of the Nineteenth Amendment, plans were laid by the New Jersey AMEZ-WHFMS to nominate Rev. Florence Spearing Randolph for the position of general secretary of missions. Organizing behind the scenes, in March 1924 an anonymous AMEZ-WHFMS state officer drafted and submitted a nominating speech to Randolph for her approval. This remarkable document illustrates the political maturity and sophistication of Randolph and her cohorts. The document stated that the Magna Carta and Declaration of Independence were important to understanding man's search for freedom. However, it noted that the women's rights movement of the 1840s was "even more significant," in that at Seneca Falls, New York, "a forward few women . . . by their declaration of sentiment in 1848 in favor of a 'Human Rights' program rolled up their sleeves and refused to 'Equivocate' or 'Retreat a single inch' until old traditions, customs, and distasteful practices surrender to the wholesome demand that woman no longer be kept in the state of a 'perpetual minor' but that she be granted the suffrage she merited." The women at Seneca Falls realized that in trying to effect change "or upset precedent, they were attempting one of the most difficult things in the world," which required courage and "sacrifice of time, energy and money" as well as "reliance upon a divine power, especially since they were actuated by the feeling that their cause was just." These AME Zion women placed themselves squarely in the tradition of the

women's rights and suffrage movements. Building on the denomination's tradition of supporting the equality of women in the polity, they
asked, "[S]hould [the AME Zion Church] not be Equal to the greater
act of giving to her women the same opportunity for self expression in
all phases of her church life that it has given to men by the engaging of
her organized powers along the lines of human endeavor in the missionary society?"

Carefully delineating the qualifications of Rev. Florence Spearing
Randolph, the New Jersey society asked AMEZ-WHFMS members
throughout the United States to support her candidacy and use their
influence for her election. "Weep, if necessary (as Dorothy Dix says)
on the second button of your husband's vest, if he has a vote, until he
promises you that he will do what he can to give you the desire of your
heart." Few men or women would question Randolph's qualifications
for the office, but most men still were not ready to elect a woman to a
general office in the denomination. It was acceptable for women to run
for offices designated for females, but AME Zion men were unwilling
to permit them to fully compete with males for all offices in the polity.
Though females were elected and served as lay delegates, they were
outnumbered by male lay delegates at the General Conference. Randolph and other women failed in their bids to compete for national
offices on denominational boards.

After 1940, AME Zion women at the local and national levels
became more involved in the interracial women's ecumenical movement led by Church Women United. As the old guard died out, AME
Zion women concentrated less on gaining access to male-dominated
positions. Though they recognized their marginalization in the AME
Zion denomination, they basked in the knowledge that they already
possessed the religious rights that women in most black and white
denominations sought. While AME Zion women were ordained and
appointed as pastors, for the most part they continued to be relegated
to small missions and poor churches. Although women participated in
the denomination's legislative bodies, they continued to be outnumbered by male clergy and lay men and had minimal influence on
denominational decisions. At the end of the twentieth century, the
episcopacy remained male, and for the most part decision-making
remained a male domain.

Black church women of all persuasions invested considerable time
and energy in the struggle for religious rights and to create and operate missionary associations and conventions. However, that is only part

of the story. What was the focus and impact of their domestic and foreign mission work, and how did it relate to the plight of black Americans and Africans—particularly women—in the diaspora? What was the relationship of church women and their missionary societies and conventions to the secular women's political movement?

CHAPTER 4

"The Relief Corps of Heaven"
Women and Missions

You can do no large great work for God in Africa unless you make *female* influence a prominent influence. Woman keeps Africa low and degraded, and hence only woman, under God, can raise Africa up.

Alexander Crummell (1870)

Some people do not like the idea of women being forward in Christian work, but what would the cause do without them? They do most of the work and they furnish most of the lives that are sacrificed in service on the foreign field. Think of the late Joanna P. Moore, who gave her life in sacrificial service. Then think of the illustrious E. B. [Delaney] and many others, some of who are still laboring in the cause and are giving the very best that is within them for the cause of missions.

Mission Herald *(1930)*

WHEN MAMIE DONOHOO referred to black church women as the "Relief Corps of Heaven," some eighty years had passed since the AME Daughters of Conference and the AME Zion United Daughters of Conference, forerunners of the national women's missionary societies, were founded. A leader in the AME Zion Woman's Home and Foreign Missionary Society, Donohoo perceptively described the much overlooked, vast philanthropic contribution of women that consisted of benevolent work and gifts. She suggested that philanthropy, with its multiple meanings and dimensions, was a central element in the lives of black women because of their social location as persons of African descent. Donohoo claimed that they engaged in Sunday school and church work, temperance, and rescue work; raised funds to build schools, orphanages, and homes for working girls and the elderly; formed auxiliaries to male organizations to raise funds for a variety of causes; and filled the coffers of denominational missionary organizations as they embraced their "special mission" to Africa. This

Young Vai Woman in Liberia, West Africa, at the beginning of the twentieth century.

"special mission," in particular the idea of redeeming or restoring the virtue of women of African descent, is a central theme that permeates most of the writings and work of black female activists during every period of African American history.

The main focus of church women's organizational activity was domestic and foreign missionary work that often fused evangelism with political and social reform. As centers of religious activity, women's missionary societies and conventions were significant nonpartisan bases of power. Their foreign work extended to Africa, Haiti, Canada, the Dominican Republic, and throughout South America. Missionary societies provided leadership, financial capital, voluntary services, and material resources to innumerable individuals and groups. As powerful networks of leaders and workers, Baptist, Methodist, and other women's religious organizations embraced a commitment to religion and racial uplift, by combining evangelism with their reform efforts and making them the central elements of their activism. Emphasizing the need for a church that was actively engaged in its community, these associations launched programs that aimed at providing basic social services. By 1900 the collective voluntary and organizational services of their "sister laborers" constituted the foundation of African American philanthropy.

Black women leaders generally agreed that foreign mission work was important and raised funds to support missions in Africa and Latin

America, but first and foremost their chief focus was home mission work, broadly defined and aimed at elevating the status of African Americans. During the late nineteenth century the majority of blacks were poor and uneducated. The 1890 census noted that more than half the black population of Georgia, Alabama, Louisiana, Mississippi, and South Carolina resided in rural areas and was illiterate. In regard to rates of illiteracy, the South ranked at the top. In 1910, 78.8 percent of the black population in the South was rural. In that year, of the 2,227,731 black illiterates in the United States, 2,133,961, or 95.8 percent, were in the South. Few southern black children received even a rudimentary education, and the majority of school facilities designated for blacks were deficient in every respect. Most children worked in the fields with their parents as sharecroppers.

In the period immediately following Emancipation several white Protestant denominations established freedmen's boards and educational programs for blacks. Northern white missionaries such as Joanna Moore traveled to the South to work among the freed people. A native of Clarion County, Pennsylvania, Moore graduated from Rockford College in Illinois in 1863 with the intention of becoming a foreign missionary. Hearing of the plight of former slaves gathered in the numerous refugee camps, she went to a "horror-stricken camp" located on an island in Mississippi where she became "a preacher, a doctor and a home-training advisor." Between 1863 and 1868, Moore worked in black orphanages in Little Rock and Helena, Arkansas, and Lauderdale, Mississippi.

Joanna Moore spent fifty years of her life working among African Americans. During the 1870s, she labored in Louisiana as an "evangelistic missionary," aiding the people in whatever way she could. Recognizing the enormity of the task, she pleaded with northern white "Christian" women for help. Her efforts led to the founding of the Woman's Baptist Home Mission Society in 1877, for which she served as the first missionary. In New Orleans, Moore organized a home for destitute elderly women. Realizing the need for providing basic training in "home duties" and teaching the Bible to black women, she set up Mother's Training Schools in several cities. To avoid racial confrontation with whites against "educating the nigger up to think they are the equals of the white folks," in 1884 Moore organized Fireside Schools, which were held in black homes. To stimulate Bible reading in the home, Moore began publishing *Hope* in 1885. In the early 1890s, Moore left Louisiana and settled in Little Rock, Arkansas. Several years later she relocated to Nashville, Tennessee, where she spent the remainder of her life until her death in 1916.

During the early years of her work among African Americans in Mississippi and Louisiana, Moore exhibited the typical prejudice and paternalism displayed by white missionaries. Living and working with African Americans in the bayou country, she developed a more positive attitude toward blacks, recognizing that their plight was related to their former status as slaves and the lack of educational and economic opportunities. Like most nineteenth-century missionary workers, Moore believed that Bible reading would promote Christianity and teach literacy, moral and social values, and self-determination to African Americans. She was especially concerned about the treatment of them by whites, emphasizing that black women were abused and disrespected by both black and white men. Working mostly among the Baptists, she organized women's missionary societies and Bible Bands. Moore commented that in some communities "secret societies had been organized in the church, and this had crowded out the mission society. These organizations do seem to hinder the religious growth of our churches very much." In the late nineteenth century, as a pioneering home missionary worker, Moore's ideas influenced numerous southern black women such as Virginia Broughton, who became active in the missionary movement. Moore's emphasis on the importance of the Bible, especially using scripture to teach reading, and also for use in defending themselves, was an important element of the Bible Band movement among black Baptist women. The work of black women in Bible Bands influenced the founding of the National Baptist Convention's Woman's Convention and women's work in the Church of God in Christ.

African Americans took great pride in the settlement work, normal schools, and colleges that developed after 1865. Given the dimensions of poverty, illiteracy, and other social problems, black churches saw it as their Christian duty to administer to the masses of black southerners. Of great concern were the black women and girls who were said to be in great need of mental and moral training. The need to improve the image of black women, and to reinforce notions of chastity and domesticity, made it imperative that women's organizations, especially their church associations, take on the task of developing the next generation of mothers. Proponents of domesticity argued that because of the enormity of the task, "[w]oman's touch is needed for the Negro womanhood and girlhood of the South, and this, the initial field of most of the Woman's Home Missionary Societies, still demands time and means and effort. To get the children is to get the older people."

Beyond the charitable work of women's religious societies there was a felt need for full-time missionary workers who would venture into rural areas and city slums and preach Christianity while engaging in "uplift" work. Alarmed by the escalating racial violence and the declining status of African Americans, NACW leader Josephine E. Holmes argued that it was time for a new and "more humane" solution, "for the ills of present day racial evolutions," and "that remedy is applied Christianity." Holmes asserted, "With such a premise, then the part of the Negro woman is clearly to be more than a nominal Christian." The need was to eliminate "racial disagreements" and speed up "the wheels of racial progress." In the common parlance of the day, this was a racial version of the Social Gospel movement. Church women's organizations such as the Baptist Woman's Convention were among those who defined their mission work as "applied Christianity."

Organizational constitutions differed in their language, but most held women responsible for raising funds to be disbursed as the male-dominated conventions and missionary boards saw fit. As evidenced in their programs, women's organizations conceived their role in broader terms, as both philanthropic and evangelical. Eschewing the label "missionary society," Baptist women organized a women's convention, whose mission was more expansive than that of their associates. Describing their work as dealing with the "religious, social, and economic welfare" of the race, Baptist women focused on a diversity of issues, including migration, lynching, education, employment, housing, suffrage, health, nutrition, child welfare, and foreign missions. As S. Willie Layten explained, "[I]t seems that whatever we do in our churches or convention work as laborers for Christ to improve our homes, our communities, our nation, would be classed as home missionary endeavor."

Given the structure of the Baptist Convention and the fact that the local church was autonomous, the NBC-USA Woman's Convention and the missionary society were separate entities. In 1928, Nannie Burroughs stated, "The missionary society is not a fixture in many of our churches and its true relationship is not definitely defined." Whereas Baptist missionary societies were purely local, the WC was national, regional, and local in structure. Burroughs emphasized that the missionary society was a local church auxiliary whose "life depends upon a few faithful women and the expenditure of its funds upon the pastor's interpretation of the purpose of a missionary society." Burroughs accurately described the situation in 1928.

In Methodist denominations the missionary society was the counterpart of the Baptist Woman's Convention. Societies were local and national in structure. In comparison to the WC, Methodist organizations were less autonomous in their functions, and focused almost exclusively on building churches, and raising funds to support preachers, foreign missions, and missionaries. Operating under the supervision of male denominational boards, Methodist women were more restricted in their operations than Baptist women. Their national programs were less oriented to social and political reform. Regardless of how much authority they possessed, women's organizations constantly defined and redefined their roles, explaining to their members that mission work was more than "helping the poor and needy in the church and community."

The Home Missionary Movement

DURING THE PERIOD 1890–1940 the home mission work of black women in the Methodist Episcopal Church was most evident in the Ladies Aid Society at the local level. The northern-based Woman's Home Missionary Society ME-WHMS at the national level was organized and operated exclusively by white women. The few black women such as Mrs. M. C. B. Mason and Margaret Davis Bowen who attended its meetings were mostly wives of prominent Methodist ministers. The ME-WHMS and the Woman's Missionary Council of the Methodist Episcopal Church, South, established a variety of homes and schools for black children, administered by white women. Very few, if any, black women were members of the MECS. A few African American women worked at the industrial homes for blacks in Louisiana and Texas. Methodist Episcopal women established missionary projects to meet the needs within the denomination's regional conferences. In 1940, after the unification of Methodism, a new jurisdictional system structured by race was organized. In December 1940, following the founding of the Women's Society of Christian Service of the Central Jurisdiction, each black conference Woman's Home Missionary Society transferred its projects to the new organization.

Among independent black denominations, because home missions work was left to the local church, it was not as "highly organized" as the foreign missionary work. But, as Rebecca Stiles Taylor noted, in the absence of local welfare agencies, black church and fraternal organizations "filled the breach as best they could" by dispensing charity to the "needy poor and outsiders as well." Evangelicalism—conversion of "heathens" and nonbelievers to Christianity—undergirded the efforts of all women's missionary societies and conventions. Denominational organizations varied in terms of the comprehensiveness of their programs, especially the emphasis they placed on secular reform. For example, the Baptist Woman's Convention was creative in its vision and incisive in program definition, emphasizing no less than a cultural transformation of American society from racist to nonracist. Though the home mission work of Methodist women was varied and extensive, it adhered more closely to their constitutional precepts.

In comparison to the programs of most black women's religious organizations, the work of the Baptist Woman's Convention was expansive and nontraditional. The primary reasons for these discrepancies lie in the nature of their legal structures, denominational histories, and the experience and assumptions of their leaders. The leaders of Methodist, Episcopal, Presbyterian, Catholic, and Pentecostal women's organizations were more inclined to be accepting of the subordination of their missionary societies to the central authority of their denominations than their Baptist counterparts. Women's missionary work in these groups tended to be traditional and primarily local.

Missionary societies were often confused about the purposes of mission work, assuming that the main goal of the missionary was to raise money. In the ongoing discourse about the primary function of the missionary, the point was often made that the most essential task was to save souls. In many churches, monies collected were used for local charity and relief. In the late nineteenth century, Mrs. H. L. Shelton, president of the AME Women's Home and Foreign Missionary Society of Georgia, asserted, "[T]hey think home means right here where they live, and most of them think that 50 percent for Home Missions ought to be used for benevolent purposes, such as paying sick benefits, burying the dead, caring for the poor members of the church, and also of the city or town where they live. . . . Home means from the Atlantic to the Pacific, and from the Gulf to the Bay." Shelton stated that the WHFMS was "willing to aid the poor and needy, but who are more in need than the poor preachers and mission churches." Members were instructed to "use the money only as the constitutions direct; boldly dare to do your duty." Ironically, though the AME, AME Zion, and CME women's organizations provided substantial support for ministers and the building of missions and churches, many ministers were reluctant to cooperate with the women, often refusing to sanction their programs. During the early years of organization, the president of most local and state organizations literally begged the clergy to support their work.

Owing to their legal structures, Methodist women's organizations lacked the level of freedom enjoyed by Baptist women in determining the nature of their mission work. At the national level, the AME and AME Zion women's missionary societies raised funds for their foreign missionary programs. At the local level, operating under the leadership of mostly clergy wives, AME, AME Zion, CME, and ME women raised funds to support local missions and churches. The discourse regarding what constituted home mission work was as much related to the class differences between clergy wives and female laity, as it was to the varying concerns of male and female laity. For example, Mrs. H. L. Shelton's chief concern in Georgia's WHFMS was raising funds to support preachers and churches, not providing general uplift to poor black Georgians.

Given the overall poverty of the majority of the AME laity, it was reasonable to expect that a portion of the money should be spent to aid the poor and improve the living conditions of their parishioners. Failure to do so could mean the loss of members to other denominations. The problem was how to reach a happy medium and satisfy the different needs of a diverse congregation. To achieve a certain balance and maintain the image of their local leadership and churches, many societies included at least one high-profile project among their multifarious activities. For example, in the early twentieth century the Tennessee Conference Branch WHFMS announced that it planned to give attention to "the health question and to all questions pertaining to the uplift of our people." The New Jersey AME Woman's Mite Missionary Society aided ministers and needy clergy widows, but also devoted "much time and some means to local work, such as visiting the sick, the jails, penitentiaries and hospitals," organizing food and clothing drives, "and doing . . . real social work."

Contrary to the wishes of the male clergy, the CME Woman's Connectional Missionary Council argued that money—fund-raising—was important, "but should not be the sole standard by which to judge our program." To their way of thinking, raising thousands of dollars was commendable, but a society that lacked an "aggressive missionary program" emphasizing social service should not be deemed a success.

Since each church and community had different human and fiscal needs, and varied in terms of numbers and quality of leadership, the council was adamantly against setting standards for its missionary societies.

The Baptist Woman's Convention informed its members that helping the poor was "indeed a very worthy thing to do, but it is not home mission work. That is our Christian Duty." For the WC, home mission work was literally anything that could be construed as having an impact on the home, community, or nation. Throughout its history, the WC emphasized the central importance of home and family life to the development of mentally, physically, and morally strong individuals whose character was shaped by Christian values. In 1914 the WC Committee on Home Missions recommended that black organizations establish local committees to canvass the homes of their members and hold joint meetings to deal with "the evil of concubinage. This practice between white men and Negro women is a prevalent evil in the South." In the public arena, the WC agenda targeted the segregation of blacks in public accommodations. The WC Executive Committee also suggested that local committees be appointed "to approach the proper authorities . . . and impress upon them the necessity of providing first-class common carriers for first-class Negro passengers."

From the beginning, Baptist women considered social and political reform work essential to black women's home mission work. For example, the YWCA movement was perceived as "a phase of home missionary work" that was "meeting a great need among young women as a preventive and constructive agency." All "Christian women" were urged to support the organization, but the YWCA initially excluded black as well as Catholic women. In the late nineteenth century black Catholics organized the Colored Young Woman's Catholic Association as an alternative to the YWCA. In the late nineteenth century, black church women in Brooklyn, Baltimore, and Philadelphia established parallel organizations to meet the needs of young black women. In 1913, the AME Zion *Missionary Seer* reported that on Thanksgiving day, fifteen hundred people gathered at the Sixth Avenue Baptist Church in Birmingham, Alabama, "for the closing of a membership campaign that had been vigorously waged for two months." The purpose of the campaign was to organize a YWCA. The recruitment attracted 1,080 applicants, and netted $806.71. The Baptist Woman's Convention went one step further; it not only encouraged its members to affiliate with the YWCA, but also created a Young Woman's Association and Young Men's Association for their members.

During World War I, Baptist and other denominational women stressed the need to work with the War Camp Community Service in supplying black soldiers with much-needed clothing. In the aftermath of the war, the WC also encouraged its members to work with the organization in the training and employment of black workers, and to develop contacts with white people in war work who could aid their cause. Cognizant of the political advantages accrued from the migration of African Americans to the North and West; the WC advised members, "Do not overlook church opportunity to supervise the political gain caused by migration." While some female migrants managed to acquire employment in shops and stores, Nannie Burroughs emphasized that "fifty-seven percent of our women [are] wage workers [employed] as domestics, and we should see that they [are] organized to increase their efficiency and give them needed protection." Burroughs was relentless in her efforts to gain Baptist support for concerted home mission work on behalf of domestic workers.

Using the theme "Home Mission Work by Women—for Women," Burroughs asked the WC to "give more serious and definite attention to improving conditions in five far-flung fields," including domestic workers, farm women, and migrants—a large number of whom were women and children. Emphasizing that the work of the WC's Red Circle and Young Matron's societies reached very few wage-earning women, she asserted, "[I]t is our business to be vitally concerned about the young womanhood of our race to whom we are looking for future leadership in the field of Christian Social Service." Burroughs believed that women in the local churches were the most "valuable assets," but she stressed that the presidents of local missionary societies and the directors of young people must be better equipped to meet the tasks.

A firm believer in education at all levels, for decades Burroughs supported leadership training in the form of summer schools, conferences, and institutes for Christian workers. She recognized a critical need to educate local leaders, many of whom were domestics, and headed organizations comprised largely of wage-earning women. Burroughs claimed, "Domestic workers constitute the largest regularly employed stable labor group within the Negro race. They carry more of our economic burdens than any other group. Their labor and sacrifices made it possible for many in the educated class to get where they are today." The "so-called educated Negro" looked down on and scorned working-class women who had "character enough to work for an honest living." Since most black churches were dependent on the financial support of domestic workers, Burroughs questioned how they would function if the women decided to "stage a stay away or sit down strike. It is high time that we were working definitely to lift as we climb, instead of making the domestic workers hold the ladder while we climb."

Attentive to issues of national and international import, and understanding the politics of race, Baptist women's concerns also encompassed the problems of other nationalities and peoples of color. The growth of the Americanization movement in the early twentieth century had an impact on the way the WC perceived its work. Similar to the methodology employed in the foreign mission work of Protestant denominations, American reformers encouraged immigrants to abandon their customs and languages and adopt white Anglo-Saxon culture. This was the traditional route that the Irish, Jews, and other European immigrants had utilized to gain acceptance as "white" in the United States. The WC added a new twist to these notions that considered the inherent nature of racism in the rhetoric of Americanization. For example, in 1919 the Baptist Woman's Convention argued that given "the relations between nations and races in America and the world . . . in our Home Missionary work we should become more interested in aliens of darker races who come to the United States— Chinese, Japanese, West Indians and Mexican. When they first come untouched by [the] prejudice of race, gain their friendship. . . . Gain them, else in a short time they are absorbed by White Americans, learn their Christianity, join with them and others opposing our advancement."

Addressing the plight of immigrants, during the 1920s the WC defined home mission work as "looking after the foreign people who come into this country, and giving the Gospel to them in destitute places; not only the Gospel of the Bible, but the Gospel of training the young people to take care of home and seeking to teach others how to live in their homes." The WC stressed the importance of conducting "community work among the lowly people, not only the lowly [of] our own, but among all people, for Jesus Christ died for all the same." The WC's "community work" also extended to Africans in the diaspora, in Africa in particular. Indeed, this was a mainstay of the NBC-USA Woman's Convention program throughout most of the twentieth century. Among black women's religious organizations, the WC was the chief sponsor of black female foreign missionaries.

Home Missions and the Great Depression

DURING THE 1930s, the Great Depression presented new problems for black denominations and their parishioners. The loss of employment, and rising poverty in rural and urban black communities, diminished church resources and impacted the nature of how missionary societies and conventions functioned. As the last to be hired and the first to be fired, African Americans felt the impact of the Depression long before most whites. At the local level there was a demand for more programs that addressed basic human needs. As the homeless rolls grew, local societies administered soup kitchens and clothing distribution centers to serve their communities.

Though the Depression touched the lives of all Americans, it had a devastating impact on the black community. In an effort to revive industry, in 1933 Congress passed the National Industrial Recovery Act, which created the National Recovery Act, an agency to oversee the drafting and operation of industrial business codes. The NIRA specified that, regardless of race, creed, or religion, all citizens employed by cooperating organizations or industries were to receive the minimum wage specified by the NRA. Throughout the South, relief programs discharged many black workers rather than complying with NRA labor requirements. In cities such as Columbia, South Carolina, African Americans protested the discriminatory practices and demanded federal action.

Government programs such as the Works Progress Administration, the National Youth Administration, and Civilian Conservation Corps, designed to deal with the widespread social and economic instability that emerged in the wake of the stock market crash of 1929, routinely segregated and discriminated against people of color. A federal relief census conducted in 1933 revealed that the majority of African Americans on relief under the age of forty-five were female. Black widows represented the largest group among the relief populations. Formal education among blacks was very limited. Half of all blacks had less than eight years of education. With little or no training and restricted economic opportunity, most African Americans on the WPA programs were relegated to unskilled labor. Two-thirds of the men and nine-tenths of the women worked at unskilled occupations. Black female heads of households, formerly employed in domestic service or farm labor and classified as "unskilled," were usually assigned to sewing projects, classified as "semiskilled" work. Thus, black workers earned less than whites employed on federal programs, but more than those employed by private industry.

The AME Zion Church operated a number of WPA and NYA training projects throughout the nation, most of which were started or administered by women who perceived their work as an extension of their commitment to home missions. In Wilkesboro, North Carolina, Esther Bingham, a revered member of the Denny's Grove AME Zion Church, started a relief program before the national programs were instituted. Bingham, a public school teacher, worked closely with the AME Zion Women's Missionary Society and other church organizations. She established an adult education class to help poor blacks develop literacy skills, and initiated a cooperative program between the public schools and the adult project.

In numerous far-flung cities and towns located in Pennsylvania, Massachusetts, Connecticut, California, North Carolina, West Virginia, South Carolina, New Jersey, and many other states, AME Zion women operated Welfare Institutes that employed all-black personnel, where students were mostly taught sewing skills. In addition to sewing, to improve the employability of former domestic servants and enable them to earn higher wages, WPA projects, such as those in Bluefield, West Virginia, taught "scientific home management," which included cooking, home care of the sick, child care, and handicraft. In South Carolina, denominational colleges supported by the AME, AME Zion, and Baptist churches sponsored NYA projects that employed black youth. In return for receiving college aid, more than four hundred young women and men earned wages working in a variety of occupations, including clerical and general office work, teaching and janitorial work, and playground supervision. At Clinton College, an AME Zion school in South Carolina, Mrs. L. Massey administered an NYA project that taught cooking, cleaning, sewing, and handicrafts.

In the 1930s and '40s the American Baptist Home Mission Society increased its support to northern black Baptist programs. Southern white Methodist and Baptist women, in particular the Women's Missionary Council of the Methodist Episcopal Church, South, and the Baptist Woman's Missionary Union, expanded their social service work among blacks. They became more proactive and creative in their efforts to ameliorate race differences, introducing programs of "interracial cooperation" that supported home mission projects. Leadership training institutes, Sunday school training classes, missionary study classes, and cooperative programs in southern black denominational schools offered courses in domestic science and missionary training. These programs lasted to the early 1950s. The WC continued to stress issues of employment and to focus more intently on the impact of federal welfare programs on the black home and family. The persistent migration of African Americans to large urban centers—Chicago, Detroit, Boston, Philadelphia, New York City, Los Angeles, Cleveland, and Washington, D.C.—increased the demand for decent and inexpensive housing and better health care. The WC emphasized these issues as well as the problems of mothers and children and seasonal migrant workers. It also established city missions, which dealt with a range of issues. Missionary societies were urged to conduct educational programs against drug addictions, a growing problem in urban black communities. Local societies were encouraged to study community problems and establish community welfare committees to work on at least one of the WC's home missions tasks.

During the first three decades of its existence, the WC was intimately involved with national movements, which had for their purpose the elimination of segregation and discrimination and the advancement of black women's national status. However, by 1930, as a result of reorganization, the WC's work was decentralized and became more focused on fund-raising for the programs defined by the all-male NBC executive board. The combination of internal struggles within the WC and the growing importance of state conventions effectively diluted the WC's power and shifted the focus from national to local work. Noting the change that occurred in the WC, in 1945 the inveterate Baptist journalist and feminist critic Rebecca Stiles Taylor alluded to the lack of WC involvement in women's postwar planning efforts nationally. Evaluating the change in the WC's program focus, she asked, "Is it only interested in itself?" While Taylor was most critical of the WC, she also questioned the absence of church women's organizations affiliated with predominantly white denominations. She asked, "Where are the national Congregational, Presbyterian, Seventh Day Adventists, Catholic, Community and other church units that control thousands of our women?" Recognizing the importance of black women's participation in "shaping the future of the world" and "in planning the peace," Taylor argued that "women should and must have a voice in policy making." Taylor was particularly concerned that women might lose many of the jobs they acquired during the war. She realized that this was a potential problem for all women—but since a large percentage of the women who were the chief breadwinners for their families were black, it would likely have an even greater impact on them. The WC's retreat from engaging political and social issues, at the national level, represented its growing subordination within the NBC.

The introduction of the Social Security Program in 1935 and the growing prominence of government and private social welfare programs in the 1930s, '40s, and '50s tended to overshadow the importance of church women's missionary work. As the government engaged private entities to organize and manage federal projects, faith-based and secular organizations often tailored their programs to accommodate government initiatives and access federal funding. The Great Society antipoverty programs of the 1960s and similar community development programs enacted in the 1970s were modified to meet the needs of the poor and working class, a large percentage of whom were black. Federal and state grants to faith-based and secular organizations were frequently related to politics and designed not only to help the poor and disabled, but also to recruit support for the political party in power at the local and national level. Thus, black religious leaders carefully assessed the programs of the Democratic and Republican parties and supported those organizations that catered to the needs of the African American community.

The Foreign Missionary Movement

BY THE LATE nineteenth century white Protestant foreign missions were located on every continent. Most denominations had established national home and foreign women's missionary associations by 1872, and by 1915 white female missionary societies had registered more than three million women. Black women's auxiliaries developed after 1874 and experienced much slower growth than those of white denominations. Aggregate membership numbers for black women's societies are unavailable, but thirty thousand members would be a fair estimate, based on miscellaneous membership statistics for the Baptist Woman's Convention and local Baptist missionary societies, and projections for Methodist and other Christian organizations in 1916. By 1945 there were at least 600,000 women enrolled in the multiple missionary societies of black denominations. The National Baptist Convention, USA, reported an enrollment of 274,225 members in its 21,091 local missionary societies.

Given the overall economic status of the African American community, the multiple religious and secular funding needs, and the fact that contributions to most church women's organizations were at the disposal of male-dominated denominational mission boards, the financial bases of black women's organizations were minimal in comparison with white associations. At the same time, they were significant in terms of black philanthropy, and substantial in relationship to black earnings during that period. For most of the twentieth century the chief base of support for church organizations was the female domestic workers who formed the majority of the members in most black denominations. As Mamie Donohoo suggested, the philanthropy of black women must be measured not just in terms of monetary contributions, but also by the extent of their voluntary services, which constituted a major unseen resource. The donation of monies and services by women and men who were largely poor suggests the level of their commitment, and the sacrifices they were willing to make to advance racial and religious ideals. In the early twentieth century, the importance of these contributions may be seen in the physical and psychological changes that occurred in many black communities at the local level and in the support for foreign missions.

Stressing the importance of racial uplift on an international scale, black missionary boards embodied two major concerns: the need for uplifting and improving the status of Africans in the motherland, and countering a white Protestant missionary theology emphasizing paternalism and racial superiority. In reality, African Americans did not generally differ from whites in their ethnocentrism, and while most African Americans recognized a kinship with black Africa and identified themselves as sisters and brothers in the flesh, they generally looked down on many aspects of Africans' cultural beliefs and practices.

In their letters, articles, missionary reports, and speeches, missionaries rarely missed an opportunity to comment negatively on traditional African religion, cultural patterns, and practices, including the Islamic faith, paganism, polygamy, polygyny, bride payment, dress and nudity, views on sexuality, child care, and attitudes toward women. Though some missionaries admired certain aspects of African life and culture, most did not. In the main, the black missionaries were thoroughly Westernized, and they viewed themselves as civilized and the

Africans as uncivilized "heathens" in need of civilization. They also had selfish reasons for wanting to "uplift" Africans. Improvement of the African condition and inculcation of Western cultural values was a strategy for racial empowerment. For example, in explaining the relation of African Americans to evangelization in Africa, Mrs. E. J. Dodson, an advocate of AME Zion African missions, asserted that improvement in the status of Africans would positively impact the plight of African Americans. Dodson held that "once Africa is filled with institutions of civilized freedom and the light of knowledge and religion, the whole Negro race is raised from its hopeless depths of degradation."

African missionary work was envisioned by some black religionists as a movement of "Divine Providence." It was God's will, and Christians had a responsibility for bringing civilization to the "heathen." Most missionaries saw it as a Christian duty, but African American leaders embraced it as a "special mission" and a significant element in the race's destiny. Mary Mason, editor of the *Star of Zion* "Woman's Column," was familiar with AME Zion Bishop Alexander Walters's oft-repeated argument that Africans were brought to America and enslaved, converted to Christianity, and educated to bring about the redemption of Africa. She recalled that in the nineteenth century, notions of "the Divine Permission of Human Slavery" had proliferated among black Christians, who "thought that we had been brought here with a deep inscrutable purpose—the redemption ultimately of the homeland, Africa." AME Bishop Henry McNeal Turner suggested that slavery was "a divine-sanctioned manual labor school" that brought heathen Africans into "direct contact with the mightiest race that ever trod the face of the earth." Though he praised white Americans for their knowledge and progress, Turner argued, "There is no manhood future in the United States for the Negro."

Like Bishop Turner, some leaders favored sending missionaries, but many questioned the feasibility of establishing missions in foreign countries. There was a concern that spending hard-earned money and sending the most promising young men and women abroad for amelioration of the problems of Africans represented poor judgment on the part of religious leaders. During the 1890s, given the limited human and monetary resources, the crushing problems created by widespread poverty and discrimination, and the escalating lynching and indiscriminate violence plaguing African Americans, some thought it foolhardy to talk about going to Africa or any other place to solve other people's problems. There was also a fear that the leadership would be decimated by the departure of persons representing the small cadre of educated African Americans capable of providing an enlightened leadership. Commenting on the decision of Rev. Charles S. Morris, "the brilliant" Baptist minister, to undertake missionary work in Africa, John Mitchell Jr., editor of the *Richmond Planet*, asserted, "He is too valuable a young man to throw his life away. A protracted stay in that country will enable him to soon advocate our cause around the throne of God. We have enough defenders in that neighborhood and need a great many more in this land of our sorrow."

The discourse on Africa and the need for African missions and missionaries was laced with discussions of the political and social alternatives facing African Americans, including the repeated calls for emigration to Africa. Bishop Turner's trenchant arguments for African emigration and missionary work, his stark portrayal of the plight of African Americans in the United States, and the impact of European colonization on Africans were like thunderous bolts of lightning in a vast sea of calm. He predicted that African Americans would never be able to fully advance in the U.S.; at best they would continue to "eke out an existence." Thus, the only alternative was to emigrate to Africa, "The Fatherland." The clarity of his arguments and the sincerity of his claims for African humanity fell on the conscience of all who encountered him, and often set the tone for the lively debates in the 1890s. As editor of the *Voice of Missions*, Turner provided a forum for articulating his arguments and engaging the most pressing social and political issues facing African Americans.

But the issue of black leadership and involvement in the African missionary movement was far more complex than this. It was also about respect, identity, destiny, self-determination, and "manhood." Rev. Solomon Porter Hood argued that the AME Church "must gain prestige and power in foreign lands." Many black Baptists and Methodists were troubled by the numerous missions established by white denominations, and the large number of white missionaries operating in Africa.

Some black leaders emphasized a link between imperialism and white "Christian" missions. In the early nineteenth century, proclaiming the need to convert and "civilize" the Africans, white Americans and Europeans organized missions throughout Africa. By 1880, however, the emphasis was less on conversion and more on partitioning Africa and establishing trusteeships and colonies. European nations engaged in frantic competition for control of African territory, dividing the entire continent up among themselves. In 1890, with the exception of Liberia and Ethiopia, all of Africa was under the control of Europe. All things considered, the argument that African mission work was the special responsibility of African Americans was compelling. There was speculation that improving the condition of their African brothers and sisters would also establish the abilities of African Americans and consequently garner greater respect for "the race." The AME Department of Missions argued in 1892, "The Department of Missions necessarily lies at the foundation of all Church extension and propagation, and no ecclesiastical denomination is entitled to any respect which is devoid of a fully equipped mission machinery."

While most African Americans did not sanction the brutality and greed that accompanied European imperialism, many were willing to overlook colonial expansion if it meant the spread of Western civilization. Reasoning that "religious education and time would work out" the problems Africans faced, in the late nineteenth and for most of the twentieth century black denominations urged their missionaries to " '[b]e subject to the power that be,' in keeping with the teachings of the Scriptures." Rev. Alexander Crummell, Episcopal priest and missionary to Liberia, praised Belgian King Leopold's expansion in the Congo, and supported English control of all of West Africa. Crummell argued that leaders should rid themselves of the notion that "the special aim of missionary zeal is to fit the soul of a heathen man for heaven." He believed that converting the heathen to Christianity was not the missionary's "finality of duty." Rather, the supreme goal should be to restructure the individual and move him from "the rude, crude, half-animal conditions in which the missionary first found him." For Crummell, and most black religious leaders, the preeminent purpose of missionary work was "progress and development."

Though sensitive to the impact of European and U.S. imperialism on people of color, in the nineteenth century African Americans rarely acknowledged the imperialistic nature of their own quest to evangelize Africans. Yet, a few leaders considered that promotion of Africa, especially Liberia, as a suitable area for black American mission development was a reflection of the African American's desire for imperialistic roles. AME Bishop Daniel Alexander Payne opposed AME involvement in foreign missions, fearing the development of an "African Methodist Imperialism" by black missionaries, who he felt would treat Africans the same as the Europeans treated them. In the 1930s an

AME Zion missionary observed, "[T]he American Negroes who colonized Liberia had set up a social system in close imitation of the one from which they had fled, except that in this case they were the masters and the unhappy natives were their slaves." The Americo-Liberians, the descendants of the African Americans who formed the original colony, were the ruling group in Liberia. This statement might also be applied to the preferential treatment given African American clergy in the administration of AME and AME Zion African missions and conferences in Africa.

Liberia, West Africa, is one of the oldest mission fields for African Americans. It was founded in 1822 by the American Colonization Society, an organization led by prominent whites, including President James Monroe and John Marshall, chief justice of the U.S. Supreme Court, as a haven for free blacks and slaves who wished to leave the United States. Some black leaders viewed the colonization movement as a scheme to rid the country of free blacks. Despite the cooperation of several black nationalists and the support of numerous white southerners, relatively few African Americans chose to migrate to Africa. However, for slaves who were promised emancipation on the condition of emigration, there wasn't an opportunity to freely choose to reject colonization, so they made the best of it.

In 1847 Liberia declared its independence and became known as the Republic of Liberia. African American emigrants modeled Liberia's constitution and government after that of the United States; however, citizenship was restricted to persons of color and whites could lease but not purchase land. The Liberian constitution also called for "the improvement of native tribes, and their advancement in the art of agriculture." Liberia was originally divided into four counties, or districts: Montserrado, Grand Bassa, Sinoe, and Maryland. The capital, Monrovia, was perceived as a gateway to Central Africa, a thriving center of trade and missionary operations. American industry, merchants, and missionary societies considered Liberia a promising field of activity. By 1880 the Presbyterian, Episcopalian, Baptist, Methodist Episcopal, Catholic, and Lutheran churches were located throughout the nation, mostly in the cities and towns inhabited by Americo-Liberians. The majority of native Liberians lived deep in the interior in areas difficult to reach. From the beginning there was conflict and dissension between Americo-Liberians and the indigenous population, as was the case between Europeans and native peoples in North and South America.

By 1890 most African American and native missionaries working in Africa were sponsored by white associations. Under the aegis of various Christian denominations and agencies, African Americans and African missionaries were located in Liberia, Sierra Leone, the Congo, South Africa, and Nigeria. In 1896 of the approximately eighty-one missions operating in Africa, only three received the support of black churches. The AME Zion and AME churches with meager resources sent several ministers to Africa and organized a few mission churches on the west coast in the late nineteenth century. The National Baptist Convention had established its first mission station at the Cape of Good Hope in South Africa in 1894. Thirteen other missions were under the control of white American denominations, including the American Baptist Home Mission Society, the Southern Baptist, Protestant Episcopal, Lutheran, Methodist Episcopal, United Brethren, and northern and southern Presbyterian churches, and the American Board of Commissioners for Foreign Missions. European Protestant denominations and the Catholic Church administered the remaining sixty-five.

By 1900, European colonial officials in Africa called for either exclusion of African Americans or marginalization and control of their activities. As the only independent African nation, Liberia welcomed black denominations and missionaries. Between 1900 and 1930, the AME and NBC churches established a number of missions in South Africa, but the bulk of their work and most African American missions were concentrated on the west coast of Africa, primarily in Liberia. AME and NBC mission stations in South Africa were operated almost exclusively by African men and women, educated in the United States at black denominational colleges.

In the early twentieth century there was a dramatic decline in the numbers of African American missionaries selected to represent mainstream denominations at their African mission stations. White missionaries and Africans reared in the missions supported by white churches were preferred. Racial incidents were common at these missions. The rise of the "New Negro" consciousness, Pan-Africanism, Marcus Moziah Garvey and the Universal Negro Improvement Association's Back to Africa Movement, and other ideologies among African Americans was threatening to European colonial powers. At the same time, white American missionaries, who feared that Africans might be influenced by "radical ideas" of racial equality and social justice, rejected educated African Americans. As European nations tight-

ened their control over most of Africa and dominated indigenous people everywhere on the continent except Liberia and some coastal
regions of Sierra Leone and the Gold Coast, few Christian organizations chose to hire African Americans, and many simply retrenched or
eliminated them from African missions.

By 1925 racial prejudice was common in many African colonial territories. In South Africa, for example, the Native Land Act of 1913 and
subsequent laws deprived Africans of most of the land in rural districts.
Moreover, the Urban Act prevented Africans from purchasing land in
any town. Whites were the recipients of 87 percent of the land, leaving
the African majority with a mere 13 percent. Missionary letters and
studies commissioned by American agencies reveal the depth of racial
hatred and jealousy harbored by whites against black missionaries. For
example, in 1930, following a fact-finding tour through remote parts
of South Africa, Angola, and the Congo, George E. Haynes, secretary
of the Federal Council of the Churches of Christ's Department of Race
Relations, commented on the "problems of relations between white
and colored in Africa." Haynes noted that whites and blacks were segregated and there were "many questions of friction and prejudice."

In 1929, in a survey of 793 missionaries sent to Africa by white
American societies, including the Presbyterian United Brethren,
Southern Baptist, and Lutheran churches, and the United Missionary
Society, the United Presbyterian Women's General Mission Society,
and the Sudan Interior Mission, W. E. B. Du Bois found that none
were African American. With the exception of the Foreign Mission
Board of the Southern Baptist Convention, which stated frankly that it
was not their policy to send Negroes as missionaries, the organizations
stressed that they were training "native helpers" and offered excuses
such as "have not had any applicants," "never formulated any policy
concerning the sending of American Negroes as missionaries," or
"never discussed the matter." The American Society of Friends (Quakers) admitted that several foreign governments, especially that of the
Belgian Congo, objected to African Americans.

Du Bois observed that while most white American missionary societies in the late nineteenth century supported the idea of sending black
missionaries to Africa to convert Africans to Christianity, they were
unwilling to accept or treat African Americans and Africans as their
social equals. Moreover, such recognition would require that African
Americans be paid salaries equal to those of whites and that they be
treated as "civilized beings." Du Bois understood that "American

white Christianity could not stand this" and therefore they changed their policies. Thus they chose to employ Africans, whom they could discriminate against in both treatment and wages without complaint. Du Bois's report followed the 1927 Le Zoute Conference, which was organized by white American denominations and held in Hartford, Connecticut. Among the mostly white attendees at the conference were AME, NBC-USA, and Lott Carey Baptist delegates. A prominent issue was the question of African Americans "entering the mission field of Africa." In general, white missionaries and many government officials did not favor black missionaries and argued that black missionary efforts in Africa were poor and had met with little success. This ruse obscured their real concerns about the threat to European imperialism posed by the presence of black Americans. However, Marcus Garvey's black nationalist movement in the post–World War I era appeared to be the driving force in the fight against black Christian missionaries entering Africa.

It is likely that Du Bois's exposé of "American white Christianity" encouraged a few organizations to send African Americans primarily to missions in West Africa. For example, in 1933 the American Board of Commissioners for Foreign Missions announced that it was supporting three black missionaries: Dr. Aaron M. McMillan, a physician; Dr. Henry C. McDowell, a minister; and Samuel B. Coles, an agriculturist. In 1940, Methodist Episcopal Church officials appointed Artice D. Banks as supervisor of the denominational schools in Monrovia. After 1940, the Methodist Episcopal Church sent a few African American missionaries to India. However, the majority of its black missionaries were sent to Latin America, not Africa. Alluding to the political changes taking place in Africa, in 1950 Sallie Lou MacKinnon, administrator for Methodist missions in Africa and Europe, wrote, "I think it is possible now to send members of the Negro race as well as of other races [to Africa]. We need doctors, nurses, teachers, social workers, architects, agriculturists, workers for urban and rural regions; in fact, I know of few skills that could not be used in Africa." Mainstream denominations assigned African American missionaries to Africa after 1960. However, by that date Africans had largely replaced foreign missionaries and the American Peace Corps attracted large numbers of persons who formerly would have sought denominational missionary positions. Some white and black denominational leaders feared that the Peace Corps would replace Christian mission work.

Women and Missionary Ideology

WOMEN'S ORGANIZATIONS PLACED a high priority on the uplift of African females, reasoning that the position of women within a society indicates the degree of civilization. They believed that Christianity could transform a society and argued that it had set women free. Distinguishing Christianity from Islam and other non-Christian or so-called "pagan" religions, Mary Mason argued, "Christianity stood forth with glory for having lifted woman out of the slough of age-old degradation; the non-Christian religions without exception stood condemned for permitting and indeed, often commanding the perpetual enslavement and debasement of the racial mother. The loss to mankind through the attitude of the pagan world toward womanhood is perhaps the most incalculable one ever sustained by humanity."

The nineteenth-century notions of domesticity and true womanhood contributed to the rise of the women's missionary movement. Ironically, the movement itself would ultimately challenge the idea that the proper place for women was in the home. For more than three centuries, the most widely used and pervasive argument for extending Christianity through missionary activities was the claim that "wherever this faith goes, its view of the sacredness of personality raises the status of womanhood." This belief became so deeply ingrained among Christians that by the twentieth century the church considered itself "a pacesetter" in the American women's rights movement. Given the widespread discrimination against women in the church, nothing could be farther from the truth.

In the 1830s and '40s mainly middle-class white Protestant women in the U.S. argued that the most significant aspect of civilizing non-Western countries was through the conversion of "heathen" women. Inculcating women in Africa, India, and China with Christian beliefs and values would ultimately change the overall society, since wives and mothers exerted great influence over men and children. Women were the culture bearers, with responsibility for shaping the personalities and the worldview of future generations. Leading black intellectuals and religious leaders such as Rev. Alexander Crummell promoted this idea in the late nineteenth as well as the twentieth century. Following almost twenty years in West Africa as an Episcopal missionary, Crummell concluded that female missionaries were of greater importance to the achievement of mission goals than males. Crummell's views were based upon close observation of two groups—the Americo-Liberians in Monrovia, and Africans in Cape Palmas. Located in the Liberian interior, Cape Palmas represented indigenous African traditions and culture. Aware of the discussions in the AME Church regarding African missions, in 1870 Crummell suggested that the denomination develop a broad-based African missions program that included "female agency." He warned AME leaders, "You can do no large great work for God in Africa unless you make *female* influence a prominent influence. Woman keeps Africa low and degraded and hence only women, under God, can raise Africa up." Crummell's thesis regarding women in Africa was closely related to notions about the need to reclaim and secure African American women's virtue, and its importance for racial uplift, and the advancement of blacks in the United States.

Male clergy were ambivalent about Crummell's suggestion regarding women missionaries, but they recognized the importance of his argument in their quest to raise funds for foreign missions. Stressing the usefulness of employing females as missionary workers and the necessity of improving the status of African women were powerful and compelling arguments that could attract and fuel women's interests in foreign missions. Crummell's belief that females were of greater importance to the achievement of mission goals than males was an integral part of the women's missionary societies' arguments for employing females as foreign missionaries and undertaking missionary work on a global scale. It was a central reason for their dedication to the Baptist and Methodist mission programs in Africa, South America, and the Caribbean. Moreover, women assuming leadership in mission work enhanced their struggle for equality within their denominations.

Whereas black and white American missionaries evinced concern for educating African girls, until the late 1920s the prime interest of Europeans—settlers, officials, and missionaries—was the education and socialization of African boys and men. European interests in Africa were driven by economic objectives. Exercising authority over millions of Africans to ensure economic profitability required military security and strict control over the African population. African males were socialized and disciplined "to obey and defer to Europeans." Education was a critical component in the plan to develop an efficient labor force. African men were essential to the diverse economic activities of European colonies, especially commerce, mining, and agricultural ventures. Males were also employed as domestic laborers for house cleaning, cooking, child care, tailoring, and so on. Thus, Europeans concentrated on the education and training of men. On the other hand, European officials and settlers viewed African girls and women as "threats to respectable European life, authority, economic activity, and homes."

The exclusion of African females from domestic employment represented an unspoken, but clearly understood, need to police white male sexual desire. In doing so, Europeans hoped to avoid conflict with African males, whose labor was sorely needed for industrial production. African women were perceived "not as people, but as dangers." For example, in the 1896–97 uprisings in Southern Rhodesia, African concubines were charged with stealing weapons and ammunition to use against soldiers. Europeans feared resistance from African males in the event that African girls or women were raped or otherwise abused by Europeans or their African employees. Between 1900 and 1930 most complaints about police abuse, schools, mission activity, and the Rhodesian Native Department's administration focused on difficulties with women.

At the heart of most white and black foreign mission movements was the belief that "Mohammedanism" or Islam must be eradicated and replaced by Christianity. Mohammedanism was not just a religion; it was a way of life and a set of beliefs and practices that defined the very essence of many African and Middle Eastern cultures. In 1908, when the AME Zion General Conference placed Bishop Alexander Walters in charge of its foreign mission work, he asserted, "My main object is to have our men help to civilize and Christianize non-Christian Africa, and this must be done quickly or Mohammedanism will overrun" the continent. Like Crummell and other leading black and white religious figures, Walters argued, "Mohammedanism encourages polygamy, which means the destruction of the home. Christianity stands for purity, which means the stability of the home and the nation." Primarily concerned with the elimination of the indigenous African practice of polygamy, Crummell reasoned that missionaries should give first priority to the education and evangelization of African girls. He emphasized that American missionaries might "educate a thousand boys, but if woman is not enlightened, [the] mission will prove a failure." African girls taught by black American women missionaries would eventually "teach in the native schools, visit the native women and force respect for woman upon these native chiefs and kings, and train the boys to respect womanhood." In time, as boys became men, they would "respect their sisters, mothers, and lastly their wives, and thus home and society," and eventually eliminate the practice of polygamy. Crummell recommended that missionary boards send two female missionaries for every male.

Crummell's conclusions were publicized in the *Christian Recorder*, the most widely circulated black publication in the 1870s. AME Bishop Richard Harvey Cain heeded Crummell's plea for female missionary teachers. The son of an African man and a Native American mother, Cain was a foremost proponent of African emigration and black American missionary work. In 1885 he asserted, "Africa is a good place to develop our manhood." He asked, "Who among our young Christian ministry are willing to go to Africa and undertake the responsibility of guiding our work there? Are there any young women who have qualified themselves [as] teachers who will go to Africa and devote their time and talents to building up character in the persons of the boys and girls of the heathen?"

Crummell's views influenced Methodist and Baptist denominations to consider female missionary applicants, and encouraged some black women to aspire to become missionaries. The employment of African American women by white foreign mission boards was not lost on black denominations, which argued that black churches must not be left behind in the worldwide efforts to evangelize Africa. Highly publicized reports of evangelist Amanda Berry Smith's missionary work in England, Scotland, India, and Africa, especially her tenure as a Methodist Episcopal Church missionary in Liberia for eight years in the 1880s and the publication of her autobiography in the 1890s, influenced the decision of black women's missionary societies to provide more support for foreign missionary work. Similarly, the published letters and reports about the status and treatment of women in the Congo, Nyasaland, Liberia, and other nations also described the beauty and exotic nature of Africa and suggested that missionary work provided an opportunity for one to fulfill her mission as a woman, and as an African American. The power of these appeals cannot be overstated. In the late nineteenth century, a few single women, such as Pinkey Davis, answered the challenge and went to Africa. Struck by the plight of her African sisters, Davis wrote, "As a missionary, woman can enter the homes of thousands whose doors would forever [be] closed to man. Woman comes with her needle work, painting, cooking and ministry to the sick." Appealing directly to her sisters, Davis pleaded, "[W]oman, think what a mission is yours. Dark Africa lies in ignorance and sin waiting your aid, only you can save her."

Crummell's argument regarding the importance of educating African girls and of recruiting females for missionary work served as a catalyst for promoting the idea of single black women as missionary teachers, and was perceived by some leaders as a way of advancing denominational efforts among Africans. Crummell's views would be reiterated by many missionaries whose cultural and religious chauvinism caused them to conclude that the indigenous Africans were "uncivilized heathens" who needed to be divorced from traditional customs and beliefs that were detrimental to women and girls and thus hampered African development. However, the male-dominated foreign mission boards of black denominations (like their white counterparts) were firmly rooted in patriarchal beliefs and practices and more interested in recruiting men for African missions, particularly clergy to work as preachers and pastors. In the nineteenth century married men were preferred, because their wives as teachers and assistants could be a profitable source of either unpaid or underpaid labor.

Women Missionaries

HOW AND WHERE did black women gain prominence in the African missionary movement and what roles did they play in mission development? Not much is known about the operation of any of these mission stations or what a typical day, week, month, or year at a mission was like. Little has been written about the ordinary activities and organization of women missionaries or the day-to-day problems they faced, especially those who chose to work in the West African hinterland. What were their views about the process of conversion and how did they effectuate them? How did they pursue their work among indigenous Africans, some of whom were suspicious of their motives and hostile to the missionaries' purposes? How did Africans react to black missionaries and missionary education? What supports or protections did indigenous peoples provide to the missions, especially those staffed mainly by women? These questions, as well as the issue of the finances for a mission group, are important to the understanding of a station's development, support, and expansion of mission activities. It appears that missions with regular financial backing remained stable and tended to flourish, whereas those without ongoing funding either had to shut down or were in a state of constant instability.

By all accounts, foreign missionary work was physically and spiritually grueling and was not for the faint of heart. Rather, it required strong religious faith, determination, and a firm resolve that one had been called by God. Above all, one needed great physical stamina. Legions of missionaries testified to the difficulties of adjusting to the African environment. The relentlessly hot climate, the overwhelming and often difficult workload, and the prevalence of exotic diseases and vicious animals were considerable drawbacks for anyone contemplating going to Africa. Considering the goals of missionary work, mission boards sought candidates who were resourceful, courageous, and possessed of the proper "mental and education equipment." Given the challenges of dealing with unexpected conditions and developments in the field, missionary work also required optimism, creativity, and flexibility—the ability to perform many things well. Since education was a primary goal, mission boards sought workers who were educated and properly trained. Missionaries were expected to have extensive knowledge of the Bible and understanding of religious doctrine, and to be able to teach both religion and English to their converts. Education was proposed as a possible method to entice "heathens" to participate in mission activities. The idea was to separate children from their families and friends, inculcate them with notions of Christianity and civilization, and educate them for missionary work among their people.

Above and beyond the normal cultural, ecological, and geographical challenges, in Africa black female missionaries confronted a society where gender and age were the markers of social distinction, and where women and children were legally defined as property. A father, for example, could claim the right of control, property and possession over his children. The so-called "bride price," which a father received in "exchange" for giving his daughter away as a wife to someone, was based on such rights. Experienced missionaries emphasized the importance of getting Africans to permit their children to leave their villages and live at the mission school, especially females. AME Zion missionary Hilda Nasmyth concluded that since polygamy was "practiced without restraint . . . the only hope for the ultimate redemption of Africa was to take girls away from their fathers, adopt, and give them a Christian name, and train them 'for God.' "

Emma B. DeLaney and other missionaries were woefully lacking in knowledge about African cultures and peoples. However, knowledge of African history and culture were not considered essential. For most black and white missionaries in the nineteenth and early twentieth centuries, it was not just a matter of neutral ignorance. Rather, their actions were driven by ideology. Missionaries invariably believed that Africans were uncivilized, and their religion and cultural patterns were dismissed as inferior. Thus, the missionary saw his or her job as one of transforming the people and the culture through evangelization, conversion, and inculcation of Christian beliefs and Western cultural values. African resistance to the missionary's efforts was often selective and frequently involved negotiation. In exchange for Western medicine and medical treatment, Africans would generally allow missionaries to organize religious services in their villages. Concern for the education of children caused some parents to allow mostly males to reside at the mission schools. However, there were villages where Islam was so strong that missionaries were literally driven away by physical threats. Some missionaries were transformed by their experiences. Others, such as Emma DeLaney, were not. Most missionaries discovered that they had to either adapt to some African cultural patterns or suffer the consequences.

Affectionately referred to by native Liberians as "God Mammies," pioneering missionaries such as DeLaney gave their lives in the cause of "saving Africa." Motivated by their desire to serve and to perform their "special duty" to their African homeland, in the late nineteenth century a number of single black women sought positions as missionaries representing white as well as black associations. Some women believed that Africa provided a new context in which to construct their racial and gender identities. Many believed that they were "called" by God, and had a "special mission" to fulfill by giving service to the "homeland." It was their duty to convert their "heathen" African brothers and sisters to Christianity, and to liberate their African sisters from a state of quasi-degradation. When queried as to why they chose missionary work in Africa, most women gave those reasons, but also related their need to vindicate the virtue of black womanhood—theirs, as well as that of their African sisters. Many had other reasons. While it was generally not prudent to state these motivations, some women entered the foreign missionary field to avoid marriage, and others sought to elevate their social status. For some, Africa was a place where they could escape from American racism. In any case, Africa provided a new context in which to construct their racial and gender identities.

Recruitment of black females for missionary work was further enhanced by the American Baptist Home Mission Society's support for formal missionary training, which was institutionalized with the 1891 establishment of a separate missionary training department at Spelman Seminary (later known as Spelman College) in Atlanta, a school for black girls and women. The two-year course of study included five months of home mission field-work, often in the most rural areas of the South. The distinguishing features of field-work were home visitations, women and children's meetings, Bible Bands, parents' conferences, and local training classes for Christian workers. Spelman's emphasis on training for home and foreign missionary work, and the subsequent graduation and placement of trained missionaries in communities throughout the South, provided high visibility for the school and its program and helped to spread the message about the importance of missionary work. It also served as an effective arm for recruiting young female students, many of whom spent at least ten years at the seminary, matriculating in the elementary and normal school program, graduating from the high school, and then pursuing further academic and/or missionary training. Spelman was a key factor in the growth of female missionaries and the feminization of the Baptist missions at Monrovia and Suehn, Liberia.

The growth and development of denominational women's organizations and the introduction of missionary training programs at colleges and universities encouraged young women and men to consider becoming foreign missionaries. Most denominational missionary societies and women's conventions were formed for the express purpose of raising funds to support foreign mission work. The Lott Carey Baptist Convention was organized in 1897 as an autonomous foreign mission association. This organization and the National Baptist Convention, USA, with its numerous mission stations throughout Africa, were in the forefront of black missionary work in the twentieth century. The problem for the black denominations, however, was how to fund these programs and extend the mission work of the church.

There are no statistics available for black female missionaries in the nineteenth century, but at least thirty or forty black women went to Africa, South America, Haiti, and several other countries as representatives of mostly white denominations. A handful were also employed by the AME and AME Zion churches. Betsey Stockton is one of the best known of the antebellum missionaries. Born into a wealthy slaveholding family in Princeton, New Jersey, around 1798, Stockton experienced conversion and became a member of the First Presbyterian Church in Princeton in 1816. It was around this time that she was manumitted by Ashbel Green, the president of the College of New Jersey (later known as Princeton University). While working as a domestic servant, she read in Green's library, studied with one of his sons, and attended Sabbath school. Betsey expressed an interest in going to Africa as a missionary, but her friends discouraged her. In 1822, she joined a company of missionaries headed for the Sandwich Islands (now Hawaii). Her contract defined her role as a missionary and servant to Rev. and Mrs. Charles S. Stewart. The American Board of Commissioners of Foreign Missions, an agency representing mainly the Congregational and Presbyterian churches in the United States, sponsored the company. As the first nonwhite female missionary in the Sandwich Islands, Stockton attracted the attention of the Hawaiian king, who requested that she teach him and his son English. She established a school with English and Hawaiian students, but she was obliged to return to the States in 1826 when her employer became ill. Though her career as a missionary was limited to two years, the publication of a version of her Hawaiian diary by Ashbel Green in the *Christian Advocate* helped to promote interest in the American Board's mission work and establish Stockton's name as a legendary black missionary.

While Betsey Stockton is widely believed to be the first black female missionary, in the 1850s, under the auspices of the Southern Baptist Convention, several African American women accompanied their husbands to Liberia, where they quietly taught school and otherwise assisted their spouses. In keeping with southern tradition, prior to the late nineteenth century the SBC did not officially appoint women to mission stations and would not consider employing single women. By the 1880s there was a steady flow of single women, which had grown substantially by the 1920s. There were also numerous unpaid missionary wives who worked as teachers, seamstresses, administrators over mission houses and schools, and assistants to their husbands in conducting religious services. Many women accompanied their spouses to Africa, India, Haiti, Demerara, the West Indies, and other far-flung places. Though they might assume the same duties as paid female workers, wives received little credit for their contributions and seldom gained positions of prominence. Far less is reported in the religious press about missionary wives who assumed roles as teachers and religious assistants. Rather, they are described as performing their functions as wives, and their husbands take credit for their work.

Among nineteenth-century missionary workers, Lucy Henry Coles exemplifies the expectations of wives who were perceived as "help-mates" to their husbands, not leaders of missions. Though women such as Coles served as workers alongside their husbands, an equal number of single women worked within established missions. Born in Richmond, Virginia, in 1865, at an early age Lucy Ann Henry assumed responsibility for the care of her disabled mother and siblings. Growing up in the Ebenezer Baptist Church, she was enthralled with the discussions about the need for African Americans to uplift their African sisters and brothers. While teaching at a subscription school, she met and fell in love with Rev. John J. Coles, an African missionary. Prior to marriage, she entered the missionary training program at the Hartshorn Memorial College in Richmond, Virginia, a school for black girls supported by the ABHMS. Lucy set sail for Africa with her husband in January 1887. At the Jundoo Mission Station in Sierra Leone, West Africa, she was in charge of the mission house, which included caring for and teaching the sixteen resident African children. Rev. D. N. Vassar, commissioner of the Baptist Foreign Mission Convention of the United States, described Lucy as the perfect "helpmate to her husband." Upon returning "from his labors among the heathens [Rev. Coles] finds his wife waiting and everything in readiness to make him happy and to give him [the] rest so necessary in that climate. Often, she accompanies him and leads the singing before and after preaching." As the children came to the mission with "not even a rag or string around the waist," Lucy painstakingly sewed all of their clothing with only needle and thread.

Between 1873 and 1895, Lucy Coles, Jane Sharp, Harriette Presley, Julia Smith, Nancy Jones, Henriette Ousley, Mrs. M. H. Garnett Barboza, Nora Gordon, Clara Howard, Anna E. Hall, Dr. Francis Davis, and Susan Collins were among the first black women missionaries in Africa. Little information about these women exists. However, their experiences are important to understanding the lives of women who chose to become foreign missionaries. With few exceptions, these pioneers were educated, married, and appointed to mission stations in Africa. Though several of these women, such as Lucy Coles, received support from local black churches, most went to Africa under the auspices of white-controlled organizations, including missionary boards and churches. These included the American Colonization Society, the American Board of Commissioners for Foreign Missions, the American Baptist Home Mission Society, the Boston Board of Donation for Education in Liberia, and Episcopal, Congregational, and Methodist Episcopal churches.

Graduating from the Boston Girls' High School in 1873, Jane E. D. Sharp was nominated by the Liberia Education Society to head the women's department at the University of Liberia at Monrovia. In this position she was responsible for educating the daughters of elite Americo-Liberians and prominent leaders of local ethnic groups. During her tenure at the university, Jane met and married Jesse Sharp, a wealthy mulatto coffee planter. After several years of teaching, she questioned the need for her services in Monrovia. Believing that there was a greater need for work among African female children, she shifted her focus to the "bush tribes." At the death of her husband, Jane Sharp purchased a 650-acre plantation at Mount Coffee, where she mastered the customs, philosophy, religion, and traditions of the Gola people. The Gola and other ethnic groups in the region were very supportive of Sharp and interested in her plans to establish an industrial training school for girls. Gola women were highly skilled in doing fine leather work, making sheaths for knives, and hand weaving fine cotton, palms, and grasses into a variety of articles. Very few Liberians engaged in farming. Most of their foodstuffs were imported from Europe and sold at high prices. Sharp felt that African girls could be taught poultry rais-

Oyoro Ashanti A.M.E. Zion Congregation in West Africa, ca. 1930s

ing, fruit culture, and preservation of pineapples, mangoes, and plums. The sale of these goods would enable them to become self-supporting and appropriately clothed. Like most foreigners, Sharp was concerned that women and girls wore little clothing. She believed that if they were properly clothed they would be less susceptible to malaria and other tropical diseases that killed so many people. Industrial training would address this problem. What was lacking was the money to erect suitable buildings and equipment on the plantation.

Unlike most foreign missionaries and Americo-Liberians, Jane Sharp did not consider Africans to be savages, nor did she believe that children should give up their native language and customs. Rather, they should be bilingual. She was impressed with the Africans' "pride of descent." Sharp noted, "Pride of descent has played an important part in the development of all races. I have seen tribes in Africa that I am only sorry that I cannot claim my descent from such as the Mandingo, Ashantee, Zulu, and others. If the colored race in America only knew their African antecedents, instead of regarding themselves as being descended from savages or slaves, they would have more self-respect, and would be encouraged to higher effort. My work is altogether for girls." In 1903, Sharp returned to the United States to raise funds for the industrial venture. The Mount Coffee Association was formed, and friends and supporters in Massachusetts rallied to the

Rev. Nora F. Taylor (third row, right end), board of directors, teaching staff, and students at the AME Girls' Industrial Institute at Freetown, Sierra Leone, West Africa, ca. 1920s

cause and organized Jane Sharp Circles. Whether or not Jane Sharp succeeded in her efforts to build an industrial school for girls is not known, but the story of her dedication and zeal is compelling and significant to the reconstruction of African American women's foreign missionary work.

By 1910 the National Baptist Convention, Lott Cary Baptist Foreign Missionary Convention, African Methodist Episcopal, and African Methodist Episcopal Zion denominations had established mission stations in Africa and had several missionaries stationed there. Though all of these groups sent missionaries to Africa—mostly to Liberia—by 1920 the National Baptist Convention, USA, was the foremost black organization engaged in the evangelization of Africa. However, even the Baptist numbers paled in comparison to those of white missionaries. By 1927, while there were scarcely fifty African American missionaries on the continent of Africa, there were approximately seven thousand whites. Black denominations knew from the outset that they would never be able to match the Europeans and white Americans in missionizing Africa. In 1900 Rev. Charles S. Morris, the NBC Foreign Mission Board's commissioner to Africa, in an analysis of the political situation in South Africa recognized that the denomination could not compete with the Europeans, who had extensive missions, and two thousand resident missionaries. Thus, he astutely argued that the NBC should organize its South African missions to be

Rev. Florence Spearing Randolph was a missionary at the AME Zion's mission at Quittah, West Africa, 1922.

"self-supporting" and have "African men and women fund and operate the missions." Morris also felt that since South Africa was "already a half-civilized nation" and Africans had far more opportunities there than on the "desolate West Coast" of Africa, it was imperative that the NBC concentrate its efforts on indigenous people in West Africa, in particular in Liberia.

A careful study of the missionary work of black denominations reveals that more black females served in the NBC-USA foreign missions in West Africa than in any other organization. Most of the AME and AME Zion missionaries were male clergy. Black Methodist denominations established churches and schools, organized African denominational conferences, and appointed mainly nonresident bishops to supervise mission work. Their goal was to develop self-sustaining missions administered by African American clergy and staffed by Africans. During the early years (1900–30), clergy wives accompanied their husbands to distant posts. However, because the death rates from tropical diseases soared and many wives and daughters died, some were reluctant to leave the United States.

At the same time, the structure of the AME and AME Zion churches hindered the missionary activities of women in foreign fields in two ways. First, since the primary focus of these denominations was the establishment of churches, ministers were more in demand. The assumption was that their spouses would perform the normal roles expected of a minister's wife whether in America or Africa. Bishops' wives were designated as "missionary supervisors" to organize and oversee the work with African women. The creation of African women's societies diminished the need for African American women as missionaries. However, there were AME Zion and AME women such as Rev. Florence Spearing Randolph and Rev. Nora Taylor, who, at their own expense, served as missionary teachers in Africa. Black American women who clamored for paid positions as foreign mission workers found few opportunities in these denominations for their services.

Relatively few AME and AME Zion women were appointed as foreign missionaries in either the nineteenth or twentieth centuries, and those who were settled mostly in urban areas. In 1889, Sarah Gorham offered her services to the AME Church as a missionary. Gorham was an ordinary woman, a laundress who became known for her marked spirituality and religious zeal, unusually powerful prayers, and prodigious missionary work in the church and in black and white communities in Boston. In recognition of her special gifts, Rev. John T. Jennifer, pastor of the Charles Street AME Church, appointed her as a class leader. Her local notoriety led to employment with the Boston Associated Charities, for which she was paid forty dollars per month, a considerable sum in the 1870s. Gorham went to Liberia at her own expense to work in the AME mission there. However, upon arrival in Monrovia she discovered that there was no mission. Rather than return home, Gorham assisted Rev. J. R. Frederick in Sierra Leone and conducted revivals in Freetown and the interior among indigenous Africans. In 1891, after a bout with malaria, she returned to the United States to regain her health and raise funds for mission work. She returned to Africa in December 1893, under the auspices of the AME Woman's Parent Mite Missionary Society, where she was appointed by the Sierra Leone AME Annual Conference to work among the Timnees people at the Magbelly station in West Africa. Within eight months the dreaded malaria claimed her life. Hailed as the first woman missionary appointed by the AME Church to a foreign field, for decades Sarah Gorham was held up as a model of what AME women could accomplish in missions.

In 1900 Rev. Levi J. Coppin was elected the first AME bishop of South Africa and assigned to the Fourteenth Episcopal District (Cape Colony and Transvaal, South Africa). Fanny Jackson Coppin, former president of the AME Woman's Mite Missionary Society and the first black female to head a major educational institution, Philadelphia's Institute for Colored Youth (later known as Cheyney State University), shared her husband's commitment to African mission work. In 1902 Fanny retired from her position with the institute and joined Bishop Coppin in Cape Town, where she worked with the Bethel Institute, the first industrial manual training school in South Africa. Since Cape Town was a modern city, the couple did not endure the hardships encountered by Emma DeLaney and missionaries working in the African interior among indigenous peoples. Food was plentiful, and the drinking water was superior to that found in other locales. Fanny organized the Mite Missionary Society in Cape Town and other towns where the AME Church had mission stations. In Cape Town, she founded the Women's Prayer Circle, a group of women who held services in the women's section of the Cape Town jail and aided the lepers' colony on Roben Island. This prayer group formed the nucleus for the first AME mite missionary society in South Africa.

In her travels with her husband to identify prospective sites for

planting AME missions, Fanny Jackson Coppin went as far as Bula-
wayo, 1,360 miles from Cape Town. In South Africa, she was both surprised and delighted to find several of her former students. In keeping
with her educational philosophy, she emphasized the uplift of African
women. Stationed in an urban area, she had an opportunity to assess
the needs of young African women in cities, whose plight was similar
to that of many black women in the United States. Fanny felt that the
only hope for the economic advancement of poor and uneducated
African women was domestic service. She was not ashamed to admit
that she had once worked as a servant, and she appealed to the young
women to free themselves from the notion that the position of servant
girl was degrading. Thus, she stressed the need for industrial training
of girls.

Though men were favored, the legal structure of the Baptist polity
did not preclude the employment of females as foreign mission workers. Baptist women were therefore more prevalent and were able to
accomplish more as individuals in foreign mission work than their
Methodist counterparts. Moreover, because the NBC-USA Woman's
Convention was able to exert some control over its program and funds,
it often provided crucial support for women as foreign missionaries. By
1925, females were appointed as teachers at most Baptist missions, and
the number of NBC-USA female missionaries exceeded those of the
males in at least two mission stations. In the twentieth century, as more
professional job opportunities in the United States became available
for black men, the numbers of male foreign missionaries declined.
However, men—black Americans as well as Africans—headed up most
of the foreign missions.

The feminization of the NBC-USA Liberian missions in Suehn
and Monrovia was related to the persistent support of the Woman's
Convention and the pioneering work of Emma DeLaney, the founder
of the Suehn Industrial Mission, and the dedication of the black Baptist women who served at Suehn and the Monrovia Carrie Dyer Hospital mission. The survival and successful development of Suehn
between 1926 and 1970 was due almost solely to the administrative
genius of Sarah C. Williamson and the exceptional women missionaries who staffed the mission. The work of Williamson, Dr. Pauline
Dinkins, Ruth E. Occomy, Ruth Morris, Phyllis Bryan Jackson, Mae
Davis, Gladys East, and Frances Watson was highly publicized in the
United States. These missionaries were supported by a number of
individuals as well as by local, state, and national Baptist organizations,

including the Woman's Convention, the NBC-USA, the ABHMS, and New York City's Abyssinian Baptist Church. The work of black women was critical to the maintenance and development of Liberian missions, and essential to the recruitment and education of Africans.

Emma B. DeLaney: Icon and Model Missionary

BETWEEN 1893 AND 1919 Spelman College graduated twenty-five young women who specialized in Christian missionary training. Nora Gordon, Clara Howard, Emma B. DeLaney, and Ada Jackson Gordon were the first graduates of Spelman to become African missionaries. Howard and Gordon founded the Lukungu Seminary in 1890, a school located at the Lukungu Mission Station in West Central Africa, near the mouth of the Congo River. DeLaney, the fourth Spelman graduate to become an African missionary, was a graduate of the high school, nurse training, and missionary training departments. Believing that conversion to Christianity was a life-altering experience, most black missionaries aimed at changing an existing community if possible, or educating individual Africans who would in turn become missionaries to their people. The best way to accomplish this goal was to establish boarding schools. Separating African children from their families by having them live at, work at, and attend the mission school allowed missionaries to convert children to Christianity and introduce

Nora Gordon (center) was a member of the 1895 missionary training class at Spelman Seminary in Atlanta, Georgia.

them to Western ways of thinking and living. Recognizing the importance of having Africans trained as missionaries, these women selected
five Congo girls for education at Spelman: Suluka and Emma Yongebloed, Lena Clark, Margaret Rattray, and Flora Zeto. Following completion of the high school course, Suluka and Emma Yongebloed
pursued degrees in medicine and nursing. A graduate of Meharry
Medical College, Suluka became a physician and settled in Fort Valley,
Georgia, with her African American husband. Emma worked as an
assistant at a Nashville hospital and married a physician. Lena Clark
and Margaret Rattray completed the missionary training course and
returned to the Congo, where Lena served as a linguist and Margaret
as a Bible teacher. Flora Zeto graduated from Spelman in 1915 and
married Dr. Daniel Malekebu, Emma DeLaney's adopted African son.
During the early 1920s Daniel and Flora Malekebu served as missionaries in Liberia prior to returning to Nyasaland (Malawi)—their
homeland—where Daniel served as a preacher, teacher, and physician
and Flora as a teacher and nurse.

Emma DeLaney's African experience in Nyasaland and Liberia is
emblematic of the difficulties many missionaries faced when they
chose to work among indigenous populations in the hinterland. Her
first tour of duty began in 1902 at Chiradzulu, British Central Africa,
in Nyasaland near the Zambesi River at the Ajawa Providence Industrial Mission Station, where she spent several years as a missionary
teacher. The mission was organized in 1899 by Rev. John Chilembwe,
an African who was mentored by Joseph Booth, a British missionary at
the Seventh-day Adventist mission station in Nyasaland who claimed
to have originated the slogan "Africa for the Africans." In 1897
Chilembwe toured the United States and Europe with Booth, who
campaigned to raise awareness of the unjust treatment of Africans by
European colonizers. Booth taught Chilembwe that Africans were
"being greatly wronged by the English settlers." Chilembwe was sent
to the U.S. in 1898 by the seven indigenous groups in British Central
Africa for the express purpose of gaining an education at the Baptist
Seminary in Richmond, Virginia. Chilembwe returned home and
secured ninety-three acres of land in the name of the National Baptist
Convention. Employing labor to make bricks and to build a school and
church, Chilembwe established the first African American mission station in Nyasaland.

During her three-year stint at Chiradzulu, DeLaney encountered white missionary opposition to Africans and black Americans leading in missionary work. White missionaries were often confirmed in their belief in white supremacy, and determined to erect structures of dominance in Africa. Some observers argued that white missionaries were in many ways the handmaidens of European colonial powers. In the name of Christianity, their role was to subdue the Africans with the Bible and make them amenable to their status as wage laborers. In British-ruled Central Africa, South Africa, Rhodesia, and other European colonies, the movement and activities of DeLaney and other black missionaries were carefully monitored. Like the free Negroes who resided in the South during the antebellum period, black Americans in Africa were considered threats to the interests of European imperialists who feared that African Americans would create havoc and incite Africans to revolt against colonialism. In 1902, while in South Africa, Fanny Jackson Coppin observed, "[T]he government had spies on hand, native spies, to observe all that was said, and report to the authorities. . . . The spirit of suspicion was everywhere prevalent, and did much for a time to retard our work." In the twentieth century, colonial government officials often opposed African Americans seeking entry to an African colony and the operation of missions by African Americans and Africans. They erected laws that made it difficult for black denominations to obtain land and establish missions.

For black missionaries who believed that they were escaping American racism and discrimination by going to Africa, those illusions were quickly shattered. Throughout the British Empire, there were racial policies designed to maintain white supremacy and ensure the "domination of the white minority over the black majority." Europeans were dependent on African labor and recognized a need to enforce strict control over Africans and black Americans. Though racial policies varied in South Africa, Southern Rhodesia, and Central Africa, by 1920 Europeans practiced segregation. In 1902, en route to Chiradzulu, Emma DeLaney missed a steamship connection and was forced to remain in Capetown, South Africa, for more than two weeks, where she discovered that the white ticket agents were not unlike those in the United States in their treatment of black Africans. She noted the "inhuman treatment of natives" by the white employees of steamer companies and concluded "that there is as much prejudice in some places in Africa as in America." DeLaney was not dissuaded by the racism she found in Africa; rather, she became more determined to pursue her mission. After all, she had braved the opposition of family and friends, and resolved to undertake what was arguably a daunting venture.

Following three and a half months of travel, including five changes of steamers and forty miles of overland travel on foot through dense bush, DeLaney finally reached her destination. Admitting that her decision to travel alone to the interior represented poor judgment, she assured friends and supporters that if it took a year to find someone to accompany her, she would "never venture to return alone." Several mission stations were located within eighty miles of the Providence Mission. Days after her arrival in Chiradzulu, DeLaney was felled by the fever associated with malaria. She felt alone in her suffering, as there was "not a civilized woman nearer than twelve miles." Between DeLaney and the nearest mission station were five streams and no bridges. Until the arrival of the Branch family at the Seventh-day Adventist mission, she was the sole black female in the region, and one of two African Americans at the only black mission station in British Central Africa. At the time of her illness, John Chilembwe was away on vacation, and Rev. L. N. Cheek, the other African American missionary, was also sick with malaria. In the face of "the horrid condition of the people," DeLaney observed that it was easy to "forget one's self, and your constant thoughts are, How can I better [the conditions for] these women especially?"

During the first three months, DeLaney apologized for visiting only six villages. In the absence of roads, travel was extremely dangerous. She stated, "[T]he grass is so high that it covers me when I am being carried through it in the *machila*; and there is great danger of animals and snakes." In fact, six lions were spotted just three miles away from the two-room mud house she occupied. The discomfiture of the house, especially having to deal with the torrential rains, the intense tropical heat, and the bone-chilling cold, severely tested one's resolve. Problems acquiring food and eating the strange and exotic traditional African fare—like the tough meat of the zebra and old ox meat—were common. Acclimation to the lack of variety in meals and the absence of typical American fruits and vegetables was difficult.

Chiradzulu was located within sixteen degrees of the equator. Standing in the door of her mud hut, DeLaney could see the snow on Chiradzulu mountain. Like many African missionaries, she never tired of writing about the multiple plagues. Greeted by lice—"not only on the natives, but all in the grass and [they] get on you despite the fact that you change [clothing] daily"—she was tempted to return to the United States. Instead of dwelling on the hardship and disappointment she encountered, however, she looked for solutions and ways to accomplish her goals. Lacking basic necessities, DeLaney found her living conditions unsatisfactory. She did not seek comforts, but "the necessary things of life." The most immediate need was to master the Nyanga language, become familiar with the area, and organize a program of education for the mission children.

The NBC-USA mission station was located in the midst of several indigenous groups: the Angonies, Yaos, and Angulus. The predominant religion was Islam. There were seven million Africans in British Central Africa, more than a million of whom lived in the district where DeLaney resided. By law, every African who owned a hut was required to pay three shillings (seventy-five cents) in tax and possess a letter from a European stating that he had worked for one month each year. The British were only interested in harnessing African labor and saw no need to educate the populace. According to Rev. Cheek, there was "not a single school" provided by the British government "for her dusky subjects."

By October 1902 DeLaney had settled into a routine. Two mornings a week she taught sewing, two evenings were devoted to voice training, and every afternoon she taught reading and writing. Admitting that there was little time "for play," DeLaney wrote about the

An outdoor mission school for girls at Ikoko, located in West Central Africa in the Congo, ca. 1900

activities that filled her life. One of her goals was to teach the girls how "to put a room in order properly." This was a difficult task, since African girls were taught that their most important function was to "make the garden and *ufa* (meal) for food." DeLaney also trained the boys to cook. She observed that they were "more apt by far than the girls. This is accounted for when we remember no girl had an opportunity to rise above [her] condition." Noting that European missions concentrated on educating the boys, DeLaney acknowledged an obsession with the plight of females. "What can I do to help the women and girls? And then with what am I to help them?" In the weekly visits to the villages, girls were invited to attend the mission church and school. Most responded that they had "no cloth to wear," but were willing to work for it. DeLaney had plenty of yard and garden work for them to do, but no money, salt, or cloth to pay them with.

African children, like the adults, required that they be paid wages, either in gold or in kind. Typically, missionaries experienced difficulty in recruiting villagers to the Sunday church services. DeLaney reported that they did not understand "a Savior who loved them so much that He died to save them, [when you as a servant] of this same Savior can't give them a dose of medicine to relieve their suffering. Yet this occurs daily with me. . . . They come to me with the blood streaming, limbs swollen, asking for medicine." Though trained as a nurse, during the first year a critical lack of resources forced DeLaney to turn away numerous people who sought medicine and medical care. Because of the environment, in particular the abundance of insects, snakes, and other predators, many wounds resulted from "jiggers" and insect bites, but most were burns. The villagers often slept around the fires built in the middle of the hut and some were badly burned or burned to death. As word spread about the medical services available at Providence, more people came in search of treatment. In November 1903 DeLaney reported, "Some of them come long distances on their hands and knees for treatment," and others were carried on the backs of fathers and husbands.

In spite of numerous problems and the backbreaking work, DeLaney took great comfort in the idea that she was training local leaders. Among the many children who attended the mission school, she favored Daniel Malekebu and his sister Ruth. The children's parents came to resent their relationship with DeLaney, describing her as "the foreign woman." DeLaney had a powerful influence over all the mission children. She was concerned that Ruth would be taken back to

her village and circumcised; at that time female circumcision, or cli-
toridectomy, symbolized the transition from childhood to adulthood.
Daniel refused to be circumcised, and despite threats from his family
would not return to his village, but Ruth clung to her mother's customs.

DeLaney reported that days before the female circumcision ceremony, the villagers engaged in "beastly dances where they danced day
and night." Since the mission was only five minutes away from the village, the drums and chanting were loud and distracting, and an
unavoidable aggravation over which missionaries had no control.
DeLaney described "a drunken revelry" that "looks bad with civilized
heathens, you can form some idea how it looks with a low grade. Last
week I went to one of their largest dances, known as the circumcision
dance. Eight hundred girls were circumcised. They are kept under this
training, as we might call it, three weeks (for girls), the last four days
being days of great debauchery for all belonging to that tribe. This so-
called pleasure to those on the outside is bought at the expense of all
those who are going through this training." Throughout Africa assort-
ments of "bush schools" were held to educate boys and girls about
African life. Varying from a few weeks or months to years, these
schools prepared females for marriage and the roles expected of them.
Likewise, males were taught how to be leaders and warriors and the
meaning of manhood. The training made no sense to DeLaney, who
described it as "heathenism and barbarism combined." Western missionaries regarded circumcision of girls as an example of "savagery."

Africans often resisted the efforts of missionaries to convert them
to Christianity and to alter their cultural values and patterns. Many
adults ignored or opposed Christian propaganda. Islam held sway
among most indigenous groups in British Central Africa and the
Congo. In 1905, the *Blue Book of Missions* estimated that there were
about fifty million adherents to Islam in Africa and 8,957,000 Christians, "including all white residents regardless of their beliefs."
DeLaney wrote, "When and where they worship God, many of the
natives have adopted the worship of Mohammed. We have them in
large numbers about us. They have their missionaries or prophets and
many schools for the natives. I am told they are well attended. The
lowest tribe has not the slightest knowledge of a Supreme Being. They
think everything is in the hand of the witch." Instead of converting
Africans to Christianity, whole villages were being "taken by the
Mohammedans." Reminding black American Christians of their dere-

liction of duty in not providing adequate support for foreign mission work, DeLaney stressed, "Someone will be on time if Christians are late." The use of medicine to reinforce Christian power was one method of engaging adults in discussions of the nature and practice of Christianity.

An encounter with an African woman illustrates the type of resistance missionaries met. DeLaney wrote, "I was talking to one of the women in the village about her need of a Savior. I talked quite a while with her (they do not like to have you speak to them individually, but as a whole). The African woman responded, 'This kind of talk is plenty trouble to me.'" When the woman requested medicine for her ailing daughter, DeLaney responded that the medicines would arrive "some day" and that "they were being sent by Christian people, and if [there] were no Christians in the world to send such help, I would not have any to give them." The African woman said, "I like to talk about medicine; I see this, but the other is all dark."

The experience of working among indigenous people in British Central Africa helped DeLaney to formulate a mission philosophy that she would use in the founding of the Suehn Industrial Mission in Liberia. In the meantime, constant bouts with malaria weakened her body to the point that she decided to leave Chiradzulu. Although the Baptist Woman's Convention had financed the building of a brick house to protect DeLaney from the elements, it could not reverse the deterioration in her health. Having spent almost three years laboring at the NBC's Providence Mission, DeLaney left Chiradzulu for the United States in June 1905.

Determined to regain her health and return to Africa, DeLaney spent several years engaging in domestic missionary work and raising funds to establish a mission school. No longer a neophyte, she possessed a deeper sense of mission and direction. DeLaney knew what she wanted and was confident that with her newfound knowledge and hands-on experience she could achieve her goal of building and administering a school for African children, who would then become leaders among their people. Most important, she recognized the need to raise the funds to make her dream a reality. Though she intended to return to Nyasaland, the Belgian government refused to issue permits to African Americans interested in settling in the Congo. Moreover, to obscure the Belgian program of forced labor and brutal atrocities against Africans, black denominations were banned from working in the Congo and white American denominations were dissuaded from employing any African Americans at their mission stations.

DeLaney went to the west coast of Africa in 1912 with the intent of setting up a mission school for girls in the Liberian interior. It was there that she founded the Suehn Industrial Mission, breaking her earlier promise not to ever again travel alone into the interior or attempt to establish a mission station there. It was through sheer determination and personal fortitude that she succeeded in establishing the Suehn mission that became a showplace for the NBC-USA.

DeLaney arrived in Monrovia in early July 1912 during the rainy season. Following a brief stopover, she departed for Arthington, Liberia, where she was forced by the torrential rains to remain until October. As the trip from Monrovia was made via the river "in an open boat through a constant downpour" and on land in an oxcart, she was soaking wet for hours—and the dreaded fever returned with a vengeance.

Locating a school in the hinterland would not be easy. Outside Monrovia, there was little development, and securing mail and basic necessities would mean long overland trips by foot, or a boat to Monrovia. Within days of her arrival she informed the NBC-USA that more money would be needed for the new undertaking than anticipated. Labor costs were ten times higher and travel was more difficult and expensive in Liberia than in British Central Africa. Travel would necessitate the purchase of a car or boat, and the school building would cost more than the estimated three thousand dollars. And there was the issue of building a house; the immediate need for a structure that would withstand the climatic conditions and prevent further deterioration of DeLaney's health posed an additional expense.

DeLaney wasted no time in getting acquainted with local conditions and traditions. Her first task was to establish a relationship with both the Africans and the Americo-Liberians, learn the Gola dialect, and locate an appropriate site for the mission school. Finding a site meant travel to distant locations, "with absolutely no conveniences for getting to them." Acquiring a place in the hinterland required getting a land grant from the Liberian government and obtaining the approval of a king and indigenous groups to establish a mission station and work among them. It appears that neither DeLaney nor the Baptist Foreign Mission Board was aware of the legal wrangling and protocol necessary for acquiring land. After a year and a half of negotiations, in late 1913

DeLaney received a grant of twenty-five acres of land from the Liberian government. An additional private donation of two hundred acres in December 1914 provided land for raising most of the mission's food and the planting of rubber trees. However, prior to establishing the mission, DeLaney needed the approval of the paramount chief in Montserrado County, Liberia.

In response to the imperialistic aims of the French and British and to avoid tribal wars and uprisings against the Liberian government, in 1905 Liberian president Arthur Barclay instituted a new system of laws. Under the new regime, the government tightened its control over the interior. Indigenous Africans were made nominal citizens, thereby strengthening the Liberian government's claim to inland territories. An African king, designated as the paramount chief, was appointed district commissioner and recognized as the official government representative of all tribal groups in a region. As a salaried employee, the commissioner was responsible for collecting taxes, settling disputes, recruiting labor, and otherwise responding to the needs of the Americo-Liberian government. The new laws were designed to ensure total control over the majority of the population and to block political coalitions among indigenous tribal groups. Following the receipt of a government grant, denominations choosing to locate beyond the coast and outside of urban areas in the hinterland were obligated to have "palaver" or engage in "breaking word" before working in a village or region. This was viewed as a formal negotiation of an agreement or contract with the local authority. DeLaney asserted, "[W]ithout 'Breaking Word' there is no working successfully in these villages. The natives give the government no thought, but whatever the king gives his consent to is law to them. This 'Breaking Word' is a kind of contract between you and the people; it is also very binding on the part of the king."

The "Breaking Word" ceremony required a payment of one shilling and a formal introduction of a missionary by someone respected by the local authority. The missionary was also required to offer a gift of white cloth to illustrate that "your heart is clean and pure toward them." In the introduction of DeLaney, Deacon Moore, an Americo-Liberian, announced, "[T]his Mammy come with God Book and want to set this mission down for them if they want it." Accepting the offerings, the Mandingo king said that he was pleased, "because this mission will bring us together. There are so many tribes and each speaks a different language. This mission school will teach us all the same thing and we can walk together." Acceptance of the twelve yards of cloth meant that the king and his "head men" assumed responsibility for protecting DeLaney if she became "dangerously ill" or died, or if war broke out, or if anything happened to the property. DeLaney believed that protection by the Mandingoes was especially necessary while the interior was in such a state of unrest. There were signs of impending warfare. She could see soldiers passing the mission, "as it is on the main road."

Since most denominational missions were located in Monrovia, DeLaney was often asked, "Why do you go up in the interior a lone woman where there are no civilized people?" She responded that the people she came to help were in the interior, and acknowledged that she had entered a very "hard" field—first, because Islam was "very strong" in one indigenous group, and second, because the other Africans were located on a large hill near the mission. The Suehn Industrial Mission was situated on one side of the road, and the men's secret order, or "Devil Bush," was on the other side. DeLaney said, "I forfeit my life if I cross the road." Directly in front of the mission was the women's secret order, or "Gree Gree Bush."

The Poro and Sande societies established bush schools for males and females. Like the African schools in Chiradzulu, the Devil Bush and Gree Gree Bush were important institutions in traditional Liberian culture. Children spent several years in the bush schools and received instruction in the secrets of the Poro and Sande societies and other matters relating to their adult responsibilities. They were taught marital duties, the use of herbs and other medicines, and practical lessons related to daily life. The bush schools were designed to strengthen governmental authority and make governance less difficult.

Though known by various names, the Devil Bush, open to males between the ages of seven and fifteen, was one of the most important social institutions of indigenous people in Liberia and other African nations. Its purpose was strictly educational. The Devil Bush's daily ritual consisted of morning training of boys to use the bow and arrow, to throw a spear, and to wield a sword. The afternoon was devoted to hunting for small game, target shooting, and throwing the spear. When the boys mastered these skills, they participated in "sham battles" and were taught the methods of warfare. After supper the boys were taught singing and dancing for sacrificial ceremony, and their duties to the gods.

The Gree Gree Bush offered basic education and industrial training. For example, girls were taught hairdressing, household arts, farming, sewing, weaving cotton, dyeing, making mats and nets, and embroidery. They were also instructed on their duty to the king, their parents, and future husbands. The expense of each bush was borne by the parents of children enrolled in the school. When a girl emerged from the Gree Gree Bush, she was well prepared to become a wife. An indigenous woman was not highly respected unless she was trained in the Gree Gree Bush.

The Poro and Sande societies were the chief socializing agencies among indigenous Liberian ethnic communities in the West Atlantic region. Secret societies held sway among all of the indigenous peoples except the Bassa, Kru, and Mandingo. The Americo-Liberian government tolerated the societies as long as they did not interfere with mission and other Western-type schools, missionaries, clinics, and other institutions. Poro was an important political entity that served as a kind of police force, controlling antisocial behavior such as murder, stealing, incest, and arson. It also monitored the behavior of women and of women "chiefs" in the absence of young warriors. Poro had the power to implement the death penalty.

Christian missionaries were indifferent to the purpose and function of the Poro and Sande societies and the Devil and Gree Gree bushes. Instead they focused on inculcating Christianity as a way of life that would eradicate bush training. Working among indigenous Africans during the 1920s, Baptist missionary Frances Watson wrote that it was advisable to get parents to give their girls to the mission to be trained before they were sent to the Gree Gree Bush. It was generally understood that when a girl entered the bush, "part or all of the purchase money has been paid for her to be some man's wife." As the Suehn Industrial Mission was the first one in the region, initially the Africans did not know what to expect. However, by September 1914 they clearly understood that DeLaney was attempting to subvert their training of children, and they resisted her efforts. DeLaney said, "Some of them feel that there is great danger in allowing their children to come to school." She noted that a man who she "always thought was above the average" reneged on his promise to bring his daughter to school. Upon investigation, DeLaney found that the man had given his daughter to his uncle as repayment of a debt for purchase of an ox. This confirmed her belief that the indigenous customs were "heathenish" and unsuitable for civilized living. DeLaney concluded, "A woman and her children may be with the husband and father today in this village and tomorrow they will be owned by some other man in a village miles away. . . . I trust that Christianity will destroy these customs in the years to come."

Founding a mission school in the hinterland was not easy. DeLaney and other NBC-USA female missionaries went "into bush areas, cleared the ground, drove down stakes, and began work for the Lord." Within two years, DeLaney succeeded in clearing the land, erecting an "iron" mission house, and establishing a school. By 1918 there were three buildings, including a girl's dormitory, a boy's cottage, and a one-room building that served as a chapel and school. Since Suehn was not near any other missions or missionaries, it was literally isolated in the bush.

Liberia was dependent on Germany for transporting mail and freight. Germany controlled all but one of the large trading places in Monrovia. The outbreak of World War I in August 1914, pitting Germany and Austria-Hungary against the Allied powers of England, France, and Russia, created havoc in Liberia. Germany closed all of its business places in Monrovia, making it difficult for the Americo-Liberians and foreign missionaries to obtain foodstuffs and basic necessities. German blockades later prohibited passage of English and French ships bound for Sierra Leone and Central Africa, preventing the shipment of munitions and other goods to European colonies in Africa. The Americo-Liberians and American and European missionaries, dependent on foreign trade, were literally starved out. DeLaney desperately needed the shipments of medicine and utensils and teaching and other materials sent by the NBC-USA Woman's Convention and other donors. News of the war did not reach the interior until a month after it had begun, so by the time DeLaney sent a messenger to Monrovia it was almost impossible to obtain basic foodstuffs, and available goods had doubled in price. Her primary concern was feeding the children on the mission. After struggling so hard to convince villagers to place their children there, she feared sending them home to their villages where they would revert to traditional patterns of African life and once again become "heathens."

Nyasaland was only a primer for what DeLaney experienced in Liberia. In 1916, during the unrest caused by World War I, she reiterated that "this is a very hard field, and being the first mission in this part of the interior, it requires time, patience, and means, before we can see great results. Christianity has not been brought to this section, hence Mohammedanism is very strong." DeLaney's observations were accurate. The Muslims constituted about one-fourth of the Liberian population, and they were highly concentrated in the hinterland. Protestants represented little more than one-tenth of the total Liberian population of roughly two and a quarter million people. Lacking knowledge about the overall makeup of the Liberian population and its geographical distribution, DeLaney had not anticipated the level of resistance she found in Montserrado. Whereas the Mandingoes had initially greeted her warmly, three years later they were countering her efforts to convert the villagers to Christianity. For example, one Sunday in early 1916, when an African worker at Suehn attempted to hold a church service in a village, the villagers formed a mob and drove them out. Moreover, they refused to even allow the missionaries to hold the services outside of the village. DeLaney noted, "We have often had them [Muslims] to absent themselves from the service, but have never had an open attack yet." She repeated her vow to stay the course, because "to close the door on the [children] here simply means that the devil will open his in the Gree Gree Bush, the Devil Bush, or the Mohammedans will get their hands on them. When I remember this, I forget [that] I am [the] only one with everything to look after."

As the war progressed, conditions deteriorated, and famine loomed over Liberia, DeLaney was forced to send fifty-five of the eighty-four students back to their villages. Within a year, as the situation worsened, DeLaney admitted that she was "on the verge of a nervous breakdown." She wrote that the incessant bouts with fever and the strain of being responsible for feeding and mothering such a large number of children were wearing her down. Suffering from sheer exhaustion, she requested a furlough. However, Lewis G. Jordan, secretary of the NBC-USA Foreign Mission Board, asked that she remain at the mission until a replacement could be found.

October 1918 found DeLaney uneasy about the growing threat of civil war among the ethnic groups in Montserrado, and more desperate than ever to leave Suehn. She reported that the people "are very excited over the prospect of war and are taking their children from the school. They are hiding and running from place to place." When DeLaney refused to give the children up, their parents stole them away. Moreover, she said, "The Country Devil told the villagers that he was going 'to eat the mission.'" DeLaney responded that he would have to "eat her first." Though she thought the Africans were simply trying to frighten her, just in case they meant business she was "well

Native Devil Parade at Vai Village in Liberia, West Africa, in the early twentieth century

armed" and prepared to defend herself and the mission. DeLaney wrote that the Africans did not know how strong her "conjure" might be. "Humanly speaking, I am not leaving a stone unturned that I can think will tide me over if any attack is made on us." Fearing an assault, she notified the Liberian secretary of the interior of the situation. The government informed the local chiefs that they would be held responsible "if anything whatsoever happens to Miss DeLaney and her mission."

Having spent almost eight long and hard years in Liberia, Emma DeLaney returned to the United States on April 17, 1920. Reflecting on those years, she said, "The fight was long, the battle fierce, but never so hot that I wanted to retreat. Disease, famine, and war all followed in rapid succession." DeLaney stressed "that no one can imagine what it meant for a lone individual to have existed as teacher, preacher, mother, doctor, builder, nurse, and farmer, the bread winner as well as the one to direct the making of it, and to be everywhere present at almost the same time." DeLaney spent the last two years of her life speaking and raising funds to support her dream of a chain of mission schools located in the interior of Liberia. In 1922 she became ill with hematuria fever, a virulent form of malaria—"her African heritage"—and died. For those who followed her, DeLaney's story became the stuff of legend.

Foreign Mission Work After 1920

BY 1920 MORE WOMEN than men were seeking foreign missionary positions. In the twentieth century many married women went to Africa with their husbands as missionaries. Though they are frequently referred to as "missionary wives," quite a few Baptist women, including Ella May Howard Caston, Emma F. Butler, and Elizabeth Coles Bouey, were bona fide, highly trained and paid missionaries. Viewing themselves as career missionaries, single women such as Lula E. Cooper, Sarah Williamson, and Ruth G. Morris felt that God had called them to do missionary work in Africa.

Though Suehn was a veritable showcase for exceptional missionaries, after 1925 it was Sarah Williamson who became the shining star. A native of Norfolk, Virginia, a graduate of the Hampton Institute and the Rochester Theological Seminary, and Girl Reserve secretary at the Dayton, Ohio, YWCA, at the age of twenty-four Williamson felt called to do missionary work in Africa. Her first appointment, in 1924, was at the Bible Industrial School in Fortsville, Grand Bassa. In 1925, barely recovered from an attack of malaria, she received a cable from Dr. James East, secretary of the NBC-USA Foreign Mission Board, stating, "Rush and save Suehn." Arriving at Suehn, Williamson found the mission abandoned. The buildings were near collapse, the road to the mission littered with dead trees, and the grounds reclaimed by the bush. Already in bad shape when DeLaney departed in 1920, by 1925 the site had fallen into almost total disrepair. Williamson "hated to leave" the Grand Bassa mission, but "because of orders I obeyed and went." Located in the interior and surrounded by hundreds of villages and small towns, Suehn was a far more difficult place to work than Grand Bassa. Given the tropical climate and the NBC-USA's limited resources, Williamson decided that the denomination "would never be able to send enough missionaries to Africa to Christianize, civilize, and educate even a tribal section of Liberia." The need was to build a school where girls and boys might receive training similar to that offered at the Tuskegee and Hampton Institute and be educated beyond an elementary level.

Williamson's success in transforming Suehn into the single most important NBC-USA mission on the continent of Africa was due to several factors: her education, tact, eloquence, administrative and organizational capability, physical attractiveness, and Hampton Institute connections. In contrast to DeLaney, who was very dark complexioned and heavy-set, Williamson was light skinned, slim, and by the beauty standards of the day considered very pretty. DeLaney also lacked the contacts and support of the black elite. Though she received support from the Woman's Convention, she was never able to garner the level of financial support from the black middle and upper classes, white philanthropists, or the denomination's foreign mission board that Williamson did. While on furlough, Williamson conducted financial campaigns, lecturing at churches throughout the United States. Aside from other contributions, the returns from her lectures averaged more than a thousand dollars per month. According to Dr. East, many missionaries were perhaps as educated and well spoken as Williamson, but they kept the money from the lectures and often claimed that the board owed them more. The Hampton Institute brought Williamson into contact with prominent alumni and established black and white leaders and philanthropists, such as Hattie M. Strong and Harper Sibley, some of whom would later aid her efforts at Suehn. Unlike DeLaney, after the initial shock of finding that the conditions in Africa were beyond description and impossible to capture in words or even in photographs, instead of constantly complaining about the horrible conditions, dire poverty and suffering, and "uncivilized heathens," she wrote positive letters that often praised the denomination for its support and illustrated the actual progress of the mission and plans for further development.

More missionaries were assigned by Dr. East to Suehn than to any of the other Baptist missions in Africa. He also ensured that the Suehn missionary salaries were paid on time. The paramount chief and other villagers sensed Williamson's humility and dedication to helping them, and unlike the situation with DeLaney never felt challenged or threatened by her presence. Williamson rarely made disparaging comments about African culture in her published letters. Even more interesting, the Africans did not refer to Williamson as a "God Mammy," but, rather, as "God Sister." (Perhaps she did not fit their definition of a mammy and they viewed her more as a sister, not a mother figure.) In 1932, Williamson ended her first tour of duty in Liberia and returned to the United States to marry Matthew Shields, a Dayton attorney, and head up the newly created NBC-USA Women's Missionary Department, organized as a stopgap to meet the mission board's funding needs during the Great Depression.

Williamson's role in developing and administering the NBC-USA's most successful black mission in Africa led to suggestions that she should succeed the recently deceased Dr. James East as the secretary of the Foreign Mission Board. However, the male clergy favored a man. In 1940 she accepted a missionary appointment to South Africa. Returning to the foreign field, Williamson criticized the denomination, especially the clergy and local churches for their lack of support of foreign missions. She wrote, "It is serious business when whole areas of missionary territory are abandoned as in Liberia, Nigeria, Gold Coast, West Africa. . . . To what phase of our missionary work are you going to dedicate more of your thought, time and money?" In part, Williamson's criticism was related to the lagging support of Rev. Joseph H. Jackson, secretary of the Foreign Mission Board, for her work in South Africa. Jackson had no intention of embellishing Williamson's already stellar credentials. He was well aware that Williamson's name had been put forth in 1934 for the position he now occupied.

Though the NBC-USA Foreign Mission Board wanted women to accompany their missionary husbands and be helpmates, many had other goals. As more females journeyed to Africa, in particular Liberia, and became highly visible as educators and medical missionaries and in evangelistic roles, they were seen as a threat to the masculine image of African missionary work. In 1929, Dr. East, as editor of the *Mission Herald*, voiced his concern that more women than men were "leaping into the ocean of heathen darkness to rescue perishing souls." Moreover, East proclaimed, "[I]t is to our everlasting disgrace, as a group, that at this present day we cannot count fifteen ordained ministers of male missionaries who are engaged in the rescue of these perishing people." Black Baptist leaders had real cause to be alarmed. Whereas Methodists, Pentecostals, and women from many religious traditions were found in a number of capacities as evangelists and ordained preachers, Baptist women rarely were. They could choose to work with the various women's conventions and auxiliaries and as domestic field-workers, but some Baptist women sought what they perceived as more challenging roles. Foreign mission work offered a range of possibilities, including the opportunity to travel, explore new lands and cultures, and broaden one's experience.

Foreign missionaries, similar to black women in all professions, were always in competition with black men for employment. Unlike white men, educated black men had limited professional opportunities. This, as well as the prevailing nineteenth- and early-twentieth-century views regarding a woman's place, was an important factor in the preference of black male clergy for missionary positions. In the nineteenth century the missionary was considered to be a member of an "elite corps." If the position provided an elevation in status for white men, it might be seen as a pinnacle for a black man. Thus, men such as Alexander Crummell and Charles S. Morris sought and were sought after for missionary service. In the twentieth century many males of the caliber desired by black religious denominations found more lucrative employment opportunities in the United States and increasingly rejected the offers for service in Africa.

As it became more difficult to recruit black males, denominations made every effort to place men in charge of the missions, with women working in subordinate positions. However, for the Baptists, this too was problematic. Because of the superior education and experience of the women at some missions—such as Suehn—it was not easy for denominations to enforce this rule. It was no secret why women with an intense religious commitment chose missionary work—lacking the professional opportunities available to their male counterparts and excluded from holding leadership roles in the religious polity, many gravitated toward this kind of service. As missionaries in foreign fields, women like DeLaney had considerable authority. Sheer distance and the lag in communications from male-dominated mission boards granted women a significant degree of independence. In Africa, female missionaries regularly held evangelistic services. At stations such as Suehn they were the teachers, evangelists, nurses, doctors, and dentists.

The issue of staffing African missions was not limited to women. Among black Methodists—the AME and AME Zion—it was understood that bishops would head up the African American episcopal districts, and that the male clergy would oversee the churches and mission stations. In accordance with church practice, wives served as teachers and supervisors of African women. Cultural clashes, as well as exclusion of Africans from leadership roles, forced mission boards to grapple with charges of paternalism and issues of dominance that reeked of discrimination. Albeit for different reasons, white and black missionaries and foreign boards in the late nineteenth century argued that African youth should be sent to Europe and the United States and educated in denominational colleges and universities to become missionaries to their people. African girls and boys—such as Charlotte Manye, Charles Dube, Delia Rudolph Sisusa, Adelaide Tantsi, James Aggrey,

Frank Ato Osam Pinanko, Charity Zomelo, Anna Ruth Malekebu, Daniel Malekebu, Flora Ethelwyn Zeto, and Amanda Mason—came from many places in Africa, including South Africa, the Belgian Congo, Nigeria, Nyasaland, and Liberia, to study at black colleges. They were enrolled at a number of black institutions such as Wilberforce, Livingstone, Spelman, the Hampton Institute, Benedict College, Lincoln University, and the National Training School for Girls and Women. Upon their return to their homeland, most African students became missionaries, ministers, and teachers. Daniel Malekebu, Robert Sisusa, and a few others became medical doctors. Osam Pinanko was among those who sought leadership positions in the AME and AME Zion African conferences. Under colonization, European denominations regularly placed Africans in charge of missions.

During the 1920s and '30s African repatriates often criticized the churches for failing to heed the demand for African bishops and to elevate African missionaries to positions of leadership in African conferences. For many Africans the tendency of mostly Methodist denominations to favor African American leadership over that of Africans was a form of discrimination. On the other hand, most black American Methodist leaders argued that as the administration of African missions was centralized in the United States and overseen by an American bishop, there was no need for African bishops. In the heat of the debates, AME Zion Bishop William Matthews contended that because of "certain tribal conditions," Africa should remain under American supervision. In many places, Africans were in charge of the day-to-day operation of Methodist missions. The wives of African clergy served as presidents of the women's missionary societies. Bishops usually resided in the United States and rarely visited the churches under their supervision.

Throughout the early twentieth century denominations debated the question of whether bishops should pay yearly or quadrennial visits to Africa. Concern about how the funds they raised were being managed also led the women's missionary societies and their leaders to conduct fact-finding tours of their mission stations. The central problem was money. Strapped for funds to finance domestic and foreign mission work—in particular to build, operate, and maintain African churches, missions, schools, and homes for girls, and to pay the salaries of African missionaries—few denominations relished the expense of having either field supervisors or resident bishops who required regularized travel to African episcopal districts. However, as more African students returned to the homeland, the demand for local leadership increased in all African countries where missions existed, but especially in South Africa, Nyasaland, and other nations that excluded African Americans. Even worse, some Africans abandoned the black Methodist churches and created independent institutions. Others joined white Methodist missions. For example, Charity Zomelo, a young African from Keta, East Gold Coast, West Africa, who was raised and educated in the United States by Rev. Florence Spearing Randolph, upon returning home refused to teach in the poorly supported AME Zion Mission School and joined the white Methodist mission.

In 1933, in a scathing critique of black denominations, AME Bishop E. D. W. Jones argued that black churches were supporting too many enterprises, most of which were poorly funded and operated. He warned that continuance of these churches' destructive competition with each other would limit black progress. Citing the numerous denominational publications that competed with black secular weeklies that were "printing more church news than church papers," "too many poor schools," and foreign missions that were "just existing" with "poorly paid missionaries in Africa," Jones asserted that denominations needed to stop carrying their "fanatical differences to Africa" and "dividing Africa into denominational factionalism" and work collaboratively for the good of the race. What Africa needed was "a united Negro America . . . the entire Negro American Christian United Church . . . behind Africa as one." Jones concluded that the foreign mission projects were "far more costly than is justified by the good accomplished."

After 1930, under pressure, the AME and AME Zion denominations appointed Africans to leadership positions in foreign conferences. The experience of attending black colleges and universities, exposure to the teachings of Marcus Moziah Garvey, Pan-Africanism, and the African American struggle for civil rights in general impacted generations of African students, some of whom developed a new racial consciousness and visions of Africans participating in local and world affairs in their homelands. African students were exposed to new ideas and political movements that propelled them to embrace the burgeoning ideas of African nationalism. Many students were inspired to become involved in secular politics, and in doing so aided the politicization of future generations. African students in Europe were influenced by the political currents of the time, in particular European and African intellectuals in Europe. Embracing the doctrine of self-determination and espousing nationalism, African intellectuals who came of age between 1930 and 1960—an era of decolonization and post-World War II African liberation movements—gave voice to the mounting aspirations for freedom and independence.

World War II and the establishment of the United Nations had the effect of altering the power relations among nations. The dominance of Third World nations in the UN Security Council gave people of color a powerful voice in foreign affairs and hastened the downfall of European colonialism. However, of the twenty-four resolutions passed at the UN in 1945, only three were against race slavery in colonial territories and peonage in the American South—and Great Britain, having dominion over two-thirds of all people of color in the world, managed to insert a clause that stated, "[T]here shall be no domestic interference against the nations represented at the 'Peace Table,' in their colonies." This clause provided a loophole for continued European domination of Africans and others. Walter White, W. E. B. Du Bois, and Mary McLeod Bethune, the only black American representatives admitted to the 1945 UN founding convention, pledged to fight for the removal of the clause. Linking the freedom of black Americans in the U.S. with that of Africans, they were determined to continue the struggle to end colonialism. At the same time, given the status of most Africans, they recognized the need for continued mission work.

In 1950 the Africa Committee of the Foreign Missions Conference of North America, an interracial group comprising a diverse group of scholars, journalists, and representatives of foreign mission boards, met to map out plans for a survey of social, economic, and political conditions in Africa as the prospect and reality of decolonization became apparent. The committee's main concern was to determine the actual status of African missions and the denominations' plans for continuing their foreign mission work in Africa. The ACFMC had long been aware of the soaring nationalism and demands for self-government in Nigeria and other British colonies. Widespread unrest was manifest not only in Africa, but "in the attitudes of African students in Europe and America. Labor conditions in the Gold Coast, race riots in South Africa and in other parts of the continent [could no longer] be ignored by the missions."

Surveying the plight of the AME Zion's missionary field in 1955,

Bishop William J. Walls called for the Board of Foreign Missions to take action and shore up its African missions. Walls pointed out that except for one bishop, the denomination did not have a single American missionary in Africa. The AME Zion Church's call for men and women to teach in the AME Zion's secondary schools fell on deaf ears. The church was even in danger of losing control of the Aggrey Memorial Zion College at Brafo Yaw near Cape Coast, Ghana. If that were not enough, Walls pointed out that "no systematic effort [was] being made to train young people to carry on the work of the Church." Dr. J. W. DeGraft Johnson, an African and the denomination's legal adviser and attorney, warned that failure to address these pressing needs might mean that the church would "be compelled to competition and inanition to close down shop and retreat from the field." Johnson argued that under the circumstances, it was "a perfect disgrace to the cause of Zion." He questioned the lack of interest in foreign mission work and intimated that were it not for the white churches, Africa might be left to "grope in the dark." In recognition of the criticism and to shore up its mission work in Africa, in 1960 the AME Zion Church elected Rev. Solomon Dorme Larte of Monrovia, Liberia, as its first African bishop. Bishop Larte presided over Liberia until 1968, when he became the episcopal supervisor of the entire AME Zion Church work in Africa, a position he held until his death in 1969.

For years Claude Barnett, editor of the *Chicago Defender* and a member of the ACFMC, had given extensive coverage to African affairs, particularly issues regarding the role of religion in missions, and he critiqued the programs of white and black religious organizations. African Americans during the late nineteenth century did not have the same access to information on Africa as they did in the twentieth century. As a result of the Great Migration, several national newspapers were spawned and others such as the *Baltimore Afro-American* expanded to address the needs of a burgeoning urban black population. First published in 1912, by 1920 the *Chicago Defender* was widely read in the United States and abroad. It was known for its in-depth and critical analysis of racism as well as sexism.

Etta Moten Barnett, a noted actress and a prominent member of the AME Church and the Alpha Kappa Alpha Sorority, was an influential and highly respected figure among African Americans. As the wife of Claude Barnett and an acknowledged social activist, Etta Barnett gained entry to church councils and spoke out on many issues. In 1947, in a speech before the AME Women's Missionary Society, she was highly critical of the AME missions in Liberia, Sierra Leone, and the Gold Coast. At the same time, Claude Barnett secretly advised women leaders on what to say in articles for publication in the *Chicago Defender*. For example, in 1947 he informed Christine S. Smith, "What you want to do is to point out the backwardness of the church in its business relationship, the obtuseness of the bishops. . . . Too, there is the matter of their absolute failure to do a decent job in missions. If some analysis were made of what really happens to mission money, it would be revealing. I sent a reporter to Dr. [Leonidas] Berry [AME secretary of foreign missions], but he did not give us the information desired." Barnett made reference to allegations that bishops misused foreign mission funds and diverted them to other causes.

As a team, Claude and Etta Moten Barnett exerted their power and constantly brought attention to the plight of African Americans and people of color throughout the world. In exchange for publicizing their achievements and organizational programs, Claude Barnett prodded the leaders of black women's missionary organizations to provide him with insider data on their denominations' foreign programs. In this manner, he was able to obtain much valuable information for publication. In 1950 Annie Heath, president of the AME Women's Missionary Society, informed him that the AME Church had not had a bishop in South Africa for at least a decade, and that it had been years since a bishop and his wife had occupied the episcopal residence in West Africa. Exposing the problems inherent in the foreign mission programs of white and black denominations encouraged groups such as the Episcopal and Methodist bishops and the NBC-USA to take a hard look at their mission work and make improvements. In 1950 Barnett acknowledged that all of these groups were "right on the job and [were] developing wonderful work. . . . The AME work lags way at the end of the procession, but it's better than it was three years ago. . . . AME Missions raise money. The trouble lies in the administration."

African Missions in the Post-Colonial Era

THE END OF European colonialism impacted the traditional relationships between foreign missionaries and Africans. By 1960 indigenous African missionaries were in the majority on the continent. Colonialism left the African continent in a state of near social, political, and economic devastation. Poverty, disease, and ignorance abounded. Lacking the requisite fiscal and human resources required to make a seamless shift from colonization to modernization was difficult. During the 1950s and '60s Africans celebrated their newfound freedom and African Americans took great pride in their African heritage. By the early 1960s African American cultural nationalism could be seen in the adoption of natural hairstyles, African fashions, dances, naming patterns, and an embracement of everything African. It was a special moment in the history of African Americans when the slogan "Black Is Beautiful" became a mantra to celebrate black skin color and challenge those who valued a light complexion and straight hair over a dark skin and nappy hair. In the euphoria of the moment, many African Americans anticipated African nations reclaiming their glorious heritage and prospering. Few suspected that within less than two decades many African nations would be wracked by civil wars, poverty, unimaginable devastation, and a death-dealing disease such as AIDS.

With the elimination of most formal colonial systems, the question most black denominations confronted was how to justify and maintain foreign missionary programs that required great outlays of capital. The black Baptist, Methodist, Pentecostal, and other foreign mission programs were never well supported or funded. In fact, given the multiplicity of programs sponsored by black denominations, including churches, schools, camps, and domestic missionary work, and the paucity of financial resources at their disposal, it was a sheer miracle that they accomplished as much as they did.

Recognizing the dominance of African missionary leadership and the demands for self-determination, George Napoleon Collins, as bishop in the Eighteenth Episcopal District, advised the AME Church in 1963 to change its outlook and policy on African missions. Being pragmatic, he recommended that the denomination conduct "serious study and meditation on the plight of the AME Church in a changing Africa." Collins argued for the establishment of a "clearing house" in Africa to oversee and finance African missions, the organization of an African bishops' council, and the founding of an African general board—all of which would function as subsidiaries of the parent boards. Centralizing African mission work in Africa under African control would mean that church literature would be printed in the languages and dialects of the various ethnic groups and better facilitate AME evangelization efforts.

Collins felt that the clearinghouse or African mission center would "render incalculable service" by employing Africans and properly training them for the jobs. The old policy of sending a few African students to the United States for training was slow and costly. The need was to build a "strong theological center"—an AME college, staffed with teachers from Africa and the U.S.—and to educate missionaries in Africa, not America. Collins warned, "[T]his may not be what some of us would like to hear and believe, but there is no way of separating the struggle for civil autonomy from that of religious autonomy. They both go hand in hand, and there is no-good reason for us to try to avoid seeing it by burying our heads in the sand." Collins was concerned about the AME Church's indifference toward the uprisings and unrest in the Congo and other parts of Africa in the early 1960s. In a rather pointed critique of AME patronage, he argued that the church must send qualified bishops to all foreign mission fields. Education and preaching ability were not enough; bishops and their wives needed to possess a certain "spirit, zeal, mind-set, attitude, adaptability, reverence, and devotion to the charge."

Collins offered the unvarnished truth about the actual situation in Africa. The picture he painted was not as rosy as that regularly fed to the denomination through the reports about the activities of AME bishops and their wives in Africa. The problems described by Collins could easily be imputed to the Baptist and other black denominations that lacked the wherewithal to address the pressing issues of the times. In 1976, AME historian Rev. Howard D. Gregg frankly stated, "Our entire missionary enterprise, especially in the foreign fields, should be restudied and perhaps restructured." Gregg reiterated much of what Collins had said at least a decade earlier. Specifically referring to the African Episcopal districts, Gregg noted that the AME Church boasted of five "so-called missionary areas," two of which were in South Africa, and one each in West Africa, Central Africa, South America, and the West Indies. "Candor suggests that we recognize as a Church certain difficulties in our missionary enterprise. First and foremost is our poverty as a Church. . . . At the present time and in the foreseeable future the AME Church does not have the funds to adequately support its work in foreign fields." Bishops appointed to each of these districts rarely resided in or even went to Africa. This pattern of neglect fueled the long-standing demands of Africans for indigenous leadership. To this long list of issues Gregg added that bishops and their wives were often ill-trained to assume responsibility as supervisors of African episcopal districts.

Like the AME Church, the NBC-USA and AME Zion denominations also evaluated the fiscal and programmatic needs of their mission programs during the 1960s and considered making adjustments in their methods. However, very little substantive change was made either in their attitudes about Africa and Africans or in their methods. Overly biased views regarding the need for conversion to Christianity and the elimination of traditional African cultural practices continued. Denominational efforts to bring education and medicine to the continent also continued. Though a denomination might admit that its missionary program was lacking in many respects, few were willing to totally abandon the enterprise. As entities that competed with each other and sought respect from whites, black denominations were reluctant to follow that course. The leaders of the NBC-USA, AME, and AME Zion churches simply acknowledged problems of finance and waning interest in foreign missions.

During the Civil Rights Movement, mission boards experienced even greater difficulty in raising funds for foreign missions. Symbolic of the times, to dramatize the critical need for financial aid some institutions—such as the Canaan Baptist Church in Philadelphia—adopted catchy slogans: "A Penny a Day Keeps the Witch Doctor Away." However, some leaders thought that it was not just the witch doctor who needed to be feared, but the growing power of Islam. One Baptist missionary observed that the postcolonial era was "a very dangerous period in the development of Africa." Of particular importance was the growing concern about the relationship of African independence to Christianity and education. There was a need to teach Africans how to use the Bible for solving problems in their daily lives as well as political difficulties. Though Islam had been present in Africa for centuries, decolonization accelerated its growth. The missionary asserted that, "faced with Islam's confidence in the Koran, the unsure, halting Christians, particularly . . . in West Africa—are falling back."

Having focused for decades on a program of expansion, in 1964 William J. Harvey, the head of the NBC-USA Foreign Mission Board, admitted that the denomination was facing a challenge "unlike any it has faced in the last twenty-five years." As he explained, because of prior emphasis on expansion, little attention was paid to general maintenance of buildings and facilities, and recruitment of missionaries was increasingly difficult. In line with the overall NBC-USA policy stressed by President Joseph H. Jackson, Harvey also articulated the pressing need for the masculinization of all Baptist mission work, both domestic and foreign. The flagship mission station at Suehn, expertly operated by an all-female staff, would require major renovation at a cost of approximately $300,000. In South Africa, fifteen churches, at a cost of at least $250,000, were needed to replace those demolished by the government when Group Area laws created apartheid and mandated separate residential places for Africans. Other African and South American missions required attention as well, and new methods were sought to resolve the problems. Whereas in 1960 white and black denominations had feared that the burgeoning Peace Corps could cause the destruction of the African mission enterprise, by 1963 Baptist missionaries such as Mattie Mae Davis, principal of the Suehn Industrial Mission, realized the importance of acquiring Peace Corps teachers to "lighten the load" of understaffed mission stations. The addition of two white Peace Corps couples to the mission proved to be a boon to the financially strapped NBC-USA Foreign Mission Board.

In the 1960s, Edra Mae Hilliard, supervisor of the AME Zion Church's WHFMS foreign mission work, described Nigeria and Ghana as nations with millions of indigenous people who lived in the interior. Hilliard asserted that the first concern was "to accept the challenge of the 'need for education' " and to erect churches to support student enrollment. For Hilliard the success of the AME Zion's missionary program could readily be seen. She proudly noted that formerly impassable village roads were now paved with "asphalt and composite"; clay and thatch-roofed buildings were replaced by cement and steel; witchcraft was being supplanted by clinics and hospitals; public school education was becoming compulsory; and opportunity abounded for girls as well as boys. For her, civilization was triumphing! However, Hilliard failed to point out that traditional patterns of African life prevailed in vast areas of these nations. She and her colleagues maintained the denomination's earlier vision of spreading Christianity and "civilization."

Similar to the Baptist and AME women's associations, the AMEZ-WHFMS's missionary projects in the 1960s and '70s were extensions of their traditional programs. For the AME-WHFMS this meant education—scholarships to prepare "young men" for the ministry, a professorship of missionary education at Livingstone College, a student-loan program, and the "Second Mile Offering Project," for miscellaneous domestic and foreign activities. By 1970, the Nigerian government had taken over the operation and support of all public education at the elementary and high school levels, and most of the AME, AME Zion, and Baptist schools in Liberia were receiving government aid. However, these denominations continued to support schools in Ghana, Angola, and South Africa.

At the end of more than a century of foreign missionary work in Africa, most Methodist and Baptist denominations acknowledged the deficiencies in their programs, especially their inability to raise the level of funding required to maintain and operate quality schools. However, the churches, run by mostly Africans, continued to seek new converts and extol the virtues of Christianity. For African American religionists these institutions represented their "personal symbolism of love," evidence of their ties to people they considered "kith and kin," and brought the respect for their denominations that they had craved.

CHAPTER 5

"Righteous Guidance"

Religion and Politics

[T]he obstacle that is thrown in [church women's] way is prejudice. Yes, a prejudice against them. But it is the same prejudice that does not allow women to have political suffrage. The same that objects to women being anything but housekeepers or butterflies.

Rev. Nicholas B. Stewart (1898)

The Negro woman inherited the ballot. The inheritance of a large fortune carries with it temptations and dangers. The prodigal son, dazzled by sudden riches, spent his life in riotous living; he squandered his birthright. We said to [the Woman's Convention] in our last annual report that Negro women by their silence did as much to hasten the enfranchisement of women as did the white women by their activity. We kept comparatively quiet because our activity would have muddled the waters and delayed the happy consummation of a long struggle.

Nannie H. Burroughs (1921)

Now, politics is one form of public activity that needs righteous guidance. To urge this is the work assumed by the Suffrage Department of [the Woman's] Convention. Our object is A Christian Polity with a Christian Policy. Our aim is to re-create in the church a keen interest in the political affairs of the community, the state and the nation. . . . [T]he interpretation of suffrage which interests us most [is] the right or power to participate in electing public officials, and adopting or rejecting legislation. . . . Jim Crow laws do not express the wish of the majority of the citizens of those states where they are in force; but they are the expressed will of the few who schemed and got them on the statutes of their states. The anti-lynching bill is not the will of the few who believe in mob violence, the Ku Klux Klan; but it expresses the will of the majority, the will of all true American citizens, and will go upon the federal statutes, if we do our duty.

Gertrude Rush (1922)

Frances Ellen Watkins Harper, abolitionist and feminist reformer. Raised in the African Methodist Episcopal Church, she later affiliated with the Lutheran Church, a hotbed for abolitionists and political activists.

WOMEN'S MISSIONARY ORGANIZATIONS and conventions and ministers' and bishops' wives associations were hotbeds for political activists. Methodists, Baptists, Presbyterians, Episcopalians, Bahá'í, and Catholics all had their share of black club women who were active in the NACW, the WCTU, the YWCA, the NAACP, the League of Women Voters, and the Urban League at the local, state, and national levels. Suffrage and political study clubs, the National League of Colored Republican Women, and other politically oriented organizations were led by women who were also leaders in their denominations, and by 1900 most church women's organizations were engaged in social reform. Irrespective of their religious affiliations, many leaders engaged in some form of political activity within their communities and their secular and religious associations. However, the Baptist Woman's Convention was the most politically active of all the church women's organizations. As a group, the WC was not as active in the women's interracial church movement as AME and AME Zion women. This was in part related to their relationships with white Baptist women's organizations such as the American Baptist Home Mission Society and the Woman's Missionary Union. Between 1880 and 1960 the WC maintained a biracial relationship with the northern-based ABHMS. In the 1930s, the WC established a similar relationship with white women in the Southern Baptist WMU. The WMU provided financial aid, material support, and volunteer services for southern black women's education and various WC projects.

When women gained the vote in 1920, Nannie Helen Burroughs told the members of the Woman's Convention that it was a victory for black women, who were equal partners with white women in the struggle for women's suffrage. Burroughs revealed that African American women leaders had made a conscious decision not to conduct an organized national protest against white women's organizations that excluded them from the movement, and against congressmen who argued that black women were undeserving of the franchise. Anxious to add the ballot to their arsenal of social justice weapons, Burroughs suggested that black women leaders had carefully calculated their strategy to achieve the desired result of suffrage for women.

African American women recognized the connection between race and suffrage and realized that without the ballot their ability to influence government policy would be minimal, and the economic and material survival of African Americans would be placed in jeopardy. For black feminists, suffrage was a "political vehicle" useful for obtaining broad freedoms. As a theoretical concept it undergirded their resistance to multiple oppressions, including racism, sexism, economic and political exploitation, and lynching. In 1866 at the American Equal Rights Association meeting, Sojourner Truth and Frances Ellen Watkins Harper had argued, albeit for different reasons, in favor of women's suffrage. In 1873, Harper, speaking before the American Woman Suffrage Association, declared that as "much as white women need the ballot, colored women need it more." This rationale would be reiterated by black women suffragists for many years. Between 1850 and 1920, black women participated in suffrage activities at the local and regional levels. For example, forty-three black women, mostly professional women and Howard University students, participated in the 1913 suffrage parade held in Washington, D.C., and a small number affiliated with the AWSA and the National Woman Suffrage Association. Ida Wells-Barnett, through her own volition, forced her way into the parade and marched with the all-white Illinois Equal Suffrage Association delegation. Thus, African American women believed that the ratification of the Nineteenth Amendment was as much a victory for black women as it was for white women.

In 1894 Fannie Barrier Williams noted that black women in several western states possessed "fragmentary suffrage." By this she meant that women were being granted token suffrage in a number of areas. Williams said that in Chicago women were "getting a taste of politics." The Illinois state legislature granted women the right to vote for trustees at the state university. Women were nominated by the Republican and Democratic parties and an election was held. Williams emphasized that although these were nonpartisan offices, suffragists availed themselves of the opportunity to pursue the political process. As white suffragists eagerly solicited their votes, Williams cautioned black women not to be put "in the humiliating position of being loved only for the votes we have." Williams argued that black women should question the sincerity of white women, who had always "scorned our ambitions and held themselves aloof from us in all our struggles of advancement." She advised black women to work with "the best" white women "inside or outside of party lines" and use the franchise to force white women's candidates and women party managers "to relent their cruel opposition to our girls and women in the matter of employment and the enjoyment of civil privileges," and never to forget that the exclusion of black women and girls from places of "respectable employment is due mostly to the meanness of American women." Williams's assessment represented the common consensus of most black women leaders, who understood the ambivalent nature of their relationships and work with white women and knew that the struggle for equality and justice would not be easy.

Religion was not viewed by black women as a barrier to political involvement. African American women leaders reasoned that as Christians it was their duty to see that justice was done, and there was no better way to do that than to become involved in politics. After all, as Gertrude Rush, a prominent attorney from Des Moines, Iowa, and the chair of the WC's Suffrage Department, explained, "[P]olitics is one form of public activity that needs righteous guidance." In 1919, in an address before the Woman's Convention entitled "What the Ballot Can Do," Rush revealed that she had "joined [the] law to the gospel." As she explained, "The Ballot can save or destroy us; can regulate labor's hours; can get better wages; secure fair opportunities in business; regulate moral and sanitary conditions; secure better educational advantages; and wipe out all forms of discriminations; secure justice in the courts; and abolish lynch law." Rush concluded, "The Ballot when used religiously can make this country a democracy in reality, and not in name only."

Burroughs and Rush perceived politics as a major avenue through

As president of the Woman's Era Club, Josephine St. Pierre Ruffin
issued the call for the First National Conference of Colored Women,
which was held in Boston, July 1895.

which black women could impact American public policy and achieve
their gender and race goals. Years before women's suffrage became a
reality WC leaders argued that the vote would permit black women to
fight for the rights of African Americans and provide them protection
from abuse and male domination. WC leaders recognized that eliminating segregation, lynching, and the rape of black women was a matter of exerting political power through the use of the ballot and legal
redress in the courts. In Alabama, a white suffragist asked Burroughs,
"Why, what will colored women do with the ballot, if they get it?" Burroughs replied, "What could they do without it, if white women get
it?" Based on white women's history as slave mistresses, employers of
black domestic servants, and supporters of the so-called "southern
way of life," Burroughs and other black women leaders did not trust
them to speak and act on behalf of black women and their families.
Similarly, WC President S. Willie Layten argued that black women
"were self-supporting and independent so much longer than white
women . . . [and] the vote will mean more to them than to white
women." The issue of voting rights formed part of the WC agenda
from the beginning. Mary Mossell Griffin, a leading political operative
in Philadelphia, an activist Congregationalist, and the chair of the
NACW's Legislative Department during the 1920s, argued, "The
Afro-American woman had a two-fold purpose in view. The securing

of the ballot meant not only the future of the women of color in America, it also meant the correcting of many evils which if corrected would mean a new day for the American Negro." Thus, black church women saw no conflict between their acceptance of Christianity and their involvement in social reform and political activities.

In the 1870s the political agenda of black church women organizing at the local and national levels included an array of social reform activities defined as home missionary work. In the 1880s Methodist women, in particular, began to focus more intently on their rights within the church: ordination, suffrage, and equal representation in the denominational polity. As the times changed, so too did the needs of black women and the African American community. Traditionally black women's agenda has included a number of specific concerns, such as education, employment, housing, temperance, women's suffrage, rape, protection of women and children, prison reform, international affairs, lynching, peace, the poll tax, and voting rights. These and other concerns came into sharp focus by 1900 and continued throughout the twentieth century. From the antebellum period to the present, black women's agenda has, of necessity, included women's rights, civil rights—equal treatment under the law, and the elimination of segregation and discrimination in all areas of American life, including public accommodations. The aim of church and club women was to acquire and use power for the purpose of improving their lives and protecting their children, families, and communities. Major strategies for achieving their political goals included the ballot, networking in black and white organizations, and the use of organized protest to influence public policy.

The NACW, Religion, and the "New Woman" in the Public Sphere

DECADES BEFORE THE RATIFICATION of the Nineteenth Amendment, when confronted with widespread lynching, verbal attacks on "the virtue of black womanhood," exclusion from membership in mainstream white women's organizations, and a general deterioration in the economic, social, and political position of African Americans, black women founded the National Association of Colored Women. Assessing the political climate and the status of black Americans, Josephine St. Pierre Ruffin, president of the Boston Women's New Era Club, reasoned, "The time for resistance, wise resistance has come. Our hope for creating public sentiment grows dimmer and dimmer, and patience and humility have ceased to be virtues." From the beginning the NACW was a political entity with a specific agenda aimed at influencing public policy as it affected the status of black women and their families. Envisioned as an organization of black women's clubs throughout the nation, it consisted of a variety of groups, including religious and secular associations. Unlike organizations that focused on a single issue, the NACW incorporated an expansive agenda representing the multiple concerns of black women. As NACW historian Elizabeth Lindsay Davis explained, "[W]hen the [NACW] came into being in Washington, D.C., our women faced new conditions, differing from [those of] church and fraternal organizations." Davis alluded to a number of issues, including the challenges black women faced in their struggle to escape rape and forced seduction by white men, especially in the South, that had dominated the lives of enslaved women and continued after the Civil War.

As black women and men struggled to rebuild their lives and establish viable communities, they challenged traditional attitudes about black sexuality and called for legislation requiring white men to support the million or more mulatto children they had fathered. They recognized slavery as a destructive experience under which sexual exploitation of black women was common. It was a form of violence used to maintain social control and to break the will of enslaved men and women. W. E. B. Du Bois asserted that after the Civil War, "Negroes were still being threatened, women were prostitutes to their white owners. . . . The state and the government were aware of the mistreatment of Negroes in the South, but nothing was done to stop it." White men's control of black women's sexuality caused marital and familial instability, and engendered fear in the black community. Few whites were willing to acknowledge the practice. Rather, they blamed black women for their plight. With few exceptions, white journalists, as well as noted political and social leaders, led the movement to defend the South and white men's so-called "honor." The defense was frequently couched in terms that pitted the whites against blacks, challenged the credibility of all African Americans, and stripped black women of any claim to virtue.

The most famous and highly publicized statement of the white defense against these assertions was made in 1895 by John W. Jacks, a white editor and the president of the Missouri Press Association. Refuting Ida Wells-Barnett's charge that the majority of African Americans who were lynched were not rapists, Jacks claimed, "The Negroes in this country are wholly devoid of morality, the women are prostitutes and all Negroes are thieves and liars." Jacks's statement created a furor among African American women leaders, who felt that what was needed was an organization to speak "in defense of black womanhood." The national and international publication of the statement was the catalyst that led to the founding of the National Association of Colored Women. The NACW developed a multipronged strategy to address the gender and race stereotypes, improve the image of black womanhood, defend black women's virtue, and fight for African Americans' political and civil rights.

In 1895, the Boston Women's New Era Club organized the First National Conference of Colored Women, which brought together representatives of black women's organizations. Delegates to this meeting included a broad range of women's organizations, denominational groups, and interdenominational associations, such as the Woman's Christian Temperance Union and the King's Daughters. Methodist and Baptist women's organizations and individual churches sent delegates and letters of support to be read at the conference. Among the many leading church women supportive of the meeting were Eliza Gardner and Alice Felts. Gardner, a leader in the antebellum abolitionist movement, a member of the executive committee for the Massachusetts Woman's Suffrage Association, the founder of the AME Zion Woman's Home and Foreign Missionary Society, and an officer in the Women's New Era Club, was intimately involved in the planning and execution of the Boston meeting. Gardner was also a key figure in the AME Zion women's struggle to gain suffrage and lay rights in their denomination. Alice Felts was a prominent AME leader, suffragist, and outspoken proponent of church women's rights, and was involved in the pre-conference planning and submitted a paper entitled "Social Purity."

From the outset, black church women made clear their support for the founding of the NACW and clarified their political position on the controversial Jacks letter. Hannah Jones, a delegate representing "One Thousand Afro-American Women of Bethel AME Church in New York City," was said to have "attracted much attention" at the Boston meeting. In a letter addressed to the conference organizers, the AME women strategically aligned themselves as equals with other black women's organizations in the movement, and asserted the preeminence of black women's work among "the masses" prior to 1895. Stating that African American women "were actively at work . . . long before the base slanders, born in the vile mind of a common Missouri white man, were uttered," the AME women requested that the conference not give credence to the idea that the Jacks statement was the event that spurred black women to action, and that it not be the cause for defining their future work.

The AME women were quite accurate in their portrayal of black women's community work before 1895. Female church organizations, mutual aid associations, and secret societies were the forerunners of the independent black women's club movement. Women's clubs began in the antebellum period among free black women and developed rapidly after the Civil War, especially in the 1880s and '90s, as women banded together to support literary and charitable organizations, schools, day nurseries, orphanages, churches, homes for the elderly, cultural endeavors, and community improvements. During the early 1890s, black feminists in Washington, D.C., Kansas City, Missouri, Chicago, Toledo, Denver, Baltimore, St. Louis, and Charlotte established women's clubs. Eventually independent local organizations were organized into state and national federations. For example, the National League of Colored Women, formed in Washington, D.C., in 1892, was a coalition of 113 associations. Similarly, at the state level, the Maryland Federation of Christian Women brought together women's organizations. These groups formed the core of the National Association of Colored Women at its founding in 1896.

The Bethel AME Church women also vocalized their displeasure and concern about the behavior displayed by black men at their gatherings, and asked that the women meeting in Boston demonstrate to the world that there was a large constituent group of black women who were free from the impulsive and unpredictable "disposition" that was "the fatal defect" in black men's conventions. This criticism was obviously directed at both the religious and secular gatherings of black male leaders that excluded black women. By 1895 the resistance of AME women to male authority and domination, and their struggle to participate in the denomination's General Conference, was well known. The Boston gathering provided AME women an opportunity to demonstrate their power, publicize their protest, and send a message to male leaders that black women were on the move. One of the reasons the letter was signed "One Thousand Afro-American Women of Bethel AME Church" was to assert their power. In the conclusion, the AME women stressed that their work was "among the masses," and declared, "We can and will lend powerful support to such enterprises as promise true good to the race." Because the majority of AME women were poor and southern, and most of the "One Thousand" Bethel AME Church women were working-class women who labored as domestic servants and washerwomen, it was important to emphasize that the focus of their work was the "masses." Thus, their message to the elite leaders of the Boston Conference certified their solidarity with all black women, and at the same time reinforced their class concerns.

Also listed among the delegates to the Boston Conference were representatives of the Concord Baptist Church of Christ in Brooklyn, New York. To attract black church and fraternal women who often served as auxiliaries to organizations directed and controlled by men, and to allay fears of racial divisiveness, Josephine St. Pierre Ruffin carefully crafted the opening address she presented at the 1895 meeting. She proclaimed that the work of the organization also would include men, but she emphasized that the leadership and control would be centered in women. Ruffin asserted, "Our woman's movement is a woman's movement in that it is led and directed by women for the good of women and men, for the benefit of *all* humanity, which is more than any one branch or section of it. We want, we ask the active interest of our men, and, too, we are not drawing the color line; . . . we are not alienating or withdrawing, we are only coming to the front, willing to join any others in the same work and cordially inviting and welcoming any others to join us." As Florida Ruffin Ridley later explained, the conference organizers aimed to not only bring together "the outstanding women alone, but [appealed] for the support of the ordinary woman" also. Decades later Ridley described the movement as "bolder" and "more courageous" than women in the 1930s could imagine. Reflecting on the conditions faced by black women in the 1890s Ridley disclosed that "women's clubs were tabooed, ridiculed and discouraged by the majority of men," and that most clubs "were church and benevolent societies where women were generally allowed to cook the suppers and help raise the money to pay the men officers and heads."

In the aftermath of the Boston meeting, desiring to capitalize on the support of church women and anxious to have the backing of the powerful national church women's organizations, Margaret Murray Washington, the newly elected president of the National Federation of Afro-American Women, sent out a special appeal to the leaders of these organizations asking that they give their "hearty cooperation" to the movement. As Washington explained, "Any woman or body of women, after forming an organization . . . founded upon a definite plan of work for a definite purpose, and having a president, secretary and other officers, if needed, may become a part of our National Federation."

In December 1895 the first National Congress of Colored Women met in Georgia at the Atlanta Cotton States and International Exposition. Originally conceived as a feature of the Negro Department of the exposition, and designed as a forum for discussing issues of relevance to African American women, the Congress was actually an extension of the First National Conference of Colored Women. Black women's leaders representing twenty-six states and the District of Columbia elected Lucy Thurman president of the Congress. Many of the delegates had attended and participated in the Boston meeting. However, there were an unusual number of prominent church women present, including the wives of AME bishops and ministers, such as Fannie Jackson Coppin, Mary A. Campbell, Sarah Elizabeth Tanner, Martha Dewitt Turner, Hattie Wayman, Christine S. Smith, and Lillian Derrick, who did not participate in the earlier conference. The Congress also attracted a large contingency of AME women, such as Sada Anderson, Rebecca Aldridge, and Sarah Early, who were leaders of episcopal district missionary associations. Among the CME women present were Fannie B. Blount, Julia A. Patterson, and Anna L. Beasley. Noted evangelist Amanda Berry Smith, Presbyterian reformers Lucy Craft Laney and Lottie Wilson Jackson, and a host of Baptist women, including Mary V. Cook and Georgia De Baptiste, were among the many leading figures present.

At the first National Congress of Colored Women, the discussion centered around issues related mostly to southern racism, specifically lynching, mob violence, prison reform, and railroad segregation. A special appeal was made to southern white women to assist black women in their struggle for justice. However, Lucy Thurman and others also used the gathering to bring attention to the concerns of the NFAAW and to emphasize the need for a national secular organization. The point was stressed that black women in the past had "never advanced to the front save through religious channels," and that black men throughout the nation had discouraged women from being involved in "public work."

The support of the AME and other denominational women for the Boston conference, the National Congress of Colored Women, and

First National Congress of Colored Women

The First National Congress of Colored Women held in Atlanta, Georgia, in November 1895 at the Atlanta Cotton States and International Exposition

the founding of the National Association of Colored Women suggests that black women did not abandon their religious, literary, and fraternal associations; they simply created a national interdenominational organization that could focus more broadly on public issues and accommodate a more diverse group of women and clubs. The support of prominent religious women for organizing the NACW was also a loud protest against the gender proscriptions and male clergy's dominance in black churches. In a short history of the NACW, Mary Church Terrell wrote, "Owing to conditions which confronted them and obstacles which they had to surmount, colored women had reached a point in their development where they decided they must work out their own salvation as best they could."

The timing of the Boston and Atlanta meetings coincided with the struggles of black women in the AME, AME Zion, and CME denominations for ordination and lay rights. Equally important was the antagonism they met in trying to create national missionary organizations. By 1895 many Methodist and Baptist women had concluded that the struggle to obtain recognition and the right to participate in the governance of their churches would be long and protracted. The NACW offered them an opportunity to escape from the confines of their religious domains, freely express their views, fully engage the political issues of the day, and actively participate in an organization that gave full vent to their talents. In 1901, after attending the annual convention of the Michigan State Federation of Colored Women's Clubs, Mary Taylor Blauvelt, a white journalist, observed, "The women who attended this convention are . . . for the most part religious women, but with them religion is no mere sentiment or emotion—no mere intellectual conviction even—but a strong ethical impulse. Their religion consists not so much in singing of the joys of the future world as in working to make this present world better." Thus, the NACW represented a free and less compromised space than their churches, where their gifts could be recognized and used to bring about the social and political reform they envisioned.

In 1900, Alberta Moore-Smith, a member of the Illinois State Federation, the second vice president and only female officer of the newly founded National Business League, and the organizer of the first businesswomen's club in Chicago, contended that as American society had become more complex women were "forced into all works of reform and social improvement." Expressing a belief in gender equality, Moore-Smith asserted, "It is gradually being conceded that woman is man's equal intellectually. . . . [She] is only in need of a broader education to constitute her a dangerous competitor to him." She argued that the organization of women's clubs had propelled women to a new level "of significance and power in the community," but none existed for "us along any line of work other than the home and church."

As a member of Chicago's Third Ward Republican Club, Alberta Moore-Smith helped organize the vote for Republican candidates. In 1897 she was rewarded with an appointment to a position as deputy collector in the South Chicago municipal office. At the beginning of the twentieth century Chicago boasted of twenty-four clubs, ten of which were very popular and all of which were affiliated with the Illinois State Federation. These included the Institutional AME Church Woman's Club, the Civic League, and the South End Women's Political Club. The inclusion of a club affiliated with a specific church and the NACW suggests that women such as Moore-Smith and Ida Wells-Barnett were seeking an uncontested public space where they could function outside the control of their religious institutions and yet be identified as an organic and supportive part of a denomination. More-

The First Annual Convention of the National Federation of Afro-American Women, held in Washington, D.C., July 20–22, 1896, at the 19th Street Baptist Church. The National Association of Colored Women was founded at this meeting. Harriet Tubman (second row, sixth from right) attended the meeting.

over, as part of the Illinois Federation the women could expand their boundaries and engage in any number of reform activities, including politics, which were sometimes outside the scope of their missionary societies programs. The members of the Institutional AME Church Woman's Club evidenced an interest in "The Civic Responsibilities of Women," including political reform that spoke to the needs of African Americans.

Following the founding of the NACW in 1896, many talented women divided their time and energy between their church groups and the NACW and discovered new ways of cooperating with other organizations, including those of black men and white women, to achieve their objectives. It was not easy for these women to pursue such a course, and at first they were resented and castigated by their pastors for not concentrating their energies exclusively on church issues—in particular fund-raising. Beginning in the late nineteenth century and continuing well into the twentieth century, veteran club leader, suffragist, political activist, and journalist Rebecca Stiles Taylor asserted that "there was a certain amount of hostility on the part of pastors of churches toward what was then called *the* 'FEDERATION,' so much so, that many of those selfish, untrained and uninformed pastors—in no uncertain terms—denounced *the* 'Federation' for they felt that *the* 'Federation' was undermining them and their means of living." Taylor said, "[I]n the beginning of the 'Woman's Movement' the church elders insisted on being present in the women's meetings lest the silly women would pray for something they did not need." Taylor concluded that although the ministers "were more antagonistic at the outset," they later "converted" and realized the value of women's organized work. As a leading figure in the NACW, longtime devoted member of the Baptist Church, and intimate associate of numerous church leaders, Taylor had firsthand knowledge and was privy to the attitudes and political rows common to the Baptists and other denominations.

Taylor's observations regarding the reaction of the clergy to the women's movement, especially the NACW, could be applied to the experience of the Baptist Woman's Convention. At the founding of the WC in 1900, S. Willie Layten and Nannie Burroughs were elected to the positions of president and corresponding secretary. As outspoken leaders of the WC they experienced the deep-seated resentment and hostility of some ministers—leaders in the National Baptist Convention—who wanted total authority over the Woman's Convention. The internal struggle for control of the WC and the National Training School for Girls continued unabated throughout the twentieth century, ending only with Burroughs's death in 1961. After that date the WC functioned solely as a "department" of the National Baptist Convention, a denomination whose membership was more than two-thirds female. Neither the tension between the WC and the NBC nor intermittent verbal attacks on the WC's political agenda affected the activism of the Baptist women during the early twentieth century.

As a forum for discussion of contemporary issues and program development, the WC invited prominent women and men, including experts on a variety of subjects, organizational leaders, and ministers, to speak and deliver sermons at the WC's annual meetings. Baptist ministers and laymen were divided in their views about women's roles. However, some interjected their opinions about women's political activism and made clear their disdain for women's suffrage. W. E. B. Du Bois, editor of the *Crisis*, was among those who encouraged Baptist women to support the women's suffrage movement, "for their victory [means] victory for our race." Black church women were seemingly unfazed by the suggestions of some clergy that their proper role was as mother and wife in the home, and not in politics. Woman's Convention and other women leaders felt that both were important and saw no conflict between the two. Instead of withdrawing or curtailing their activism, they boldly stated their position on women's suffrage, praised their supporters, and answered their critics. WC leaders agreed with the NACW's call for "the women of the race [to] set their faces like a flint against the political methods of our men." Burroughs spoke out about the charge that some black men were selling their votes. She asserted, "If women cannot vote, they should make it very uncomfortable for the men who have the ballot but do not know its value." Burroughs contended that black women needed the ballot to obtain the political and economic rights that the race had lost as a result of black men's misuse of the vote. The WC moved forward with great confidence, buttressed by the "new woman" ideology, and enthusiastic about their advance in the women's movement. In less than two decades after the founding of the NACW black church women dominated the leadership of the organization and had created an interlocking directorate that included most of their religious and secular organizations, and key black male and white female strongholds, such as the NAACP and the YWCA.

The "New Woman" Movement

NOT A FEW BLACK church and club women leaders who came of age in the 1890s embraced the concept of the "new woman." While they differed somewhat in their perceptions of what constituted a new woman, Belle Dorce, Sarah Pettey, Dora J. Cole, Fannie Barrier Williams, and S. Willie Layten are examples of feminists who viewed themselves as part of the "new woman" movement. The "new woman," essentially a term used between 1890 and 1930, described a woman who had discovered "her capabilities, powers, and responsibilities" and was willing to engage in new forms of public behavior and gender roles. These women argued that education had made a difference in women's lives, giving them a new sense of their self-worth and perception of their equality with men. They saw no reason why they should not have careers, be public figures, and be accorded all of the rights and privileges available to men. They also asked, "Why not give woman a voice in the legislative body of the church?" Among black and white women, discourses on the new woman marked a shift from bourgeois Victorian ideals of true womanhood. Elements of the new woman identity included partisanship, education, and reform work as a career. The new woman ideology emphasized scientific efficiency and social science analysis of issues. As a feminine ideology that postulated gender differences and a superior moral responsibility among women, it reinforced the need for separate women's organizations that were devoted to varied interests and maintained concern for the improvement of the individual and the community. African Americans, male and female, debated its meaning for black women. For many male religionists it meant women seeking clergy and lay rights.

In 1895, following the extension of religious suffrage to the female members of St. Thomas Protestant Episcopal Church in Philadelphia, a prominent layman declared that "he fervently hoped that he should never live to see the day when one of these 'new women' was seated in the convention." However, like Alberta Moore-Smith, Dora J. Cole, a leading figure among black Episcopalians and a founding member of the NACW, thought it was "the same *old* woman, the eternal feminine, only the outward visible sign has changed somewhat." Ada Sweet, also an Episcopalian, revealed that one "prominent representative of the New Woman school" referred to God as "She." Upon hearing this, Sweet told Cole that it "was the first time I had ever heard the Deity referred to as feminine, and I will admit that I was shocked." Cole felt that "in the light of recent intellectual and spiritual growth there is every propriety in contemplating the Deity as feminine." Obviously, some women no longer saw the perception of God's maleness as an impediment to their advancement in the polity or society.

Belle Dorce, Sarah Pettey, Fannie Williams, and S. Willie Layten saw within the new woman a potential for power. Dorce was among the first black women to comment on the changes that had occurred in women's attitude and status. Other than being the wife of an AME minister, little is known about Dorce. As a contributor to several AME publications, including the *Christian Recorder*, Dorce astutely observed that most writers who wrote about the American girl "seem to include the white girl only. The time is not come when one can write on a general subject without distinguishing the black from the white." Dorce clarified that in her references to "the American girl," she included "the Afro-American girl; for she is just as much of an American as the Anglo-Saxon." Though the "opportunities of the Afro-American girl are far behind those of her white sister," all women suffer discrimination. For example, she said, "We do not hear so much of woman's power because most of the editors of the leading papers and magazines are men, and they are actually too jealous to recognize them as great lights." Dorce explained, "Certain positions are denied them, but this simply shows the absurd weakness of some of our leading men." As to women's political acumen, she asserted, "Now, we do not mean to say that woman is such a power that she would reconstruct the whole government; but we do mean to say that some of the perils that reflect on this grand government would be eradicated." Dorce's views were not unique; rather, they were representative of any number of black women in the late nineteenth century who recognized their worth and saw themselves as the equals of white women, and black and white men.

Sarah Pettey, a native North Carolinian, the wife of Bishop Charles C. Pettey, and a leading AME Zion feminist, described the new woman as "unpretentious," and a "thorough-going political campaigner" who engaged in grassroots political organizing among working-class women. Like Fannie Williams and S. Willie Layten, Pettey was educated and came from a fairly privileged background. Williams's feminist views and sense of self-worth had been carefully cultivated in Brockport, New York, in the predominantly white community where she was born and raised. Although she grew up in a Baptist Church, following her marriage to S. Laing Williams, an attorney, and subsequent move to Chicago, she affiliated with a white Unitarian church. Well known among the black educated and social elite, Fannie Williams was catapulted to national fame following her speeches before the World's Parliament of Religions and the World's Congress of Representative Women at the Columbian Exposition of 1893. Celia Parker Wooley, pastor of a Unitarian church in Geneva, Illinois, was among the leading white women who were impressed with Fannie Williams's intelligence and arguments against racial discrimination. In 1894, Wooley suggested that Williams join the all-white Chicago Woman's Club and the Unitarian Church and promote "her race prejudices principles." The tension surrounding the debates over desegregating the Chicago Woman's Club made Williams an instant celebrity.

Illustrating her own metamorphosis, in the late 1890s Williams described the "New Colored Woman" in relationship to the changes that had occurred in the consciousness of middle-class black women in the years between 1885 and 1895. She opined that in the past, "the interest of colored women in each other was personal or individual," but by 1895 African American women were focused on racial and social issues. Williams spoke of the founding of the NACW as a watershed event that "possibly means more to the social order and improvement of the colored race in this country than anything yet attempted outside of the churches." Simply put, Williams envisioned the "new" black woman creating the NACW as a potential force for exercising the individual and collective power of African American women.

S. Willie Layten was more specific in linking the new woman movement to what she viewed as women coming of age and claiming the rights that were naturally theirs. In 1895 Layten attended the second Woman's Congress of California, an interracial gathering that included noted white suffragists Susan B. Anthony and Rev. Anna H. Shaw. Commenting on the congress's deliberations, Layten observed that the "new woman . . . demonstrated her intellectual fitness and cleverly proved herself able to use her brain. . . . Women have finer brain power than men and will improve government." Following that meeting black women in Los Angeles attended the Woman's Parliament, where the main discussion focused on the issue of women's suffrage and women in politics. Layten commented, "I am certain no woman listening to these logical arguments . . . questioned the need of the ballot for women."

For Layten and her counterparts the new woman was a feminist who was outspoken about the equality of women with men and the need for women in politics. On the heels of the Woman's Congress, Layten organized, in Los Angeles, the first Colored Woman's Club in California. Responding to the plea of a black minister that the Woman's Club grant membership to men, Layten noted that "while some of us favor co-relative work the majority are vindictive and decree that what has been sauce for the goose shall now be served to the gander." The new woman was determined to be free, independent, and equal, not subordinated to the control of men—at least, that was the rhetoric espoused by some women in the movement. The question was how African American women would assume their roles as "new" women. One thing was clear: they would work assiduously to ensure that women acquired the vote, fight discrimination on all fronts, build a powerful free-standing secular national organization—the NACW—create a base of influential religious organizations, and fully assert their leadership in the church and community.

Layten and other black suffragists emerged in 1920, at the end of the "woman's era," as full-blown politicians and expert organizers. Layten, Burroughs, and their cohorts organized independent local Republican leagues in Philadelphia, the District of Columbia, and several other cities, and in 1924 founded the National League of Colored Republican Women. The new woman movement was not limited to traditional black women's organizations, or to the middle class. Rather, it was embraced by women in radical race organizations such as the United Negro Improvement Association. Explaining the "Black Woman's Part in Race Leadership," Eunice Lewis, a member of the Chicago branch of the UNIA and a disciple of Marcus Garvey, observed that "the true type of the New Negro Woman was bent on tackling those problems confronting the race" and determined to "learn all of the essentials of leadership." Black women would not abandon their responsibilities to their homes and families. However, they would participate as equals with men "in the office as well as on the platform," while working for the rebirth of Africa in America and abroad. And they would "demand absolute respect" from black and white men. Saydee E. Parham, also a member of the UNIA, summed up the success of the new woman: "In the political world she is the source of all reform legislation and the one power that is humanizing the world." Most of the women Parham referred to were part of the post–Civil War generation whose political activism spanned a period of at least sixty years, from 1890 to 1955.

Political Activism Before 1920

THE YEAR 1920 represents a major turning point in black women's history. It ushered in a period in which many African American women actively engaged in electoral politics. However, the reality is that black women's political activism predated the ratification of the Nineteenth Amendment. The question is, how should black women's political activities before 1920 be defined? Prior to 1920 black women advocated for women's suffrage, participated in electoral politics, and engaged in a diversity of political activities frequently categorized as social reform. In *Gender and Jim Crow*, Glenda Gilmore argues that black women's denominational organizations, under the guise of "missionary work," created a vast and invisible network throughout the South in which they engaged in activities that resulted in community activism targeted to improvements in education and health.

African American women's work was invisible only in the sense that most whites had direct contact with their servants and were largely unaware of and generally indifferent to the world blacks inhabited. The patterns described by Gilmore were operative throughout the nation. However, while some southern black women, for good reason, were somewhat clandestine in their political activities, others were not.

Adella Hunt Logan, a pioneering suffragist, served as NACW's national director of suffrage. Logan passed for white and attended the National American Woman Suffrage Association's conventions in the segregated South. She shared information from those meetings with leaders of NACW.

To engage openly in political activities challenging the white South was dangerous, particularly in some states and locales. In areas of the South where lynching and other forms of intimidation were most prevalent, black women clearly understood that the threat of violence to their persons and their families was never far away. However, there is ample evidence that in the early twentieth century southern black women were highly visible in their fight for suffrage. For example, when the Texas legislature granted suffrage to women in 1917, black women held mass meetings to encourage women to register and vote in Galveston, Houston, and Austin. With the support of the National Association for the Advancement of Colored People, these women attempted to vote in the white primary. In 1919 and 1920 black women in Chatham County and Savannah, Georgia, formed a Suffrage Club and League of Women Voters, and organized workshops to prepare women to vote. These organizations helped to familiarize women with political issues and provided opportunities for leadership and public visibility. Lucy Craft Laney, a Presbyterian activist and the head of the Haines Institute in Augusta, Georgia, was a leader in the Georgia women's suffrage movement.

During the Progressive Era, and indeed even before 1890, black women could be found engaging in politics at every level throughout the United States. In the North and West, African American women openly professed their views, laid claim to the vote, and engaged in municipal and electoral politics. In the late 1880s, Lucy Wilmot Smith, a leading Baptist woman and journalist, "was always outspoken on woman suffrage." Answering the critics who were hell-bent on proving that the majority of women were not interested in politics, and did not want to vote, Smith wrote, "It is said by many that women do not want the ballot. We are not sure the 15,000,000 women of voting age would say this, and if they did, majorities do not always establish the right of a thing. Our position is that women should have the ballot, not as a matter of expediency, but as a matter of pure justice."

The disfranchisement of black men in most southern states, and the 1896 *Plessy v. Ferguson* Supreme Court decision upholding segregation, dealt a bitter blow to African Americans and their quest for equality and justice. However, its impact on southern blacks extended to every area of life. By 1900 segregation and discrimination, lynching, and other forms of oppression were standard features of southern life. Under these circumstances it was difficult for southern black women to be as open in articulating their political views or as public in their political activism as their sisters in other regions of the nation. Depending on the racial climate, African American women and men in some southern locales, especially middle-class leaders, tended to engage in more circumspect activities, sometimes obscured and hidden within the programs of their religious and community organizations, and actively pursued through their denominational and interdenominational networks of reform. Others prodded their liberal white allies to speak and act on their behalf.

There were women in the Deep South, such as Sarah Pettey, Lucy Craft Laney, and Adella Hunt Logan, who openly promoted women's suffrage. Logan could, and did, pass for white when she attended the segregated meetings of the National American Woman's Suffrage Association held in the South. Acting in this capacity, she was able to access and share critical information with NACW leaders regarding

NAWSA's suffrage strategies. Logan was a member of the faculty at the Tuskegee Institute and the Tuskegee Women's Club, an affiliate of the NACW. For a number of years she directed the NACW's Department of Suffrage. In 1912 Logan confirmed that there were growing numbers of black women engaged in the study of politics. As these women became knowledgeable about public affairs, they developed an understanding of the relationship between their lives and politics and an appreciation for the importance of women having the vote. Logan concluded, "Not only is the colored woman awake to reforms that may be hastened by good legislation and wise administration, but where she has the ballot she is reported as using it for the uplift of society and for the advancement of the state." Logan made specific reference to black women voting in states such as Kansas, California, Colorado, Wyoming, Utah, Idaho, and Washington, where women's suffrage was legal. In 1912 it was estimated that 13,488 black women were eligible to vote in those states. Prior to 1920, African American women also voted in Massachusetts, Missouri, Oklahoma, Nebraska, New York, and Illinois.

Though a variety of legal and extralegal methods were used to diminish the numbers of black male voters, between 1900 and the passage of the Voting Rights Act of 1965 African Americans in some southern states and counties faced little opposition in registering and voting. For example, as late as 1907 there were few bars to black voting in Alabama. In Jefferson County, Alabama, of the approximately fifteen hundred eligible black voters, six hundred were registered, and their votes were avidly sought by white politicians of every ilk. However, in any number of states, through economic and physical intimidation and a variety of ruses, including the erection of laws requiring the payment of a poll tax, the black vote was severely reduced after 1900. In some locales working-class and poor black women as well as some middle-class leaders were less circumspect in their political activism.

Between 1866 and 1910, in cities such as Richmond, Virginia, and Birmingham, Alabama, during elections women and children turned out at the polls to ensure that black men voted. Though they could not vote, black women saw themselves and their children as having a stake in the male franchise. Throughout the South, African Americans were encouraged by their leaders to register to vote and pay their poll taxes. Examples of the political activism of ordinary women in Richmond after the Civil War, and Birmingham at the beginning of the twentieth century, suggests the extent to which women felt that the vote belonged to the black community as a whole, and exemplifies their determination to see not only that their men voted, but also that they adhered to the wishes of the community. In November 1907 in Birmingham women and children thronged the polls to assert their support of the prohibition movement, in particular to ensure that the city and county liquor saloons were closed. Reportedly, a "great confusion reigned the entire day about the polling places. So thick were the places beset with women and children that the voters at times had great difficulty in reaching the polls. Women prayed, women sung, children leaped into the air and skipped along. Everyone was enthusiastic and possessed with a kind of religious fervor, and the scene was inspiring. It was a frequent sight to see the women kneeling in the streets with voters. 'Nearer My God to Thee' was hummed throughout the day." The *New York Age* asserted, "This contest showed the importance of Afro-Americans registering and paying their poll tax."

During the 1880s and '90s black women in the North and West were active in the suffrage movement, organized political clubs, participated in electoral politics, and voted in municipal elections. In 1895 Mary F. Handy, a suffragist and leading figure in the black woman's club movement, voted in the municipal election held in Kansas City. In 1892, following her husband's election as bishop and assignment to the Fifth Episcopal District comprising the Missouri, Kansas, and Colorado conferences of the AME Church, Handy became actively involved in a number of organizations. In 1895, while serving as the vice president of the AME Woman's Parent Mite Missionary Society, Handy was elected president of Kansas City's Colored Woman's League, and vice president of the National League of Colored Women. In 1896, at the founding of the NACW, she was elected national treasurer. In her position as president of the WPMMS from 1907 to 1929, Handy directed the organization's efforts to fund missionary activities in South Africa, West Africa, the West Indies, and the United States. In 1896 the Handys returned to their home in Baltimore, Maryland, where Mary provided leadership to numerous organizations in the state. Mary Handy worked with the Baltimore Colored Young Women's Christian Association, the Maryland Federation of Christian Women, and the AME Home for Aged Women. In 1920, as the superintendent of the AME home, Handy made sure that the inmates were taken to the polls, where they were expected to cast their votes for Warren G. Harding, the Republican candidate for president.

During the early twentieth century, in states such as Ohio and

Kansas, NACW women such as Waterloo Bullock Snelson, the wife of Rev. Floyd Grant Snelson (AME), were actively engaged in organizing the suffrage movement among black women. Women's suffrage organizing was most often held at churches, and sometimes black women used Woman's Day programs for the purpose of engaging women in a discussion on women's rights. For example, in 1912 at the Haven Methodist Episcopal Church in Philadelphia, Patti Caldwell of the Morris Brown AME Church spoke on "The Rights of Women." The *Philadelphia Tribune* reported that Caldwell "advocated woman suffrage, and so convincing was her argument that even some of the men were in sympathy with the cause."

Though church and club women engaged in many issues throughout the nineteenth and twentieth centuries, there are several that consistently demanded their attention. Historically, the major focus of their political agenda has been African American and women's rights. Beginning in the antebellum period with civil rights for free blacks and the abolition of slavery, their political agenda expanded to include suffrage, women's rights, and temperance. In the aftermath of the Civil War most black women continued to support suffrage for women and black men, temperance, and civil rights for all African Americans. In states where women were excluded from legal enfranchisement, black women were actively engaged in shaping the vote and influencing political decisions. During the late nineteenth and early twentieth centuries they actively participated in political meetings and organized political societies. They believed that the vote belonged to the community and that black men represented them.

Irrespective of class, following Reconstruction, African Americans paid strict attention to the legal reversals and growing violence directed at southern blacks in particular. In 1891, May M. Brown, an AME Zion woman in Cleveland, Ohio, asserted that black people were most interested in "The Race Problem, the Federal Election Bill, and the Congo Free States." Brown observed, "Although women go not to the polls, yet by their interest and influence upon those in their homes who represent them, they very often wield the elections. In such cases then, they must study and weigh well the issues at stake, look at both sides of the question most carefully, and so train their thoughts that the advice they give to others may prove useful and beneficial." Emphasizing that women exercised influence over the political agenda not only in the home but also in the church, Brown said, "We seldom go into the pulpits, but we often speak through the mouth of the preacher."

Many leaders of black women's national organizations had achieved middle-class status, a few came from elite backgrounds, and some were members of the black working class. At the local level working-class black women were leaders and members of women's religious and fraternal groups, and belonged to associations such as the NACW and, later, the National Council of Negro Women. Some, like Callie House, a Baptist washerwoman and leader of an early-twentieth-century movement of poor people that sought pensions from the federal government for former slaves, were politically active in radical and nationalist organizations. Women employed as washerwomen, domestic servants, seamstresses, beauticians, factory workers, and in a variety of skilled and service capacities, joined teachers, a small number of civil servants, entrepreneurs, and other professionals as members of the missionary societies, women's conventions, and the NACW.

By 1900 the majority of black women were engaged in domestic service. As white women, especially the Irish, relinquished positions as servants for employment in clerical positions, black women filled their slots. The Great Migration increased the numbers of black women employed as domestic servants in urban areas such as Chicago, Detroit, Philadelphia, and Washington, D.C. Between 1910 and 1940, almost three-fourths of all African American women were employed as domestic servants. At the local level, the majority of the members and some of the leaders in the missionary societies and women's conventions were working class. However, the national leadership of church women's organizations was mostly middle class.

Recognizing that the majority of black women workers, as well as their members, were in domestic service and, like other working-class women, needed to organize for protection and development in their vocation, in 1919 the Woman's Convention pledged its support for a national organization of domestic workers. In 1921 the National Association of Women Wage Earners was founded. For two years Burroughs and a small cadre of prominent women, including Maggie Lena Walker, Mary B. Talbert, Ora Brown Stokes, Sallie W. Stewart, and Violet A. Johnson, engaged in the planning to launch what they conceived of as a "great Labor Union" to be composed of wage earners. With the exception of Stewart, who belonged to the Lutheran Church, all of the organizers were Baptist. In addition to their memberships in the WC and the NACW, several of these women held national offices in the YWCA and the National Race Congress. Among the organizers, Walker and Johnson, a vice president of the WC and the New Jersey

State Federation, were the only women who had ever worked respectively as a washerwoman and a domestic servant. Like Burroughs, a few had grown up in families where their mothers, aunts, and other relatives were personal servants and household workers.

Lucy Thurman, a leading figure in the AME Church, is an excellent example of how the post–Civil War church women developed and used their influence to acquire leadership positions and launch their agendas. In 1896, at the organization of the NACW, the constitution defined as the organization's goals "to secure harmony of action and cooperation among all women in raising to the highest plane, the home, moral and civil life." Thurman, a founder and NACW officer, insisted on the insertion of the words "by the help of God." Thurman's success as a temperance organizer and lecturer with the WCTU, and her loyalty to WCTU President Frances E. Willard, ensured her a position as the WCTU's first elected Superintendent of Temperance Work Among Colored People in 1893. In 1896 she was elected president of the National Congress of Colored Women. In 1898 Thurman founded and served as the first president of the Michigan State Federation, and in 1906 she was elected the third national president of the NACW, a position she held until 1908. During Thurman's administration the NACW established a Temperance Department, passed resolutions, and actively worked in support of anti-lynching campaigns, juvenile courts, and the National Association for the Protection of Colored Women and Girls.

As president of the Michigan Federation, Lucy Thurman focused on civic issues at the local level, especially in Detroit, and national issues such as education, lynching, and prison reform, in particular the convict lease system at the state level. In 1906, under Thurman's leadership, the NACW protested the opening of *The Clansman*, a play by Thomas Dixon, which glorified the birth of the Ku Klux Klan and included vicious stereotypes of African Americans. On numerous occasions the Michigan Federation lobbied the state and federal governments to pass legislation supportive of measures that would benefit the African American community. For example, in 1900 the group petitioned President William McKinley to grant an indemnity to the family of Frazier J. Baker, a black postmaster in Lake City, South Carolina, who was lynched. The petition included a recommendation that those states where lynching persisted be expelled from the union.

As a prominent AME church woman and leader of the NACW, the WCTU, and the Michigan Federation, Lucy Thurman illustrates the centrality of the work of black church women at the beginning of the black women's club movement and their high visibility as Christian feminist activists. Thurman was one of many church women who formed the leadership of the NACW and other reform organizations at the state and national levels. As NACW president, Thurman made sure that AME and Baptist leaders such as Eva T. Jennifer, Cornelia Bowen, Emma Ransom, and S. Willie Layten were represented on the NACW's programs. These women delivered papers, participated in symposiums on topics dealing with the plight of working-class women and girls, and chaired important committees.

It was Lucy Thurman's vision, pioneering agenda, and teachings that set the tone for the work of the Michigan Federation for well into the twentieth century. Two-thirds of the clubs affiliated with the federation were located in Detroit. The Detroit City Federation was among the NACW's most politically active units. In 1939, following decades of organizing and networking with white and black associations, the federation announced its intention of having a club woman appointed to *all* Detroit municipal boards. The group asserted, "We want representation along with our taxation. It is but just. It is the law." This tactic was part of the NACW's national strategy to secure representation on the boards and commissions of important government agencies and social reform organizations. In this manner, black women would be able to access resources and participate in the development of policies and programs that impacted the lives of African Americans and women. In the twentieth century, as the National Association of Colored Women grew in stature and gained widespread recognition, its leaders were recognized and tapped by the local, state, and national governments for special service.

Similar to the interlocking religious, political, and social activities of Thurman and the Michigan women, the Illinois State Federation and the Chicago and Northern District Association drew no line between their religious and civic affairs. Organized in Springfield in 1899, by 1932 the Illinois State Federation's membership exceeded that of any other NACW state association, and the CNDA was among the largest and most powerful of the district federations in the nation. Illinois's president, Annette H. Officer, the first black woman to serve as clerk of the Illinois State Labor Department, was a founder of the St. Louis NAACP, and vice president of the NBC-USA Woman's Baptist State Convention in Illinois. In 1937 the CNDA comprised thirty-three affiliate clubs. During the 1930s the association offered a

Ida Wells-Barnett was among those religious activists who were driven by their strong belief in social justice to take on national issues such as lynching. In 1896 she was instrumental in launching an international debate and protest about lynching, and in 1922 she was a member of the NACW delegation that went to the White House to urge the President to support anti-lynching legislation.

religious training program as part of its Education Department's work. Its Civics Department included committees on interracial work, legislation, peace, and international relations.

Annette Officer, Ida Wells-Barnett, Elizabeth Lindsay Davis, Carrie Lee Hamilton, and other women embraced politics and political activism as a natural right and a duty to the race. Wells-Barnett, among the most famous members of the Chicago Federation, laid claim to her role as a pioneer in the anti-lynching movement; the organizer of the first "Colored" women's club at the 1893 World's Fair held in Chicago; and the founder of the Alpha Suffrage Club, the first suffrage and political club in Chicago for black women. Wells-Barnett stated that it was because of her political activism that the first black woman to run for the position of senator in a state legislature—Nellie D. Calloway—was from Illinois.

Elizabeth Lindsay Davis, a member of St. Mark's Methodist Episcopal Church in Chicago, was widely known for her religious work in the Sunday school and the church. During her long life she was said to have held every position in the church "except that of a licensed minister." A charter member and the national historian of the NACW, Davis was the founder and chief executive of the Chicago Phyllis Wheatley Home for Girls. She held memberships in numerous organizations, including interracial groups such as the Chicago Woman's Club and the League of Women Voters. During World War I, she was a member of the Chicago State Council for National Defense. Described by her contemporaries as active in politics before and after the ratification of the Nineteenth Amendment, Davis called for black women to study and familiarize themselves with local, state, and national politics. It was her belief that political education would enable African American women to become better citizens and to "realize the gigantic power that lies dormant in . . . Race women." Davis insisted that black women needed "wise leadership and systematic organization to become an active, potent factor in the body politic."

Carrie Lee Hamilton, a graduate of Wilberforce University, was raised in the AME tradition, and as the private secretary to Bishop Henry McNeal Turner developed an appreciation for the ways in which politics could be used to further the goals of Christianity. While serving as a teacher and private secretary to President William Hooper Councill at the Alabama A&M College in Huntsville, Alabama, she refined her speaking skills and learned how to negotiate the thickets of race and gender in dealing with whites as well as blacks. Following a fourteen-year stint in the South, Hamilton returned to her native state of Illinois, residing first in Cairo and later in Chicago, where she had a long and productive career as a Christian feminist activist. As president of the Illinois Federation (1916–18), she extended her social and political network. Skillfully applying the lessons she had learned, Hamilton immediately secured employment as the first probation officer in Pulaski County, and was elected the first president of a women's Republican club in Cairo.

Between 1910 and 1930, Hamilton was active in politics at the local level in Chicago. She worked closely with the Republican Party organization in the Fifth Ward, and campaigned for the party throughout Illinois during national elections. As the director of social service of the

Fourth Episcopal District of the AME Church, state president of the Illinois Federation, grand worthy matron of an Eastern Star chapter, and a charter member of the integrated Illinois Women's Republican Club and the Chicago Church Federation, Hamilton was able to provide "righteous guidance," exert considerable influence on the policies of these multiple organizations, and manipulate their agendas to include the NACW's political goals.

Of all the black women's religious organizations, the WC appears to have most dominated the NACW leadership at the state and national levels. Unlike any of their counterparts, the WC had a heightened sense of racial and gender self-determination that was reflected in their consistent political activism from 1900 to 1950. As a semi-autonomous group that for the most part abrogated its struggle for lay and clergy rights within the National Baptist Convention, the WC maintained a varying degree of control over its leadership, finances, and program until 1961, and the death of Nannie Burroughs. At the national level, black Methodist women's missionary societies, as auxiliaries, were subordinate to the male clergy leadership in their denominations. Between 1870 and 1960 AME and CME women fought for lay rights, ordination of women, and recognition in the church polity. Among the Methodists, AME Zion women were the only group to achieve these goals by 1895. However, this did not end gender discrimination in the denomination. Tension around the issue of women's recognition and power within these churches continued throughout the twentieth century. In the Presbyterian, Episcopalian, and Catholic denominations, black women were caught between white women and black men and continued to struggle against racism and sexism within their church organizations.

Thus, it is both the structure of the WC and the leadership of Layten and Burroughs that set the tone and defined the political philosophy of the WC for more than fifty years. The WC fought to achieve racial and gender equality in American society, and to maintain their autonomy in the National Baptist Convention. Whereas women officers in other religious organizations served for a limited period of time, Layten and Burroughs held their leadership positions as president and secretary of the WC for more than fifty years. Described as a militant and iconoclastic figure, Burroughs was the central driving force behind the WC's organizational autonomy and political activism. All of the women's missionary societies and conventions were sporadically involved in traditional forms of politics and protests, such as electoral politics, petitions, boycotts, and written and verbal appeals to justice. However, with the exception of the WC, none of these groups consistently engaged in political activism directed by their organizations. AME and AME Zion women's organizations appear to have been more active in the national interracial movement between 1920 and 1965, working first with the FCC Church Women's Committee and later with Church Women United in the struggle to dismantle racial segregation and discrimination.

Religious Leadership and the Public Sphere

LEADERS SUCH AS Rev. Florence Spearing Randolph, S. Willie Layten, Maria Lawton, Julia Mason Layton, Marie Madre-Marshall, and Nannie Helen Burroughs understood the criticality of acquiring social power or social capital, an important resource that could be used to develop and shape the collective power or cultural capital of black women and to provide a foundation for their political activities. As quintessential examples of women who skillfully merged their church, club, and political work, these women are not exceptions to the rule. Rather, they are representative of how so-called "elite" women in communities throughout the nation understood and used their organizational networks. These women exemplify how black women's political power and public activities are related to and stem from their collective work as church and club women. Florence Randolph, a minister, suffragist, anti-lynching and temperance advocate, and African missionary, founded and served as the first president of the New Jersey Federation of Colored Women, and held offices in the NLCRW, the WCTU, and the AME Zion Church.

S. Willie Layten's diverse positions as the president of the WC and the Philadelphia City Federation of Colored Women's Clubs, leader in the National League of Colored Republican Women, social worker with the National League for the Protection of Colored Women, and member of the Republican Women's Committee of Philadelphia earned her a position on the National Republican Committee of Pennsylvania.

In New York, Maria C. Lawton, an educator, journalist, and president of the NACW's Empire State Federation, combined religious and club work with political activities. The initial outlets for Lawton's political activism was her employment as a columnist for the *Standard Union* (white), leadership of the Presbyterian Conference of Workers

Among Girls, and work with the NACW and the YWCA. As one of the first black women to campaign for women's suffrage, Lawton, a lifelong Republican, was active in politics at the local, state, and national levels for more than forty years. In 1920 Lawton became a member of the "regular" New York Republican organization, and the first black woman to be elected a member of the organization's Executive Committee.

Nannie Burroughs and S. Willie Layten were part of a large cadre of politically active Baptist women, which included Mary Talbert, national president of the NACW and the leader of the NAACP's Anti-Lynching Crusaders campaign, and Maggie Lena Walker, the first female banker in the United States and the president of the Independent Order of St. Luke. These women were in large measure responsible for the WC's establishment of a suffrage committee and the appointment of Gertrude Rush as committee chair. All were major figures in the NACW at the national and local levels. The activities of Burroughs and Layten mirror those of many church women. In cities throughout America black women used established denominational and interdenominational club networks, especially those of the NACW, to challenge gender proscriptions in the black community, influence public policy, and secure a foothold in local and national politics.

Having a large number of seasoned NACW leaders and political operatives, the WC was a center for dissemination of information and a training ground for women who implemented the WC's political agenda and reform programs at the local level. The Baptist women's program of political education was similar to that of the NACW. By 1905 the NACW—and not the church, as suggested by Evelyn Higginbotham—was the chief "arena for discussion, debate" and developing strategies "for implementation of black women's social, economic and political agenda vis-a-vis white America." It was common practice for Baptist, Methodist, Presbyterian, and Episcopal women to translate and implement NACW program initiatives through their church-based community projects. The women's conventions and missionary societies had thousands of members and a diverse class base, and could reach more women in small towns and cities throughout the nation than the NACW. In some ways the NACW served as a think tank for developing strategies and defining programs that could be replicated by other women's organizations.

Irrespective of their denominational affiliations, African American women clearly understood the relationship between their religion and the public sphere. They knew that prayer was powerful and that God answered prayers. However, as Christian feminist activists they entered a covenant with God to uphold biblical tenets and provide "righteous guidance" in all of their public activity. Responding to the ratification of the Nineteenth Amendment, black women organized Republican leagues and political study clubs at the local level, and, like the NACW and the Baptist Woman's Convention, set up committees within their national religious structures to organize and coordinate their political activities.

Religion and Political Activism, 1920–1950

IN 1920, TWO WEEKS after the ratification of the suffrage amendment, Burroughs informed the delegates at the WC's annual meeting that "[w]omen must organize and educate." She explained that a significant part of the "new educational work" was teaching women to be cognizant of "the affairs of state." The WC Executive Board recommended that a suffrage club be started in every church and that three or four churches form a suffrage union. WC leaders were warned that there would be "a protest against 'Politics in the Church.' " Burroughs stressed that African American women "will not be a tool for white women; they will not sell out to white men; they will not undervalue their only weapon of self-defense." She gave three reasons why black women needed instruction in the use of the ballot. Organization was needed to oppose parties and candidates who were not supportive of civil rights for African Americans; "to fight discrimination and class legislation"; and to empower black women to "go a step further and organize to re-enfranchise Negro men." Black women were expected to vote as a "matter of principle." Thus, with faith in themselves and God, a solid determination, and no illusions about the struggle ahead, they moved forward, intent on laying claim to the ballot and exercising the rights that they felt were justly theirs.

In anticipation of the 1920 national elections, black women's organizations developed grassroots programs to educate and prepare their members to become actively involved in the political process. At its annual meeting in Indianapolis in September 1920, the Woman's Convention signaled its determination to use its influence in every state, to have black women register, qualify, and go to the polls to vote. A suffrage committee was appointed to organize the WC's voter registration campaign. At the local level, women such as Mrs. E. E. Morris provided the leadership for carrying out the national program of the WC. In 1920, in Hutchinson, Kansas, Morris urged black women to vote and carefully instructed them how to mark their ballots to ensure that their votes would not be lost. Morris was vice president of the local Colored Women's Republican Club, and had served for twenty-three years as the organist of the local Second Baptist Church. Urging black men and women to either divide their vote between the Republicans and the Democrats or support the Socialist Party, Burroughs announced that she also planned to assist the NACW in directing its Campaign for Education, which was designed to defeat the parties that had failed to assist African Americans in safeguarding their constitutional and political rights.

Thousands of black women in the North and West voted for the first time in 1920. In a relatively short period of time, southern black women discovered that they would be denied the franchise. Though they were eventually disenfranchised, and the National Woman's Party declined to support their efforts to obtain the vote, there is ample evidence that black women throughout the South escalated their interest and involvement in the electoral process. Given that black men were disenfranchised, African American women held no illusions about the possibility that they would suffer a similar plight. From the beginning they understood the tenuous nature of their relationships with white women in the women's suffrage movement. However, they did not shrink from seeking the franchise for women and civil rights for African Americans. At every turn, they met discrimination in the women's movement, but they refused to give up and simply retreat to their organizations. Instead they faced the issues directly, and developed strategies for achieving their goals.

In the aftermath of women gaining the vote, Rev. Richard R. Wright Jr., the editor of the AME *Christian Recorder*, wrote, "[W]e may expect to see them [women] more and more in politics." Aware of the thousands of enfranchised black women voters residing in the North and West, particularly in areas where the AME Church was strong, Wright asserted that there were serious questions regarding "the relation of women and politics and the church." He observed that the women best suited for political activism were denominational leaders who had received their training from the church, and it was because of the superb organizing abilities of a large number of church women that "many . . . churches [were kept] alive." Wright feared that politicians would recognize the value of these women, recruit the most talented church leaders, and "thus divide the interest of these women between the church and the state." In his view this would pose a serious danger to the church. Wright concluded that because of the exclusion of women from business and politics, their interests were confined to the home and the church. If the church failed to minister to the increasing needs of church women in the new era, it would lose their talents and services.

Wright's observations were accurate. However, what he failed to realize was that it was already too late to stop the movement of women from the church to the public sphere. The shift begun in the late nineteenth century was in full force by 1917. In fact, a decade earlier, Mamie E. Stewart, a leading NACW Baptist woman, stated, "In many of the states women have been formed into distinct organizations, by the churches or by the denominational organizations, for the purpose of doing specific work . . . and in the interest of reform movements." Similarly, in 1924 Sadie Tanner Alexander, in a Women's Day speech entitled "A Demand for Women as Executive Officers of the Church," remarked, "The Church can no longer hope to compete with other institutions that are diverting the executive and intellectual ability of the women to positions of importance."

Most church women who entered politics did not abandon their churches. They used their church-based leadership to achieve their political purposes. This was particularly true between 1915 and 1940, and less so after World War II. Between 1950 and the present women entering politics have relied more on the status and support of their feminist secular organizations than that of their churches. Beginning in the 1940s the national black secular press, in highlighting the political activities of women, rarely referred to a woman's denominational affiliation or church leadership. Rather, women's affiliations and the offices they held in the college-based and professional sororities and other prominent social and reform organizations such as the NACW, the NCNW, and the YWCA were more frequently mentioned.

Women like Nannie Burroughs, Julia Mason Layton, and S. Willie Layten used their church organizations to achieve their political goals. In 1920, while serving as the corresponding secretary for the Baptist Woman's Convention, Burroughs joined leaders of the Washington Federation of Colored Women (NACW) in organizing a League of Republican Women in the District of Columbia. Burroughs was the league's secretary and the chair of the Propaganda Committee, the association's public relations arm. Using the WC's organizational network and the writing and organizing skills she had honed as the WC corresponding secretary, Burroughs disseminated information regarding the league's activities, informed women of their political rights, and actively recruited women to the league. League leaders Julia Mason Layton and Marie Madre-Marshall—the president and vice president respectively—were, like Burroughs, also prominent figures in WC and AME women's organizations.

Described by the editor of the *Washington Bee* as "The most accomplished and polished female politician and diplomat among women," Julia Mason Layton enjoyed a remarkable career as an educator, politician, and WC and NACW leader. A nationally known activist, Layton's work with the federation began in the late nineteenth century with the founding of the National League of Colored Women, the precursor of the District of Columbia's Federation of Colored Women's Clubs. During the 1920s Layton served as chair of the NACW's Religious Work (1925), president of the District's federation, and the president of the WC and the Baptist Woman's Home and Foreign Missionary Society of Washington, D.C.; in 1921 she became the first black woman appointed to the D.C. State Republican Executive Committee.

Layton's associate Marie Madre-Marshall was a highly regarded educator and AME Christian feminist activist. As a member of the AME Woman's Mite Missionary Society, at the General Conference of 1908 she argued for the admission of women as lay delegates. Madre-Marshall earned a law degree from Howard University and was the first female president of the famed Bethel Literary and Historical Society, an AME organization founded in 1881 by Bishop Daniel A. Payne, which served as a national forum for intellectual debate of important political and social issues. Madre-Marshall, described by contemporaries as an "organizing genius," was president of the District Federation of Colored Women (1915–18), vice president of the Northeastern Federation of Colored Women's Clubs (1917–20), and the first director of the AME Church Temperance Department (1916). During the 1920s, Madre-Marshall led the largest Temple of Daughter Elks in the world. In the late 1920s, Burroughs, Layton, Madre-Marshall, and hundreds of other women used their church connections to recruit members for the newly organized National League of Colored Republican Women.

In states such as Washington, Texas, Georgia, South Carolina, Pennsylvania, New Jersey, New York, Massachusetts, Rhode Island,

Michigan, Illinois, and Kentucky, women escalated their political activism, organizing suffrage clubs and registering women to vote. During the 1920s black women, especially Christian women, discovered that politics offered them a large and open field for personal and social service. Women ministers, clergy wives, leaders of religious and interdenominational organizations, and ordinary laywomen engaged in electoral politics and ran for office. The paucity of women and African Americans in elective office did not prevent black women from being active in party politics. Like their white counterparts, they often formed the majority of canvassers and served in a variety of supportive positions at the precinct level in urban areas. Mamye L. Copeland, Geraldine Chaney, Mary Warfield, Theodora V. Jones, Betty Hill, Cora Calhoun Horne, and Mary B. Martin are representative of literally hundreds, perhaps thousands, of women who were actively engaged in electoral politics, mostly at the local level. Lethia Cousins Fleming, Rev. Florence Spearing Randolph, Fannie B. Peck, and Christine S. Smith are examples of women whose political activism was both local and national in scope.

Methodist Episcopal women such as Geraldine Chaney and Mary E. Warfield moved from the South during the Great Migration and became active in church and secular politics. In 1918, Chaney, a native of Norfolk, Virginia, relocated to Queens, New York, where she affiliated with the Brooks Memorial Methodist Episcopal Church. Between 1920 and 1935, Chaney gained visibility for her church and secular political activities, which included election in 1932 to the Brooks Memorial Board of Trustees, a position held by very few women in any denomination. During the early 1930s Chaney was a social welfare worker in Jamaica, New York, and elected chair of the Queens County Committee for Equal Rights; in 1935 she ran on the Labor Party's ticket as a candidate for alderman in the Fifty-eighth District. Believing that ministers should be in the forefront of movements "that affected the welfare of Negroes," in 1935 Chaney issued a "bitter denunciation" of black clergy in Queens. She accused ministers of "indifference, cowardice and selfishness, and cited an almost total lack of cooperation by the clergymen in the movements for slum abatement, against police brutality and discrimination, and for economic security for the race." Chaney's comments resulted from the refusal of Rev. William McKinley Dawkins of the Macedonia AME Church in Flushing, New York, to permit the use of his church for a meeting to protest police brutality.

Like Chaney, Mary E. Warfield—known as "Mother" Warfield—was very active in religious and secular politics. Born in 1872 near Anchorage, Kentucky, Warfield lived in Bloomington, Indiana, for many years before moving to Indianapolis in 1917. In Indianapolis, she became immersed in the work of the Scott Methodist Episcopal Church, which included holding several leadership positions as a stewardess, class leader, and Sunday school teacher. Widely known for her philanthropic and voluntary contributions to numerous community groups, she organized the Sisters of Charity Lodge No. 15, a benevolent organization. Warfield was a member of the League of Women Voters, the American Legion Auxiliary, and the WCTU. For a number of years she was active in Republican politics, serving as a precinct committeewoman.

No less active than their black Methodist sisters, Mayme L. Copeland and Dr. Mattie E. Coleman, as ministers' wives and political activists, were known for their feminist leadership in the Colored Methodist Episcopal Church's Woman's Connectional Missionary Council and their grassroots and state politics in Kentucky and Tennessee. In 1928, as the leader of the Colored Women's Division of the Republican Party in Kentucky, Copeland was "hard at work doing her bit to elect Herbert Hoover president of the United States." The *Christian Index* asserted that she "is a distinct honor to her church and race." For many years, Dr. Coleman was the most celebrated woman in the CME denomination. As the founding president of the Woman's Connectional Missionary Council, Coleman fought long and hard for women's right to organize a national missionary society and have a voice in the CME polity. She was widely known for her work on behalf of women's suffrage, and was largely responsible for galvanizing more than two thousand black women to vote in the 1919 municipal elections in Nashville, Tennessee.

Theodora V. Jones, Betty Hill, Cora Calhoun Horne, and Mary B. Martin are examples of Catholic, Congregational, and Bahá'í women who were actively engaged in electoral politics, mostly at the local and state level. In 1932, Jones, a twenty-four-year-old woman described as a "worker and leader in the Roman Catholic Church," was an alternate delegate with the California delegation to the Democratic National Convention. At a time when the majority of African Americans were members of the Republican Party, Jones argued that blacks should join the Democratic Party. As a student of politics, Jones recognized the changing trend in black voting patterns that began with the presidential election of 1924 and was quite evident by 1932. Emphasizing the advantages of being a Democrat, Jones asserted, "We command respect. We are not after [jobs as] janitors posing as custodians, as many Republicans do, but are seeking real positions for qualified Negro Democrats." As a senior law student at the Pacific Law Institute, Jones worked as a legal file clerk in the office of Erwin P. Werner, Los Angeles city attorney.

Moving from New York to California in 1927, and faced with the prospect of supporting herself, Jones turned to politics. "I had never done any housework," she explained. "I was not strong enough to go into service." In 1928 she organized the Thomas Jefferson Colored Democratic League, which included forty-three members. By 1932 there were nineteen branches of the league in California, with 2,500 members. In the presidential election of 1932 Jones supported Franklin D. Roosevelt. As a member of the Democratic State Central Committee, she was appointed to the subcommittee on finance. Jones also served as chair of the Democratic County Central Committee of the Sixty-second Assembly District. In 1932 she was a Democratic Party candidate for nomination to the General Assembly. In 1930, despite her political credentials, she was refused admittance to the Woman's Athletic Club, where the Los Angeles women of the Democratic Party were honoring a prominent Democrat. When Jones protested the discrimination, she was informed by Mary Kinard, a leading white female Democrat, that "the club did not admit colored women even if they were members of the party." Though Jones was offended by the rebuff, like most black women politicians she did not become disillusioned by politics nor dissuaded from pursuing her political goals. Rather, she pressed forward to become a leader in the California Democratic Party.

Described as "[o]ne of the West Coast's most prominent women, and without doubt the most powerful political figure of the Race in this section," Betty Hill was a leader in the Congregational Church and the Republican Party. A resident of Los Angeles, California, Hill was a member of the Lincoln Memorial Congregational Church, where she served on the Board of Trustees and directed the religious education program for eleven years (1929–40). Her civic activities included twenty years of service on the board of the Los Angeles NAACP, seventeen of which she served as chair. Hill worked closely with the YWCA, serving on the Los Angeles Board of Management for twelve years. By the late 1920s Hill had amassed a great deal of social and political capital, which she used to undergird her efforts to desegregate swimming pools and eliminate forms of employment discrimination in Los Angeles, including having black nurses employed and black doctors granted internships and admitted to practice at the General Hospital. Other "race" organizations had attempted but failed in their struggles to win these battles. In 1940 Hill gained national recognition as the first African American "west of the Rockies" to be elected a delegate to the National Republican Convention.

In an assessment of her career and rise to national prominence in politics, the *Chicago Defender* reported, "One of the reasons Mrs. Hill is both feared and courted by California political aspirants is that she controls one of the most unique and powerful organizations in the state, the Woman's Political Study Club." Under Hill's direction this organization, whose motto was "Justice for All," grew to include thirty-two units in California, with an active membership of five thousand. Between 1935 and 1940, members engaged in a focused study of political organizations, leaders, and strategies. The club carefully monitored legislators and legislation, singling out cases of discrimination and racism at the state and national levels. For example, in 1935, the Los Angeles club publicly denounced Congressman Arthur Mitchell for comments he made in a speech at Morris Brown College in Atlanta, Georgia. Mitchell was defending the "toothless" anti-lynching bill he had introduced in Congress. As the first black Democrat to be elected to the United States Congress, Mitchell gained notoriety for resorting to "Uncle Tomming"—ingratiating himself with white political bosses in Chicago.

In 1946 the Political Study Club sent Hill to Washington to present a resolution to President Harry S. Truman condemning discrimination in the nation's capital. This action was in response to the treatment Hill had received in 1945 when she was a delegate to a Republican Party convention in Washington. Arguing that foreign visitors "observing Washington practices" would conclude that racial discrimination was a policy of the federal government, the resolution urged that segregation and discrimination be abolished in the city. Hill skillfully used her interracial, religious, and political networks to advance her gender and race issues. Taken as a whole, these are the bases of power that led to her election in 1955 as president of the California Republican Women's Committee.

Little is known about the organized work of black women in the National Spiritual Assembly or other organizations of the Bahá'í movement. However, many well-known politically active, black club women, such as Cora Calhoun Horne, Mary Martin, and Lethia Cousins Fleming, were Bahá'í. Though the Bahá'í forbade political activities, these women did not cease their involvement in partisan politics. Horne—the grandmother of Lena Horne, the famous entertainer—was active in the suffrage movement, national politics, and the civic and social life of Brooklyn for more than three decades prior to her death in 1932. During World War I, she organized and directed a YWCA unit for the American Red Cross. In recognition of her service, Horne was appointed to New York Mayor John F. Hylan's victory committee. In 1924, during the presidential campaign of Calvin Coolidge, she was the national organizer and secretary of the eastern division of the National Republican Women's auxiliary. Horne was a member and held office in many of the most prominent social and political organizations of her time, including the NACW, the YWCA, the NAACP, the Urban League, the Big Sisters organization, the Women's International League for Peace and Freedom, and the International Council of Women of the Darker Races.

The Bahá'í faith, considered by some contemporaries to be a non-Christian and exotic cult, advocated racial equality. The organization emphasized that "[w]hen one becomes a Bahá'í, one enters a new and higher realm of reality where the world's traditional values have no influence." It presented no barrier to the political aspirations of women such as Mary B. Martin who sought election to public office. Stressing racial unity at least fifty years before segregation ended, black and white Bahá'í members held integrated meetings throughout the United States. Martin, a teacher in Cleveland, Ohio's public schools, in 1929 became the first black woman to be elected to a public office in the history of Cleveland politics. Martin won election to the school board three times, beating out two white male candidates. Martin was national chair of the NACW Education Department and a founder of the Cleveland NAACP and the Amity Fellowship League, an interracial charitable organization that fed an average of 250 persons per day during the Depression. For many years she was affiliated with the Mt. Zion Temple Congregational Church, but in the 1920s she joined the Bahá'í movement, and served as a member of the Spiritual Assembly and chair of one of the organization's committees.

Mary B. Martin's success in politics is reflective of the early interdenominational coalition efforts of white and black women taking place mostly in some areas outside of the Deep South. During the early twentieth century, Mary Church Terrell, of Washington, D.C., and Mary Martin were among the first African Americans to serve on urban school boards. Their victories followed the stunning 1890 election of Amelia Anna Allen to the school board in Salina, Kansas. Allen, the first black woman ever to be elected to a school board in the United States, like Martin received substantial white support. Allen's white Methodist Episcopal sisters and a coalition of white and black suffragists worked assiduously to put her in office. Explaining how and why Allen was elected to the office, Laura M. Johns, the white president of the Kansas Equal Suffrage Association, asserted that Allen was "not there because she sought the office—the office sought her. . . . We are all interested in her success, and will do all in our power to sustain her." However, unlike Allen and Martin, the majority of women like Terrell were appointed, not elected, to a city school board. Like Allen, Martin's success was based on support garnered from a broad base of interracial and race-specific secular and religious organizations with whom she had close connections.

Similar to Martin, Lethia Cousins Fleming was a leading figure in the Congregational Church prior to joining the Bahá'í movement. As president of the Ohio State Federation of Colored Women (1928–33), Fleming established several new departments of work, including those of Interracial Relations, Peace and Foreign Relations, Church Relations, and Fraternal Relations. She was a major force in Ohio and national Republican politics for more than four decades. Active in most of the major reform movements of the twentieth century, Fleming's activities in the suffrage movement led to an interest in politics, especially political organizing. Starting as a precinct committeewoman, ward leader, and election officer, she quickly advanced to membership on the Republican State Central Committee, and gained recognition in her appointments as director of "colored women's work" in the national campaigns of several presidential candidates, including those of Warren G. Harding (1920), Herbert Hoover (1928 and 1932), and Alfred Landon (1936).

Fleming was instrumental in organizing, chartering, and incorporating the National Association of Republican Women of the U.S. and setting up headquarters for the organization in Washington, D.C. Reputed to be the first black woman to ever serve on the Republican Party's National Program Committee before 1950, Fleming was prominent in local and national politics and a potent force in community affairs. In 1950, the *Cleveland Courier* described her as a "stern, but just Daughter Ruler of the Elks, and a tour-de-force in her church." Fleming was extremely proud of the fact that she was the first woman elected to the trustees' board of the Mt. Zion Congregational Church, and had served as vice president of the interracial Congregational Women's Clubs of Ohio and a trustee of the International Work of Federated Churches of America. She continued to be an "ardent" worker in the Congregational Church even after she developed an interest in the Bahá'í movement in 1912.

Fleming's activism in race, gender, and interracial organizations, like that of many other black women political operatives, helped her to develop an expansive base of power. She was a member of the first board of directors of the Cleveland Urban League, and a charter member of the Cleveland NAACP. Fleming held life memberships in the NACW, the NCNW, and the Ohio State Association of Elks. Little attention has been given to the economic, social, and political significance of black fraternal orders such as the Elks and its female auxiliary, the Daughter Elks. Like the Masons and its auxiliary, the Order of the Eastern Star, all of these interdenominational organizations had national and international memberships, and represented centers of power and influence. Fleming's involvement with the Elks extended over more than five decades. She was daughter ruler of Glenara Temple No. 21 from 1928 to 1949, and at the national level served more than three terms as grand trustee of the Elks, chair of its Department of Civil Liberties, and Director of Public Relations and Education.

The Elks were intricately involved in politics. In 1949, in a report of her activities as the Grand Directress of Public Relations, Fleming detailed the organization's political activism and stressed that the cooperation of each fraternal group of Elks and Daughter Elks was needed to raise the group's "set quota for this Gigantic struggle for self-preservation." (The reference to "self-preservation" alluded to the struggle of African Americans for civil rights.) Fleming's activities in 1949 included attending the national conferences of UNESCO and social workers, the Civil Rights Convention in Washington, D.C., the National Consumer's League, radio executives, and the Ohio State Association of Colored Women's Clubs' annual meeting, to gather information and make contacts for networking. Fleming also represented the Elks in their collaborations with various organizations on issues pertaining to African peoples in America and in the diaspora. In 1948 Fleming reported that eighteen hundred signatures were collected and mailed in petitions to President Truman, urging him to act immediately to free Rosa Ingram and her teenage sons, who had been accused of killing a white farmer in Georgia. During the late 1940s and early '50s, telegrams were sent to state and national political leaders urging their support of bills for funding of programs supportive of neglected and dependent children, and for the Barded Bill for Federal Aid to Education, which would benefit African Americans.

Like Fleming, Rev. Florence Spearing Randolph's social and political activism was extensive and felt at many levels in race, gender, and interracial organizations. Randolph is one of several female leaders who enjoyed careers that spanned six decades. She is an example of a minister who was a suffragist, African missionary, and temperance leader, and was active in politics for most of her life. She was among the first women to be ordained deacon and elder in the AME Zion denomination, and to be appointed pastor of a church. As a temperance organizer, suffragist, and civic reformer, Randolph became widely known for her political activism. Born in Charleston, South Carolina, in 1866, following her graduation from the Avery Institute, a school established by the American Missionary Society, Randolph moved to Jersey City, New Jersey, where she married Hugh Randolph, who worked on the railroad as a cook for the Pullman Company. She became politically active in the late 1880s following her affiliation with the WCTU in Jersey City.

As a member of the Executive Board of the New Jersey Suffrage Association, Florence Spearing Randolph was a key figure in the state's passage of the Nineteenth Amendment. She worked unceasingly to garner support for the legislation, and on several occasions testified before the New Jersey State Legislature. In 1920, Randolph was appointed by the chairman of the New Jersey Republican Party to assist Lillian Feickert, head of the Republican women's division, in organizing and getting out the vote for Warren G. Harding. Randolph had charge of organizational work among black women. In the 1930s, she became a candidate for nomination for assemblywoman on the Republican ticket. Randolph was active in most of the major white and black reform organizations of her time. She was a member and held offices in the National League of Colored Republican Women, the NACW, the Federal Council of Churches Department of Race Relations, the New Jersey Federation of Churches, and the New Jersey Women's Republican Club.

In 1915 Randolph founded the New Jersey Federation of Colored Women. She viewed the federation as an opportunity to mobilize women for the purpose of improving the status of black women and girls, and the race in all areas. Like Lugenia Burns Hope and later Mary McLeod Bethune, Randolph realized that much could be gained by having the backing of thousands of black women. In other words, similar to Hope and Bethune, she used the NACW to assert the power of black women and to open doors that were closed to the race. For example, in the aftermath of World War I, Randolph was concerned about the rising tide of racism in New Jersey and the nation. After 1920, she was extremely pained by the disenfranchisement of southern black women.

In 1920, following her appointment as head of the New Jersey Colored Republican Women, Randolph spoke at the Republican Women's Jubilee Luncheon in Trenton. In attendance were more than seven hundred white Republicans, mostly women. Randolph reminded the audience that white and black women "answered the call and went into service" for their country during the war. She said that they worked "[i]n hospitals, in suffering homes, munition plants, factories, stores, as farmers, conductors, street cleaners, . . . measuring up in every way as did our men." Having established the role black women played in the war effort, Randolph asked, "Are these same women, most of whom are wage earners and bread winners, qualified to exercise the right of franchise? Are they worthy to be called American citizens? To have any voice at all in the government by which they and their children are governed and for which they fought?" Asserting that the work of black women was a little different from that of their more "fortunate sisters," she told the audience that the fate of America was in the hands of white women, and that they had a responsibility to address the "uprisings, strikes, mob violence, lynch laws, and race riots." Concluding her speech with a reminder of the voting strength of black women in New Jersey, Randolph said, "We are 70,000 strong in this state. Our husbands and sons fought and died in the recent struggle for human rights and human liberty, just as your husbands fought and died—We bought bonds and stamps, sewed and knitted and served the country . . . all the while suffering from bitter race prejudice. And now we are asking no special favors, no Negro rights, but human rights and justice."

Randolph's interpretation of the Bible, the meaning of Jesus Christ's life, and the purpose of religion informed her political activism. She disputed claims that "the racial question is a social question, not a religious question," arguing that "religion is absolutely a social question, because every conceivable relation between individuals is involved in religion." She believed that two things were needed to bring about change: a solid belief in Christianity, and a willingness to engage the political process in every way. Successfully joining religion and politics, Randolph preached a message of black liberation in which Jesus Christ was the chief liberator. She took every opportunity to weave this message into her sermons and speeches. For example, in 1928, in a speech before the AME Zion Woman's Home and Foreign Missionary Society in New Jersey, she commented on two "horrible" lynchings, and wondered how and why such things could occur in a great country such as America. She "decided it was because we know not God," and argued that "the only thing that needs to be stressed, anytime and anywhere, among church groups is the need of a clear interpretation of Jesus Christ and his teaching."

For Randolph, Jesus's life was about the responsible use of power, and also about being a servant of God. The idea that power and responsibility go hand in hand is stressed in the Bible, and found in many religious traditions. Randolph evoked this theme to argue the importance of politics as an instrument to effect change. Randolph informed the women that the newly elected governor of New Jersey was not what blacks anticipated and that they should not expect anything from him. She also reminded the AME Zion women of their political accomplishments. Randolph said, "As church women you have organized against greed, graft, and corruption, and double dealing—you are clamoring for clean government, for honesty and respect for law, [and] you are working to get the right men and women in public office. How are you going to do it? . . . What is our objective? . . . What are we driving at? Are we dissatisfied with city and county conditions, with state and national conditions . . . ? If we are, I am asking what are we going to do about it? Who is responsible?"

Randolph used every means available to challenge the prejudice, segregation, and discrimination against African Americans. Like Frances Harper, Nannie Burroughs, and other black women leaders, Randolph did not believe that black women were powerless without the vote. Though she knew that the vote was extremely important, she also felt that informed and militant leadership, organized protest, and interracial coalitions were essential to racial adjustment at all levels of the society. During her long tenure as pastor of the Wallace Chapel AME Zion Church in Summit, New Jersey, the *Summit Herald* frequently published her letters to the editor, in which she singled out the racism and discrimination that existed in the city and responded to unjust charges made against African Americans in the newspaper. On one occasion Randolph spoke out against what she viewed as a "growing unrighteous, unjust, unfair attitude against the colored people of Summit." She related that a white woman had visited her at the Wallace Chapel parsonage and asserted that because of the actions of a few black workers, a group of housewives in Summit and Short Hills, New Jersey, "planned to dismiss all colored help and to spread propaganda to discourage those who were employing them." At first, Randolph considered the incident a "flare up" that would rapidly dissipate. However, as weeks passed, the issue gained momentum and many black workers were fired. Indignant over the treatment blacks were receiving, Randolph questioned the motives of whites: "[W]hat are you trying to do, make criminals out of Negroes—force them to steal to keep soul and body together, so that an entire race might suffer from the desperate acts of a few starving people, discriminated against for no other reason [than] that God Almighty created them black?"

Like many women preachers, some clergy wives, in their roles as leaders of missionary societies and secular organizations, were politically active. Fannie B. Peck, the wife of Rev. William Peck, a prominent Detroit AME minister, formed the Detroit Housewives' League in 1930 for the purpose of developing support for black businesses and professionals, and increasing the employment opportunities for blacks in the city. This is an example not only of economic nationalism, but also of the political activism of black women. During the Great Depression, many black businesses closed their doors or laid off employees, and blacks were refused employment by white-owned establishments located in the black community. As a leader of the Detroit Civic Rights Committee, the "most militant and active agency of black protest," Rev. Peck challenged the city's overall segregation and racial employment policies. The committee felt that if it "could properly organize" Detroit's 81,000 eligible black voters, black employment opportunities would increase. The committee's political activities contributed to the growth of the black electorate, which led to the rise of black Democrats like Charles Diggs. An important but often overlooked element in the 1930s black struggle for political power were the "Don't Buy Where You Can't Work" campaigns, which included the neighborhood boycotts of white businesses sponsored by the Housewives' Leagues.

Fannie Peck believed that the Housewives' League's goals could be achieved by directing the spending power of African Americans to black businesses. The Housewives' League, organized as an auxiliary to the National Negro Business League, was part of a network of quasi-political consumer associations established by black women in Harlem, Chicago, Philadelphia, Baltimore, and other large cities during the Great Depression. Beginning with fifty members in 1930, within a year the Detroit Housewives' League included 5,500, and within four years the organization's membership increased to ten thousand. Peck's ability to attract members was directly related to her religious leadership and her husband's prominence as the pastor of the Bethel AME Church and president of the Booker T. Washington Trade Association. The league, in collaboration with the trade association and a grocery cooperative known as "Your Store System," strove to create an economic power base. Peck used her extensive religious network to recruit members and build the organization. In 1929 Peck was elected president of the Ruth Woman's Mite Missionary Society, an office she held for at least fourteen years. In 1936 she organized a credit union, an affiliate of the Consumer-Cooperative Organization, in the Bethel AME Church. Peck served as president of the Detroit Housewives' League from 1933 to 1943, and in 1943 was elected president of the National Housewives' League.

The Detroit Housewives' League, an adjunct to the Detroit NACW, was primarily an interdenominational network of ordinary, working-class women, who neither owned nor had any connection to local black businesses. The league was reflective of the black population in Detroit, which was 99 percent working class and 1 percent professional class. It was divided into units identified by number, and represented in black neighborhoods throughout the city. The league made a special effort "to coordinate the club program with religious life in the community." To establish and maintain good relations between league members and churches, monthly visits were made by a unit to all of the churches in its area. Stressing that many of the members were housewives and working-class women who had no "professions of their own," Helen Malloy, the organization's publicity chairman, explained, "These women work daily unselfishly striving to do their bit to help put the job over."

The Detroit Housewives' League required no dues or other assessments other than national dues. It relied on the support of the business and professional people it supported. An annual scrapbook contest involving junior units, created for youth, illustrated the diverse business ventures and professions in which blacks engaged. Contest winners received books and other prizes, purchased from the Association for the Study of Negro Life and History. The league sponsored three major projects—the annual spring and fall "Trade Week" campaigns, and the Annual Trade Guide for homes and business establishments. Trade Week campaigns required door-to-door canvassing and distribution of trade bulletins. The league also conducted spending drives to increase support for black businesses and professionals. Other activities included member teas, radio programs, and monthly educational programs held in churches.

Christine S. Smith, elected president of the AME Woman's Parent Mite Missionary Society in 1931, worked closely with Fannie Peck and used her local and national prominence to promote the programs of the Detroit Housewives' League. Reflecting on the struggle of black women for equal rights, Smith pointed out that "through organization we gain the privileges to which we are entitled." As one who had risen from the depths of poverty—working as a domestic servant, washerwoman, and ironer—to the highest office a woman could hold in a denomination, she understood the struggles of black women. Her marriage in 1888 to Dr. Charles Spencer Smith, an ordained minister, a member of the Alabama House of Representatives during Reconstruction, and an AME bishop (1900–22), increased her already substantial base of contacts and provided her additional visibility. Prior to marriage, Smith was employed as an assistant vice principal in the State Normal and Industrial School in Normal, Alabama, headed by Rev. William Hooper Councill, a leader in the AME Zion Church. Smith was a seasoned political activist whose record of leadership included most of the major reform movements between 1890 and 1950. Her religious work—including service as president of the Michigan Woman's Mite Missionary Society, president of the Michigan NACW, chair of the Committee of Management of the Lucy Thurman Branch YWCA, member of the Executive Board of the Detroit Urban League, and the first female to serve on the Michigan Republican Committee—was part of the enormous social and political capital she had accumulated by 1931, which she used to develop a national network of Housewives' Leagues.

In a speech to Baltimore businessmen, Smith combined feminism with domesticity to argue for the organization of a Housewives' League in that city, stressing that although most "husbands believe they are the masters in the homes," women exert the power, controlling the operation of both husband and home and directing the spending of most of the home budget. Therefore, "if business men want to direct the channel through which the vast expenditures of the home must flow, it must be done through the organization of these women." Smith also made clear the league's intention to bend merchants to their will and see that they maintained clean grocery stores, stocked the foods and other goods league members required, and sold their products at a fair market price.

The Detroit Housewives League, in cooperation with a local white women's consumer group, organized citywide strikes and protested against merchants who charged exorbitant prices. In 1935 the interracial coalition conducted a strike against the high prices for meat. The group elected a delegation of five women to go to Washington, D.C., to demand action of President Franklin D. Roosevelt and Secretary of Agriculture Henry Wallace in connection with the meat-packing industry, which was responsible for the price gouging. The delegation, consisting of Irene Thompson and four white women, demanded an investigation of the meat packers for alleged profiteering and asked for a 20 percent reduction in meat prices. The results of this meeting are unknown, but the success of the Housewives' League during the 1930s and '40s owed a great deal to the organizing skills and volunteer work of Detroit's church women, whose political astuteness and hard work not only increased the number of businesses owned and operated by blacks in Detroit and created employment, but also was used to impact the electoral process. White politicians could not help but notice the success that the organization was having, as well as the potential voting power of the group. Also, the political activism of the Detroit Housewives' League and the Detroit City Federation led to the appointment of black women to important municipal boards by 1940.

Similar to Randolph, Peck, and Smith, Mary B. Talbert used her organizational network, including the NACW and the Baptist Woman's Convention, to raise funds for the Anti-Lynching Crusade she led under the auspices of the NAACP. Anti-lynching, a staple NACW issue from the beginning, was actively promoted by the Northeastern Federation of Colored Women long before the NAACP crusade was launched. In 1912 the federation issued a call for anti-lynching legislation. The District of Columbia, New York, Massachusetts, and New Jersey associations, as members of the Northeastern Federation, emphasized anti-lynching as part of their political agenda. In July 1917, under the leadership of Nannie Burroughs, the federation in Washington, D.C., organized a campaign against lynching and

Mary Burnett Talbert was president of the NACW and national director of the NAACP's Anti-Lynching Crusaders' campaign for congressional legislation to abolish lynching during the 1920s.

mob violence to protest the riots in East St. Louis, in which many blacks were killed and injured. In October the federation held a mass meeting at which Ida Wells-Barnett delivered a stirring speech, telling blacks to "Agitate—Then Act." Wells-Barnett revealed that she had been commissioned by the NACW to organize anti-lynching clubs as auxiliaries to the national federation, and delegated to represent the organization before the Department of Justice and congressional committees in the investigation of the East St. Louis riots. At the NACW's convention in 1918, Burroughs presented a report on lynching and other abuses that had occurred throughout the United States. In 1919 the New York Federation, headed by Maria Lawton, sent a letter to Congress protesting lynching and urging support for anti-lynching legislation. During that year, the New Jersey Federation, under the leadership of Rev. Florence Spearing Randolph, authorized a letter to President Woodrow Wilson refuting the traditional justification—the alleged rape of white women—for lynching black men.

At the 1922 Spring Conference of the NAACP, held in Newark, New Jersey, U.S. Congressman Leonidas C. Dyer of Missouri suggested that black people organize a national campaign against lynching and agitate for the legislation that he drafted. The House of Representatives passed the Dyer Anti-Lynching Bill, but the bill was stalled in the Senate. Sixteen black women from five states immediately formed the Committee of Anti-Lynching Crusaders, set up a permanent organization and elected Mary Talbert as national director of the campaign. At the NACW convention in August 1922, the Anti-Lynching Department recommended immediate action. An anti-lynching delegation was appointed, representing the pivotal states in the fall congressional elections, to meet with President Warren G. Harding. Ida Brown, an officer in the New Jersey Federation and the AME Zion Women's Missionary Society, as the spokesperson for the NACW reminded the president that in 1920 he had run on the Republican Party platform, which pledged to take steps to abolish lynching. In his first message to Congress, Harding recommended support for passage of the Dyer Anti-Lynching Bill.

To undergird and strengthen the efforts of the Anti-Lynching Crusaders, Talbert appealed to her Baptist sisters for support. In December 1922, in an address to the Women's Convention called "The Cause of the Crusaders," she asked members to return home and organize "a band of Crusaders, to pray and pay, that our race might receive justice at the hands of our country." The need was to raise funds to aid the NAACP in its legal campaign to outlaw lynching. Burroughs reinforced Talbert's message by emphasizing the WC's outreach and power to effect change. She asserted, "We are in direct touch with more women than any other organization of Colored women in the world. United and determined we are invincible." Burroughs suggested that the WC appoint a committee of one hundred to cooperate with the NAACP. The WC appointed a director in each state, and each town had its "key women." The state directors and key women were part of the NACW and the black religious organizational network. The majority of meetings and numerous fund-raising events were held in churches. At a meeting in Buffalo, New York, Helen Curtis, the state director, explained, "[T]he women will begin with prayer at a sunrise, and end with prayer at a sunset—in between they will do a much more sweaty work than praying." Stressing the need to include all classes of black women, Curtis stated, "Of course there should not be a colored

American woman from the wash pot to the university who will not want to 'count [as] one' in this crusade." Buffalo is an example of the format used by the WC in other states for organizing essentially working-class church women to raise funds to support the anti-lynching campaign.

In late December 1922, when it was announced that the Dyer Anti-Lynching Bill had been defeated, Mary McLeod Bethune, a prominent member of the Methodist Episcopal Church and the president of the Southeastern Federation, stated, "[C]olored women of the South are bitterly disappointed. . . . Nevertheless we are urging our people not to lose hope. God is stronger than all the combined powers of injustice and wrong. He is at the helm; and these cruel practices that find victims in both races must and will cease." Bethune announced that black women would continue to fight to end lynching. Through the efforts of Talbert, the Anti-Lynching Crusaders, and others, the NAACP raised more than $45,000 by 1924. As the national president of NACW (1924–28) and the founder and first president of the National Council of Negro Women (1935–49), Bethune continued to emphasize anti-lynching and to fight for an end to segregation and discrimination in the United States.

Though African American women's political agenda concentrated on issues of national significance such as employment, segregation, suffrage, and lynching, it was also transnational in that it included an international focus. Traditionally, church women's organizations sponsored programs and provided support for their denomination's foreign missionary programs in Africa and the Carribean. However, the founding of the International Council of Women of the Darker Races in the 1920s represented a new level of interest and an effort to expand on and internationalize their concerns. The ICWDR was an interdenominational coalition developed by leading NACW women such as Nannie Burroughs, Addie Dickerson, Mary McLeod Bethune, Margaret Murray Washington, and Mary Church Terrell, most of whom possessed years of experience working with their denominational organizations to improve conditions for people of color in Africa, Haiti, Puerto Rico, the Phillippines, and Brazil. Many ICWDR women also held membership in the Women's International League for Peace and Freedom. Similar to the YWCA, the WILPF included a network of prominent white women with powerful connections to the major social, political, and economic networks in the United States. Black women saw the potential for using the league to achieve their international goals. The ICWDR served as an educational forum, a base from which they could form significant links with other women of color in the diaspora, and a think tank to flesh out international issues. Like the YWCA, the WILPF served as a conduit for achieving some of their international goals.

Viewed through a national prism, the political activism of African American women between 1920 and 1950 was multidimensional and sectional in orientation. Northern, southern, and western strategies existed for achieving the overarching goal of racial and gender justice in America. Segregation and rank discrimination defined every area of American life, especially in the South. Southern black women such as Charlotte Hawkins Brown, Mary Jackson McCrory, Lucy Craft Laney, Mary McLeod Bethune, and Lugenia Burns Hope knew that their strategies for addressing racism and dismantling the southern structure of dominance had to be subtle, covert, interracial, and exacting. However, there was also a national strategy for attacking the root causes of lynching, racial segregation, and discrimination, and for accessing the human and fiscal resources necessary to carry out a larger reform agenda in the black community. In addition to securing political suffrage, the national and sectional strategies of African American women were incisive in their focus on the importance of engaging white leaders, especially white women, in the struggle for racial justice. They recognized that white women were at the center of progressivism and had the ear of many powerful white men—their fathers, husbands, brothers, sons, and lovers. All black women, especially those employed as domestic servants in the homes of white people, were encouraged to "use their influence for the good of the race"—to convert whites to the cause of justice.

In the years before the formal beginning of the interracial movement, black women openly plotted strategies for reaching and using white women and their organizations as tools to achieve justice and equality and to acquire resources. At the same time, though they showed little interest in equal rights for blacks, progressive southern white women and men were concerned about being a mediating influence between African Americans and whites, primarily to control and contain black people and to quell the threat of racial violence, which was never far away. Because of these and other concerns, black and white women engaged in a concerted effort to develop a cross-racial dialogue related to lynching, racial discrimination, and economic and political reform. At the center of that dialogue in the South were the Methodist Episcopal Church Woman's Missionary Council, and the NACW's Southeastern Federation. The Southern Commission on Interracial Cooperation included representatives of these groups and provided an avenue for black women to pursue aspects of their political agenda.

At the national level, white Methodist women and their organizations represented the largest and most powerful group of denominational women in the United States. Southern Methodist women worked closely with black Methodist women of all persuasions, in particular those affiliated with the CME and Methodist Episcopal denominations, developing local social reform programs. However, it is their work in the interracial movement that had the greatest impact. Black and white Baptist, Episcopalian, and Presbyterian women also developed modes of communication and interaction through their organizations. As noted, the WC cooperated with both the ABHMS and the WMU. At the center of the national dialogue were the YWCA, the NACW, and the Church Women's Committee, a unit of the Federal Council of the Churches of Christ's Department of Race Relations. The NACW, as the national and interdenominational voice of black women, was effective because it could engage issues of national and sectional importance through the leadership of diverse entities and interests, including its city, state, and regional federations. Between 1920 and 1960, these organizations, the NCNW, the black women's missionary societies and conventions, and Church Women United, an interdenominational organization of women, would form the core of the women's interracial movement and have an impact on the modern Civil Rights Movement that emerged in the 1950s.

CHAPTER 6

"Across the Divide"

The Interracial and Interdenominational Movement, 1880–1940

Hath not the bond-woman and her scarce emancipated daughter done what they could?

Will not our more favored sisters, convinced of our desires and aspirations because of these first few feeble efforts, stretch out the helping hand that we may rise.

Gertrude Bustill Mossell (1894)

The next long step towards the solution of the race problem must be taken by white women. . . . We will not get anywhere with our race relations program and interracial cooperation schemes until white women decide that this roasting of human beings alive, this lynching and burning in America must stop. . . . White Christian women in America meet annually, appropriate large sums of money for the education and Christianization of peoples in all lands and for Negro education in America. But these Christian women have never raised their voices in protest against the inhuman, barbarous practice of their own people in this "land of the free and home of the brave." The white women are the only sentiment makers in this country and until they speak boldly and bravely the white men who are working at this Race Relationship Program might as well spend their time counting the stars by night and sweeping the sun out of their path by day as to hold conferences to discuss how two races can develop more natural respect for each other.

Nannie Helen Burroughs (1921)

Realizing that interracial action must be preceded by interracial thinking, we find the women of our church need to learn to work with rather than for the Negro. We believe that existing church organizations constitute the best channel for creating this attitude.

Committee of the Interracial Conference of Church Women (1926)

THE TWENTIETH-CENTURY interracial movement was officially launched in 1919 by the Federal Council of the Churches of Christ in America, a Protestant organization founded in 1908. The movement engaged thousands of churches and religious organizations and extended to many secular associations. Among the thirty-three denominations originally affiliated with the FCC were the African Methodist Episcopal, the African Methodist Episcopal Zion, the Colored Methodist Episcopal, and the National Baptist Convention. These organizations included more than 90 percent of the membership of black churches. From the beginning African Americans were represented in the FCC. However, their voices were not being heard and their issues were not being directly addressed. Although the FCC was cognizant of racial issues, during the first decade of the organization's existence its programs were primarily supportive of domestic and foreign missions that served a diverse minority population. Calling for racial toleration and the elimination of racial violence, the FCC became the moral voice of America. Stressing education and dialogue on issues of race, its main concern was the elimination of racial tension and amelioration of the social conditions confronted by racial and ethnic minorities. The movement launched by the FCC and subsequent interracial organizations helped to lay the groundwork for the modern Civil Rights Movement of the 1950s and '60s.

W. E. B. Du Bois's prophetic prediction that the color line would be the problem of the twentieth century fell on deaf ears. For many Americans the abolition of slavery and the freeing of almost four million enslaved persons was the beginning of a new era that called for a restructuring of expectations and relationships between white and black people. In 1865 most African Americans had enthusiastically looked forward to a life of freedom that held the possibility of unprecedented educational and economic advancement. At the same time many white Americans were apprehensive about the social, political, and economic changes that would surely alter life as they had known it. As America became industrialized, the North and South forged new economic and political alliances and closed ranks around the Supreme Court's ruling in the 1896 *Plessy v. Ferguson* case, which gave legal sanction to racial segregation. The *Plessy* decision provided the base for building a system of segregation and discrimination that would engulf the United States for decades to come and provide a platform for the interracial movement.

The majority of African Americans in the South lived in poverty. Generations of blacks lived in one- and two-room shacks on the plantations where their enslaved forebears resided. The interracial movement brought together white and black church women who created an extensive network of local projects designed to improve living conditions and ameliorate racial differences.

Launching the Interracial Movement

THE INTERRACIAL MOVEMENT was launched at the end of World War I, during the Great Migration and in the wake of urban riots that occurred in several northern cities during the summer of 1919. A complex of social movements and a change in the external conditions of African Americans altered their material condition and transformed their consciousness. As a result of the migration, thousands of blacks from small towns moved to urban industrial centers, where, for the first time, many were gainfully employed and earning fairly decent wages. At the same time, in the midst of rising black expectations and escalating racial tensions, 400,000 black soldiers returned to the United States and civilian life. The clash between black and white ideals and aspirations and the surging African American race consciousness posed a threat to many whites. To offset what some black and white leaders viewed as a potentially dangerous racial situation, on September 4, 1919, the Home Missions Council, which comprised a coalition of Protestant missionary societies, called a conference to discuss their concerns.

With the approval of the conference and the FCC Committee on Negro Churches, in 1919 the FCC issued a statement to its members entitled "A Race Crisis," in which they declared, "We must face frankly the fact that a most dangerous interracial situation now threatens our country. The problems growing out of the presence of two races in America are clearly seen to be nationwide and the adjustments must be . . . made on the basis of national responsibility. The migration of thousands of Negroes to the North emphasizes this fact. The outbreaks in several cities and the persistence of the anarchy and treason of lynch-law imperil our democracy." Asserting the preeminence of the Christian church in averting conflicts, the FCC called on its affiliates to provide "the ideals, the program and the leadership" in the crisis. Churches were warned that if they failed to assume their "obligation," leadership would "pass not only to secular agencies, economic or socialistic, but to forces that are destructive of civilization." The FCC also called for "A Constructive Program for Just Interracial Relations," and recommended that the government take action against mob violence and lynching, and ensure equal employment opportunity and access to decent housing, adequate educational facilities, and the franchise. In simple language that was clearly understood by white and black Americans of that time, the FCC spoke about the need to ensure "the protection of the sanctity of the home and womanhood"— alluding to the sensitive issue of rape. This statement was read in various ways. For some white Americans it meant protecting white women from black brutes. African Americans used the statement to make their case about the historic rape and forced seduction of black women. African American women in the interracial movement continued to reiterate this concern.

The FCC Department of Race Relations

IN THE AFTERMATH of the 1919 pronouncement, churches and related social reform agencies held numerous meetings and conferences to discuss issues of race. In 1921 the FCC set up the Commission on the Church and Race Relations, which became known as the Department of Race Relations. Under the leadership of George Edmund Haynes, the full-time executive secretary, and Will W. Alexander, the director of the southern Commission on Interracial Cooperation, the FCC launched a national interracial movement and became the catalyst for the development of numerous local, state, and national organizations whose goal was to eliminate denigrating racial stereotypes and allay the fears, hatreds, suspicions, and misunderstandings surrounding the issue of race, especially as it related to black Americans. In establishing the Department of Race Relations, the FCC envisioned the churches serving as conduits through which its program of education and social action could be disseminated at the local level and eventually to the nation as a whole. The DRR would define the methods and techniques and aid the churches in utilizing them to apply the Christian ideal of social justice to change racial attitudes and patterns, and to improve relations between black and white people.

George Haynes, a prominent black sociologist and a cofounder of the Committee on Urban Conditions Among Negroes (the forerunner of the National Urban League), helped organize the FCC's Department of Race Relations and was employed as its first executive secretary. His associate, Will Alexander, a noted white reformer, southern Methodist preacher, and former YMCA executive, was not actively involved in the day-to-day operation of the DRR. However, the FCC defended its choice of having both a black and a white heading up the department. It was important from the outset for the FCC to send a message that the department would be interracial in its operations. Also, the FCC recognized the need to build a base of support that included black and white leaders from different geographical regions. This was of special importance since the FCC did not operate to any extent in the South.

Because of its liberal image and policies, few southern churches held membership in the FCC. In appointing Alexander, the FCC emphasized the work and principles of the CIC, and supported the CIC's efforts to organize local interracial committees in the South. And the CIC anticipated attracting more members of FCC's affiliate churches to its local and state interracial committees. To address questions regarding the relationship between the FCC and the CIC, in 1925 the FCC explained that one of the reasons for establishing the DRR was to provide additional support for the CIC's southern work. The Commission on Interracial Cooperation, a voluntary association of southern leaders, was organized in Atlanta in 1919 under the leadership of Will Alexander and John Eagan, a southern Presbyterian layman. It was the first interracial organization in the United States. Although the DRR and the CIC were independent entities, they were perceived as interdependent agencies whose cooperative efforts could be mutually beneficial, particularly in the South, where the CIC operations were concentrated.

Interracial Work Among Church Women

THE FIRST EFFORTS to develop interracial work among church women occurred in the southern Methodist Episcopal Church in 1921 under the leadership of Carrie Parks Johnson. Johnson also served as chair of the CIC's Women's Committee, which was organized in 1921 and was the model for the FCC's Church Women's Committee on Race Relations, established in 1927. Johnson, like many black and white female leaders, used her religious and secular organizational bases to develop a powerful political bloc of support among white women, who formed the rank-and-file workers in the larger movement for social reform and were instrumental in organizing the first interracial local committees in the South. Growing up during the late nineteenth century, Johnson learned firsthand that the most important channels for dealing with social reform issues were the church and the Woman's Christian Temperance Union. Thousands of women, black and white, became involved in the temperance movement, the majority of whom were Methodist women. Focused on social reform, not just alcohol, by 1892 the WCTU was the largest and most dominant organization of women in the nation.

The WCTU was headed by Frances Willard, a Methodist educator who understood the relationship between reform and politics. It provided a vehicle for expanding the role of women and mobilizing their leadership for social reform. Protestant churches, especially the black and white Methodist women's missionary societies and the Baptist women's organizations that sprang up during the 1870s, were actively involved in the temperance movement and in church reform, especially women's struggle for ordination and laity rights. Alcohol and related social problems crossed racial, ethnic, religious, and geographical lines, bringing together American women of all persuasions to work for a single cause. The WCTU officers and leaders were predominantly Methodist women. In effect, the WCTU created extensive ecumenical cooperation among women from diverse missionary societies, which served as an organizing model for the interracial efforts of church women through the FCC, the CIC, Church Women United, the National Council of Churches, and the Civil Rights Movement of the 1950s and '60s.

The Methodist Woman's Missionary Council

PROTESTANT CHURCH WOMEN, particularly those in the Woman's Missionary Council of the Methodist Episcopal Church, South, developed an extensive program of educational and social service work among African Americans and other minorities that provided a model useful for launching a national interracial movement. The Methodist Church was the largest and wealthiest Protestant denomination in the United States. In 1920 Methodist women along with the YWCA formed the most powerful bloc of women in the United States. Thus, with Carrie Parks Johnson as head of both the CIC Women's Committee and the MECS's Commission on Race, and a Methodist woman in charge of the YWCA, Methodist women wielded an inordinate amount of power in the interracial movement. Under Johnson's leadership, Methodist missionary societies created an extensive network of local committees that developed detailed surveys of housing, sanitation, and recreational facilities in African American neighborhoods and established church study groups on black achievement and progress. This knowledge prepared them to work on social issues and improvement projects in black communities. Between 1922 and 1927, the number of these committees grew from 110 to 606. Methodist and CIC women leaders were intimately involved with the YWCA, which was an important institutional means for including black women in the interracial movement. During the early years of the interracial movement the most important avenue for reaching African American women of all persuasions was the National Association of Colored Women. As a national organization of black women's clubs, by 1910 the NACW had developed a network of local, state, and regional federations that included the leaders of most black religious and secular organizations, including the YWCA.

The National Association of Colored Women's Clubs

BETWEEN 1890 AND WORLD WAR I African Americans became painfully aware of the discrepancies between the reality of their lives and the ideologies of democracy and freedom espoused by the United States. The ever-tightening reins of segregation, humiliating discrimination, escalating numbers of lynchings, and bloody race riots of 1919 convinced black leaders of the need for direct and open communication with white leaders—potential allies who would aid in organizing a massive attack on racism in the United States. From its inception in 1896 as the first national black secular organization to unify black women's clubs, the NACW, through its departments of work, concentrated on issues related to the welfare of the race in general and black women in particular. Civil rights issues, including suffrage, segregation and discrimination, peonage, and lynching, were given priority. These concerns were part and parcel of the NACW philosophy of racial uplift. The establishment of Evangelistic Work and Interracial Relations departments to facilitate the development of programs, as well as to ensure NACW representation and involvement in activities and issues of importance to its membership, illustrates the extent to which the organization was involved in American life and culture and its importance to the black community.

By 1915 African American leaders were actively soliciting the help of white religious and secular moderates in organizing the southern attack on racism. Prominent black women leaders in the NACW's Southeastern Federation of Colored Women's Clubs—such as Lugenia Burns Hope, Mary McLeod Bethune, Charlotte Hawkins Brown, Margaret Murray Washington, Elizabeth Ross Haynes, Lucy Craft Laney, Janie Porter Barrett, Grace Towns Hamilton, Marion Wilkinson, Minnie Lee Crosthwaite, Juliette Derricotte, and Eva D. Bowles—believed that by working with upper-middle-class white women they could gain support for their agenda in southern black communities. Most of these women agreed with S. Willie Layten's claim that "[t]he white women of the South are the power behind the throne and dictate conditions. They are more powerful than the law makers in our congressional halls." Forming themselves into an unofficial black women's caucus, these leaders used their religious and secular organizational networks to make contacts with white and black women who were willing to actively involve themselves in the identification of resources and aid in opening the doors of communication with other white leaders. To effect their agenda, the black women's caucus first approached the YWCA, one of the few white organizations that provided black women access to a national network of influential white Christian women who were prominent leaders in their local communities.

The YWCA membership comprised women from Christian religious traditions. Its community-based contacts included the poor, immigrants, Asians, a variety of persons of white ethnicity, African

Lucy Craft Laney, as principal of the Haines Normal and Industrial Institute, was the only black woman at the head of a major school affiliated with the Presbyterian Church. A suffragist and member of the NACW and YWCA, she chaired the Colored Section of the Interracial Commission of Augusta, Georgia.

Americans, college students, and church leaders. The YWCA was strongly influenced by the Social Gospel movement, with its ethic of social reform. While black women leaders recognized the YWCA's potential for doing significant interracial work, they knew all too well the racial pitfalls and barriers, including segregation and racism, that existed at all levels of the organization. Because of the bureaucratic nature of the YWCA, it took an inordinate amount of time to get action on any initiative. Casting an eye toward the Methodist Episcopal Church's Woman's Missionary Council—the second most promising organization through which African American women might advance their agenda—black women noted the MECS's work in establishing the Bethlehem Centers (settlement houses) in black communities, and its stand against lynching.

John and Lugenia Burns Hope are excellent examples of how black leaders used white allies to accomplish their goals. John Hope was the first black president of Morehouse College and later the president of Atlanta University. Lugenia Burns Hope founded the Neighborhood Union, a settlement house and community project administered, supported, and controlled solely by black women. Establishing residence in Atlanta in 1897, by 1915 John and Lugenia Hope had created a broad personal and political network that included white and black leaders. In 1919, they succeeded in getting Will Alexander to agree to work with them to organize an assault on racism. Alexander's previous work coordinating YMCA war relief work provided him access to YMCA funds and a network of white leaders. In 1919 Alexander, as a cofounder of the Commission on Interracial Cooperation, played a key role in choosing the twenty select white leaders who served on the CIC Board of Directors. The CIC's central concern was improving relations between the races. Like the FCC, at its founding the CIC did not seek equal rights for African Americans or the elimination of segregation. Moreover, the CIC met for a year before deciding to include African Americans. A product of its time, the CIC was paternalistic and sometimes condescending to its black members.

Will Alexander, despite his conservatism on the issue of race, proved to be a faithful ally whom Lugenia Hope used to gain access to the leaders of the Methodist Woman's Missionary Council. At Hope's insistence, Alexander used his Methodist connections to approach the leaders of the MECS and to introduce them to the NACW's southern black women's caucus. In 1920 Belle Harris Bennett, the president of the Methodist Woman's Missionary Council, convinced the organization to appoint a Commission on Race Relations for the purpose of "studying the whole question of race relationships, the needs of Negro women and children and the methods of cooperation by which better conditions might be brought about." For the members of the MECS, Christianity could be a powerful force for addressing racial differences and interracial crises.

Crossing the Divide: Meeting at Tuskegee Institute

SARA ESTELLE HASKIN and Carrie Parks Johnson, members of the MECS Executive Committee, initiated the research on race relations by attending the NACW's national meeting at Tuskegee Institute. Haskin, the former supervisor of the Nashville Bethlehem House and a YWCA leader, had put forward the motion to create the MECS commission. Carrie Parks Johnson was appointed chairman of the group. Hearing of the creation of the Methodist commission, Lugenia Hope extended an invitation to Haskin and Johnson to attend the biennial conference of the National Association of Colored Women at Tuskegee Institute in July 1920. Arriving at Tuskegee, Haskin and Johnson discovered a world, and a black woman, that they did not know. In the NACW body of eight hundred women they found "orators, writers, poets, artists, business women, teachers, secretaries, lawyers, bankers, etc." A leader in the NACW's Southeastern Federation of Colored Women's Clubs observed, "[A]s they listened to the addresses and debates and witnessed the splendid executive ability of those educated Negro women, they realized that in that body was massed a potential power of which they had little dreamed."

Prior to the conference, Lugenia Hope had asked a select group of women, leaders in the Southeastern Federation, to remain after the close of the biennial for a special meeting with the representatives of the Methodist commission. In that meeting, black women spoke frankly and with great confidence about their concerns. Reflecting upon her experience, Carrie Parks Johnson said, "I had a new world opened to me, a world I had never conceived before." Unlike the white women, the black women were ambivalent about the Tuskegee meeting and uncertain about what could be accomplished. Leaders such as Charlotte Hawkins Brown rightly suspected that the white women's concern regarding "Negro Betterment" was related to their interest in developing a larger and more efficient black cadre of domestic servants. The meeting was somewhat tense; the air was filled with the black women's hostility, and given the southern racial protocol that governed black and white relationships, there was some confusion as to the proper etiquette. This was the beginning of a relationship between the Methodist Woman's Missionary Council, the CIC, and the Southeastern Federation of Colored Women's Clubs that would be fraught with much struggle as white and black women worked to peel back the layers of racism and develop a mutual respect based on their common concerns for addressing a multiplicity of difficult issues including lynching, the treatment of black women, and racial tensions.

Haskin and Johnson reported their findings to Will Alexander and the MECS, revealing how startled they were to find so many educated, confident, articulate, and refined black women whose oratorical skills and knowledge of parliamentary procedures equaled those of white women leaders. In *Southern Women and Racial Adjustment*, Lily H. Hammond stated, "This discovery of the educated colored woman is of deep significance. It is she who must lift her people, but she can do so little without our help!" Hammond summed up the feelings—and the paternalistic views—of most white women leaders. Encouraged by the MECS commission's report, and pressured by Haskin and Johnson to set up a separate CIC women's committee, Will Alexander convinced the CIC of the need to finance a meeting composed of the leaders of all the denominations and Christian agencies of white women in the South, and representatives of the Southeastern Federation of Colored Women's Clubs. Alexander was fearful of the publicity that the gathering might invite, and its potential impact on the CIC. Thus, in planning for the conference Alexander arranged for the meeting to be held in a small, dingy room in the Memphis YMCA, and sent out a vaguely worded invitation that simply stated that the gathering would consider "important problems." The conference was held in Memphis, Tennessee, on October 6–7, 1920, and was attended by one hundred women from all southern states, a majority of whom were the general and state officers of white women's missionary organizations representing members of the MECS, and the presidents and social service superintendents of Methodist conferences located in areas with large black populations. Four black women, representatives of the NACW's Southeastern Federation of Colored Women's Clubs—Margaret Murray Washington, Jennie B. Moton, Elizabeth Ross Haynes, and Charlotte Hawkins Brown—were invited to attend and speak to the gathering.

The Crossroads of Race: The Memphis Meeting

IN THE AFTERMATH of the Tuskegee meeting, the Southeastern Federation of Colored Women's Clubs drafted a statement setting forth the reasons for existing racial conditions. Believing that the position paper would serve as a basis for the launching of the MECS's new race relations program, the African American women's caucus presented a broad range of black issues: working conditions for black women domestics, child welfare, segregation and discrimination on public transportation, education, lynching, inflammatory and misleading representations of blacks in the white press, and the right to vote. Though the statement addressed matters pertinent to all African Americans and included specific recommendations, it was very pointed in its discussion of what Rebecca Stiles Taylor, the inveterate club woman and journalist, described as "the many unjust and humiliating practices [of] which colored women in the South have been victims." At the Memphis conference, the black delegates were surprised to find Carrie Johnson reading a revised and somewhat watered-down version of their statement to the conference. The lynching discussion was changed to include a preface suggesting that black men, by their actions, were responsible for exciting "the mob spirit." The suffrage resolution calling for white women to "indicate their sanction of the ballot for all citizens" was omitted. And Johnson removed the preamble that demanded for black women "all the privileges and rights granted to American womanhood."

Following Johnson's speech, Washington, Brown, and Haynes spoke on "What It Means to Be a Negro," "The Negro in His Home," and "The Difficulties of the Daily Life of the Negro People." The black women delegates were upset by the changes made to their statement; however, they heeded the advice of Margaret Murray Washington, an advocate of accommodation, tempered their speeches, and were silent at the meeting. They left the Memphis meeting feeling betrayed and determined to have the Southeastern Federation of Colored Women's Clubs' original statement published in the MECS's proposed pamphlet. After much negotiation, and the MECS's decision to abandon the project, the federation at its June 1921 meeting voted to adopt and publish the black women's statement, in pamphlet form, as the platform of the federation. Published under the title "Southern Negro Women and Race Co-Operation," the pamphlet did not include the original preamble and suffrage plank, and the discussion of lynching was toned down. Agreements to these changes represent the compromises that the black women agreed to among themselves. This was just one of the many accommodations that African American women leaders in the twentieth-century interracial movement would agree to in order to move their feminist and racial agendas forward.

In the context of 1920, Carrie Johnson and the MECS leaders were "liberals." For many whites, these women were radical. To confront traditional white attitudes, prejudices, racist practices—and, indeed, lynching—was a radical move on the part of a southern white woman. On the other hand, black women bristled at the continued compromises and accommodations they had to make to what they viewed as blatant racism. But black and white women recognized that there could be no change without negotiation and compromise. White women emerged from the experience with a new understanding and appreciation for educated black women and their concerns, and African American women were more determined to fight for the rights of black women and their families. The Memphis conference helped black and white women to begin the crossing of the divide.

News of the Memphis meeting spread rapidly, and within months, both the Southeastern Federation's pamphlet and the MECS's recommendations were published and reprinted in the white and black press. The reception in the black press was generally laudatory and reflected the hope of most African Americans that their struggle for racial equality would be addressed. The FCC's newly organized Commission on the Church and Race Relations was elated over the news, and predicted that the Memphis conference would "do more to bring the womanhood of the South into active service in behalf of the race than any other yet held." The MECS and NACW leaders and the CIC were acclaimed as "the strongest force yet organized in the nation in behalf of the colored race." The black women's caucus made some compromises, but there was a general feeling that black women, in particular the members of the Southeastern Federation, were the victors. For many years afterward, at the annual meetings of the federation, the leaders asserted that one of the "three planks in the platform of the Southeastern [Federation]" was interracial relations, and that it was their federation that "laid the foundation for the great interracial program now existing today in the southland." This attitude undoubtedly carried over to the Civil Rights Movement of the 1950s.

Church Women and the Interracial Movement:
The CIC Women's Committee

THE SUCCESS OF the Memphis meeting encouraged the MECS to move forward with its interracial agenda, and convinced Will Alexander and the CIC that the time was ripe for the establishment of a CIC Women's Committee. Carrie Johnson was the linchpin that brought together the MECS and the CIC; in her dual role as the chairperson of the MECS's Commission on Race Relations (1921–26) and director of the CIC's Women's Committee (1921–25), funded jointly by MECS and the CIC, Johnson was able to build a network comprised initially of women's missionary societies. In the beginning the base of support for the CIC Women's Committee came from white Methodist women and their local associations, many of whom were members of the

YWCA and the WCTU. Laying the groundwork for expanding the southern women's interracial movement, the Memphis conference established the Continuation Committee, composed of ten white women, seven of whom were appointed by the women's church organizations in the South. This committee, in cooperation with the CIC, was responsible for organizing southern white women. Similarly, the Southeastern Federation of Colored Women's Clubs established the Interracial Committee, which was comprised mostly of women who formed the black women's caucus.

In October 1922 the Continuation Committee invited the Interracial Committee of the Southeastern Federation to a meeting in Atlanta, where they were asked to nominate seven black women for membership on the CIC Women's Committee. Among the eight black women who were nominated and elected were Margaret Washington, Mary McLeod Bethune, Charlotte Hawkins Brown, Lugenia Hope, Mary McCrorey, Lucy Craft Laney, Janie Porter Barrett, and Marion Wilkinson. Although all of these women belonged to the NACW's Southeastern Federation, they were also affiliated with several religious traditions and Christian organizations, including the Methodist Episcopal, Baptist, and Presbyterian churches and the YWCA. White and black members of the CIC were responsible for disseminating CIC plans in their churches and through their missionary organizations, and for seeing that local, state, and district groups implemented programs designed to improve race relations.

NACW women carefully developed strategies to promote their agenda through the CIC. For example, to address the issue of black girls who were arrested for minor offenses being placed in prisons with hardened criminals, the Southeastern Federation decided to raise funds and develop their own institutions. By 1920 the NACW had succeeded in building institutions for delinquent black girls in Alabama, South Carolina, North Carolina, Georgia, and several other states. Once established, these facilities required continuous support. Believing state governments were obligated to provide "separate but equal" institutions for blacks, NACW leaders promoted this agenda through the numerous interracial organizations and committees. In 1925 Lugenia Hope and Selena Sloan Butler, members of the Georgia NACW state federation, used their positions on key interracial boards and committees to promote an agenda that included having the Georgia state legislature enact laws and provide support for an anti-lynching law, an institution for delinquent black girls, support for improved housing, education, justice in the courts, and better travel conditions. Selena Butler, as a member of the Executive Committee of the Georgia CIC, and co-head of the "colored" section of the committee, was instrumental in seeing that the committee's agenda correlated with that of the NACW.

As the women's interracial movement progressed between 1922 and 1950, NACW women throughout the United States could be found serving on local, state, and national committees, as well as on the boards of national organizations such as the FCC's Church Women's Committee, and Church Women United. Like Butler and Hope, Helen Sayre, a noted Episcopal woman from Chicago, was a pioneer in the club movement. In 1896, as president of the St. Louis, Missouri, Woman's Club, Sayre was a delegate to the NACW founding meeting in Washington, D.C. Known for her work with the Illinois League of Women Voters, the Chicago Woman's Republican Club, the YWCA, and other national organizations, as an NACW devotee Sayre was among the numerous black women who recognized the importance of networking in the interracial movement during the early twentieth century.

In 1929 Jessie Daniel Ames became director of women's work for the Commission on Interracial Cooperation. Carrie Parks Johnson first encountered Ames in 1922 at a meeting of Texas white women interested in working with the newly formed Texas Interracial Commission. Ames was outspoken in her opposition to the Ku Klux Klan and supported education for African Americans. Impressed with her potential for leadership, Johnson appointed Ames chairman of the Texas commission's woman's committee. Ames was also elected to membership on the CIC Women's Committee. In 1930 Ames, as the most prominent white woman in the southern interracial movement, founded the Association of Southern Women for the Prevention of Lynching. With the support of the CIC Women's Committee, the women's missionary societies of the Methodist Episcopal Church, South, and black and white branches of the YWCA, Ames mounted a campaign for racial justice. Soon after assuming leadership of the women's committee, Ames sought to extend the CIC's contacts with black women in the southern states. During the 1920s Ames had attended several of the interracial meetings sponsored by the Federal Council of Churches and other organizations. These meetings brought her into contact with prominent black women leaders, such as Nannie Burroughs, whom she would later engage with in her work with the CIC. In March 1931 Burroughs was informed of her election to membership in the CIC. During the next three years Burroughs and Ames discussed strategies to secure the franchise for African Americans. Ames believed that many problems could be solved if women participated in local political and judicial processes.

In early January 1934, Ames wrote a letter to Burroughs in which she argued that Burroughs and black leaders such as Mary McLeod Bethune and Charlotte Moton should set up an organization to hold citizenship classes in the South and help secure the franchise for blacks. Burroughs agreed that black women should lead the fight and indicated her willingness to meet with Ames, Bethune, and Moton to discuss the issue. As a member of the CIC Women's Committee, Ames had worked with Bethune and Moton for several years before assuming the position as director, but she did not feel comfortable approaching them directly on this issue. Historian Jacqueline Dowd Hall suggests that Ames's "relationships with individual black women such as Bethune seem to have been based on mutual, if distant respect. Yet it is equally clear that Ames seldom saw blacks as equals even in the struggle against their own oppression." Ames did not consider black women for membership in the ASWPL, and "felt no obligation to be responsive to black agendas for reform." The question is, why was Ames so solicitous of Burroughs's help in getting support from southern black women leaders for a black suffrage campaign? Perhaps the answer lies in Ames's need to avoid growing conflict with NAACP head Walter White and other black leaders because of her refusal to support a federal anti-lynching lobbying campaign during the congressional hearings of 1934. Her overtures to Burroughs, Bethune, and Moton appear to be more of a ruse to deflect attention away from her personal politics and to engender the support of black women for the ASWPL's program of local and regional intervention, amelioration, and political education. Ames was far more liberal than most white southerners; however, like most white liberals of the time, she could be condescending and paternalistic in her treatment of black Americans.

The Roots of Black and White Women's Work in the Interracial Movement

MOST STUDIES OF WOMEN, including those on religion, have ignored the roots of black and white women's work in the interracial movement, and have paid little attention to the important and complex networks women developed to consolidate their power. A careful study of the executive boards of women's religious and secular reform organizations such as the YWCA, the NACW, and the WCTU reveals patterns of membership and leadership in these organizations that led to the creation of interlocking directorates. This was no less true among the major black organizations. Claude A. Barnett, founder of the Associated Negro Press, observed in 1924, "Colored America is better organized than ever before. Interlocking, group leadership is proving effective, and it is a well-known fact that the time is here when Colored America can send an effective message from one end of the nation to the other in twenty-four hours through various organized bodies." Barnett noted that the NAACP, the National Urban League, the National Business League, and the NACW were critical networks, "not mere paper bodies seeking occasional publicity, but they are well organized, functioning bodies giving vital assistance to a people's development."

The leaders of the women's committees affiliated with mixed-gender organizations such as the FCC, the CIC, the NAACP, the National Urban League, and other reform organizations frequently crossed organizational boundaries to achieve their goals. For example, Rev. Florence Spearing Randolph—founder and first president of the NACW's New Jersey Federation of Colored Women; an officer and member of the AME Zion Women's Missionary Society, the WCTU, the NACW, the NAACP, the YWCA, and the New Jersey Republican Women; a delegate to the first national Interracial Conference of Church Women; and a member of the FCC's Church Women's Committee and Church Women United's executive committee—effectively used her religious and secular organizations as conduits for implementing her gender, racial, political, and interracial goals. In 1928 she helped organize the first state interracial conference in New Jersey. Randolph used her extensive network, including the New Jersey Federation, which worked closely with the state interracial council, to implement civil rights programs. Randolph was also an active force in the New Jersey Interracial Committee of Church Women.

The FCC, Church Women, and the Interracial Movement

THOUGH THE FCC provided leadership for the interracial movement among women in the North in the late 1920s and sponsored the first national interracial conference of women, from the beginning few women were involved in the organization. The FCC constitution required that each denomination select a certain number of persons for membership in the FCC. Few churches chose women as representatives of their institutions. Male clergy formed the bulk of the membership from FCC constituent denominations. When the FCC was founded, the Church Council program was designed exclusively for the men of the churches. The FCC established a network of local councils whose work was coordinated by the Commission on Councils of Churches. FCC community programs were implemented by cooperating churches through the local councils.

In 1921 the FCC, in its annual report, stated, "The Commission must gather up the experiences of the cities in which the women are taking a more active part of the work." The FCC was concerned that church women, who were traditionally restricted to missionary work, were devoting more of their time to organized club work because their talents were not recognized by the church. In 1925 the FCC Executive Committee requested that the Administrative Committee investigate the possibility of a constitutional provision that would open the door for "adequate representation of women in the work of the Council." Frustrated with the denominations' refusal to appoint women, in 1936 the FCC Executive Committee reiterated its request that the FCC remind the denominations of "the opportunity to designate a larger proportion of women to membership in the Federal Council." And in 1940 the FCC's Appraisal Committee stressed the importance of having greater representation of women in the FCC and on the Executive Committee who would be more active in the work of the FCC. Given the denominations' reluctance to grant recognition to women within the church, and the pattern of selecting delegates who were primarily ministers, the FCC throughout most of its history was an organization dominated by males. Like most mixed-gender organizations, the FCC attempted to address the issue through the establishment of special women's committees. However, members of the committees, who did not hold an FCC denominational membership, were restricted from serving on other FCC committees.

The FCC recognized the problem, but it had no authority to order denominations to appoint women. Ministers viewed representation and participation in a national body such as the FCC as an honor and a symbol of their standing in the national religious community. In some denominations, women were denied the clergy and lay rights enjoyed by men. To appoint women as denominational representatives with men would confer a certain degree of authority, power, and status to them that could create what some ministers felt were unusual expectations about their roles within local parishes. Women, by and large, were confined to work in missionary societies segregated by gender, and rarely held membership or served on denominational boards with men. While some missionary societies were independent, others were auxiliary to the general boards of the denominations, and some few were composed of men and women on an equal basis. To maximize their power and coordinate their home and foreign missionary work, white women organized the Federation of Woman's Boards of Foreign Missions of North America (1897) and the Council of Women for Home Missions (1908). AME women, leaders of the Woman's Mite Missionary Society, were among the first black women to participate on the conference programs of the Woman's Boards of Foreign Missions. However, prior to the 1920s, black women's organizations were excluded from membership in white women's associations. In 1921, in response to the interracial movement among church women, and possible pressure from the MECS, the Council of Women for Home Missions, an organization comprising nineteen boards, extended membership to the Woman's Connectional Missionary Society of the CME Church, the smallest and least influential of the black Methodist women's organizations.

Responding to the concerns of the FCC's small cadre of female members, as well as the success of the CIC Women's Committee in organizing women for interracial work at the local level, in 1923 the FCC's Executive Committee considered setting up a church women's committee as a division of its Department of Race Relations. The Executive Committee was persuaded that promotion of its interracial work in the North would be enhanced if northern church women could be enlisted to work with the movement in a way similar to that of the southern women. The Executive Committee noted that the CWHM had voted unanimously to "take an active interest" in interracial work in the North and to cooperate with the FCC'S Department of Race Relations. The CWHM suggested that the Department of Race Relations hire a field-worker to arrange meetings between white and black church women, and to bring these women and their organizations into the FCC's interracial movement.

Interracial Versus Biracial Work:
Tensions Between Southern and Northern Women

IN 1924, THE FCC voted to hold a conference between representatives of the FCC Department of Race Relations, the Council of Women for Home Missions, and the CIC Women's Committee. The CWHM agreed to initiate interracial work in the North, but CIC leaders were against the idea. Southern white women leaders in the CIC were apprehensive about working with northern black women, whom they viewed as aggressive and less accommodating than southern black women. George Haynes revealed that the delay in promoting the FCC's women's work was specifically related to the "feeling of suspicion among women, from both the racial and sectional angles." Angered, hurt, and publicly embarrassed by the response of black women leaders representing the NACW at the 1920 biracial conference sponsored by the CIC in Memphis, Tennessee, and weary from their struggle to work with black women in establishing the CIC Women's Committee, southern white leaders, such as Carrie Johnson, demonstrated little enthusiasm for real interracial work.

Carrie Johnson and her cohorts envisioned a biracial work, similar to the pattern established by the MECS and the CIC General Women's Committee, in which white women would organize local and state organizations and then identify black women to form a "parallel committee." Many white women were paternalistic in their treatment of African Americans, and were more comfortable with the traditional patterns of race work that were employed between 1865 and 1920. The MECS formed the Race Relations Commission and developed a "standard interracial program" that included committees in all of its local missionary societies. By 1926 the MECS boasted of six thousand committees, with a total membership of 250,000 women. Focusing its attention mostly on the so-called "lax morality of blacks," the MECS's concern was "the purifying and uplifting of the negro [sic] home." Ignoring segregation and discrimination as the root causes of poor health conditions, high black mortality rates, lack of education, and political disfranchisement, the MECS's Race Relations Commission emphasized the development of vocational skills and disseminated information about morality, health, sanitation, and nutrition.

Following emancipation, white Protestant churches worked on the periphery of what was called "the Negro problem." This work, frequently referred to as "interracial," might be more accurately described as a part of home mission philanthropy. Likewise, a great deal of the CIC and MECS work referenced as interracial between 1920 and 1940 was biracial. The term "interracial" as it was used in the early twentieth century is misleading. Often committees, conferences, and work referred to as interracial simply meant that the focus of the activity was on how to improve relations between the races. It did not mean that the group favored integration, or that it was interested in abolishing segregation. Interracial could mean that black and white men and women occupied the same space and presented their points of view, or talked about their experiences. It did not mean that black and white people functioned as equals in defining the issues or making decisions about an organization's agenda, or that African Americans were actively involved in the initiation of programs. Also, an "interracial meeting" could mean having an African American speak to an all-white gathering.

During the late nineteenth and early twentieth century most religious organizations developed a separate work that was titled "colored work." African Americans were thought of and treated as a group by themselves—people who had certain needs and should be ministered to, but who were separate from the main life of the organization. Thus, in their organizational work with blacks, the Methodist, Baptist, Presbyterian, Episcopalian, Catholic, and other religious and secular associations such as the YWCA developed specific patterns of interaction that were often defined by unwritten codes of social etiquette. In this manner white people became accustomed to doing work on behalf of black people, not with them. World War I, or the period between 1917 and 1920, witnessed the rise and spread of a biracial type of work. In an illustration of the biracial work of the Catholic Church, W. E. B. Du Bois asserted that while the " 'old guard' of Catholic priests and sisters teaching in the colored South deserve all credit for their unselfish work . . . [t]he Catholic Church in America stands for color separation and discrimination to a degree equaled by no other church." He criticized white priests and sisters for refusing "to work beside black priests and sisters or because they think Negroes have neither brains nor morals enough to occupy positions open freely to Poles, Irishmen and Italians."

It was during the early twentieth century that numerous white organizations became very conscious of African Americans as a group,

Charlotte Hawkins Brown, founder and president of Palmer Memorial Institute in North Carolina, and Baptist leader Nannie Helen Burroughs were prominent figures in the NACW and the interracial movement.

and that the so-called Negro branches of established associations, such as the YWCA, came into existence. Similar to the YWCA, "liberal" white religious associations viewed themselves as groups of black and white women working side by side on common interests, but not working together. Following the 1920 CIC women's biracial conference,

NACW leaders such as Charlotte Hawkins Brown and Lugenia Hope made it clear that the old attitudes and patterns of interaction were unacceptable and that African American women intended to speak for themselves, be treated as equals with white women. The widespread publicity given this incident, combined with other events of national significance, helped to launch the women's interracial movement.

Summarizing the difficulties encountered by the FCC in attempting to introduce a program of interracial work among northern women, George Haynes indicated that there was also a great deal of "inertia, and some indifference among white women of the North," but that there was evidence of interest among some church women who had enrolled in the FCC mission study courses in race relations. Haynes also lamented the fact that the Race Relations Department lacked the funds to hire a competent female field-worker to organize the northern work. The FCC was unwilling to set up a church women's committee until they had the support of prominent white women leaders and their organizations. Given the CIC experience, the FCC understood the importance of involving white women's organizations who had engaged in interracial work with black women. The FCC's interest in having influential white women's organizations affiliated with the DRR was motivated in part by the FCC's need for funds to support its work. Though the FCC could boast of a large Protestant church affiliation, it was constantly in need of funds. Like its member denominations, the FCC recognized the need to bring women's organizations, such as the Council of Women for Home Missions, into the association to help fund the FCC projects. What the FCC wanted was a northern-based women's organization, similar to the MECS, that would provide funding and an organizational base through which an FCC women's committee and the DRR could implement the FCC's interracial program.

The First National Interracial Conference

WHILE THE FCC women struggled to get organized, in April 1925 the Commission on Interracial Cooperation and the FCC's Department of Race Relations cosponsored the first National Interracial Conference held in the United States. The meeting, held in Cincinnati, Ohio, was attended by an array of prominent black and white church leaders, educators, and social reformers. Two white women leaders, but no black women, participated on the program.

A number of black women leaders attended the conference as delegates, but the names of the most prominent and outspoken southern
black women—including Mary McLeod Bethune, Nannie Helen Burroughs, Charlotte Hawkins Brown, and Lugenia Burns Hope—were
not included on the list. Speakers at the first National Interracial Conference traced the history of the interracial movement and touched on
essential race issues.

The first National Interracial Conference opened with a discussion
of the role of the white media in the formulation of public opinion
about African Americans. Of specific concern was the lack of balance
in the reporting of black crime as opposed to black heroism and
achievement. Dr. Herbert A. Miller, a white professor of sociology at
Ohio State University, told the gathering that facts did not support the
belief in the inferiority of black people and the notion that the Japanese could not be assimilated in the United States. Moreover, Miller
argued, "[I]t is proven by statistics that excessive Negro criminality is
a myth." Dr. C. V. Roman, a black lecturer on public health at Fisk
University and Meharry Medical College, alluded to the hypocrisy
inherent in religion. Roman asserted, "Christians have morals with
reservations. We preach one thing and practice another." Industry and
race relations, the courts and race relations, and schools and colleges and race relations were discussed by two prominent African
Americans—Forrester B. Washington, executive secretary of the
Philadelphia-based Armstrong Association, and John Hope, president
of Morehouse College—and Judge John F. Hager, a white jurist from
Ashland, Kentucky. Mary van Kleeck, director of the division of industrial studies at the Russell Sage Foundation, presided at a session in
which the discussion centered on the interracial movement, social
agencies, and race relations.

The First National Interracial Conference
of Church Women

THE SUCCESS OF the first National Interracial Conference convinced
FCC women that the time was ripe for a national interracial conference of church women. Working behind the scenes, they were able to
garner enough support to launch the project. At a meeting of the FCC
Executive Committee held in April 1926 the FCC women's proposal
to hold the first Interracial Conference of Church Women was
approved. The conference, initiated by FCC women and in coopera-

tion with the Council of Women for Home Missions and the National Board of the YWCA, was held at Eagles Mere Park, Pennsylvania, on September 21–22, 1926. The YWCA, with black and white branches located throughout the United States, had shifted, at least rhetorically, from a biracial to an interracial stance. It was an excellent replacement for the CIC. The YWCA included in its membership and leadership most of the southern black women involved in the Tuskegee and Memphis conferences, and in the organization of the CIC General Women's Committee. It also boasted of many prominent northern and western black women. In fact, African American women religious leaders, NACW officers, and YWCA and FCC members were frequently one and the same. In this manner, black women were able to maintain a consistent agenda and use their multiple organizational bases to achieve their goals.

The first National Interracial Conference of Church Women brought together black and white church women from the North and South. Although southern white women CIC leaders did not support the FCC's efforts to organize an interracial conference, Jesse Daniel Ames was one of three women representing the CIC and was listed as a participant in two of the conference sessions. Estelle Haskin, as the representative of the MECS, also participated on the conference program. Unlike the CIC women's Memphis meeting, which included only four black women and ninety-six white women, the Eagles Mere conference consisted of eighteen black women and thirty-two white women from fifteen states. FCC women were determined from the outset that, if possible, all of their "interracial" conferences would include an equal number of black and white women participants on the program, as well as an equal number of delegates.

The Eagles Mere delegates represented national church women's organizations with a total membership of four million women. The conference program was arranged in a manner that permitted involvement of all delegates in the proceedings. African American women participated fully, serving as conference speakers and panelists, and openly voicing their viewpoints as delegates. This pattern of engagement was absent at the CIC women's Memphis meeting, where the four black representatives were expected "to interpret to the meeting the viewpoint and needs of colored women and children," and were not involved in the overall conference program. Mary Westbrook, a member of the FCC and the YWCA's Council on Colored Work, set the tone for the Eagles Mere conference by renouncing patterns of racial interaction that failed to reinforce equality. Westbrook asserted, "No longer can one group work for another, . . . the time has come when all groups must work together." The conference included open forums. Topics discussed at the Eagles Mere conference were: "Experience in Interracial Work Among Women"; "How Can Organizations of Church Women be Used for Local Interracial Work"; "Conditions of White and Colored Women in Employment"; "Concrete Methods of Work in Race Relations"; "Concrete Interracial Projects for Local Church Women's Groups"; "The Problem of Housing Segregation in Cities"; "What Church Women Can Do to Create Wholesome Racial Attitudes"; and "Contributions of Each Race to Better Race Relations." Discussions on these topics were led by experts including Mary Anderson, director of the U.S. Department of Labor Women's Bureau, and prominent black women such as Charlotte Hawkins Brown, Elizabeth Ross Haynes, Nannie Helen Burroughs, and Josephine Humbles Kyles.

The FCC Church Women's Committee

FOLLOWING THE EAGLES MERE conference, FCC women formed the Continuation Committee of the Interracial Conference of Church Women and proceeded to organize and seek FCC authorization as a permanent department of the council. In March 1927 the FCC officially recognized the Church Women's Committee on Race Relations as one of four divisions of the FCC's Department of Race Relations. Membership on the CWCRR was open to women executive officers of the FCC boards and organizations, women representatives of other organizations concerned with race relations, and FCC women members at large. Mary Westbrook, YWCA president, served as chairman. Initially, the Continuation Committee was comprised of the small number of women appointed to the FCC by their denominations, many of whom were members of the DRR. Not all denominations were represented by women in the FCC. To address this issue, the CWCRR Personnel Committee recommended that denominations, without official representation of church women, appoint women to the CWCRR. Because there were far more white female members, the Personnel Committee paid special attention to the recruitment of African American women. For example, the committee undertook a study of the process used by the FCC for soliciting the names of prospective black members, and requested additional time to review the CWCRR's suggested lists of black women. The committee recognized the importance of having black women who represented different perspectives. To ensure a black presence at the monthly meetings, the Personnel Committee also suggested that the CWCRR select additional black church women in the New York area who could aid in the interpretation and promotion of the committee's interracial program.

Among the few black women members of the FCC prior to the establishment of the CWCRR were Eva D. Bowles (Episcopal), Juliette Derricotte (Presbyterian), and Elizabeth Ross Haynes (NBC-USA). These women had been actively involved in the FCC for some time as representatives of the YWCA. In February 1927, Reverend Florence Spearing Randolph (AME Zion), Josephine Humbles Kyles (AME Zion), Christine Smith (AME), and Rossie Hollis (CME) were accepted as members of the CWCRR. Subsequent to the February meeting, invitations were extended to other prominent black women, including Mary McLeod Bethune (ME) and Annie Malone (AME). During the fifteen-odd years of the CWCRR's existence, membership on the committee averaged about seventy women, a third of whom were black.

Between 1927 and 1942, at least thirty-five black women actively participated in the CWCRR's deliberations. Although there were a few black representatives of mainstream denominations, such as the Presbyterian and Episcopal churches, the majority of African American FCC members belonged to the historically black Methodist and Baptist denominations and the YWCA. The CWCRR also extended membership to prominent African American social and political activists associated with secular organizations whose work was related to the CWCRR's agenda. For example, in 1931, when Fisk University's Dean of Women Juliette Derricotte died as the result of an automobile accident following which she was refused hospital care, the CWCRR established a committee to consider ways to provide better health services and medical training for African Americans. Mabel K. Staupers, the president of the National Association of Colored Graduate Nurses, and Ida Louise Jackson, the supreme basileus of the Alpha Kappa Alpha Sorority, were invited to join the CWCRR because of their prominence as leaders in the black health movement and the relationship of their organization's work to the CWCRR's efforts to desegregate hospitals and nursing schools. Staupers and the NACGN, as foremost advocates of the training and placement of black nurses and doctors, and Jackson's leadership in Alpha Kappa Alpha's Mississippi Health Project, brought national attention to black public health issues. AKA's political activities, in particular its establishment in 1938 of the Non-Partisan Lobby for Economic and Democratic Rights, to monitor and lobby for congressional legislation that affected the African American community, could be useful to the CWCRR in the promotion of its political agenda.

Among the African American women who served on the CWCRR were Louise Congo, Creole B. Cowan, Ida L. Wallace, Abbie Clement Jackson, Mrs. B. C. Robeson (AME Zion); Mrs. S. Joe Brown, Helen Curtis, Kay Bailey Nichols, Lucy M. Hughes, Mary E. Jackson (AME); Mrs. E. T. Woods, Mrs. Channing H. Tobias (CME); Eunice Jackson, Isabel Powell, Nannie Burroughs (NBC-USA); Lillian H. Bragg (Episcopal); Juanita Jackson (ME); and Cordelia Winn, Marion Cuthbert, Grace Towns Hamilton, Josephine Pinyon Holmes, Juanita Saddler (YWCA). Representatives of the NACW included Mrs. Orrin Judd, Charlotte Hawkins Brown, Lugenia Hope, Clara Burrill Bruce, Susie W. Yergan, and Ella Barksdale Brown (New Jersey Federation, chairman of the Committee on Interracial Affairs). Recognizing the importance of the NACW, the CWCRR reserved an official membership slot for the president. Between 1927 and 1942, a succession of NACW presidents served on the women's committee, including Mary McLeod Bethune, Sally W. Stewart, Mary F. Waring, and Jennie Moton.

Unlike any other women's interracial committee or most women's organizations of the time, the CWCRR was determined to demonstrate that it not only argued for integration, but practiced it. Throughout the committee's history, an effort was made to ensure black women's equal participation in every aspect of the FCC and its affiliate women's organizations. For example, in 1939 Katherine Gardner presented recommendations to the National Committee of Church Women illustrating ways in which it could promote work in race relations. First and foremost she urged the "integration of members of racial minority groups in the ongoing interdenominational programs of church women." Practicing what it preached, each year the CWCRR elected a white and a black woman to fill the positions of chairman and vice chairman of the committee. Between 1931 and 1939 all of the chairmen were white and all of the vice chairmen were black. However, from 1939 to 1941, Josephine Humbles Kyles served as the first black chairman. The predominance of black Methodist women in the FCC and on the CWCRR was evident in the selection of AME, AME Zion, and CME women leaders. Black Baptist denominations appointed very few women to the FCC, and even fewer were members of the CWCRR. Elizabeth Ross Haynes, the first African American elected to the YWCA National Board, Nannie Helen Burroughs, the Corresponding Secretary for the NBC-USA Woman's Convention, and Isabel Powell, an actress and the wife of Congressman Adam Clayton Powell, were among the small number of black Baptist women whose names appear in the CWCRR records. Black Methodist, YWCA, and NACW women appear to be among the most active black participants in the CWCRR.

A major concern of the CWCRR was how to involve more black Americans in the interracial movement. For example, in May 1937 the discussion focused on how to reach people who were not knowledgeable about the interracial movement, especially in the black churches. The CWCRR recommended getting white speakers with the right kind of personality and message to speak before such groups. At a CWCRR conference held in Asbury Park, New Jersey, it was suggested that African Americans take more initiative in the planning and hosting of interracial activities. Responding to this concern, in 1938 Rev. Florence Spearing Randolph hosted a World Day of Prayer program in Summit, New Jersey, at Wallace Chapel, the church she pastored. In 1939, the AME Zion Annual Conference in North Carolina sponsored an interracial meeting that was attended by a number of white church leaders. And, in 1941, Randolph wrote the text for the Women's Program for Race Relations Sunday observance, used in worship services organized by church women's organizations throughout the United States. There were many reasons for the low African American response to the interracial movement. Frequently race relations programs and other activities were planned and organized by whites, and blacks were informed or brought in later. The CWCRR recommended that African Americans be included in the initial planning. For other blacks the expense of attending a regional or national conference was prohibitive. The CWCRR recommended that articles on the importance of black participation be placed in the black religious press.

Issues and Problems:
The FCC's Church Women's Committee

THE CWCRR OPERATED as a division of the Department of Race Relations for fifteen years. During that period, with Katherine Gardner as secretary, the committee held a number of local and national conferences, acted as a catalyst for bringing together organizations at the local level for interracial work, and encouraged direct action. However, the CWCRR was hampered from the beginning by its location as a unit of the DRR, and lacked the level of support from the FCC to function as a national entity. In fact, the CWCRR came into being as a result of the Continuation Committee's simple assertion of its existence. Rejection of the CWCRR would have placed the FCC in a difficult position, especially since it had initiated the idea and the Eagles Mere conference was so successful. The FCC's placement of the CWCRR under the poorly funded Department of Race Relations created problems and tension between the DRR administrator, George Haynes, and Katherine Gardner, the executive secretary of the CWCRR. Haynes made it clear from the outset that the CWCRR was expected to raise money for its operations. Following her employment, Gardner joined Haynes in the yearly incantation to the CWCRR of the need to raise funds to support their work. Many of the CWCRR members were heads of church women's organizations or other associations, for which they were responsible for raising funds. The expense and difficulty of traveling to New York City, as well as the expectation that members would organize and work with local interracial committees, placed a heavy demand on women who were already overburdened. In a few instances, George Haynes recruited wealthy women such as Annie Malone, the black beauty culture pioneer known for her philanthropy, for CWCRR membership.

Between 1926 and 1928 local interracial conferences and committes were organized to address racial concerns. Many black and white women served on FCC state committees and local interracial committees—fostered by city, county, and state government agencies, and by federations of churches and local institutions. Interracial committees worked under the auspices of church federations, joint committees of local religious and social agencies such as the YWCA, the YMCA, church women's federations, and interdenominational ministerial alliances. By 1928 the Church Women's Committee included forty-four women, representing twenty-eight denominations and national organizations, with a full-time secretary, Katherine Gardner.

In 1928 and 1930 the second and third national conferences were held to assess the progress of the interracial movement and evaluate the extent to which black and white women were forming productive relationships and working across racial and sectional lines. In preparation for the 1928 conference a special committee gathered suggestions from women throughout the nation, which were used to shape the program. Topics discussed were "The present status of the Negro in the cultural life of America"; "Negro achievements, handicaps and cultural opportunities in America"; "How Sunday Schools and other religious educational organizations can be used for developing friendly, racial attitudes"; "The problem of interracial relations in our mission schools"; "Racial relations and religious education"; and "Mental and moral attitudes involved in interracial contacts." More than four hundred national, state, and district organizations of church women were invited to send delegates. Many prominent women leaders of church and affiliate organizations, as well as experts such as anthropologist Margaret Mead, were invited to participate on the program. Among the black women who participated were Florence Spearing Randolph (New Jersey Federation), May Belcher (YWCA), and Mrs. M. C. Slutes (ME Women's Home Missionary Society), who gave reports on the work conducted by their organizations. African American women who participated in the discussions were S. Willie Layten (NBC-USA's Woman's Convention), Cordelia Winn (YWCA National Board), Addie W. Dickerson (attorney, and ICWDR officer), Alice Dunbar Nelson (American Interracial Peace Committee), Howard University Dean of Women Lucy Slowe (National Association of College Women), and Dr. Sarah W. Brown (Women's Division of the Council of National Defense).

The 1928 conference demonstrated how far the women's interracial movement had come since 1920. The open forums included frank discussions in which black and white women expressed their views and gave detailed factual reports and critiques on the attitudes, patterns of interaction, and discrimination that existed at all levels of society and in religious institutions and programs. Sensitive issues were discussed. James Eichelberger, director of the AME Zion Church's Educational Department, spoke about the racial issues in higher education and mission schools. He emphasized that white teachers "of inferior attainments and experience should not be sent to colored schools because [they were] willing to work for a low salary." The practice of placing only white representatives on the mission boards dealing with problems related to black people was assailed. Women leaders gave concrete examples of ways in which local interracial committees could work to improve housing, health, public school situations, recreation, and amusement. The conference admitted that church organizations were not promoting a liberal and firm policy on interracial issues.

In 1930 the Third General Interracial Conference of Church Women was held in Ohio at Oberlin College. Women representing FCC denominations met to discuss what church women could do to "bring about more Christian attitudes in regard to race relations." This was the largest interracial conference of church women ever to be held. The list of delegates included women from states such as Texas, Massachusetts, Florida, Missouri, Minnesota, and Iowa. Various phases of black and white race relations were discussed. The conference findings and recommendations were specific and indicative of how far the movement had progressed since the first meeting at Eagles Mere in 1926. After four years of discussions and participating in a variety of activities in which blacks and whites met face-to-face and got to know each other, many felt that what was needed was a program of education, study, and direct action.

The 1930 conference recommended that the FCC Church Women's Committee employ a research organization to study the racial policies and practices of the denominations in their training of black leaders for church activities at home and abroad; to evaluate patterns of employment, such as salaries, living conditions, and opportunities for advancement of black women missionaries; and to define ways to include African Americans on denominational committees for preparation and criticism of race relations curriculums. It also emphasized the importance of promoting local and state interracial conferences. Local interracial units were asked to examine the interracial committees to ensure adequate representation of all groups and to gain the confidence of all elements of the local community. Rather than addressing questions of race relations in the abstract, or merely sponsoring special events, the conference asserted that better results could be obtained by dealing with concrete situations in the local community. The FCC committee was asked to study how groups arrived at successful solutions and to make the reports available to local organizations. The conference called for churches to be more cognizant of the importance of laity in the development of public opinion related to race relations and in supporting individual members who took unpopular stands. Churches were asked to insist upon the inclusion of representatives of all racial groups on planning committees. Local groups were requested to study ways in which the press might be used to influence public opinion on race relations.

By 1930 local "interracial" activities were popular throughout the nation, especially in the North and West and in border states. Groups met for a variety of purposes related to education, labor, housing, lynching, and racial tensions. From the outset much was written about the interracial movement and the racial concerns of diverse groups. With few exceptions the record is silent about the sexual harassment of black women in the movement, a dilemma confronting mostly middle-class black women at the local level. When faced with sexual harassment by prominent white men, most women opted for silence. Albeit for different reasons, silence among both blacks and whites on issues of rape and sexual harassment was a fact of American life, especially when it occurred between employer and employee, or when a prominent white male was involved. While black men and women sometimes referenced these practices in their speeches and writings, rarely did working-class and poor black female servants in white households or black religious workers and professional women in the interracial movement publicly acknowledge the existence of such behavior. For black women, historically labeled as oversexed and prone to sexual immorality, this was a complex and dangerous matter. Indeed, it was a double-edged sword and required careful thought and judicious consideration. Among black women, the decision to bring public charges against a white man could pose a serious threat to one's life, family, and livelihood. In any case, it would certainly be a life-altering experience.

In 1930, a black woman from "a large Western city" broke the silence, detailing the habitual sexual harassment she encountered as a member and officer in three interracial organizations. In a letter to W. E. B. Du Bois, the NAACP editor of *Crisis*, the woman granted permission to publish the communication, stipulating, "My name must not be appended." Referencing three incidents, she carefully described the circumstances surrounding the harassment, the approaches used by prominent white men, and her initial reactions and feelings about the encounters. In the first instance, "[a] group of representative citizens, nine white and three colored," concerned about local educational conditions, met to elect a nonpartisan ticket for the school board. A well-known white attorney engaged her in conversation about conditions in the black schools. At the close of the meeting, as individuals continued to converse in groups of two and three, the attorney "lowers his voice and interrupts 'I'm perfectly crazy about you, I want you to come to my office. Here is my telephone number.' " Shocked by this overture, the woman recalled being "too dazed for words. Surprise, resentment, hot anger, each struggle within me, all the fiercer because I know I have in no wise brought upon myself this affront." Like most middle-class black women she had been schooled in ways to avoid unwanted attention from men, especially white males. Examining her appearance and behavior, she concluded, "I am positive there is nothing in my appearance or actions that would lead any man to feel I would respond favorably to his advances. I am considered attractive. . . . But my manner is serious and conservative, often to the point of stern-ness. . . . Why then, does this man misjudge me? Yet I realize I cannot afford even to look conscious." Riding home with the other colored woman at the meeting, "I do not mention the experience to her."

The second and third encounters occurred under different circumstances. As a member of the board of directors of a local branch of a "well-known Negro charitable organization . . . made up of representative persons from both races," she received "subtle advances" from a new white board member who was undeterred by her attempts to ignore him. As the harassment continued, she received unwanted telephone calls to her home and anonymous gifts, and finally "a Negro chauffeur stops at my door and hands me a note soliciting an appointment and assuring me of safety in the arrangement." She is offended by the note, and "the chauffeur's suggestive smile and knowing look . . . infuriate me. The primitive in me rushes to the surface. I tear the note into pieces and fling them in the Negro's face. I vent all my rage toward his employer on him because he and I are of one blood and his insult in my opinion is the greater."

The third and final incident, which convinced the woman to withdraw from participation in civic and community affairs, occurred at her home and came at the hand of a white minister, "the most outstanding one among" the members of the Civic Betterment Group, which included "[s]uch splendid white men and women, I have never before met." As a member of a committee with the minister and two others, the woman worked on an important survey. She described the contact between the minister and his wife as "pleasant." They exchanged books and articles, and she and her husband accepted an invitation to attend a lecture at the minister's church. When the group met at her home she was shocked as a conversation with the minister shifted abruptly from "casual remarks, . . . and then before I realize it he is telling me in rapid impassioned words how he has come to admire me and how much he wants me to mean in his life. A flood of horror rushes over me. Disgust and disappointment struggle for utterance. The deference and respect he had shown me were but masks for this dreadful thing. I want to scream, tear my hair, and yet I sit dumb as if paralyzed." Yet, she maintained her silence and quietly withdrew from all interracial activities. Her husband was perplexed by her "indifference and lack of interest, especially when cooperation between the races is desired." But she asserted, "What would he think if he knew the reasons for it?" This is only one example of the emotional and psychological abuse that a black woman might have endured in her efforts to represent the "race," to bridge the racial gap, and to address some of the racial problems in her community.

There is nothing in the CWCRR or other organizational records to indicate awareness of sexual harassment of black or white women at any of the numerous interracial meetings. It is likely that such reports were handled discreetly and the issue was not discussed. There was concern among black and white leaders that the mere suggestion of sexual impropriety could seriously damage the movement, and possibly invite crude stereotypes about black women's virtue and insinuations about the so-called rapacious sexual appetite of black males and their desire for white females. During the 1930s the CWCRR continued to promote interracial meetings, and in 1937 the group decided to hold sectional conferences to plan strategies for taking the race relations movement to another level.

The principal goal of the FCC's Department of Race Relations was to bring together men and women—representatives of various types of social, educational, civic, business, fraternal, and religious organizations—to discuss issues and develop strategies to ameliorate racial tension and conflict. Delegates in attendance at the FCC conferences possessed broad experience in dealing with racial and community problems at the local level. However, given that the interracial committees and the conferences were drawn mainly from the middle and upper classes of whites and blacks, they never attracted or made over-

tures to the grassroots masses. Moreover, members of the black Pentecostal, Holiness, and Spiritual churches and of the various religious
traditions designated as cults and sects, which were representative of
the working class and poor, were not affiliated with the FCC.

As a Protestant organization, the FCC excluded Jewish churches
from membership and was silent about race relations between Jews and
African Americans. Urban blacks often encountered Jews in their day-
to-day activities. The Jewish entrepreneur who operated a variety of
small businesses as well as theaters and other entertainment venues was
a solid fixture in the black community. Jews frequently owned businesses in the black community and downtown in major urban centers
that charged exorbitant rates and employed only whites. Jews maintained theaters exclusively for blacks in African American communities. Jewish-owned downtown theaters that either excluded or
segregated blacks were a frequent target of black protest in cities such
as Washington, D.C., Philadelphia, Chicago, Baltimore, and New
York. Jews, in turn, labeled black Americans who spoke out about Jewish patterns of segregation and discrimination as anti-Semitic. The
question of placing greater emphasis on relations with Jewish and
Asian groups was discussed at CWCRR meetings on several occasions
during the early 1930s, but until 1939 no firm decision was made about
how to handle the issue.

Of all the concerns to be raised within the CWCRR, perhaps the
thorniest and most difficult to engage was the Jewish question. In the
early 1930s and for several years afterward the CWCRR grappled with
two major issues: the matter of expanding the CWCRR's work to
emphasize relations with Jewish and Asian groups, and the growth of
anti-Semitism. The minutes of CWCRR meetings do not reveal the
full intensity of the committee's discussions, but suggest the CWCRR's
frustration in not being able to take any meaningful action. Clearly the
women wanted to become actively involved in providing aid for the
Jewish Holocaust refugees from Nazi Germany. The CWCRR
stressed the need for the DRR and the FCC to take a more proactive
role in the effort to suppress anti-Semitism and improve relations
between Christians and Jews. When the issue of including Jews and
Asians as members in the CWCRR was first discussed in 1934, the
decision was made to work with the National Conference of Jews and
Christians to cover Jewish groups, and to simply include more information on Asians in the CWCRR's newsletters. In 1935, the CWCRR

voted to go on record as opposing the participation of the United States in the 1936 Olympic games if they were held in Germany.

As the Jewish situation in Europe became more critical and Jewish refugees were pouring into northern cities, the CWCRR became concerned about the growing black fear of economic competition with the refugees and what the committee perceived as "the existing anti-Semitism among Negroes." The situation reached a boiling point by 1934. The onset of the Great Depression and deepening black unemployment and poverty exacerbated an already difficult situation. A subcommittee, which included Eva Bowles of the YWCA, was appointed to assess the situation and make recommendations. In its report the subcommittee revealed that a number of denominations were working on anti-Semitism and developing strategies to establish friendly relations with the Jewish refugees. In point of fact, the CWCRR worked assiduously to educate the FCC's affiliate women's organizations about the situation. In meetings with associational leaders Gardner stated that "special study and action is urged on the subject of anti-Semitism because of the world situation and growth of this feeling throughout our country." Considering what it described as an "acute crisis," the subcommittee recommended that the CWCRR broaden "the basis of its work to include other racial and minority groups."

To avoid conflict with the DRR and the FCC, the CWCRR authorized the subcommittee to meet with George Haynes and Samuel McCrea Cavert, the FCC director, to discuss ways to address the Jewish situation. Following the meeting, Eva Hills Eastman, the cochairman of the DRR, sent a letter to the members of the CWCRR in which she discussed the ongoing debate within the Church Women's Committee regarding whether to launch an anti-Semitism campaign. She advocated not becoming involved, because it would take time, money, and staff away from existing projects. Eastman argued that white-black relations affected a larger proportion of the population and the women should continue their efforts in this area. Also, she reminded the women that they were part of the FCC and could not act independently. Eastman's letter did not quell the CWCRR's concerns. In January 1940, in an effort to put an end to the ongoing debate, George Haynes told the women that because Jews were not represented on the FCC, they could not be members of the CWCRR. However, Jews could participate in a joint program of action. In March 1940, the CWCRR agreed not to take an active role in Jewish refugee placement, but to confine their efforts to a program of education, with possible activities to bring together white and black women with Jewish and other non-Aryan refugees.

Successes and Failures:
The FCC Church Women's Committee

DURING THE FIRST five years of its existence, the CWCRR concentrated on developing a speaker's bureau, race relations study classes, and interracial committees and conferences. The CWCRR received requests from many women's organizations to recommend speakers to "present the interracial question" at their meetings. Along with the biracial work and "Colored Departments" of work associated with national organizations, the 1920s saw the rise of African American speakers who were known as "race interpreters"—persons who spoke to white audiences about the black community and its people, institutions, and cultural values. Their goal was to present blacks as hardworking, safe, and nonthreatening people who had the same goals and aspirations as white Americans. The DRR and the CWCRR encouraged race interpretation and identified speakers such as Crystal Byrd Fauset who developed considerable expertise and recognition as race interpreters.

The popularity of race interpreters aided the CWCRR in the promotion of its objective to "integrate" and find employment for African Americans in white religious organizations. Race interpretation was utilized by mainstream predominantly white denominations, such as the Presbyterian, Episcopalian, and Methodist Episcopal churches, as a race relations tool to promote better relations between their segregated congregations. For example, in 1940, following the establishment of the Methodist Episcopal Church's all-black Central Jurisdiction, Florence L. Dyett, an employee with the Department of Negro Work of the Methodist Episcopal Church's Board of Home Missions and Church Extension, explained, "I go often to speak to church people of the opposite race. My message is about an untouched area, a new task for a new church. . . . My mission is interpretation." Although race interpretation was viewed as an important element in the race relations programs of most organizations, including the CWCRR, in 1932 the CWCRR chairman, Caroline Chapin, asked the committee to consider whether its program was too much directed toward white people. The CWCRR decided to invite more black leaders of religious education to sit in on its committee meetings and discuss this issue with its members.

A considerable portion of the CWCRR's work was concerned with the promotion of interracial work among women in the FCC-affiliated denominations. Through its committee members, conferences, and national women's organizations, the CWCRR distributed educational materials—including pamphlets, brochures, programs, articles, and condensed reports of conference discussions—for publication in religious periodicals and journals. At the CWCRR meetings, held five times a year, information was channeled through the denominational representatives to the women of the churches. Race Relations Sunday, the anti-lynching program, the Interracial News Service, and other parts of the Department of Race Relations work were also promoted among the women. However, during the early years, because the CWCRR meetings drew only a fraction of the members, Gardner experienced some difficulty in getting its program on the agendas of national organizations, and in developing work at the local level throughout the United States. To address this issue, the CWCRR decided to enlarge the committee to include women from strategic areas around the country and women who resided in areas near New York City who could be counted on to attend meetings and assist the CWCRR's program.

Under the leadership of Katherine Gardner, the CWCRR pursued an independent agenda that was defined and initiated by Gardner and the committee members. While the CWCRR operated as a subsidiary of the Department of Race Relations, both Haynes's and Gardner's positions carried the title of secretary. Indeed, Gardner did not function as a subordinate to Haynes. Though she supported the DRR program and in some instances worked very hard to see that CWCRR affiliate organizations were involved in its implementation, she also took the lead in defining and launching initiatives. The CWCRR took on a number of concerns related to segregation and discrimination in public accommodations, especially hotels, restaurants, hospitals, employment, World War II defense programs, and religious organizations and institutions. For example, it was largely through the insistence of the CWCRR that the FCC adopted a policy banning the holding of conferences in hotels where segregation was practiced.

Most of the issues the CWCRR chose to engage with were closely related to their efforts to have African Americans integrated into denominational programs, and to the specific interests of CWCRR members and the state and local interracial committees. For example, the matter of hotel and restaurant discrimination emerged in 1928 as a result of a resolution passed by the FCC Executive Committee urging all of their church organizations to make sure that provisions be made for African Americans when selecting meeting places. This was especially important for churches such as the Methodist, Presbyterian, Episcopal, and other mainstream denominations that African Americans affiliated with. The concern for hotel and restaurant discrimination developed as a result of the FCC's decision to sponsor interracial conferences and meetings. For years religious denominations and associations had met in cities where African Americans were excluded from hotels and restaurants. There were black hotels in a number of cities, but most were small, and few were first-rate. The majority of black conference delegates made arrangements to stay in private homes, boarding houses, and at the YWCA and YMCA, and took their meals at their boarding places, at churches, or in black eating establishments. Discrimination in public accommodations was a key issue for African American women, especially the NACW, which took every opportunity to challenge the treatment of blacks on public transportation and in hotels. A number of the concerns engaged by the CWCRR coincided with the agendas of the NACW and black church women. The CWCRR brought the FCC resolution to the attention of the authorities of various denominations.

Through its program of education and a system of careful monitoring, the CWCRR succeeded in making FCC affiliates aware of the criticality of negotiating with hotels and restaurants prior to choosing a city for the holding of a convention or conference. In instances in which an organization had already chosen a meeting place where black delegates were not accepted, the CWCRR prevailed upon the group to either cancel the meeting or make other arrangements. In January 1930 the Federation of Women's Boards of Foreign Missions changed their meeting place in Atlantic City to a hotel where African Americans were accepted. In May 1930 the CWCRR sent a letter to the Council of Women for Home Missions in regard to their congress, which was scheduled to be held in Washington, D.C. Discovering that the CWHM had given no thought to the issue, the CWCRR agreed to cooperate with the group's Committee on Arrangements and approach Washington hotels regarding accommodations for black delegates.

In some instances the CWCRR took positions antithetical to those of the FCC and the DRR, and against FCC policy. For example, in

1930 CWCRR members voted to urge the FCC to endorse the protest on lynching sent to Texas Governor Daniel J. Moody by the Society of Friends. The FCC Administrative Committee made it clear that the FCC steered clear of anti-lynching protest, and instead "urged denominations to place special responsibility on ministers to avoid lynchings." Gardner and the CWCRR thought otherwise. In 1932 the CWCRR voted to form a special committee to explore how church women could be more effective in the anti-lynching campaign. Ignoring the FCC directive, the CWCRR proceeded to define a strategy and to become actively involved in the protest against lynching. In 1933 the women decided to send a telegram to Governor James Rolph, Jr. of California condemning a recent lynching and urging him to apprehend the criminals who did it.

Between 1934 and 1939 the CWCRR lobbied for the passage of the Costigan-Wagner Anti-Lynching Bill. It disseminated literature, including letters, brochures, and flyers explaining the bill, and offered suggestions for individuals and group action to promote the bill. In 1935 the CWCRR distributed 25,000 fliers, entitled "What You Can Do to Stop Lynching," nationwide through the YWCA, the YMCA, interracial committees, denominations, the Association of Southern Women for the Prevention of Lynching, black colleges, and other organizations. The CWCRR's efforts resulted in the endorsement of the anti-lynching bill by many organizations and individuals. Also, in 1935 the CWCRR was a sponsor of a mass meeting at the Broadway Tabernacle in New York. The CWCRR worked with the NAACP to visit and interview each U.S. senator and representative about his or her stance on the Costigan-Wagner bill and circulated a letter illustrating the position taken by various senators on the bill. A hundred and thirty influential women and representatives of national organizations were signatories to a CWCRR open letter addressed to Senator Dixie Bibb Graves urging her "to join women of the South and the rest of the country in war against mob-murder." (Graves had spoken against the measure.) In 1938 the CWCRR drafted a resolution and sent a letter to the U.S. Senate deploring the filibuster of the Costigan-Wagner Anti-Lynching Bill.

The CWCRR never developed a successful relationship with the Southern Commission on Interracial Cooperation's General Women's Committee. The two groups differed in their philosophies and strategies for achieving racial justice. Although cordial in its relations, the CIC's Women's Committee, under the leadership of Carrie Parks

Johnson and Jessie Daniel Ames, kept its distance from the CWCRR. Though black women held membership and had a voice on the CIC committee, they were outnumbered by white women and, like black male members of the CIC, were not in a position to dictate the organization's policies and strategies. In October 1928, following the success of the second Eagles Mere conference and in anticipation of attending her first CIC meeting, Katherine Gardner outlined a plan of cooperation with the CIC. The members of the CWCRR felt that it was "important to do nothing that can be misunderstood by the southern group," but the committee agreed to encourage FCC members of southern denominations to back interracial work. As a result of the reports presented at a November 1928 CIC Atlanta meeting, Gardner gained greater insight into the differences in the race problems of the North and South and was convinced that the FCC must act more aggressively in order to maintain stable race relations. She became more aware of the impact of the migration of southern blacks and whites to the North and was impressed with the CIC's introduction of race relations courses in one hundred colleges and the formation of interracial forums among college students.

In 1929, at the suggestion of CIC director Will Alexander, Katherine Gardner was appointed as the representative of the CWCRR to the CIC General Women's Committee. In 1930 she attended the annual CIC meeting in Atlanta. Gardner was impressed with the range of race relations work carried on by church women's groups under the leadership of Jessie Daniel Ames, the CIC's director of women's work. For example, the Presbyterian church women worked with the CIC Women's Committee to set up interracial committees. The number of Southern Baptist church women's societies engaged in specific race relations work tripled in one year. The Methodist Episcopal Church, South, developed an extensive network of leadership training schools and daily vacation Bible schools for African Americans. And the Protestant Episcopal Church established a successful course in race relations in Suwanee, Georgia. Gardner was also impressed with the fact that the CIC committee had contracted with Charles S. Johnson, noted Fisk University sociologist, to prepare a study of segregation.

Sensing an opportunity to develop a cooperative relationship with the southern women, Gardner suggested that the CIC adopt the CWCRR's mission study and race relations materials for use in the various schools and training programs. A representative of the Southern Baptist Church explained to her that "material prepared with the northern churches in mind [would] not be used by many southern groups." In spite of this rebuff, Gardner's view was that the CIC did not own the South and that the CWCRR would continue its efforts to find ways of working through and with the CIC and other southern women's organizations. In discussing the CWCRR's plan of work for 1933, the committee members asked Gardner to write Jessie Daniel Ames to ask for the CIC women's cooperation on the Scottsboro case, in which nine young black men had been arrested and jailed in Scottsboro, Alabama, and sentenced to death on charges of raping two white women on a freight train. The CWCRR endorsed the stand taken by southern women, urged the support of FCC women's organizations, and reprinted and endorsed the ASWPL declaration against lynching. During the late 1930s the CIC developed cooperative projects with the Methodist Episcopal Church, South. However, as of 1939 the FCC did not operate to any extent in the South. Few southern churches chose to affiliate with the FCC.

One of the CWCRR's most difficult challenges was how to overcome the dominance of the DRR, especially with regard to its subsidiary status. Following its organization, for a short period of time the CWCRR adopted the race relations agenda set by the DRR. Instead of defining its own program and creating a separate organizational structure, it initially functioned more as an auxiliary to the DRR than as a "national group in the field [of interracial relations]." The CWCRR was required to present its recommendations and resolutions to the DRR, which in turn would present them to the FCC Administrative Committee for adoption. The CWCRR brochure included a vague statement of purpose, indicating that its goal was "to promote interracial goodwill and cooperation through united thought and action." In 1933 Caroline B. Chapin, the CWCRR chairman, "spoke of her feeling that the Women's Committee has never defined its full objective in the matter of race relations" and requested that "major time" be set aside at a meeting to discuss this issue.

Chapin appointed the Special Committee on Techniques to clarify the CWCRR's purpose, define an agenda, and bring recommendations. Concentrating on race relations and racial integration in religious denominations and organizations, including the FCC, local church federations, and other interdenominational groups, the committee recommended: 1) the inclusion of African Americans in the planning and execution of special observances, such as the World Day of Prayer, Race Relations Sunday, Brotherhood Day, Armistice Day, and other special days that engaged the church community; 2) integration of blacks on boards in religious organizations having an interracial constituency; 3) integration of African Americans in all of the work of local church federations and other interdenominational groups and activities of the community; 4) employment of blacks in offices of religious organizations, including denominational and interdenominational groups that they were affiliated with, and church boards and agencies that had no black membership; 5) opening of white churches to African Americans who wished to become members; and 6) integration of black synods and conferences in denominations that included a black constituency. Most of these recommendations duplicated the findings of the 1930 conference.

Chapin's call for the CWCRR to define its purpose was perhaps related to pressure from George Haynes and the DRR to bring the CWCRR back in line with its original purpose, which was to cooperate with the work of the Department of Race Relations as a whole. However, it was also a reflection of Chapin's frustration in trying to establish a unified focus and purpose that would distinguish the CWCRR from other women's committees and force the CWCRR to concentrate on achieving a few specific goals, rather than attempting to address so many disparate issues. The CWCRR's seeming lack of focus and eclectic race relations agenda was related, in part, to its location under the DRR, and the original expectation that it would aid in carrying out the DRR objectives through the multiple women's entities represented on the CWCRR. At the same time, it reflected the critical issues of the time.

The CWCRR's success in becoming a national interracial committee of women was hampered by the growth of any number of women's interracial committees that were affiliated with organizations such as the Council of Women for Home Missions, the National Council of Federated Church Women, and the National Commission of Protestant Church Women. Even more disturbing was the fact that these organizations were affiliated with the FCC, and, in the case of the NCFCW, were organized by the FCC. To minimize conflict and avoid duplication of program efforts, the CWCRR invited the leaders of the organizations to either coordinate their race relations activities with the CWCRR or have their race relations committees function under the auspices of the CWCRR. As a tactical move to ensure greater cooperation between these organizations and the CWCRR, membership was extended to the leaders of these organizations.

For all intents and purposes, the CWCRR was a committee of prominent church women, not an organization of church women. The CWCRR was most successful in its organization of the national and local conferences, and in its development of cooperative projects with other women's organizations. In a few states, such as New Jersey, the CWCRR succeeded in bringing together a variety of organizational leaders who became actively engaged in civil rights activities that meshed with the agendas of the DRR and the CWCRR. This occurred when members such as Rev. Florence Spearing Randolph succeeded in having their church and club organizations adopt the FCC programs. In 1929, the state of New Jersey was chosen by the CWCRR for special work because it contained the largest proportion of African American residents in a northern state.

As a result of the 1929 and 1930 conferences held in New Jersey, a permanent statewide committee was formed that represented interracial groups of church women in more than a dozen communities, mostly in northern New Jersey. In April 1932 the New Jersey Church Women's Committee held a conference in Trenton, attended by 113 women. During the conference, the women held the city's first interracial banquet. The largest and most successful World Day of Prayer was held in March 1938 in Summit, New Jersey, at Wallace Chapel, Rev. Florence Spearing Randolph's church. This event encouraged greater cooperation between black and white women and led to the formation of an interracial committee of church women in Summit. The New Jersey Church Woman's Committee also disseminated information about the state's civil rights law and argued for its enforcement. The committee worked to secure nurses' training for blacks in New Jersey hospitals. A committee of black and white women visited the directors of hospitals who were receptive to the idea. The committee succeeded in getting one hospital to integrate its nurse's training program and another one to employ trained black nurses. In 1939 and 1940 the efforts of the Interracial Council of Newark to secure opportunities for black doctors and nurses in Newark City Hospital were less successful, but did encourage the city to provide greater support for the city's small black hospital.

The upsurge of discrimination following the beginning of World War II spurred the CWCRR's concern about the problems of African Americans in national defense. The committee investigated the treatment of black nurses and soldiers and the problems they faced. Two members of the CWCRR, Rev. Florence Spearing Randolph and Ella

Barksdale Brown, cooperated with the New Jersey Church Woman's Committee and the New Jersey Federation of Colored Women's Clubs to work out an interracial program for the benefit of the black enrollees at Fort Dix. As a result of the efforts of these groups, who also worked with the American Red Cross, soldiers received books, clothing, supplies, and other necessities, and were favored by recreational programs. The group also targeted the practice of racial discrimination in hotels and other public facilities in New Jersey. Reporting on the success of the New Jersey venture, Haynes stated that the New Jersey Church Woman's Committee succeeded in keeping together black and white church women, who "learned to work together on matters of common interest and gradually overcame the barriers of race." Haynes also thought it significant to "note that a natural relationship has come about with no suspicion on either side of any desire for patronage or subservience."

Like in New Jersey, the CWCRR maintained a strong and visible program in New York City. Committee members in New York were instrumental in the development of a number of group projects that encouraged fellowship across racial lines. New York, a center of entertainment and culture, offered opportunities for general participation in theater projects and exhibitions. During the 1930s the CWCRR sponsored discussions of plays with themes of social and racial importance. Likewise, the CWCRR sponsored visits to exhibitions of black art, teas with presentations of black artists and poets, and visits to Harlem to sample aspects of black life. To some extent these "fellowship" activities were instrumental in softening racial attitudes.

As a secondary unit of the FCC, the CWCRR was least successful in getting the FCC to implement its recommendations. The CWCRR could make recommendations to the FCC, but it had no power to intervene or mediate in any situation at the local or national level. However, the CWCRR could take a position on a particular issue and urge its members to work through their groups to organize support and/or protest an issue or event. For example, in 1930 Katherine Gardner urged women to contact their local theaters to prevent the motion picture *Birth of a Nation* from being shown during its revival. The CWCRR could lobby for legislation and seek endorsements from the organizations represented by committee members. However, in most cases, women representatives of denominations did not speak for their organizations, which generally appointed men as their official representatives to the FCC. Still, CWCRR women, as representatives of independent secular organizations, had tremendous influence and could work through their local and state organizational networks. This was important, since the members of organizations such as the NACW, the Alpha Kappa Alpha Sorority, and the National Association of Colored Graduate Nurses were representative of all of the major black and mainline religious traditions and held memberships in other organizations such as the YWCA.

In spite of all its successes, the CWCRR's position in the church women's movement was seriously hampered by its relationship with the FCC, its location in the DRR, and the FCC's promotion of competing women's commissions within the council. The CWCRR's greatest strength was Katherine Gardner, who infused the CWCRR with her vision, independence, organizing skills, determination, and commitment to racial justice. Gardner skillfully used the CWCRR's relationship, in particular its access to church women's leaders and their organizations throughout the U.S. She understood the need to collaborate with other organizations engaged in race relations and civil rights activities, such as the YWCA, the YMCA, the NAACP, and the Urban League, in order to achieve the CWCRR's objectives. In many ways, the CWCRR and Katherine Gardner helped to promote the development of Church Women United, which as an independent organization built on and expanded the CWCRR program and in effect took the church women's race relations and civil rights agenda to another level.

In January 1942 Katherine Gardner resigned from the FCC, ostensibly because of an injury to a nerve in her spine. The CWCRR voted to dissolve the Church Women's Committee; to place the members of the CWCRR on various DRR standing committees; to have the CWCRR Committee on Race Attitudes in the Home and the Committee on Conference Meeting Places made standing committees of the DRR; to recommend that the FCC integrate women of various racial groups into all its committees; and to have Church Women United serve as the channel through which race relations in local women's interdenominational groups could be promoted. The Department of Race Relations adopted the recommendations from the CWCRR "that women of various racial groups who are competent be integrated into all of the Federal Council's activities," and agreed that the CWCRR should be channeled into the CWU. However, the DRR expressed the hope that the Church Women's Committee would continue to function. Dr. Samuel McCrea Cavert, the FCC president, accepted the CWCRR's recommendations and requested a list of black women who would be helpful in other FCC departments. He also said he hoped the CWCRR would continue the rest of the year, in spite of Gardner's resignation.

Following Gardner's departure, the CWCRR continued to function for several months. During that time the CWCRR explored the feasibility and possibility of connecting itself with the CWU. The CWU, wishing to avoid problems with the FCC, skirted the issue, stating that they had a race relations committee, of which Katherine Gardner served as secretary. In October 1942, noting that women had been integrated into the structure of the DRR and were participating in the FCC, the CWCRR voted to discontinue the committee. The issue of what entity should, or would, carry forward the agenda and work of the CWCRR did not end with the dissolution of the committee, however. In November 1943 Louise Young, the chair of the CWU Committee on Social, Industrial and Race Relations and a former member of the CWCRR, wrote Dr. Cavert stating that her committee planned to study the social education and social action program of the major women's denominational groups, and that her committee's mission was to carry forward the program formerly developed by the CWCRR. Katherine Gardner, Eva Hills Eastman, and Helen Wilkins, all former CWCRR officers, had been invited to serve on the committee. Cavert responded that the FCC did not abandon the program of the CWCRR, but thought of it as permanently incorporated into the work of the DRR. Cavert also informed the CWU that Gardner, Eastman, and Wilkins should not be considered liaisons with the DRR.

The demise of the CWCRR forced the FCC to integrate women more fully into the Department of Race Relations and the FCC. Many former CWCRR members continued to work in the FCC, but were affiliated with the CWU. Black denominations after 1940 appointed more female delegates to the FCC. This is in part related to the existence of the Fraternal Council of Negro Churches. Leading black clergymen and their denominations established their own political agenda and pursued goals that they defined. As black male clergy no longer maintained the same level of competition for the FCC delegate positions, the numbers of black female delegates increased. However, as late as 1948, there were no female members of the FCC Executive Committee from black denominations. In that year, Nannie Helen Burroughs was appointed to the Executive Committee.

The Fraternal Council of Negro Churches

QUESTIONS REGARDING BLACK PARTICIPATION in the interracial movement were not exclusive to the FCC, the CWCRR, or any other organization. African American leaders were not slow to respond to the suggestions that they were remiss and unconcerned about race relations. The black response was direct, and highly critical of what many African Americans had long seen as white hypocrisy, in particular as it related to American Christianity. In 1896, Rev. Reverdy C. Ransom, an AME minister and advocate of the Social Gospel, had pointed to the escalating patterns of lynching, rape of black women, disfranchisement of black men, and the depressing social and economic conditions under which most African Americans were forced to live, and charged that American Christianity was "hypocritical and cowardly." Ransom asserted,

> American Christianity is brutal. While human beings have been burned within the shadow of its churches, its only solace for the writhing agony and groans of the dying have been demoniac cheers. . . . It has uttered no protest. . . . American Christianity has comforted the Negro by pointing his weary eyes to "Gates of pearl and mansions in the skies," but has refused him an opportunity to find employment in the wealth producing industries of the country in order that he might possess a cottage on earth.

Richard H. Bowling, a *Norfolk Journal and Guide* columnist and a social critic, in 1934 summed up the thoughts of most African Americans about the interracial movement when he asked, "What bearing has the Christian doctrine of human brotherhood on the present bald faced economic exploitation of Negroes? On the denial to them by first one subterfuge then another of their Constitutional rights to equality of opportunity for earning a living, acquiring property and enjoying the peaceable possession thereof?" Bowling's critique of the interracial movement followed the widely publicized national meeting of a committee, headed by Bishop Reverdy C. Ransom and representing the five largest black denominations, to discuss the formation of a national federation of black churches. Ransom and other black Methodist and Baptist leaders, as members of the FCC, were dissatisfied with the FCC's conservatism and reluctance to move beyond its program of education and fellowship to address black concerns in a more substantive manner.

As a result of several meetings and extensive public dialogue in which the pros and cons of creating a black version of the FCC were debated, in August 1934 the African Methodist Episcopal, African Methodist Episcopal Zion, Colored Methodist Episcopal, National Baptist Convention-USA, and National Baptist Convention of America (Unincorporated) founded the Fraternal Council of Negro Churches and selected Bishop Ransom as president. The organization rapidly expanded to include twelve Protestant groups, including the Church of God in Christ and the Central Jurisdiction of the Methodist Episcopal Church. Weighing in on the debate about the need for a national black ecumenical organization, Bishop Ransom raised the question, "Has [the] Negro Church the Vision to Speak with a United Voice?" Ransom argued that while the voice of the black church had remained "inarticulate, educators, politicians, organizations and even white men have assumed to represent the voice of the five million Negro Christians in the United States."

It is possible that the idea of organizing a Council of Negro Churches was spurred by the activities of black church women during the early 1930s. While there is little evidence that African American women attempted to organize a national council of black church women, there is one example of a movement in this direction. In April 1931, the Negro Welfare Council of Richmond Virginia organized the Negro Council of Church Women, composed of two members from each black church representing every black denomination in the city. The organization met every third Monday in the month to discuss the welfare problems of blacks in Richmond and "the betterment of racial conditions among the race." This group appeared to be modeled on the CWCRR. Having observed that the FCC's Church Women's Committee operated primarily in the North, and that local interracial committees were limited in terms of their knowledge, understanding, and commitment to the black community, blacks in Richmond decided that their local organizations were best suited to address the issues and conditions found in their city.

During the late 1930s the FCNC struggled to unite all black Christian denominations. The organization, open to any denomination with a membership of ten thousand or more, focused on a broad-based program that addressed internal and external issues of religion and race in a national and international context. The creation of the Chicago Interdenominational Council of Negro Churches was unprecedented. The Chicago Council was considered to be the most representative FCNC body, including "every religious faith of protestant churches" in the membership and leadership of the organization. For example, in addition to the traditional black Baptist and Methodists denominations, the Church of God in Christ, the Holiness Church, and the Metropolitan Community Church were prominent participants in this group.

While the leadership of the Fraternal Council was predominantly male, during the interim period of organization the executive committee of thirty-nine members included two females: Belle Hendon from Chicago, representing the National Baptist Convention of America, and Rev. Ida Mae Miller, representing the Community Church. In 1935 Rev. Miller was one of fourteen persons serving on the FCNC Executive Committee. Nannie Helen Burroughs and Josephine Humbles Kyles were among the first nationally known black women leaders who actively participated in and supported the organization.

From the beginning women were included on the FCNC's annual programs. Following the traditional church format for female inclusion, an afternoon was set aside for presentation of a women's program. Many prominent women appeared on the programs and spoke on subjects related to race and gender. For example, in 1936 Addie Dickerson, president of the International Council of Women of the Darker Races, spoke on "The Negro Woman and World Peace," and Sadie Tanner Alexander, the well-known AME political and social activist who was the assistant solicitor of Philadelphia, spoke on "The Challenge to Church Women." During the late 1940s and early '50s there is evidence of an attempt to involve more women in the organization. The well-known black women leaders Burma Whitted, Dr. Dorothy Boulding Ferebee, and Jane Spaulding were cochairs of important committees. Typical of black male–dominated organizations, in 1949 the FCNC approved the establishment of women's auxiliaries in several states. There is little evidence that these divisions were established. However, in 1950, at the behest of Nannie Burroughs and several black women leaders, a women's auxiliary was organized at the national level. Women were highly visible as presenters and volunteer workers, but absent from the FCNC's policy-making boards.

The activism and pronouncements, which came out of the annual meetings of the Fraternal Council of Negro Churches, fueled the growing dissatisfaction of black religious leaders with the FCC and the interracial movement. The FCC's reluctance to make a public statement opposing segregation, to support anti-lynching legislation, and to condemn the Ku Klux Klan, as well as the 1932 retraction of its preliminary investigation findings into a brutal lynching that occurred in Salisbury, Maryland, fueled the criticism of the FCC by black clergy and other public figures. In 1939 and 1940 the argument became very heated as black leaders raised their voices in protest against the inaction of interracial committees. Noted sociologist E. Franklin Frazier accused interracial committees of being "sentimental in their attitudes toward the Negro," and alleged that the committees "did not possess power or did not care to use it in changing the status of the Negro in any fundamental sense." Frazier argued that fellowship and "goodwill" would not change the African American's status as long as the race remained in a "condition of complete economic dependence upon the whites."

By 1940 the FCNC had achieved recognition as the voice of the black denominations. Impressed by the success of the Alpha Kappa Alpha's Non-Partisan Council's political activism, especially its congressional lobby, in 1941 the FCNC established a lobby in Washington, D.C., to press for the passage of federal legislation favorable to African Americans. Focusing on the appointment of blacks to federal positions on the Supreme Court—as assistants to the president, correspondents in the White House press corps, aides to the secretary of the Navy, officers in the military, and physicians and nurses in base hospitals—elimination of all discrimination in the competition and hiring for federal civil service positions, and employment of blacks by the Federal Bureau of Investigation, the FCNC embraced an ambitious civil rights agenda. The FCNC also called for legislation to inaugurate a free public school hot lunch program, social security benefits for all Americans, and old-age pensions and unemployment insurance for ministers, domestic workers, and farm laborers.

It was easy for the FCNC to define a program, but difficult to implement it. From the outset, the FCNC confronted many problems, not the least of which was internal dissension among leaders, and issues of turf involving competition with the agendas of established national organizations such as the NAACP and the National Urban League. One of the reasons for the failure of the male-dominated FCNC to achieve its goals during the 1940s and '50s was the lack of commitment of its member denominations to its policies, and "sectarian feuding." During the late 1940s the FCNC launched what many viewed as a "militant program," calling for the support of President Harry S. Truman and the Congress for federal aid to education, housing, health, agriculture, and better representation of blacks in the Veterans Administration, passage of a federal anti-lynching law, and the end of "Jim Crow." Though the FCNC continued to function, by the 1960s it was supplanted by new organizations such as the National Council of Black Churchmen and the Southern Christian Leadership Conference.

CHAPTER 7

"Womanpower"—
Religion, Race, Gender

Consolidation of a Movement

The most grievous interracial problem in America is that of Negro-white relations. In many American communities fellowship is denied Negroes in American churches; they are segregated and given inferior accommodations in the train, in the bus, in the station and on the boat, although they pay the same fare as others; their educational opportunities are far inferior to those of whites; they are paid less than other Americans for the same work; they may not hold certain positions even when they are well qualified; they have little or no voice in the government under which they live although they are native born Americans.

In all of these things, the Gospel we profess challenges us to proclaim and practice the way of brotherhood in race relations. In the face of difficulties many churchwomen and churches have taken up this challenge.

The Church Woman *(1941)*

The churches in Christian America have not tackled their most serious problems—right here at home. They talk "Brotherhood," Fellowship and Justice—here and there and on high occasions but we have more ingrained racial prejudice than we have religion. We have more contempt for people of color than we have love for Jesus Christ.

The churches in America have over seventy-eight million members, but their influence and actions on questions of Justice and Brotherhood are nothing like as effective as is their stand against racial equality.

Nannie Helen Burroughs (1952)

More and more I was conscious of the continued patterns of segregation and discrimination. The difference between the North and South was not a difference in basic philosophy. In the South the weapon was a meat axe; in the North, a stiletto. Both are lethal weapons. It was a long time before I knew that they are as lethal to the wielders as to the victims.

Anna Arnold Hedgeman (1964)

FOLLOWING MANY DECADES of organizing and social activism, Protestant women moved beyond the strictures and structures of their local and national religious institutions, and their separate church women's organizations, to establish the first purely autonomous, national organization of Christian women independent of male or denominational control. Founded in 1941 as an interdenominational organization, by 1950 Church Women United represented ten million women in seventy Protestant denominations and more than seventeen hundred affiliated state and local councils. An inclusive organization, CWU admitted to membership any woman who supported the goals of the local organization. This included women who did not represent a denomination, or even belong to a church.

CWU represented an aggrandizement of Christian "womanpower" that united and moved women beyond a mere focus on their denominational and organizational interests. CWU women maintained their loyalty to their individual churches and religious traditions, however, in the 1940s and '50s they began to tackle major social and political problems such as race and women's status in the church and society. In doing so, they developed a Christian feminism that crossed the boundaries of race, creed, ethnicity, and nationality, and surmounted their geographical and political differences. Though at the local level CWU enjoyed an uneven and limited success, its contributions to laying the groundwork for racial ecumenical cooperation were significant. In 1946, Nannie Helen Burroughs prophesied that in the future the interracial "movement is destined to reach down and influence public education, improvement in wages, travel, health and civil rights. It will not come in a day, but the religion of Jesus Christ improves everything it touches."

Church Women United arrived at a time when Christian women were poised to move to another level. As an interdenominational organization that argued for social reform and gender equality and reached out to southern white women, CWU acted as a bridge between black and white people and males and females. In response to the growing racial tensions throughout the United States, the interracial movement was being pressured, by mostly African Americans, to shift its strategy from one of remedial action to one of preventive action. In many ways, CWU challenged the denominations and the FCC to recognize women as equals. Women's attitudes and legal status had undergone significant changes since the beginning of the twentieth century. Women had overcome many barriers, and white women had full access to the vote. Yet gender discrimination still existed in every area of American life. Women were not afforded equal opportunities in education and employment, and were generally excluded from decision-making positions in most mixed-gender organizations, including the church. However, one of the most important changes that had occurred was in the way they perceived themselves and their organizations, and their sense of women's worth and importance. Reflecting on the evolution in church women's attitudes, Gladys Gilkey Calkins observed that women discovered that they "had a larger potential contribution to make to the total life of the Church than had ever been realized." Moreover, they recognized their power, and that it could only be exercised in an organization controlled solely by women. In a 1939 editorial published in *The Church Woman*, the issue was clearly stated: "Women are ready to stand by the church, to minimize its obvious weaknesses and to emphasize its latent powers; to give to it, to work for it, to pray that it may be a tool of God. Church women form a group of more than 15,000,000 in the U.S.A., yet they are without a voice. The voice of the official church is still largely a man's voice, for what church is governed equally by its men and women members?" Calkins noted that this was true "even in so liberal an organization as the Federal Council of Churches, where women sat on boards and committees."

The Struggle Within:
Laying the Groundwork for
Racial and Ecumenical Cooperation

M ANY OF THE VICTORIES of the 1950s and '60s attributed to the Civil Rights Movement resulted in part from the groundwork laid by church women's organizations during the 1920s and '30s, including the National Association of Colored Women, the Young Women's Christian Association, the National Council of Negro Women, the Methodist Episcopal Church, South, the Woman's Missionary Union, and the women's committees associated with the CIC and the FCC, especially the CWCRR. The extensive network of local projects designed to improve the living conditions of African Americans and ameliorate racial differences at the local level brought black and white women together and helped to create communications networks that would be useful in the 1940s and '50s, and particularly during the turbulent '60s. Through a long and somewhat protracted struggle, black and white women leaders of religious and secular organizations had learned to talk and listen to one another and had developed professional relationships that, although not perfect, at least opened up avenues for airing their disagreements and for discussing difficult issues.

In 1943 Nannie Helen Burroughs wrote about "The Dawn of a New Day in Dixie," in which she praised the Southern Baptist Woman's Missionary Union and similar organizations of "forward-looking southerners" for the progress they were making "along the Christian way in race relations" in their own communities. Burroughs asserted, "I have always contended that when it comes to the race problem in the South, that the southern white woman is the molder, shaper, and changer of attitudes, sentiment and actions of the whites of that entire section. She holds the key to the solution of the race problem in Dixie. Her word is law and gospel to southern white men. . . . Whatever the South is, or whatever it becomes depends upon her vision, attitude, teachings and desires." Burroughs's purpose was to recognize the larger movement of Christian women in CWU, reiterate the message that black women were holding *all* white women—their "sisters"—accountable for seeing that segregation and discrimination ended, and to encourage white women's continued financial support of community projects that benefited the African American community.

In reality, CWU was not a new organization; rather, it had evolved from several organizations that dated back to the beginning of the twentieth century. Most immediately, it represented a merger of three organizations: the National Council of Federated Church Women, the Council of Women for Home Missions, and the Women's Committee of the Foreign Missions Conference. As the largest and most important organizations of mostly white church women, these entities included women from all walks of life. Significantly, all of the groups had worked closely with the FCC's Department of Race Relations and were represented on the CWCRR. In 1929 these associations agreed to set up race relations committees within their organizations, which became extremely important to implementing the DRR and CWCRR's program initiatives. The majority of the early race relations committees engaged in race history study programs. In 1939 the NCFCW requested that the CWCRR make recommendations for ways to "promote work in race relations." Katherine Gardner had worked closely with the NCFCW, serving as the chair of the organization's Race Relations Committee. Gardner suggested that the

NCFCW begin with the integration of women representing racial minority groups into the existing interdenominational programs of church women. This included Jewish, Asian, and African American women.

CWU brought together an extraordinary aggregation of women who possessed extensive experience and expertise in working together across denominations, in female and mixed-gender secular organizations on projects at the local, state, regional, and national levels in the varied FCC, CIC, and MECS women's and race relations councils, federations, and committees. Some of these women had participated in the first women's interracial conferences. Moreover, in the decades preceding CWU's founding, many national organizations created internal interracial committees that carried on education-and-action programs among their members. For example, the NACW established an Interracial Department, and the YWCA's Interracial Committee disseminated educational materials, sponsored interracial forums, and conducted studies to determine the impact of race on black women.

The CWU benefited greatly from the programs and strategies initiated by the CWCRR to challenge and dismantle the structures of racial dominance that undergirded the American system of apartheid. Following the demise of the CWCRR, many of its members affiliated with CWU and an inordinate number assumed leadership of the organization. However, given the rancor inherent in FCC President Samuel McCrea Cavert's letter to CWU, in which he stated that Katherine Gardner, Eva Hills Eastman, and Helen Wilkins, former CWCRR officers, should not be considered as Department of Race Relations liaisons, CWU rarely mentioned or credited the CWCRR for the important role it had played in promoting interracial relations and social justice. It was as if the CWCRR never existed. From the outset, CWU announced that it would represent Protestant church women in their relationship with the Federal Council of the Churches of Christ, the Council of Women for Home Missions, the Foreign Missions Conference of North America, and other organizations important to the work of women.

By 1940 there was a well-organized web of women's networks and contacts ready to spring into action and respond to any crisis in the society. In this network were many women leaders of religious and secular organizations, including black women educators, wives of black male leaders, and working-class black women. In addition to the numerous church women, the wives of some of the most prominent and well-situated white political leaders were intimately involved with CWU and its successors. Some women, such as Dorothy Tilly, helped facilitate the efforts of civil rights workers, Freedom Riders, and other organizers of the civil rights campaigns that took place in the South during the 1950s and '60s. Beginning with her 1929 appointment as director of the Paine College summer Leadership Training School in Augusta, Georgia, Tilly's involvement in the interracial and Civil Rights Movement spanned more than four decades.

As a social activist, Dorothy Tilly was a member of the Association of Southern Women for the Prevention of Lynching and the Commission on Interracial Cooperation, a CWU leader, a field-worker, and, later, the director of women's work for the Southern Regional Council, which succeeded the CIC in 1944. In 1945, she was one of two women appointed to President Harry S. Truman's Committee on Civil Rights. In 1949, Tilly created the Fellowship of the Concerned, an annual forum for southern white women interested in race relations. Tilly's work with black women was well known. In some instances, influential white women were able to use their personal contacts to intercede when there was either violence or the threat of such an action. Other women in the network served as behind-the-scenes mediators during some of the most critical racial crises that occurred during the Civil Rights Movement throughout the United States, but particularly in the South.

Founded thirteen years before the formal advent of the Civil Rights Movement, CWU had at least a decade to solidify its position as the most prominent and powerful organization of church women, to strengthen the bonds between and among women at all levels of society, and to focus women's minds on issues of race and gender. It was no easy task to get white women to integrate their local councils and develop at least a tacit acceptance of black women as intelligent human beings who wanted the same things for their children and families that white women did for theirs. Many of the most liberal white women and men harbored prejudices and did not appreciate what it meant to be black. Like most white persons of "goodwill," many continuously asked the question, "What do Negroes want?" This ubiquitous question was invariably followed by a second query, phrased in various ways: "Don't you agree that intermarriage is bad for Negroes and whites?" Discussions of this sort with persons of "goodwill," usually ended with white leaders counseling African Americans to be patient.

White fear of intermarriage between blacks and whites was the chief reason for the continued separation of the races, and was the driving force behind segregation and discrimination in public education, public accommodations, courts of law, and employment. During the 1940s Swedish sociologist Gunnar Myrdal, in an extensive survey of American race relations, wrote, "Fears of personal and social equality of joint use of schools, of voting, of use of public places, of equality in law courts, of equal economic opportunity are all secondary to this fear of intermarriage." Mincing no words, perhaps, Benjamin E. Mays, the noted theologian, public intellectual, and president of Morehouse College, best summed up the reason for southern white opposition: "[T]he white man is bitterly opposed to total desegregation because 'he has always had his way with colored women, and now fears that colored men will begin to have the same way with white women. Miscegenous cohabitation has always been a way of life' for the white man."

In 1943, George S. Schuyler, a prominent journalist, socialist, and conservative black intellectual, in a class analysis of race relations in the United States noted that, historically, African Americans had turned to middle- and upper-class whites to help solve the problems of segregation and discrimination. However, he argued that it was precisely that class of whites, persons of "goodwill," who introduced and enacted discriminatory legislation, controlled the broadcast and print media, produced motion pictures, ran every branch of the government, and instigated the residential covenants that created and perpetuated the urban ghettos that sickened and gouged "poor colored folk" with high rents. Schuyler concluded, "In our effort to escape from the trap, we have very largely ignored the white masses (who have historically been more friendly), and left their minds to those who would keep us enslaved. Too often we 'fell' for the master class propaganda about 'poor white trash.' " Schuyler reasoned that it was the " 'poor white trash' and the poor colored folk who have managed with not much difficulty to sit down and plan things together in sharecroppers' unions, steel workers' unions, longshoremen's unions, seamen's unions, coal miner's unions, auto workers' unions and other mass organizations." Schuyler asserted that these types of interactions rarely existed among the black and white middle class, since few blacks were members of chambers of commerce, country clubs, and other such economic and social organizations.

Schuyler touched on a sore point among many of the interracialists who firmly believed that change would only come by dealing with those who controlled the reins of power, middle- and upper-class whites of "goodwill." During the 1940s there were numerous vocal black critics of the interracial movement who were tired of talking and whose patience had worn thin. Most of these critics were male, rather than black female leaders. There were elements of truth on both sides, but the reality was that eradicating the doctrine of white supremacy from the white psyche and eliminating the structures of racism were complex issues that threatened the very base of the United States's economic, political, and social institutions. It would require a conglomeration of internal and external forces to bring change—including international pressure. With that understanding, two questions remain: How did issues of gender, sex, race, and religion factor in the struggle for racial equality? And what role(s) did church women and their organizations play in the dismantling of legal segregation and eradication of some of the most overt patterns of discrimination?

A key element in the Protestant interracial movement and the civil rights struggle was the status of white women in the church and in society. In the nineteenth century the women's rights and suffrage movements targeted the issue of sex discrimination in the American legal system. However, in deference to southern white women, racial discrimination as an issue was excluded. Prior to the 1940s few white women considered the relationship between gender and racial stereotyping or between sex and race discrimination. Through a long process of education, by conducting studies and raising issues about the legal and social status of women, organizations such as the YWCA educated women about the nature of gender and sex discrimination. As more white women became cognizant of how their sex was used to deny them their legal and institutional rights, they recognized the relationship between race and sex discrimination. It took decades of education about the patterns and effects of race and sex discrimination, and the relentless prodding by black women, for white women to recognize parallels between the two and to call attention to the contradictions inherent in addressing one and not the other.

Adding religion to the mix gave a new dimension to the arguments for racial and gender equality. Marion Cuthbert, the first black member of the YWCA's leadership division, reasoned that most women's organizations, such as the YWCA, operated "as religiously motivated programs of social work." Because many of these organizations were founded by Protestant denominations, Christianity continued to be a dominant force in their programs. Cuthbert argued that the

"Protestant expression of Christian faith" is concerned with "the search for truth and with the love of all men. It is a program of behavior as well as of faith and belief. . . . In the hands of women, this concern has expressed itself in ways consistent with woman's approach to life in our society." Cuthbert suggested that Christian women were more religious and flexible than men, and that women reflected and acted on their religious beliefs more often than men. Women fused their religious beliefs with their concepts of inclusiveness and leadership. The willingness of many women's organizations to engage in self-study, and to reorganize programs in light of their findings, enabled them to make hard decisions and eventually modify institutional structures and practices perceived as oppressive.

The YWCA's argument that it was a Christian organization and that Christian principles must be observed was a compelling moral strategy but could not by itself propel the association to pass sweeping legislation that would restructure and transform the organization. Lucy Miller Mitchell, a black community leader, related how she and a group of pioneering YWCA student leaders desegregated the Boston YWCA during the 1940s. Mitchell revealed that what made the difference was the constant pressure placed on the organization by black women at every level. She said, "We just kept talking. At every meeting we would raise issues, we kept bringing them up, and presenting the rationale and reasonableness and moral power of our arguments. Eventually our position prevailed." Cuthbert and Mitchell's analysis of how and why the YWCA succeeded in becoming one of the first national organizations to take a direct and forceful stand against racism and discrimination within its ranks is applicable to the way change came about in other organizations such as CWU. In fact, much of CWU's work was undergirded by black and white women's reform networks, particularly women's denominational and interdenominational organizations, the YWCA, the NACW, and the NCNW.

For black women the Civil Rights Movement would be the culmination of a long and often bitter fight for freedom and autonomy within white-dominated organizations such as the YWCA. They also struggled to gain respect as black women, equal rights for all African Americans, and equality and recognition within their own denominations. Though they fought on many fronts, black women emphasized that racial segregation and discrimination was the first line of battle. However, from the beginning of the black women's club movement, African American women articulated a feminist and race agenda. As practical feminists, or womanists, circumscribed by their race and gender, black women did not waste any time quibbling over which should be first. What they knew was that neither they nor their families would ever be free until every vestige of racism—legislation, policy, and practice—was removed. They recognized that, in the aftermath of segregation, their paths would be strewn with gross inequities, for without education, suffrage, economic and political power, and a proverbial "head start," the struggle for parity with whites would be extremely difficult. Thus, black women sought every avenue possible to maximize and achieve their goals. They perceived the YWCA as an organization through which they could advance their feminist and racial agendas. As an association steeped in Christian philosophy and replete with the language of evangelical Christianity, the YWCA meshed with black women's moral beliefs and values. And, given the YWCA's commitment to working-class girls and women, it was an association that could accommodate African American women's needs and concerns.

YWCA: A Model for Racial Adjustment

MANY MEMBERS AND LEADERS of the FCC, CWU, the NACW, the NCNW, and the white-only General Federation of Women's Clubs were affiliated with the YWCA, which formed a significant part of the interracial foundation church women built prior to the 1950s. Philosophically speaking, the YWCA from its beginnings in the late 1860s "desired that *all* girls and young women might share in the 'abundant life.'" Though the organization professed an interest in "colored work," it was not until the first decade of the twentieth century that the association became actively engaged in biracial branch work, which it labeled "interracial." In 1898 seven black college student associations were affiliated with the YWCA. Between the 1890s and 1918, black women in New York, Brooklyn, Baltimore, Washington, Philadelphia, and Dayton formed independent organizations expressly for African American working women who were excluded from YWCA city associations. These groups used the title YWCA, and their organizers held memberships in the YWCA; however, they were not affiliated with the national organization. Following the 1906 establishment of the YWCA National Board, the fledgling black associations became a concern.

In the fall of 1907 Addie Waites Hunton, a prominent Episcopal woman, became the first African American to be hired at the national level of the YWCA. As the wife of William Alphaeus Hunton, the first black international secretary for the YMCA, she was chosen in part because of her education, high visibility, and prominence in the NACW. As the national organizer of the NACW, Addie Hunton traveled throughout the nation, establishing branches of the organization. The YWCA National Board considered her extensive contacts with whites and blacks and knowledge of southern race relations distinct assets that would be useful in her new position. Reflecting on the relationship between the NACW and the YWCA, one observer noted that the "[YWCA's] task of securing good leadership was facilitated because of the splendid work which the Federation of Colored Women's Clubs has done in arousing a social consciousness among its members." Hunton's first assignment was to visit and investigate all black city and college associations, and to reorganize and recommend associations for affiliation with the National Board. She was also asked to choose a young woman to serve as secretary to the board for "colored work." In May 1908, Hunton chose Elizabeth Ross, a teacher in the Normal School in Montgomery, Alabama, to be the first student secretary for work among black women. The board confirmed Ross's appointment.

Between December 1907 and August 1908, Hunton also worked to establish a YWCA Colored Women's Department and to reorganize the Fifty-third Street black YWCA in New York City. Ross continued the investigation and wrote a report that revealed a struggle between the black organizations and the National Board. The question has been raised as to why black women chose "to remain with the YWCA in light of other possibilities for organizing." Black women who struggled with racism and gender discrimination in all areas of their lives felt that the National Board's racial policies and practices were not unlike those of other national organizations, religious and secular, with which black women affiliated. However, African American women recognized that the YWCA was the largest and one of the most influential of the women's organizations in the nation. Though its structure was biracial and its internal configuration represented the racial status quo, many years before the founding of CWU it was one of the few national women's organizations that accepted black members. Also, in addition to its support for working-class women, black women were attracted to the YWCA's interdenominational structure, which made it possible to work with women from different religious traditions.

Realistically assessing their position, whether in the YWCA, the CIC, or the FCC, or working with other white-controlled organizations, black women relied on their faith in God and themselves, and maintained a continuing commitment to stay the course and bit by bit to educate white women about race and racism. They were determined to transform the political and economic systems that oppressed black people, including racist institutional structures that deemed them inferior and treated them and their families as second-class citizens. Few black women leaders were disillusioned by the attitudes and positions taken by white leaders, many of whom advocated the social gospel but abhorred the idea of integration, and were adamantly against interracial sex and marriage—or, as some called it, "amalgamation." Irrespective of white attitudes, black women were rooted in their faith that change would come if they persisted in their search for racial justice. Though they recognized the personal and sometimes professional costs inherent in their quest, they understood the power of constituency and volunteer leaders to shape the issues and to exert internal and external pressure on white organizations and institutions. The power of a constituency was in numbers. The power of volunteer leaders was money and influence. The offense was led by the constituency, which was constantly pushing for change. The consistent press for change by black women leaders and their white allies, through a barrage of internal and external interactions and protest as well as a well-oiled publicity machine, effectively influenced the directives of the YWCA and similar organizations. Some of the YWCA's most significant racial compromises came out of conflict.

African American women of all religious persuasions, and a significant number of NACW members, saw the YWCA as an important beachhead in their struggle to implement their larger agenda. They sought greater voice and involvement in white organizations such as the YWCA and the MECS that delivered services to their communities. Summing up the philosophy of NACW women, in 1907 Victoria Graham, a leader in the Minnesota Federation, observed, "Clubs can be a means of power for the accomplishment of work, for the universal good, not only of ourselves, but our men and children." The YWCA is an example of how the NACW's influence was used by black women leaders to leverage power in other organizations. Social and political activists such as Lugenia Burns Hope, Lucy Craft Laney, Fannie Barrier Williams, Charlotte Hawkins Brown, Annie Malone, and Rev. Florence Spearing Randolph worked to develop YWCAs that served black women and to eliminate discrimination in the organization.

Emma Merritt, an AME activist, public school educator and

administrator, founding member of the NACW, and president of the NAACP in the District of Columbia (1930–33), clearly understood the need for black women to invest their time and energies in developing strong black YWCA branches that could engage in "uplift" as well as leadership development. In 1918 Merritt was the chair of the black YWCA membership campaign in Washington that reported 1,262 new members. In a statement of the association's purpose, Merritt aligned the NACW's philosophy with that of the YWCA and invoked the image of the "true woman" to appeal to middle-class black women. She asserted, "The work of the Y.W.C.A. is the uplifting of girls and women of our race, and preparing them to rightly fill their places in the world. The land cannot become safe for democracy unless our women are on the same basis with other women, intellectually, morally and spiritually. To accomplish [this] our association needs and solicits the assistance of every true woman of Washington."

Similar to Merritt, Lugenia Hope, a veteran social activist in the NACW, the CIC, and many other organizations, recognized the YWCA as a powerful entity that could be used as a conduit for helping black women to reach their "highest development." Realizing how high the stakes were, Hope was willing to fight tooth and nail for African American autonomy in the YWCA, to ensure that the voices of black women were heard, respected, and heeded at all levels, and to guarantee that African American women exercised real power in the association through participation in administration. A deeply religious Baptist woman who often reminded the YWCA of its Christian philosophy, Hope made it clear that her motives for fighting for the rights of black "womanhood" were related to her "aspirations for [black women's] freedom and spiritual enlargement." At one point, Hope and her southern counterparts threatened to withdraw from the YWCA and "return to their churches as bases of support." Between 1915 and her death in 1947, Lugenia Hope was a central force in transforming the YWCA and ensuring that it respected the right of black girls and women to self-determination.

In 1915, with the consent of the Southeastern Federation of Colored Women's Clubs, Hope submitted a petition to the National Board stating that she represented "300,000 Negro women of the South." Comprehensively listing what she considered discriminatory practices and policies, Hope requested an investigation of the YWCA work among African American women in the South and defined the remedies sought. This petition was a response to the National Board's acceptance of the findings of a Subcommittee on Colored Work that, among other things, specified the pattern of organization and administrative protocols for the relationship between the local white and black city associations. White members of the boards of directors would serve as chairs of colored work; black women could serve on committees of management; and affiliating committees would comprise three white and three black women, "who [would] act in the capacity of advisers and counselors." Black branch secretaries would be appointed by the staff of the all-white central association, with the approval of the branch.

African American women used their religious and secular organizational networks to exert their collective power and protest the YWCA National Board's action at the local and national levels, and won their fight. By 1920 black women occupied administrative positions at the local level, and in 1924 Elizabeth Ross Haynes became the first black person to serve on the National Board. During World War I, the War Work Council of the YWCA provided funding for expanding and accelerating the organization's work among black women. However, segregation and discrimination continued to be a factor at all levels of YWCA operation. For example, in 1920 black women leaders attending the YWCA's national meeting in Cleveland, Ohio, were not invited to the annual banquet held in the Hotel Statler. Southern white delegates objected to their presence, and members of the YWCA's organizing committee told black delegates that the hotel waiters threatened to strike if any African Americans entered the dining room.

While the YWCA argued that dual associations were necessary in communities where there was legal segregation, it mandated separate branches and separate Negro Girl Reserve clubs where there was no legal requirement. The continued protest of black women against YWCA policies of racial dominance, segregation, and exclusion began to bear fruit in the 1930s. During that period the Council of Colored Work was eliminated from the YWCA, and the local Committees on Colored Work, with their biracial structures, increasingly were yielding to the FCC and other church-related interracial committees. At the national level the effect of the FCC on the YWCA's racial practices is clear. The impact of the establishment of the FCC Department of Race Relations and subsequently the initiation of the Church Women's Committee, chaired by a YWCA leader, could be seen in the evolution of the YWCA's Council on Colored Work into an Interracial Committee and a Race Relations Committee. Between 1932 and 1942 the

YWCA introduced recommendations adopted in biennial conventions that reflected its movement toward an interracial agenda and signaled its ascendancy to a position as a major player in the Civil Rights Movement. Specifically, the YWCA program included a public relations campaign designed to change the attitudes of its members, particularly in the South, about lynching and mob violence; to influence state and federal legislation designed to deter lynching; to support legislation for improvement of economic opportunities for blacks; to ensure equal treatment before the law and enforcement of the law, regardless of race; and to improve the status of African Americans, Indians, Mexicans, and Asians.

Between 1915 and 1946, African American women were highly successful in their efforts to transform the YWCA. The association was forced to grapple with and respond to the strong, offensive activity of black women—constantly putting forth an agenda—at the local and national levels. The YWCA also was endlessly redefining its relationship with black women. White women in the YWCA such as Carrie Johnson and her CIC cohorts wanted to retain control at all cost. They saw the need to improve African Americans' material conditions, fund special projects defined by black women, and make other adjustments designed to temporarily abate racial friction. Unlike the YWCA, the FCC lacked a critical mass of black women leaders who could mount a powerful offense. And, although the black male clergy registered their dissatisfaction with the FCC, prior to the 1950s they had no clear agenda and sustained no strong offensive activity within the FCC. Instead, they formed a separate organization, the Fraternal Council of Negro Churches of America.

Unlike black church women, the black male clergy lacked a national interdenominational organization such as the NACW, which included women from diverse secular associations who worked together and defined agendas and strategies for achieving their racial and feminist goals. By the 1920s the NACW could literally deploy their troops to infiltrate a white organization, such as the YWCA, and speak in one voice. Of course, black women leaders disagreed and had personal differences, but they were largely unified on the central issues of racial segregation and discrimination. Black and white women differed in their understanding of the place and function of race in the United States, and even the most liberal white women in the CIC, the CWCRR, and the YWCA could not accept African Americans as their equals. But they found ways of coexisting and were willing to engage in long-term struggle and compromise on many issues.

Black women accepted racism as a fact of life and were not deluded into thinking that they would ever develop anything other than professional "friendships" with the white women they engaged with in the interracial movement. Even Eleanor Roosevelt and Mary McLeod Bethune were unable to transcend that barrier. Their "friendship" developed out of political necessity, during Franklin Delano Roosevelt's presidency. Bethune was of great value to the Roosevelt administration for attracting black voters to the Democratic Party. Bethune also needed Eleanor to achieve personal and professional goals. Bethune never became an intimate of Eleanor Roosevelt, and when Roosevelt left the White House, Bethune privately lamented that she never saw her. The fact of the matter is that black and white women leaders and their organizations were generally ahead of men on questions of race. Also, the NACW and the NCNW included many women leaders who were master strategists persisting in their efforts to achieve specific goals and, when necessary, regrouping and pursuing other courses of action until they obtained results.

Because of its constant engagement with black women leaders, the YWCA National Board was prodded to take action on controversial issues and became more amenable to change. Like the CWCRR and CWU, the YWCA did not shy away from critical analysis and evaluation of its policies and practices. Although discrimination abounded in all of these groups, and racial incidents often occurred within the organizations and at the national meetings, the leadership continued to articulate a philosophy, adopt policies, and engage in social activism that gradually changed the attitudes of many of their members and prepared them for the political and social upheaval of the 1950s and '60s. In 1944, the YWCA took a hard look at the impact of segregation on blacks within the organization and in the United States.

Following a detailed and critical examination of racial practices in the nation and at every level of operation within its organization, YWCA leaders concluded that it was not enough to simply talk about eliminating discrimination within the YWCA; it also needed to be eradicated within the American society. In a remarkably candid statement about the history of its interracial practices, in 1944 the YWCA admitted that it had "groped" and was still "groping" for ways to address issues of race within and outside of the organization. It announced that the National Board was opening a new chapter in the YWCA's history by adopting a statement on black-white relationships. It affirmed the group's commitment to work for "the elimination of the heavy injustices experienced by the Negro people," and promised to make an "honest examination" of its interracial practices to determine whether or not they were "Christian and democratic." The statement concluded with a powerful pledge to make democracy real within the organization: "In the life of the nation we can be a cross-section group in which there will be no racial discrimination, no crippling prejudices. As we strive to achieve this in our organization, we shall be an effective witness to democracy in our communities."

The Seventeenth National YWCA Conference, which met in Atlantic City in March 1946, adopted a thirty-five-point program for the National Board and local associations to implement. The new program included complete integration of African American women and girls on the boards and staff and in all YWCA activities. The program was accepted almost unanimously by the more than three thousand delegates attending the convention. This was the most far-reaching action taken by any organization in the United States. By unanimous vote the convention adopted the National Interracial Charter, formally recognizing that all women of "minority races" affiliated with the YWCA had a legitimate claim to the association's "understanding and support," and pledging that "wherever there is injustice on the basis of race, whether in the community, the nation or the world, our protest must be clear and our labor for its removal vigorous and steady. And what we urge on others, we are constrained to practice ourselves." Having enacted such legislation, the task before the organization was to convince white women in the local branches to integrate their facilities and provide equal treatment and access to administrative positions to African American women. This would be the most difficult task the association ever confronted. However, it would be one that would engage the whole network of church women and their multiple organizations, especially CWU.

Anticipating the passage of the Interracial Charter, Dorothy Height, the secretary for interracial education of the YWCA National Board prepared "Step by Step," a booklet explaining how to develop programs in interracial relationships. Height was assigned to work with YWCA branches to implement the recommendations in the Interracial Charter. Between 1946 and 1954 she traveled throughout the nation, especially the South, holding interracial meetings. Following the Supreme Court's decision, in the 1954 landmark *Brown v. Board of Education* case, outlawing segregation in public schools, the YWCA encouraged associations to fully participate in the desegregation of schools. Concerned about the slow pace of change within the organization as well as society, in 1963 the YWCA paired Height with a white southerner to determine how they could impact public policy as it related to racial segregation, discrimination, and integration in both the society and the YWCA. In 1965 the YWCA established the Office of Racial Justice with Height as director. Her task was to lead a "massive campaign to eradicate discrimination." Given that many YWCA women belonged to CWU, the NAACP, the NACW, the NCNW, and numerous other organizations, Height mobilized branch associations at the local level to support local desegregation campaigns throughout the South.

Race, Gender, and Religion in the 1940s

THE 1940S MAY BE CHARACTERIZED as a transitional decade. Following on the heels of the Great Depression, it was a period of tremendous change for all Americans, but especially African Americans and women. The decade opened with the bombing of Pearl Harbor in December 1941 and the launching of World War II. The war impacted every area of American life and brought far-reaching economic, political, and social changes. Between 1900 and 1940 the percent of the total black population of the United States residing in the South decreased from 89.9 to 77 percent, and to 64 percent by 1947. This change in the southern black population was accompanied by greater urbanization of African Americans.

As a result of the Great Migration, the black population was no longer concentrated in one region, but distributed throughout the United States. Therefore, by the mid-1940s, the racial problems formerly associated almost exclusively within the South were confronted by the whole of American society. The U.S. government was keenly aware of the international significance of the growing unrest in the Third World among people of color seeking freedom from the European colonial powers. As black labor became more concentrated in northern and western cities, and steadily moved into industrial jobs, issues of racial prejudice became more prevalent and tensions between African Americans and white ethnic minorities grew. The competition for jobs and housing—especially the location of blacks in crowded urban ghettos with predominantly white merchants and landlords who often overcharged and sometimes insulted their black customers—was causing great tension and unrest. The frequently reported beating, shooting, and killing of African Americans and charges of police brutality created the conditions for the riots that occurred in Harlem in 1935 and Detroit, Atlantic City, Mobile, Alabama, and Beaumont, Texas, in 1943. The Detroit riot, lasting thirty hours, resulted in the killing of twenty-five blacks and nine whites and the injuring of seven hundred persons. Metropolitan cities in the West and other northern cities feared that they would suffer the same fate. City governments quickly appointed interracial committees to intercede, prevent conflict, and quell the tensions. In the midst of all of this, African Americans protested that they were not receiving equal treatment or an equal share of the benefits being dispensed on behalf of the war effort.

In the 1940s women experienced new opportunities and moved out of the home into the workforce in greater numbers. The effect of World War II on white and black women was apparent in their movement into nontraditional jobs and roles and their involvement in many aspects of public life. The demand for more men in the military coupled with the need for women's services to keep the government running created an atmosphere of acceptance and support that women had not known before. The impact of the war on black women's labor was especially dramatic. Prior to World War II, with few exceptions, the only work available to the majority of African American women was domestic and common labor. By 1945 there were more than two million black women in war work. Employed in a variety of positions at different levels, including specialists and executives, they worked in factories, steel mills, foundries, shipyards, aircraft plants, and in the transportation and other civilian industries, and served in the armed forces.

The extensive educational programs, leadership training institutes, conferences, and networks created by church women's organizations prepared women mentally and philosophically to assume new roles and laid the groundwork for advancing their struggle for freedom and equality in the church and society. By 1940 many black and white women were poised to take advantage of the new opportunities and to seize the moment to consolidate their power, not as separate entities, but through group strategies and actions. For African American women and their organizations, the 1940s and '50s was a time of achievement and advancement of their causes. Women such as Mary

McLeod Bethune, Anna Arnold Hedgeman, Sadie Tanner Mossell Alexander, Christine Smith, Annie Heath, Creola Cowan, Rossie Hollis, and Abbie Clement Jackson gained greater visibility as they took the reins of leadership and articulated the goals of the African American women's movement.

The NACW, which was once the alpha and omega of black women's organizations, was both challenged and weakened by the founding of the National Council of Negro Women in 1935 by Mary McLeod Bethune, a former NACW president and a leader in the Methodist Episcopal Church. The rise of the NCNW and Bethune to major positions of prominence and influence hastened the decline of the NACW. In the 1940s black Methodist women's organizations, in particular the AME and AME Zion groups, escalated their push for equality and participatory democracy within their denominations and actively worked in the civil rights and women's religious reform movement represented by the NAACP, the Urban League, and CWU. Though individual women were active in the Civil Rights Movement, and in local branches of the latter organizations, CME women concentrated mostly on their internal denominational struggle for women's religious rights.

Black college-educated women of all Christian religious traditions were affiliated with the local and state church federations, the FCC, and secular interracial committees, including the interracial programs created by black sororities. Elizabeth Fouse, Blanche Williams Anderson, and Sadie Tanner Alexander, featured in *Crisis*'s 1943 "First Ladies of Colored America" series, are among the many examples of deeply religious social activists who worked and networked within multiple black and white organizations. Elizabeth Fouse, a leader of the NBC-USA Woman's Convention and the Kentucky NACW, organizer of the Phyllis Wheatley YWCA branch in Lexington, Kentucky, and member of CWU, the Kentucky Interracial Commission Executive Board, and the American Teacher's Association, also held membership in the Zeta Phi Beta Sorority. Blanche Williams Anderson, an influential Presbyterian woman, was a founder of the Friends' Interracial Fellowship of Philadelphia and a member of the NAACP, the NCNW, and the Alpha Kappa Alpha Sorority, and served as a charter member of the Southwest Leadership Training School for Christian Education. Sadie Tanner Alexander, attorney for the AME Church, lay representative of the AME Church to the FCC, member of CWU, secretary of the National Urban League, a founder of the Friends' Interracial Fellowship of Philadelphia, a director of the Philadelphia-based Armstrong Association, the Wharton Settlement, and the Women's International League for Peace and Freedom, and the first national president of the Delta Sigma Theta Sorority, was chairman of the Interracial Committee of Philadelphia.

By 1940 black women's sororities were a central part of the black women's organizational base, a powerful interlocking network of racial, religious, and gender-oriented organizations. However, Alpha Kappa Alpha was by far the leader in the political arena. Founded in 1908, AKA was the first Greek-letter sorority established by black college women. Claiming its religious roots, sorority leaders asserted, "We A.K.A. women acknowledge Christianity. Our Sorority is founded upon its underlying principles." From the beginning the organization pledged itself to find solutions to "the problems of girls and women," and committed the membership to "action related to the needs, interests, and potentialities of the community in which the group is situated."

In 1921 Lorraine Richardson Green, as AKA's Supreme Basileus, challenged sorors to "make A.K.A. an organization of gigantic power whose ultimate purpose is the improving of the social status of our people, raising the moral standards, and increasing educational efficiency." As a leading figure in the affluent Episcopal Church, during the 1920s Green worked closely with the interracial movement in Chicago. With incisive insight she perceived the importance of the sorority and its members working cooperatively with others to tear down the walls of intolerance and forge a new society. For Green, the nation was entering an "era of mighty achievement, nationalization and unification of all interests into harmonious cooperating associations," and it was important for AKA sorors to "ally themselves with far-reaching powerful associations," change agents important to AKA's vision of racial and gender social justice. Green worked closely with the Women's Division of the Chicago Federation of Churches and served as co-chairman of the Woman's Division of the Chicago branch of the Conference of Christians and Jews.

During the 1930s and '40s AKA developed programs and projects to dismantle racist structures and often implemented its programs at the local level working in conjunction with NACW city and state federations, the National Council of Negro Women, and local interracial committees affiliated with the FCC, the YWCA, and women's missionary societies and conventions. In 1935 AKA's Mississippi Health

Project organized the Traveling Clinic, which covered hundreds of miles providing services to thousands of children and adults. In 1938 AKA established the Non-Partisan Lobby for Economic and Democratic Rights and later the AKA Non-Partisan Council on Public Affairs. AKA was the first black organization to hire a full-time representative to monitor and lobby for legislation and other governmental action on behalf of African Americans. Thomasina Johnson Norford, the council's legislative representative, appeared on the programs of the NACW, the NCNW, women's missionary societies, and other organizations. During the 1940s, in conjunction with its interracial and legislative work, the sorority focused on discrimination in organized religion. In the AKA *Legislative Digest*, the sorority stated, "Christianity vs. the color line" was "public issue number one."

Interracial Work of Baptist and Methodist Women's Organizations

BLACK BAPTIST WOMEN and their organizations were represented on the CWU board and continued to form a major part of the NACW leadership. Black and white Baptist women had a long history of working cooperatively on educational and self-help projects benefitting the African American community. During the late nineteenth century the New England–based Woman's American Baptist Home Mission Society established the Atlanta Baptist Female Seminary (renamed Spelman), a school of higher education for black women. Similarly, in 1883 the ABHMS responded to the pleas of black Baptist minister Walter H. Brooks and established Hartshorn Memorial College in Virginia for the purpose of educating black women. Spelman, Hartshorn, and other schools created by northern white Baptist women helped to produce black leaders, including many ministers and teachers, some of whom filled the ranks of the ABHMS schools for blacks.

Prior to the 1930s, the Woman's Missionary Union of the Southern Baptist Church maintained a biracial work with the Baptist Woman's Convention, assisting black women in forming and conducting missionary societies. In 1902 the WMU and the WC agreed to a policy of cooperation in which they would jointly fund the salaries and expenses of two African American women missionaries in the South. The missionaries worked solely under the direction of the WC, organizing conferences and affiliate societies of the WC, and distributing religious tracts and other literature. This was the beginning of a relation-

ship between the WMU and the WC that would continue for most of
the twentieth century. In a few instances the cooperative work was
extended to include social service projects. For example, in Baltimore
white Baptist women operated industrial schools for black children,
which were eventually turned over to black women.

Throughout its history, mindful of the regional identity and conservative position of the Southern Baptist Convention on issues of race
and gender, the WMU exercised great caution in its work with African
American and feminist organizations—being careful not to breach
"regional mores." For example, at the local level, to avoid identification with "even slightly controversial causes," WMU members worked
unofficially with CWU. In 1930, at a meeting in Atlanta sponsored by
the Commission on Interracial Cooperation, the WMU turned down
an invitation to work cooperatively with Katherine Gardner and the
FCC's Church Women's Committee's interracial program. Gardner's
suggestion that the Southern Baptist women adopt and use the mission
study and race relations materials created by the CWCRR were
rejected. Not wanting to be left out of the growing women's interracial
movement, Una Roberts Lawrence, WMU mission study editor, made
a special effort to meet Nannie Burroughs, a member of the CIC's
Women's Committee.

Following the CIC meeting, Burroughs and Lawrence developed a
relationship based on their special interests and needs. Lawrence
stressed the importance of southern white women engaging in "interracial" work at the local level. However, what Lawrence envisioned
were white women utilizing the NBC-USA Woman's Convention as a
vehicle to reach large numbers of black women through the teaching
of Bible and mission study courses, dissemination of religious education materials similar to those used by the WMU, and the provision of
social welfare services in accordance with the needs of local black communities. Southern Baptist women were most concerned about reaching and controlling the large working-class black population through
religious propaganda, and were not interested in either promoting
racial justice or addressing racial problems. They also realized that
since the classes would be filled by mostly Baptist women who were
servants, they could teach them skills that would improve their ability
to serve their white employers.

By 1930, Burroughs was desperately in need of financial support
to keep the National Training School for Women and Girls open, and
to publish the now-defunct *Worker*. Under attack from the male-

THE WORKER

WORK === SUPPORT THYSELF === TO THINE OWN POWERS APPEAL

VOL. ...   LINCOLN HEIGHTS, WASHINGTON, D. C., FEBRUARY, 1915.   No. 2

WHAT THE BELGIANS DID TO THE NEGRO.

Here is a bit of Ancient (1905) History that we recite not because we like to recall unpleasant things, but because almost before the deed is recorded in cold type, that declaration in the matchless sermon on the Mount that "With what measure ye meet, it shall be measured to you again," is being fulfilled right before our eyes.

CONGO VICTIMS

This is God's declaration; this is God's doings and what can we say except that He moves in a mysterious way, His wonders to perform.

Beginning in 1884 and running through a period of over twenty years all America and thirteen European States endorsed or tolerated a most inhuman, atrocious, and outrageous policy in the Congo. This policy placed the Congo in trust and made Leopold the agent.

His "pals" and "pimps" were all Belgians. For twenty years he ruled a fruitful domain, four times as large as Germany, inhabitated by over twenty-five millions of black people. These natives gathered ivory and rubber under compulsion of lash, bullet, fire and starvation. When they were short of their tasks, through hunger, sickness and ceaseless exhausting labor without rest, the Belgian soldiers would hunt them down, butcher them, and burn their villages. These Belgians wiped a nation of friendless creatures out of existence. Persons who were present at the very first hearing of the Congo Commission said, "Men of stone would have been moved by the stories of outrages by these "Congo Butchers." It is further estimated that if the innocent blood shed in the Congo State were put in buckets and the buckets placed side by side, the line would stretch four thousand miles; if the skeletons of the FIFTEEN MILLIONS who were butchered would rise and march in a single file it would take them NINE months and FOUR days to pass a given point. These "Congo Butchers" cut off heads, hands and feet of innocent women and children. One district of FORTY THOUSAND was reduced in a few months to EIGHT THOUSAND. The natives received an average of TWO cents each week for their labor. The Belgians received in turn for their labor MILLIONS of guineas.

Misisonaries, the Congo Commission, the late W. T. Stead, and others worked faithfully, to arouse the Christian world to go to the relief of the defenseless, homeless, friendless millions but little sentiment and no definite concerted action was taken in behalf of our kinsmen.

With the blood of FIFTEEN MILLIONS slain dripping from their records the Belgians are now seeking shelter in the homeland of the kindred of the people their gallant soldiers slew. Are these soldiers and their off-springs coming to join hands in making this a better America? Let us pray that though they slew us in the Congo to the number of FIFTEEN MILLIONS; burned up our villages, destroyed the last vestage of hope; that they will not turn again to smite us and lynch us in America.

People Who Are Doing Things.

The women of Spokane, Washington have organized a Nannie Burroughs Art Club with the following officers: Mrs. P. L. Powell, President; Mrs. George Clay, Vice-President; Mrs. P. Bagby, Secretary; Mrs. William Brazil, Corresponding Secretary; Mrs. F. Minnes, Treasurer.

We trust that these good women will make their Club a source of real up-lift by making beautiful things and selling them to help foster some worthy cause.

Mrs. Julia Nichols and Mrs. E. W. McAden of Buffalo, New York, sent through Dr. Nash, five dollars ($5.00) for our work. They are zealous young women and we are happy to know that they are going to keep on doing something definite for the work here. Hundreds of young women could get together in groups, two or five to a "Bunch," and help our deserving institutions.

The Women of Washington will soon be called to form a District Union of Baptist Women. The Ministers Union endorsed the plan and the promotors are now at work, framing a constitution and outlining a plan of operation. We believe the churches will be pleased with this new organization. There is a great need of an efficient organization embracing all Baptist women, who desire to be of service, as well as those who want to catch a wide and clear vision of the field and its needs, and to have before them constantly the facts about all phases of denominational work. These facts are to be so attractively presented that they will make their own appeal. We mean to push a campaign of education and present causes in which Baptists must be interested and to which they must give through their *already established* channels.

We shall simply present each cause in a most attractive way every three months and we know the people will give more. Intelligent information is the key to intelligent giving

Miss Violet A. Johnson, of Summit, New Jersey arranged, through the President of the Missionary Society of the Baptist Church (white), a special meeting for Miss Burroughs. Miss Johnson is doing much for our work. We have added to our list of friends as a result of this meeting.

The Worker was a missionary and educational quarterly established in 1912 by Nannie Helen Burroughs, president of the National Training School for Women and Girls. As editor of the publication, Burroughs stressed the need for domestic and foreign missionary work and exposed the brutalities inherent in European colonialism and African American racism, especially lynching and segregation.

dominated NBC as well as from S. Willie Layten and her WC cohorts, Nannie Burroughs nurtured a relationship with Una Roberts Lawrence in order to secure financial support from the WMU. In 1933 the WC agreed to participate in the WMU's proposed program of "Christian Interracial Cooperation," which provided the WC with financial support for a number of home mission projects, including leadership training institutes, missionary training schools, and special projects. These statewide training programs were conducted mainly by WMU leaders in cooperation with the WC state convention presidents. Classes were organized by WC leaders and taught by local white women. The work of the WMU with black women varied according to state. However, in most states there was an interest in training and recruiting women for domestic work. Special effort was made to improve and provide material aid for the domestic science programs in public schools. In the Texas WMU women provided training for black Baptist women—mostly working-class women—who attended the workshops and classes held in churches. In 1936 Olivia Davis, treasurer for the WMU in Texas, reported that throughout Texas mission studies classes were held on Thursdays, "the day that practically all maids have their day off." In the morning they were taught handicrafts—"sewing, knitting, crocheting, etc."—and in the afternoon WMU Bible teachers discussed the Sunday school lesson.

The price of the "interracial cooperation" with the WC—or, rather, the support of the WMU for Burroughs and her school— would not be cheap. It would require that Burroughs agree to share editorial control of *The Worker* with Una Roberts Lawrence. Lawrence was above the average white person in her knowledge and understanding of race and her acceptance of African Americans. She also understood the thinking of most whites on issues of race and racial etiquette. Lawrence knew that white Baptist women would not support any project with black women that offended their sensibilities or compromised the conservative identity of the Southern Baptist Convention.

Like most white religionists, including the Catholics, Presbyterians, Episcopalians, and Methodists, Southern Baptist women were more interested in evangelizing blacks than challenging white racism. As the chair of the WMU's Co-operation Committee, Lawrence took great pains to explain to Burroughs that the WMU believed *The Worker* was weak in its presentation of devotionals and missionary programs, and that its topics were not home mission themes but "the problems of Christian living and conduct, and of personal service."

Burroughs had selected three topics for the July–September 1934 issues that interwove themes of missions with racial issues that often suggested the hypocritical nature of white people's use of the rhetoric of Christianity while practicing racial discrimination. In their stead, Lawrence proposed subjects such as "The Christian looks at America," which would include statistics regarding the unchurched, immigrants, social and economic conditions in cities and rural areas, and "un-Christian attitudes and practices."

Una Lawrence argued that a focus on "Under-privileged Peoples of America" would illustrate that blacks were not the only Americans who were underprivileged. She felt that "it would be wholesome for our Negro people to realize that by comparison their lot is much better than" that of most Americans, including Indians, Cajuns, and Creoles, Mexicans and other migrant workers, and whites in Appalachia. Lawrence further explained the importance of a topic such as "The Transforming Power of the Gospel" for illustrating the widespread "interracial cooperation" work conducted by the Southern Baptist Convention in Cuba and foreign fields, as well as with blacks in America. Finally, Lawrence informed Burroughs, "It would mean everything to the Baptist white women of the South to learn that Negro women were interested in exactly the same things, face the same sort of problems and are carrying on the same kind of work as the white women of the South. And, I believe it would have a fine psychological effect on the Negro women as well."

Nannie Burroughs believed in compromise, not accommodation or capitulation to white demands. Her response to Lawrence was thoughtful, but firm in its insistence on black self-determination. Burroughs wrote Lawrence that only a few of the topics she suggested were suitable for most black Baptist women. It was important to interest African Americans in "other peoples and their problems," but the approach would have to be different and the information simplified. Burroughs explained that there were other "underprivileged people who [were] not Negroes," who "might be having a hard time, but they are not being lynched, Jim-crowed and penalized because they happen to belong to another race or another class."

During the first six months of the WMU/WC collaboration, for the most part Burroughs adhered to the rules defined by Lawrence and made little mention of race. However, in April 1935, Burroughs's editorials, covering seven pages, included extensive references to race problems that demonstrated the culpability of white Christians. For example, in "What Is Home Missions," Burroughs defined in great detail "what it is not." Among other things, she said, "God has been too good to the Anglo-Saxon race for it to prostitute the Christian religion to the inglorious service of lynching, persecuting and robbing other races of their birthright," and "[t]he average Church is deadly silent on the question of justice. The new fad of preaching brotherhood (Race Relations) one Sunday in the year and giving the Negro the devil three hundred sixty-four days in the year is a shameful gesture."

Lawrence and the WMU were not amused by what they read in *The Worker*. In June 1935 Lawrence discussed the need to keep the publication free from any factional fights. She criticized the editorials written by Burroughs and noted that she (Lawrence) might have to relinquish the chairmanship of the Co-operation Committee because of what Burroughs wrote. Lawrence stated that to avoid alienating the white readers, not a single race problem should be mentioned in *The Worker*. Burroughs's responded that the WMU should not hold Lawrence responsible for anything that she (Burroughs) said or did. Burroughs stressed that she would always try to be patient and tolerant, but that she had to speak the truth. Assuring Lawrence that *The Worker* would not be as controversial the following year, Burroughs asserted, "I love your race a great deal more than they love mine." Between July 1935 and 1943 Burroughs tempered her language and rarely served up direct indictments of white Christians or referred to race problems.

While *The Worker* continued to hold African Americans accountable for their condition, to maintain the support of WMU, for many years it was to a great extent sanitized of all charges of racism. However, Burroughs's scathing criticism of white American racism, publicized through the black press, continued to be heard throughout black America. Meanwhile, Burroughs and Lawrence developed a very close relationship based on mutual trust. Over a period of years, they became intimates, jointly developing strategies to handle the internal organizational problems they confronted in their dealings with white and black Baptists and in their efforts to achieve their mutual goals. Lawrence later admitted that she had been "educated" about the Negro.

White organizations such as the MECS and the WMU invariably chose to support ameliorative programs rather than attack systemic problems of racism. In 1934 the WMU approved the "Open Door" program, which proposed to expand their cooperative efforts with black Baptists in "larger" southern towns and cities by focusing on problems of "delinquency, poverty and ignorance." This project, similar to many of the "interracial" plans launched by white church women, aimed at improvement of local community conditions. In establishing day nurseries, mother's clubs, and other so-called "cooperative" enterprises described as problems of "childhood and motherhood," the WMU, not unlike many white organizations and institutions, suggested that racial problems were related to "delinquency, poverty, and ignorance" instead of the white racism that denied African Americans economic, political, and social equality. Unfortunately, the WMU to some extent took some of its cues from Burroughs, an extremely complex woman, who argued forcefully against lynching, segregation, and discrimination while simultaneously broadcasting that the "crux of the [Negro] problem is in the home."

By 1945 the WMU had established biracial committees in a number of southern states. Burroughs indicated that white women were more willing to work with black women in cooperative projects in South Carolina and Virginia than in some other states primarily because they were more accommodating in their manner. For the most part these committees engaged in cooperative programs of missionary education. In Virginia the Baptist Woman's Missionary Union funded the Missionary Training School at Virginia Union University, a black Baptist school. The Department of Leadership and Missionary Training were operated as divisions of the university's School of Religion.

In the 1940s and '50s, southern black Baptist women at the local and state levels were more apt to be engaged in implementing their educational and social reform programs and less likely to be directly involved in civil rights and women's religious reform. In the North and West, the pattern of interracial cooperation was usually one of Christian fellowship. For example, in 1945 several white Baptist associations in Pittsburgh sponsored a Christian Fellowship House that was run by a staff of blacks and whites who organized interracial cultural events. The first Fellowship House was established in Philadelphia in 1941 by the Society of Friends Race Relations Committee and youth leaders representing national denominations. As a result of this pioneering effort, similar centers were opened in Pittsburgh, New York City, Chicago, and Detroit. The Philadelphia Race Relations Committee's

Christmas Celebration at the Bethlehem Center House in Nashville, Tennessee, ca. 1913. As a part of its home mission program, the Methodist Episcopal Church Women's Society established black settlement houses known as Bethlehem Houses in a number of southern cities to address issues primarily related to poverty.

program evolved from a series of supper meetings with lectures on race in 1931 to a Cooperative Council that worked on civil rights issues in 1942.

The patterns of interracial cooperation that defined the WMU and WC relationship in the South, as well as the Baptist Fellowship Houses developed in the North to promote racial understanding through knowledge of black culture and achievement, were nonthreatening to white Americans. In neither case were African Americans demanding racial equality, racial justice, and integration; rather, they enjoyed a mutual fellowship with whites, worked cooperatively on community improvement projects, and attempted to create feelings of goodwill through the development of personal relationships.

White Methodists, similar to the Baptists, had a long tradition of home mission work among African Americans. In 1912, in Augusta, Georgia, the Methodist Episcopal Church, South, founded its first social settlement for African Americans. MECS black settlements became known as "Bethlehem Houses." The first Bethlehem House was opened in Nashville around 1913. During the 1920s and '30s Bethlehem Houses were established in Birmingham, Chattanooga,

Winston-Salem, Spartanburg, Atlanta, Macon, and Memphis. Influenced by Dorothy Tilly, in 1938 the Augusta Bethlehem House was one of the few that maintained an integrated board comprising both black and white women. The programs at these houses included a sewing school, mother's club, cooking classes for girls and mothers, industrial girl's club, clubs for boys, night schools for working men and women, day nurseries, Bible schools, summer camps for boys and girls, and other activities. Sara Estelle Haskin, supervisor of the Nashville Bethlehem House, developed an intimate knowledge of black community issues and problems, and was well known among CME women leaders.

The work of settlement houses and centers, especially those created and funded by white denominations, were referred to as interracial work; however, in reality, they were really extensions of the home mission programs, related primarily to resources needed by the black community. As was the case for the Nashville Bethlehem House, where Mother Sallie Hill Sawyer, a black woman, approached the southern Methodist women, the reform agendas were usually defined by African Americans and jointly carried out by black and white women. White women who did not think of black women as their social equals claimed credit for the initiatives and could still boast that they were engaged in interracial reform. In her analysis of the program the MECS carried out with CME women, historian Mary Frederickson reveals a widespread pattern of "interracial cooperation," in which white and black church women developed nonthreatening relationships "based on neither collaboration nor enmity but mutual dependence." Frederickson argues that some black women and their organizations, like Sawyer, employed this strategy to achieve their racial goals, which she calls a "process of transformation."

The relational pattern described by Frederickson was not limited to the MECS's dealings with the CME women; it also describes the way northern and southern white and black Baptist women—the ABHMS, the WMU and the WC—functioned between 1930 and 1950. Southern protocols defining racial etiquette required that African Americans defer to whites. Obviously this was not the kind of methodology employed by black women leaders in the YWCA and CWU, whose strategies to change those organizations were more direct. However, unlike the YWCA, the CIC, and CWU, CME and WC women were not members of the MECS and the WMU. Thus, black church women saw the critical need to work both sides of the religious street. They worked with white church women's denominational organizations on specific projects for community improvement and education, and also utilized interdenominational Christian organizations to achieve social and political goals.

YWCA women leaders like Lugenia Burns Hope sought a form of transformation that would carry over into the American society and dismantle the whole structure of racism. They possessed the solid commitment and spiritual discipline necessary to involve themselves in the radical process of institutional transformation. In supporting educational, religious, and other social programs, white women unwittingly laid the groundwork for the development of a black leadership class that would fill the ranks of the black professional class, and black and white organizations such as the NAACP, the NACW, the YWCA, the NUL, the CIC, and CWU, as well as the sororities, interracial committees, and, eventually, the Civil Rights–Black Power Movement. Thus, although their style was less confrontational, the "process of transformation" employed by CME and WC women was equally as important as that used by African American women in the YWCA, the CIC, and CWU.

Nannie Burroughs and S. Willie Layten, leaders of the WC for almost half a century and members of CWU, concentrated their efforts on education and moral reform within the black community. As members of the NACW and National League of Colored Republican Women, these women were known as shrewd political operatives, actively engaged in electoral politics at the local and national levels. The work of these women, especially that of Burroughs, in the biracial and interracial movements is significant. The impact of Burroughs on the consciousness of black America was singular. For almost half a century, Burroughs's widely publicized and trenchant commentary on intraracial and interracial politics, racism, sexism, and classism in the church and society, and individual and institutional hypocrisy, exposed the ambition, avarice, and pettiness of many leaders and organizations. Burroughs worked within the broader interracial movement to eradicate legal segregation, and with the WMU to obtain special support for the WC's mission work and the National Training School for Women and Girls. Her chief concern was the education and self-improvement of working-class black girls and women, who formed the bulk of the black female population. Much later, in the 1960s, under the leadership of Mary O. Ross, a member of the CWU board, the

Christian Shoecraft Smith worked assiduously to eliminate sexism and racism in all areas of American life. Through her service and activism at the helm and on the boards of numerous organization such as the the AME Woman's Parent Mite Missionary Society, NACW, YWCA, CWU, Urban League, and Race Relations Commission of the Federal Council of the Churches of Christ, she fought for equality and justice for African Americans and women.

NBC-USA Woman's Convention became more actively involved in CWU.

In the 1940s, along with black women in the Methodist Episcopal Church's Central Jurisdiction, many AME, AME Zion, and CME women affiliated with the NCNW. Perhaps this was related to Mary McLeod Bethune's prominence as a member of the Methodist Episcopal Church, which provided extensive financial support for Bethune-Cookman College, an institution founded by Bethune. Baptist women do not appear to have been as active in the NCNW. In any case Methodist women tended to gravitate toward the NCNW and Baptist women continued to hold on to the NACW. By the mid-1960s the NACW was a shadow of what it had been and no longer a significant factor in many social movements. Bethune was very active in the CIC during the 1920s and '30s, and CWU in the 1940s. As a member of the boards of these organizations she had an opportunity to influence policy, and also to make important contacts with wealthy whites whom she hoped would contribute money to her causes—Bethune-Cookman College and the National Council of Negro Women. Under the leadership of Bethune and her successors—Dorothy Boulding Ferebee,

Vivian Carter Mason, and Dorothy Height—between 1940 and 1970 the NCNW was prominently involved in the interracial and Civil Rights movements.

Charting a New Course:
Church Women United in the 1940s

CWU's LIBERAL STANCE and forceful actions on issues of race, especially racial violence and discrimination, attracted black women to its membership. Methodist women—members of the AME, AME Zion, CME, and ME churches—were among the most active members of CWU. Leading figures such as Abbie Clement Jackson and Christine Smith had worked with local and state church federations and the FCC interracial committees, and some had served as FCC delegates and members of the Church Women's Committee on Race Relations. By 1945 a number of black women had joined CWU and established separate councils. Church Women United, like the YWCA and other predominantly white organizations, experienced difficulty in getting local white councils to integrate and include African American women in the leadership. In 1944, following a national tour and meetings with members of local councils, Jessie Daniel Ames indicated her disappointment in finding that there were so few black women in the national leadership. In CWU's official organ, *The Church Woman*, there were numerous articles on the progress of women in religious and secular life, the impact of war on society, discrimination, delinquency among girls, world and race tensions, postwar rehabilitation and reconstruction, literacy, and education. To inform its members about matters of race and sex, and to illustrate how some organizations had dealt with internal and external issues of discrimination, *The Church Woman* also publicized program initiatives. Black and white women were invited to write about their experiences in desegregated councils and in working together at the local and state levels on issues of race.

In 1941, in an article entitled "Erasing the Color Line," Ella Barksdale Brown discussed what it was like "[l]ooking from the colored side of the picture." In addition to describing how she developed her race consciousness, she spoke about her work in interracial organizations in New Jersey. Brown, a former member of the CWCRR and an organizer of the FCC's first statewide Interracial Conference of Church Women (1928), held memberships in the AME Zion Church, the New Jersey State Federation of Colored Women, the Interracial Committee of Church Women in New Jersey, and the state Federation of Church Women. She stated that, following her acceptance of an invitation to join the Federation of Church Women, she discovered that "[m]ost of the women in the organization were unaccustomed to Negroes in any position other than domestics and laborers. They were a bit offish at first but the president was a woman of force and determination." Brown suggested that the organization invite the principal of Bordentown, a state-supported educational institution for African Americans, to speak. The white women were not enthusiastic about the suggestion, but agreed to invite him. Following this event, the white women revealed that the principal's talk, and the music rendered by the school's quartet, "meant more in changing their racial attitudes than anything that had happened to them."

In describing the work of the New Jersey Interracial Committee of Church Women, Ella Barksdale Brown stressed that, like the committees in some northern and midwestern states, the organization brought together representatives of various interracial associations throughout the state to exchange ideas and information and to develop strategies for improving racial conditions and relationships. She noted, "It was our committee that first opened the doors of New Jersey hospitals for training Negro nurses." Brown explained how easy it was for the black and white members to work together and, in doing so, how they forgot race and became friends. Brown also emphasized that "oftentimes members of my own race are critical."

Reflecting on the history of AME women's relationship with CWU, Anna Burns Lynem, a leader in CWU and the AME Women's Missionary Society, recalled that "many of us have suffered embarrassment and humiliation. But the *Cause* was too great for an individual to consider personal feelings. Every time one of us appeared at anytime— anywhere, we realized we represented our racial group. It has been a long difficult way to the present." Lynem remembered the time when the CWU president, Mrs. Harper Sibley (1946–48), spoke in Louisville, and white and black CWU members held separate meetings—"because of a Church Federated group's influence, the church where she was speaking would not admit our race." Addressing the question of why AME women remained within CWU, Lynem stated, "We realize that Church Women United can do more to alleviate the evils of the world than a single group can do." As one of a very few black women to head local and state interracial councils, in 1950 Lynem was elected president of the Lexington Council, and in 1959 was vice president of both the Lexington CWU and the Kentucky State Council. Between 1945 and 1966, Lynem represented the AME Women's Missionary Society on the CWU National Board of Managers at various ecumenical institutes, and on many occasions as a speaker at CWU meetings.

Black women leaders refused to be treated or to assume roles as racial ornaments in CWU. From the beginning they were outspoken, open, and honest in articulating the position of African Americans and calling attention to discrimination in the broader American society and in CWU. Women such as Christine Smith, president of the AME Woman's Parent Mite Missionary Society (1931–44) and the NACW (1945–52), had worked within the interracial movement since the 1920s and had dealings with most of the white women leaders. Carefully honing their political skills and working closely with other black women leaders, Smith, Bethune, and others, operating behind the scenes, developed a unified group strategy to achieve their goals. Smith, a CWU vice president, was among the few African American women to serve on the organization's first Board of Managers, which had a token representation of black members, including Mary McLeod Bethune, Creola B. Cowan, Anna Arnold Hedgeman, Hazel Gomez, and S. Willie Layten. Recognizing the need to explicitly define the interracial character of CWU in 1942, Smith argued for a revision of the bylaws. Her recommendation was rejected with the reply that CWU's interracial character would develop naturally, since the organization included women who were members of churches affiliated with the FCC, some of which were black denominations.

The predominantly white CWU Executive Committee discussed the need for a race relations committee, concluding that the black-white paradigm was no longer operable and that CWU must address the problems of all races. Feeling that "the name 'RACE' Relations" was resented and that it suggested a "barrier," the committee voted to incorporate the "principles and workings" of the CWCRR into the program of CWU. Of course, this did not happen, and it was apparent that CWU needed to clearly define its structure to ensure the involvement of minority women at all levels and the proper handling of race issues. During the years since its founding, CWU had dealt with any number of race issues related to World War II, including postwar employment discrimination against minority women, and the evacuation from their homes and internment in concentration camps of more than 110,000 Japanese, two-thirds of whom were American citizens.

Mary McLeod Bethune was a noted educator and organizer. She was a president of the NACW and the founder and first president of the National Council of Negro Women. As a member of the Commission on Interracial Cooperation and Church Women United boards, she pressed white women leaders to embrace an ambitious social justice agenda.

In 1943 CWU announced the establishment of a Committee on Social, Industrial, and Race Relations, and in 1944 it hired Miss Kawano, a former Japanese intern in the Minidoka Relocation Camp, as its director. In 1945, with the help of Katherine Gardner and members of the former CWCRR, CWU finally organized the Committee on Race Relations. The creation of this committee was directly related to a substantial gift from the Rosenwald Fund for the purpose of race relations and to several embarrassing incidents in which some CWU local councils were exposed because of their intolerant and racist practices. This was obviously a problem for a national organization such as CWU that sought to unite all women.

In 1942, at the first CWU Assembly, when the question of the relationship of black councils to CWU was raised, Christine Smith said,

"Why do we feel in the Christian church that we must draw racial lines? . . . The new social policy is to work *with* and not *for* people. We Negro women are anxious to work *with* you but we do not want you working *for* us. . . . Negro Church women have all of the machinery needed to enable them to work together and do not need nor want any type of separate councils set up for them, and what is more we will not have them." In 1943 Jessie Daniel Ames, as the CIC director of field work, had a unique opportunity to assess the attitudes and practices of women at the local level, in particular CWU and the various denominations, in relationship to African American women. Ames was concerned that in the aftermath of World War II it would be important for church women "to apply the Christian principles of brotherhood without which the foundations of peace cannot be laid." She asked, "Are they prepared to admit into their councils on a basis of equality their Negro sister church women?" Relating a particular experience, Ames said, "In a certain city recently one woman advanced the proposition that the white church women of her city should admit Negro church women to their meetings without discrimination. So antagonistic was the reaction to the proposal that it extended to the woman who dared by implication to indict their Christian sincerity."

In the 1940s and '50s separate black and white councils were generally the rule in the South. Although black and white women participated in CWU meetings, there were any number of embarrassing racial incidents that challenged the Christian creed in which CWU women professed to believe. Following her arrival in Montgomery, Alabama, in 1951, Virginia Foster Durr recalled attending a CWU meeting at YWCA Camp Grandview, where Mrs. Cooper, a member of the CWU National Board and the wife of an AME Zion minister, spoke. The YWCA informed CWU that Mrs. Cooper could participate in the meeting but she could not be served dinner, because she was black. Anticipating that Cooper would be discriminated against, Mrs. Rutledge, a white woman, had brought dinner for Mrs. Cooper, but was told by the camp's director that it was against the law, and Cooper could not eat her meal there. Cooper and Rutledge were forced to leave the grounds and eat elsewhere. Humiliated and reduced to tears, Cooper determined that she would return and participate in the meeting. Cooper's return was embarrassing to some white women who considered themselves to be liberal, nonracist Christians. One woman spoke out. "Mrs. Cooper, I don't want you to think we are prejudiced on account of color. We want to stay separate, but you see I am almost as black as you are, so it's not color." The woman rolled up her sleeve and displayed her sunburned arm, and said, "It's just that you-all have such different church services. Your services are so emotional—people screaming and hollering and throwing themselves around in church. We don't like those kind of services." Mrs. Cooper responded, "Well, many black churches don't have those kind of services and some white churches do." Durr said that it was a very upsetting evening for both white and black women.

As a result of constant prodding by the CWU national leadership, by the late 1940s more councils were desegregated. However, in some cities and states, such as Pasadena, California, and Texas, CWU leaders found that it was much easier to organize an integrated council than to desegregate an existing one. For example, in Pasadena, when the all-white council learned that black churches in the city planned to have their own observance of the World Day of Prayer, it was suggested that the black woman organizing the program be invited to join the council's planning committee. Subsequently, black churches were invited to join in one united service. Several weeks later Minnielee Dames, the wife of an AME minister, was asked to join the Pasadena Council and to fill the recently vacated position of secretary. In 1946 Dames was the sole black member of this council.

The members of the Pasadena Council, not wishing to change the character of their local association, organized an interracial women's club, whose purpose was to offer people of similar cultural interests the opportunity to meet across racial lines, and also to expose them to the achievements of other racial groups. The club was organized by six white and six black women who each invited five interested women to a tea party. Forty women met at the YWCA and voted to organize the Pasadena Interracial Women's Club. By June 1947, six months after its founding, the club had 125 members, and by September 1949 reported a membership of two hundred, including "Caucasian, Negro, Japanese, Mexican, Indian, and Chinese members." The only problem was that the club was not affiliated with CWU. Although the Pasadena Council continued to be, for all practical purposes, an all-white organization with one token black member, it proudly announced that it not only had opened the door for Mrs. Dames to make many white friends for herself and her race, but also, by organizing the interracial women's club, provided an opportunity for women of different races to become members of civic and church groups that had formerly been closed to them. The discussion—of how to involve minority women in the Pasadena Council's activities—was filled with condescension. In 1949 the Texas Council reported the organization of several interracial councils. The Pasadena and Texas councils are examples of how CWU's call for integration of local councils was treated, and illustrate the deep resistance of many white Christians.

Local Council Activism

LOCAL COUNCILS WERE not well integrated in any area of the United States. By the mid-1940s, some councils worked on issues related to race relations, protested legal segregation and discrimination, lobbied against discriminatory legislation, and, in some cases, engaged in civil rights protest. For example, in 1946 the Augusta, Georgia, Council of Church Women launched a brief, well-organized campaign against the Georgia Cracker Party for their bigoted political platform. During that year, the council also condemned the lynching of two black men and their wives by a white mob in Monroe, Georgia, and demanded legal action. In 1948 the Atlanta Council of Church Women adopted a resolution condemning the activities and organization of the Ku Klux Klan and commending organizations and individuals who took action to prevent Klan demonstrations in their communities. In 1949 the group pledged to work against the Klan and all other "hate" organizations. More than one hundred members endorsed the Atlanta Junior Chamber of Commerce's recommendation that policemen be barred from Klan membership and called for the city of Atlanta to adopt an anti-mask ordinance.

Atlanta was one of the jewels in the CWU's crown when it came to civil rights activism. The leadership in Atlanta benefited greatly from the influence of women such as Grace Towns Hamilton and Dorothy Tilly. Hamilton, Georgia's first black female legislator (1966–84), held a series of jobs related to the early interracial movement. During the 1930s she was employed by the Works Progress Administration to survey black workers in Memphis, and worked for the YWCA developing interracial programs on college campuses. As a legislator, Hamilton spearheaded fair housing legislation, fought to dismantle legal discrimination in employment, and lobbied for desegregation of Atlanta's Grady Memorial Hospital. She was the architect of the Atlanta city charter that made possible black self-government through district voting. Hamilton's efforts paved the way for the election of African Americans to the Atlanta City Council in 1966 and Maynard Jackson as the first black mayor of a major southern city.

Tilly, like Hamilton a lifelong evangelical social reformer, believed that it was the duty of the church and state to build "goodwill and understanding." She felt that the church could achieve this goal through its pronouncements and the fellowship of black and white Christians. However, in 1950, as a member of President Truman's Committee on Civil Rights, Tilly argued, "Overcoming prejudice in one phase at one time in a community does not [ensure] that it will not rise again. By education and legislation, patterns must be set so that whatever the prejudice of an individual may be, he will be forced to react according to the pattern." She recognized that legal remedies, such as those sought by the NAACP, could not eliminate prejudice. However, she believed that "many of the evil practices which are visible manifestations of prejudices can be brought to an end through proper government control. So we work for legislation!" Whereas in the 1920s and '30s Tilly believed that through its collective power the church could be a powerful force in effecting social change, in the 1940s she placed her faith in the legal system. Before the introduction of federal legislation to abolish the poll tax, Tilly, as the president of the MECS, joined the Southern Women's Committee to Repeal the Poll Tax. By the late 1950s she was highly critical of the religious establishment and its silence on "interracial matters."

In September 1949 Tilly organized the Fellowship of the Concerned. This group, which drew its members from churches and synagogues in twelve southern states, developed a sweeping program aimed at achieving civil rights for African Americans. The FOC plan called for a canvass of twelve southern states to obtain the signatures of thousands of persons who felt that, as a matter of religious conviction, there must be equal justice under law. The program also called for white church women, many of whom held memberships in CWU, to accompany their black employees to the polls and to registration places as a means of safeguarding black voting privileges and to help defeat political schemes designed to deny African Americans their civil rights. The FOC supported the monitoring of the judicial system, particularly its activities related to minority discrimination, and actively recruited women to sit in county courts, offices of the justice of the peace, and police courts, and to appear before grand juries when necessary. Tilly believed that if prominent white women attended the trials of blacks and stared down the judges, prosecuting attorneys, and juries, African Americans would be treated more fairly.

By the late 1940s some local councils in other areas of the United States also engaged in civil rights activities. In 1949 the Lincoln, Nebraska, Council protested the University of Nebraska's policy of refusing the admission of Japanese and black American students to dormitories. The council urged individuals to send letters to the Board of Regents requesting that the discrimination stop. The Lincoln *Journal* reported on the protest, and four days later the regents voted to change the policy.

Some northern and midwestern councils, and their state interracial committees, focused on issues of employment and educational opportunities for blacks. For example, in 1949, the Connecticut state interracial committee reported that African Americans received better employment and educational opportunities in 1948 than ever before. They noted that the Hartford, Connecticut, department stores were second only to New York in the hiring of qualified young black women. The Rhode Island Council opposed racial segregation in Washington, D.C., and voted to send copies of "Segregation in Washington" to the state's congressional delegation and sponsor three radio programs on race relations during Negro History Week. The Interracial Committee of the Elkhart, Indiana, Council of Church Women was instrumental in having the city's one all-black public school closed. The African American pupils and their teachers were absorbed in the school system. The Portland, Oregon, CWU voted unanimously to endorse a civil rights ordinance supportive of "equality of educational opportunity."

The Georgia Council of Church Women, like most state and local councils, supported numerous projects designed to provide community services for black children and teenage girls and boys. Between 1930 and 1940, members of the Georgia Federation of Colored Women raised funds to build a suitable home and training school for delinquent black girls, whom the state of Georgia either incarcerated or turned loose on the streets. By 1937 several thousand dollars had accumulated for that purpose. With the aid of the WPA, the federation erected a suitable facility outside the city of Macon. Following the pattern established by other NACW state federations, the women offered the plant to the state of Georgia, free of charge. The state legislature accepted it without authorizing an appropriation, and for four years the facility stood empty while scores of delinquent girls were sent to jail or placed on the streets. In 1941 the Georgia Council organized a successful campaign to bring pressure on the state legislature to appropriate funds to open the facility.

Numerous local councils supported programs related to addressing the problems of delinquent children. The Washington, D.C., Council paid the salary of a social worker in the Juvenile Court. At Christmas a committee of black and white women placed Christmas trees in each of the inhabited alleys of the city, conducted Christmas services, and sponsored parties for young and old poor people. The council opened a summer camp for eighty-seven of the "worst Negro boys of the city," and organized a traveling toy library that included toys and games for indigent children. Summer programs were quite popular among local councils. One of the purposes of these programs was to keep poor children off the streets and out of mischief—many cities did not provide public parks, playgrounds, or other recreational facilities for African Americans. The New Orleans Council sponsored a child care center during the summer months. The center's success was attributed to the cooperative effort of several groups, including the Red Cross, African American public school students, and the New Orleans Public Health Service, who contributed materials, equipment, and special services.

CWU had no control over local and state councils, but through resolutions, policy statements, race relations, and program surveys, as well as other directives, it was able to exert some influence. Periodically CWU sent out questionnaires to local and state councils in which it asked leading questions designed to elicit information and to reinforce program initiatives. The publication of the councils' responses, as well as reports of the work of local and state associations, prodded many groups to be more productive. Local councils worked on diverse projects related to issues of concern to their members and local communities. The geographical location, as well as the level of commitment of local council members to racial social justice and their previous involvement in interracial organizations, determined the kind of programs and projects a council would support. For example, in states such as Michigan and Indiana, where there were heavy influxes of poor black and mostly Hispanic migrant workers, councils tended to develop projects related to the needs of the migrants.

In large urban areas, in the North and Midwest, fellowship and friendship programs were popular. The need for more informal contact among the races was emphasized in the program initiatives generated by CWU. Projects such as the Summer Porch Parties sponsored by the Rochester, New York, Council stressed the building of interracial friendships. Middle-class women came together once a week at ten-thirty a.m., brought lunches, and spent the day reading and discussing articles in *Time, Fortune,* and other magazines. They also studied history, architecture, communion services, and symbolism as related to their denominations. Included in the project were visits to the Catholic Cathedral and Jewish Synagogue. Many organizations, like the Indianapolis Council, sponsored interracial teas that brought together women of varied races and nationalities who normally had no contact. The Albion, Michigan, Council held a cooperative luncheon at the Methodist church with a program of "interracial understanding" that included having an attorney speak about interracial problems and the need for a better understanding about what constituted "justice and fair play" for all persons regardless of race or color.

Among the many different projects and programs sponsored by local and state councils, perhaps the most prevalent and traditional activities were the social welfare programs—reminiscent of the home mission programs of the early twentieth century—in which the predominantly white council provided the black community with services, resources, facilities, and material assistance. Many councils, whose members were accustomed to working on behalf of poor African Americans, preferred social welfare work to interracial fellowship and civil rights projects that brought them into direct contact mostly with middle-class, educated black women who were their equals. It was one thing to provide services and resources for improving the living conditions of poor black people, and another to have direct social contact with middle-class and educated African American women. Also, many white CWU members who supported social service programs did not favor civil rights for African Americans and were not willing to risk being ostracized by their families and friends for fraternizing with blacks.

Many of the "friendships" established between white and black women were professional relationships in which individuals worked on committees and special projects and socialized at teas and interracial meetings—events where they "fellowshipped." Typically these were professional "friendships" that did not include visits to each other's homes, memberships in white or black clubs, or residing in each other's neighborhoods. Beyond CWU, black and white women lived and functioned in separate worlds. In fact, one of the most segregated institutions in America was the church. At no point in the twentieth-century interracial movement did the racial barriers fall within American churches. It was commonly said that the most segregated hour during the week occurred on Sunday during the worship service. Given the difficulty of desegregating existing churches, some persons decided it was easier to organize interracial churches. This decision compromised the integrity of members committed to integration, but avoided the issue of desegregating existing institutions.

In the 1940s, CWU, as an advocate of integration, equal treatment, and opportunity for African Americans and other minorities, carried forward most of the program initiatives of the CWCRR. For example, as a result of the continuing refusal of hotels to accept reservations from black female delegates, CWU boycotted cities and hotels in which this type of discrimination was practiced. In 1944 and 1946 the CWU Assembly passed resolutions on segregation and lynching, and, in 1948, during its Fourth Assembly, CWU passed a resolution supporting the elimination of segregation in public schools and in every area of American life. These resolutions were implemented through the efforts of some local councils. At the end of its first decade, it could truly be said that CWU, through its national focus on race relations and its willingness to challenge segregation and discrimination at the local level, had played a significant role in laying the groundwork for the launching of the modern Civil Rights Movement.

Similar to the NACW women's earlier assessment of the value of the YWCA and its potential usefulness in advancing their agenda, by 1945 black women leaders and their organizations recognized CWU's power and its importance to the civil rights struggle. Thus, by the late 1940s we find a growing number of black women, representatives of many black Protestant religious and secular organizations, affiliating with CWU. In fact, it was considered a badge of honor to be selected as a representative to CWU's national assemblies, and a mark of high status to serve on CWU's national board. Black women saw CWU as another structure through which they could build leadership within the race, implement their political agendas, leverage their organizational power to deliver much-needed resources to the black community, and engage in fellowship that helped to eliminate traditional stereotypes and negative attitudes about African Americans.

Working within and utilizing organizations such as the YWCA and CWU was a part of the preparation to achieve the ultimate goal of integration. The extensive work of CWU at the national and local levels helped to lay the foundation for the next stage of the Civil Rights

Movement. CWU, through its intricate network and its diverse membership, had linkages to every organization in the United States and was an integral part of the fabric of American social, political, and economic life. By 1950 CWU was arguably one of the most powerful organizations in the United States.

CWU-NCC: Race and Sex in the 1950s and '60s

IN 1950 THE Federal Council of the Churches of Christ in America was enlarged and renamed the National Council of the Churches of Christ in the USA. The NCC united twenty-nine denominations and eight interdenominational agencies, including Church Women United, and linked thirty-two million church members in 150,000 churches. Following a lengthy internal debate, CWU reluctantly gave up its autonomy to become a department of the NCC. The reorganization effectively removed the barriers that prevented the affiliation of Eastern Orthodox denominations and proposed ways to fraternize and have consortia with the Roman Catholic Church. By 1960 the NCC, with thirty-three denominations representing Orthodox and Protestant groups (half of all Protestants), included thirty million Christians. It was the largest ecumenical organization in the United States. African Americans constituted one-fourth of the NCC membership. The FCC's change in structure affected women in several ways. First and foremost, CWU accepted an invitation to join the NCC, therefore eliminating the need for separate women's organizations. Many FCC women also belonged to CWU and were actively involved in local, state, regional, and national projects administered by CWU affiliates.

In the NCC, women and African Americans were often relegated to subordinate roles. In 1970 Thelma Stevens, a longtime Methodist activist and CWU leader, deplored the fact that so few women were represented in the thirty-three church delegations to the NCC General Assembly. For example, thirteen denominations had no female delegates, and the total number of women representatives was less than one hundred. Stevens said, "If men from outer space should come to earth and see the Assembly, they would conclude that the Churches were composed, for the most part, of white skinned male clergy over forty." The reluctance of the denominations to select women as representatives to the NCC Assembly was simply a continuation of the earlier pattern of discrimination prevalent in the FCC. A review of the 1954 and 1959 lists of the NCC's AME delegates illustrates how blatant—and class-based—the practice of gender exclusion was. In 1954, out of the forty-six AME delegates, only four were women, two of whom were the wives of bishops. In 1959 there were no AME women delegates in attendance at the NCC meeting in St. Louis.

The CWU's national program emphases in the 1950s and '60s reflected the key issues of the time—Communism, the end of European colonialism in Africa and the Caribbean, women's rights in the church, civil rights, and the rise of the laity. Though CWU's status changed when it affiliated with the NCC, its relationship to the programs of the local councils remained the same. However, as a general department of the NCC, it was forced to operate as a unit and work cooperatively within the larger organization. While CWU worked inside the National Council of Churches, it also defined its programs and launched projects without the official sanction of the NCC. CWU was much more in sync with movements at the local level than the NCC. Through extensive surveys and feedback from its local councils, CWU was able to evaluate the progress of race relations and to assess the attitudes of its white and black members. This information was highly useful for designing new projects to advance its integrationist agenda.

Race, as an issue in the United States, entered a new phase during the 1950s. At the beginning of the decade, black-white relations throughout the United States were defined by legalized and de facto systems of segregation. As a result of the litigation carried out by the NAACP, a number of legal victories were won during the 1930s and '40s that paved the way for the 1954 Supreme Court decision in *Brown v. the Board of Education* that declared the separate but equal doctrine enunciated in *Plessy v. Ferguson* unconstitutional. The *Brown* decision was aimed at public school education, but it was used by the NAACP and others to attack legal segregation in all areas of public life.

Brown ushered in a new period of public debate and activism. Anticipating the *Brown* decision, in November 1953 CWU went on record favoring the desegregation of public schools, and then responded to the decision by calling a conference on June 21, 1954, in Atlanta of the chairmen of the Christian Social Relations committees of fifteen southern, border, and midwestern states to develop strategies for implementing the change. In 1955 CWU published a pamphlet, "This Is How We Did It," that provided descriptions of the methods, procedures, and experiences of local councils in eighteen states throughout the nation, not just the South, handling the issue of desegregation during the first year after *Brown*. While public schools throughout the South were segregated, this was not the case in most northern and western cities. Thus, where public school desegregation was not an issue, cities developed programs aimed at race relations improvement and desegregation of public accommodations, where segregation was not mandated but practiced. In southern and midwestern states such as Louisiana, Georgia, and Missouri, education was the focus of council women's efforts.

In New Orleans, Louisiana, the state council initiated a workshop on the implications of *Brown* and defined the steps to be taken in New Orleans and throughout Louisiana to integrate the schools. In Fayette, Missouri, one of "the two most rabid places in the whole state in the matter of anti-Negro feeling," the school board voted to bus Fayette's black high school students to another town rather than have them attend the newly built school. Upon hearing of this action, the CWU president and the pastor of the local Methodist church, both members of the Committee for Better Schools, notified the superintendent of schools of their resignation. Fearing that others would follow their lead, the superintendent immediately took the matter back to the school board, which voted to desegregate the school and admit black students. And the Atlanta CWU challenged a Georgia State Board of Education ruling "revoking forever" the license of teachers who held membership in the NAACP, and anyone "in sympathy with this organization." Reasoning that the time might come when teachers would not be permitted to join CWU, the Atlanta Council passed a resolution stating its opposition. It was published on the front page of the *Atlanta Constitution*. Within ten days, in a blazing front-page headline, the newspaper reported, "Board Backs Down on Teacher Firing."

In Ohio, Virginia, Rhode Island, and Montana, some councils targeted discrimination in public accommodations. For example, in Barberton, Ohio, upon learning that African Americans could not attend the two movie theaters, the local council attempted to obtain a meeting with the theater managers. For several months they wrote letters and sent telegrams and registered letters protesting the discrimination against blacks. Their efforts resulted in the theaters being opened to black people. With a victory in hand, the Barberton Council turned its attention to employment discrimination. In Arlington, Virginia, the church women mounted a successful protest to have the "white only" restroom signs removed from several newly opened large branch department stores. In Rhode Island, CWU was one of several state organizations that developed strategies for eliminating segregation and discrimination in public housing. In Billings, Montana, CWU organized the Montana Committee for Equal Rights, an interfaith, interracial, and intercultural group that secured support from the Montana Council of Churches and local councils of church women for legislation to desegregate all public accommodations in the state, including swimming pools, restaurants, hotels, and theaters. They succeeded in getting part of the legislation passed and determined to press on until they achieved total victory.

CWU also sponsored interfaith workshops in different parts of the country in which council women discussed strategies for dealing with the issues raised by the *Brown* decision. In many cases, local councils held meetings and World Day of Prayer programs at the YWCA. CWU and the YWCA worked cooperatively on many interracial programs during the civil rights era. In 1957 the Fund for the Republic awarded CWU a $10,000 grant for "educational work in race relations." CWU used the money to hold thirty workshops around the country to teach women how to deal with controversy and improve race relations in their communities. The myriad of local and state projects initiated by CWU between 1954 and 1960 provided the foundation for the organization to launch "Assignment: RACE, 1961–1964," the most important race relations project ever undertaken in its history. The idea for the project originated with the Methodist women, who felt that CWU was the most appropriate place for such an ambitious undertaking.

Financed in part by a Field Foundation grant of $66,000 to CWU, Assignment: RACE was defined as a three-year pilot project aimed at bringing an end to discrimination and segregation within mainstream local churches and denominations; CWU's state and local councils of church women; and community institutions and businesses. Assignment: RACE was the first large-scale project, involving twelve million Protestant and Orthodox church women in America, aimed specifically at local desegregation. The plan called for CWU to hold annual workshops in eight different clusters of states throughout the country, to train leaders from local councils in thirty-four states. Participating denominations assumed responsibility for an "action program" within their local communities.

Assignment: RACE was not limited to women. Denominations were responsible for determining whether the project would be exclusive to women or include women and men working together. CWU directed the interdenominational action programs and served as a clearinghouse for information on all programs. Project committees were designated to work with community leaders. While the male-dominated NCC argued over the feasibility of becoming involved in direct-action protest, the independent and more flexible CWU launched Assignment: RACE to illustrate how the local councils and denominations could provide leadership and bring about racial change nonviolently. Instead of embracing the idea and cooperating with the women, the NCC and male clergy dismissed the program as simply something the women were doing.

In launching Assignment: RACE, Mrs. David Baker, the CWU associate general and editor of *The Church Woman*, stated that the program emerged out of the concerns of many church women that the existing efforts at achieving "racial justice . . . however good, are insufficient for the task and the time." Baker's statement was both a critique of the NCC's failure to construct a meaningful program to address the issue of desegregation at the local level and a commentary on the rapid changes taking place in the Civil Rights Movement, especially in the South. The launching of the sit-ins and boycotts, the founding of the Student Nonviolent Coordinating Committee in 1960, and the beginning of the Freedom Rides in 1961 opened up a new phase of the movement, defined by nonviolent direct-action techniques at the local level and designed to test court decisions that declared segregation unconstitutional. Between the spring of 1960 and the fall of 1961, these activities, combined with the existing voting rights campaigns in Alabama, Georgia, Louisiana, and Mississippi, although nonviolent, drew violence. These events, occurring in communities with established church and human relations councils, and church federations, as well as respected community figures who held prominent positions in their local and national denominations, posed a hefty challenge to Christian leaders who for years had conducted race relations dialogues and other projects designed to allay racial tension.

To evaluate and determine the effectiveness of phase one of Assignment: RACE, CWU conducted a detailed survey of 2,200 councils throughout the United States. The survey—or "experience inventory"—was divided into four parts, the first three of which included questions related to what the local council accomplished in its work with the Council of Church Women, the local church, and the community. The fourth group of questions related to particular aspects of the project. More than one thousand replies were received, 976 of which were used for the summary analysis. Reports from councils indicated that, within the first two years, sixty-four local councils had desegregated, and that there was increased activity in the community surrounding issues of equal rights in housing, employment, education, and civil rights legislation. However, the survey also revealed some deep and troubling attitudes about race and integration among white Christians, and fissures in otherwise stable churches.

An important aspect of the first phase of Assignment: RACE was work to achieve full participation of all races in the local church. More than half of the councils reported "progress toward racial inclusiveness." This could mean many things, but what it did not mean was racial integration. It simply meant involving the churches, in which participating local councilwomen held membership, in some aspect of the project. For example, some councils reported "making public statements in support of the inclusive church" as evidence of the "progress" they had made, while others indicated their work to "create a favorable climate; helping churches to understand the issues; and encouraging efforts to work *with*, rather than *for* . . ." African Americans. Many councils employed education and study programs to achieve their goals. These included books, films, panel discussions, speakers, small group discussions, and other programs. Their greatest efforts were directed toward getting churches to simply open their doors to racial minorities. Annual CWU observances such as May Day, Fellowship Day, World Day of Prayer, and World Community Day provided the only opportunity for interracial worship or fellowship in some locales. Local councils confronted the intransigence of conservative church councils and white ministers who might be willing to participate in the education and study aspects of the race relations programs and contribute to philanthropic endeavors aimed at minority community improvement but were less interested in desegregating or otherwise changing the racial character of their churches. Some clergy feared criticism and censorship from community leaders as well as their congregations, and worried they would risk losing their jobs if they went against the wishes of their communicants and community.

CWU anticipated that local councils would encounter problems in trying to involve local churches in the first phase of the project, particularly as it related to racial inclusiveness. However, the organization knew that the only way to move forward was to directly confront the issues. In April 1961, at the beginning of the project, *The Church Woman* published an article—"How Free Is This Church?"—in which

Elizabeth Lee Haselden requested that church women take a careful look at their churches and "ask pertinent questions concerning its freedom to proclaim the whole gospel." Haselden's prophetic description of a fictitious all-white church, located in a small midwestern city and comprised mostly of middle-class citizens who were "not seriously concerned about obvious social ills or the morality of city life," illustrated some of the problems that councils and churches would actually confront. Theologically speaking the church was fairly liberal, but was politically conservative. The church held forums and attempted to study interracial and interdenominational issues, including housing, employment, and economic discrimination. As information about the discussions was filtered to the broader community the interracial meetings were severely criticized. Business and society leaders exerted pressure on the church to end the project and launched a "whispering campaign" against the minister and church, charging them with being "soft on communism." Community pressure devastated the program and forced the minister to resign. This was a case in which secular cultural values and intolerance had won out over Christian insights and morality. Haselden concluded that it was a "subtle web of conformity"—the fear and suspicion of those who dared to take a stand on racial issues—that led some Christians to see "all issues as Communist and anti-community."

There were numerous northern and midwestern cities like that described by Haselden. It was generally assumed that desegregation was a problem exclusive to the South, but this was not the case. While legal segregation was not a factor in many areas in the North, Midwest, and West, de facto segregation and blatant discrimination were. For example, in 1962 members of CWU in Shippensburg, Pennsylvania, were shocked to learn about an incident of racial discrimination in which a man from Pakistan was denied hotel accommodations because of the color of his skin. Months before this incident, Lynn Crowding, president of the city's CWU, had warned the all-white local council of the possible consequences if they implemented the theme "One Family Under God" through Assignment: RACE. In the aftermath of the highly publicized racial incident, Crowding called a meeting of the council's executive committee.

To determine how prevalent discrimination was in Shippensburg, Crowding invited a black church woman to the meeting. White church women were "shocked" by the detailed account of discrimination in their city given by the African American woman, who explained that blacks confronted widespread employment discrimination that relegated them to only the most menial of jobs; that black men were forced to travel twelve miles for a haircut; and that there was only one restaurant where blacks were served. She also emphasized that the African American community was offended by the black-faced minstrelsy that was a prominent feature of the "dark-town units" in the annual parades and fairs. To address some of these issues, CWU held a meeting with the Human Relations Commission of Pennsylvania and submitted a formal request to the Shippensburg borough manager requesting that the "darktown brigades" be eliminated from future public events. Reports of their meetings and actions were front-page news. In a joint meeting with representatives of CWU, the Council of Churches, the executive director and deputy director of the Human Relations Commission, and three black community representatives who spoke about the widespread discrimination in housing, public accommodations, and employment, plans were made to desegregate the city. Like the white church women, a white minister on the Council of Churches said he was unaware of "these pockets of discrimination in Shippensburg."

The Shippensburg story and Haselden's description of the events that occurred in a fictitious church and community were typical of what was occurring in many communities outside of the South, and they demonstrate two different approaches to the issues and problems. In a very positive report to the NCC on the first two years of the project, CWU provided brief statements on the types of action taken by local and state councils to desegregate, and what the organization had discovered in its national work. Specifically, CWU emphasized three things members had learned that suggest the difficulties of achieving their threefold integration goal. CWU stressed that church people tended to be "hearers rather than doers of the Word." Local organizations frequently perceived a program in race relations as having speakers deliver lectures about the issues, and not in terms of developing a plan of action to effect change. Second, as seen in the foregoing examples, whites had little contact with members of other racial groups. And third, CWU lamented that there was no deep sense among whites that there was a need for "Christian urgency" to address the racial injustices clearly evident in society. Though there were many successes, and numerous councils chose to work on civil rights projects, a much larger number preferred traditional programs. With dogged determination, CWU was sure that it could achieve a much higher result with a follow-up project that would require that councils engage in a self-study of what was accomplished and what "unfinished business" needed attention.

At the completion of Assignment: RACE and immediately following the passage of the 1964 Civil Rights Act, at its Tenth National Assembly CWU launched Assignment: RACE 2. In its announcement of phase two of the project, CWU asserted that the original project had achieved "significant results" and provided church women "a channel for concerted and more effective action for racial justice." The goal of phase two was to create "equal opportunity now for all citizens." CWU defined tasks that were necessary to complete its "unfinished business" in the church and community. Councils were asked to concentrate their efforts on securing compliance with the 1964 Civil Rights Act; develop programs to increase job opportunities for minorities; work for open housing and equal education for all people; work for enactment of civil rights legislation at the local, state, and national levels; transact business with and patronize nondiscriminatory commercial entities; protest the unwillingness of local authorities to negotiate with minority groups; assist in voter registration; and work to eliminate police brutality, especially as it affected women and girls in the Civil Rights Movement.

During the second phase of Assignment: RACE, CWU and its members participated in the Wednesdays in Mississippi project. The idea for the project came from Polly Cowan, a white friend and former YWCA colleague of Dorothy Height, the associate director of leadership services of the National Board of the YWCA, and NCNW president. Between 1957 and 1971, Height skillfully used the NCNW to implement YWCA project initiatives related to desegregation of the YWCA in the South. The NCNW enlisted prominent women— members of the YWCA, the National Council of Jewish Women, CWU, the League of Women Voters, and the American Association of University Women—as participants on the weekly teams to go to Mississippi in 1964 and 1965 during July and August. The women flew to Jackson on Tuesday and spent all day Wednesday in nearby communities visiting student summer projects.

The Wednesdays in Mississippi Project involved bringing an interracial coalition of northern women leaders to Mississippi to show support for student civil rights workers and to help allay the fears of the community about the young volunteers. The women attempted to build a bridge between black and white women of the South and between northern and southern women of both races. The project brought together more than four hundred northern and southern black and white women. WIMS was designed to have a "multiplier effect." This was accomplished by having women on each team who were officers in national women's organizations and could do effective follow-up. Participants included the presidents of the NCNW, the National Council of Jewish Women, Minnesota's CWU, Alpha Kappa Alpha and Delta Sigma Theta, and the executive assistant to the National Council of Catholic Women.

Assessing WIMS's accomplishments, Polly Cowan asserted that the participants were able to share new information with women in Mississippi, since the news reports carried by the broadcast and print media in the state were biased. Open and honest discussions among women leaders often elicited differences of opinion, but many southern women insisted that change must be effected and that it could only be achieved by outside intervention. As a result, many southern women worked cooperatively with other women who were either endeavoring to keep the public schools open or to educate their churches and organizations about the problems and issues. The WIMS experience also affected northern white women, who admitted that their attitudes had changed and that they realized the need for work in their cities and states to ensure that the Civil Rights Act of 1964 was implemented.

Phase two of Assignment: RACE brought to the fore in stark reality the views of most white Christians on race. In 1966 CWU concluded that there were several "pervasive" forces that dictated the behavior of many local councils and churches, which were for the most part white and in "racially isolated communities—distorted and deprived by overt and covert racial discrimination in housing." At the end of phase two, most councils and churches remained, for all intents and purposes, segregated or racially inclusive only in the sense that they had a few token black members.

During the mid- to late 1960s black women became less interested in race relations dialogues and more concerned with racial justice and equity. Invitations to meet for fellowship with white women or attend white churches was not a major priority for most African American women. Many black women worked and could not attend the meetings, which often were held during the day. CWU acknowledged the need for educational materials, but felt that local councils needed much more assistance. The total membership needed information and training, and more attention was required to address the needs of "nonwhite" church women. Apart from the issue of integrating churches and councils, CWU concluded that major fiscal resources would be needed and new approaches would be necessary to achieve the goals defined in Assignment: RACE. The organization recognized that massive leadership training, as well as total membership training, would be required to sensitize and educate white people about how to approach and treat racial minorities, in particular African Americans. And perhaps for the first time, CWU realized the necessity of addressing "the needs of nonwhite churchwomen."

The End of an Era

CHURCH WOMEN UNITED'S success in bringing about change in some cities and towns was related in part to its practice of developing a grassroots movement led by local leaders, rather than attempting to impose a specific program on all city and state councils. In contrast, the NCC's program of involvement in the Civil Rights Movement might be described as operating from the top down and not connecting with grassroots leaders.

The NCC's program of direct involvement in racial matters began in 1963 with the first national Conference on Religion and Race held in the United States. It was organized by the three major faith associations—the National Council of Churches, the National Catholic Welfare Conference, and the Synagogue Council of America. The conveners hoped to galvanize American denominations into action on racial problems. In January 1963, seven hundred Protestant, Catholic, and Jewish religious leaders assembled in Chicago to discuss the moral responsibility of organized religion in the ensuing racial crisis. Churches and synagogues admitted that for decades they had done little besides meet and talk. Like the ubiquitous interracial meetings of the 1930s, '40s, and '50s, the conference was long on rhetoric and short on proposals for programs of action.

Dr. Benjamin E. Mays—the chairman of the conference—and Dr. Martin Luther King Jr. were the sole black speakers during the three-day meeting. Members and representatives of black congregations and denominations and leaders were not involved in the planning of the meeting, and the conveners gave little thought to the inclusion of black religious leaders on the plenary sessions, in the workgroups, or on the panels as discussants. From the outset, black leaders charged that not enough African Americans were represented on the planning or steering committees and as platform speakers. CME Bishop B. Julian Smith asserted, "Negroes felt they were spoken to and not listened to."

Anna Arnold Hedgeman, the NCC's director of Ecumenical Action, was concerned about the failure of the Conference on Race and Religion to acknowledge the "distinctive history and theology" of the African American church. She observed that "Catholic, Protestant, and Jewish religious leaders had presented the three faiths and their moral responsibilities in the racial crisis," but there was "no presentation of the Negro church, no basic realization" that black people had left "the balconies and other segregated parts of the major [white] denominations in order to find dignity for its members and their worship." She added that there was also no recognition of the sheer existence of the black church or "its lack of communication with the total church, [and] its distrust of the Christianity of the white communions." Hedgeman criticized Mays for not speaking about the need to include black leaders in the dialogue about racial problems and their solutions.

Like the earlier interracial meetings and conferences, the Conference on Religion and Race ended with an "Appeal to the Conscience of the American People." Religious leaders returned to their cities and towns feeling enlightened, but without a concrete program of action that could be carried out at the grassroots level. Martin Luther King Jr. foresaw an "eclipse" of the church's "spiritual power" if it failed to take a "bold stand" on "the question of racial justice." William Stringfellow, a prominent white Episcopalian and attorney, sent shock waves through the conference when he informed the assembly that what they proposed was "too little and too late," since the "initiative on the race issue had passed from whites to Negroes." In other words, by 1963 black leaders at every level, national and grassroots, were calling the shots, and the Civil Rights Movement was largely driven by their actions.

In 1965 the National Council of the Churches of Christ downgraded Church Women United and introduced new restrictions that challenged and curtailed the organization's independence. On September 26, 1969, CWU separated from the NCC and once again became an autonomous organization. By 1970 the interracial movement was all but dead. The NCC and mainline denominations had retreated from their 1960s liberal race relations stance. The 1970s symbolized the beginning of a new era dominated by the demands of "black power." The white Protestant establishment retreated from its former racial policies and either severely curtailed or reversed and downsized the staff and programs associated with racial issues. Like the nineteenth-century abolitionists who worked to set the slave free, many liberal whites felt that once legal segregation was eliminated their work was done. The 1970s witnessed the emergence of conservative evangelical churches that showed little or no interest in racial matters. In contrast, CWU's national leadership continued its liberal stance, and shifted its emphasis to accommodate new ideologies emerging out of the women's movement, black power and the demands of its black members for equity within the national organization, and desegregation of local councils. However, at the local level, many of its members embraced the religious conservatism permeating their religious traditions.

CHAPTER 8

Jesus, Jobs, and Justice

The Black Women's Agenda

Not a few people think that the height of the Negro's ambition is to be white. They think that our fight against the Jim Crow laws is a fight for a seat beside a white person.

The height of our ambition is to have what we pay for. When we fight the Jim Crow car or segregation in any form, we are not fighting color— we are fighting a condition against which our very sense of decency revolts and our sense of justice cries out.

Nannie Helen Burroughs (1919)

[I]t is [the AME Women's Missionary Society's] purpose to find our place and reinterpret our role in the present age. What support can we give the sit-in demonstrations—our brothers and sisters who have been incarcerated, beaten, and in other ways persecuted because they insist upon their rights at the polls and their rights to the complete services of establishments that take their money, or first class citizenship?

Octavia Dandridge (1962)

What has happened among middle class people is a black revolt within the white churches. Many black, middle class women are disillusioned with church integration. Second-class churchmanship is the order of the day, as whites insist on integration on the terms they dictate. White racism, our national sickness, finds some of its most virulent forms in organized religion that is white, Anglo-Saxon, and Protestant (WASP).

Clarie Collins Harvey (1970)

It is important to remember, particularly for women themselves, that the Black women's agenda in the church, as in society, is different in many respects from that of white women struggling to claim some prominence in the Anglican Communion. The Black women's agenda is largely focused on developing and strengthening the community so that the total community benefits. Black women and other women of color cannot be seduced by the personal power games often blatantly operative in some sectors of the feminist movement.

Rev. Barbara Harris (1985)

A FULL ASSESSMENT of black women's work in the Civil Rights Movement must of necessity consider organizational and individ-ual contributions. Driven by their faith and belief in social justice and equality, Ella Baker, Septima Clark, Fannie Lou Hamer, and others used their considerable talents to fight against racial injustice. It was their leadership and that of countless others that made the difference in the civil rights struggles that emerged in Alabama, Mississippi, Georgia, and other southern states during the 1950s and '60s. The cel-ebrated successes of the NAACP, the Southern Christian Leadership Conference (SCLC), and the Student Nonviolent Coordinating Com-mittee owe a great deal to the dedication and commitment of these and other, lesser-known women. The willingness of many women to work within mixed-gender civil rights organizations to develop and imple-ment strategies and programs, and organize grassroots leadership for which they received little recognition or remuneration, speaks to the strength of their character and dedication to the movement. The work of individual women leaders and numerous foot soldiers was but-tressed by that of the women's missionary societies and conventions in black churches and secular organizations such as the NACW and the NCNW. The modern Civil Rights Movement also benefited from the pre-1954 work of black women and their associations.

Beyond the celebration of the leadership of individual women and their organizational contributions to the movement, we must look to the thousands of unknown women whose individual acts of commit-ment formed a wall of resistance that made possible the work of those on the front lines of the struggle. In order for any movement to suc-ceed there must be persons willing to perform different functions at every level. When speaking of the Montgomery bus boycott, the SNCC- and SCLC-led voter registration campaigns in Mississippi, Georgia, and Alabama, or the numerous NAACP legal challenges, organized protests, marches, economic boycotts, and acts of civil dis-obedience, we also must look incisively at the roles played by numer-ous ordinary women. In the diverse southern communities where the SNCC workers and other volunteers lived while laboring for the cause of freedom, single as well as married women were willing to risk their homes, jobs, and lives to secure freedom and justice. It was risky busi-ness to provide lodging, cook free meals, and serve as surrogate moth-ers to the young crusaders.

In giving up her house to the college students who converged on Mississippi for the Freedom Summer project of 1964, Annie Mae King exposed herself to violence. Three attempts were made to bomb or burn down her house. Rather than being afraid and abandoning her home, King relied on her faith and grew more determined to challenge the white South and American racism by doing "whatever little I can to help." In her damaged living room, with one window boarded up, SNCC workers typed affidavits and mapped strategy while King fried chicken in the kitchen to feed the students. This is resistance at the core! King and others like her might be viewed as a solid phalanx of persons working secretly from within and at the base of society to undermine and indeed help overthrow a system of oppression, which had long denied their humanity. These single acts of courage, the "housing and feeding of civil rights workers," were considered by many whites "to be politically subversive acts." After all, black women who willingly provided these services were aiding and abetting persons deemed to be enemies of the state. Participants and observers attested to the dedication and commitment of southern black women at all levels and praised them for being the "backbone" of the movement.

Women and the Montgomery Bus Boycott

THE IMPORTANCE OF the charismatic leadership of Dr. Martin Luther King, Jr. and other male leaders cannot, of course, be dismissed. Nor can the work of individual women who designed and carried out the projects and programs of national civil rights organizations simply be ignored and attributed to male leaders. Obviously, these were important factors in the success of the movement, but this is only part of the story. Neither of these could have accomplished their goals without the substantial participation of local people, formal and informal leaders of religious and secular groups, and the support of women's organizations in faith-based communities.

One of the best examples of the interdependent nature and diversity of participants who constituted the movement at the local level is the Montgomery bus boycott. The Women's Political Council, organized in Montgomery, Alabama, in the fall of 1946, played a crucial role in initiating the bus boycott of 1955–56 and provided the network for organization and support of the movement. The WPC was the brainchild of Mary Fair Burks, a self-described feminist, who as a teenager had waged a "personal war" of defiance against the Jim Crow practices in Montgomery and was determined to find a way to challenge segregation. One Sunday morning, following her arrest for cursing at a white woman, Burks found the answer in a sermon delivered by Rev. Vernon Johns, the controversial pastor of the Dexter Avenue Baptist Church. Rev. Johns, Dr. King's predecessor, was a firebrand known widely for his political activism. According to Burks, Johns "mounted one of his scathing attacks on the complacency of his affluent membership." Convinced that her individual acts of resistance would not eliminate discrimination or segregation, Burks left the church with the idea of creating a women's organization to address some of the city's racial problems.

As a teacher at Alabama State College, like most members of her church and the middle-class women she socialized with, Mary Fair Burks lived a life very different and much removed from that of the majority of African Americans in Montgomery, who were poor and uneducated. Typical of many southern cities, Montgomery's black community consisted of a small black middle class, comprising ministers, morticians and small business owners, and teachers at the all-black Alabama State College and the city's African American public schools, but the rest of the blacks were poor servants—domestics or "yard men" who worked for less than $5.00 per day. However, Burks recognized that she and her cohorts were as vulnerable to abuse, violence, and death as the poorest and most despicable black person. Acknowledging that class differences did not matter when it came to racial segregation and discrimination, Burks felt impelled to take the first step and organize a group that would create a movement involving both the "classes" and the "masses" of black people.

The WPC's first project was to have its members register to vote. The Fifteenth and Nineteenth Amendments had granted suffrage to African Americans and women, but between 1890 and 1920, the majority of blacks in the South were disenfranchised through violence, intimidation, election schemes, and an elaborate system of laws requiring literacy tests and poll taxes. Prior to the passage of the 1965 Voting Rights Act, a small number of black people voted in locales throughout the South. Through persistence—especially the willingness to repeatedly take the literacy tests—eventually all of the WPC members were allowed to register to vote. In the early 1950s the WPC, with the cooperation of ministers, established citywide voter registration schools in local churches. Weekly meetings were held in which people were taught how to write and to fill out registration forms. When applicants were ready, WPC members accompanied them to the courthouse to fill out the forms, and returned with them to check on the results. The WPC succeeded in having enough persons registered to have an impact on the outcome in close elections.

Members of the all-white Montgomery, Alabama, League of Women Voters were invited to attend WPC meetings and discuss the issues and policies supported by the political candidates. The WPC used this process to select candidates, whom they recommended for bloc voting. Mary Fair Burks, as chairman of the Political Action Committee of the Dexter Avenue Baptist Church, at the conclusion of the Sunday-morning services would read the names of the candidates considered the least objectionable. This action was repeated in the various churches that WPC members belonged to throughout the city. The WPC also provided leadership training for black youth. The Negro Youth City program was instituted at the black high schools. Modeled after the white Youth City, the program taught senior students how to run for political office, and the meaning of democracy. Burks said, "[O]n the surface we were merely imitating, but in reality we were using subversive tactics to serve our own ends." The students registered to vote at twenty-one, and the program inspired some to pursue careers as lawyers, judges, and state legislators and become active in politics.

The success of these projects encouraged the WPC to take on the task of opening the Montgomery public park to African Americans and to address the abuses blacks received on the city buses, which included "insults, vulgar affronts, and disparaging remarks." Black women were called "niggers, black apes, black cows, and worse epithets by bus drivers." In most southern cities segregation prevented blacks from using parks and other public accommodations, such as libraries. The WPC met with city commissioners and argued that African Americans paid taxes that supported playgrounds, parks, and other public facilities and therefore had a right to use them. The commissioners refused to open the Montgomery park to blacks, but agreed to let them walk through it on their way to work for whites. On the issue of the buses, the WPC recognized that the 1896 Supreme Court decision in the *Plessy v. Ferguson* case had legalized segregation. While in 1954 *Brown v. Board of Education* had struck down the precedent of "separate but equal" established by *Plessy*, the later ruling dealt with public school desegregation and had no immediate effect on segregation in public accommodations. The WPC's initial concern was the abusive treatment of black

passengers traveling on city buses—since African Americans constituted the majority of bus patrons, the WPC felt they should receive
more respect.

The forcible removal and prosecution of two teenage girls,
Claudette Colvin and Mary Louise Smith, from Montgomery buses in
March and October 1955 presented the NAACP the potential test
cases needed to challenge the bus segregation laws. The WPC had met
with the city commission numerous times prior to these arrests.
Though Colvin and Smith were willing to fight the charges, as
teenagers coming from working-class backgrounds they were not the
role models the NAACP and WPC were looking for. Initially Colvin
was considered as a potential candidate for launching a test case. However, it appears that the WPC and other black organizations changed
their minds following an allegation by E. D. Nixon, the president of
the Montgomery NAACP, that Colvin was pregnant. It is likely that
Nixon used this ruse, as well as other misrepresentations, to eliminate
Colvin and Smith from consideration. The fifteen-year-old Colvin was
the daughter of a mother who worked as a maid and a father who
mowed lawns for a living. Smith was an eighteen-year-old Catholic
who was employed as a domestic. Colvin later commented that she
believed that NAACP leaders rejected her because they felt she would
not appeal "to the adults and to middle-class people . . . [because] I'm
dark-skinned." Prior to Nixon's revelation, the Colvin arrest had
brought together WPC representatives, Dr. King, and members of the
city's Ministerial Association, who met with and engaged in a very
heated discussion with the city commission, and alluded to the possibility of a boycott.

On December 1, 1955, Rosa Parks, a seamstress at the Fair Department Store in Montgomery, triggered the protest that lasted for more
than a year, when she refused to surrender her seat and move to the
back of the bus when commanded to do so by a white bus driver. Parks
was perceived as the perfect candidate for a test case. Nixon asserted
that she was "morally clean [and] reliable, nobody had nothing on her,
[and] she's got the courage of her convictions." In a very astute analysis
of why Parks was chosen, historian David Garrow said that Rosa Parks
"was a 'bridge between classes' in Montgomery's black community
[which was] blue collar by trade, but middle class in 'tone.' " Garrow
asserted that this ensured that African Americans in the city "would
work together as they might not have had another person been chosen." Parks, described as a "stalwart" member of the St. Paul AME

Church, and the secretary of the Montgomery NAACP, was well known. For years she had worked with the NAACP Youth Council and other civic causes. She was highly respected by all classes, and in fact for a short period of time had served as a mentor to Colvin, who had joined the NAACP Youth Council after her arrest and told her story to Parks.

The Parks arrest outraged the black community, but it was the WPC that voted to launch a boycott and proceeded to prepare and distribute leaflets, in which they explained the situation and asked that all black people boycott the buses for one day. Thus the Montgomery bus boycott was initiated by an organization comprising upper-middle-class black Baptist and Methodist women. However, it was the Montgomery Improvement Association, organized after the boycott began, that took over the leadership and directed the protest. The spokespersons for the boycott, whose images appeared in the press and were flashed on television, and whose names and exploits are written in bold strokes on the pages of most civil rights histories, were black males, mostly clergy. The majority of persons attending the crowded church rallies were working-class church women. Most of the movement leaders did not ride the buses and therefore were not subject to the daily abuses. Mary Fair Burks later paid tribute to the "nameless cooks and maids who walked endless miles for a year to bring about the breach in the walls of segregation." At the same time, members of the WPC, the MIA, and others who owned mortuaries, taxi services, and other businesses, supplied funds, used their automobiles to form a car pool, and served as an escort service to deliver domestic workers, common laborers, and other service workers, mostly women, to their jobs. Eighty-five percent of the city's black population was working class, and 11.5 percent were in the professions, which included mostly teachers and clergymen. The movement in Montgomery and other southern cities often cut across class, gender, and racial lines and involved a variety of persons who were bound together by their deep religious faith and their belief in racial justice.

The 1950s divide between the black "masses" and the "classes" was not as deep as some have suggested. Rather, at the local level there was an unspoken understanding between the two that they shared a heritage of slavery and white racism and that each had a role to play in the civil rights struggle. It is probable that many of the leaders and participants in the boycott had heard about the Montgomery bus boycott of 1902, in which the city's black population succeeded in their fight to have city buses desegregated. When black workers decided to walk and not ride the trolley, the local company almost went bankrupt. Faced with financial disaster, the company permitted African Americans to sit in any part of the trolley cars they desired. Stories about this earlier encounter were undoubtedly passed down to succeeding generations.

Women and Youth in the Movement

IN 1964, IN AN ANALYSIS of the relationship of class status to participation in the movement, Bess Baliff, a twenty-year-old woman from Denver, Colorado, informed the readers of the AME *Christian Recorder* that many African Americans were in favor of civil rights protests, but the majority of middle- and upper-class southern and northern blacks were reluctant to get involved for fear of jeopardizing their jobs and status. Though Baliff made specific reference to the large number of young people who participated in the 1963 Mississippi voter registration campaigns organized by the SNCC, her observations are relevant to the changes that followed the launching of the sit-in movement and the founding of the SNCC in 1960. After that date, the numbers of students participating in the struggle soared. In 1954, none of this applied to women such as Mary Fair Burks, Jo Ann Robinson, and other WPC women employed as teachers at Alabama State College and in the public schools. Like Rosa Parks, these women risked being fired from their jobs—and, indeed, this is what occurred. Baliff suggested that one reason why the civil rights struggle was mostly a youth movement was because black adults, especially those in the middle class, feared economic reprisals. She articulated what was obvious to many of the leaders and participants in the movement after 1960: the visible presence of a large number of children, teenagers, and women in the direct-action protest activities that occurred in cities throughout the nation, but especially in the South.

Black ministers such as Dr. King, and Ralph David Abernathy, and other leaders of churches and economically independent institutions, were not exempt from white violence and other reprisals. However, they were less threatened by the loss of their livelihoods. This was also true of men and women such as Ella Baker, Septima Poinsette Clark, and Dorothy Cotton, who were employed by the NAACP and the SCLC. Therefore, most of the spokespersons for the movement were black preachers and representatives of civil rights organizations such as the NAACP, the SCLC, the National Urban League, and the Congress of Racial Equality. Middle-class black and white church women's organizations such as the missionary societies, women's conventions, Womanpower Unlimited, and Women in Community Service rarely engaged in direct-action protest. Their civil rights programs and activities were geared primarily toward dealing with the effects of racial discrimination, poverty, and lack of education. Their protests were largely confined to writing articles, speaking, petitioning, organizing support for the specific campaigns defined by civil rights organizations and CWU, providing philanthropic support for the NAACP's legislative activities, and cooperating with interracial coalitions supportive of ameliorative projects for nonwhites, including Native Americans and Hispanic migrant workers.

During the 1930s and '40s Mary McLeod Bethune, Mary Church Terrell, and Nannie Helen Burroughs had served as role models for women such as Mary Fair Burks, who had grown up reading about and listening to the speeches of these women and held memberships in organizations such as the WC, the NACW and the NCNW. Bethune, Terrell, and Burroughs lived to see the fruits of their labor and made their final contributions during the 1950s and '60s before passing from the scene. It is their assessments and voices that are heard at the beginning of the struggle. In response to the *Brown* decision in 1954, seasoned leaders like Bethune were pragmatic in their evaluation of its impact. Assessing the political context that framed the decision—in particular the international implications related to the end of colonialism, the growing political impact of Third World nations on world affairs, and America's involvement in the United Nations—Bethune reasoned, "Very few people were surprised by the recent decision by the Supreme Court." However, she cautioned, "[w]e must expect that the enemies who dwell within, will do all within their power to circumvent the Court decision. We must not expect that they will accept full citizenship for all the people—just as they have been unable to accept the complete social doctrine of the church." Bethune informed black Americans that they must move forward to implement the decision. "This must be done with common sense and Christian forbearance. But it must be done! And within this simple fact lies the long road ahead." Though she would not live to see the decision implemented, or the many changes that would occur in the years to come, Bethune had a deep and abiding faith in her God and in her people and fervently believed that freedom was in sight. However, it would take more than a decade to remove the legal barriers to freedom.

NBC-USA Baptist Woman's Convention and Missionary Societies

THROUGHOUT HER CAREER, as a public intellectual Nannie Burroughs had utilized the press to educate, shape, and influence black public opinion. As president of the Woman's Convention, during the 1950s she employed *The Worker* as a tool to inform black Baptists about the *Brown* decision, discuss the meaning of citizenship rights, and present news about the Civil Rights Movement. For most black women leaders, "good citizenship" meant a careful consideration of all issues of vital concern to the welfare of African Americans. A chief concern was the solution of the labor problem. For many years, Burroughs, Mary Church Terrell, and their cohorts had argued that labor discrimination disposed black youth to a life of poverty and crime. In July 1954, in an insightful editorial, Burroughs asserted, "The United States Supreme Court has at last spoken on the second basic Constitutional requirement for building a democracy." She explained that the four basic requirements for a democracy are freedom, an equal opportunity to education, an equal opportunity to employment, and an equal right to public accommodations. Burroughs concluded that America was not a democracy, because African Americans were denied the last three of these "democratic rights." In her usual fashion, she argued that justice and equality are "Divine gifts," bequeathed by God, not man. While the right to work and to have equal access to "public places" and "public carriers" are God-given "basic democratic rights," Burroughs insisted that they "must be made constitutional." Denial of these rights to blacks was "the grossest insult to personal dignity."

In January 1955, just weeks after the Montgomery bus boycott was launched, Burroughs met with the WC Board of Directors. She observed, "[W]e are facing a social crisis in America and we must be able to spell [it] out and make people see it." Citing the bus boycott as an example, Burroughs said, "The Negro is not going to ride on the street cars. If the Negro *class[es]* spell it out the Negro *mass[es]* will do it." Explaining that "[w]e can beat race prejudice to a frazzle but you've got to know how," Burroughs stressed the need to develop educational materials for missionary societies, who would provide training for the masses at the local level.

Burroughs and black Baptist women rejected segregation and its doctrine of separate but equal. In the early twentieth century, Burroughs argued that Christian women in "God's Army" need to be organized to fight "a condition." The WC's continuous attack on lynching and Jim Crow laws throughout the early twentieth century exemplified the traditional black "discourse of resistance," first articulated at the national level by the NACW in its protests against the violence directed to African Americans and the abusive and humiliating treatment black women were forced to endure on railways, street cars, and other public conveyances during the 1890s. Decades before Martin Luther King, Jr. and the black leaders of the 1960s Civil Rights Movement, Josephine St. Pierre Ruffin and other nineteenth-century NACW leaders argued, "If laws are unjust, they must be continually broken until they are killed or altered."

In the early twentieth century, as Jim Crow laws and practices became a factor in all areas of American life, the NACW took the position that it would do everything in its power to end legal segregation, but in the interim the organization's protest was directed to making white America accountable for "equal" though separate accommodations. This strategy was accepted and articulated by black women leaders of religious and secular organizations throughout the nation, including the Baptist Woman's Convention, and with the founding of the NAACP it was accepted as a basic tactic of the African American struggle. At the same time, black organizations continued to urge Congress to enforce the Fifteenth Amendment in every state, and the NAACP worked assiduously to legally reinstate all parts of the Fourteenth Amendment. While blacks fought for equal accommodations during the Jim Crow era, this was a strategic and temporary stopgap measure, useful until the battle for full equality was won. In challenging the treatment of blacks on Montgomery's buses, Mary Fair Burks and the WPC represented a long-held tradition among African Americans, especially black women activists.

Unlike the leaders of Methodist women's organizations, Burroughs ruled the NBC-USA Woman's Convention with an iron fist. She was revered and respected by Baptist women and the masses of working-class African Americans, who viewed her as a champion of their rights. In September 1955, at the annual convention of the WC, Burroughs

announced that "Home Missions and Race Relations" would constitute a major part of the organization's program for 1956. Burroughs
felt that it was important for the WC to take the lead in organizing an
interracial conference comprising black and white Baptist women to
discuss the issues. Having served on the boards of the Commission on
Interracial Cooperation and Church Women United, and cooperated
with the northern and southern white Baptist women in the American
Baptist Home Mission Society and the Woman's Missionary Union,
like most black church women she continued to believe that black and
white Christian women could make a difference in the ensuing struggle. In 1955 Burroughs asserted that since the WC represented "quite
three million Christian women" and was the largest organization of
black Christians in the world, it had a responsibility to work with the
American Baptist in the North and the Woman's Missionary Union
and Southern Baptist Convention to teach black and white Christians
how to work together. At the same time, Burroughs was clear about the
black women's agenda and the specific needs of African Americans. She
declared, "The Negroes must have Jesus, Jobs, and Justice."

Like many church men and women, at the beginning of the
student-led sit-in movement Burroughs questioned the feasibility of
direct-action tactics. However, within months of its launching she
decided that it was one of the most significant strategies devised. To
signal her support and encourage Baptist women at the grass roots to
support the students in their efforts, Burroughs devoted the July–
August 1960 issue of *The Worker* expressly to the sit-in movement. In
September 1960 at the WC's annual meeting she said that black people
"must decide that they are done with satisfied ignorance and second
class citizenship," and stressed the importance of sit-ins and the Civil
Rights Movement. Listening closely to the young black militants and
adopting their language, Burroughs said in "the parlance of the
street . . . , the Churches and the government have certainly 'ganged
up' on the Negro to keep him in his so-called place." By December
1960, just months before her death, Burroughs recognized that the day
that she had hoped for had finally arrived. She said, "The day of
protest has come. It has come out of centuries of suffering." Condemning the government and the white church establishment for their
complicity in keeping black Americans in a "low economic, social,
moral and spiritual condition," Burroughs explained that the
"weapons" of black "warfare must not be frustration and hate." Rather,
African Americans must use the "weapons" of education, improvement

of home and family life, and Christian living to achieve their goals. These were the cornerstones of her philosophy, and the values she had proclaimed during most of her lifetime.

Black Methodist women's missionary societies and the NBC-USA Woman's Convention were among the most active of the church women's organizations in the Civil Rights Movement of the 1950s and '60s. However, while historically Methodist women perceived their civil rights activities as a dimension of their home mission work, before 1950 the WC separated missionary work from political activities. The Woman's Convention had always functioned as a feminist organization that fully accepted the idea of women's equality in the larger society, while at the same time opting for a separate auxiliary status in the NBC. This was part of their strategy as black American women who believed that, given the race's struggle for sheer survival, it was important for the Baptist Church to function as a bulwark against racism in the United States. WC leaders were concerned that constant direct challenges and demands for clergy and laity rights for women might divide the church as a whole. In reality, the WC had more power and, for many years, was more independent than any other national black church women's organization. Though AME Zion women possessed full religious rights, similar to the AME and CME women, their national missionary society lacked the formal power and authority invested in the WC. Until 1961, the WC was the only church women's organization that had consistently retained some degree of control over its finances and program throughout its history.

The bitter internal struggle in the NBC for control over the WC's resources began during the first decade of the WC's existence and escalated after 1915. The WC leadership became seriously divided after the death of S. Willie Layten. As president, Burroughs was placed in an extremely defensive position. Her attention was divided, and she expended a great deal of energy and time fighting the male clergy and trying to hold the WC together. During its early years, the WC had created suffrage and legislative departments that focused specifically on voting rights for women and lynching. Between 1950 and 1961, the WC had no explicitly designed political agenda, or civil rights program. The WC's national program did not specify national civil rights projects or other political activities that its members should support or participate in. Rather, under Nannie Burroughs's leadership it continued to emphasize interracial work with white women. After 1961, under the leadership of President Mary O. Ross and Corresponding

Secretary Georgia Gayton—wives of prominent NBC-USA clergy—
the WC sanctioned the position of Rev. Joseph H. Jackson, president
of the NBC-USA.

Perhaps the WC's reluctance to announce or engage in a specific
program was related to the official position taken by Jackson following
his election in 1953. Having risen to the pinnacle of his success, and
believing himself to be the most powerful black man in the United
States, Jackson made no bones about his personal dislike for Martin
Luther King, Jr. and bluntly stated that he did "not feel that the church
should be active in the field of civil rights." Jackson was intensely jealous of and felt threatened by the young King, the head of the SCLC
and the most recognizable spokesman for black Americans between
1955 and 1965. As leader of the largest and arguably the most influential black denomination in the United States, Jackson believed that he
deserved the attention that King was receiving. Asserting that "a great
people must do more than protest, they must produce," in 1964, at the
height of King's popularity, Jackson proposed to the NBC-USA that
the denomination establish a "Ten Million Dollar Education Foundation" to support black Christian institutions, instead of protesting and
depending on white largesse to deliver the race. Jackson disagreed with
the National Council of Churches, King, and other denominational
leaders who regarded the church's attitude on race prejudice as a theological matter. In other words, religious leaders had a moral responsibility to speak out on issues of social justice.

Jackson viewed sit-ins, freedom rides, and direct-action protest as
rabble-rousing and castigated those who engaged in such activities.
Following his reelection as NBC-USA president, in 1963, in response
to the National Council of Churches' establishment of a commission
to encourage negotiations, demonstrations, and direct-action campaigns in places of crises, Jackson proposed the founding of a separate
civil rights commission for the Baptists, which would set up a lobby in
Washington, advise local communities, push voter registration, beau-
tify black neighborhoods, and encourage churches to find jobs for
African Americans. The Congress of Racial Equality picketed outside
of the NBC-USA convention to criticize Jackson for not supporting
the Civil Rights Movement. SNCC officials John Lewis and James
Forman challenged Jackson's assertion that African Americans
should keep their struggle for civil rights within the framework of
law and order or anarchy would result, arguing that unjust laws had
to be destroyed before black Americans could become full citizens.

Lewis and Forman also said that "creative chaos" was necessary to bring about a new order.

At the local level Baptist women often organized and participated in civil rights projects related to their individual concerns. For example, Baptist women such as Ollie Weeks and Lillian Naomi Wortham worked with the NAACP Youth Council in Indianapolis between 1940 and 1960. In 1941, Weeks joined A. Phillip Randolph's March on Washington to protest racially discriminatory hiring practices by defense contractors and government agents during World War II. In 1962, the *Indianapolis Recorder* described Weeks as an "active sit-inner." Having participated in numerous sit-in demonstrations to desegregate local eating facilities, Weeks became the target of threatening calls, letters, and other literature from "race haters." Like Weeks, Mrs. Harry Wallace was active in civil rights at the local and national levels. Described as a "staunch supporter of integration," Wallace fought for implementation of the Fair Employment Practices Act in industry. In Indianapolis, as an employee at the Allison Division of General Motors, she was a member and officer of a United Auto Workers union in Indianapolis. In 1956 she represented the union at the National Civil Rights Conference held in Washington, D.C. All of these women were active members and workers in the Baptist Church.

The WC's assertion of its independence during the early twentieth century allowed it to concentrate on a separate political agenda. While Burroughs fervently engaged in politics, at the same time she held African Americans partially responsible for their plight. She believed that even if the laws were changed, white Americans would continue to exclude the race unless blacks exemplified values and behavior acceptable to middle-class white Americans. Burroughs maintained that integration would fail unless blacks changed their behavior. In her opinion, the majority of black children and young adults were "ill-bred, coarse, rude, common and vulgar." She reasoned that if parents taught their children "the rules" of behavior, they would succeed in their "new integrated relationships." These views were remnants of an earlier era when there was a strong belief that advancement of the race was dependent on self-improvement and education.

During the late nineteenth century, the white mission philanthropy dispensed by mostly northern missionaries and teachers to southern freedmen and women emphasized that black Americans, as well as European immigrants, could gain white acceptance if they became "civilized." In programs sponsored by the American Missionary Association, the American Baptist Home Mission Society, and other white religious organizations, women such as Sarah Sawyer emphasized the importance of training "ignorant," loud, and "uncouth" black girls to be teachers who would later instruct other members of the race on moral and physical cleanliness. Some middle-class African Americans, such as Sawyer, believed that if black women and men were educated and comported themselves in a "respectable" manner, acceptable to whites, they could gain the respect of white Americans. This theme reverberated through generations of African Americans who were taught to practice what St. Clair Drake and Horace Cayton identified in the 1930s as "respectability." Drake and Cayton argued that the middle class is distinguished from the lower class "by a pattern of behavior expressed in stable family and associational relationships," and their "great concern with 'front,' . . . 'respectability,' " and "drive for 'getting ahead.' " Drake and Cayton asserted that the objective measure of "respectability" is one's "standard of living—the way people spend their money, and [their] *public behavior*."

During the late 1950s many older black women leaders such as Rossie T. Hollis, the former president of the CME Woman's Missionary Council and the editor of the *Missionary Messenger*, were concerned about white Americans' perceptions of black boys and girls as unfit to attend public schools with white children. Though most did not openly express the same level of obsession with black behavior as Burroughs did, many were concerned about how black people, in particular children, represented themselves and the race as they entered the recently desegregated schools. Hollis commented that she, like other African Americans, hated

> segregation in public schools because we have for many years seen it in operation and we know how segregation and discrimination have gone hand in hand to keep the Negro child and Negro teachers working against odds which pure prejudice created. Those of us who went to Negro schools in the little Negro one room churches, because no school houses were provided for Negro children . . . remember how we walked miles on the cold mornings to a school with one small stove which often smoked until water ran out of our eyes.

Hollis observed that following the Supreme Court decision declaring segregation in public schools unconstitutional—and "of course we know unChristian"—there were those who still hated to see black children attending school with white children. Hollis was responding specifically to the comments of a white woman who said that she had "no objection to Negro children going to schools with my children but Negro children have so little culture." Confusing "culture" with public behavior, and equating culture with access to white creativity and intellect, Hollis said, "I had to admit that many of them have no culture to be sure, . . . but who made the laws that barred them from people who had the culture? Who kept Negro children and their parents so underpaid for their labor that they could not afford books to read nor time to read if they had books? Who shut the doors of colleges to Negroes? Until poor Negro churches could organize some poorly equipped colleges and poorly prepared teachers, there was no opportunity for culture. Who is to blame that some Negroes are not as cultured as some white people." Hollis concluded that although whites had oppressed them, black people must forget the past and move forward. She advised young "Negro girls and boys standing at the door of opportunity" to be on their best behavior and not let anyone "be more polite, more courteous, more industrious, more studious than you are. Go the second mile in good behavior. . . . Keep clean in person and clean in the inner parts. Nothing is gained by profane language. Work hard, study hard, be fair and you will be bound to win."

Concerns about the public behavior of women and working-class and poor blacks were not new; rather, it was a cornerstone reform strategy, embraced by many well-to-do free blacks during the antebellum period, that continued to resonate among the black middle class, as well as the upwardly mobile working class, for well into the twentieth century. Among African American leaders—male and female—there were those who believed that some racial problems could be solved, or at least ameliorated, if the masses were educated and exemplified middle-class white American cultural values. Middle-class and working-class concerns about the acceptance and maintenance of normative behavior in the black community persisted into the late twentieth century. However, few black leaders publicly emphasized such beliefs after 1940. While many recognized that cleanliness, honesty, industry, and good behavior were important, they emphasized that segregation, discrimination, lynching, and ill treatment was meted out equally to poor, working-class, and middle-class blacks.

In the 1950s and '60s, the middle-class black girls and boys who attempted to enroll in previously all-white colleges, universities, and public schools in Little Rock, Arkansas; Prince Edward County, Virginia; Clinton, Tennessee; and other places were not rejected or excluded because of their speech, manners, or appearance, but because they were black and posed a threat to the accepted white social order and stirred white fears of miscegenation. Moreover, white supremacy still held forth as the central philosophy of most white southerners—and, for that matter, many white Americans throughout the United States. Nevertheless, Burroughs was correct in her assessment of the need for African Americans to become educated, develop skills, and excel in whatever they did. She accurately predicted that though the doors might open, without proper training many would not be prepared to enter and take advantage of the new opportunities.

Women: Ecumenicalism and Civil Rights

WOMEN IN THE Baptist and Methodist denominations, as well as the Church of God in Christ, worked cooperatively with Church Women United and often read *The Church Woman*. Methodist women, in particular, embraced CWU's considerable feminist agenda. In doing so, they became even more sensitive to issues of sexism and began to raise more explicit questions and aggressively challenge the male clergy on issues of women's rights in the church. The internal struggles of black Methodist women's missionary societies against the sexism in their denominations demanded a great deal of their attention. These concerns were not new. However, they escalated in the 1950s and '60s. Assertions of their "womanpower" and the push for women's rights created internal struggles within Methodist churches. At the local and national levels, in the churches and in civil rights organizations such as the SCLC, Martin Luther King, Jr. and other male clergy leaders discouraged female leadership, believing that men should take the lead in the movement as spokesmen for the cause. King, Abernathy, C. T. Vivian, and other leaders in the SCLC and other civil rights organizations accepted the norms and practices of the Baptist Church and saw no reason to change their views regarding the role and place of women.

For the most part women were relegated to support roles in the majority of civil rights organizations. Leaders and organizers such as Ella Baker and Septima Clark, who defined strategies and implemented major civil rights programs for the Southern Christian Leadership Council, were often kept in the background and were rarely given public recognition for their accomplishments. It is primarily for these reasons that most church women leaders and their organizations continued to engage in civil rights activities that occurred outside of their denominations and were related primarily to their work with race-specific civil rights and interracial organizations. Most prominent was their work with CWU, the YWCA, the NCNW, and the NAACP. At the same time, hundreds of rank-and-file working-class black church women participated in the grassroots activities initiated by the SCLC and organized by Baker and Clark, and avidly worked with the SNCC and CORE projects. However, CWU was the single most significant organization in defining the civil rights agenda for middle-class white and black women's associations. Many of the themes selected by missionary societies, as well as the local and national projects that engaged religious and secular groups, were those sanctioned by CWU. Decades of interracial organizing contributed to the extraordinary level of cooperation that existed between black and white women leaders during the Civil Rights Movement.

During the 1950s and '60s seasoned black church women became even more involved in CWU. At the national level CWU was outspoken and unequivocal in its support for African American civil rights. At no point did the organization abandon the cause or equivocate on the issues. However, in an assessment of church support for the *Brown* decision, CWU President Cynthia Wedel pointed out that "while in principle all of the churches support the decision, in practical application, there are differences of opinion." Wedel noted that this problem was not exclusive to the South, but existed in the North as well. More than a decade later, in 1970 Clarie Collins Harvey, a prominent member of the Methodist Episcopal Church and a leader in CWU, confirmed that many middle-class black women "consistently used the fellowship of Church Women United as a medium through which to function." However, Harvey stressed that blacks who joined white churches and CWU found that "racism and the caste system are still the Eleventh Commandment of White Christianity. . . . [T]oo many local units of Church Women United still are gatherings where women smile at each other and discuss issues but never get to the levels of mutual hostility which they really feel. They play roles, they give lip service to integration, but they fail to make any really basic changes in their attitudes and practices."

Part of the significance of CWU lay in the dogged determination of its national leaders to stay the course and continue to push for legislation and equal rights for all minorities. It did not matter that member organizations and local churches did not fully embrace the CWU program. At the national level the leadership utilized political and "Christian" means to bring about change. CWU was one of the few predominantly white female organizations in which black women were well represented in the national leadership. In 1953 African American women served on the CWU Board of Managers, which included the presidents of national denominational women's organizations and councils. Also on the board were seventy-five additional women, representatives of denominations and state and local councils. Still, few CWU chapters in the South were integrated.

AME Women and Civil Rights

CHURCH WOMEN'S ORGANIZATIONS were active in campaigns before and after the 1950s to protest discrimination in education, employment, voting, public accommodations, and housing. For example, in 1942 the New York Conference Branch of the Woman's Mite Missionary Society of the AME Church made clear their approval of President Franklin Roosevelt's policy during World War II relevant to the war and the position he took against discrimination in the hiring of African Americans in industries handling defense contracts. They also urged Roosevelt to support the passage of legislation providing for the inclusion of domestic workers in the Social Security Act, and requested the appointment of a black person to the National Labor Relations Board. Between 1954 and 1965, the AME Women's Missionary Society passed resolutions denouncing violence and other tactics designed to prevent the passage and implementation of the *Brown* decision and the various civil rights acts, participated in economic boycotts, organized voter registration drives, provided leadership training for implementing legislation, raised funds to support civil rights organizations and student activists, and engaged projects launched by CWU and other women's organizations.

In 1954, CWU leaders—including AME and other black Methodist and Baptist women from fifteen southern states—met in Atlanta and pledged to work for "a Christian society in which segregation is no longer a burden upon the human spirit." At that meeting the discussion centered around the challenges presented by the *Brown* decision and the question of how they might work with ministers and government and community agencies to address the issue of segregation in the South. The group identified three specific problems needing immediate attention: the establishment of private parochial schools by some white churches to avoid desegregation; an upsurge in the efforts of white parents and public school teachers to instill prejudice in white children; and the plight of black teachers in segregated schools who faced dismissal and possible difficulties in finding teaching positions in desegregated schools. Given their numbers and dominance in the black press, Methodist and Baptist women were more visible in the movement than Episcopalian, Presbyterian, Catholic, and other black church women.

As the twentieth century advanced, definitions of home mission work changed. In the 1960s, Mary E. Frizzell, director of promotion and missionary education for the AME Women's Missionary Society, noted that missions had become more complex, and the problems were more acute. Between 1824 and 1964 the focus, as well as the methods of achieving their organizational goals, had changed in response to the issues and conditions found in the different regions where the denomination was located. Answering the critics who argued that the AME women's work was static and did not relate to the times, Frizzell declared, "[W]hen education is one of the motives of missions, [our work] can be defined in several ways." For example, she noted that the purpose of the religious education program was to help people to understand and adjust themselves to a changing world. Included in this definition was a broad-based work at the local level designed to train rank-and-file members to assume responsibility for the promotion of "better citizenship." This included voting, political activism, and sponsoring training programs, forums, and panel discussions on the 1964 Civil Rights Bill. It also meant cooperating with other organizations for specific purposes—for example, to acquire legislation. Frizzell concluded that missionary education provided an opportunity for total "consideration of the many different subjects facing the world . . . , such as race, labor, housing, technology, and ecumenicity."

During the 1950s and '60s, though individuals and local AME churches might choose to support or participate in some aspect of the Civil Rights Movement, the denomination remained aloof and "denounced" direct-action protests as "remedial methods employed by the populace." Asserting the AME Church's historical role in "the Negro's fight for liberation and freedom," denominational leaders emphasized that its involvement with civil rights began in 1789 when Richard Allen walked out of St. George's Protestant Episcopal Church in protest of racism. Moreover, AME leaders claimed that historically

the church was "in the vanguard of those fighting for freedom, liberation, and civil rights." The problem with this argument was that
almost two centuries later blacks were still being deprived of their civil
rights and were fighting for equality and justice. Additionally, contemporaries focused less on the past and more on the unfolding struggle in
the late twentieth century.

Under pressure to clarify the denomination's position, in 1961 the
AME General Conference passed a resolution supporting the freedom
rides. However, questions continued to be raised about the role of
the AME Church in the Civil Rights Movement. Responding to the
National Council of Churches' call for its thirty-one member denominations to stage nationwide demonstrations against racial discrimination, in 1964 the AME General Conference passed "A Resolution on
Civil Rights," endorsing "all properly sponsored and well planned
nonviolent demonstrations against racial prejudice and segregation"
and encouraging AME officers and laity to participate in the planning
and implementation of such demonstrations. The resolution made
clear that while the denomination approved of the activities of the
NAACP, the National Urban League, and the Southern Christian
Leadership Conference, it did not support "extreme radicals," Com-
munists, or "Black Nationalists." By inference, this could apply to any
number of organizations, such as the Student Nonviolent Coordinating Committee, the Congress of Racial Equality, the Black Panther
Party, and many other groups that included substantial numbers of
young people.

Similar to women affiliated with other religious traditions, individual AME women—such as Daisy Bates, president of the Arkansas
NAACP, and high school and college students such as Minnie Brown
and Diane Nash—made choices based on their personal philosophies.
Crying out in pain because of the failure of the AME Church to not
only commit itself to the civil rights struggle but to place its human
and fiscal resources behind members who chose to stand for freedom,
Bates castigated the church for its lack of courage. In 1959, in an
address at the AME Connectional Laymen's Convention, Bates
revealed that as president of the Arkansas NAACP and a staunch member of the AME Church, her pleas for AME clergy support in 1957 and
1958 during the crisis surrounding the NAACP efforts to desegregate
Central High School in Little Rock, Arkansas, fell on deaf ears.
According to Bates, only two ministers—Rev. Z. Z. Dryver, pastor of
the Union AME Church, and Rev. Dunbar Ogden, a white Presbyter-

ian who was president of the Interracial Ministerial Alliance—"showed up" to walk with the nine black children, six of whom were members of the AME Church, through the rabid white mob to the line of National Guardsmen.

Bates also scolded AME men for not joining the volunteer guard program to protect members like herself, whose property was invaded and houses were bombed. Indignant about what she viewed as the AME Church's failure to support its own members, she asserted, "We must let our young people and the world know that we stand united in this struggle for freedom and whenever a member of our church is intimidated, boycotted as many of us have been for daring to stand up for human dignity, we must let them know that they are not alone but that the entire resources of the AME Church are behind them." Pained by what she perceived as a lack of courage among AME men, Bates asked, "Have we no angry voices to challenge forces of evil? Is there no Thomas Paine to fan the flames of freedom and stir the imaginations of men toward human dignity? Is there no one to emulate Jesus and rid the temple of money-changers? Where are God's angry men?"

Lacking a definition of what they considered either proper or "sufficient" to dismantle American structures of racism and dominance, throughout the 1950s and '60s AME Church leaders argued that "evil for evil is not sufficient." A. Beatrice Williams, editor of the *Women's Missionary Magazine*, asserted that in spite of the gains that black Americans had made through "token integration," and legal and congressional action, "the basic attitudes of man toward man remain the same." Williams noted that nonviolent protests "reverted to violence and white and black power philosophy. The margin of tolerance has not been increased." She proposed that the AME denomination and the WMS adopt a "positive mission" and actively work to change the hearts of white Americans and Europeans throughout the world. Thus, like the NBC-USA's Woman's Convention, the AME Women's Missionary Society defined a program of support for civil rights at the local and national levels.

In 1950 the national missionary societies called for detailed study and review of "Missions at the Grass Roots." Between 1960 and 1962, the West Tennessee Conference Branch Missionary Society provided aid to black farm families in Fayette and Haywood counties who were evicted from the land they worked as sharecroppers. The evictions were related to the farmers' participation in the voting rights campaigns and boycotts of white businesses which opened up the opportunity for black residents to vote for the first time in 1960. The evicted farmers moved into Freedom Village, a tent city. In answer to the pleas of the Emergency Relief Committee of Fayette County, AME women joined other organizations in providing food and clothing to the evicted farm families. The Conference Branch also sponsored a scholarship for one young woman from Freedom Village to attend college. In response to the success of the SCLC's grassroots literacy program designed by Septima Clark to teach illiterate and semi-illiterate blacks the basic reading and writing skills necessary for registering to vote, the East Tennessee Missionary Conference Branch engaged volunteer teachers to work with persons who could neither read nor write.

Responding to the rapid changes occurring in the Civil Rights Movement, especially the direct-action programs of the SNCC, which often were accompanied by violence, church women reassessed their purpose and considered ways in which their organizations could be of more help to those on the front line of the struggle for freedom. Octavia Dandridge, a leading figure in the AME Women's Missionary Society in 1962, asked, "[J]ust what is Mission's role in the present age?" She asserted, "[I]t is our purpose to find our place and reinterpret our role in the present age. What support can we give the sit-in demonstrations—our brothers and sisters who have been incarcerated, beaten, and in other ways persecuted because they insist upon their rights at the polls and their rights to the complete services of establishments that take their money, or first class citizenship?" Dandridge also stressed the need for women to vote "intelligently" on the candidates and issues. Having refined their focus by 1963, the WMS chose a new theme, "New Dimensions in Missions," which would permit them to expand their definition of mission work.

In 1963 the WMS of the Northeast South Carolina Conference agreed to implement the organization's national theme by endorsing President John F. Kennedy's stand for civil rights and launching a voter registration drive in 1964. Protesting the bombing of the Sixteenth Street Baptist Church in Birmingham, Alabama, and the killing of four black girls, in 1963 the WMS State Conference branches throughout the nation sent telegrams to President Kennedy requesting that he take immediate action to apprehend and bring the guilty parties to justice. Responding to the church burning and incidents of white intimidation that had taken place in Hattiesburg, Mississippi, Earline Boyd, the director of the AME's Young People's Department, announced that women in that city were "fighting for Civil Rights and . . . have pledged not to buy anything from any dress store downtown who will not treat Negroes as first class citizens."

Some women such as Evangelist Mary Lou Henderson and Mrs. Peter G. Crawford, the wife of an AME minister, made personal commitments to challenge local customs by testing the new laws. Henderson was among the few AME women fortunate enough to have been appointed to pastor twelve different churches during her long career as a minister. During the 1960s, while serving as an assistant pastor of a church in London, Ohio, she undertook a successful campaign to desegregate public accommodations in Barnesville, Cumberland, Circleville, and Gallipolis, Ohio. Similar to Evangelist Henderson, Crawford took the initiative and became the first person in Memphis, Tennessee, to test the Civil Rights Act of 1964. She took a calculated risk by going alone to the Cafeteria, an exclusive restaurant that had adamantly refused to desegregate. The *Commercial Appeal* reported that Crawford was served without incident. Like Rosa Parks, Ollie Weeks, and Lillian Wortham, Crawford worked with the NAACP Youth Council of Memphis and Shelby County and counseled young girls and boys to be courageous in asserting their rights. Now it was time for her to stand up and be a role model for the youth who looked up to her. Crawford was well known as a leader, having served several years on the Virginia, North Carolina, and Tennessee CWU Board of Directors, and as a leader in the WMS.

The majority of AME women's political organizing and direct-action activities related to their cooperative work with race-specific and interracial organizations such as the NAACP, the Southern Regional Council, Church Women United, and the National Council of the Churches of Christ. In 1965, Loretta Randolph, the director of public relations for the WMS, observed that as a result of working with CWU, most church women's organizations had changed the way they functioned. "No longer is missionary work concerned only with individual denominations, but with humanity. No longer are churches striving as a single unit to reach out to those in need, but by uniting their efforts as the National Council of Churches and United Church Women, they are doing a better job together than could be done alone." Randolph cited the Migrant Ministry as one example of cooperative work on behalf of people who were poor.

In response to the NCC, the WMS adopted the migrant project in 1964, following a discussion of the need for long-term activities to involve the Cook County, Illinois, Christian Training School for Indians in the "total civil rights movement." At the Illinois Conference Branch WMS's annual meeting in August 1966, Mrs. Miguela Sierra Molina, a nurse and migrant worker from Moline, Illinois, was invited to speak about the plight of the migrant workers and the need for churches and communities to support them in their efforts to overcome racism and improve their living conditions. Through special service projects, AME women continued to work on behalf of migrants and their children for several years. In 1967 Mary Frizzell confirmed the organization's shift to "new concepts of missions" emphasizing "Christian Growth on the part of persons, social structure, and cultures." Stressing the need for AME women to become more involved in ecumenical work, Frizzell asserted, "We must be in the world with other forces. The Women's Missionary Society must work with these groups in helping to bring about adjustments and shaping decisions in education, business, government, labor, etc. This new Quadrennium emphasis will stress more community action."

Changing Directions

WITH THE ENACTMENT of the Civil Rights Act of 1964 and the Voting Rights Act of 1965, the civil rights movement had achieved most of its objectives—the end of legal segregation, and the restoration of first-class citizenship rights to African Americans and other nonwhite minorities. By all accounts the nonviolent phase of the movement was over. However, the struggle for equality and social justice had not ended. At the National Council of Negro Women's annual meeting in November 1964, journalist Alice Dunnigan predicted that the struggle would shift from the South to the North, and that the battle "must be waged increasingly on economic and social issues which cut across racial barriers." Urging NCNW delegates to return to their communities and "form a militant mass movement," Dunnigan acknowledged, "In spite of all the legal equality of the North, the colored man to a great extent is still herded into teeming [rat-]infested racial slums because of his economic condition. . . . His unemployment rates are twice those of the whites because of his lack of training. And his characteristic occupations are menial and ill paid because he has no skills." Dunnigan also noted the importance of the Neighborhood Youth Corps, authorized by Congress to be established under the anti-poverty bill, and the need for training and retraining of persons

Arenia Mallory and Pauline Coffey, leaders in the Church of God in Christ's Women's Department, accompanied a delegation to the White House during the National Council of Negro Women's annual convention during the 1940s.

under the Manpower Development and Training Act established in 1962.

Alice Dunnigan's speech was directly related to her appointment as an educational consultant to the President's Committee on Equal Employment Opportunities. Nationwide, women were already engaged in devising means of implementing their organizational programs around the War on Poverty. President Lyndon Johnson had appointed Jeanne Noble, a noted black educator, as director of the Office of Economic Opportunity to plan and develop the Job Corps for Girls for the War on Poverty program. Noble, an Episcopalian activist, advised women's organizations on ways to implement their work. In October 1964 at the annual convention of the National Association of Business and Professional Women's Clubs, Noble spoke about all facets of employment and advised the leaders of national organizations, representatives of leading churches, and other prominent figures that race and color were no longer a factor in obtaining employment. She informed the group that there was a demand for trained women to fill a variety of jobs. Participants on the program included NCNW President Dorothy Height, COGIC leader Arenia C. Mallory, journalist Ethel Payne—the vice chair of the Democratic National Committee—and Alice Dunnigan.

The most prevalent civil rights programs among national black women's organizations in the late 1960s were those related to the War on Poverty. Organizations such as the Alpha Kappa Alpha Sorority and the NCNW were poised to take advantage of the government funding that was available for launching projects that dealt with the problems of urban slums and impoverished rural areas. In May 1965 AKA received the first and largest award, a two-year federal government grant of $4 million to establish a residential job training center for women. In 1966 the Department of Health, Education, and Welfare awarded the NCNW a grant of $150,000 for the development of a job training program for low-income African Americans in Washington, D.C. Similar to AKA, other organizations, such as Women in Community Service, also looked for ways to aid and alleviate the racial tensions and to contribute to the struggle for social justice.

In July 1963, President John F. Kennedy called a national conference of the leadership of national women's organizations to find ways to solve America's social problems. Two months prior to that meeting CWU, the YWCA, the NCNW, the National Council of Catholic Women, and the National Council of Jewish Women held "a private meeting" in Atlanta with white and black women, representing eight southern states, to discuss what their organizations could do to alleviate the problems, especially the tension resulting from the direct-action protests. The group decided to send teams of women to racially divided cities to "build bridges between white and colored women." All of these organizations had units in the South, but it was difficult for an individual or a group to fight against racism and to singlehandedly handle the threats against their lives and businesses. The leaders of these groups had faith that their united efforts would provide the strength needed to organize a major program. In the months that followed, plans were made to launch the program. An interracial and interdenominational meeting, comprising fifty women from more than twenty-five southern cities, was held in Atlanta, Georgia, in June 1964 to determine the possibility of united action. At the insistence of

Dorothy Tilly, the Southern Regional Council's director of women's work, provided leadership for the meeting. At that meeting, Tilly told the group, "Women must act as shock absorbers."

According to the Women in Community Services historian, Judith Weiner, the women who participated in the Atlanta conference "did so at great risk." Though some feared physical reprisals, the "risk" Weiner made reference to had more to do with the women's concerns for the economic reprisals and other harassments they and their families might be subject to if their identities were revealed. This was not the first interracial meeting to be held in Atlanta. Rather, it was a continuation of the tradition established by the CIC, the Southern Regional Council, and CWU. The significance of this meeting was that it brought together women from different groups to work across organizations at the local level and it included Jewish and Catholic women. Also, unlike the earlier interracial meetings, this one was held at a hotel located in downtown Atlanta. To avoid publicity, protect their identities, and prevent harassment and possibly violence, the group chose a "nonthreatening name," the Women's Inter-Organizational Committee (renamed Women in Community Service), to list on the hotel's calendar of events. The three-day meeting was filled with testimony from experts on prison reform, and young black women activists who spoke of the brutality and indignities they had suffered during their imprisonment in Atlanta, Mississippi, and other places where they had participated in direct-action protests. Margaret Mealey, executive director of the National Council of Catholic Women, felt that WICS could begin with "the injustices inflicted on young women, the young black women in the South who were arrested, thrown in jail and abused because they participated in peaceful demonstrations for the cause of justice and civil liberties."

At the conclusion of the meeting, Mealey observed that one of the reasons for the strong bond among WICS organizations was because the motivation was not simply humanitarian, "it's also a spiritual motivation." The organizations constituting WICS comprised twenty-seven million women, including the vast membership and outreach of CWU, the National Council of Catholic Women, the National Council of Jewish Women, and the National Council of Negro Women. The purpose of this coalition of Protestant, Catholic, Jewish, black and white, poor, middle-class and affluent women was to bridge the racial, religious, cultural, and economic gaps separating Americans. For years, many of the WICS leaders, including Dorothy Tilly, Dorothy Height, Polly Cowan, and others, had worked together in the YWCA and CWU for civil rights legislation, voter registration, equal educational opportunity, and open housing. However, though a small number of Catholic women were represented in CWU after 1960, Jewish women were not.

The Wednesdays in Mississippi Project resulted from the Atlanta meeting. During the summer of 1964, several teams of women were sent to Mississippi, where they spent up to two months. Arriving from Boston, Chicago, Minneapolis, Washington, Baltimore, New York City, New Jersey, and St. Paul, Minnesota, the women centered their activity in Jackson, but worked in Ruleville, Canton, Hattiesburg, Meridian, and Vicksburg. WICS relied upon member organizations that had chapters in different locales to take the lead in target areas. Clarie Collins Harvey, a prominent Jackson, Mississippi, businesswoman representing Womanpower Unlimited—a local interracial organization comprising church and civic leaders that provided resources and services for freedom riders and SNCC activists—served as spokesperson at the first WIMS meeting, held in July 1964. Harvey had organized Womanpower Unlimited for the explicit purpose of providing aid to the freedom riders when they were released from jail. The group housed and fed the protesters, gave them free beauty parlor and barber services, and bolstered their waning confidence. Successive waves of militant protesters, including the hordes of SNCC student workers who descended on Mississippi, led protests and demonstrations in Jackson and other cities, and participated in the Freedom Summer project, received similar services. Womanpower Unlimited was flexible and remained ever ready to do whatever was necessary to aid the civil rights workers.

Four local white women met with Harvey, NCNW representatives, and an interracial WICS team, consisting of mainly northern leaders, to discuss how to "build bridges of communication" between black and white communities and work to offset tension and possible violence that might erupt during the Freedom Summer Project. This project, launched by the Council of Federated Organizations and the National Council of Churches, brought students from across the United States to Mississippi to set up freedom schools and voter registration drives. Reflecting on the WIMS experience, one participant observed that it was of special importance to WICS leaders because "it broke down barriers peacefully, through association, and helped to set the stage for the marches and other historic demonstrations yet to come."

Though WIMS lasted for only two summers, its significance cannot be overemphasized. Mississippi was one of the few states in the South where there had been little or no interracial organizing. It was considered to be among the most violent places in the United States, and was known for the most virulent racism. Unlike Montgomery, Atlanta, and some other cities in the South, black and white women leaders in Mississippi had very little contact and hardly knew each other. WIMS played an important role during the summers of 1964 and 1965 in establishing an interracial network of mostly black and white church women in Mississippi, and creating a larger base of support for the SNCC students working with the grassroots voter rights campaigns in the state.

The Mississippi experience, especially the relationships and mutual understandings that developed among the leaders, would be extremely valuable to the future work of WICS. In 1965 the group was formally incorporated as a nonprofit organization, for the express purpose of recruiting and training young women sixteen to twenty-one years old for Job Corps Centers in all states. This was an important initiative spearheaded by the federal government. However, like so many programs of the time, it addressed only a small part of the enormous problems confronting African Americans and the poor. President Johnson's anti-poverty program dealt with some concerns, but could not solve the mountains of problems caused by decades of neglect, racism, segregation, and discrimination. It would take several generations of education and economic and social advancement to level the playing field and bring African Americans up to a position equal to that of whites.

In 1965 the urban ghettos exploded with anger and violence. The nation was awestruck by the riots that erupted in the Watts section of Los Angeles in 1965 and in Newark and Detroit in 1967. Young blacks rejected Dr. King's call for nonviolence and his goal of an integrated society. Changes in the philosophies and protest tactics of existing organizations such as the SNCC, and the growth of more militant leaders and organizations such as Malcolm X and the Black Muslims, the Black Panthers, and the call for "black power," signaled the beginning of a new era. The assassinations of President John F. Kennedy, Malcolm X, and Dr. King left the nation emotionally drained and in a state of shock.

Black Power, Black Theology, and Women's Liberation

THE WOMEN'S LIBERATION and Black Power Movements, as well as the public discourse surrounding them, influenced the political consciousness and social activism of African American women of every social class, religious tradition, and region of the country. Impressed by the success of the Civil Rights Movement, in 1966 a coalition of leading feminists, including Pauli Murray and Aileen Hernandez, founded the National Organization of Women to combat sexism and discrimination in all areas of American life. In the 1970s NOW was a powerful voice in defense of women's rights. Few black women joined the organization, viewing it as racist and unsupportive of the issues that defined the lives of most African American women and their families. Extensive media coverage and the constant controversy surrounding the organization and its leaders contributed to its visibility and ascendancy.

The rise of NOW coincided with the call for women's liberation, the earliest name for the second-wave feminist movement that began in the 1960s. The word "liberation" was first used to describe the attempts of Africans and other Third World people to free themselves from colonial occupation. In the United States, it was utilized by many groups as a symbol of rejection of traditional values, roles, restraints, and expectations. The phrase "women's liberation movement" appeared in March 1968 as the title of the movement's national newsletter. Similar to NOW, the movement was predominantly white, middle class, and educated. Initially it was split into two branches—"women's rights" and "women's liberation." In the women's rights group were the older, more established national organizations, such as CWU. As the press used "women's lib" to ridicule and demonize the movement, it was replaced by the term "feminist." Though many persons accepted that women were discriminated against, there was little agreement among most groups as to what that meant in relationship to them. The majority of black women and men rejected the terms "women's liberation" and "feminist," labeling them racist and unrelated to the black struggle for liberation from race oppression.

In the 1960s and '70s black women activists of all persuasions raised their voices to challenge the chauvinism and sexism in male-dominated organizations, and significant changes in social practices were brought about. Young black women denounced the conservatism of traditional black female organizations, civil rights groups, and community institu-

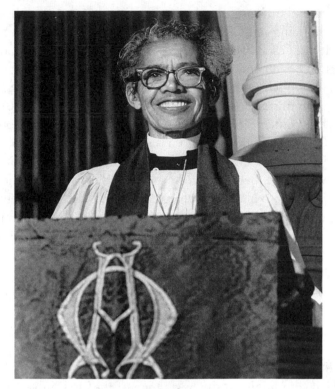

Pauli Murray, an attorney, civil rights and women's liberation activist, and the first black female priest in the Episcopal Church, spoke out against sexism in the Civil Rights Movement and criticized organized religion for its treatment of women.

tions. Many of the issues and programs developed by the black power and black feminist organizations were gradually incorporated and became part of the thrust of more established groups that saw themselves as trying to gain the liberation of all black people. Though some leaders of established civil rights and social welfare organizations, such as NAACP and NCNW leaders Roy Wilkins and Dorothy Height, rejected and labeled the slogan "black power" as divisive, in 1966 a coalition of some forty-eight leading black Christian leaders known as the National Committee of Negro Churchmen issued the "Black Power Statement," declaring, "From the point of view of the Christian faith, there is nothing necessarily wrong with concern for power. At the heart of the Protestant Reformation is the belief that ultimate power belongs to God alone and that men become most inhuman when concentrations of power lead to the conviction . . . that any nation, race or organization can rival God in this regard."

This statement represented a break with the coalition that existed between the King-led Civil Rights Movement and the white Protestant theological establishment represented by the National Council of Churches. The tendency toward nationalism and shifting ideas of identity are implicit in the change of the organization's name from the National Committee of *Negro* Churchmen to the National *Conference* of *Black* Churchmen. The separation occurred at the NCC conference on "The Church and the Urban Crisis" held in Washington, D.C., in September 1967. Young members of the NCBC exhibited little patience with white members of the NCC and insisted that the conference be divided into black and white caucuses. The NCC meeting was the impetus for the 1970s establishment of race and gender caucuses in the predominantly white denominations, which dealt with issues of black identity and black power. Similarly, the "Black Manifesto," which served as the catalyst for the development of a black nationalist religious thesis known as black theology, was a result of the 1967 meeting.

The Black Manifesto developed out of the National Black Economic Development Conference, which met in Detroit in April 1969. The purpose of the conference was to discuss economic development in the black community as the next stage of the civil rights struggle. It called for African Americans to identify with Africa and to reject capitalism and imperialism. In short it demanded the overthrow of capitalism and the establishment of a socialist society led by black people. It asked for $500 million in reparations to African Americans to be paid through the BEDC by American white Protestant and Catholic churches and Jewish synagogues, and argued that they were a central element of the capitalistic system. The Black Manifesto was threatening to most whites because it defined an infrastructure for institutionalizing black power in the United States. It was a road map for the development of racial pride, solidarity, and self-determination as a basic step toward a plan for gaining control of the black community's institutions and resources. Most of the program defined in the manifesto was not new. However, it included the new rhetoric of black power and Third World revolution and was threatening to whites. Moreover, it was a comprehensive plan for liberation, not a piecemeal strategy addressing a few problems.

The Black Manifesto and other confrontations revealed the problems within the black organizations, and of black caucuses within white denominations. In order to succeed, African Americans needed ecumenical unity. They needed a united response to white Protestant and Catholic churches and Jewish synagogues. However, the greater significance of the manifesto was that it provided the boost necessary to launch the theological movement that became known as black theology. The need was to develop a theological thesis, grounded in scripture and the black experience, that would integrate black power into black religion. In 1967 the NCBC created a commission to outline a new theological perspective. Many clergy felt that King's nonviolent, redemptive suffering ethical position was inappropriate. What was needed was "an interpretation of historic black faith grounded in the experience of suffering and struggle, but also in a realistic appraisal of the depth of white racism and the possibilities of black consciousness and power." While some black women sanctioned the basic tenets of the Black Manifesto, they were offended by the sexism implicit in the organization's name, which referenced only "Churchmen" and thus ignored the very existence of church women. Anna Arnold Hedgeman, the coordinator of special projects for the NCC Commission on Religion and Race, organized the 1966 NCC conference on "The Church and the Urban Crisis." She was the sole woman invited to sign the 1966 Black Power Statement.

During the 1960s and '70s the ongoing debate among Christian theologians about various oppressed peoples' liberation movements generated an important body of literature, variously referred to as "theology of liberation," "theology of revolution," and "theology of hope." Although most of the writing emanated from Europe and Latin America, black theology, feminist theology, and womanist theology, produced in the United States, emerged out of the black liberation and women's liberation movements. In the midst of all the debate, an unknown religious scholar appeared. In 1969 James H. Cone published *Black Theology and Black Power*, in which he demonstrated how a historically accurate interpretation of the Bible leads to the conclusion that black power is a legitimate expression of the gospel in a particular situation of oppression. Utilizing the philosophies of Paul Tillich, Franz Fanon, and Albert Camus, Cone emphasized that black power is the affirmation of black being against white racism. Thus, black power was indispensable to the formulation and practice of a black theology, and essential to a Christian understanding of freedom and humanity. Cone's highly controversial book and the emergence of the women's liberation movement changed the nature of the discourse among black religionists, especially women, and led to the publication of several seminal works that analyzed and critiqued the black power and feminist movements, which ignored the special plight of black women in the church and society. Pauli Murray, an attorney, civil rights activist, and the first black female priest in the Episcopal Church, argued that the common theme connecting all of the liberation theologies was "the relation between Christian theology and social action."

An avowed feminist and a lesbian, in 1963 Pauli Murray was among the first to speak out against the sexism in the Civil Rights Movement and to assail organized religion for its treatment of women. Murray's early analysis of sexism among black male civil rights and religious leaders would become a full-blown public conflict by 1970. Her scathing critique presaged the women's liberation movement and fueled some of the later debates about African American women's role in black liberation and women's liberation. In the fall of 1963, in a speech called "The Negro Woman in the Quest for Equality," Murray expressed black women's frustrations over their treatment by male civil rights leaders. As the only female member on the Committee for the 1963 March on Washington, Anna Hedgeman petitioned the six black men involved—namely, A. Phillip Randolph, the director of the march, Martin Luther King, Jr., Roy Wilkins, James Farmer, Whitney Young, and John Lewis—to include at least one black woman speaker. Her request was denied. In the aftermath of the march, Murray asserted that it was "bitterly humiliating" for black women to have been excluded from making at least one of the speeches and not to have been invited to be part of the delegation of leaders who met with President Kennedy at the White House.

In an incisive analysis of their historical role in American society, Murray detailed "The Heritage" and "The Dilemma" of black women. Suggesting that black women were placed in "double jeopardy" as they carried "the dual burden of Jim Crow and Jane Crow," Murray argued that the civil rights revolt of the 1960s revealed a major fissure in race solidarity—the "backlash of a new male aggressiveness against Negro women." She said that in their effort to gain recognition of their manhood, civil rights leaders were assigning women "a secondary ornamental or 'honoree' role instead of the partnership role . . . earned by their courage, intelligence and dedication." In a statistical analysis of the status of black women as related to education, marriage, mortality rates, and employment, Murray demonstrated that black women were disadvantaged and at risk in every area. She concluded that black women could no longer "postpone or subordinate the fight against

[race] discrimination" or sexism, "but must carry on both fights simultaneously." However, she advised black women to insist on a partnership role in the Civil Rights Movement.

Though it began in 1968, the full impact of the women's liberation movement was not felt until 1970. Using marches, parades, and outrageous tactics such as burning brassieres, and adopting black power slogans and symbols, the movement gained critical media attention, and support. As a coalition of predominantly white feminist, gay, and lesbian groups, the movement called for government-supported babysitting for working mothers, legalized abortion, equal pay for equal work, and fair employment. *Ebony* magazine reported that few African American women were attracted to the movement, which one black woman critic described as "[j]ust a bunch of bored white women with nothing to do—they're just trying to attract attention away from the black liberation movement."

Black women harbored a diversity of nuanced views about women's liberation. Phyllis Bedford, the president of the CME Woman's Missionary Council, commended Dorothy Height for the response she gave to the question of women's liberation during her appearance in August 1970 on NBC's *Today* show. Bedford agreed with Height and others who opposed the women's liberation movement, perceiving it as a rejection of black women's concerns and a challenge to the black male. Speaking for CME women, Bedford said, "We too are still concerned about the Black man, because a race cannot rise any higher than the respect it has for its male." In the nineteenth and first half of the twentieth century most black Americans had endorsed the concept that the race could rise no higher than its women. In the 1960s, with the masculinization of the Civil Rights and Black Power Movements, conservative women leaders such as Height and Bedford spoke in defense of black men. They did not heed Pauli Murray's advice that black women must fight racism and sexism at the same time. CME and Baptist women's organizations were among the most conservative of the black religious traditions on this issue.

The most spirited debates about women's liberation and black power occurred among black women in the AME Church. AME Zion and WC leaders, once in the forefront of black feminist movements, after 1950 receded into the background. Most of the stalwart and outspoken activists such as Florence Randolph, Eliza Gardner, Christine Smith, S. Willie Layten, and Nannie Burroughs had either passed from the scene or been replaced by younger women whose leadership focused more on internal church issues. However, this was not the case with black women in the AME Church and the predominantly white Methodist, Catholic, Episcopalian, and Presbyterian churches. In April 1969, Myrtice H. Goree, the AME "Woman's Page" editor, urged black women to study the issues "of greatest concern" to the race—"survival and liberation of the Black community." She argued that if black people were going to survive "emotionally, psychologically, and physically," they must be aware of the "Black Revolution, [and] fully understand the demand for Black Power." Beginning in the late 1960s and continuing into the early 1970s, the "Woman's Page" of the AME *Christian Recorder* was filled with articles illustrating the diversity and division on social and political issues among women in every denomination, and the debates on black power and women's liberation taking place within women's organizations. Black and white women engaged in a critical discourse on the meaning of these movements for them.

Among the first black women to grapple with the issues of racism and identity in the white church were black Catholic nuns. Saundra Willingham, the only black nun in the Sisters of Notre Dame Convent in Cincinnati during the 1960s, spoke about the impact of the Civil Rights Movement on her decision to quit the convent. In an effort to "establish an inner principal strong enough to be a bulwark against what seemed to me intolerable (racial) pressure . . . I used to read such men as Dr. King, Mohandas Gandhi and Thomas Merton." The 1963 March on Washington, the assassination of Malcolm X, and the bombing of the Sixteenth Street Baptist Church in Birmingham had "embittered" Willingham; increasingly she became angry and resentful of "the casual attention" given these events by white nuns. She attended lectures on the Civil Rights Movement held at Dayton University in Ohio, and realized "how backward" and ignorant she was about African American history and the overall struggle of black people.

Willingham observed that young people with less experience than she were more knowledgeable about the Civil Rights Movement and "were able to argue and challenge while I could only sit back in ignorance. I was humiliated at my state of mind: it was white." Seeking solace and support from her superiors, Willingham said that "on every front I met only paternalism, protectiveness and color blindness." White nuns encouraged her to ignore race and read other books. At one point she was forbidden to read any more "race books." Willingham became "increasingly more vocal and more militant with some undertones of bitterness, becoming detectable." Reflecting on her epiphany she said, "As I watched black heads being bashed in from St. Augustine to Detroit, as I listened to black voices crying 'Freedom now!' and 'Black Power,' as I contemplated the commitment unto death of Dr. Martin Luther King, Jr., I began to ask myself some very basic questions." Having had her consciousness raised and become educated about the history of racism in America, it was clear to Willingham that she had to "make a choice between the white authority-bound institution into which I had put myself and the black race into which I was born." For a long time she believed that her choice was "both undesirable and unnecessary," and fervently hoped that the two were not "mutually exclusive." "However, time and exposure to both institution[al] and individual racism both in the [Catholic] Church and the nation forced the inevitable choice."

Though Willingham chose to withdraw from the convent, the majority of black nuns and black Americans in white-led churches stayed and fought for change within their institutions. Many older black women in these denominations accepted their separate status and second-class treatment, while younger women such as Willingham challenged their churches to live up to the Christian creed they espoused. Willingham's descriptions of the numerous incidents of racial prejudice and covert and subtle acts of discrimination, as well as the lack of concern she faced in her religious community, were not unlike the experiences of other black nuns. Sister Barbara Ann Moore, of Avila College in Kansas City, Missouri, was one of many black Catholic activists who participated in the marches and other protests of the 1960s. For the most part white Catholics steered clear of the movement and questioned the need for direct action. Some Catholic insiders suggested that the Catholic Interracial Councils and other organizations be restricted by the church from making decisions on their own as to "whether or not to take part in public demonstrations. The future clearly indicates less freedom of action, but greater strength and unity with respect to the total diocese." By 1960 the bulk of white Catholics had fled the cities and had little contact with black Americans except as "floor-sweepers" in the white business establishments they patronized in suburban areas. Many argued that "there are no Negroes in many suburban parishes and hence there is no racial problem."

Very few Catholics were involved in the demonstrations and protests that occurred before 1965. It was Martin Luther King, Jr.'s call to the nation's clergy to participate in the Selma to Montgomery March that brought numerous white and black Catholic priests and nuns into the Civil Rights Movement for the first time. Sister Moore joined other Catholics and civil rights activists on that fateful march, where they were brutally attacked by Alabama state troopers and local police on the Pettus Bridge on what became known as "Bloody Sunday."

At the local level Sister Moore was a member of a Catholic committee supporting Kansas City legislation on open housing. She felt that the "worst kind of racism was the unconscious kind practiced by people who would not dream that they had any racist feelings." It was "the person who is blind to his racism . . . who perpetuates the system." She believed that the Catholic Church had played a significant role in the history of racism in the United States. It is for these reasons that Moore joined the 156 women representing seventy-five Catholic communities in twenty-two states who met in Pittsburgh at Mt. Mercy College in August 1968 and formed the National Black Sisters' Conference. The organization was called a conference rather than a caucus to avoid all suggestions of conflict with Catholic ecclesiastical authorities and to avoid comparison with the Black Catholic Clergy Caucus formed several months earlier, and other black caucuses in predominantly white denominations such as the Presbyterian, Episcopal, and Methodist Episcopal churches. The NBSC incorporated "black cultural, political, and economic liberation" at the center of their mission and developed programs to implement their liberationist goals.

Described as "an awakening of Black Nun Power," the NBSC was organized by Sister Martin de Porres, a member of the Sisters of Mercy, who believed that black nuns had a responsibility to ensure the development of strong black communities. Sister de Porres, as the only woman present at the April 1968 Black Catholic Clergy Caucus meeting, responded to the urging of the priests to organize black nuns. As a predominantly white institution, the Catholic Church catered to white communities. However, since the racial problem in America was caused by white racism, Sister de Porres believed that black religious women must assume the responsibility of educating white clergy and white nuns about white racism, "so [that] they in turn can teach their people the truth." Sister de Porres made it clear that the conference of black nuns was different from that of the priests, because "our chief purpose is largely educational." In the nine demands presented to white American bishops, black priests focused exclusively on their subordinate status in the Catholic Church. They primarily sought equal representation in the diocesan polity, recruitment of more black clergy, the establishment of a separate Catholic Conference under black leadership, and the right to employment in Catholic institutions situated in the black community. No mention was made of the plight of black nuns.

While black nuns felt that the church should give them more power in black communities, they argued that principals of Catholic schools in black communities should be "if at all possible, black males." Sister de Porres asserted that racism in the convents was expressed in "very subtle ways." She felt that many black nuns had identity problems and needed to understand their own attitudes about black people. When asked why white nuns were not invited to participate in the dialogue, she explained that black nuns must get themselves together before they confer and dialogue with others. Though they received little support from white nuns and church officials, most of the nuns at the conference were excited by the new spirit of militancy and black consciousness permeating America during the late 1960s. Determined not to be left behind, black nuns met to discuss how they could become more "relevant" to the issues and needs of the African American community.

Proudly wearing buttons stating "I Am Proud to be BLACK, Black is BEAUTIFUL," black nuns spent a week discussing how they could become more responsible to black people, the Catholic Church, their religious communities, and the nation. In bitterly frank dialogues with black power activists, students, educators, and social workers who presented their interpretations of what was happening in black America, nuns and speakers confronted each other. The conference succeeded in solidifying the bonds between black nuns and in eradicating many of the stereotypical views held by the American public and the black community about them. The Catholic establishment and white sisters were surprised by the forthrightness, militancy, and willingness of the black nuns to challenge racism in the Catholic Church.

Unlike black women in other mainstream churches, most black nuns exhibited little concern for women's liberation and feminist theology; rather, they supported the elevation of black male clergy to positions of leadership in black Catholic schools and asked only that women be allowed to play a more prominent role in the African American community. However, Sister Mary Roger Thibodeaux not only embraced the doctrine of black power, but also spoke about the racism of white nuns. She recognized sexism in the black movement and racism within the Catholic sisterhood and argued, "[T]he Black nun will have to continue the struggle against injustice both from within and from without." Black power elicited a strong emotional response and permitted black Catholics to engage with issues of their identity in a white-dominated church. Like black Presbyterians, Episcopalians, and United Methodists, they struggled with the question of what it meant to be black and Catholic.

One of the most significant voices in the debate about women's liberation was that of Theressa Hoover, the first black head of the Women's Division of the United Methodist Church's (formerly known as the Methodist Episcopal Church) Board of Global Missions, the policy-making body for 1.8 million women in 36,500 Women's Soci-

Theressa Hoover, a significant voice in the women's liberation debates, was the first African American to head the Women's Division of the United Methodist Church's Board of Global Missions.

eties of Christian Service and Wesleyan Service Guilds. At the June 1970 meeting of the Methodist women's assembly, Hoover asserted that women were "awakening to a new awareness and militancy, especially in the context of Christian principles, but men do not need to feel threatened. . . . They have no reason to fear for their positions. We're not going to take over the church. We don't want it that badly." Comparing women's liberation and black liberation, Hoover said, "We've got the laws—women, like blacks—but how do you clothe them with reality?" She offered that the first step was to "end the oppression of women and blacks."

Among white women, the Woman's Division of the Methodist Episcopal Church was the leading liberal religious organization. Beginning in the 1920s with Carrie Parks Johnson, Sara Estelle Haskin, and Dorothy Tilly of the Woman's Missionary Council of the Methodist Episcopal Church, South, and extending to the Woman's Division of Christian Service in the 1940s and '50s, white Methodist women had a history of involvement in the civil rights struggle. In 1960, they called on the General Conference to "take clearly defined steps to remove the pattern of segregation from the structure of the church and from its total program and practices." Under Hoover's leadership, by December 1970 women in the United Methodist Church were expressing strong support for the women's liberation movement. Hoover organized a meeting devoted solely to a consideration of the movement. She warned Methodist women against judging the movement by what they read in the "Male dominated communications media." Hoover emphasized that United Methodist women's organizations were not attracting younger women because they were not dealing with the issues related to their interests.

United Presbyterian Women, at their triennial meeting, held in August 1970, like the Methodist women grappled with the issues of the time and adopted resolutions on abortion, the Vietnam War, and women's rights. The resolution on women's rights urged local churches to form task forces to work "toward the full liberation and equality of women in church and society." Mrs. Roy Denham, an American Indian, was elected president of UPW. Denham was the first nonwhite to serve in this position. Similarly, among white Baptist leaders at the northern-based American Baptist Convention, women were said to have gotten "behind the cause of the feminist movement" following the assertion of Rev. Dass French that "fewer family problems would arise if women stayed at home where they belong." A national officer of the American Baptist Women's association countered French by presenting a history of "what she described as female exploitation."

After weeks of extensive reporting on the worldwide reactions of mostly white women's organizations to issues of women's equality and liberation, the editor of the AME *Christian Recorder*'s "Woman's Page" asserted that the central question raised by men that had created a lot of discussion was "What Is It Women Really Want?" According to the editor, men did not understand why women wanted to be equal with them when they felt that they were unequal to women. They argued that since little boys were taught that girls were superior and extraordinary human beings, as men they were expected to cater to women by opening doors, buying lunches and dinners, giving up their seats on buses, assuming the role of breadwinner in the family, and so on. Readers were informed that the Equal Rights Amendment passed by the U.S. House of Representatives on August 10, 1970, might remove some of the basic protections women enjoyed under the state and federal laws dealing with employment and marriage. Arguing that sex discrimination no longer existed, the editor asked black women how they would handle their "God given right of being a mother . . ."—would they join white women and practice birth control and continue to neglect their "duty" of "strengthening black family life?" Since black women were supposedly "liberated" the editor asserted that they should be more concerned with their working-class and poor sisters. Women were urged to "go forth and accomplish [their] God given task." This traditional view of the role of black women in the black community and society, which combined domesticity with feminism and evidenced a concern for poor and working class black women or what black women theologians would soon define as one aspect of womanist theology, continued to be articulated by some of the leaders in black denominational associations, particularly the wives of bishops and some prominent ministers.

Women's liberation as an ideology was alien to the majority of poor black women, who had always worked and often assumed total responsibility for the financial support of their families. Pauli Murray noted that in 1962 one out of every eight of the more than three million women in the labor force was nonwhite. At least three-fifths of that number were household employees (domestics) or other service workers, compared to the national average of 25 percent of all women in these jobs. Alma Trotter was one of the women included in the statistics Murray quoted. Comparing her life to that of middle-class white females who advocated women's liberation, Trotter, a disabled retired domestic worker, stated,

> I never liked working for them (white women) when I was a domestic. . . . I didn't get much formal training, so I had to do it, but I didn't enjoy going out of my house to dust their houses. Anyway, most black women wish they could stay home. Another thing is that white women don't respect you. I raised a many of their children and slept with them and still they treated me like I was nothing. I had a house and a man that I could never take care of for taking care of their house and their men and children. We always been apart from our men and children. It's time now for black women and their men to get together.

Trotter and others like her could be found every Sunday morning in the pews of Baptist, Pentecostal, Apostolic, and other churches that attracted large numbers of working-class black women.

By 1971 the black theology movement was shifting from local black congregations and the masses in the streets into the academy. For some, the transition that occurred in the movement during the late 1970s was particularly distinguished by the "theological repudiation" of the sexism in black theology by African American women. The 1970s represent a turning point in the struggle of black women for equality in the church and society. Historically, black women had pre-dominated in the pew, but not in the pulpit or other leadership positions. However, almost a century of protest had brought legislative changes that made it technically possible for women to occupy any position they desired. As religious barriers were removed, more women enrolled in seminaries and sought positions as ministers, religious educators, and administrators.

During the 1970s and '80s an overwhelming number of young women, such as Jacquelyn Grant, Katie Cannon, Prathia Hall Wynn, Cheryl Townsend Gilkes, Cheryl Sanders, and Vasti Murphy McKenzie, entered the seminary and acquired religious training. By 1980 the voices of a new group of seminary-trained women were raised as they assumed positions mostly as assistant pastors, religious educators in black churches, and academicians.

Young seminarians like Jacquelyn Grant were in the vanguard of those who came of age at the height of the debates about black power, women's liberation, the feminist movement, and black theology.

Keenly aware of the issues and the struggles of black women, Grant was among the first to raise questions about the role and place of African American women in these movements and to frame out a new philosophy. As a seminarian studying under James Cone at the Union Theological Seminary in New York City, Grant was particularly sensitive to Cone's failure to recognize that black women were among the most oppressed of the oppressed. As the controversial author of *Black Theology and Black Power*, Cone was quite right in his argument for a black theology. However, he was, as he later admitted, remiss in overlooking the special oppression of black women in the church.

In 1979 Jacquelyn Grant questioned black men and their adoption of the values and definitions of white patriarchy as it relates to women. She took black male theologians to task for adopting the views of the same white theologians they condemned, and for excluding women from theological scholarship. Grant demonstrated the relationship between racism and sexism and illustrated how they operate as forms of oppression in the black community. Observing that Cone's thesis suggested that either black women had no place in black theology or black men were capable of speaking for them, she argued that both of these assumptions were false and should be discarded. Grant asserted that in a male-dominated society, African American men perceived themselves as the legitimate spokespersons for the black community, ignored black women's views, and exhibited little concern for the oppression of black women in the church and the community. She questioned the authenticity of a theology that presumed to speak for a population that represented more than 50 percent of the black community and more than 70 percent of the black church.

While internal issues of racism and sexism continued to engage black religionists, the white male clergy leadership in the National Council of Churches was disillusioned with blacks and their push for black power. To appease and avoid alienating conservative council members, NCC leaders ignored feminist causes. The NCC was particularly concerned about losing the support of the conservative Orthodox Catholic churches, which were admitted to the council in the late 1960s. Unlike the NCC, CWU leaders refused to retreat into a conservative shell; rather, they accepted the challenge of black power, embraced the concept of women's liberation, and elected Clarie Collins Harvey as the first black president of CWU. Harvey's rise to power and the womanist theology movement that emerged in the 1980s owed a great deal to the issues and struggles that framed the civil rights, black power, black theology, and women's liberation movements of the 1960s and '70s.

In an address before the CWU Ecumenical Assembly in 1971, Harvey asserted, "Never once did I think nor imagine I would be chosen by you to face the sun as the . . . President of Church Women United, for all of the years of my life until six short years ago the doors of CWU were closed to me as a Black living in Mississippi. . . . Months of soul searching, study, receiving of counsel, and prayer preceded my giving an affirmative answer. I needed to know it was God's plan and purpose for my life and for the life of the movement which is Church Women United that I serve Him in this way." As president of CWU, Harvey represented thirty million Christian women. In effect, she became the most influential black woman in America. Her election coincided with African American women's disaffection with the interracial movement, and the escalating militancy of black Episcopalians, Presbyterians, Catholics, and others who held membership in the so-called "interracial churches." The white liberal establishment's reaction to the growing militancy of blacks was visible in many interracial organizations, such as Church Women United and the United Methodist, Episcopal, and Presbyterian denominations, that either excluded African Americans from the upper echelon of the leadership hierarchy or placed them in lesser positions. However, some of the women's organizations associated with these and other religious traditions moved swiftly to address the absence of minority women in their hierarchies by selecting women such as Hoover, Denham, Collins, and others as their leaders.

Having engaged in the struggle for racial and gender equality for over half a century and worked unceasingly in the interracial church movement, by 1970, as Clarie Collins Harvey explained, "Many black, middle class women are disillusioned with church integration. Second-class churchmanship is the order of the day, as whites insist on integration on the terms they dictate. White racism, our national sickness, finds some of its most virulent forms in organized religion that is white, Anglo-Saxon, and Protestant." Harvey argued that though most black women "speak with affection and without self-consciousness of 'The Lord,'" many middle-class black women had left the church because of sexism and other practices, and that they found fulfillment outside of their homes and jobs "in bridge clubs, sororities, politics, and other social and civic activities." However, those who had not lost their faith in organized religion continued to engage the fellowship of

Church Women United, but were less involved in their denominations.

The Black Women's Agenda and Womanist Theology

EMBATTLED AFRICAN AMERICANS in predominantly white denominations were in the forefront of the struggle with white religionists. In the aftermath of the Civil Rights Movement black caucuses developed in most of the predominantly white denominations. For years blacks within the Presbyterian, Episcopalian, Methodist Episcopal, and Catholic churches were treated as stepchildren, segregated and discriminated against within these denominations. The civil rights, black power, and black theology movements brought their long-standing disagreements and disenchantment with their treatment to the surface. In order to address the dilemma of black leadership in white churches, between 1965 and 1970 black clergy and laity organized themselves into black caucuses for the purpose of challenging the white religious establishment and its official theology. Following the general pattern of sex discrimination that had prevailed in the church, in most mixed-gender organizations, and in the Civil Rights Movement, women were assigned secondary, supportive roles in the caucuses. The leadership consisted of mainly male clergy who made most of the decisions. In black churches, women dealt with sexism; in the white denominations they confronted racism and sexism. The creation of women's task forces and other groups to deal with the role of women in the church further marginalized black women, who realized that their issues were not being addressed by either group.

Whereas the 1970s was a period in which black theology emerged as a foundational theological philosophy that built on the Black Power Movement of the late 1960s and provided the nexus that realigned the left wing of the southern Civil Rights Movement with northern black Christians, the 1980s witnessed the rise of the womanist theology movement. This movement was profoundly influenced by the struggles of black women with black theology and white feminism. An unforeseen but highly significant result of the challenges posed by the masculinized black theology and feminist movements to black women theologians was the emergence of the "black women's agenda," which emanated from the struggle of black Episcopal women for self-determination. Coincidental to this development was the emergence in the early 1980s of a cadre of young female theologians and

Bishop Barbara Clementine Harris was elected a suffragan bishop of the Massachusetts Diocese in 1988 by the Episcopal Church. She was the second black woman bishop in the United States and the first female bishop in more than four hundred years of tradition in the Anglican Communion.

university-trained scholars who possessed the intellectual creativity, spiritual zeal, and commitment to not only do black theologies, but to build on the black women's agenda and create a new theological perspective—womanist theology—that asserts the value of black women's history and experience in the context of their historical struggles with racism, sexism, and classism in the churches and society. The ideology of womanist theology was first defined and articulated as the "Black Women's Agenda" by the black Episcopal women's task force during the early 1980s.

At the 1985 Afro-Anglicanism Conference held in Barbados, Rev. Barbara Clementine Harris, a priest in charge of the St. Augustine of Hippo Church in Norristown, Pennsylvania, discussed the history of "Black Women in the Anglican Communion." Referencing the political agenda of white women in the feminist movement of the time, she asserted that in the Episcopal Church and the Anglican Communion, the "Black Women's Agenda is largely focused on developing and strengthening the community so that the total community benefits. Black women and other women of color cannot be seduced by the personal power games often blatantly operative in some sectors of the feminist movement."

In 1973, as a result of women's dissatisfaction with their overall treatment in the church, the Episcopal Church established a Task Force on Women. The only entity within the denomination's executive council structure that was concerned with empowering women, the task force's public program included three national conferences held in St. Louis (1977), Cleveland (1979), and Indianapolis (1981), to identify and address "personal and structural blocks that inhibit women's full response to the Gospel."

According to Janette Pierce, a member of the three-person Episcopal Church's conference subcommittee, in planning for the Indianapolis meeting she recognized "the tension between racism and feminism as a major block for women, the church, and society in general." Since there was only one black person on the task force and the conference organizers were all white, Pierce questioned how the issue could be addressed in a valid manner to gain acceptance in the black women's community. The subcommittee envisioned a discussion between a black woman and a white woman on the issues of racism and sexism. In hindsight, Pierce said that the fact that "this would have modeled, [and] incarnated, the very split we were trying to bridge never really entered our minds." Fortunately an advisory committee to the Black Ministries at the Episcopal Church Center recommended having a separate session with black women speakers.

At the 1981 Indianapolis conference, Rev. Harris, Dr. Deborah Harmon Hines of Nashville, Mattie Hopkins of Chicago, and Myrtle Gordon of Atlanta spoke forcefully about their distrust of the feminist movement and unveiled what became known as "The Black Women's Agenda," a hefty challenge to white feminism. Hines, who later headed the Union of Black Episcopalians, explained that because of racism, black women's issues and concerns were different from those of white women. She said black women "unequivocally see their roles as maintaining, strengthening and uplifting our race, our families, our culture and heritage, our men and ourselves. And, these women see racism as their archenemy in this struggle." In four separate presentations, entitled "Racism Breeds Stereotypes," "Bigotry 'Fashionable' Again,"

"Other Struggles Seducing Blacks," and "You Don't See Most of Us," Hines, Gordon, Hopkins, and Harris presented an analysis of the Black Women's Agenda in which they alluded to the problem of racism in the church and feminist movement, and in graphic terms systematically laid out the overall concerns of black women. Pierce reported that the audience was totally surprised by the open, honest, and frank presentations of four black women, and that "the white women, had to deal with the pain, anger, frustration, even tears that many thought had been put behind by the mid-seventies." Following the conference, a separate black women's task force was organized. Its purpose was to advise the Episcopal Women's Board about the concerns of black women.

The Black Women's Agenda articulated by African American females in the Episcopal Church put in place a comprehensive analysis of the history, status, and concerns of black women. Broken down into its simplest elements, there was nothing new about what the women said that had not been stated by black foremothers such as Anna Julia Cooper, Frances Ellen Watkins Harper, Mary Church Terrell, Fannie Barrier Williams, Hallie Quinn Brown, Christine Smith, Mary McLeod Bethune, Pauli Murray, Theressa Hoover, and many others too numerous to name. Murray and Hoover were among the first black women "theologians" to criticize black male theology. However, the timing and context of the Black Women's Agenda, most importantly the publication and wide dissemination of their messages, stimulated a broad discourse among black seminarians, female clergy, and others seeking to find their voices and solidify their concerns into a movement. While black Episcopal women provided a comprehensive analysis and philosophy upon which black female theologians could build a movement, Alice Walker provided the name—"womanist"—that spoke to the unique angle of vision and special brand of feminism exemplified in the black woman's experience.

The publication of Alice Walker's book, *In Search of Our Mothers' Gardens: Womanist Prose* (1983), and her widely acclaimed novel *The Color Purple* (1982) helped launch the womanist theology movement. Katie Geneva Cannon, the first African American woman to be ordained a minister in the United Presbyterian Church in the USA (1974) and to earn the Doctor of Philosophy degree from Union Theological Seminary in New York (1983), is the progenitor of womanism as a movement within the American Academy of Religion. Among the first generation of womanist scholars were Jacquelyn Grant, Delores

Williams, Cheryl Townsend Gilkes, Diana Hayes, Toinette Eugene, Renita Weems, Jamie Phelps, Shawn Copeland, Emily Townes, Clarice Martin, and Marcia Riggs. Including women from all religious traditions, in the 1990s the womanist thought expanded and encompassed the voices of black women theologians, historians, writers, and philosophers. Though it is difficult to identify a specific date for the beginning of the womanist theology movement, it is safe to say that it was under way by 1985 and was in full bloom by the 1990s.

Womanist Theology

WOMANIST THEOLOGY EMERGED out of the black theology movement. While it affirms the liberation theology of black male theologians, it also critiques it. Womanists join with African American men in the struggle against white church dominance, which by extension includes white feminist theologians. However as black feminists, womanists align themselves with white feminists in the struggle against male dominance. Womanists acknowledge their relationship to both black male theologians and white feminist theologians, but they reserve the right to define and name their own experience and to construct a system of doing theology that is "accountable to the survival and liberation of Black women." The designation "womanists" is derived from the term "womanish," which Alice Walker used in *In Search of Our Mothers' Gardens*. Walker explained that a womanist is "[a] black feminist or feminist of color. From the black folk expression of mothers to female children, 'You acting womanish,' i.e., like a woman. Usually referring to outrageous, audacious, courageous or *willful* behavior. Wanting to know more and in greater depth than is considered 'good' for one." A womanist is "[c]ommitted to survival and wholeness of an entire people, male *and* female. Not a separatist, except periodically, for health." A womanist is also a "woman who loves other women, sexually and/or nonsexually."

By the late 1990s the term womanist had been adopted by some black women historians, religious scholars, and political and social activists, and was being included in many women's studies and black studies courses. Of all these groups, the womanist theologians have been the most creative in tweaking and refining the philosophy to fit their specific purposes. While some womanist theologians do not consider black feminist as a synonym for womanist, many black women historians do. For black womanist theologians the term specifically describes a woman of African descent, who may or may not be a Christian. Womanist theologians incorporate a multidimensional theological analysis to black women's experience that includes race, class, gender, and heterosexism.

Delores Williams defines womanist theology as "a theology of the Spirit informed by Black women's history, culture, and religious experience." Survival is a theme found in the writings of all womanist scholars; however, it is the principal focus in Williams's theology. Her provocative study of the relationship between African American women's experience, and that of the biblical figure Hagar, is affirmed in the writings of black religious foremothers and forefathers. Williams's trenchant analysis of the Bible and its interpretational importance to the African American experience, and her deep understanding of the uniqueness of black women's experience and their historical explication and embracement of biblical women, led her to conclude that Hagar's story is the "most illustrative and relevant to Afro-American women's experience of bondage, of African heritage, of encounter with God/emissary in the midst of fierce survival struggles."

In many ways the 1980s represented the culmination of a long struggle for legal, race, and gender equality in society and the church. For African Americans and women, it represented the dawning of a new era in which they would seek to actualize the gains they had made. The struggle to advance and move forward economically, politically, and socially and achieve *full* equality would present new challenges. Between 1990 and 2008 black women and men, in their separate and collective struggles, would realize that, while they had won monumental battles, the war was not yet over.

Coda

With some denominations, when the pastor has done all the vile things he can do, has taken advantage of all the weak girls in his flock, and become beastly intoxicated, the church "splits" the majority (women of course) following the "herd." In other denominations when the "hero" has broken hearts and homes, stolen funds, and frequented places of questionable character, the bishops transfer them to another conference, and dumps the garbage down on another congregation. . . . If the women of every Negro congregation would demand that the pulpits be filled with men of clean character, and refuse to support any other kind, the heads of the churches would awaken to their duty and their false position and cease to encourage rascality by giving them larger congregations.

Dorothy, "Woman's World"
Indianapolis Freeman *(1908)*

The black church currently is faced with a serious crisis of gender relations. More than any other African descended group in the New World, the black communities and churches in the United States have been shaped by the status and agency of women. . . . This womanist infrastructure finds itself facing an emergent militant black manhood that is highly ambivalent about the importance of the church's women's history.

Cheryl Townsend Gilkes (1998)

There are numerous gay people in the Black church who are still closeted, and people know that they are gay and aren't bothered by it. They love them and treat them well. But if they try to make a big issue out of it and try to force general church acceptance of them, right now the Black church hasn't yet reached that stage of understanding. Individually gay Black church members are embraced and accepted, but the church as a whole isn't ready to take an official position on formally recognizing and accepting gay people. There are musicians and preachers and others in the church who are gay and people know it, but nobody makes a big issue out of it.

Mozella G. Mitchell (2001)

As the twentieth century ended, African American women had much to be proud of. They entered that century with the intention of breaking down the barriers of racism and sexism and ended it with an impressive array of victories. They were determined to bring an end to Jim Crow, be active participants in local and national party politics, and to have a voice and play a meaningful role in the churches they had literally bought and paid for. One by one, they hammered down the barriers that at one time were overwhelming. Fighting segregation and discrimination at the local and national levels, organizational leaders and laywomen contributed to the struggle for social change. In most Protestant churches, progress has been difficult, slow, and sporadic. By the 1990s the majority of Protestant denominations had granted women religious suffrage, full clergy rights, and the right to be elected and participate in the chief legislative bodies. For Baptist, Catholic, Church of God in Christ, Pentecostal/Holiness, and Spiritual women, there is still much to be accomplished. Among Baptist denominations, while some women have been ordained by their pastors, the ordination, placement, and promotion of women called to ministry remains problematic. Sandra E. Crouch, a Grammy-winning gospel artist, was ordained an elder in the New Christ Memorial Church of God in Christ in 1998. Ordinarily COGIC women are not employed as pastors, but Elder Crouch was appointed co-pastor of the church. Women's ordination continues to be an issue in COGIC, and in some Pentecostal/Holiness religious traditions as well.

At the opening of the twenty-first century black women accounted for 12 percent of clergy and 50 percent of all ordained female clergy in mostly independent Holiness and Pentecostal churches. A relatively small number of women are employed as pastors in white and black churches, and are professors in seminaries and university departments of religion. In the late twentieth century, fourth-generation women clergy managed to expand their preaching base and secure a few positions as bishops in mainstream denominations. Concerns for ministerial appointments as pastors and the elevation of several women to the most coveted ecclesiastical positions influenced the debates of the late twentieth century. Legislative barriers to advancement in the polity have diminished, but in 2008 women were still underrepresented in the religious hierarchy. In 2009 the selection of Leslie D. Callahan as the first woman to lead the historic St. Paul's Baptist Church in Philadelphia was viewed by many as "leading the way for others to break down old barriers" in Baptist churches. While there are female

Baptist ministers, pastors are a rarity. As a sign of the changes occurring in the United States, also in 2009, Alyssa Stanton was ordained as the first African American rabbi by Hebrew Union College—a mainstream Jewish seminary.

With all of their successes—large and small—women still struggle with the forces of sexism, and are limited in their opportunities to advance in the religious polity. Their plight is similar to that of African Americans who won the legal struggle for civil rights—the barriers restricting participation in all areas of American society have been removed, and the "Colored" and "White" signs have disappeared, but black Americans have not achieved full economic or political equality. In Barack Hussein Obama, we have the first African American president of the United States, and African Americans and women now occupy positions of authority in the church and society that once were unthinkable. But there is only token representation in most areas. Females continue to perform most of the work of the church, while

Vashti Murphy McKenzie was the first female to be elected bishop in the African Methodist Episcopal Church, and in the historically black denominations.

males hold the majority of leadership positions. In the National Baptist Convention, USA, the largest black denomination, the Woman's Convention has actually lost ground. Once a powerhouse of Baptist women's self-determination, the WC is now under the control of the male-dominated National Baptist Convention, USA, Inc. Among black Methodists, the African Methodist Episcopal Church is presently viewed as the most progressive. Whereas for decades the most advanced black church in terms of women's rights and religious leadership was the AME Zion denomination, by 1990 it had been overtaken and surpassed by the AME Church.

Targeting positions traditionally held by men, in the late twentieth century AME women made incremental but significant gains. In 1964 three women sought offices formerly designated for males. Rev. Carrie Thomas Hooper was a candidate for bishop—the first female in the history of the AME Church to run for this office—and Octavia Douglass ran for the office of historiographer. Though Hooper and Douglass were not elected, they made history by simply running for these offices. Hooper did not think that she would be elected. She stated that "her campaign was an expression of the spirit of the times and age when women have the right to aspire to do whatever men do." Alma Polk was elected director of the Office of Public Relations, and became the first female general officer in the history of the AME Church. In the 1980s and '90s, Jayme Coleman Williams and Paulette Coleman were the first of their sex to serve as editors of the AME *Church Review*. At the beginning of the twenty-first century the AME Church made national news with the election of three AME women to the episcopacy—the first females to hold the title of bishop in any major black denomination. The elections of Vashti Murphy McKenzie (2000), Carolyn Guidry (2004), and Sarah F. Davis (2004) were unprecedented. More recently, in 2008, the AME Zion Church elected Mildred Hines as its first female bishop.

A woman bishop was not remarkable among mainstream Protestant denominations, since the office was open to female clerics in the Episcopal Church, United Methodist Church, and Evangelical Lutheran Church in America. Vashti Murphy McKenzie, scion of one of America's most prominent black families, was the first female bishop in the historically black denominations, but not the first black woman to become a bishop. That distinction belongs to the United Methodist Church, which elevated Rev. Leontine Kelly to the bishopric in 1984. While Kelly was the first black woman in any denomination to be elected bishop, she was the second woman to occupy that position in the United Methodist Church. In 1988 the Episcopal Church elected Barbara Clementine Harris a suffragan bishop of the Massachusetts Diocese, making her the second black woman bishop in the United States and the first female bishop in more than four hundred years of tradition in the Anglican Communion—and a symbol for the 2.5-million-member Protestant Episcopal Church and Anglicans throughout the world.

Before the dust had settled on the McKenzie election, in November 2003 Rev. Leah Gaskin Fitchue was chosen as president of the AME Church's much esteemed and historic Payne Theological Seminary. Fitchue became the first woman president of Payne Seminary in its 160-year history, the first female to serve as president of a historically black theological seminary, and the first black American woman president of a fully accredited seminary that held membership in the prestigious American Association of Theological Schools.

In many ways, the advance of clergywomen was facilitated by the Commission on Women in Ministry. Established in 1989 by AME clergy women, in 1992 the COWM was admitted as a conference organization to the General Conference, where it fought for the elevation of women clergy to the bishopric and to high-level administrative posts.

While AME women have clearly broken down barriers and ascended to levels of leadership unheard of in the past, Rev. Fitchue argues that it is too soon to claim that the " 'glass ceiling,' which subordinates the role of women in the church and the secular world, has been shattered," since "the cuts and bruises on my body gained while trying to maneuver around the jagged edges that remain in place say otherwise." She admits that "there is a crack in the ceiling through which more and more women are emerging through," but Fitchue says, "if the glass ceilings were shattered, it would mean that the original structure that successfully kept women in their places for centuries would no longer exist and we would be so plentiful in leadership positions that there would no longer be a discussion of the 'first woman' to accomplish this or that." Quoting Rev. Jacquelyn Grant Collier, Fitchue emphasizes that "we have a long way to go." She also acknowledges that women could not and did not achieve these accomplishments by themselves—they were aided by men who believed in "gender justice." Of course, she is right. AME men such as Bishop Richard Allen Hildebrand, Bishop John Richard Bryant, Robert

Vaughn Webster, Zedekiah Lazett Grady, Bishop Vinton Randolph Anderson, and a host of others removed some of the obstacles that allowed Fitchue to accomplish her goals.

Today, the primary issue in black Episcopal, Presbyterian, and Catholic churches is their status in mostly white- and male-dominated denominations. African Americans in these institutions continue to be conflicted about their relationships to a white leadership, and about their place among the historically black denominations. Black Presbyterian and Episcopalian pride in having achieved a largely middle-class status is set aside by their collective guilt over being in minority churches that have traditionally catered to elite black congregations. Preoccupied with a middle-class bias and their concerns for equality in the polities of their denominations, their congregations have often found it difficult to engage with the issues of the masses of poor blacks. Gayraud S. Wilmore captures the ambivalent nature of African Americans in the Presbyterian and Episcopal denominations, as well as the historical perception of most black Americans that these churches "are too snooty for most Black people." While African Americans are aware of blacks in the Catholic Church, they are less knowledgeable about black Presbyterians and Episcopalians.

Wilmore's riveting example of the reaction of one black woman in Hattiesburg, Mississippi, to black Presbyterian ministers who participated in the United Presbyterian Church, USA's 1964 voter registration project speaks volumes. This woman, who volunteered to provide "additional housing for the project in her two-room tar-paper shack," asserted, "I seed some White Pedestrians downtown, but I ain't never heard of no *colored* Pedestrians." When told that there were many black Presbyterians in the South, and some in Mississippi, "[s]he replied that although it wasn't her business, colored people were supposed to be either Baptist or Methodist." Responding to a suggestion that she should visit a black Presbyterian Church, she stated, "It ain't likely I'd be goin' to no Pedestrian church, Reverend, ya'll too high class fo' po' folks like me."

Following the Civil Rights–Black Power Movement, African Americans in mainstream denominations were concerned about their blackness—specifically, the ways in which they differed from traditional black denominations. The music, worship, and communal life of Presbyterian, Episcopal, and Catholic churches were viewed as cold, sterile and often lacking in emotion. In short, they were too "white," or, in the parlance of the time, "not black enough." There was a growing demand for clergy and laity to recognize their unique history and contributions to the development of their denominations, and to ensure that their churches embody the cultural beliefs and practices of African Americans. Under these circumstances, concerns for women's status in the Presbyterian and Episcopal churches tended to take a backseat to issues of race. Toward the end of the twentieth century, black Catholics became increasingly disaffected by the church. Many felt that the mostly white bishops failed to meet the needs of black Catholics or place them in decision-making positions in the church. Father Bryan Massingale, professor at the St. Francis Seminary in Milwaukee and the Institute for Black Catholic Studies at Xavier University, stated, "We don't like to speak of these things, the pain and grief, the hurt and the disappointment of belonging to a church in which we sometimes feel orphaned and abandoned."

Jacqueline Wilson, former president of the National Association of Black Catholic Administrators, was among the first to speak about the church's inordinate "attention and emphasis on Hispanic needs and concerns," which caused many to "feel that issues in the African American community are ignored." She added that many black Americans "still view the church as a racist institution." The National Black Catholic Clergy Caucus, the National Black Sisters Conference, the National Black Catholic Seminarians Association, and the National Association of African-American Catholic Deacons see the issue as "[i]mplicitly, racism" and are concerned about the extent to which black Catholics are excluded from the hierarchy and decision making.

In response to the concerns of black Catholic deacons in the Chicago Diocese about the sparse involvement of black men in their parishes and the recruitment efforts of the masculine-oriented Promise Keepers in the black community, a one-day meeting was held in Chicago to discuss "the image and role" of black Catholic men. Dexter Watson of the Holy Angels Parish said, "This is just ludicrous. . . . it was 'terrible,' " that there was not "a black man in any position in the church in the Archdiocese of Chicago in 1998. . . . There are qualified black men to lead in this church." As a leader in the black Catholic community in the 1970s and '80s, ten years before Watson and others challenged the bishops to hire African American and other people of color as diocesan personnel, Sister Thea Bowman, a member of the National Black Sisters' Conference, the founder of the Institute of

Black Studies at Xavier University in New Orleans, and a pioneer in the movement for black Catholic history, spoke out about the discrimination in the Catholic Church.

After 1970, African Americans in most mainstream denominations were faced with an identity crisis, in that they felt distant and outside of the religious culture of what was defined by some as "authentic" black American Christianity. As they struggled to find themselves in an ever-changing society, modifications were made in the preaching, music, polity, liturgy, and patterns of congregational life. In 1989, Father George Augustus Stallings, pastor of a Catholic church in Washington, D.C., introduced the "African-American Catholic Congregation" at a service held at the Howard University School of Law. At least four thousand people attended the ceremony, which included an African-based liturgy and chants to African saints and ancestors. Father Stallings was suspended and later excommunicated for violating the laws of the Catholic Church. Stallings created quite an uproar with his charges of racism in the Catholic Church and the subsequent creation of the Imani Temple. During the 1990s, his black Catholic congregation spread to a number of cities, including Baltimore, Philadelphia, Richmond, New Orleans, and Columbia, South Carolina. Significantly, Father Stallings recognized the need for the new Catholic Church to represent the interests of women and gays. Along with African-centered liturgies and support for the marriage of priests, the Imani Temple upheld the right of women to ordination to the priesthood, the use of contraceptives by females, and the acceptance of homosexuality. Father Stallings also stressed African contributions to Christianity and used the Bible to emphasize that Jesus was a person of color.

During the 1970s black Catholic women became more organized and conscious of their identity as black females in a white and male establishment. The National Black Sisters' Conference, led by a series of highly committed nuns, kept the issues of black women before the denomination. Though the NBSC initially shunned identification with the feminist liberation movement, for many years it has been the voice of nuns and laywomen. In the 1980s and '90s a cadre of black Catholic female scholars and womanist theologians arose and gave voice to black Catholic women through their presence, lectures, and writings. Women such as Diana Hayes, Jamie Phelps, M. Shawn Copeland, and Diane Batts Morrow refuse to allow the history of either black Catholic women or blacks in the Catholic Church to be excluded from African American or Catholic religious history. These scholars have written about black Catholic women and elevated them from the margins of Catholic and women's history.

In August 2001 the National Black Sisters Conference sponsored the first National Gathering for Black Catholic Women to focus solely on issues of importance to female laity and nuns. Sister Patricia Chappel, president of the NBSC, informed the gathering of more than eight hundred women that "solidarity, health, spirituality and political empowerment, economic development and vocations" were the key issues. In her keynote address, "The State of Black Women in the Catholic Faith," Diana Hayes claimed, "Despite racial, gender, class and religious biases, black Catholic women's spirituality still exists because of their female ancestors' commitment to Catholicism. . . . Being forced to sit in the back pews of churches, being last in line to receive Communion, even being denied the opportunity to send their children to diocesan schools didn't dissuade them." Like black women in other denominations, they "persisted in their faith . . . and helped raise money to build their own churches and schools." However, Hayes expressed concern that black Catholics were leaving the church to become Muslims, Protestants, and Buddhists. She also accused the Catholic Church of being racist and sexist and pitting "one group against another," in particular Hispanics and black Americans.

The National Gathering for Black Catholic Women infused the laity and other female leaders with a greater zeal to speak out about racism in the Catholic Church and to make their voices heard on issues regarding the paucity of black priests and nuns, the closing of black Catholic schools in numerous dioceses, the imprisonment of black men, and poverty and HIV/AIDS. In 2002, at the meeting of the National Black Catholic Congress, Sister Anita Baird, president of the NBSC, voiced the sentiments of many black Catholics who refused to vilify Cardinal Bernard Law of Boston, a symbol of the Catholic Church's inability to stop the sexual abuse of children and women by priests. Baird stated that while black Catholics felt that "people should be held accountable" for wrongdoing, they remembered that Law had placed blacks in positions of authority and made himself available to black leaders. Baird stressed that "the black Catholic community has issues that are broader. . . . There's too many of our boys and women who are dying or going to prison. That's foremost in our minds as black Catholics." For the first time in the history of the Catholic Congress, Africa was a major subject on the agenda.

The rapid growth of Catholicism in Africa had implications for black Catholics in the United States. In 2002 black Africans constituted 130 million members, 601 dioceses, and 27,000 priests. The discussion of Africa was raised in part because of the resistance African priests encountered in black American parishes. Sister Baird acknowledged that African priests were meeting resistance and explained that it was because they came "from a culture that puts priests on a pedestal and does not view women as equal." She asserted that the African priests and sisters "will adjust when they understand that just being black is not enough." By 2003 black Catholic women were voicing their disagreement with the Catholic Church's policies on abortion, birth control, the role of women, and same-sex marriage.

African American women in traditional black Christian churches continue to grapple with sexism and a deeply embedded, virulent religious masculinity. These issues were evident in the nineteenth century, nurtured throughout the twentieth century, and gained sustenance and were expanded during the Civil Rights–Black Power Movement. Cheryl Townsend Gilkes aptly describes the "emergent militant black manhood" dominated by baby boomers who are "highly ambivalent about the importance of the church's women's history." The rhetoric of the African American church has always been masculine. However, between 1965 and 1968 black power advocates and the leadership of the Nation of Islam, with their deafening emphasis on "the Black Man" and their "male centered analysis" of the African American condition, thrust black women into a defensive public stance where they felt the need to justify their femininity. As black women have continually fought for their religious and secular rights, they have been accused of being masculine and of emasculating black men. Women such as Ida Wells-Barnett had to defend their right to speak out against lynching and to engage in religious and civil politics. For decades women leaders and their organizations answered these charges and often claimed superiority to black men.

Historically, white America has paid little attention to what black men and women have done as long as their rhetoric and actions do not threaten white institutions and authority and their activities are confined to the black community. All of this changed with the modern Civil Rights–Black Power Movement of the 1950s, '60s, and '70s, and its demands for social justice and economic equality. In defense of its social policies, and to justify the economic and social plight of many black Americans, the U.S. government issued a series of reports targeted to the black family and the historic role of black women in their families and society. The most devastating of all the public documents was the Moynihan Report, which exonerated the government and blamed the black family—in particular the black woman—for the economic and social conditions inherent in the black community. A national debate ensued over the credibility of the report, and African Americans were deeply divided over this issue. The accusation that the black community was dominated by a matriarchal structure inadvertently fueled the existing masculine thrust. The hyper-concerns of young black males heightened their efforts to assert their manhood. Many of these black men disavowed any connection with the black church during the 1960s. However, as they approached middle age, in the '90s, they returned to their religious institutions.

Fired up by the Nation of Islam's Million Man March, numerous local churches developed programs to attract more men. In 1995, Minister Louis Farrakhan, head of the Nation of Islam, organized the march, touted as a day of atonement and healing for African American men. Black women had mixed feelings about the rally. Some believed that it was a reflection of the religious masculinity associated with the Nation of Islam. Others felt that the march was a positive event that presented diverse models of black men and brought attention to black males' plight. Most agreed that a more balanced portrait was needed to offset the widespread and dangerous daily media depictions of black men as criminal, deranged, and irresponsible. While black women generally supported the Million Man March and agreed with the issues presented, they felt that black women also needed to be heard.

In the aftermath of the Million Man March, Philadelphia activists Phile Chionesu, a businesswoman, and Asia Coney, a local housing activist, organized the Million Woman March to address the specific concerns of black women. On October 26, 1997, thousands of women gathered in Philadelphia to hear a diversity of speakers with backgrounds in religion, civil rights, and community affairs assert the need for black women to use their collective power "to solidify family relationships and solve the ills that plague their communities." In addition to traditional concerns of education, drugs, crime, and poverty, the march emphasized personal responsibility and the need for self-love, and focused on human rights abuses against African Americans, a demand for an investigation into the alleged role of the CIA in the crack cocaine trade in black communities, and the need to counteract the negative stereotypes of black women in the media and pop culture.

Speakers included well-known women such as U.S. Rep. Maxine Waters, Winnie Madikizela-Mandela, Dorothy I. Height, and Sister Souljah, as well as men such as Dick Gregory and U.S. Rep. John Conyers Jr. However, for the most part the speakers were unknown black women from diverse walks of life. Religious women such as the noted Chicago civil rights activist Rev. Willie Barrow spoke about the power of black women. Barrow told the gathering, "We are not as divided as we are connected." Chionesu emphasized that a major purpose of the march was to "convince women of African origin that they should recognize their own economic, social and political might to overcome the ills of their communities." She stressed that women do not realize that they possess the power to bring change.

Following the Million Man and Million Woman marches, Bishop T. D. Jakes rose to power and prominence stressing self-help and personal accountability. Jakes provides instructions to help men discover who they are and reclaim their lives, while teaching women how to support men during their transformation. He is the founder of T. D. Jakes Ministries and the pastor of the Potter's House, a nondenominational church in Dallas, Texas, that draws ten thousand or more worshippers to its two Sunday services. Bishop Jakes is a nationally acclaimed pastor, author, and playwright, and his conferences and books, targeted at women, have been extremely successful. Jakes's ministry focuses on issues such as child abuse, domestic violence, unhealthy sexual relationships, and gender roles. His "Man Power" and "Woman, Thou Art Loosed" conferences—now called "God's Leading Ladies"—attract more than fifty thousand attendees.

Cheryl Townsend Gilkes argues, "The black church currently is faced with a serious crisis of gender relations." The black church in the new millennium accepts its responsibility to the new urban, black poor by engaging with issues of poverty, black males, black families, and education of black youth. It recognizes the continuance of institutional and interpersonal racism as dangerous and damaging to the lives of African Americans. Urban black male clergy, in particular, are actively engaged in finding ways to resolve the problems of black male violence, and they provide a diversity of much-needed services to inner-city poor blacks. However, both traditional and mainstream denominations continue to ignore critical issues of gender and sexuality.

Lurking just beneath the surface of many black churches are problems of sex and sexuality, subjects long held as taboo. Hidden deep in old church records and boldly reported on the historic pages of the black press are stories of clergy malfeasance. Clergy malfeasance is being employed as a rubric to define any type of wrongdoing or misconduct by a church official. Misuse or theft of church money or property, rape, sexual abuse of any kind, and sexual harassment are the key issues here. Ministers and priests are held in high regard and are expected to be a cut above the average person in wisdom and morality. Congregations usually trust their religious leaders more than politicians, government officials, and other prominent leaders. However, that trust has been shattered by widespread press reports of clergy malfeasance. Highly publicized and scandalous charges of sexual and financial abuse, exploitation, indictments, and imprisonment of Catholic priests and ministers such as Praise the Lord televangelist Jim Bakker and NBC-USA President Rev. Henry J. Lyons shined the spotlight on patterns of behavior and practices that were previously shrouded in secrecy. Few church officials or members are willing to go on record and air the dirty linen of either their church or their denomination. They prefer to handle such matters privately. Thus, perpetrators have often been exonerated or forgiven for criminal behavior.

What constitutes clergy malfeasance, and how and where does it most often begin and occur? Most Protestant churches require that clergy confine sex to monogamous marriage. Sexual contact outside of marriage—coerced or consensual—between clergy and laity is taboo because it is a violation of church morality. Christian moral teaching as defined in the Bible condemns promiscuity and the sexual violation of minors. Perhaps more than anything else are the formal and informal patterns of patriarchal dominance of denominational structures that have permitted certain behaviors to exist. For example, since male clergy have maintained strict control of the polity, rarely do churches hold clergy accountable for immorality, outright theft, or misuse of funds.

Church authorities may choose to ignore obvious cases of theft, but pedophilia, gender-based violence, and, more recently, sexual harassment are defined in civil law as criminal behavior that may be prosecuted by the state. Women who were reluctant to report sexual harassment, rape, and forced seduction by male clergy are no longer silent. Though their numbers remain small, they are beginning to emerge from the shadows of ecclesiastical dominance. Women who speak out and seek legal redress risk being labeled as traitors, shunned, harassed, and forced out of their churches. Rarely are the male clergy—ministers, priests, and bishops—who are found guilty of these acts ousted, even for the most egregious of charges. Offenders who are tried and convicted in a civil court may be forgiven and appointed as pastors of other churches or, in the case of bishops, assigned to other dioceses and episcopal districts.

Among the earliest and perhaps most scandalous examples of this pattern of clergy malfeasance in a black denomination occurred between the late 1860s and 1884. In 1872, 1876, and 1883 AME Zion Bishop William H. Hillery was charged with acts of intemperance and immorality. In 1876, at the time of Hillery's elevation to the episcopacy, clergy knew of his flagrant violation of church law. However, they voted for him. In 1876, at the Annual Conference in San Francisco, several persons testified to his "drunkenness and other immoral acts. . . . That after being made Bishop, it was sworn to and proven in court, that Bishop Hillery encouraged his ministers in adultery and to defraud each other. That Bishop Hillery was often seen in the streets of San Francisco in a beastly state of drunkenness."

For almost two decades, there was dissatisfaction in the denomination over the publicity and rumors that continued to surface about Hillery's behavior. In 1883 two charges were brought against Hillery for drinking whiskey at a public grocery bar and failing to pay a liquor and grocery bill. In preparation for Hillery's 1883 trial, AME Zion Bishop James Walker Hood traveled to California to investigate the charges. He uncovered a wealth of information. According to Hood, "[T]here had been an accusation against Bishop Hillery for tearing the drawers off a girl, and attempting to commit rape upon the wife of a minister. The matter had been crushed out, and it was intimated to [Hood] that the ministers had smothered 'an accusation that members of the Kentucky Conference had received [pastoral] appointments for a price.' "

In spite of Hillery's well-documented record of malfeasance, the 1883 trial conducted by the Committee of Bishops, ended in a hung jury. Ministers and bishops were concerned about the considerable damage to the denomination's reputation and the loss of members on account of Hillery's notoriety. Hillery's behavior at the 1883 trial convinced Bishop Hood that he was incorrigible. Prior to the trial Hood admonished Hillery and suggested that if he "mended his ways" he would do all he could for him, but Hillery ignored the warning and continued to drink and act irresponsibly. Public outrage over his behavior reached a peak and could no longer be ignored. Given the new accusations, Hood felt that he had no choice but to bring formal charges against Hillery at the 1884 General Conference. The bishops selected "the mildest" of incidents and formulated them into charges.

As the presiding bishop and chair of the Committee of Bishops, authorized by the General Conference to conduct the trial, Hood explained that incidents of Hillery's misconduct included attempts to rape, sexual harassment, misuse of church finances, alcoholism, and possession of armed weapons. Complaints against Hillery began when he was an elder. Although there was indisputable evidence against Bishop Hillery, including the attempted rapes, the prelate over the California episcopal district ignored the accusations and never referred these or any other charges to the Quarterly Conference. Therefore, in accordance with church law, the original and perhaps most damaging charges could only be mentioned, not adjudicated by a Committee of Bishops. Despite confirmation of the attempted rapes and the willingness of the females to testify, no depositions were ever taken. During the 1883 trial there was evidence of intimidation. Hood asserted, "It was hinted, if things did not go to suit Bishop Hillery, there would be several dead bishops. While I was in the chair, Bishop Hillery stood over me in a threatening attitude, and when I asked him to sit down, he paced the floor like a mad bull. . . . Shot guns were thought to be necessary during that trial to protect me and my friends. As we were fighting the battle of the church, we meant to do or die." Though Hood was vilified by some ministers and bishops for questioning Hillery's fitness for the bishopric, Hillery was defrocked and formally removed from his episcopal office by the 1884 AME Zion General Conference.

There is much to be learned from the Hillery affair. The question is, why did it take the AME Zion Church so long to deal with Hillery's malfeasance? The clergy, laity, and general public were aware of his misdeeds. Why did AME Zion leaders continue to either ignore his behavior or argue on his behalf? Moreover, at the General Conference of 1872, the clergy elected Hillery to the office of general secretary— in effect, he was rewarded for his immorality and intemperance. In analyzing the behavior of black- and white-male-dominated polities, when faced with similar circumstances of gross clergy malfeasance, one might ask why it is that, historically, clergy leaders have tended to close ranks around offenders and protect them until a crisis arises. In cases of sexual abuse and theft, is it because the behavior is such an integral part of the fraternity of male clergy that it is acceptable, and exposure of one individual might threaten others who engage in similar behavior? What kind of attitude prevails among those male clergy and ministerial groups who perpetuate a predatory ideology? For example, why did the Catholic Church allow the sexual abuse of children to continue for decades? Their records document a pattern of insidious behavior that was known to the hierarchy. Yet they did absolutely nothing until the victims began to speak out and institute legal action against the denomination. These are difficult questions that cannot be fully addressed here.

It is clear from existing data that the Hillery affair and the Catholic Church scandals are not aberrations. Rather, similar patterns of behavior may be found in other denominations. While the reports of corruption in the church escalated in the early twentieth century, it was not because more clergy were engaging in reprehensible behavior; it was related to the declining status of clergy, and the widespread exposure of malfeasance by the press. By 1920 the number of national black newspapers had soared. The press came of age during an era of rampant corruption and excesses in corporate America and government. Newspapers grew by leaps and bounds as they exposed unethical practices in every area of life. By the 1920s the intellectual leadership in the nation was no longer dominated by ministers, but by college professors, editors, organizational leaders, and professional people, who often deprecated the corruption associated with the church and suggested that what was needed was a better-educated ministry. Crusading journalists avidly wrote about the private lives and lifestyles of prominent black leaders and leaked stories about the inner workings of black organizations and institutions. It was no longer possible to hide unflattering reports about theft, sexual abuse, and, in general, the immoral behavior of so-called Christian leaders.

In the early 1930s, at least fifty years after the Hillery affair, Ralph Matthews, a Baltimore *Afro-American* columnist, asked, "Can We Save the Bishops?" Matthews raised this question during a time when the African Methodist Episcopal Church was having to deal with numerous cases of immorality and malfeasance. In 1930 a bishop was sued for alienation of affections, and another bishop barely escaped imprisonment on charges of selling jobs while holding a political appointment by dying; in 1931 a third bishop was accused of fathering the child of a minor. National exposure of the scandalous behavior of some of its clergy was impacting the AME denomination's image and membership. Many of Matthew's readers—loyal members of black churches—responded pessimistically that in spite of their willingness to unceasingly work on behalf of their religious institutions, they believed "that the church has wallowed so long in its own . . . peculiar heathenism" that reform was unlikely. Others optimistically believed that "with all their deviltry clergy men are not beyond redemption."

Matthews also reported the national scandal associated with a white bishop "whose greed and avarice" were "just as pronounced as that possessed by our own right reverends of the cloth." However, unlike black clergy, white bishops invested church funds in stocks and accepted large sums of money from political parties in exchange for votes. In this manner, they were "able to keep above the more disreputable means of increasing the family larder employed by our pulpit pounders of color." White clergy had broader opportunities to line their pockets and "make grand killings in the more legitimate marts of trade" closed to black clergy. Matthews charged that black bishops resorted to extorting money from the pastors in their districts in exchange for appointments to prosperous churches. If a minister failed to bring a certain amount of money to the conference, he would receive a less desirable appointment. The power to appoint was referred to as "the big whip that prelates use to keep men who dare express their convictions groveling in the dust." Bishops often used those funds for personal purposes. Matthews charged that the AME denomination had been "reduced to a feudal system in which the pulpit pounders are mere tax collectors whose duty it is to squeeze the mob for all the shekels they can get and dump them into the coffers of their overlords." Matthews failed to mention that church women's organizations raised money for missionary work that was sometimes used for other purposes.

By 1930 exploitations in some black denominations had reached an intolerable level. The onset of the Great Depression added to the already existing problems. While Hillery appears to be the only bishop or ecclesiastical leader of that rank ever to be officially removed from office by a black denomination, in every period between 1920 and 2006 there are examples of pastors and other church officers being expelled. In the African Methodist Episcopal Church and the National Baptist Convention, USA, there are several cases of malfeasance that compare to the Hillery affair. At the beginning of the 1930s, the AME Church was overwhelmed by widespread, scandalous reports of immorality and misuse of church funds by its bishops. Albeit for different reasons, in 1931 the white and black secular press took careful notice of the court case in Geneva, Alabama, involving AME Bishop Robert Alexander Grant's relationship with Ollie Glass, a seventeen-year-old clergyman's daughter. According to Glass, in 1930 she was seduced and subsequently impregnated by Bishop Grant. In an effort to hide his infidelity from his wife and the AME Church, Grant signed a contract with the girl and her parents in which he agreed to pay $2,000 in ten equal installments. When Grant failed to pay an installment, Glass and her parents sued for the balance. Bishop Grant was arrested in Birmingham, Alabama, while conducting the AME Church's North Alabama Conference. He was jailed for several hours until the posting of a cash bond for $1,000 to guarantee his appearance at a preliminary hearing.

During the interim, pending the court trial, Bishop Grant was a full participant in the AME Council of Bishops meeting, where he conducted devotional exercises and sang "Down at the Cross." In anticipation of the firestorm at the General Conference—namely, charges of malfeasance against bishops William T. Vernon and Joshua A. Jones—the council, including Bishop Grant, voted against the inclusion of language in the episcopal address stating that "No man who is not sincerely convinced of the necessity of adequate fitness for the gospel ministry should be accepted in this service," and for the deletion of all references to women's ordination. The council opened the way for an AME minister of the New England Conference who was expelled from his church, convicted by a Massachusetts court, and sent to jail for stealing trust funds, to be reinstated as a minister. In other words, the Council of Bishop's favored keeping women out of the fraternity of clergy while supporting men accused of immorality and fiscal malfeasance.

Growing up in the South, Bishop Grant was a student of southern white thought. All-white southern male juries generally believed that black women were loose and lascivious. The common assumption was that no black woman could be raped. More than anything, they resented the interference of white and black northerners and were protective of those blacks who "knew their place." Southern black bishops were well known to the white establishment. As long as they counseled patience and did not press for civil rights or pose a threat to white supremacy, they were tolerated. Bishop Grant, like most black pastors, established relations with whites whom he trusted and called upon for help when necessary. The Alabama white lawyer hired to defend Bishop Grant understood the southern white psyche. Thus, the main points of the defense's argument were that the bishop was a "good Southern Negro and deserved protection" from the attacks of "North-

ern Negroes and newspapers [who] were interfering with the relations" that existed between black and white southerners.

The jury did not consider the most important piece of evidence—
the contract and documents certifying that Bishop Grant had paid part
of the note. The jury found Grant not guilty as charged. The general
opinion of most African Americans in Geneva, Alabama, was that the
jury believed that it was not the responsibility of white men and courts
to protect Ollie Glass if the AME Church, in which her father served
as a pastor and she was a member, did not take action against Bishop
Grant. In other words, it was "colored folk's business." Carl Murphy,
editor of the Baltimore *Afro-American*, asserted that if the "accuser of
Bishop Grant had been white, would any Southern mob have spared
him? Would a Geneva court have set him free? Women pay a price for
being black in the South. Bishop Grant has brought shame and disgrace upon the church he serves, no matter what the criminal courts of
Alabama say."

According to local blacks in and around Geneva, Ollie Glass "sustained an excellent character until the exposure of the alleged relations
with Bishop Grant." During the trial, Glass testified that she was
impregnated by the bishop during the time that he was a guest in her
father's house. The incident occurred when Ollie carried a breakfast
tray to the bishop's bedroom. She said that "he enticed and embraced
her." Rev. James B. Glass stated that when Ollie became pregnant and
identified Bishop Grant as the father, he entered into an agreement
designed to provide support for his daughter and "keep the scandal
from hurting the church." The bishop never denied having sex with
the girl or signing the agreement that was photostated and reprinted in
several newspapers. Prior to the court trial, the trial board of the AME
Church in Mobile, Alabama, found Bishop Grant not guilty. AME
ministers in different locales sent telegrams to Grant congratulating
him "on his vindication" by the courts of Alabama. Irrespective of the
fact that Grant was found not guilty of fathering the child, neither
the leaders of the AME Church nor most of its ministers questioned
the impropriety of a married bishop having sex with a minor and signing a contract to keep the matter secret.

The avalanche of reports about clergy malfeasance, including those
published in the *Allenite*—an AME publication—and the highly publicized and unflattering articles in secular newspapers detailing the
indiscretions of bishops, were embarrassing and a blow to the pride of
the AME laity, who reveled in the heroic tales of Richard Allen and the

founders of the denomination. The five hundred ministers and lay delegates at the 1932 AME General Conference came with an agenda—mainly, to reclaim at least a part of the denomination's prestige. Charges were brought against three bishops: William Tecumseh Vernon, Joshua Jones, and William Decker Johnson. Grant narrowly escaped being suspended—the justification being that he was exonerated of the bastardy charge by an Alabama court. Bishop Johnson was spared as well. However, in spite of the great tumult and disorder that lasted for two hours, the General Conference voted to suspend Vernon and Jones for four years for misuse of conference funds amounting to $17,360 and $15,000 respectively. According to Bishop Reverdy C. Ransom, the most damaging complaints against Vernon were the "subtle references to his known affections for his women church members." Bishop Vernon wept and cried, "Nobody wants me with the reputation of being a thief. I am disgraced for life." To no avail, Bishop Jones appealed to the body to retire, not suspend him. Following his untimely death several months later, the denomination removed the suspension. Since subsequent General Conferences declined to reinstate Vernon, in reality he was defrocked.

At the AME General Conference, Bishop Grant maintained a low profile and declined to speak about the paternity suit. However, his wife "talked freely." She made it clear that even if he were guilty she would support him. Mrs. Grant stated, "[T]he bishop told me all about it, and I told him I believed in him. . . . When these things happen, we should get together and hush them up. They hurt the church. . . . The Glass family who accused him are of extremely low class. Ollie Glass appeared in court sloven and dirty. My husband is modest. He doesn't drink. He is careful and honest in handling of conference moneys. So they tried to put this thing on him and they failed." As for the suspensions of bishops Vernon and Jones, Mrs. Grant asserted, "It was wrong to expose that to the world. Laymen, hearing that a bishop received $17,000 illegally, cannot be persuaded to give money to the church. It will close their pocketbooks. If they got all the bishops who accepted more money for themselves than the law allows, few would be saved."

Many AME leaders agreed with Mrs. Grant that it was dangerous to publicly air the church's dirty linen. However, in defense of her husband, Mrs. Grant proceeded to detail the widespread malfeasance of bishops and confirmed what many already believed. She failed to mention that the bishop did not deny having sex with Ollie Glass, nor did she explain why he agreed to pay the family $2,000 to keep the matter quiet. Typical of clergy wives thrust into the position of defending the infidelity of their husbands, she blamed the women, who she claimed threw themselves at prominent men.

During the early 1940s, Rev. D. V. Jemison, president of the National Baptist Convention, USA, was concerned about racial hatred in America and the proliferation of reports about the "morals and character of ministers and church members alike." He believed that Christians had abandoned the teachings of Jesus Christ. The subject of his annual address was "The Deplorable Conditions of the Visible Church of Our Day, the Cause and the Remedy." In actuality the church was no better or worse off during the 1940s than at any other period of its history; the difference was that religion, religious leaders, and the church as an institution no longer held the same meaning for many black Americans as it had in the nineteenth and early twentieth century.

As African Americans became more educated and urbane, the church was no longer the center of their lives. They were less dependent on their churches for defining who they were. Of utmost importance was the rise of the laity as a force within black denominations. Powerful lay organizations in the AME, Baptist, and AME Zion churches were more critical and demanded greater accountability of their bishops, ministers, and other leaders. As the laity claimed more of the general offices and exercised their voice and vote in their legislative bodies, more clergy were tried and expelled from their churches. The emphasis on civil rights during the period 1950 to 1990 tended to overshadow clergy malfeasance. Although Martin Luther King's infidelity made national and international news, black Americans resented what they perceived as J. Edgar Hoover, the FBI, and the federal government's efforts to besmirch his image and destroy him and the Civil Rights Movement.

In the 1990s and at the beginning of the twenty-first century the spotlight focused more intently on clergy malfeasance. Though sexual harassment of women was not new, it was no longer acceptable after the women's liberation movement. Reference to a woman's anatomy, sexual innuendo, and unwanted touching, feeling, or kissing was defined as sexual harassment. Laws were enacted making sexual harassment illegal and subject to prosecution in a court of law. As more women were ordained and employed as pastors, assistant pastors, and religious educators, they were more frequently in closer contact with bishops, elders, pastors, and other male clergy. Rev. Marcia Y. Riggs argues, "[W]omen stand in, yet outside the gates of the black church; they control relatively autonomous women's departments of the church but their authority in other spheres of the church's life and acceptance in leadership roles must be negotiated and approved by male gatekeepers." Like Riggs, more female ministers are speaking out about the abuse of women by male clergy. For example, Rev. Marcia L. Dyson has detailed the exploitation of women by "preachers that prey."

An excellent example of the sexual harassment and abuse of female ministers is the case of Kansas City, Missouri, Councilwoman Saundra McFadden-Weaver, a former pastor at the Mariah Walker AME Church in Kansas City. Rev. McFadden-Weaver accepted the call to the ministry at age thirteen. She was first ordained at St. Mary's Grand Holy Tabernacle at the age of sixteen, and at seventeen she was licensed by St. Mary's National Council of Churches. In 1987 she received her first pastoral appointment. From 1990 to December 1996 she was a minister at the Mariah Walker AME Church. McFadden-Weaver filed a lawsuit in 1998 claiming that Rev. Ronald Williams, the senior pastor at the church, sexually harassed her and demanded sexual favors in exchange for his support of her ordination. When she complained to Elder Prince Albert Williams (no relation to the pastor), he pressured her to accede to the pastor's wishes. When she refused to do so and continued to lodge complaints against the pastor, Elder Williams attacked her professionally. According to McFadden-Weaver, in 1996 Elder Williams "grabbed and squeezed her breasts" in the church lobby in the presence of other ministers. This was the "final straw." McFadden-Weaver's complaints to Bishop Vernon Byrd about the elder's sexual harassment and the breast-grabbing incident led to her excommunication, "12 days before Christmas."

Following her dismissal from the AME denomination, McFadden-Weaver founded the Community Outreach Christian Fellowship in Kansas City, a nondenominational church. She also determined that no other woman should have to undergo years of physical, psychological, and emotional abuse. In the 1998 lawsuit filed against the AME Church and Elder Williams, she sought actual and punitive damages for sexual harassment and the "intentional failure" of the AME Church to supervise clergy. In December 1999, a jury ruled in favor of McFadden-Weaver and ordered Elder Williams to pay her $15,000 in actual damages and $1 million in punitive damages, and the AME Church to pay her $25,000 in actual damages and $5 million in puni-

tive damages. The punitive damage award against the AME Church
was later reduced to $4 million.

The AME Church and Elder Williams appealed the decision. The
Missouri Court of Appeals reversed the verdict and threw out the $5
million jury award against the AME Church on the grounds that
McFadden-Weaver failed to prove her "claim of intentional failure to
supervise clergy." However, the court sustained the $1 million punitive
damage award against Elder Williams. McFadden-Weaver lacked the
documentary evidence required to prove that the AME Church was
knowledgeable of the dangers presented by Elder Williams and that it
took no action to rectify the situation. In other words, there were no
witnesses and no written evidence. Though she might have verbally
informed Bishop Vernon Byrd, head of the AME's Fifth Episcopal District, or others in the AME hierarchy about the sexual harassment, she
lacked the written evidence required by the court to substantiate her
claims against the denomination. As for Elder Williams, there were
witnesses to the breast-squeezing incident.

The process for redressing the grievances of members and church
personnel is clearly defined in laws set out by each denomination. At
each level there is a process for adjudicating complaints. In the
McFadden-Weaver case, the presiding elder was responsible for handling the charge of sexual harassment brought against the pastor.
When he failed to do his duty and proceeded to employ the same tactics, McFadden-Weaver had no choice but to report the elder's moral
laxity to Bishop Vernon Byrd, leader of the AME Church's Fifth Episcopal District. In an effort to resolve the problem, McFadden-Weaver
exhausted the denomination's judiciary system. Consequentially, she
was fired and expelled from the denomination. The unspoken message
to every AME woman, especially female preachers, was that you must
either accept the sexual overtures and capitulate to the wishes of male
clergy who seek sex in exchange for their support, leave the church, or
risk expulsion. Though it may be common knowledge that a certain
clergyman has a history of sexually harassing women, in most cases,
when women complain or seek legal redress, their character is
assaulted and they are blamed and run out of the church. Thus, many
women suffer in silence, fearing that they will be charged with
besmirching the denomination's name and damaging its image.
Women also fear being shunned and marginalized by family, friends,
and others in their community.

It is possible that McFadden-Weaver's case might have received widespread publicity if it had not been upstaged in 1997 by tales of clerical sex and theft in the National Baptist Convention, USA, and in 2000 by the widely publicized election of Rev. Vashti Murphy McKenzie to the bishopric. The timing of the McKenzie elevation to the episcopacy could not have been more perfect. Coming several months after the December 1999 $5 million judgment against the AME Church in the McFadden-Weaver case, some suspected that Rev. McKenzie was in some ways the beneficiary of the court's decision. Given the internal denominational politics and the real concern that the image of the AME Church might be besmirched by the McFadden-Weaver affair, it is likely that the case had some effect on not only the elevation to the episcopacy of Rev. McKenzie, but also that of Rev. Carolyn Guidry and Rev. Sarah F. Davis.

Second only to the scandals of the Catholic Church were the shocking allegations of theft and adultery by Rev. Henry J. Lyons, president of the 8.5-million-member National Baptist Convention, USA. Following his 1994 election as president of the denomination, Lyons gained national visibility by allying himself with President William Jefferson Clinton, refusing to endorse Nation of Islam leader Louis Farrakhan's Million Man March, preaching "economic self-sufficiency," and founding Trusted Partners, an organization similar to the Promise Keepers. At the height of his success, Rev. Lyons was indicted for grand theft and racketeering, including federal charges of bank fraud and tax evasion. He resigned his position as NBC-USA president and worked out a deal with prosecutors in which he pleaded guilty to five federal charges of tax evasion, fraud, and falsifying information, for which he was sentenced to five years in prison.

In 1997, Lyons's malfeasance was uncovered quite by mistake when his wife discovered that he had secretly purchased a $700,000 home with Bernice Edwards, his mistress and the public relations director for the NBC-USA. Investigation revealed that Lyons used his position to filch millions of dollars to finance his lavish lifestyle. He stole $4 million to purchase luxury homes and jewelry and to support a bevy of mistresses. Set free in 2003, Lyons remained on probation for three years on federal charges and owed $2.5 million in damages. Upon his release from prison he was met by NBC-USA clergy leaders who welcomed him back into the Baptist fold and presented him with his robe and a position as pastor of a prominent church. Though the denomination was well aware of Lyons's much-discussed malfeasance, he was never held accountable for his misdeeds or required to pay back one cent of the money he stole.

At the dawning of the twenty-first century the American public, particularly black Americans, were saddened by the disclosure about another NBC-USA minister and civil rights leader—namely, Rev. Jesse Jackson's adulterous affair with Karin Stanford and his confession that he was the father of her two-year-old daughter. It was no secret that Jackson had an eye for the ladies. For years, rumors abounded about his alleged involvement with other women. However, until the Stanford affair, there was no hard evidence to confirm the reports. As one of the most gifted and astute leaders of his time, Jackson knew that the best thing to do was to admit to his wrongdoing. His public confession came days before the *National Enquirer* planned to break the story. To avoid a racially divisive debate over the rumors and to spare his family, church, and Rainbow/PUSH Coalition activist organization from further embarrassment, Jackson promptly confessed. His confession did not quell the disappointment of countless Americans who held him in high esteem.

News of the Jackson affair came at a time when many Americans were inured to reports of adultery by public figures. As the public was bombarded by news of President Clinton's affair with Monica Lewinsky and reports of his alleged sexual exploits with other women, the Jackson affair simply added fuel to the growing debate about the quality of American leadership. Most agreed that moral and religious leaders, such as Jackson, should be held to a higher standard. Equally disturbing was the fact that Rev. Jackson was engaged in the affair at the time he served as pastoral counsel to President Clinton during the Lewinsky scandal. Jackson not only appeared on television praying with Clinton, but also took Karin Stanford, his pregnant mistress, to the White House. Jackson's numerous black and white supporters hoped that the scandal would not destroy his standing as a preeminent spokesperson for human rights and arguably the most effective voice for African Americans and other people of color. As with the Lyons case, some blacks blamed Jackson's problems on a Republican conspiracy to destroy black leaders. The Jackson scandal broke during the divisive debate over whether or not George W. Bush and the Republicans had used illegal methods to secure the presidential election in 2000.

African Americans held mixed views about whether or not Jackson could rebound from the scandal. George Wake, a Philadelphia businessman, predicted that African Americans would be "less forgiving of Jackson." Numerous black pastors, such as Rev. Simms of the Morris Brown AME Church in North Philadelphia, counseled forgiveness. Referencing the Bible, Simms stated, "Let those without sin cast the first stone." Most African Americans were troubled by Jackson's affair with Stanford and recognized it as "spiritual hypocrisy," but they were disinclined to judge him on the basis of a single mistake.

Within days of his confession, Jesse Jackson—the quintessential politician—in an effort to retain his leadership perch and the media attention that had been critical to his rise as a national social and political leader, entreated prominent ministers and public officials to come and speak on his behalf at the Canaan Baptist Church of Christ in Harlem. As the pastor of Canaan Baptist, Rev. Wyatt Tee Walker agreed to the event with the understanding that it would be a "Service of Penance" on Jackson's behalf. Walker could not attend the event, and was extremely concerned that in his absence Jackson would use it for personal purposes to boost his image. Walker informed Jackson that only clergy should speak, and that Jackson should not speak "unless you made some kind of statement that was an apology for your behavior and ask for prayers and understanding." Ignoring Walker's wishes, Jackson turned the event into a rally and media event. Walker was embarrassed and felt betrayed by Jackson when he saw the live broadcast. He asserted that the event "became a circus with photographers standing on the pews in our Sanctuary. The live broadcast reenforced the image, in the general community, that people of African ancestry have little sense of morality." Walker was particularly concerned about the statements made by some politicians. He stated, "How crass of Charlie Rangel, in light of your [Jackson's] fathering a child outside of your marriage, declaring again and again from my pulpit, *Get over it!* My personal credibility and that of my Church has been terribly scarred by all that transpired." Making the connection between Jesse Jackson's malfeasance and that of Rev. Henry Lyons, Walker claimed that Jackson "created [as] much pain for all clergy persons as did Henry Lyons."

These examples of clergy malfeasance at the highest levels of church leadership are mere microcosms of the behavior of mostly male clergy for almost a century and a half. Nor should it be assumed that such acts of immorality are limited to black clergy. As illustrated in the recent explosive and titillating disclosures about the widespread sexual abuse of children—mainly boys—by mostly white Catholic priests, immorality has no color, and is not restricted to a particular denomination. However, the concern here is with gender relations and clergy malfeasance in the African American church. Also, there is similarity between the attitudes as well as the ways in which black and white male clergy leaders have handled incidents of clergy malfeasance. The Catholic Church was well aware of the extensive sexual abuse prevalent in innumerable parishes, but showed little interest in addressing the widespread documented immoral behavior of its priests. Moreover, as in most black denominations, Catholic bishops ignored the behavior and took no action until it was publicized and threatened to damage the image of the church. They simply reassigned priests to other parishes. It was only when the victims determined that enough was enough, and that it was time to speak out about the long-standing abuse of parishioners by spiritual leaders, that any action was taken. Ironically, many white parishes, like their black counterparts, chose to support their priests and bishops and were reluctant to remove an individual who they felt met most of their needs.

While the Catholic Church grapples with charges of pedophilia and homosexuality and seeks ways to resolve its problems and heal the open wounds caused by the breach in its code of ethics by rogue priests and bishops, black churches have buried their heads in the sand and refused to acknowledge the existence of either sexism or homosexuality in their midst. Kelly Brown Douglas, an Episcopal priest and womanist theologian, argues that there is a relationship between homophobia and heterosexism in the African American community, and that one reason why it refuses to acknowledge sexism is that it would lead to a discussion of black sexuality and resurrect the historical stereotypes about African Americans. A common expression among blacks is that "Homosexuality is a White thing." Of course, there is no logic to this assertion, as anthropologists have found evidence of homosexuality in all human cultures, including Africa. And black lesbians and gay men have always been a part of the black community and represented in its leadership. Others argue that the predominance of black female-headed households encourages the development of homosexuality in black males.

The denial of homosexuality in the black community and its institutions is related to a number of factors. Homosexuality is considered a threat to the black family and the image of black manhood, and a hindrance to racial progress. During slavery, in order to justify the widespread sexual abuse of black women by white men, and to obfuscate and prevent sexual liaisons between white women and black men, whites created an image of black men and women as sexually deviant. Myths about black deviance have been widely disseminated in literature, popular culture, and the broadcast and print media. It has been endlessly perpetuated and is now considered dogma. The rise of the white evangelical right and its support of the Republican Party's anti-gay message strengthen the resolve of the black middle- and upper-class church and community leaders to steer clear of issues dealing with homosexuality and instead promote values stressing the importance of marriage and the family.

In 2003 the African Methodist Episcopal Church felt compelled to make clear the denomination's position on ordaining gay clergy. In an article titled "God Have Mercy on His Church," *USA Today* stated that the AME Church supported the ordination of "openly gay clergy." The Council of Bishops, including Bishop Vashti Murphy McKenzie, responded by publishing an announcement on the AME Church's official website and a one-page statement in the *AME Church Review*, and sending a pastoral letter to be read in all AME churches denying the report. The announcement stated that the Council of Bishops held a special session on August 7, 2003, in Dallas, Texas, and noted "with indignation and great offense, the published statement appearing in . . . *USA Today* that the AME Church ordains openly gay clergy. This statement is incorrect. The Council of Bishops has ruled and affirmed on several occasions—and the AME Church through position papers and public statements—that the Church does not support the ordination of openly gay clergy. To do so is to take action contrary to our theological interpretation of the scriptures."

As the issue of gay marriage became a national matter, in 2004 dozens of black pastors rallied to protest legalizing such unions. Many black clergy were outraged by the gay rights movement's comparison of their struggle with that of black Americans for racial equality. A delegation of thirty pastors presented a declaration to the Georgia legislature stating that same-sex marriage was not a civil right, and that marriage between a woman and a man was required for raising children. Speaking before a crowd of about 250, Bishop William Shields of the Hopewell Baptist Church crystalized the issue by stating that gay marriage was "a threat to who we are and what we stand for." Most black religious and community leaders believe that the continuance of female-headed households, out-of-wedlock children, criminal behavior, and homosexuality stigmatizes black Americans and prevents the race from achieving social acceptability and a level of normalcy acceptable to white America. This argument negates the existence of systemic racism and suggests that those blacks who have not been able to escape poverty are somehow at fault for not adhering to societal norms.

Whether or not black churches and communities are more homophobic than their white counterparts is debatable. The problem is that homosexuality is real, and will not disappear. It is a fallacy to blame black homosexuality on whites and to suggest that individuals can choose to be either gay or straight. The greater problem for African American church and community institutions is that some black homosexuals are no longer content to remain in the closet. Most black churches have no problem with accepting lesbians and gay men as long as they pretend that they are heterosexual and do not flaunt their homosexuality. Women who feel called to preach have always been suspected of being lesbian, particularly if they are single. And, even if they are not, in some instances they have been labeled as such, simply because they sought a position designated for black males.

When Rev. Irene Monroe made the decision to train for the ministry, she decided that since she had been raised in the African American church and intended to be a black Baptist minister, the best place to go was a black seminary. She applied to Howard University's Divinity School and the Interdenominational Theological Center in Atlanta. Monroe was rejected by both institutions because she was a lesbian. The ITC contacted Monroe regarding her application, in particular her reference to being "a born-again Black lesbian Christian." The admission's committee was impressed with Monroe's academic record and would admit her if she "would agree to be closeted in the program." Monroe commented that she didn't believe that she would be the only lesbian at ITC. She was informed that if she revealed her sexuality, she would receive no support from students or faculty and would not be accepted for field placement by any church in Atlanta. When Monroe asked, "What about King's church, what about Ebenezer Baptist Church," the female official responded, "Girl, please!"

Rejected by the black seminaries, Irene Monroe went on to graduate from the Union Theological Seminary and pursue a PhD at the Harvard Divinity School. While at the seminary, she served as pastor of several urban black Presbyterian churches. According to Monroe, race was a major factor in her acquisition of these appointments. "Nobody—Black or white—wants to pastor them." The few black men who manage to complete the Presbyterian ordination process receive the choicest appointments, and white ministers are not wanted in black churches. Thus, as in other denominations, black women are sent to the "struggling, dying Presbyterian Churches."

Though there are black ministers who have become outspoken supporters of gay people, for years Rev. Jesse Jackson has been the best-known pro-gay black clergyman. Among the African American religious leaders—ministers, scholars, and church administrators representing diverse denominations—who are leading in the efforts to integrate lesbians, gay men, bisexuals, and transgendered people into their congregations, seminars, and universities are James A. Forbes Jr., James H. Cone, Jacquelyn Grant, Cornel West, Michael Eric Dyson, M. Shawn Copeland, Yvonne V. Delk, Emilie M. Townes, Mozella G. Mitchell, Irene Monroe, Renee L. Hill, Marjorie Bowens-Wheatley, and Edwin C. Sanders II. These individuals feel that the oppression of any group of people has no place in black church or religious institutions, which represent the epitome of the centuries-long struggle of African Americans for freedom.

In recent years the Christian right has courted black conservatives and encouraged them to mount anti-gay political campaigns. For example, in the presidential election of 2004, President George W. Bush pursued black pastors, dangled faith-based grants before them, and wherever possible took advantage of photo opportunities with ministers of prominent churches who often competed for the publicity that came with a presidential visit. In the black community it is a symbol of power to have your pastor appear on television and be featured with the president on the front page of a city's major mainstream publication. For the minister, it could mean an expansion of church membership, greater recognition in one's denomination and community, and an opportunity to gain federal funding. The stakes are high for those who are outspoken about the so-called evil of homosexuality.

Like Peter Gomes, the noted scholar and professor of Christian morals and minister of Memorial Chapel at Harvard University, many black religious leaders believe that it will take several decades for the African American church and community to even consider embracing homosexuality. Most black churches will not even tolerate discourse on the issue. Meanwhile, there are clergy activists who have not only lent their names to the cause but are also organizing ministries to homosexuals. Rev. A. Cecil Williams of San Francisco's Glide Memorial Church pioneered in the launching of a support movement for gay men and lesbians in 1962. During the 1970s, Troy Perry, a gay Pentecostal minister in Los Angeles, founded the first Christian denomination for homosexuals, the Universal Fellowship of Metropolitan Community Churches. Since that time other churches have been founded for lesbians and gays. Although relatively few in number, these institutions represent safe harbors for black women and men seeking affirmation of their lives, relationships, and families.

The majority of black denominations have steadfastly refused to acknowledge homosexuals and homosexuality and have for many years steered clear of discussions on HIV/AIDS. In July 2000, the Black Church Initiative, a multicultural program of the Religious Coalition for Reproductive Choice, sponsored a three-day National Black Religious Summit on sexuality at the Howard University School of Divinity. In attendance were several hundred church leaders, laity, health professionals, and young people. Ministers spoke openly about sex and acknowledged that the issue had been ignored. Rev. Susan Newman, a minister at the First Baptist Church in Atlanta, asserted, "What most of us were taught about sex by our parents and ministers was 'Keep your dress down, keep your pants up, and don't bring any babies home.' " Prior to the twenty-first century, preaching about abortion, safe sex, and HIV/AIDS was taboo in black churches. However, in 1999, 80 percent of the five hundred black pastors surveyed agreed that these issues should be addressed by churches.

In 2000 black Americans accounted for almost 50 percent of the AIDS cases in the United States. In 2006 Rev. Derrick Harkins, pastor of the historic Nineteenth Street Baptist Church in Washington, D.C., said that during the last decade and a half he has buried people who had AIDS. He felt that the growing number of AIDS victims and the rise in teen pregnancy was causing black ministers to speak out. A report covering the years 2001 to 2006 stated that one in every twenty of the District of Columbia's residents was infected with HIV, and 80 percent of the identified infections were in African American men, women, and children. Nine out of ten of the infected were black women. In 2008 the face of AIDS is black and primarily female. Approaching the end of the first decade of the twenty-first century, AIDS is the number one killer of black women in the United States between the ages of twenty-five and thirty-four. The discourse over issues of sex and sexuality, HIV and AIDS, and same-sex marriage is not likely to end in the near future. But the most hopeful sign is that at least these issues are finally in the open and are being discussed by black religious leaders.

It is difficult to predict what the twenty-first century holds for black women and their churches. But if the past is a predictor of the future, then we can expect black women to continue in their support of their churches and ministers. In an ethnographic study of the role of spirituality in the lives of African American women in northeastern North Carolina, a poor and rural southern area, Marla F. Frederick said, "In spite of the problems within the church, women not only remain members, they worship, participate, teach Sunday school, usher on the ushers' board, give their tithe, form community outreaches, and in a large sense undergird the entire operation of the church." Irrespective of geographic location, this is probably typical of a number of black churches. However, changing patterns of religious affiliation indicate a growing dissatisfaction with the leadership of traditional black denominations. The shift appears to be driven by the need for a more authentically black religious ritual as well as for churches that can serve the multiple needs of black communities. The growth of nondenominational and mega-churches, as well as the expanding membership of Pentecostal/Holiness and Islamic churches, and the rise of the New Age and other religious movements attracting the attention of black women and men, suggests the changes that are taking place at the beginning of the twenty-first century.

Historically, African American women have been sustained by their faith in God and their ability to prevail. They have been imbued with a hope that surpasses time. At the end of the nineteenth century, Carrie M. Green, an obscure CME woman, wrote, "Hope is something unseen. . . . When all else fails us, hope still abides with us. Reasonable hope is endowed with a vigorous principle; it sets the head and heart to work and animates one to do his utmost, and thus by perpetually pushing and assuring, it puts a difficulty out of countenance and makes a seeming impossibility give way."

It may be that womanist theologian Jamie Phelps reflects the historical pragmatism and the hope that will continue to sustain black women of all religious persuasions in the twenty-first century. Phelps states, "I've watched changes and growth over 40 years, and I'm realistic. We do not have a perfect church, nor a perfect society. But I have lived long enough that I believe, in God's own time, we are moving forward, not backward." One hopes that Phelps is right. However, the disappearance of the old black women's network of religious and secular organizations that focused church women on the problems of oppressed people not only in the United States but in Africa and other far-flung places has created a void, and the expansion and diversification of the black leadership in the latter part of the twentieth century diminished the significance of the black minister in the larger society. But decentralization of black denominations strengthened the position of the local minister. Thus, church women now focus more intently on the internal issues related to their local churches and communities.

In the interim, as change occurs, albeit at a slow pace, black women must continue to hold their institutions and leaders accountable and demand that women be elevated in the polity and be treated fairly as clergy and parishioners, that they no longer be relegated to just being the "backbone" of the church, but also serve as the head. They must continue to challenge church bureaucrats and theological dogma that deem them less than men and that relegate them to service but exclude them from leadership. They must raise their voices and demand justice for those whose voices have been silenced by sexism, racism, and classism—in the church and in society. Their hope of complete freedom and equality—an aspiration in slavery and through Jim Crow—persists into the twenty-first century.

Acknowledgments

WRITING THIS BOOK, I have traversed centuries, moved into unimaginable worlds, delved into people's lives, and immersed myself in areas of darkness and light that enlightened me in ways difficult to describe. Twenty years ago, if I had fully known the sacrifices I would have to make and the inordinate time it would require to reconstruct the history of so many organizations, lives, and worlds, I might not have undertaken such a huge project. Having done so, I am immensely grateful for the experience and the opportunity to grow in ways that I could not have perceived.

This book is based on extensive research in archival collections, religious and secular periodicals and newspapers, widely scattered and unorganized denominational church records, the papers of ecumenical organizations, the manuscript census, organizational and other little-known histories, and interviews with church women and their descendants. The papers and correspondence of relatively few black women leaders have been collected and placed in archives. In 1987 I undertook a survey of national libraries and archives. The survey revealed that few repositories had developed finding aids for black women, or religion, and that the records of most black denominations, religious women, and their organizations were either uncollected or scattered in a variety of places. The belfries and basements of black churches, colleges, religious and secular organizations' headquarters, and the basements and attics of private homes are treasure troves of information.

Identifying women leaders and their organizational work required a painstaking reconstruction of their lives and institutions that involved a major effort of systematically reading and indexing at least thirty or more newspapers and periodicals, organizational proceedings, and library and microfilm clipping files covering two centuries of African American life and culture. Obituaries, autobiographical notes, personal correspondence, and newspaper articles were important sources—sometimes the only sources—of information about a woman, an event, and the activities of an organization. Long before I conceived the idea of writing a history of African American women and religion, I had begun the search for women and their organizations, carefully constructing biographical and organizational files of miscellaneous women, their clubs, and activities in all periods of time. By 1987 I had collected a wealth of information about black women in virtually every period and organization. By 1990 I had a clear understanding of the individuals and associations, newspapers and periodicals, primary and secondary sources, and archival collections that required research.

The earlier survey of archives and libraries paid large dividends, in that many archival administrators recognized the need to collect the records of black religious organizations and black women at the local and national levels, and to identify and develop finding aids for data on women in existing collections. The invaluable organizational minutes of ecumenical and women's organizations like Church Women United, the Federal Council of the Churches of Christ, the Woman's Missionary Union, and the National Association of Colored Women became available after 1995. These and many more collections made it possible to document the interactions and political activism of black and white women in the interracial movement. The growing collections of black religious and secular newspapers and periodicals available on microfilm aided in the reconstruction of black church biography and history.

I received exceptional support from the Lilly Endowment and the Ford Foundation for the research and writing of this book. During the late 1980s, Lilly funded a planning grant to determine whether or not there were "enough data" to write a history of black women and religion. Satisfied by the findings, Lilly funded the bulk of the research conducted during the 1990s. The Ford Foundation provided generous support for research on women in the interracial movement. At the writing stage, I received a National Endowment for the Humanities and Rockefeller Foundation Fellowship from the National Humanities Center, and a Lilly Endowment grant that provided me an absolutely golden year of writing in North Carolina at the National Humanities Center. Lilly Endowment and Ford Foundation grants supported a one-year fellowship at Princeton University's Center for the Study of Religion. I also received a modest research travel grant from the Episcopal Women's Research Project. Temple University provided invaluable space for the Black Women and the Church Project.

I owe a huge debt of gratitude to Jacqui Burton, the Lilly Endowment program officer who suggested that I write a history of African

American women and religion, and to C. Eric Lincoln (deceased), Lawrence H. Mamiya, Vincent Harding, AME Bishop John Hurst Adams, Delores Carpenter, Larry Doss, and other members of the Lilly Endowment panel of religious scholars who supported the project from the beginning. Lilly Endowment Vice President Craig Dykstra and program officers Jacqui Burton, Sister Jeanne Knoerle, SP, and Jean Smith provided encouragement and unstinting support at every stage of this monumental project. Were it not for their belief in the project and me, and the Lilly Endowment's generous support of the total project, this book would not have seen the light of day. Program director Constance Buchanan and President Susan V. Berresford were my angels at the Ford Foundation who recognized the significance of religious women to the twentieth-century interracial movement and generously supported the research to unearth that data.

The onsite research encompassed archives and special collections in innumerable colleges, universities, seminaries, and special collections in public libraries, as well as state and federal archives, private homes, churches, and organizational headquarters. Literally hundreds of staff at the Fisk University Library's Special Collection; Spelman College, Hampton University, Johnson C. Smith University Library; Carnegie Library and the Heritage Hall, Livingstone College; Tuskegee University Archives, Hollis Burke Frissell Library; Payne Theological Seminary, Wilberforce University in Xenia, Ohio; Barber Scotia College Library; the Urban Archives and Paley Library at Temple University; Trevor Arnett Library, Atlanta University Special Collection; the Shaw University Library; Rutgers University's Alexander Library; the Presbyterian Historical Society; the General Commission on Archives and History of the United Methodist Church at Drew University; the Virginia State Archives; the Tennessee State Archives; the American Baptist Center in Valley Forge, Pennsylvania; the Samuel Colgate Historical Library in Rochester, New York; the Southern Baptist Historical Library and Archives in Nashville; Virginia Union University in Richmond; the AME Church Headquarters in Washington, D.C.; the AME Sunday School Union in Nashville, Tennessee; the Mother Bethel AME Church Historical Commission in Philadelphia; the Christian Methodist Episcopal Church Archives in Memphis, Tennessee; the Southern Historical Collection, University of North Carolina Library; the Western Reserve Historical Society, Kelvin Smith Library, Case Western Reserve University; the National Archives for Black Women's History, Mary McLeod Bethune

Council House National Historical Site in Washington, D.C.; the Moorland-Spingarn Research Center, Howard University; the Amistad Research Center, Tulane University; the Virginia State University Johnston Memorial Library; the Avery Research Center for African American History and Culture, College of Charleston; the Schomburg Center for Research in Black Culture, New York City Public Library; the Boston Public Library; the Arthur and Elizabeth Schlesinger Library, Radcliffe College; and the World Methodist Council Headquarters in New York contributed in various ways to this history.

Among the many institutions that responded to requests for interlibrary loans of microfilm, provided generous assistance, and facilitated numerous requests for documents and articles were the Young Women's Christian Association Papers, Sophia Smith Collection at Smith College; the National Archives; Manuscripts Division, Library of Congress; the Chicago Historical Society; the Indiana Historical Society; the Virginia Historical Society; the Virginia Baptist Historical Society; the Balch Institute Library; William Perkins Library, Duke University Library; the University Archives, Van Pelt Library, University of Pennsylvania; the Historical Society of Pennsylvania; the Library Company; the University of Louisville Archives and Records Center; the University of South Carolina; the Memphis Historical Society; the Chicago Historical Society; the Oblate Sisters of Providence Manuscript Collection; the Sisters of the Holy Family Manuscript Collection; the Pentecostal Assemblies of the World, Inc.; the National Council of Churches of Christ; the Yale University Divinity School Library; the Lutheran Theological Seminary; the New York Theological Seminary; the Union Theological Seminary; the American Theological Seminary; the Garrett Evangelical Seminary; the General Theological Seminary; the Eastern Baptist Theological Seminary; the Interdenominational Theological Center; the Summit, New Jersey, Public Library; the New York City Public Library; and the Moody Bible Institute.

It is not possible to list the names of all of the persons who facilitated the research, sent articles, pamphlets, and books and recommended sources to consult. Thanks to Rev. Jeffrey N. Leath, Ruby C. Boyd, Randall Burkett, Dennis C. Dickerson, Rebecca Hankins, Joyce Howard, Kenneth E. Rowe, Jocelyn Rubinetti, Harold Dean Trulear, Louise Roundtree, Uvelia S. A. Bowen, Rev. Willie Aldrich, Elizabeth Mosby, Marvin Delaney, Jessie Carney Smith, Beth Howse, Janet Sims

Wood, Donna Wells, Thomas Battle, Phillip Lapsansky, Wilma Gibbs, Lucius Edwards, William N. Flemister Sr., Minnie Clayton, Bishop Clyde Williams, Mamie Williams, Anice Johnson Ward, Diana Lachatanere, Florence Moody, Sherry Dupree, Elder Minerva Bell, Rev. Lawrence L. Reddick, Cynthia Mason, Rev. Cyprian Davis, Karen Watson, Laura Thomas, and Margaret Jerrido.

I will never be able to thank all of the persons who contributed in some way to this project. Special thanks especially to Fatima Aliu and Danielle Smallcomb for their exceptional research. As research assistants they spent years reading newspapers and church minutes on microfilm and microfiche, digging through dusty records in church basements, homes of senior citizens, and southern black colleges, painstakingly clipping and filing newspaper and magazine articles, filing interlibrary loan requests, and traveling and living in hotels, motels, and dormitories throughout the United States. Though Debbie Skoh's time as a research assistant was brief, it was invaluable to this undertaking. Her careful research and wonderful insights about women in the AME Zion Church and her meticulous handling of the transcription of the sermons of Rev. Florence Spearing Randolph were much appreciated. Patricia Parkman's research on Presbyterian and Episcopalian women was very helpful. Richard Woodland, Joanne Hawes Speakes, and Marie McCain supported this work in a myriad of ways. Among the numerous Temple University undergraduate students who read, copied, clipped, and mounted articles from diverse newspapers and periodicals were Duana Faust, Tonya Eason, Auraneittia Durham, Rochele Felder, Michael Duson, Keya Epps, Laishon A. Gooding, Tammi R. Hawes, Angela Johnson, Benedict Thomas, and Lauren Wells.

Several scholars read and commented on chapters in the book. My colleagues Kenneth Kusmer, Harvey Neptune, and Teshale Tibebu graciously consented to read a chapter, and Genna Rae McNeil, Peter Paris, Patricia Sullivan, Judith Weisenfeld, and V. P. Franklin took time out of their busy schedules to read and comment on at least two or more chapters. My colleague Elizabeth Varon not only read four chapters but also provided sage advice and much-needed encouragement on days when I felt down and discouraged. Each of these scholars raised critical questions and helped to bring clarity to the book. My literary agents Charlotte Sheedy and Neeti Madan prodded me to write this book. My wonderful editor at Knopf, Victoria Wilson, immediately recognized the significance of this work and continued to encourage me to produce a book that was accessible not only to scholars but also to a broad audience.

I am always thankful for the love and support of my family, Joseph T. Collier Jr., Thelma Collier, Charles Gary Collier, Carlton Collier, Nathaniel Collier, and Ann Collier. Second only to family are the friends who have provided moral support and encouragement when I most needed it, especially V. P. Franklin, Sharon Harley, Kenneth Kusmer, John Hope Franklin (deceased), Giles Wright (deceased), Cheryl Townsend Gilkes, Patricia Sullivan, Gloria Dickinson (deceased), James Turner, Rosalyn Terborg Penn, and Bettye Gardner.

My husband, Charles Thomas, was the single most important catalyst that spurred me to write this work. His unflagging support, constant questions, and unique insights have been a tremendous help to me. To keep me abreast of contemporary religious issues, events, and personalities for a period lasting over a decade, he has consistently read a battery of newspapers and magazines and clipped articles, book reviews, obituaries, and anything else that he thought important to this history. Charles has always been there for me, and for this I am immensely grateful.

Abbreviations

ABHMS	American Baptist Home Mission Society
ABCFM	American Board of Commissioners for Foreign Missions
ACFMC	Africa Committee of the Foreign Missions Conference of North America
AME	African Methodist Episcopal Church
AME-PHFMB	African Methodist Episcopal Church Parent Home and Foreign Missions Board
AME-WHFMS	African Methodist Episcopal Church Women's Home and Foreign Missionary Society
AME-WMMS	African Methodist Episcopal Church Woman's Mite Missionary Society
AME-WMS	African Methodist Episcopal Church Women's Missionary Society
AME-WPMMS	African Methodist Episcopal Church Woman's Parent Mite Missionary Society
AME ZION	African Methodist Episcopal Zion Church
AMEZ-WHFMS	African Methodist Episcopal Zion Church Woman's Home and Foreign Missionary Society
ANP	American Negro Press
ASWPL	Association of Southern Women for the Prevention of Lynching
AWSA	American Woman's Suffrage Association
BCH-NHS	Bethune Council House, National Historical Site
BEDC	Black Economic Development Conference
CAB-J	Claude A. Barnett Papers, Series J
CCC	Civilian Conservation Corps
CME	Colored Methodist Episcopal Church
CME-WMS	Colored Methodist Episcopal Church Woman's Missionary Society
CIC	Commission on Interracial Cooperation
CICWC	Commission on Interracial Cooperation Women's Committee
CNDA	Chicago and Northern District Association
COFO	Council of Federated Organizations
COGIC	Church of God in Christ
CORE	Congress of Racial Equality
COWM	Commission on Women in Ministry
CWCRR	Church Women's Committee on Race Relations
CWHM	Council of Women for Home Missions
CWU	Church Women United

CWU-GCAH	Church Women United Collection, General Commission on Archives and History
DRR	Department of Race Relations
FABC	First African Baptist Church
FCC	Federal Council of the Churches of Christ in America
FCC-CWCRR:PHS	Church Women's Committee on Race Relations Collection, Presbyterian Historical Society
FCC-DRR:PHS	Department of Race Relations Collection, Presbyterian Historical Society
FCC-WCC	Women's Cooperating Commission
FCNC	Fraternal Council of Negro Churches
FSRC	Florence Spearing Randolph Collection
ICWDR	International Council of Women of the Darker Races
LC	Library of Congress
LCFC-WRHS	Lethia Cousins Fleming Collection, Western Reserve Historical Society
MCT-LC	Mary Church Terrell Collection, Library of Congress
ME-WHFMS	Methodist Episcopal Church Women's Home and Foreign Missionary Society
ME-WHMS	Methodist Episcopal Church Woman's Home Missionary Society
MECS	Woman's Missionary Council of the Methodist Episcopal Church, South
NAACP	National Association for the Advancement of Colored People
NACGN	National Association of Colored Graduate Nurses
NACRW	National Association of Colored Republican Women
NACW	National Association of Colored Women
NAWSA	National American Woman Suffrage Association
NBC	National Baptist Convention
NBCA	National Baptist Convention of America (Unincorporated)
NBC-USA	National Baptist Convention, USA, Inc.
NBSC	National Black Sisters' Conference
NCBC	National Conference of Black Churchmen
NCC	National Council of the Churches of Christ in the USA
NCCW	National Council of Catholic Women
NCFCW	National Council of Federated Church Women
NCJW	National Council of Jewish Women
NCNW	National Council of Negro Women
NFAAW	National Federation of Afro-American Women
NHB-LC	Nannie Helen Burroughs Collection, Library of Congress
NIRA	National Industrial Recovery Act
NLCRW	National League of Colored Republican Women
NLPCW	National League for the Protection of Colored Women
NUC-AU	Neighborhood Union Collection, Atlanta University
NUL	National Urban League
NWSA	National Woman Suffrage Association
NYA	National Youth Administration

UBC Union Baptist Church
UNIA United Negro Improvement Association
UPW United Presbyterian Women
URL-SBHL Una Roberts Lawrence Collection, Southern Baptist Historical Library
WC Woman's Convention
WCFMC Women's Committee of the Foreign Missions Conference
WCMC Woman's Connectional Missionary Council
WCTU Woman's Christian Temperance Union
WICS Women in Community Service
WILPF Women's International League for Peace and Freedom
WIMS Wednesdays in Mississippi
WMU Woman's Missionary Union
WMS Women's Missionary Society
WPC Women's Political Council
WSCS Women's Society of Christian Service
YMCA Young Men's Christian Association
YWCA Young Women's Christian Association

Notes

Prologue

xvi *In 1888 she became:* Ellen McKenzie Lawson and Marlene D. Merrill, *The Three Sarahs: Documents of Antebellum Black College Women* (New York: Edwin Mellen Press, 1984), 149–67, 176–82.

xvii *Many of the women:* Paula Giddings, *When and Where I Enter: The Impact of Black Women on Race and Sex in America* (New York: Morrow, 1984); Darlene Clark Hine and Kathleen Thompson, *A Shining Thread of Hope: The History of Black Women in America* (New York: Broadway Books, 1998). Each of these works emphasizes traditional figures and well-known themes. Little attention is paid to religion, and though Giddings mentions the interracial movement, Hine and Thompson do not.

xvii *"It was the conviction":* Virginia Simmons Nyabonga, "The Twentieth Century Woman," *AME Church Review* 68:174 (October 1952): 64.

xviii *Expanding far beyond:* Ruth Bogin and James Loewenberg, *Black Women in Nineteenth Century American Life* (University Park, Pa.: Pennsylvania State University Press, 1976), 7.

xviii *Scholarly work:* Deborah Gray White, *Too Heavy a Load: Black Women in Defense of Themselves* (New York: Norton, 1999). White's study of black club women utilizes five national women's organizations to examine black women's conflict between feminism and nationalism. Discussing class and gender tensions inherent in women's clubs, White deconstructs monolithic notions of a unified "black womanhood." Exploring what it meant to be a club woman, scholars such as White have centered their work on the NACW and several secular women's organizations. Concentrating exclusively on aspects of the association's early history, few studies discern or explore the NACW's relationship to women's religious organizations and its connections to a broader national network of white and black organizations. This is critically important for analyzing the ways in which NACW leaders networked in black and white organizations, at the local and national levels, to create a unique power base and to implement the NACW's broad agenda. In addition to White's examination of feminism as a major theme in the NACW's history, numerous scholars reference the NACW and provide brief discussions of the organization's early history. Among the most important studies of the NACW are Tullia Kay Brown Hamilton, "The National Association of Colored Women, 1896–1920" (PhD diss., Emory University, 1978); Stephanie F. Shaw, "Black Club Women and the Creation of the National Association of Colored Women," in *"We Specialize in the Wholly Impossible": A Reader in Black Women's History*, ed. Darlene Clark Hine, Wilma King, and Linda Reed (Brooklyn, NY: Carlson Publishing, 1995), 433–47.

xviii *or, more recently:* Evelyn Brooks Higginbotham, *Righteous Discontent: The Women's Movement in the Black Baptist Church, 1880–1920* (Boston: Harvard University

Press, 1993); Jualynne E. Dodson, *Engendering Church: Women, Power, and the A.M.E. Church* (Lanham, Md.: Rowman and Littlefield Publishers, Inc., 2002); Bishop Othal Hawthorne Lakey and Betty Beene Stephens, *God in My Mama's House: The Women's Movement in the CME Church* (Memphis: C.M.E. Publishing House, 1994). These three book-length studies examine women's participation in the National Baptist Convention, AME, and CME churches. Each of these works stresses the central importance of religious women's organizations. Higginbotham discusses the history of the Woman's Convention during the first two decades of its existence. In a sociological study, Dodson examines how women acquired and utilized power within the AME Church. Although written for a lay audience, in *God in My Mama's House* Lakey and Stephens provide insight into the leadership roles of women in the CME Church.

xix *Bishop Othal Hawthorne Lakey:* Lakey and Stephens, *God in My Mama's House.*

xix *In the recently published:* Anthea Butler, *Women in the Church of God in Christ: Making a Sanctified World* (Chapel Hill: University of North Carolina Press, 2007).

xxi *Imbued by ideas:* Martin Summers, *Manliness and Its Discontents: The Black Middle Class and the Transformation of Masculinity, 1900–1930* (Chapel Hill: University of North Carolina Press, 2004). An excellent source for examining the struggle between black men and women over the meaning of masculinity and femininity after 1920 is White, *Too Heavy a Load.* For an exploration of the "woman question" among African Americans see Martha Suzanne Jones, "The 'Woman Question' in African-American Public Culture, 1830–1900" (PhD diss., Columbia University, 2001).

xxii *The YWCA is an example:* The first YWCA opened in New York City in 1858. Throughout the United States women organized city associations to provide housing and religious instruction to single young women. The YWCA of the USA was founded in 1906. In the late 1890s black women established several separate institutions. YWCA affiliate "Colored branches," also known as Colored YWCAs, were established in the early twentieth century. For a brief history of the YWCA see Susan Lynn, "YWCA," in *The Reader's Companion to U.S. Women's History*, ed. Wilma Mankiller et al. (Boston: Houghton Mifflin, 1998), 657. There is no book-length history of black women and the YWCA; however, the following studies examine the role of black women in the organization's history. See Adrienne Lash Jones, "Young Women's Christian Association," in *Black Women in America: An Historical Encyclopedia*, vol. 2, ed. Darlene Clark Hine (Brooklyn, NY: Carlson Publishing, 1993), 1299–1303; Judith Weisenfeld, *African American Women and Christian Activism: New York's Black YWCA, 1905–1945* (Cambridge, Mass.: Harvard University Press, 1998; Nancy Marie Robertson, *Christian Sisterhood, Race Relations, and the YWCA, 1906–46* (Urbana: University of Illinois Press, 2007).

xxii *Organized in 1873–74:* Kathryn Kish Sklar, "Woman's Christian Temperance Union," in Mankiller, et al., *The Reader's Companion*, 641.

xxii *However, temperance and prohibition:* The contributions of black women to the WCTU have been overlooked by most historians. However, given the leadership role of Frances Ellen Watkins Harper in the WCTU, the contributions are included in books and essays discussing Harper's reform work. See Bettye Collier-Thomas, "Frances Ellen Watkins Harper: Abolitionist and Feminist Reformer, 1825–1911," in *African American Women and the Vote, 1837–1965*, ed. Ann D. Gordon et al. (Amherst: University of Massachusetts, 1997), 55–60; Glenda Elizabeth Gilmore, *Gender and Jim Crow: Women and the Politics of White Supremacy in North Carolina, 1896–1920* (Chapel Hill: University of North Carolina Press, 1996), 46–59; Rosalyn V. Cheagle, "The Colored Temperance Movement: 1830–1860" (MA thesis, Howard University, 1969).

xxii *Black religious women:* Higginbotham, *Righteous Discontent*, 17.

xxiii *Though largely overlooked:* Susan M. Hartmann, *The Other Feminists: Activists in the Liberal Establishment* (New Haven: Yale University Press, 1998).

xxiii *However, class:* Bart Landry, *The New Black Middle Class* (Berkeley: University of California Press, 1987).

xxiv *"saw themselves as ambassadors":* Gilmore, *Gender and Jim Crow*, xix.

xxv *the Great Migration:* St. Clair Drake and Horace R. Cayton, *Black Metropolis: A Study of Negro Life in a Northern City*, 4th ed., rev. and enl. (Chicago: University of Chicago Press, 1993), 614, 641–46; C. Eric Lincoln and Lawrence H. Mamiya, *The Black Church in the African American Experience* (Durham: Duke University Press, 1990), 124–25; Victoria W. Wolcott, *Remaking Respectability: African American Women in Interwar Detroit* (Chapel Hill: University of North Carolina Press, 2001), 64–66,189–92.

xxv *Slave owners:* Albert J. Raboteau, *Slave Religion: The 'Invisible Institution' in the Antebellum South* (New York: Oxford University Press, 1978). Raboteau illustrates that slave masters were unable to keep blacks from shaping and using the Christian faith to serve their spiritual and psychological needs.

xxvi *By 1890:* Bettye Collier-Thomas, "The 'Relief Corps of Heaven': Black Women as Philanthropists," in *Philanthropy in Communities of Color: Traditions and Challenges*, ed. Pier C. Rogers, ARNOVA Occasional Paper Series 1:1 (summer 2001): 25–39.

xxvii *Women variously strove:* For an excellent discussion of the relationship of church women to the development of secular reform organizations see Mamie E. Steward, "Afro-American Woman and the Church," and Josephine E. Holmes, "The Negro Woman and Religion in Problem Solutions," in "Woman's Part in the Uplift of the Negro Race," *Colored American Magazine* 12:1 (January 1907): 53–61.

xxviii *As long as white America:* See chapter 2, "Exploring the Community Connection: Race, Class, and Women's Agency," in Cheryl Townsend Gilkes, *'If It Wasn't for the Women': Black Women's Experience and Womanist Culture in Church and Community* (Maryknoll, NY: Orbis Books, 2001), 28–39.

xxix *They administered primarily:* In addition to Butler, *Women in the Church of God in Christ*, the best published works on Pentecostal/Holiness women are Cheryl Townsend Gilkes, "Together and in Harness: Women's Traditions in the Sanctified Church," *Journal of Women in Culture and Society* 10:4 (1985): 678–99; Cheryl Townsend Gilkes, "The Role of Women in the Sanctified Church," *Journal of Religious Thought* 43:1 (spring-summer 1986): 24–41.

xxx *It is not easy:* Diane Batts Morrow, *Persons of Color and Religious at the Same Time: The Oblate Sisters of Providence, 1828–1860* (Chapel Hill: University of North Carolina Press, 2002); Grace Sherwood, *The Oblates' Hundred and One Years* (New York: Macmillan, 1931); Cyprian Davis, *The History of Black Catholics in the United States* (New York: Crossroad Publishing Co., 1996). Other than *Persons of Color*, there are no book-length publications, and very few scholarly articles, published on the Sisters of the Holy Family, the Handmaidens of Mary, or other black Catholic sisterhoods. Morrow's study of the Oblates mentions several organizations of Catholic laywomen, organized in the early nineteenth century. Cyprian Davis's history of black Catholics includes information on most of the sisterhoods as well as some laywomen.

xxx *Thus the organizational work:* Diana L. Hayes, *Hagar's Daughters: Womanist Ways of Being in the World* (New York: Paulist Press, 1995); Diana L. Hayes, *And Still We Rise: An Introduction to Black Liberation Theology* (New York, NY: Paulist Press, 1996); Diana L. Hayes, "Strong, Faith-Filled Black Women Enrich U.S. Catholic Church," *National Catholic Reporter*, February 21, 2003; Jamie T. Phelps, ed., *Black and Catholic* (Milwaukee: Marquette University Press, 1997).

xxx *"all members must be connected":* Carrie Brice, "Woman's World," *Philadelphia Tribune*, July 17, 1915.

xxx *However, most middle-class:* "Belief in God Necessary in Direction of Race, Judge Terrell Tells Elks," *Washington Post*, April 7, 1922.

xxxi *"political and social involvement":* Based on the earlier sociological studies of black churches by scholars such as Benjamin Mays, E. Franklin Frazier, and Sinclair Drake and Horace Cayton, Gayraud Wilmore argues that the black church and clergy were "deradicalized" by the 1930s. See Gayraud Wilmore, *Black Religion and Black Radicalism: An Interpretation of the Religious History of African Americans* (Maryknoll, NY: Orbis, 1998). For a discussion of the "deradicalization thesis" and evidence refuting this assertion, see Lincoln and Mamiya, *The Black Church*, 209–11.

xxxi *in 1924 a cadre:* Evelyn Brooks Higginbotham, "In Politics to Stay: Black Women Leaders and Party Politics in the 1920s," in *Women, Politics, and Change*, ed. Louise Tilly and Patricia Gurin (New York: Russell Sage Foundation, 1990).

xxxii *Numerous women joined:* Weisenfeld, *African American Women*. Weisenfeld's study of the Harlem YWCA suggests the need for additional studies of black YWCAs in other cities, such as Atlanta, Richmond, Philadelphia, Washington, Baltimore, Chicago, and Detroit.

xxxiii *However, the majority:* Hartmann, *The Other Feminists*. There is little published work on the political activism of Church Women United during the 1940s and its involvement in the Civil Rights Movement of the 1950s and '60s. Hartmann illustrates how women working outside the mainstream feminist establishment in four liberal organizations, including the National Council of Churches, influenced the "Second Wave" feminist movement of the 1960s and '70s, and demonstrates how organizations such as the American Civil Liberties Union, the NCC (CWU affiliated with the National Council of Churches in 1950), and the Ford Foundation were more supportive of black feminists than the National Organization of Women and other white feminist groups. She also examines the relationship of civil rights to women's rights and the different experiences of black women within the Second Wave. See also "Lillian Smith, Author of 'Strange Fruit,' Praises Southern White Women," *Chicago Defender*, December 15, 1945. Smith points out that although Governor Ellis Arnall received the credit for the passage of legislation repealing the poll tax in Georgia, church women had been "working quietly" for twenty-five years (1920–45) "first to change the mind about lynching, and then to change its mind about other things also. The poll tax was just one of them."

xxxiii *Some black women's organizations:* Bettye Collier-Thomas and V. P. Franklin, *Sisters in the Struggle: African American Women in the Civil Rights–Black Power Movement* (New York: New York University Press, 2001), 22.

xxxiv *As African American men:* James H. Cone, *Black Theology and Black Power* (New York: Harper and Row, 1969).

xxxiv *During the last two decades:* Deborah Harmon Hines, "Part 1: Black Women's Agenda," *The Witness* 65:2 (February 1982): 5–8; Janette Pierce, "Black Women's Agenda," ibid., 4; Marjorie Nichols Farmer, "Different Voices: African American Women in the Episcopal Church," in *Episcopal Women: Gender, Spirituality and*

Commitment in an American Mainline Denomination, ed. Catherine M. Prelinger (New York: Oxford University Press, 1992), 224–26; Stacey M. Floyd-Thomas, ed., *Deeper Shades of Purple: Womanism in Religion and Society* (New York: New York University Press, 2006), 4.

CHAPTER 1 *"Soul Hunger"*

4 *"keep them ever so ignorant"*: "Narrative of James Curry, a Fugitive Slave," *Liberator*, January 10, 1840.

4 *As enslaved women and as free:* Historically black-controlled Christian denominations have been independent of white denominations in the United States. For a discussion of organization and development of these institutions, as well as the general use of the term, "the Black Church," by scholars and the general public, see C. Eric Lincoln and Lawrence Mamiya, *The Black Church in the African American Experience* (Durham: Duke University Press, 1990), 1.

4 *Generations of Africans:* For a discussion of African religious traditions, see Albert J. Raboteau, *Slave Religion: The "Invisible Institution" in the Antebellum South* (New York: Oxford University Press, 1978), 5–16.

4 *"the slaves' deep resentment"*: Ira Berlin, Marc Favreau, and Steven F. Miller, eds., *Remembering Slavery: African Americans Talk About Their Personal Experiences of Slavery and Emancipation* (New York: New Press, 1998), 165; Lincoln and Mamiya, *The Black Church*, 17.

5 *This did not mean:* According to Albert Raboteau, "The majority of slaves . . . remained only minimally touched by Christianity by the second decade of the nineteenth century." Raboteau, *Slave Religion*, 5–7, 46–47, 71, 149.

5 *In the context:* Toinette M. Eugene, " 'Lifting as We Climb': Womanist Theorizing About Religion and the Family," in *Down by the Riverside: Readings in African American Religion*, ed. Larry G. Murphy (New York: New York University Press, 2000), 435.

5 *Loathing the sight:* Thelma Jennings, " 'Us Colored Women Had to Go Th[r]ough a Plenty': Sexual Exploitation of African-American Slave Women," *Journal of Women's History* 1 (winter 1990): 45–74; George P. Rawick, *The American Slave: A Composite Autobiography* (Westport, Conn: Greenwood, 1972), 55, 134–35.

5 *To justify slavery:* Ira Berlin, *Many Thousands Gone: The First Two Centuries of Slavery in North America* (Cambridge, Mass.: Belknap Press, 1998), 9.

6 *"moral and spiritual"*: Cheryl J. Sanders, "African Americans, the Bible, and Spiritual Formation," in *African Americans and the Bible: Sacred Texts and Social Textures*, ed. Vincent L. Wimbush (New York: Continuum, 2000), 589; Katie Geneva Cannon, "Slave Ideology and Biblical Interpretation," *Semeia* 47 (1989): 15–17.

6 *"On Sundays"*: Berlin, Favreau, and Miller, eds., *Remembering Slavery*, 102; Charles L. Perdue Jr., Thomas E. Barden, and Robert K. Phillips, eds., *Weevils in the Wheat: Interviews with Virginia Ex-Slaves* (Charlottesville: University of Virginia Press, 1992), 183. For interview with Sallie Blakely see George P. Rawick, Jan Hillegas, and Ken Lawrence, eds., *The American Slave: A Composite Autobiography*, suppl., ser. 1, vol. 3, *Georgia Narratives: Part 1* (Westport, Conn.: Greenwood Press, 1977), 65. Hereafter cited as Rawick, *Georgia Narratives*, SS 1:3.

6 *In these meetings:* Raboteau, *Slave Religion*, 212–19. For Della Briscoe's slave testimony, see George P. Rawick, ed., *The American Slave: A Composite Autobiography*, parts 1 and 2, vol. 12, *Georgia Narratives* (Westport, Conn.: Greenwood Press,

1972), 127. The WPA slave testimonies invariably use the term "arbor" rather than harbor. Scholars often substitute the term "harbor." It is possible that the interviewers spelled the word as it was articulated by their subjects.

7 *"Go Down Moses":* Miles Mark Fisher, *Negro Slave Songs in the United States* (Ithaca, NY: Cornell University Press, 1953), 130. For a discussion of how the biblical story of Exodus resonated and was broadly interpreted by African Americans during the antebellum period, see Eddie S. Glaude, Jr., *Exodus!: Religion, Race, and Nation in Early Nineteenth-Century Black America* (Chicago: University of Chicago Press, 2000).

7 *They taught their children:* Darlene Clark Hine, "Rape and the Inner Lives of Black Women in the Middle West: Preliminary Thoughts on the Culture of Dissemblance," *Signs* 14 (summer 1989): 912–20.

7 *"[I]t was death":* Octavia V. Rogers Albert, *The House of Bondage or Charlotte Brooks and Other Slaves,* in *The Schomburg Library of Nineteenth-Century Black Women Writers,* ed. Henry Louis Gates Jr. (New York: Oxford University Press, 1988), 9, 28, 31, 40.

7 *"Don't look down":* Nannie H. Burroughs, "Only God, and Negroes Can Understand Negro Philosophy," *Baltimore Afro-American,* September 27, 1930.

8 *"tell the priest":* Albert, *The House of Bondage,* 68–69.

8 *By the mid-eighteenth century:* Quoting Vincent L. Wimbush, "The Bible and African Americans: An Outline of Interpretive History," in *African Americans and the Bible,* ed. Wimbush, 702.

8 *Literacy was a highly valued:* Janet Duitsman Cornelius, *When I Can Read My Title Clear: Literacy, Slavery, and Religion in the Antebellum South* (Columbia, SC: University of South Carolina Press, 1991), 92–93; see also Allen Dwight Callahan, *The Talking Book: African Americans and the Bible* (New Haven, Conn.: Yale University, 2006), 4–20.

9 *"I'm no man's nigger":* Bert James Lowenburg and Ruth Bogin, *Black Women in Nineteenth-Century American Life: Their Words, Their Thoughts, Their Feelings* (University Park: Pennsylvania State University Press, 1976), 40.

9 *Harriet Tubman firmly believed:* Ibid., 10; for biographies of Tubman see Catherine Clinton, *Harriet Tubman: The Road to Freedom* (New York: Little, Brown and Company, 2004); Kate Clifford Larson, *Bound for the Promised Land: Harriet Tubman, Portrait of an American Hero* (New York: Ballantine Books, 2004).

10 *Albert illustrated:* Albert, *House of Bondage,* 130, xxviii, xxi.

10 *Coppin, like Albert, saw her work:* Lowenburg and Bogin, *Black Women in Nineteenth-Century American Life,* 7.

10 *Belief in Jesus:* Jacquelyn Grant, "Womanist Theology: Black Women's Experience as a Source for Doing Theology, with Special Reference to Christology," in *Black Theology: A Documentary History,* vol. 2: *1980–1992,* ed. James H. Cone and Gayraud S. Wilmore (Maryknoll, NY: Orbis Books, 1993), 283; Harold A. Carter, *The Prayer Tradition of Black People* (Valley Forge: Judson Press, 1976), 47.

10 *"Many times I have bowed":* Albert, *House of Bondage,* 55–56.

10 *"Just so it is":* Ibid., 16.

11 *"All I want is Jesus":* Rawick, ed., *Georgia Narratives,* SS 1:3, interview with Rev. W. B. Allen, 10.

11 *"Our troubles":* Rawick, *Georgia Narratives* SS 1:3, 17.

11 *In this sermon:* Grant, "Womanist Theology," 283.

11 *Enslaved women rarely:* During the 1920s, Fisk University interviewed former slaves. These slave narratives, bound and published in mimeograph form, reveal

how the enslaved converted God to meet their needs. See Paul Radin, "Status, Phantasy, and the Christian Dogma," in *God Struck Me Dead*, Social Science Institute (Nashville, Tenn.: Fisk University, 1945), vi.

11 *Given the African background:* Carter, *Prayer Tradition*, 47–48.

12 *"the miracle of Black women's survival":* Toinette M. Eugene, "There Is a Balm in Gilead: Black Womanist and the Black Church as Agents of a Therapeutic Community," *Women and Therapy: A Feminist Quarterly* 16:2–3 (1995): 68–69.

12 *These clandestine meetings:* During the 1890s, as black leaders searched for ways to solve the myriad economic and social problems that beset African Americans, much attention was given to the impact of slavery on moral behavior. Professor Eugene Harris of Fisk University argued that "much of the moral laxity which exists among us today arose out of slavery." Harris cited the physical abuse of women, the breakup of slave marriages by masters, slave breeding, and rape as factors influencing the social behavior of blacks in the postbellum period. See Eugene Harris, "The Physical Condition of the Race: Whether Dependent upon Social Conditions or Environment," in *Atlanta University Publications*, no. 2, ed. W. E. B. Du Bois (Atlanta: Atlanta University Press, 1897), 25; Albert, *House of Bondage*, 11–12, 17, 23.

13 *When they sang:* Albert, *House of Bondage*, 10, 36. Slave testimonies reveal that it was common practice for the enslaved to place large empty iron pots, sometimes filled with water, in the center of the cabin's floor to absorb the sounds of their voices. Some slaves believed that if a big pot were turned upside down no sounds would escape from a room. For additional discussion and examples of this practice see George P. Rawick, ed., *The American Slave a Composite Autobiography: From Sundown to Sunup: The Making of the Black Community*, vol. 1 (Westport, Conn.: Greenwood, 1972), 41; Rawick, *Georgia Narratives 1*, SS 1:3 (1977), 4; Social Science Institute, "Preacher from a 'God-Fearing' Plantation," in *God Struck Me Dead*, 156.

13 *"Fare you well":* As quoted in Deborah Gray White, *Ar'n't I a Woman?: Female Slaves in the Plantation South* (New York: W. W. Norton), 123.

13 *"[A]dult female cooperation":* Ibid., 121.

13 *Shouting was a religious role:* Jean E. Friedman, *The Enclosed Garden: Women and Community in the Evangelical South, 1830–1900* (Chapel Hill: University of North Carolina Press, 1985), 74.

13 *"All of my people":* Social Science Institute, "Preacher from a 'God-Fearing' Plantation," 154–55.

14 *Sinda's prediction:* White, *Ar'n't I a Woman?*, n. 17, 189–90; 131.

14 *"Do I believe":* Rawick, *Georgia Narratives*, 52. It is not clear what constituted a "puppy." It is possible that the reference was to a "puppet," which refers to a doll whose acts were controlled by an outside force or influence. Conjurers were fond of using dolls to represent the person upon whom the spell was being placed.

14 *"I don't believe":* Social Science Institute, "There Ain't No Conjurers," in *God Struck Me Dead*, 76.

15 *"Slaves believed":* For discussion of the history and uses of African religious traditions in Africa and the diaspora, including Vodun, and conjuring practices among African American slaves, see Raboteau, *Slave Religion*, 5–42, 75–87, 275–78, and Charles Joyner, " 'Believer I Know': The Emergence of African-American Christianity," in *African American Christianity: Essays in History*, ed. Paul E. Johnson (Berkeley: University of California Press, 1994), 34–36.

15 *These three women:* Theophilus G. Steward, *The Haitian Revolution, 1791 to 1804*

(New York: Thomas Y. Crowell, 1914), 24–38; Raboteau, *Slave Religion*, 77, 79; Christopher Phillips, *Freedom's Port: The African American Community of Baltimore, 1790–1860* (Urbana: University of Illinois Press, 1997), 70–71.

16 *She merged Catholic beliefs:* Virginia Gould, "Laveau, Marie (c. 1790–1881)," in *Black Women in America: An Historical Encyclopedia*, vol. 2, ed. Darlene Clark Hine (Brooklyn, NY: Carlson Publishing, 1993), 701; Latin Catholicism, particularly as practiced in Haiti, Cuba, Martinique, and New Orleans, appears to be more amenable to the incorporation of African religions, including those that emanated from Vodun, than other religions, such as that of the Methodist and Baptist. For an excellent discussion of the lives of the two Marie Laveaus see Martha Ward, *Voodoo Queen: The Spirited Lives of Marie Laveau* (Jackson: University Press of Mississippi, 2004).

16 *Following the death:* Raboteau, *Slave Religion*, 79.

16 *A woman born:* Social Science Institute, "Sixty Five Years a 'Washer and Ironer,' " in *God Struck Me Dead*, 188.

17 *"They had a white man":* Social Science Institute, "Stayed with 'Her People' After Freedom," in *God Struck Me Dead*, 198.

17 *All of this:* See Aunt Charlotte's slave testimony in Albert, *House of Bondage*, 79; for patterns of worship and church attendance in the South, see Social Science Institute, *God Struck Me Dead*, 188; Rawick, ed., *Georgia Narratives 1*, SS 1:3, 64, 92, 114, 122, 170, 238; for discussion of African American women who attended and held membership in white Methodist churches during the late eighteenth and early nineteenth centuries, see Cynthia Lynn Lyerly, "Religion, Gender, and Identity: Black Methodist Women in a Slave Society, 1770–1810," in *Discovering the Women in Slavery: Emancipating Perspectives on the American Past*, ed. Patricia Morton (Athens: University of Georgia Press, 1996), 202–26.

18 *She succeeded:* Robert Russa Moton, "Religious, Educational and Economic Progress of Negro," *New York Age*, September 3, 1921; Lyerly, "Religion, Gender, and Identity," 203, 205. During the period 1750–1820 a few black women joined the Moravian Church, a Protestant group founded in 1457. In 1740 Moravian settlers founded a religious community in Northhampton County, Pennsylvania. Moravians, like some Methodists, were concerned about the souls of their slaves, and manumitted some persons who evidenced deep religious beliefs. For an autobiography of a black Moravian woman who lived in Philadelphia and Bethlehem, Pennsylvania, during the late eighteenth and early nineteenth centuries, see "Magdalene Beulah Brockden," in *Moravian Women's Memoirs: Their Related Lives, 1750–1820*, trans. Katherine M. Faull (Syracuse: Syracuse University Press, 1997), 77–78, 145n24; see also Jon F. Sensbach, *Rebecca's Revival: Creating Black Christianity in the Atlantic World* (Cambridge, Mass.: Harvard University Press, 2005).

18 *The black membership:* In Baltimore and Philadelphia, respectively, African Americans affiliated with the Strawberry Alley, Lovely Lane, and St. George Methodist Episcopal churches. William J. Walls, *The African Methodist Episcopal Zion Church: Reality of the Black Church* (Charlotte, NC: AME Zion Publishing House, 1974), 40, 47.

18 *"the blessed chapter":* A. Mott, comp., *Biographical Sketches and Interesting Anecdotes of Persons of Color* (New York: M. Day, 1839), 110–14.

18 *However, black churches:* Sharp Street Methodist Episcopal Church, "Register of Trials and Church Decisions, 1823–1846." This one-ledger volume includes membership lists, with remarks, that constitute a record of removals, deaths, and dismissals. "Removals" refers to free black and slave members who left the Sharp

Street Church and either became affiliated with other churches or left Baltimore because they were sold by their slave owners or were fugitive slaves captured and returned to their owners. This record also includes details of several church trials.

18 *Conversion, a central element:* For a discussion of the holiness tradition among African Americans and the role of the Methodist Church in the holiness movement see Bettye Collier-Thomas, *Daughters of Thunder: Black Women Preachers and Their Sermons, 1750–1979* (San Francisco: Jossey-Bass, 1997), 12–18.

19 *Inherent in their personal testimonies:* Lyerly, "Religion, Gender, and Identity," 208–09.

19 *The Methodists were:* Berlin, *Many Thousands Gone,* 272; for black membership in southern evangelical churches from 1790 to 1836, see Christine Leigh Heyrman, *Southern Cross: The Beginnings of the Bible Belt* (New York: Alfred A. Knopf, 1997), 263–65. According to Heyrman, in 1790 there were 8,640 black Methodists and 4,012 black Baptists. By 1813 there were 30,223 and 22,710 Methodists and Baptists respectively. And by 1836, 72,898 and 58,028 African Americans held membership in southern white Methodist and Baptist evangelical churches.

20 *Parents, especially mothers:* Lyerly, "Religion, Gender, and Identity," 213–17.

20 *"shape a gender identity":* Ibid., 219–20.

21 *However, in the upper South:* Ira Berlin, *Slaves Without Masters: The Free Negro in the Antebellum South* (New York: Pantheon, 1974), 175–77, 180; Leonard P. Curry, *The Free Black in Urban America, 1800–1850: The Shadow of the Dream* (Chicago: University of Chicago Press, 1981), 7–9, 252–54.

21 *Some women:* Edward Byron Reuter, *The Mulatto in the United States* (New York: Haskell House Publishers, 1969), 139–43.

21 *"The black females":* W. E. B. Du Bois, ed., *The Negro Church: Report of a Social Study Made under the Direction of Atlanta University; Together with the Proceedings of the Eighth Conference for the Study of the Negro Problems held at Atlanta University, May 26th, 1903* (Atlanta: Atlanta University Press, 1903), 4.

21 *Commenting on how:* Social Science Institute, "Preacher from a 'God-Fearing' Plantation,' " 150, 174–75; for a thorough discussion of how slave women were sexually exploited, see Jennings, " 'Us Colored Women Had to Go Th[r]ough a Plenty,' " 45–74.

22 *After the whipping:* Julia A. J. Foote, *A Brand Plucked from the Fire: An Autobiographical Sketch,* in *Sisters of the Spirit: Three Black Women's Autobiographies of the Nineteenth Century,* ed. William L. Andrews (Bloomington: Indiana University Press, 1986), 166.

24 *"gladly received":* Sarah J. W. Early, "The Great Part Taken by the Women of the West in the Development of the AME Church," in Lawson A. Scruggs, *Women of Distinction: Remarkable in Works and Invincible in Character* (Raleigh, NC: L. A. Scruggs, 1893), 148.

24 *"[A]s black institutions":* James Oliver Horton, *Free People of Color: Inside the African American Community* (Washington, DC: Smithsonian Institution Press, 1993), 102; see also James Oliver Horton, "Freedom's Yoke: Gender Conventions among Antebellum Free Blacks," *Feminist Studies* 12:1 (spring 1986): 51–74.

25 *Sojourner Truth:* Collier-Thomas, *Daughters of Thunder,* 15, 44, 48, 49, 53, 57, 58.

25 *In the South:* Heyrman, *Southern Cross,* 167.

26 *Essentially, in spite of church law:* Collier-Thomas, *Daughters of Thunder,* 17.

26 *As part of their journey:* For spiritual autobiographies written by antebellum black women preachers, see Jarena Lee, *The Life and Religious Experience of Jarena Lee, a Coloured Lady, Giving an Account of Her Call to Preach the Gospel. Revised and Cor-*

rected from the Original Manuscript, Written by Herself; Zilpha Elaw, *Memoirs of the Life and Religious Experience, Ministerial Travels and Labours of Mrs. Zilpha Elaw, an American Female of Colour: Together with Some Account of the Great Religious Revivals in America*; Julia A. J. Foote, *A Brand Plucked from the Fire*, in *Sisters of the Spirit*, ed. Andrews; and Amanda Berry Smith, *An Autobiography: The Story of the Lord's Dealing with Mrs. Amanda Smith* (Chicago: Christian Witness, 1893).

27 *"dramatic experience"*: Charles S. Johnson, introduction to Social Science Institute, *God Struck Me Dead*, iii.

27 *It was also common practice*: Heyrman, *Southern Cross*, 181; for discussion of black preaching women and charges of mental instability, see Collier-Thomas, *Daughters of Thunder*.

28 *Some female exhorters*: Collier-Thomas, *Daughters of Thunder*, 19–20.

28 *She died in 1832*: Mott, *Biographical Sketches*, 74–82; Sylvia R. Frey and Betty Wood, *Come Shouting to Zion: African American Protestantism in the American South and British Caribbean to 1830* (Chapel Hill: University of North Carolina Press, 1998), 170.

29 *It was in this manner*: Collier-Thomas, *Daughters of Thunder*, 45, 47.

29 *By 1820, practically all*: Bettye C. Thomas, *History of the Sharp Street Memorial Methodist Church, 1787–1820* (Baltimore: Sharp Street Memorial Methodist Church, 1977); Frey and Wood, *Come Shouting to Zion*, 176.

29 *The African Methodist Episcopal*: Walls, *African Methodist Episcopal Zion Church*, 43, 48.

30 *Women were instrumental*: Walls, *African Methodist Episcopal Zion Church*, 44, 133; Jualynne E. Dodson, *Engendering Church: Women, Power, and the AME Church* (Lanham, Md.: Rowman and Littlefield, 2002), 7, 8; Horton, *Free People of Color*, 102.

30 *"[i]n all-black churches"*: Frey and Wood, *Come Shouting to Zion*, 172; see also 243n116.

31 *In Virginia and South Carolina*: Frey and Wood, *Come Shouting to Zion*, 163–64; for comments on the impact of the Great Awakening and the Second Awakening on African Americans see Miles Mark Fisher, "The Negro Churches," *Crisis* 45:7 (July 1938): 220.

31 *Enslaved women also*: Frey and Wood, *Come Shouting to Zion*, 165.

31 *Class meetings provided*: Walls, *African Methodist Episcopal Zion Church*, 98.

32 *In most black churches*: Rev. T[heophilus] G. Steward, "Work for the Women of the Church," *Christian Recorder*, March 20, 1890.

33 *"never [being] disciplined"*: "Her Death Mourned," *Savannah Tribune*, December 5, 1903.

34 *The church claimed*: For a discussion of these practices in Virginia's black Baptist churches see Mechal Sobel, *Trabelin' On: The Slave Journey to an Afro-Baptist Faith* (Westport, Conn.: Greenwood Press, 1979), 206–08. During the antebellum period, AME and AME Zion denominations adhered to the discipline of the Methodist Church. Prior to 1800, in accordance with the views of John Wesley, "a pastor was responsible to God for the purity of the flock—hence, he should judge as to the guilt or innocence of the accused member." In 1800 the discipline was amended, giving the authority to "pronounce the guilt or innocence of accused members" to a specially appointed committee. Under church law, as defined by the discipline, women had no status, lacked religious suffrage, and were ineligible to fill any position. Thus they could not serve as members of a committee for trial. This pattern of male dominance would continue in most religious traditions for well into the twentieth century. The AME Zion Church was

among the first to admit women to the polity (see discussion in chapter 2), and to strike the word "male" from the discipline, granting women equal rights in the church. See John B. Small, *Code on the Discipline of the African Methodist Episcopal Zion Church* (York, Pa.: York Dispatch Print, 1898), 52, 53. By 1895 few urban churches held trials for infringement other than that of adultery, and only women were tried for this offense. See "Men and Measures of the AME Church," *Indianapolis Freeman*, June 11, 1897.

34 *Margaret Philips was then expelled:* Sharp Street Methodist Episcopal Church, "Register of Trials and Church Decisions." Similar to Frederick Douglass and other slaves, who were permitted by their masters to hire their time in the city, Louis Philips was able to make choices, and freely mingle with free blacks in Baltimore.

34 *unmarried enslaved women:* Frey and Wood, *Come Shouting to Zion*, 188–89.

35 *It became an important part:* Ronald Takaki argues that the English aided in the creation of the ideology of the "racialized savage," which defined male and female persons of color as oversexed and possessed with insatiable sexual appetites. Takaki states that *The Tempest*, the seventeenth-century play authored by William Shakespeare, aided in the spread and acceptance of the notion of Native Americans as racialized savages who could not be civilized. These beliefs were imputed to Africans, Asians, and Hispanic peoples. Winthrop Jordan also traces the widespread acceptance of this notion among Europeans. See Ronald Takaki, *A Different Mirror: A History of Multicultural America* (Boston: Little, Brown and Company, 1993), 31–32; and Winthrop D. Jordan, *White over Black: American Attitudes Toward the Negro, 1550–1812* (Chapel Hill, NC: University of North Carolina Press, 1968), 3–48.

35 *For example, it was used:* Alfreda M. Duster, ed., *Crusade for Justice: The Autobiography of Ida B. Wells* (Chicago: University of Chicago Press, 1970), 64–65.

35 *Community activities:* Shirley J. Yee, *Black Women Abolitionists: A Study in Activism, 1828–1860* (Knoxville: University of Tennessee Press, 1992), 74, 78; See also Mary R. Sawyer, "Black Religion and Social Change: Women in Leadership Roles," in Murphy, *Down by the Riverside*, 304–05.

35 *The second organization:* "The Women's Missionary Society of the AME Church: Over a Century of Commitment and Service," *National Black Monitor*, June 1985, 4, 5, 8–10, 12–13; "Angels of the Church: Quadrennial," *Christian Recorder*, July 9, 1963; Mary E. Frizzell, "Missions," ibid., February 18, 1964. According to Jualynne Dodson, the Daughters of Conference, began in 1816 and later formed into a national association, coincided with the founding of the African Methodist Episcopal denomination. However, numerous AME sources dispute Dodson's undocumented claim; see Dodson, *Engendering Church*, 41. In his monumental history of the AME Church, Bishop Payne asserted that at the AME General Conference held in 1828, "we hear for the first time of the existence of that noble and useful band of women called 'Daughters of Conference.'" See Daniel Alexander Payne, *History of the African Methodist Episcopal Church* (Nashville: AME Sunday-School Union, 1891), 56.

35 *"commonly called Daughters of Conference":* "Memoir of Elizabeth Harris," *Christian Recorder*, July 28, 1866.

36 *By 1830, branches:* Ibid., "Our Daughters of Conference," *Christian Recorder*, April 17, 1873.

37 *Roberts was responsible:* Bettye Collier-Thomas, " 'The Relief Corps of Heaven': Black Women as Philanthropists," *ARNOVA* 1:1 (2001): 26; Aurora Evans, "Origin and Work of the Daughters of Conference and Kindred Societies," *AME*

Zion Quarterly Review (January 1898): 66–67; "She Hath Done What She Could," *Star of Zion*, April 9, 1931; Walls, *African Methodist Episcopal Zion Church*, 47, 48, 50, 133–37.

37 *Free women also:* The term "sister laborers" was coined by Mamie Donohoo, to describe the multifaceted philanthropic work of African American women. See Mamie Donohoo, "Woman as a Philanthropist," AME Zion *Quarterly Review* (October 1899–January 1900): 45–48; Walls, *African Methodist Episcopal Zion Church*, 28. One of the few works to include a discussion of antebellum black church women and their role as social activists is Yee, *Black Women Abolitionists*. This work explores the relationship between black women's social activism and religion.

38 *It also provided assistance:* Dorothy Sterling, ed., *We Are Your Sisters: Black Women in the Nineteenth Century* (New York: W. W. Norton, 1984), 107.

38 *The society required:* "Constitution of the Colored Female Religious and Moral Society of Salem," *The Liberator*, February 16, 1833.

38 *The Daughters of Africa:* Sterling, *We Are Your Sisters*, 105; "The Rush Society," *Christian Recorder*, March 16, 1861.

38 *Renamed the Love:* "On the Death of Anna B. Bedford, Formerly Anna B. Powell," *Christian Recorder*, February 23, 1861. Began as a female organization, the Daughters of Africa was later opened to males.

38 *The organization collected:* "New York African Free School," *Freedom's Journal*, March 7, 1828.

38 *Dorcas societies:* "History of the New York African Free Schools," *Genius of Universal Emancipation*, April 1830, 10; "Improvidence!" ibid., October 1837, 114.

39 *Named in honor:* "For the Genius of Universal Emancipation," *Genius of Universal Emancipation*, February 1834, 34; "The Female Lundy Society," *New York Age*, June 28, 1890.

39 *The Female Benevolent Firm:* Elizabeth Lindsay Davis, *Lifting as They Climb: A History of the National Association of Colored Women* (Washington, D.C.: National Association of Colored Women, 1933), 5.

39 *Many women held:* "The Condition of the Coloured Population of Baltimore," *Baltimore Literary and Religious Magazine* 4 (1838); Sterling, *We Are Your Sisters*, 107–08; James Oliver Horton and Lois E. Horton, *In Hope of Liberty: Culture, Community, and Protest Among Northern Free Blacks, 1700–1860* (New York: Oxford University Press, 1997), 128; Linda Perkins, "Black Women and Racial 'Uplift' Prior to Emancipation," in *The Black Woman Cross-Culturally*, ed. Filomena Chioma Steady (Rochester, NY: Schenkman Books, 1992), 318–19.

39 *For example, during:* *Anglo African*, January 6, 1860; Phillips, *Freedom's Port*, 171.

40 *During the 1830s:* Mott, *Biographical Sketches*, 240.

40 *The society, named:* "Garrison Society," *Liberator*, February 16, 1833, 26.

40 *For example, in 1832:* Quoted in Yee, *Black Women Abolitionists*, 77.

41 *Some societies were:* Ibid.; Sterling, *We Are Your Sisters*, 113, 114.

41 *She imbued her son:* Yee, *Black Women Abolitionists*, 29, 21.

41 *As a free person:* Clinton, *Harriet Tubman*, 20–21, 30–31, 217–18; Larson, *Bound for the Promised Land*, 263, 279.

41 *However, Harper maintained:* Bettye Collier-Thomas, "Frances Ellen Watkins Harper: Abolitionist and Feminist Reformer, 1825–1911," in *African American Women and the Vote, 1837–1965*, ed. Ann Gordon et al. (Amherst: University of Massachusetts Press, 1997), 41–65.

41 *During her lifetime:* Collier-Thomas, *Daughters of Thunder*, 53–54.

42 *"ridicule and sarcasm"*: "Independent Lectures," *Frederick Douglass Newspaper*, December 23, 1853; "Mrs. Stowe on Female Orators," ibid., February 9, 1854; "Sallie Holley," ibid., February 19, 1852.

42 *When Katy Ferguson:* "A True Woman," *Frederick Douglass Newspaper*, December 22, 1854.

43 *True men did not: Freedom's Journal*, launched in the 1820s, was the first newspaper to be owned and published in the United States by a black person. Numerous articles defining women's roles and critiquing the public behavior of black women appeared in the paper. For examples of articles extolling "true" womanhood, see "Woman's Role," *Freedom's Journal*, February 14, 1829; "Hints to the Ladies," ibid., July 18, 1828. For advice articles relevant to married and unmarried women, see ibid., April 11, June 20, and July 25, 1828.

44 *As a woman who had:* "The Late Mrs. Maria W. Stewart," *People's Advocate*, February 28, 1880.

45 *"basic Christian principles"*: Ibid.; Yee, *Black Women Abolitionists*, 26, 112–15; also see Stewart's address in Sterling, *We Are Your Sisters*, 156–57.

46 *Following her marriage:* Yee, *Black Women Abolitionists*, 33. See also Jim Bearden and Linda Jean Butler, *Shadd: The Life and Times of Mary Shadd Cary* (Toronto: University of Toronto Press, 1995); Jane Rhodes, *Mary Ann Shadd Cary: The Black Press and Protest in the Nineteenth Century* (Bloomington, Ind.: Indiana University Press, 1999).

47 *"For by one Spirit"*: "Katy Ferguson: Or What a Poor Colored Woman May Do," *Christian Recorder*, May 25, 1861.

48 *A contemporary recalled:* Mrs. John W. Olcott, "Recollections of Katy Ferguson, Founder of the First Sunday School in New York City," *Southern Workman* 52:9 (September 1923): 463.

48 *For forty years:* Ibid., "Catherine Ferguson's Work to be Fittingly Commemorated," *New York Age*, April 11, 1907; "A True Woman," *Frederick Douglass Newspaper*, December 22, 1854.

49 *In the absence:* Monroe N. Work, "Fifty Years of Negro Progress," *Southern Workman* 42:1 (January 1913): 11; Phillips, *Freedom's Port*, 164–65.

49 *In 1859:* Dodson, *Engendering Church*, 50. The growing numbers of women teaching Sabbath school is likely related to the disproportional number of black women in Baltimore who were free and literate by 1850. Possessing the largest urban free black population in the United States, the city boasted of at least fifteen schools for blacks.

49 *Among the most:* "American Convention," *Genius of Universal Emancipation*, March 1, 1828; "Negro Religious Sisterhoods," *St. Elizabeth's Chronicle* 1:8 (October 1928): 26; for a discussion of the Oblate Sisters of Providence, see Diane Batts Morrow, *Persons of Color and Religious at the Same Time* (Chapel Hill, NC: University of North Carolina Press, 2002).

49 *Jane Crouch began:* "Reports from Virginia Colored Teachers," *Southern Workman* 10:8 (August 1881): 86.

50 *A cadre of African American:* Bettye Collier-Thomas, *Black Women Organized for Social Change, 1800–1920* (Washington, DC: Bethune Museum-Archives, 1984), 25; "Constitution of the Colored Women's Union Relief Association for the Benefit of Wild's Colored Brigade," *Christian Recorder*, July 4, 1863; "Thanks! Thanks!!," ibid., February 11, 1865; "The Freedmen," ibid., March 4, 1865; "Gone to the Front," ibid., April 8, 1865; "Camp William Penn," ibid., April 8, 1865; "From Camp Wm. Penn," ibid., April 15, 1865.

51 *Between 1862 and 1864:* Collier-Thomas, *Black Women*, 25. The work of these associations has received little scholarly attention. The emphasis has been more on the organizing efforts of white Americans.

51 *While black men:* Ibid.

52 *Similar work was:* Ibid.; for reports and discussions of the work of the Ladies Soldiers' Aid societies in these cities, see "First Female Contraband Aid Society of Alexandria," *Christian Recorder*, March 21, 1863; "Letter from H[enry] Matnell (sic) Turner," ibid., September 13, 1862; "Hard at Work," ibid., October 4, 1862; "Societies in Washington, D.C., for the Benefit of the Contraband," ibid., November 1, 1862; "Letter from Chicago," ibid., October 24, 1863; "Louisville Correspondence," ibid, November 5, 1864; "The Second Annual Report, of the (Col.) Ladies' Union Aid Society of Leavenworth," ibid., May 21, 1864; "Union League of Bridgeport, Conn.," ibid., April 8, 1865; "Nashville, Tennessee," ibid., March 18, 1865; "Brooklyn Correspondence," ibid., October 1, 1864; "Report of Ladies Union Association," ibid., August 6, 1864; "Washington Correspondence," ibid., June 4, 1864; "Colors for the Mass[achusetts] 55th," *Liberator*, June 12, 1863; "Encouragement to Labor for Freedom," ibid., September 25, 1863; "Sanitary Fair of Colored Ladies," ibid., October 21, 1864; "The Fair in Aid of Colored Soldiers," ibid., November 18, 1864.

52 *In March 1865:* Collier-Thomas, *Black Women*.

52 *A great deal:* Information about Sabbath schools is sparse. For a brief discussion of the development of the Sabbath school system in the South after the Civil War, see James D. Anderson, *The Education of Blacks in the South, 1860–1935* (Chapel Hill, NC: University of North Carolina Press, 1988), 10–15. Citing the first Freedmen's Bureau reports, Anderson discusses the educational activities of former slaves prior to the inauguration of public schools. Church-sponsored schools were operated at night and on weekends to teach the basic skills of reading and writing. Many Sabbath schools continued long after Reconstruction. Anderson states, "[I]n 1868 the AME Church enrolled 40,000 pupils in its Sabbath schools. By 1885, the AME Church reported having '200,000 children in Sunday schools' for 'intellectual and moral' instruction." Though the Bible was used, the most popular book was the blue-back spelling book.

CHAPTER 2 *"Taxation Without Representation"*

55 *Second in numbers:* Whereas at the beginning of the Civil War, there were approximately 275,000 black Methodists and 250,000 Baptists, by 1898 black Baptists constituted 1.5 million, and Methodists represented a little more than a million persons. Presbyterians numbered about thirty thousand, the Disciples of Christ 18,578, and the Episcopal bodies had fewer than five thousand members. See U.S. Bureau of the Census, *Negro Population: 1790–1915* (Washington, DC: Government Printing Office, 1918), 25, 32–33, 55–57; H. F. Kletzing and William H. Crogman, *Progress of a Race: Or the Remarkable Advancement of the Afro-American Negro* (Atlanta: J. L. Nichols and Co., 1898), 423–24. For the role of black women in the development of churches in the West see Sarah J. W. Early, "The Great Part Taken by the Women of the West in the Development of the AME Church," in Lawson A. Scruggs, *Women of Distinction: Remarkable in Works and Invincible in Character* (Raleigh, NC: L. A. Scruggs, 1893), 148.

55 *Almost a decade:* Mary Helm, *The Upward Path: The Evolution of a Race* (New York: Young People's Missionary Movement of the United States and Canada, 1909), 241–42; H. K. Carroll, "The Negro in His Relations to the Church," in *Africa*

and the American Negro: Addresses and Proceedings of the Congress on Africa, ed. J. W. E. Bowen (Atlanta: Gammon Theological Seminary, 1896), 217–18.

55 *After the war:* As early as 1816, Bishop Benjamin W. Arnett had used "Manhood Christianity" to describe the organizing conference of the AME Church. For a discussion of the slave preacher and the independent black church as important "models of manhood," see William H. Becker, "The Black Church: Manhood and Mission," in *African American Religion: Interpretive Essays in History and Culture*, ed. Timothy E. Fulop and Albert J. Raboteau (New York: Routledge, 1997), 179–95. This essay was originally published in the *Journal of American Academy of Religion* 40 (1972): 316–33. It does not discuss manhood in relationship to issues of gender.

56 *"As a people":* See J. Harvey Anderson, "Editorials: Negro Womanhood," *Star of Zion*, December 11, 1919, for an excellent discussion of how black women were "brutally outraged" and used as sex objects by white men during slavery, and the impact of the practice on black women's "virtue." Anderson emphasizes that while "their sons and their male companions were powerless to defend them . . . black women in thousands of instances struggled for their honor and black men faced death in their defense." "Appeal to the Colored People of the State of Pennsylvania," *Christian Recorder*, December 24, 1864. The National Equal Rights Association was organized in 1864 at a national convention held in Syracuse, New York. Following the meeting, the Pennsylvania State Auxiliary League was formed. The "Declaration of Wrongs and Rights," signed by thirty-five leading black men, was a detailed ideological statement of what the organizers believed was the position of African Americans. This document outlined the wrongs heaped upon free blacks and slaves, stated the rights due all African Americans, and called for an end to slavery. Though women were not included among the organizers, the constitution prohibited discrimination on the basis of "color or sex" in the formation of county leagues. Please note that the "Declaration of Wrongs and Rights" was published by the National Convention of Colored Men almost three months before the Pennsylvania State Auxiliary League was organized. See "Proceedings of the National Convention of Colored Men, Held in the City of Syracuse, N.Y., October 4, 5, 6, and 7, 1864; with the Bill of Wrongs and Rights, and the Address to the American People," in *Minutes of the Proceedings of the National Negro Conventions, 1830–1864*, ed. Howard Holman Bell (New York: Arno Press and the New York Times, 1969). See also Reverdy C. Ransom, "Deborah and Jael, Sermon to the I[da] B. W[ells] Woman's Club at Bethel A.M.E. Church, Chicago, Illinois," ca. 1899, Reverdy C. Ransom Collection, Ohio Historical Society, Columbus, Ohio.

57 *However, beginning in the late:* The *Christian Recorder* is the only black newspaper consistently published between 1854 and 1885. It is the best source for assessing the attitudes of black church women in the period immediately after the Civil War. After 1885 there are several black religious and secular newspapers, and other publications that include the writings of well-known as well as obscure women. These include the *New York Age*, *Christian Index*, and *Star of Zion*. For discussion of issues regarding black "manhood" and "womanhood" rights, see Bettye Collier-Thomas, *Black Women Organized for Social Change, 1800–1920* (Washington, DC: Bethune Museum-Archives, Inc., 1984), 30–31. Historian James T. Campbell argues that there was "a virtual obsession with racial manhood, beginning in the 1840s and '50s and peaking in the decades after the Civil War." He asserts that many AME leaders interpreted "the whole history and meaning of their movement in its light." Though I agree with Campbell's asser-

tions regarding the prewar period, the data does not support his conclusion that religious masculinist beliefs and practices waned during the postwar era. See James T. Campbell, *Songs of Zion: The African Methodist Episcopal Church in the United States and South Africa* (Chapel Hill: University of North Carolina Press, 1998), 50–51. Unlike Campbell, Julius H. Bailey emphasizes how the construction of domesticity relied on conceptions of manhood and masculinity as well as femininity and the home after the Civil War. See Julius H. Bailey, *Around the Family Altar: Domesticity in the African Methodist Episcopal Church, 1865–1900* (Gainesville: University Press of Florida, 2005).

57 *The founding of the National:* Between 1866 and 1869 five Baptist conventions were established in North Carolina, Alabama, Virginia, Arkansas, and Kentucky. By 1898 there were fifteen southern state conventions. Kletzing and Crogman, *Progress of a Race*, 428. For historical overviews of black Baptists see C. Eric Lincoln and Lawrence H. Mamiya, *The Black Church in the African American Experience* (Durham, NC: Duke University Press, 1990), 20–46; Henry M. Mitchell, *Black Church Beginnings: The Long-Hidden Realities of the First Years* (Grand Rapids, MI: Wm. B. Eerdmans Publishing Company, 2004).

57 *After the war:* For historical overviews of the African Methodist Episcopal and African Methodist Episcopal Zion denominations see Kletzing and Crogman, *Progress of a Race*, 428–33; Lincoln and Mamiya, *The Black Church*, 47–75.

57 *Northern blacks:* James Melvin Washington, *Frustrated Fellowship: The Black Baptist Quest for Social Power* (Macon, GA: Mercer University, 1986), 108–09. Washington describes the development of sectional tensions and rivalries in the Consolidated American Baptist Missionary Convention.

58 *A relatively small percentage:* Larry G. Murphy, J. Gordon Melton, and Gary L. Ward, *Encyclopedia of African American Religions* (New York: Garland Publishing, Inc., 1993), 164–67, 250–53, 584–85, 612–14, 719–20; Cyprian Davis, *The History of Black Catholics in the United States* (New York: Crossroad Publishing Co., 1996); Kletzing and Crogman, *Progress of a Race*, 433–34; Lincoln and Mamiya, *The Black Church*, 78–84, 124.

58 *The largest and most prominent:* The National Baptist Convention (Unincorporated) was founded in 1895. In 1915, as the result of a split, the original organization was renamed the National Baptist Convention of America, and the National Baptist Convention, USA, Inc., was formed. The Progressive National Baptist Convention was organized in 1961 as the result of dissension in the National Baptist Convention, USA, Inc., that led to a split. For historical overviews of these denominations, see Lincoln and Mamiya, *The Black Church*, chap. 2, "The Black Baptists," 20–38. See chap. 3 for a full discussion of the 1915 split in the National Baptist Convention.

58 *He claimed that:* "The Value of Training for Home Life," *Southern Workman* 30:10 (July 1901): 379; "Washingtonians Look Back on Half Century," *Washington Afro-American*, January 7, 1950. Much was written about the importance and place of the church in black life and culture. For example, see "The Place of the Negro Church in the Life of the Negro," *Christian Index*, May 19, 1938; see also Evelyn Brooks Higginbotham, *Righteous Discontent: The Women's Movement in the Black Baptist Church, 1880–1920* (Cambridge, Mass.: Harvard University Press, 1993), 16. Higginbotham argues that because the black church was "open to both secular and religious groups in the community [it] came to signify a public space." Thus it was a "public dialogic site."

59 *Since black women:* For an estimate of the percentage of female members in the

black church during the nineteenth century, see Theophilus G. Steward, "Work for the Women of the Church," *Christian Recorder*, March 20, 1890. For commentary and numerical breakdowns on the disparity between the sexes in black religious institutions during the nineteenth and twentieth centuries, see Alice S. Felts, "Women in the Church," *Christian Recorder*, February 18, 1886; F. M. Hamilton, "Editorial," *Christian Index*, July 14, 1888; Mrs. N. F. Mossell, "Work for Women of the Church," *Christian Recorder*, January 19, 1893; S. N. Vass, "Progress of the Negro Race," *Colored American Magazine* 11:16 (December 1906): 265–68; Alice M. Dunbar, "What Has the Church to Offer the Men of Today," *AME Church Review* 30:1 (July 1913): 5–12; "More Females Than Male," *Chicago Defender*, October 17, 1914; "Western Letter," *Star of Zion*, December 1, 1898; "Our Women and the Church," *New York Age*, May 11, 1905; Charles E. Hall, "African Methodist Episcopal Zion Church: 1916–1926," undated two-page typescript, Bureau of the Census, Washington, DC; "None but Women Members in this Carolina Church," *Norfolk Journal and Guide*, August 1, 1925; "Percent of Negro and White Men and Women in Church, 1926, 1916, and 1906," in Monroe Work, *Negro Year Book, 1931–1932* (Tuskegee, Ala.: Tuskegee Press, 1933), 264; J. B. Adams, *Allegheny Conference A.M.E. Zion Church, Pittsburgh, Pennsylvania, October 15–20, 1947 at Wesley Center A.M.E. Zion Church* (Charlotte, NC: A.M.E. Zion Publishing House, 1947), 48; Thomasina Hayward, "Mother Bethel Gets Legal Name," *Christian Recorder*, May 7, 1953; Michel McQueen, "AME Church Seeks More Men Members," *Washington Post*, July 10, 1981; Higginbotham, *Righteous Discontent*, 7.

59 *"The Negro Church":* Nannie H. Burroughs, "Black Women and Reform," *Crisis* 10:4 (August 1915): 187.

59 *Within its pages:* Renita J. Weems, "Reading *Her Way* through the Struggle: African American Women and the Bible," in *Stony the Road We Trod: African American Biblical Interpretation*, ed. Cain Hope Felder (Minneapolis: Fortress Press, 1991), 64–65.

59 *Often referred to:* Rebecca Stiles Taylor, "Activities of Women's National Organizations," *Chicago Defender*, February 13, 1943.

59 *Male clergy often:* In each generation, lay and preaching women assailed the use of scripture to assert women's inferiority; see discussion of this issue, as well as the sermon by Pauli Murray, "Male and Female He Created Them," in Bettye Collier-Thomas, *Daughters of Thunder: Black Women Preachers and Their Sermons, 1850–1979* (San Francisco: Jossey-Bass Publishers, 1997), 234–39, 281.

59 *Among the few leaders:* "Ladies Magazine," *Voice of Missions* 2:2 (February 1894).

60 *Rather, he argued:* James Walker Hood, "The Woman Question," *Star of Zion*, January 12, 1899.

60 *Though he was not:* "Miscellaneous," *Christian Recorder*, September 25, 1869; Collier-Thomas, *Daughters of Thunder*, 15; Nancy Hardesty, Lucille Sider Dayton, and Donald W. Dayton, "Women in the Holiness Movement: Feminism in the Evangelical Tradition," in *Women of Spirit: Female Leadership in the Jewish and Christian Traditions*, ed. Rosemary Radford Ruether and Eleanor T. McLaughlin (New York: Simon and Schuster, 1979), 227–29.

60 *The assumption was:* In a study of black churches in Philadelphia from 1890 to 1940, historian Robert Gregg comments on gender roles in the AME Church. He asserts that "service was associated with women and prestige (or power) with men." However, the evidence does not support his conclusion that "African Methodist women, . . . seldom if ever confronted the notion of separate spheres

directly." Robert Gregg, *Sparks from the Anvil of Oppression: Philadelphia's African Methodists and Southern Migrants, 1890–1940* (Philadelphia: Temple University Press, 1993), 105, 108.

60 *Bible women such as:* For examples of references to Bible women by black women from diverse denominations, in different venues and for varied purposes, see "Odd-Fellowship," *Savannah Tribune*, August 20, 1898; Lillie Mae Owens, "He Is Risen from the Dead," *National Baptist Union Review*, January 23, 1915; Lillie Carson, "Calvary—It is Finished," ibid., January 16, 1915; Mary Williams, "Missionary News—Louisiana," *Star of Zion*, February 26, 1953; Addie E. Etheridge, "Women of Metropolitan Raised 1,372.93," ibid., November 30, 1950; Naomi Joiner, "What Is Happening in the First District?" *Christian Recorder*, March 19, 1959; Helen B. Suber, "Beautiful Nite in White and Parade of States at North Ohio Conference," ibid., January 14, 1969; for an analysis, discussion, and examples of black women preachers' use of Bible women, see Collier-Thomas, *Daughters of Thunder*.

61 " 'the hand that rocks' ": "Odd-Fellowship," *Savannah Tribune*, August 20, 1898. The Household of Ruth, organized in 1857 in Harrisburg, Pennsylvania, by 1889 numbered five hundred Households (chapters), with a total membership of approximately twelve thousand. The organization was known for its domestic and foreign philanthropic activities. In 1915 the group endorsed women's suffrage. For discussion of its founding and activities, see "Items of G.U. of O.F.," *Washington Bee*, July 7, 1888; "What Our Women Are Doing," *Indianapolis Freeman*, December 26, 1914; "Colored Women Endorse the Enfranchisement of Women," ibid., August 28, 1915; "Household of Ruth Pays $108,000 for Home in North Carolina," *New York Age*, May 30, 1925; "Mrs. Anderson Elected Head of Household," *Chicago Defender*, September 22, 1923; "Women in Odd Fellowship Outnumbers and Appear More Progressive Than the Men," *New York Age*, November 4, 1939.

61 *The most frequently cited:* Collier-Thomas, *Daughters of Thunder*, 8–9, 50; for a discussion of how black Baptist women used the Bible to create a "feminist theology," see Higginbotham, *Righteous Discontent*, 120–49.

62 *By the late 1880s:* According to historian Carroll Smith-Rosenberg, white women also created a space for their social activism by transposing "the Cult of True Womanhood to suit their needs." Carroll Smith-Rosenberg, *Disorderly Conduct: Visions of Gender in Victorian America* (New York: Oxford University Press, 1985), 173. See poem "She Hath Done What She Could," in Alice Parham, "To the Ladies of the Woman's Missionary Society of Missouri and Kansas," *Christian Index*, October 27, 1888. In 1926 Mrs. W. A. Lewis, president of the AME Women's Home and Foreign Missionary Society of Tennessee in a "sermonette" entitled "Woman's Mission in the World," used as a text, "She hath done what she could," see "14th Episcopal Dist[rict]," *Christian Recorder*, May 20, 1926.

62 *Though the titles:* Amanda Turpin, "Female Influence," *Christian Recorder*, August 20, 1864; Lyda C. Tolbert, "The Influence of Woman on the Christian World," ibid., May 4, 1893.

62 *Within the question:* Ibid.

62 *Thus, the place:* Lillie Devereux Blake, *Woman's Place Today: Four Lectures, in Reply to the Lenten Lectures on "Woman" by the Rev. Morgan Dix, D.D.* (New York: John Lovell Company, 1883).

62 *Relying on the Bible:* Ira F. Aldridge, "Female Seminaries," in *Minutes of the Sixteenth Session of the North Carolina Conference of the African Methodist Episcopal*

Church, Held at Durham, N.C., November 14th to 21st, 1883 (Greensboro, NC: Thomas, Reece and Co., 1883), 69–71.

62 *In their writings:* For examples of how male clergy used the Bible to reinforce women's inferiority and define their role in the church and society, see Rev. J. W. Smith, "Woman's Place and Work," *Star of Zion*, August 2, 1900; Rev. A. B. Adams, "The Light House," *Pittsburgh Courier*, June 6, 1931.

63 *Johnson concluded that:* James H. A. Johnson, "Woman's Exalted Station," *AME Church Review* 8:4 (April 1892): 402–06.

63 *The argument that:* For examples of the use of this line of reasoning, see Dora J. Cole, "Pennsylvania," *Woman's Era* 2:3 (June 1895): 6–7; Rev. W. H. Davenport, "Women," *Star of Zion*, May 23, 1929; " 'Women' Subject of Dr. Sockman's Address," *Baltimore Afro-American*, September 20, 1930. Sockman articulates the concern of many men who reacted to women's assertion of their rights and their movement from a private to a public sphere.

63 *Ministers such as:* Bonnie Thornton Dill, "The Dialectics of Black Womanhood," *Signs: Journal of Women in Culture and Society* 4 (spring 1979): 543–55; Elsa Barkley Brown, "Mothers of Mind," in *Sage: A Scholarly Journal on Black Women* 6:1 (summer 1989): 7.

63 *Though they clearly:* Johnson, "Woman's Exalted Position."

64 *"quite a reputation":* Mrs. N. F. Mossell, "Our Woman's Department," *New York Freeman*, July 31, 1886.

65 *"the full recognition of women":* Alice S. Felts, "Women in the Church," *Christian Recorder*, February 18, 1886. Felts was the wife of Rev. Cethe C. Felts, the presiding elder in the AME Philadelphia Conference in 1884 and 1885.

65 *"I have long been":* Bishop Campbell was one of several AME clergy who debated the propriety of ordaining women during the late 1880s. Campbell died one month before the publication of Alice Felts's article. For biographical data on Campbell, see Fannie Jackson Coppin, "In Memory of Bishop Jabez Pitt Campbell," *AME Church Review* 8:2 (October 1891): 152–53. For Campbell's views see Jabez P. Campbell, "The Ordination of Women: What the Authority for It?" *AME Church Review* 2:4 (April 1886): 351–61. For Felts's reference to Bishop Jabez P. Campbell, see Alice Felts, "Women's Rights," *Christian Recorder*, December 10, 1891.

65 *Felts concluded that:* Felts, "Women's Rights." Alice Felts's comments were also meant as a reminder to the male clergy of the "educated suffrage" argument launched by the National and American Woman's Associations in support of women's suffrage on the nativist and racist grounds that educated native-born white women were more deserving of the vote than immigrant and illiterate black men. For discussion of this issue, see Bettye Collier-Thomas, "Frances Ellen Watkins Harper: Abolitionist and Feminist Reformer, 1825–1911," in *African American Women and the Vote, 1837–1965*, ed. Ann D. Gordon et al. (Amherst: University of Massachusetts, 1997). Founded in 1886 in New York City as an interdenominational organization of Christians, the International Order of the King's Daughters and Sons comprised a membership of women representing diverse denominations. The association differed from other groups in that it did not define a specific work to be done other than "it must be work for King Jesus." By the 1890s there were numerous local organizations located in the towns and cities of Indiana, Ohio, Maryland, Mississippi, Texas, Kentucky, Georgia, and New York that engaged in charitable work ranging from aiding the sick and poor, engaging in rescue work for girls and women, building homes for working

women and the elderly, providing proper burials for the indigent, and raising funds to support the education of "worthy and needy" black youth. In the early twentieth century some King's Daughters clubs also affiliated with NACW state federations. For example, in Mississippi the Faithful Few Circle of the King's Daughters belonged to the Mississippi State Federation of Women's Clubs. For quote above, and information regarding the organization's founding, see "King's Daughters," *HOPE* 6:66 (May 1891): 3. For discussion of black groups between 1890 and 1910, see "The Baltimore Letter," *Indianapolis Freeman*, April 12, 1890; "Monumental City Sparks," ibid., January 16, 1892; "The 'King's Daughters,'" ibid., November 10, 1894; "Darien Dots," *Savannah Tribune*, June 26, 1895; W. E. B. Du Bois, *Atlanta University Publications* 14 (1909), 63. For a brief history of the organization, see "International Order of the King's Daughters and Sons," http://www.iokds.org/index2.html.

66 *Therefore it was only fair:* Theophilus G. Steward, "Work for the Women of the Church," *Christian Recorder*, March 20, 1890.

66 *They were key participants:* Albert G. Miller, *Elevating the Race: Theophilus G. Steward, Black Theology and the Making of an African American Civil Society, 1865–1924* (Knoxville: University of Tennessee Press, 2003), 98–113; Albert G. Miller, "Her Children Shall Rise Up and Call Her Blessed: The Use of Rebecca Steward as a Paragon of Female Domesticity," *AME Church Review* 118:385 (January–March 2002): 48. Miller suggests that Theophilus Gould Steward and Alice Felts were at odds over the issue of women's ordination. However, I have found no evidence to substantiate this claim. To the contrary, in 1890 Steward argued for women occupying any and all leadership positions available to men. See Steward, "Work for the Women of the Church." While Theophilus Gould Steward claimed that his mother, Rebecca Steward, "was an uncompromising opponent to women's preaching," there is no evidence that he shared her views. For quote, see Theophilus Gould Steward, *Memoirs of Mrs. Rebecca Steward* (Philadelphia: AME Publishing Department, 1877), 44. Ironically, though Theophilus Gould Steward supported women's equality in the church, in the late 1890s he opposed the admission of women to membership in the prestigious American Negro Academy. See Dorothy Sterling, ed., *We Are Your Sisters: Black Women in the Nineteenth Century* (New York: Norton, 1984), 436–37.

66 *"The greatest trouble":* Rev. C. S. Whitted, "The Mission of Woman," *Star of Zion*, January 22, 1903.

67 *In the case of the AME Church:* Collier-Thomas, *Daughters of Thunder*, 22–23. Acknowledging that AME women were granted some religious rights before the end of the nineteenth century, Gertrude Bustill Mossell emphasized women's "faith to believe" they would be granted "much more" in the twentieth century. See Mrs. N. F. Mossell, "The Quarto-Centennial," *Christian Recorder*, June 6, 1889; Gertrude E. B. Mossell, *The Work of the Afro-American Woman* (Philadelphia: George S. Ferguson Co., 1908).

67 *"triple jeopardy":* Theressa Hoover, "Black Women and the Churches: Triple Jeopardy," in *Black Theology: A Documentary History*, vol. 1: *1966–1979*, 2nd ed. rev., ed. James H. Cone and Gayraud S. Wilmore (Maryknoll, NY: Orbis Books, 1993), 293–303.

68 *Cooper concluded that:* Charles Lemert and Esme Bhan, eds., *The Voice of Anna Julia Cooper* (Lanham, Md.: Rowman and Littlefield Publishers, Inc., 1998), 65–66.

68 *For many decades:* "Three Colored Sisterhoods," AME *Church Review*, 12:1 (July 1895): 167–80; "Negro Religious Sisterhoods," *St. Elizabeth's Chronicle* 1:8 (October 1928): 26; for quote and discussion of black Catholic religious commu-

nities of women in the nineteenth century and black men in the priesthood, see Cyprian Davis, *The History of Black Catholics in the United States* (New York: Crossroad Publishing Company, 1996), 102, 98–115, 146–62, 240–41; for a history of the Oblate Sisters of Providence in the nineteenth century, see Diane Batts Morrow, *Persons of Color and Religious at the Same Time* (Chapel Hill, NC: University of North Carolina Press, 2002); Rev. Raymond George Hill, "Social Works of the Colored Sisterhoods: An Historical Study," (MA thesis, Catholic University, 1932). Since black men were largely excluded from the priesthood until the twentieth century, the parishes were headed by white priests and likewise the sisterhoods were supervised by them. There are no published histories for any of the black Catholic women's religious orders that discuss their development in the twentieth century. For a brief history of their growth and expansion see Work, *Negro Year Book: 1931–1932*, 265–66; in 1929 there were only four black priests in the United States. See Theodore A. Thomas, "Changing the Color Line," *St. Elizabeth's Chronicle* 2:6 (June 1929): 19.

70 *However, black Christian:* In a detailed study of African American religion, Du Bois found that black denominations had the same doctrinal beliefs, systems of government, and disciplines as their parent bodies, differing only in the race of their communicants. See W. E. B. Du Bois, ed., *The Negro Church: Report of a Social Study Made Under the Direction of Atlanta University; Together with the Proceedings of the Eighth Conference for the Study of the Negro Problems Held at Atlanta University, May 26th, 1903* (Atlanta: Atlanta University Press, 1903). For discussion of the survival of African religious traditions, see chapter one.

70 *Most black Methodists:* In 1954 the Colored Methodist Episcopal Church was renamed the Christian Methodist Episcopal Church. For the purposes of this study when the full denominational title is referenced the original name will be used for the period 1870 to 1960. In general the church will be referred to as CME between 1870 and 2005. Othal Hawthorne Lakey, *The History of the CME Church* (Memphis Tenn.: CME Publishing House, 538–42).

70 *Though the General Conference:* For quote, see Richard R. Wright, *The Negro in Pennsylvania: A Study in Economic History* (Philadelphia: AME Book Concern, n.d.); quoted in Jualynne E. Dodson, *Engendering Church: Women, Power, and the AME Church* (Lanham, MD: Rowman and Littlefield Publishers, 2002), 22.

71 *It is responsible:* Ibid., 52–58. For substantiation of the constitutional rights conferred upon women by the Methodist quarterly conferences and specification of requirements for holding office in the Methodist Episcopal, AME, AME Zion, and CME denominations at varying points in time, see the disciplines for each denomination. Like the United States Constitution, amendments to denominational constitutions reflect the social and political changes occurring in women's status in the larger society. Also, though women might gain certain rights, there was no guarantee that they would participate in the polity.

71 *Beginning with several:* Antebellum churches founded by slaves were not "independent." By definition they could not be. Rather, they required the oversight of their slave master or his representative.

72 *Among most Baptists:* For a detailed discussion of the histories and structures of the black Baptist, Methodist, and Pentecostal churches, see Lincoln and Mamiya, *The Black Church*; for discussion of the Full Gospel Baptist Church, see Kenneth C. Ulmer, *A New Thing: A Theological and Personal Look at the Full Gospel Baptist Church* (Tulsa: Vincom, Inc., 1995). The process for becoming a preacher varies among Baptist churches, and may include the notification of one's pastor of receiving a "call," preaching an initial or trial sermon, or authorization by a local

congregation to receive a license following the delivery of a sermon. Baptists are among the most flexible religious traditions in their requirements for ministers. Though this examination includes the major patterns, it does not reference all of the possible variations that may be found among the Baptists.

72 *After the Civil War:* For a historical overview of the holiness tradition among African Americans and a discussion of women preachers in the nineteenth-century movement, see Collier-Thomas, *Daughters of Thunder*, 12–13, 46–55, 57–60, 62–63, 66–68; for a discussion of the healing tradition and examples of black women healers, see Sharla M. Fett, *Working Cures: Healing, Health, and Power on Southern Slave Plantations* (Chapel Hill: University of North Carolina Press, 2002); Rosemary D. Gooden, ed., *Faith Cures, and Answer to Prayer: The Life and Work of the First African American Healing Evangelist* (Syracuse: Syracuse University Press, 2002); "A Healer of the People," *Indianapolis Freeman*, February 13, 1897; "Colored Woman Is Divine Healer," *Star of Zion*, October 26, 1922; " 'Sister,' Who Claims Divine Power to Heal Afflicted Draws Mammoth Crowds," *Pittsburgh Courier*, September 1, 1923; "Harlem 'Boobs' Fleeced in Name of Jesus by 'Sister' Harrell, Is Claim," *Amsterdam News*, March 11, 1925; "Teacher's Sight Restored by Faith Healer," *Norfolk Journal and Guide*, February 17, 1934; "Bishop M. L. McLeod Jewell," *Kansas Plaindealer*, August 27, 1943.

72 *"leading [Baptist] advocates":* Virginia W. Broughton, *Twenty Years' Experience of a Missionary* (Chicago: Pony Press Publishers, 1907), 79.

72 *In the twentieth century:* For a historical overview of black Holiness, Pentecostal, and Apostolic movements, see William C. Turner Jr., "Movements in the Spirit: A Review of African American Holiness/Pentecostal/Apostolics," in *Directory of African American Religious Bodies: A Compendium by the Howard University School of Divinity*, ed. Wardell J. Payne (Washington, DC: Howard University Press, 1991), 41–48.

73 *Holiness devotees emphasize:* Collier-Thomas, *Daughters of Thunder*, 28.

73 *Worship style:* Ibid., 178–79, 184–93.

73 *Among the visitors:* Ibid., 29; Lincoln and Mamiya, *The Black Church*, 76–84; Cheryl Townsend Gilkes, " 'Together and in Harness': Women's Traditions in the Sanctified Church," in *Signs: Journal of Women in Culture and Society* 10:4 (1985): 682, 684, 688–89; Jualynne E. Dodson and Cheryl Townsend Gilkes, "Something Within: Social Change and Collective Endurance in the Sacred World of Black Christian Women," in *Women and Religion in America*, vol. 3: *1900–1968*, ed. Rosemary Radford Ruether and Rosemary Skinner Keller (San Francisco: Harper and Row, 1986), 87.

73 *The early movement:* Turner Jr., "Movements in the Spirit."

73 *During the first decades:* Drake and Cayton, *Black Metropolis*, 640.

74 *Blacks in white-controlled:* Miles Mark Fisher, "The Negro Churches," *Crisis* 45:7 (July 1938): 239.

74 *There is great diversity:* Robert W. Prichard, *A History of the Episcopal Church* (Harrisburg, Pa.: Morehouse Group, 1999).

74 *It legislates for:* Lefferts A. Loetscher, *A Brief History of the Presbyterians*, rev. ed. (Philadelphia: Westminister Press, 1958), 49–54; for information pertaining to black Presbyterians, see Andrew E. Murray, *Presbyterians and the Negro* (Philadelphia: Presbyterian Historical Society, 1966); Gayraud S. Wilmore, "Identity and Integration: Black Presbyterians and Their Allies in the Twentieth Century," in *The Presbyterian Predicament*, ed. Milton J. Coalter (Louisville: Westminister/John Knox Press, 1990); Clarence L. Cave and Kermit E. Overton, "Varieties of Ministries," in *Periscope 2: Black Presbyterianism Yesterday, Today, and Tomorrow*

(New York: Program Agency of the United Presbyterian Church in the U.S.A., 1983), 40.

76 *"many of the hardships"*: Mrs. R. A. Hurley, "The Minister's Wife," *Christian Recorder*, September 9, 1886.

76 *"selecting a partner"*: Charles H. Phillips, "Editorial," *Christian Index*, December 19, 1891.

77 *Burroughs warned that:* Bessie E. Batchelor, "Church Engaged My Husband, Not Me," *Star of Zion*, January 24, 1901; Mrs. M. Guile, "The Ideal Minister's Wife," *AME Church Review* 30:4 (April 1914): 304–05; Mary F. Handy, "The Minister's Wife," *AME Church Review*, ibid., 29:4 (April 1913): 337–38; Mrs. D. L. Furgerson, "The Minister's Wife," *Star of Zion*, July 29, 1920; Mrs. Luke M. Bleakney, "The Minister's Wife," ibid., September 13, 1920; Nannie H. Burroughs, "The Minister's Wife," ibid., August 8, 1929. Whereas most of the articles published in the 1920s represented the views of laywomen, in the 1930s the majority of articles were written by a clergy wife; see Cora E. Moseley, "The Minister's Wife," ibid., September 29, October 27, November 17, December 1, 1932; March 30, April 20, June 29, September 7, 1933; November 29, 1934.

77 *In 1868 white missionaries:* For 1868 quote from the *American Baptist* regarding the role of the "church mothers" in New Orleans black Baptist churches, see Washington, *Frustrated Fellowship*, 109. For examples of "church mothers" in Methodist, Baptist, Pentecostal, and Holiness denominations, see "A Mother in Israel Gone," *Star of Zion*, July 18, 1901; "A Very Large Number Attend 'Mother' Jordan's Funeral," *Philadelphia Tribune*, February 14, 1914; "Woman Church Leader Passes," *Pittsburgh Courier*, April 20, 1940; "Georgia, Florida Churches Plan Merger," *Pittsburgh Courier*, May 4, 1949; "Union Holiness to Host Christ Holiness Confab," *Norfolk Journal and Guide*, July 21, 1956; Dr. J. W. Yancy II, "People on Waco Streets Saying—'Mother Sherman'—Now," *Christian Recorder*, July 21, 1970.

77 *The title was extended:* Cheryl Townsend Gilkes, *If It Wasn't for the Women: Black Women's Experience and Womanist Culture in Church and Community* (Maryknoll, NY: Orbis, 2001), 61–75, 103. Gilkes explains that "church mothers" are usually spiritual and moral leaders who have participated in varied missionary society activities or held offices as deaconess and stewardess. The honorific title of church mother appears to predominate in Baptist, Methodist, and Holiness/Pentecostal churches.

77 *Women leaders:* Shirley J. Yee, *Black Women Abolitionists: A Study in Activism, 1828–1860* (Knoxville: University of Tennessee Press, 1992), 114. For additional sources regarding the appropriate role for women leaders, see "Women as Clergy," *Star of Zion*, January 9, 1936.

77 *Indeed, women exceeded:* Mamie Donohoo, *AME Zion Church Quarterly* 9 (October–December 1899): 45–48; for a comprehensive history of black women's philanthropic efforts, see Bettye Collier-Thomas, "The 'Relief Corps of Heaven': Black Women as Philanthropists," *Association for Research on Nonprofit Organizations and Voluntary Action* 1 (2001): 25–39.

78 *However, Felts spoke:* Felts, "Women in the Church"; Alice S. Felts, "A Timely Reminder," *Christian Recorder*, May 24, 1894; M. R. Mitchell, "Reply to Mrs. Felts," ibid., June 14, 1994.

78 *The realization that:* For a discussion of how women used their power in the AME Church during the late nineteenth century, see Dodson, *Engendering Church*.

78 *The question was:* Roswell Field, "Church Federation—Plans to Reform the Nation," *National Baptist Union*, February 20, 1909; during the early period of its

organization, the association was called the Male Forward Movement. Following two years of organizing, the movement was formally launched in 1911. "Missionary Jubilee," *New York Age*, October 26, 1911.

79 *However, the movement:* "Missionary Jubilee"; C. H. Johnson, "How the Laymen May Best Cooperate with the Minister for Spiritual and Social Ends," *AME Church Review* 29:4 (April 1913): 360–63; for discussion of the AME Laymen's League between 1920 and 1950, see chapter 3. L. G. Jordan, "How to Interest the Individual in Missions," *Mission Herald* 16:12 (December 1910): 1, 3; L. G. Jordan, "The Men and Religion Forward Movement," ibid., 16:4 (November 1911): 2. See also Gail Bederman, " 'The Women Have Had Charge of the Church Work Long Enough': The Men and Religious Forward Movement of 1911–1912 and the Masculinization of Middle Class Protestantism," *American Quarterly* 41:3 (September 1989): 432–65. Bederman acknowledged that she found no analysis of "the relation between gender and masculinity in the black churches during this time period," or "evidence that black churchmen felt any impetus to masculinize their churches." Bederman theorized that racism may have precluded the development of masculinization as an issue for black churches. However, the reasons for this development among black male Protestants were more related to their status as a disfranchised minority in a patriarchal society. Black men sought recognition and validation of their manhood in a society that privileged manliness and masculinity. In 1925 as president of the Alabama Baptist State Convention and a leader in the Baptist Laymen's Movement, Jemison breathed new life into the organization with his prediction that it would eventually be a major force in the denomination. For Jemison's pronouncements regarding the future of the Laymen's Movement, see NBC, *Journal of the Forty-fourth Annual Session of the National Baptist Convention, U.S.A., Inc., Held in Baltimore, Maryland, September 9–14, 1925* (Nashville: Sunday School Publishing Board, 1925), 106.

79 *Turner acclaimed women:* Bishop Turner not only articulated these views, but also acted on them. For example, in 1893, during his long stint in Africa, he employed Mrs. C. E. Young as the manager and editor of the *Voice of Missions*. He informed readers that Young's "scholarship and wide reading [singly] fits her for almost any position where learning and thought are required." Similarly, in 1898, Turner hired Mrs. Blanche B. Saunders, a medical student at Central Tennessee College, as secretary; see "Remarks by Bishop Turner," *Voice of Missions* 1:7 (July 1893); and "No Secretary," ibid., 6:8 (August 1898).

80 *As a result:* Comparisons of black men with black women and struggles over the meaning of black masculinity and femininity were quite common in the nineteenth and twentieth centuries. For the quote by Turner, see "Editorial," *Voice of Missions* 4:9 (September 1896): 2; for examples of the widespread commentary, see "The 'Calamity Howler,' " *Indianapolis Freeman*, August 17, 1895; "Rev. Dr. N. B. Steward on the Defense and Rights of Women Workers in the AME Church," *Voice of Missions* 6:12 (December 1898); Rev. J. Harvey Anderson, "Searchlight Scenes," *Star of Zion*, June 15, 1899; Pauline Hopkins, "Our Noble Womanhood," *Colored American Magazine* 7:8 (August 1904): 530; W. Calvin Chase, "Men vs. Women," *Washington Bee*, March 17, 1906; "Our Women in the Cause of Missions," *Mission Herald* 33:8 (September 1930): 6; Rayford Logan, "Seven Noted Women," *New York Age*, January 23, 1932; "Worries About New He-Women," *Chicago Defender*, January 3, 1943; Ellis Cose, "The Black Gender Gap," *Newsweek*, March 3, 2003, 46–50. For a sample of the criticism and defense of Ida Wells-Barnett, see Rev. G. W. Clinton, "Miss Wells in England," *Star of*

Zion, June 14, 21, and July 19, 1894; "Notes and Comments," *Christian Recorder*, April 26, 1894; "Personals," ibid., June 14, 1994; Rev. J. G. Robinson, "Miss Ida B. Wells and the Governor of Missouri," *Indianapolis Freeman*, July 7, 1894; A. J. Lowe, "Georgia School Teacher's Association," ibid., July 21, 1894; "Local Notes," *Huntsville Gazette*, July 7, 1894; W. Calvin Chase, Editorial, *Washington Bee*, June 12, 1919. For a discussion of the role of NACW leaders in the ensuing discourse, see Deborah Gray White, *Too Heavy a Load: Black Women in Defense of Themselves, 1894–1994* (New York: W. W. Norton, 1999), 59–60, 65.

80 *By 1905:* Among the most prominent secular women's national organizations were the Woman's Christian Temperance Union (1873), National Council of Women (1888), the National American Woman Suffrage Association (1890), the General Federation of Women's Clubs (1891), and the National Association of Colored Women (1896). For brief historical overviews of these organizations, see Wilma Mankiller et al., eds., *The Reader's Companion to U.S. Women's History* (New York: Houghton Mifflin, 1998), 641, 577–81, 242, 392.

80 *"were the legitimate prey":* Du Bois, *The Negro Church*, 4.

81 *Unlike their AME:* In 1900 the Methodist Episcopal Church voted to admit women as members to the General Conference. This action was ratified by two-thirds of the members of the ME Annual Conference as required by the denomination's constitution. As class leaders, ME women were already members of the Quarterly Conference. However, they were not eligible to participate in the district meetings, and the Annual and General conferences. See "For and Against Women," *Star of Zion*, November 10, 1898; "Triumph at Last," *Christian Index*, January 25, 1902; "Women in the General Conference," ibid.; for discussion of St. Elizabeth's Catholic Church, see "The Carnival," *St. Elizabeth's Chronicle* 1:2 (April 1928): 13, 23.

82 *However, a deaconess:* Whereas in Methodist and Episcopal denominations the deacon was the first order of the ordained clergy, among Baptists male deacons were ordained, but were not clergy. They are considered spiritual officers. "Baptist Deaconess Work," *Spelman Messenger* 24:7 (April 1908): 2; "The Feminist and the Churches," *Star of Zion*, March 6, 1930; "Funeral Rites Held for Mrs. Currey, 75," *Amsterdam News*, January 26, 1935; "Thomaston, Ga.," *Indianapolis Recorder*, June 10, 1939.

82 *It was debated:* Rev. J. W. Smith, "A Deaconess," *Star of Zion*, August 25, 1898; "Deaconesses in the AME Church," *Christian Recorder*, July 14, 1898. For an excellent history of the origin of the deaconess position, see H. U. Weitbrecht, "Deaconesses," *Woman's International Quarterly* 4:2 (January 1916): 74–81; World Council of Churches, *The Deaconess: A Service of Women in the World of Today* (Geneva: World Council of Churches, 1966); Harold Nichols, *The Work of the Deacon and Deaconess*, rev. ed. (Valley Forge: Judson Press, 1964), 9–14.

83 *"If this is all":* "Our Woman's Column," *Christian Recorder*, May 26, 1887.

83 *Like that of the stewardess:* "Women as Clergy," *Star of Zion*, January 9, 1936. Though the constitutional definition of a deaconess might differ slightly among the denominations, and some included the term "ordination," the roles were remarkably similar. Unlike the black Methodist denominations, the Protestant Episcopal and Methodist Episcopal disciplines stated that women could be ordained as deaconesses. However, they made it clear that only men could be ordained as clergy. In these two denominations, deaconesses simply received the title of "Reverend" and were assigned specific functions separate from those of the clergy.

83 *The religious activism:* Collier-Thomas, *Daughters of Thunder*, chap. 1, "Women

Who Paved the Way," 41–60. For discussion of Lena Mason and Nora Taylor, see Sylvia G. L. Dannett, *Profiles of Negro Womanhood*, vol. 1: *1619–1900* (Chicago: Educational Heritage, Inc., 1964); "Mrs. Lena Mason Celebrated Woman Preacher Dead," *Norfolk Journal and Guide*, September 20, 1924; Elizabeth Howard, "The Passing of Lena Mason," *Christian Recorder*, November 27, 1924; Nora F. Taylor, "An Address to the Chicago Union Mite Missionary Society," *AME Quarterly Review* 38:3 (January 1922): 109–12; "The Responsibility of Womanhood," *Chicago Defender*, July 1, 1911; "Allen AME Church," *Philadelphia Tribune*, April 6, 1912. Mason, Small, Randolph, and Taylor represent the second generation of black women preachers; however, their careers extend into the twentieth century and overlap with those of the third generation.

84 *AME Zion women:* Collier-Thomas, *Daughters of Thunder*, 69–72, 91–94, 101–06.

84 *The growing ranks:* "Race Gleanings," *Indianapolis Freeman*, February 4, 1905; for biographies and details regarding these women's ministerial careers, see Collier-Thomas, *Daughters of Thunder*, 194–207, 173–93.

84 *"incessant worker":* "Rev. Mary E. Lark Hill," *Chicago Broad Axe*, October 10, 1903; "Chips," ibid., October 31, 1903; "Rev. Mary E. Lark Hill," ibid., June 17, 1905; Rev. M. E. L. Hill, ibid., December 1, 1906.

86 *Continuing their long quest:* For examples of clergywomen's organizations, see "Women's Ministerial Union," *Baltimore Afro-American*, April 20, 1912; "Notice to the Women," ibid., September 30, 1916; "Women's National Evangelistic Conference," ibid., May 30, 1919; "Women's National Evangelistic and Missionary Headquarters," ibid., March 7, 1931; "The Women's Minister's Alliance," *Philadelphia Tribune*, July 12, 1913; "State President of Women Evangelists and Missionaries," *Norfolk Journal and Guide*, July 30, 1927; "Evangelists to Meet Here Again Next Year," ibid., August 13, 1932; "Evangelists in 2-Day Meeting at Union Church," *New York Amsterdam News*, May 7, 1938; "Ordain Pastor's Wife at Little Mt. Carmel," *Philadelphia Afro-American*, December 16, 1944; "Women's Evangelist Alliance Closes Year," *Indianapolis Recorder*, November 23, 1940; "Planning for Evangelist Conference," *Detroit Tribune*, June 21, 1941; "The National Association of Pentecostal Women," *Chicago Defender*, July 1961; "National Association of Clergy Women, Inc.," Eastern Baptist Theological Seminary, Philadelphia, Pennsylvania, August 4, 1990, printed program in possession of the author; A. B. Williams, "The Spirit of Evangelism," *Christian Recorder*, August 20, 1953; "Evangelist Federation," ibid., January 8, 1963; "Fourth Episcopal District Union of Evangelists," ibid., June 8, 1965.

86 *Methodist conferences reported:* Editorial, *Christian Recorder*, October 26, 1950. To address this disparity, denominations developed plans and made concerted efforts to recruit young men to the ministry. In 1950 a black Methodist minister found "many youth of ability and character are preparing for medicine, law, pharmacy, engineering, journalism, dentistry, and like secular pursuits, but only a few are interested in religion." Even more disturbing to him was the lack of concern, among young black men, for what some denominations viewed as "an alarming situation."

86 *In a study:* Kathleen C. Berkeley, " 'Colored Ladies Also Contributed': Black Women's Activities from Benevolence to Social Welfare, 1866–1896," in *The Web of Southern Social Relations: Women, Family, and Education*, ed. Walter J. Fraser Jr. et al. (Athens: Ga. University of Georgia Press, 1985), 181–203.

87 *Commenting on the chief:* "The AME Conference," *Chicago Broad Ax*, May 14, 1904.

87 *"On the Lord's Day":* For discussion of similar membership patterns in the Bed-

ford, Pennsylvania, AME Zion Church, see AME Zion, *Journal of the 54th Session of the Allegheny and 7th Session of the Allegheny-Ohio Annual Conference of the AME Zion Church, Held in Pittsburgh, Pennsylvania, October 22–28, 1902* (York, Pa: Dispatch Publishing Co., 1902), 42; for discussion of membership patterns in Chicago at the beginning of the twentieth century, see Lisa Gail Materson, "Respectable Partisans: African American Women in Electoral Politics, 1877 to 1936" (PhD diss., University of California, Los Angeles, 2000), 92; Anna Arnold Hedgeman, *The Trumpet Sounds: A Memoir of Negro Leadership* (New York: Holt, Rinehart and Winston, 1964), 38; for additional information on Hedgeman, see Paula F. Pfeffer, "Hedgeman, Anna Arnold (1899–1990)," in *Black Women in America: An Historical Encyclopedia*, vol. 1, ed. Darlene Clark Hine (Brooklyn, NY: Carlson Publishing, 1993), 549–52.

87 *In 1901, while arguing:* Benjamin F. Lee, "The Roanoke Deaconess Home," *Christian Recorder*, March 21, 1901.

87 *In 1904, 85 percent:* Emmett J. Scott, "The Tuskegee Negro Conference," *Voice of the Negro* 1:5 (May 1904): 179.

87 *Most black settlements:* The early American settlement movement virtually excluded African Americans. The movement began in the late 1880s to accommodate the needs of the masses of European immigrants who were crowding into the slums of major cities. White settlement workers were concerned with helping white immigrants. A few welcomed blacks among Russian Jews, Slavs, Irish, and Italians, but most either excluded them or opted for segregated facilities. For black women and their organizations settlement work was part of their overall program of self-help and institution building. Major scholarship on the settlement movement cite very few of the early settlements for blacks. The best sources for information about black settlements are black newspapers, journals, biographies and autobiographies, and related organizational and personal collections. For examples of black organized settlement work, see Margaret Murray Washington, "Social Improvement of the Plantation Woman," *Voice of the Negro* 1:7 (July 1904): 288–90; "White Rose Mission Settlement," *New York Age*, July 6, 1905; Fannie Barrier Williams, "Growth of Social Settlement Idea," ibid., August 3, 1905; "Washington Poor People," ibid., July 18, 1907; Janie Porter Barrett, "Social Settlement for Colored People," *Southern Workman* 41:9 (September 1912): 511–15; Edward Franklin Frazier, "Neighborhood Union in Atlanta," ibid., 52:9 (September 1923): 437–42; "Work of Uplift Shows Results," *Baltimore Afro-American*, August 31, 1912; Floris Barnett Cash, "Radicals or Realists: African American Women and the Settlement House Spirit in New York City," *Afro-Americans in New York Life and History* 15 (January 1991): 7–17; Sarah Collins Fernandis, "Social Settlement Work Among Colored People," *Charities and the Commons* 21 (November 21, 1908): 302; "Social Settlements for Negroes," in *Negro Year Book*, ed. Monroe Work (Tuskegee, Ala.: Tuskegee Institute, 1913), 271–72. See also Robert A. Woods and Albert J. Kennedy, *Handbook of Settlements* (New York: William F. Fell Co., 1911), 6, 8, 30, 50, 97, 121, 171, 178, 267, 270, 287, 298; see also Allen Davis, *Spearheads for Reform: The Social Settlements and the Progressive Movement 1890–1914* (New York: Oxford University Press, 1967), 95. In speaking of black settlements, Davis incorrectly states, "In almost every case the initiative for the settlement came from interested whites rather than Negroes."

88 *The movement included:* Ralph E. Luker, *The Social Gospel in Black and White: American Racial Reform, 1885–1912* (Chapel Hill: University of North Carolina Press, 1991).

88 *"extra parochial"*: Rev. H[utchens] C. Bishop, "How to Hold the Young People in the Church," *Southern Workman* 27:9 (September 1898): 179–80; "Old Landmark Sold," *Indianapolis Recorder*, February 26, 1910.

88 *Helm believed that:* Helm, *The Upward Path*, 281–82, 286–87.

89 *He regretted that:* Steward, "Work for the Women of the Church." A few churches such as the Union Bethel AME Church in Washington, D.C., elected a male and female superintendent to supervise Sunday school classes segregated by gender. See *People's Advocate*, April 19, 1979.

89 *However, Mixon did not:* W. H. Mixon, "Against Women Preaching," *Christian Recorder*, March 18, 1886.

89 *"so much for them":* Rev. L. J. Coppin, "Women to the Front," *Christian Recorder*, March 15, 1888.

89 *As a result:* Collier-Thomas, *Daughters of Thunder*, 26–27. "Philadelphia and Vicinity," *Christian Recorder*, June 30, 1898; Mary C. Palmer was among the most noted AME evangelists of the Philadelphia conference who was well known for the Holiness meetings and conventions she regularly held at the Mission House located at 918 Locust Street in Philadelphia during the 1890s and early twentieth century. For information related to Palmer, see "Personals," *Christian Recorder*, October 15, 1891, January 20, and March 12, 1896, April 26, 1900, October 17, 1901, and March 20, 1902.

90 *The resolution passed:* Stephen Ward Angell, "The Controversy over Women's Ministry in the African Methodist Episcopal Church during the 1880s: The Case of Sarah Ann Hughes," in *This Far By Faith: Readings in African American Women's Religious Biography*, eds. Judith Weisenfeld and Richard Newman (New York: Routledge, 1996), 95–97.

90 *In 1887 the North Carolina:* Collier-Thomas, *Daughters of Thunder*, 27.

90 *Full clergy rights:* Collier-Thomas, *Daughters of Thunder*, 20, 26–27, 32.

90 *Women were appointed:* For a discussion of the stewardess position in the AME Church, see Dodson, *Engendering Church: Women, Power and the AME Church* (Lanham, MD: Rowman & Littlefield Publishers, 2002), 58–59.

90 *"it is conceded":* "Deaconesses in the AME Church," *Christian Recorder*, July 14, 1898.

91 *Whereas Slater was:* "Deaconesses in the AME Church," *Christian Recorder*; Bethel AME hired Sarah Slater when it became known that a white church in Philadelphia had offered her a position. Since Slater was a member of Bethel and wished to serve in her own church, it would have been an embarrassment for the AME Church to ignore her request. However, her expenses and entire support for the year were raised and paid for by her white friends and admirers. For a discussion of Amanda Smith's role, see Grant, "Deaconess Manual"; for consecration of AME women as deaconesses, see "Chicago Annual Conference," *Christian Recorder*, October 8, 1925; David Johnson, "Bishop A. L. Gaines Holds Record Breaking Conference," ibid., October 21, 1926.

91 *"arm of rescue":* Lee, "The Roanoke Deaconess Home"; "Connectional, Religious, Personal," *Christian Recorder*, February 19, 1901; "A Deaconess' Home," ibid., March 21, 1901; "Report of Committee on the State of the Church," ibid., May 16, 1901. The deaconesses' home envisioned by Bishop Lee never materialized. See "A Missionary Department for the Women of Our Church," *AME Church Review* 4:152 (April 1922): 199–200.

91 *As the position was popularized:* For example, the Indiana State Deaconess Association, founded in 1921, held annual conventions throughout the state. See "AME

Deaconess Close Successful Convention," *Indianapolis Recorder*, August 26, 1944; "Indiana State Deaconess Ass'n to Have Session Aug. 9," ibid., August 4, 1945.

91 *All five hundred:* "The AME Conference," *Chicago Broad Ax*, May 14, 1904.

91 *For example, although:* This legislation was passed at the Twenty-fourth Quadrennial Session of the AME Church meeting in Louisville, Kentucky, in May 1924. See "AME Session Closed on Wednesday," *Baltimore Afro-American*, May 23, 1924; "Report of Lay Delegate W. C. Overton to Long Island Dist. Churches," *New York Age*, May 31, 1924; "Bethel Women Members May Get Church Vote Right," *Philadelphia Tribune*, October 14, 1950; Thomasina Hayward, "Mother Bethel Gets Legal Name," *Christian Recorder*, May 7, 1953.

92 *In 1944 Alexander:* "AME Bishops Name Woman as Attorney," *Indianapolis Recorder*, June 3, 1944; for information regarding Sadie Tanner Alexander and Willie Roundtree, see "Laymen of AME Church Check Power Long Held by Bishops," *Pittsburgh Courier*, May 29, 1948; Francille Rusan Wilson, "Sadie T. M. Alexander: A 'True Daughter' of the AME Church," *AME Church Review* 119:391 (July–September 2003): 40–46; Theresa Snyder, "Sadie Alexander (1898–1989)," in Smith, *Notable Black American Women, Book I*, 5–8.

92 *It would be eight years:* "Our Women," *Christian Recorder*, July 16, 1926. Legislation was introduced at the 1928 AME General Conference meeting in Chicago granting the presidents of the WPMS and the WHFMS the right to be seated as delegates of the General Conference. See AME, *Journal of the Twenty-eighth Quadrennial Session, General Conference of the AME Church, May 7–23, 1928* (Philadelphia: AME Book Concern, 1928), 98.

93 *Finally, in 1960:* "Women Will Ask for Change in AME Discipline," *Pittsburgh Courier*, April 25, 1936. A bill for ordination of women who possessed four years' experience as ministers, had completed a four-year course of study in a theological seminary, and had passed the AME elder's examination was defeated at the AME General Conference of 1936. A key figure in the struggle for full clerical rights for women, Rev. Martha Jayne Keys, was a prominent leader in the Woman's Parent Mite Missionary Society. See Collier-Thomas, *Daughters of Thunder*, 34–35; Dennis C. Dickerson, "Martha Jayne Keys and the Ordination of Women in the African Methodist Church," *AME Church Review* 118:385 (January–March 2002): 72–83.

93 *She organized and served:* "841 Delegates Certified to Next AME General Conference," *Baltimore Afro-American*, February 27, 1932. Carrie Hooper, born in 1894, died in New York in 1996 at the age of 102. For information concerning her life and career, see "Evangelist Writes Book," *Pittsburgh Courier*, January 14, 1933; F. B. Livingstone, "First Female Candidate to Aspire for the Office of Bishop," *Christian Recorder*, July 14, 1964; Carrie T. Hooper, "A Vision," ibid., November 12, 1963; funeral program, "A Service of Praise and Thanksgiving 'Obsequies' for the late Rev. Dr. Carrie T. Hooper, 1894–1996," December 20, 1996, AME Church Records, Department of Research and Scholarship, AME Sunday School Union, Nashville, Tennessee.

93 *Though Hooper failed:* For quote, see Dr. J. W. Yancy II, "Women in the Spirit of the Age," *Christian Recorder*, August 4, 1964; Dennis C. Dickerson, " 'The Making of a Female Bishop': From Jarena Lee to Vashti Murphy Mckenzie," *AME Church Review* 116: 377–378 (summer 2000): 14–16.

93 *Foote was the second:* Collier-Thomas, *Daughters of Thunder*, 22–24.

93 *The ordination of Julia Foote:* Julia Foote was ordained deacon by Bishop Hood on May 13, 1895, and not on May 20, 1894, as originally cited in William Jacob

Walls, *The African Methodist Episcopal Zion Church: Reality of the Black Church* (Charlotte, NC: AME Zion Publishing House, 1974), 111, and repeated in subsequent publications, most notably in Lincoln and Mamiya, *The Black Church*, 285, and Sandy Dwayne Martin, *For God and Race: The Religious and Political Leadership of AMEZ Bishop James Walker Hood* (Columbia, SC: University of South Carolina Press, 1999). For correct citation, see AME Zion Church, *Minutes of the New York Conference African Methodist Episcopal Zion Church, Seventy-fourth Session, Held at AME Zion Church, Newburg, N.Y., May 8th-13th, 1895* (Salisbury, NC: Livingstone College Press, 1895), 21, 31, 58.

94 *At eighty-two years:* In Collier-Thomas, *Daughters of Thunder*, 23, Julia Foote's age at the time she was ordained to the diaconate is incorrectly cited as "seventy-one"; her death certificate cites her age at death as eighty-eight in 1901. Therefore she was eighty-two at the time of her ordination. See New Jersey State Department of Health, Julia A. J. Foote, "Report of Death," Document 27111, November 24, 1901.

94 *She was widely known:* At the time of her ordination, and until her death in 1901, Julia Foote resided with Bishop Alexander Walters and his family. Foote developed a close relationship to Walters during the early 1880s when she assisted him in his ministry at the Stockton Street AME Zion Church in San Francisco. Walters was elevated to the episcopacy in 1892. See Collier-Thomas, *Daughters of Thunder*, 23, 59; "Personal Mention," *Star of Zion*, August 22, 1895.

94 *Her primary gain:* Collier-Thomas, *Daughters of Thunder*, 23.

94 *"they had power":* Mary J. Small was ordained on Sunday, May 19, 1895; see J. W. Smith, "Philadelphia and Baltimore Conference," *Star of Zion*, June 6, 1895; "Rev. Mary J. Small," Ibid., November 17, 1898.

94 *Guinn (1899) was the third:* "The Missouri Conference," *Star of Zion*, September 20, 1894; "News from Kentucky," ibid., December 20, 1894; Bishop W. J. Walls, "Mary Elizabeth Taylor," ibid., April 21, 1955; Collier-Thomas, *Daughters of Thunder*, 105; AME Zion, *Minutes of the Second Joint Session of the Allegheny and Ohio Conference, September 21, 1898*, 21; Sarah Pettey, "Woman's Column," *Star of Zion*, November 2, 1899.

95 *At the Missouri Annual Conference:* "The Missouri Conference," *Star of Zion*, September 20, 1894.

97 *But she argued:* "Some of Our Noble Women," *Star of Zion*, November 12, 1896; Josie C. Mayes, "Our Women Preachers and Their Influence," *AME Zion Church Quarterly* 9 (October–December 1899): 53–56. This article was published only months after the controversy over the ordination of Mary Small as an elder ended.

97 *The* Star of Zion *reported:* "Wife Wants to Come," *Star of Zion*, September 29, 1898.

97 *Declaring that the men:* Mrs. Rev. W. L. Moore, "Eyes of Jealousy," *Star of Zion*, July 28, 1898; Mrs. F. A. Clinton, "Take My Advice," ibid., August 10, 1899; Carissa Betties, "Let Rev. Mrs. Small Alone," ibid., December 15, 1898.

99 *Hughes began her ministry:* For discussion of Sarah Pettey, Marie Clinton, and Victoria Richardson and their leadership in the AME Zion Woman's Home and Foreign Missionary Society, see Glenda Elizabeth Gilmore, *Gender and Jim Crow: Women and the Politics of White Supremacy in North Carolina, 1896–1920* (Chapel Hill: University of North Carolina Press, 1996), 154–55. For an excellent discussion of Sarah Hughes and the AME controversy surrounding her ordination, see Angell, "The Controversy over Women's Ministry," 95.

99 *In the aftermath:* "Female Elders," *Star of Zion*, October 27, 1898; for biographi-

cal information on James Walker Hood, see Walls, *The African Methodist Episcopal Zion Church*, 578; and Martin, *For God and Race*.

99 *Like most WHFMS officers:* "Bishop C. C. Pettey D.D. of the AME Zion Church Cut Down by Grim Death," *Star of Zion*, December 13, 1900; Rev. B. J. Bolding, "Mrs. S. F. C. Pettey," AME Zion Church, *Minutes—1897, Sixty-ninth Session of the Philadelphia and Baltimore Annual Conference of the AME Zion Connection Convened in St. John's AME Zion Church, Chambersburg, Pennsylvania, Wednesday, May 19th, 1897* (Harrisburg, Pa.: William Howard Day, 1897), 7, 85–86; Dannett, *Profiles of Negro Womanhood*, 303. See also Gilmore, *Gender and Jim Crow*, 154.

100 *Walters was extremely:* Alexander Walters, *My Life and Work* (New York: Fleming H. Revell Company, 1917), 12–13, 22.

100 *Bishop Clinton's wife:* "Mrs. George W. Clinton," *Baltimore Afro-American*, April 29, 1911. Under Marie Clinton's leadership, the North Carolina federation, representing women from various Protestant denominations, discussed "important subjects" such as "The Relation of the Club Women to the Church." See "Personals," National Association of Colored Women, *National Notes* 15:3 (December 1911): 3.

100 *He was a staunch supporter:* For biographical data on Alexander W. Walters, Charles C. Pettey, John Bryan Small, and George Wylie Clinton, see Walls, *The African Methodist Episcopal Zion Church*, 580–86; "The Late Bishop Alexander Walters," *Star of Zion*, February 5, 1920; George M. Miller, "The Social Mission of Bishop Alexander Walters," *AME Zion Quarterly Review* 83:2 (summer 1976): 117–23; B. F. Wheeler, "The Late Bishop J. B. Small, D.D.," ibid., 4:2 (February 1905): 34–38. For Bishop Small's support of his wife's ordination as an elder, see Bishop John Bryan Small, "Mrs. Small's Case," *Star of Zion*, June 16, 1898, and "Woman Ordination," ibid., August 11, 18, 25, and September 1, 1898.

100 *It was conceded:* Rev. J. Harvey Anderson, "Searchlight Scenes: Ordination of Women and the General Conference," *Star of Zion*, September 29, 1898; Bishop J. W. Hood, "Female Elders," ibid., October 27, 1898; Rev. S. A. Chambers, "He Has Killed It," ibid., November 10, 1898; AME Zion Church, *Official Journal of the Daily Proceedings of the Twenty-first Quadrennial Session of the General Conference of the African Methodist Episcopal Zion Church, Held in Metropolitan AME Zion Church, Washington, D.C., May 2 to 22, 1900* (York, Pa: Dispatch Print, 1901), 76.

100 *Though many AME Zion:* Margena A. Christian, "AME Zion Church Elects First Female Bishop," *JET*, August 18, 2008.

101 *For many decades:* Collier-Thomas, *Daughters of Thunder*, 15, 27; Lakey and Stephens, *God in My Mama's House*, 70; Harry V. Richardson, *Dark Salvation: The Story of Methodism as It Developed Among Blacks in America* (New York: Anchor Press, 1976), 225–26; Randall Albert Carter, "Southern Methodism's Oldest Daughter," *Christian Index*, May 25, 1939.

102 *Between 1870 and 1935:* Carter, "Southern Methodism's Oldest Daughter." The first conferences were organized in Tennessee, Mississippi, Alabama, Georgia, Kentucky, Arkansas, Texas, and South Carolina. During the Great Depression, the CME Church made a conscious decision to follow its membership to Detroit, Cleveland, Indianapolis, Philadelphia, Pittsburgh, Chicago, Newark, New York, Kansas City, Kansas; Springfield, Massachusetts; Kansas City, Missouri; and other cities in the North and West, where it established missions and churches. By 1945 it was located in eighteen states in the North and West, and by 1989 it reported a membership of 900,000 in the United States and 75,000 overseas. For discussion of conference development, see Richardson, *Dark Salvation*, 226–27; Lincoln and Mamiya, *The Black Church*, 60–65; for discussion of the CME

Church's reaction to the Great Migration, see "The C.M.E. Church Reacts to the Migration," in CME, *Minutes of the Fourteenth General Conference and the Fourteenth Quadrennial Session of the C.M.E. Church, Held in Lane Tabernacle C.M.E. Church, St. Louis, Missouri, May 3–16, 1922* (Jackson, Tenn.: CME Publishing House, 1922), 18–21.

102 *They were denied:* Collier-Thomas, *Daughters of Thunder*, 27; Lakey and Stephens, *God in My Mama's House*, 72; Lakey and Stephens (a CME bishop and a laywoman), absolve the CME Church, in particular the bishops and male clergy, from all blame and responsibility for their attitudes and treatment of CME women as second-class members, undeserving of any rights. The authors suggest that CME women quietly accepted their plight, when in fact they did not. Lakey and Stephens argue, "It is in the light of the need for and their commitment to survival—the survival of their families and their race during the years of Reconstruction and Reaction—that we are to understand the role of women in the black church generally and the CME Church specifically. The responsibilities those turbulent times thrust upon African-American women, however, demanded that the needs of the race be placed above their rights as women. Priority had to be given to duties that had to be performed rather than positions that might be earned. The quest for leadership both within the church and without was bequeathed to their daughters and grand daughters. For the most part women in the CME Church served in the shadows, unknown and without recognition."

102 *Since women were:* Ibid. CME, *The Fifth Session of the General Conference of the Colored Methodist Episcopal Church in America Convened in the Trinity C.M.E. Church, Augusta, Georgia, May 5, 1886* (Memphis, Tenn.: CME Publishing House, 1886), 316, 321; CME, *The Sixth Session of the General Conference of the Colored Methodist Episcopal Church in America Convened in Miles Chapel, Little Rock, Arkansas, May 7, 1890* (Jackson, Tenn.: CME Publishing House, 1890), 404–05.

102 *CME bishops were certain:* CME, *The Eighth Session of the General Conference of the Colored M.E. Church of America Convened in Collins Chapel, Memphis, Tennessee, May 2, 1894* (Jackson, Tenn.: CME Publishing House, 1894), 481, 532.

103 *These appeals:* Ibid., 500–01.

103 *The licensing of Roberts:* Ida E. Roberts, "More About Clergy Rights for Women," *Christian Index*, December 26, 1946, 2; Collier-Thomas, *Daughters of Thunder*, 26–27.

103 *In that year:* Collier-Thomas, *Daughters of Thunder*, 27–28; "Williams Temple Nets $3,700 during Jubilee," *Philadelphia Afro-American*, October 14, 1944.

103 *Though they were responsible:* A. J. Cobb, "Some Issues of the Forthcoming General Conference," *Christian Index*, February 1, 1902.

104 *Thus, the bishops:* Charles H. Phillips, Editorial, *Christian Index*, May 17, 1902. Please note that Lakey and Stephens, in *God in My Mama's House*, 86, incorrectly state that the 1894 legislation provided for the office of stewardess automatically included women "in the membership of the quarterly conference and gave women the right to vote on all church officers, persons seeking licenses to preach, matters of property, and delegates to district conferences." Legally, this is so; however, in reality, women were not permitted to participate in the Quarterly Conference, which is why the question was raised at the 1902 General Conference. Lakey and Stephens provide no documentation for the data they present on this issue.

104 *In this manner:* CME Church, *Doctrines and Discipline of the Colored Methodist Episcopal Church in America*, rev. ed., 1902 (Jackson, Tenn.: CME Publishing House, 1902), 53–54.

104 *Though limited in number:* CME, *Minutes of the Sixteenth General Conference and the Fifteenth Quadrennial Session of the Colored Methodist Episcopal Church, Held in Jamison Temple C.M.E. Church, Kansas City, Mo., May 5–18, 1926* (Jackson, Tenn.: CME Publishing House, 1926), 195; CME, *CME Quadrennial Address of the Bishops of the Colored Methodist Episcopal Church to the Eighteenth Delegated General Conference Assembled in Hot Springs, Arkansas, May 1938,* 48.

105 *Agreements made:* "How the Baptists Do It," *Union Signal,* June 14, 1888. For an excellent example of how Baptist ministers in the District of Columbia attempted to centralize power in a local conference and establish standard rules to be followed by all member churches, see "Citizen Flays Baptist Conference for Attempting to Abrogate Rule," *Washington Tribune,* January 19, 1935; George Howard Mack, "Danger to Church's Independence Seen in Spread of Ministerial Power," ibid., February 2, 1935. In this case, lay church members organized and challenged the authority of the Baptist Conference, arguing that because of the sovereignty of each church, the conference had no power to legislate for its members. The laity perceived the Baptist Conference as an attempt by the clergy to seize power and override congregational authority.

105 *For example, in 1895:* "Brevites," *Savannah Tribune,* November 2, 1895. The First Bryan Baptist Church founded in Savannah, Georgia, and the First African Baptist Church, during the late eighteenth century, claimed to be the oldest black Baptist churches in the United States. "F.A.B. and F.B.B. Churches Celebrate 132nd Year—Both Churches Enjoy Distinction of Being Oldest," ibid., January 17, 1920; "First Bryan Church Has Fine Celebration," ibid., January 26, 1928.

105 *Rev. Harvey Johnson:* "Dr. Johnson Laid to Rest," *Baltimore Afro-American,* November 17, 1917; Union Baptist Church, "Minutes of Regular Church Meeting," June 1, 1910, 283; April 27, 1911, 307, recorded in the Union Baptist Church, Baltimore, Maryland; *Minutes, Vol. II, October 28, 1897, to March 26, 1919,* Union Baptist Church, Baltimore, Maryland (hereafter cited as UBC). The Union Baptist Church minutes consists of two volumes. Volume I, November 3, 1872, to June 3, 1874, contains twenty-seven miscellaneous loose-leaf pages. Volume II is complete. Minutes are very brief and rarely provide details regarding discussions and debates.

106 *Women's participation:* For examples of the patterns cited, see "A Useful Woman Gone," *Savannah Tribune,* July 16, 1898; UBC, I and II; First African Baptist Church, Richmond City, Minutes, Book I, II, and III, 1841–1859 and 1875–1930, Virginia State Library and Archives, Richmond, Virginia (hereafter cited as FABC). In the late nineteenth and early twentieth centuries all church correspondence, minutes of meetings, and records were kept by the church clerk, who was cited in the Union Baptist and First African church minutes as male. In each of these churches there was no position designated as "secretary" until the 1920s and '30s.

106 *However, in the case:* Mechal Sobel, *Trabelin' On: The Slave Journey to an Afro-Baptist Faith* (Westport, Conn.: Greenwood Press, 1979), 208.

106 *Though women had a voice:* For the reference to Rev. Peter Randolph, see Higginbotham, *Righteous Discontent,* 120. There are no known extant records of church meetings at the Ebenezer Baptist Church. However, the *Richmond Planet* regularly reported on the activities at local churches. For information regarding women voting on the pastor at Ebenezer, see "God Called the Pastor," *Richmond Planet,* September 14, 1901.

107 *The petition was tabled:* See FABC, I, II, and III; Petition of Mrs. Margaret Osborne et al., "To the deacons and members of the First Baptist Church," dated

April 15, 1880, and presented at the "regular church meeting," June 27, 1880, FABC, II, 141–42. The petition of the First African Baptist women to vote on the hiring and firing of the minister is one example of nineteenth-century protests of black church women for suffrage and other "rights" in their religious traditions. These women were influenced by a number of internal and external factors, including the ongoing discourse and demands of women for participatory democracy and equality in the church and society. My research findings agree with those of Jacquelyn Jones, who asserts that black men, "like other groups in nineteenth-century America, . . . believed that males alone were responsible for—and capable of—the serious business of politicking." Elsa Barkley Brown, "Negotiating and Transforming the Public Sphere: African American Political Life in the Transition from Slavery to Freedom," in *The Black Public Sphere: A Public Culture Book* (Chicago: University of Chicago Press, 1995), 111–13; Jacquelyn Jones, *Labor of Love, Labor of Sorrow: Black Women, Work, and the Family from Slavery to the Present* (New York: Basic Books, 1985), 66.

107 *Mired in national:* For a detailed discussion of the divisive issues precipitating the struggle over the election of a pastor for the First African Baptist Church, see Ann Field Alexander, *Race Man: The Rise and Fall of the "Fighting Editor," John Mitchell Jr.* (Charlottesville: University of Virginia Press, 2002), 117–30.

108 *"worse than a minstrel show":* The regional, class, and generational divisions characterizing First African Baptist Church were typical in black denominations at the beginning of the twentieth century. Debates about the significance of the black church in the black community were quite common. In his monumental history of "the Negro Church," Carter G. Woodson concluded that the church was deeply divided over issues of doctrine, music, and styles of worship. Conservatives held fast to the pre-war patterns of worship, and theology, whereas religious progressives—more interested in assimilation—embraced more mainstream styles of worship and theology. See chapter 12, "The Conservative and Progressive," Carter G. Woodson, *The History of the Negro Church*, 3rd ed. (Washington, DC: Associated Publisher, 1921; reprint, 1972), 224–41 (page citations are to the reprint edition). For discussion of the church meetings and the important role of women in the election of the pastor of the First African Baptist Church, see "Did God Call the Pastor?" *Richmond Planet*, July 6, 1901; "First Baptist Church Trouble," ibid., July 13, 1901; "Hot Times There," ibid., July 20, 1901; "The First Church Muddle," ibid., July 27, 1901; "Stormiest of All the Meetings," August 10, 1901; "Editor Mitchell's Statement: A Review of the First Baptist Church Trouble," ibid., August 17, 1901. Maggie Lena Walker, a leader in the NACW and the first woman banker in the United States, similar to other elite NACW leaders like Anna Julia Cooper, Mary Church Terrell, and Alice Dunbar Nelson detested what Cooper described as "the rank exuberance and often ludicrous demonstrativeness" and the "semi-civilized religionism" found in numerous black churches. Anna Julia Cooper, *A Voice from the South: By a Black Woman of the South* (New York: Oxford University Press, 1988 [1892]), 34–35; Mary Church Terrell, Diary, May 24, 1936, Mary Church Terrell Papers, Library of Congress; Gloria T. Hull, ed., *Give Us Each Day: The Diary of Alice Dunbar-Nelson* (New York: W. W. Norton, 1984), 179, 224; For biographical information on Maggie Lena Walker, see Gertrude W. Marlowe, "Walker, Maggie Lena (1867–1934)," in *Black Women in America*, vol. 2, ed. Hine, 1214.

108 *There was a particular:* Lawrence W. Levine, *Black Culture and Black Consciousness: Afro-American Folk Thought from Slavery to Freedom* (New York: Oxford University Press, 1977), 162–70; Du Bois and other black intellectuals argued that "the

curious custom of emotional fervor" was no longer attracting young people and thus was detrimental to the development of the church; see Du Bois, *The Negro Church*, 207–08; Dexter Avenue Baptist Church in Montgomery, Alabama, is an excellent example of a black middle-class church that abhorred revivals and shouting, and disdained spirituals. For discussion of Dexter Avenue's beliefs and practices, see Taylor Branch, *Parting the Waters: America in the King Years 1954–63* (New York: Simon and Schuster, 1988), 11.

108 *In some states:* During the late 1930s, camp meetings, reminiscent of the antebellum period, continued to hold sway among African Americans in rural Virginia. The typical camp meeting was described as "a great festival of shouting and song, where old-time songs are sung as slave ancestors knew them. . . . Far into the night the worshipers shout, while backsliders proclaim their sins." As their bodies moved to the sway of the music and exhibited "the frenzy of the 'jerks,' " they shouted and pranced as they confessed "the joy of being 'born again.' " See Work Projects Administration Virginia Writers' Program, *The Negro in Virginia* (New York: Hastings House Publishers, 1940), 254–55.

109 *The minister blamed:* "Blood Flowed," *Cleveland Gazette*, July 1, 1905; for other examples of the laity challenging the authority of Baptist ministers in Boston and the District of Columbia, see " 'Hub' Baptists Air Troubles," *New York Age*, March 29, 1917; "Church Case Again in Court," *Washington Tribune*, September 16, 1922.

110 *"All business meetings":* "Rev. Taylor's Trial Tuesday Women Tell of True Conditions in Church," *Washington Tribune*, February 25, 1922; "Rev. Taylor Makes Desperate Attempt to Win Public Sympathy," ibid., February 11, 1922.

110 *At the local level:* See Mack, "Danger to Church's Independence." In terms of structure, there are many variations that a church might adopt. For example, some churches have constitutions, whereas others do not. In case of squabbles, challenges may be brought on the basis of the local constitution.

110 *These men—similar:* For an example of how deacon boards exerted their power, see R. T. Lockett, "Resignation of Pastor Requested," *Philadelphia Tribune*, April 26, 1924. For discussion and analysis of the careers of Adam Clayton Powell Jr., Martin Luther King Jr., Ralph Abernathy, Jesse Jackson, Calvin Butts, and Floyd Flake, see Wil Haygood, *King of the Cats: The Life and Times of Adam Clayton Powell, Jr.* (New York: Houghton Mifflin, 1993); Clayborne Carson, *The Autobiography of Martin Luther King, Jr.* (New York: Warner Books, 2001); Ralph David Abernathy, *And the Walls Came Tumbling Down: An Autobiography* (New York: HarperCollins, 1991); Barbara A. Reynolds, *Jesse Jackson: America's David* (Washington, DC: JFJ Associates, 1985); USA Weekend, "Special Reports: Religion, Rev. Calvin Butts," USAWeekend.com; Religion and Ethics News Weekly, "Profile: Floyd Flake," September 24, 2004, episode no. 804, www.pbs.org/wnet/religionandethics.

111 *Female evangelists were:* "The Interdenominational Missionary Convention . . . ," *Star of Zion*, June 22, 1906; "Prominent Among Women Leaders," *Norfolk Journal and Guide*, November 18, 1916; "Union Revival Meetings," *Washington Bee*, March 23, 1912; "The Great Evangelist," ibid., February 7, 1914; *Baltimore Afro-American*, January 26, 1923; "First Annual Convention of the Second Emancipation League," *Philadelphia Tribune*, October 26, 1912; P. J. Tay, Letter to the Editor, *National Baptist Union Review*, September 7, 1918; "Tribute to Late Mrs. Devereaux," *Savannah Tribune*, April 2, 1925; "Berean Baptist Church," *Norfolk Journal and Guide*, April 18, 1925; "South Dakota," *Chicago Defender*, August 21, 1926; "Girl Evangelist Sends Greetings to Many of Her Friends," *Pittsburgh*

Courier, January 6, 1934; "Rev. Mrs. Howard Conducts Revival," ibid., "Evangelistic Singer Returns," *Indianapolis Recorder*, September 13, 1941; "News of the
Churches," ibid., November 1, 1941; "Come to Church," ibid., March 18, 1944;
"Coppin Chapel," ibid., April 8, 1944; "Mrs. V. Belcher Presented at 17th St.
Baptist," ibid., May 20, 1944; "Madeline Shank at First Baptist, North Indianapolis," ibid., November 18, 1944; "Evangelist Dies," *People's Voice*, December
15, 1945; "Evangelist in Her 4th Annual Service," *Indianapolis Recorder*, January
3, 1948; "Rev. Mrs. Nadine Coleman," ibid., October 2, 1950; "A Spiritual Feast
at Mt. Pleasant Baptist Church Sunday 3:30," ibid., January 9, 1954;
"Evang[elist] Talley Speaks at Coppin," ibid., June 11, 1966; "Evangelist Rice
Guest Speaker at Pathway Baptist," ibid., October 16, 1971.

111 *Fearful of alienating:* Lewis G. Jordan, "Women Preachers," *Mission Herald* 19:7
(July 1913): 2. Jordan was editor of the *Mission Herald*, and corresponding secretary for the Foreign Mission Board of the National Baptist Convention. Though
Jordan opposed women preaching, he supported the organization of the Baptist
Woman's Convention. He viewed it as a vehicle to raise funds for foreign missionary work. See Higginbotham, *Righteous Discontent*, 156. For examples of how
domesticity was used by male clergy and other leaders in the twentieth century,
see "Baptists Get New Definition of Sin," *Washington Afro-American*, May 3,
1941. Jordan's comments came at a time when the male-led National Baptist
Convention was trying to force the Woman's Convention into a subordinate
position as a board that answered to the all-male NBC-USA board. See discussion in chapter 4.

112 *As a member:* "Tribute to Late Mrs. Devereaux," *Savannah Tribune*, April 2, 1925.

112 *Taylor-Birchmore belonged:* "Thousands Pay Tribute to Remains of Mrs. Birch-
more," *Pittsburgh Courier*, April 12, 1941.

112 *To attract more males:* "Baptists Ban Women Preachers," *Indianapolis Recorder*, May
26, 1934. At present, there are no studies documenting the history of black Baptist women preachers. Higginbotham's study of black Baptist women, covering
the period 1880–1920, makes no mention of Baptist women as preachers or evangelists. See Higginbotham, *Righteous Discontent*. For Ella Eugene Whitfield, an
example of a Baptist missionary preacher, see Collier-Thomas, *Daughters of
Thunder*, 5–6, 153–61.

112 *In the presidential election:* "Prominent Among Women Leaders," *Norfolk Journal
and Guide*, November 18, 1916; "Record of Attendance for Alice L. Waytes,"
Moody Bible Institute, 1904, Moody Bible Institute Library, Chicago, Illinois.

113 *Even if they favored:* "Blazing Trails in Her 50 Years as a Minister," *Philadelphia
Inquirer*, May 14, 2000. Rev. Toland's influence among Baptist ministers in
Philadelphia resulted in the ordination of other women. In 1951 Bessie Sim-
mons, the assistant pastor of Good Shepherd Church, was ordained by Rev. Joel
F. Frazier, Toland's successor at Enon. See "Woman an Ordained Minister,"
Philadelphia Tribune, October 23, 1951. Among the earliest Baptist women
preachers in Philadelphia were Mary Tribbitt, the first woman to be licensed by
the First African Baptist Church, and Rev. Mrs. G. R. King, who was ordained in
1915. King was the wife of Rev. Dr. J. C. King, pastor of the Second Baptist
Church in Frankford, Pennsylvania. For information on Tribbitt and King, see
"First African Baptist Church," *Philadelphia Tribune*, May 18, 1912; "City Federation Holds One Day Conference," ibid., June 13, 1929; "Rev. Mrs. King Feted
on 25th Anniversary," ibid., October 31, 1940.

113 *In the 1960s:* "Rev. Mrs. Charles O. Trimm Elected Pastor at New Testament,"
Chicago Defender, November 6, 1965; "The Holy War of the Rev. Trudie

Trimm," *Ebony* (September 1969), 72–77. During the early 1980s Rev. T. J. Jemison, president of the National Baptist Convention, USA, Inc., claimed that the denomination "has had three women pastors within the past twenty-five years," including Trudie Trimm, a Chicago woman who took charge of a church during the illness of her husband, and Rev. Flora Bridges, the assistant pastor of Grace Church in Mount Vernon, New York. See Lincoln and Mamiya, *The Black Church*, 296.

114 *A graduate of Emerson College:* The American Baptist Churches in the USA is a predominantly white, but multiracial, denomination of more than 1.5 million. For brief biographical information on Rev. Suzan D. Johnson, see Ella Pearson Mitchell, ed., *Those Preachin' Women: Sermons by Black Women Preachers* (Valley Forge, Pa.: Judson Press, 1985), 119. Founded in 1913 and held annually in Hampton, Virginia, the Hampton University Ministers Conference was an interdenominational gathering of clergy from diverse denominations. During the early part of the twentieth century it was billed as a "Man-Building Program." Ministers assembled to partake of lectures and participate in discussions on numerous topics concerning sermon development, program development, vital social issues of the time, and interreligious cooperation. For a discussion of the Hampton Ministers' Conference, see William Anthony Aery, "230 Ministers Meet at Hampton," *Amsterdam News*, July 11, 1923; "Hampton University Ministers' Conference," *Christian Century*, July 31, 2002.

114 *It was her feeling:* "Sisters of the Cloth: African-American Women Try to Break the Clerical 'Old Boy Network!' " in Howard University, *Alumni Magazine* (June 1993): 51. In June 2002 Rev. Suzan D. Johnson Cook was elected the first female president of the ten-thousand-member Hampton University Ministers' Conference, the premier interdenominational organization for black clergy. Cook noted that in 1980 she was one of only ten senior pastors in attendance. At that time women were not invited to lead any of the sessions. President William Jefferson Clinton appointed her to the Domestic Policy Council (1994) and the President's Advisory Commission on Race (1997). See Joy Duckett Cain, "Suzan D. Johnson Cook: Cracking the Stained-Glass Ceiling," *Essence* (February 2003).

115 *In 1895 these groups:* Lincoln and Mamiya, *The Black Church*, 23–30; Higginbotham, *Righteous Discontent*, 64–65.

115 *Throughout its history:* Higginbotham, *Righteous Discontent*, 65–66.

115 *A small number:* According to Evelyn Higginbotham, of the 213 delegates present at the ANBC Convention in 1892, thirty-two were women. These included Mary V. Cook, a professor at the State University of Louisville, who was elected recording secretary of the NBEC. Cook and Elizabeth A. Garland of Virginia served as members of the NBEC's first executive board. Between 1887 and 1892, women were most active in the ANBC, serving on a separate women's committee, participating with men on other committees, and holding a few offices. Mary Cook was a member of the ANBC's executive committee. Julia Mason (Layton) of Washington, D.C., served on the executive board of the ANBC Bureau of Education. Amanda V. Nelson and Lucy Wilmot Smith, leading figures in the Kentucky women's state convention, held positions as statistical secretary and historian. See Higginbotham, *Righteous Discontent*, 64–65, 250n59.

115 *"rose up in their churches":* Virginia W. Broughton, *Twenty Years' Experience of a Missionary* (Chicago: The Pony Press Publishers, 1907), 34; Higginbotham, *Righteous Discontent*, 68–70.

116 *Similar to the women:* Higginbotham, *Righteous Discontent*, 71.

116 *Some churches shunned:* Using data culled from the federal census, Dr. Samuel A.

Steuffer, a University of Chicago professor, detailed the reasons why blacks migrated out of the Deep South to the North and West as well as to border states. Steuffer argued that in the two decades preceding the Depression they left to find jobs in northern industry. But during the Depression not only were blacks "losing out in southern agriculture," but they were the hardest hit by the Depression and received less in relief than white southerners. The North offered higher relief bounties and thus many of the 403,000 persons who migrated between 1930 and 1940 were in search of relief. See "Says Relief Drew 403,000 Negroes from the South," *Kansas Plaindealer*, May 23, 1941; see also Collier-Thomas, *Daughters of Thunder*, 33. For discussion of the role of women in the Pentecostal/Holiness movement in Chicago, see Drake and Cayton, *Black Metropolis*; and Wallace D. Best, *Passionately Human: No Less Divine* (Princeton, NJ: Princeton University Press, 2005).

117 *Healing was one:* For a brief discussion of Tate, see Sherry Sherrod DuPree, *African-American Holiness Pentecostal Movement: An Annotated Bibliography* (New York: Garland Publishing, Inc., 1996), 509. For discussion of blacks and the healing arts, see Fett, *Working Cures.*

117 *It is for this reason:* Dupree, *African American Holiness*, 266, 509. Lightfoot's church was originally called the King's Chapel. For a discussion of Ida Robinson's life and career and examples of her sermons, see Collier-Thomas, *Daughters of Thunder*, 194–207.

118 *As founders and pastors:* For discussion of the careers and doctrinal differences among these women, see Collier-Thomas, *Daughters of Thunder*, 173–207. For Elder Lucy Smith, see Best, *Passionately Human*, 149–80.

118 *"have charge of a church":* Collier-Thomas, *Daughters of Thunder*, 29; Gilkes, "Together and in Harness," 684, 688–89; "With, Without Female Clergy," *USA Today*, May 24, 2006.

118 *The CWC's annual meetings:* Willa Thomas, "1500 Women of Churches of God in Christ Here for Meet," *Indianapolis Recorder*, August 4, 1962; "Church of God in Christ Set Annual Women's State Convention," ibid., September 18, 1971.

119 *The Women's Department:* "Church of God in Christ Closed Convocation at Memphis," *Chicago Defender*, December 30, 1939; for quotes, see Anthea Butler, "A Peculiar Synergy" (PhD diss., Vanderbilt University, 2001), 2, 5.

119 *"Most modern religion":* Linda Faye Williams, "Power and Gender: A Glass Ceiling Limits the Role of Black Women in the Civil Rights Community," *Emerge* (December–January 1995): 63–65.

CHAPTER 3 *"A Woman's Church Within the Church"*

120 *"We have been taught":* Mrs. Dr. J. R. Porter, "Prophecy Woman's Club," *Voice of Missions* 5:3 (March 1897).

121 *For many black women:* In 1899 the Boston-based Woman's Era Club, an affiliate of the NACW, announced a public meeting to discuss the worldwide impact of U.S. and European imperialism on people of color. See "Territorial Expansion and its possible effect upon the Colored Peoples of the world," handbill announcing a meeting of the Woman's Era Club at Revere Street M[ethodist] E[piscopal] Church, on March 20, 1899, Boston Public Library, Special Collections. The term "race" woman was used during the late nineteenth and early twentieth centuries to identify black American political and social activists who worked to advance people of African descent. For examples of the use of the

expression, see "Tributes to the Life and Work of Miss Mary R. Hoyt of Albany," *New York Age*, November 23, 1905.

121 *In an assessment:* Elise Johnson McDougald, "The Double Task: The Struggle of Negro Women for Sex and Race Emancipation," *Survey* 53 (March 1, 1925): 689–91. Elsie Johnson McDougald, a native of New York, pioneered in the field of Vocational Guidance. As a member of the Alpha Kappa Alpha sorority during the early 1920s she established the sorority's national Vocational Guidance program. Elise Johnson McDougald, "Vocational Guidance—A Professional Field for the College Woman," *Ivy Leaf* 3:1 (May 1924): 48–49.

121 *Black women:* In March 1988, at the AHA Conference on Women in the Progressive Era in a presentation on "The History of the National Association of Colored Women," I used "practical feminism" to illustrate how black women pursued and defined their feminist efforts and to counter the assertions of women historians who argued that because black women privileged race over sex they could not be considered feminist. The term "womanist" was "appropriated" by black women theologians, from novelist Alice Walker, who presented the concept as a way of defining the difference between black and white women's feminism. Womanist proponent Delores S. Williams explained that many black women used the term "as a way of affirming themselves as *black* while simultaneously owning their connection with feminism; and with the African-American community, male and female. The concept of womanist allows women to claim their roots in black history, religion, and culture." Delores S. Williams, "Womanist Theology: Black Women's Voices," in James H. Cone and Gayraud S. Wilmore, *Black Theology: A Documentary History*, vol. 2 (Maryknoll, NY: Orbis, 1993), 265–66. See chapter 8 for a discussion of the womanist theology movement.

121 *Thus, their feminism:* Patricia Hill Collins states, "Race, class, and gender represent the three systems of oppression that most heavily affect African-American women." But, whereas black women must grapple with all three, "white women are penalized by their gender but privileged by their race." Patricia Hill Collins, *Black Feminist Thought: Knowledge, Consciousness, and the Politics of Empowerment* (New York: Routledge, 1991), 224. See also Paula Giddings, *When and Where I Enter: The Impact of Black Women on Race and Sex in America* (New York: William Morrow and Company, 1984), 6–8.

121 *The masses of Protestant:* For discussion of movements such as social Darwinism and eugenics that buttressed notions of white supremacy, see Christine Rosen, *Preaching Eugenics: Religious Leaders and the American Eugenics Movement* (New York: Oxford University Press, 2004); Richard Hofstadter, *Social Darwinism in American Thought* (Boston: Beacon Press, 1992). For discussion of the linking of racism with eugenics, see Mark H. Haller, *Eugenics: Hereditarian Attitudes in American Thought* (New Brunswick, NJ: Rutgers University Press, 1963), 144–76.

122 *"In some denominations":* E. P. Murchison, "The Freedom of Women," *Christian Index*, January 30, 1947.

122 *Speaking in the context:* There are no book-length studies of black women in the Episcopal and Presbyterian churches, and very few articles that trace the history of women and their organizations in these denominations. For quote and analysis of black Episcopal women's attitudes and concerns during the latter part of the twentieth century, see Marjorie Nichols Farmer, "Different Voices: African American Women in the Episcopal Church," in *Episcopal Women: Gender, Spirituality and Commitment in an American Mainline Denomination*, ed. Catherine M. Prelinger (New York: Oxford University Press, 1992), 231, 222–38.

123 *"The women who wash"*: Nannie Helen Burroughs, "Baptist Women's Edition," *National Baptist Union*, August 8, 1903.

123 *As members of segregated:* In 1883 the Woman's Home Missionary Society of the Methodist Episcopal Church (WHMS) organized "bureaus" of work administered by white women for Native Americans, Mexicans, Chinese, "illiterate" southern whites, Mormons, and "Colored People in the South." This work represents an early form of what was later referred to as "interracial work"—representing white women working on behalf of the "Negro." Though limited in its discussion of black women, one of the best sources for discussion of the early organizing efforts of Methodist Episcopal women is Ruth Esther Meeker, *Six Decades of Service, 1880–1940: A History of the Woman's Home Missionary Society of the Methodist Episcopal Church* (New York: Continuing Corporation of the Woman's Home Missionary Society, 1969).

124 *The growing power:* For the quote and a history of COGIC's Women's Department, see Anthea D. Butler, "A Peculiar Synergy" (PhD diss., Vanderbilt University, 2001), 165; Cheryl Townsend Gilkes, "Together and in Harness: Women's Traditions in the Sanctified Church," *Signs* 10:4 (1985): 678–99.

124 *The majority of men:* Alexander Crummell, "Letter," *Christian Recorder*, November 19, 1870.

124 *For example, in the late:* Mrs. N. F. Mossell, "Work for Women of the Church," *Christian Recorder*, January 19, 1893; D. A. Graham, "Indiana Women's Mite Missionary Convention," *Voice of Missions* 5:7 (July 1, 1897).

125 *In 1904, for example:* "Treasurer's Report," *Home Mission Monthly* 9 (July 1904): 220–22.

125 *" 'break up the effort' ":* NBC, *Proceedings of the Twenty-fourth Annual Session of the Woman's Convention, Auxiliary to the National Baptist Convention, U.S.A., Inc., Held in Nashville, Tennessee, September 10–15, 1924* (Nashville: Sunday School Publishing Board, 1924), 324.

125 *Patterns of opposition:* "Ministers and Women," *New York Age*, March 12, 1908.

125 *"harness the full strength":* NBC, *Journal of the Forty-fourth Annual Session of the National Baptist Convention, U.S.A., Inc., Held in Nashville, Tennessee, September 10–15, 1924* (Nashville: Sunday School Publishing Board, 1924), 78.

125 *"movement will fill":* NBC, *Journal of the Forty-fifth Annual Session of the National Baptist Convention, U.S.A., Inc., Held in Baltimore, Maryland, September 9–14, 1925* (Nashville: Sunday School Publishing Board, 1925), 106.

126 *Wright claimed that:* "Bishop Offers Program to Revamp AME Church," *Pittsburgh Courier*, February 21, 1948.

126 *Locust revealed that:* O. M. Locust Sr., "Wayside Pulpit," *Mission Herald* 60:11 (March–April, 1958): 3; Rev. William J. Harvey III, "Men and World Missions," ibid., 67:5 (March–April 1965): 28. As the corresponding secretary for the NBC-USA's Foreign Mission Board, Harvey was alarmed by the "indifference and non-participation of men" in missionary work. He asserted that there was an "unwritten exclusion of men" practiced by most Baptist churches. Beatrice Birdsong, "Chattanooga District Holds Area Missionary Meeting," *Christian Recorder*, February 8, 1966. In a sermon entitled "Master Missionary," AME minister Rev. George Knight stated, "The Lord told both men and women to go into the vineyard and work and whatever was right He would pay. If this great missionary work was only for women, only women would be paid."

127 *Not a few men:* Evelyn Brooks Higginbotham cites a controversy that occurred among Arkansas Baptists during the 1880s in which women's right to organize

separately was challenged for these reasons. For quote, see Higginbotham, *Righteous Discontent*, 68.

127 *These experiences helped:* For biographical data on S. Willie Layten and Nannie Burroughs, see Jessie Carney Smith, ed., *Notable Black American Women, Book II* (New York: Gale Research, 1996), 403–06; Darlene Clark Hine, ed., *Black Women in America: An Historical Encyclopedia*, vol. 1 (Brooklyn: Carlson Publishing, 1993), 137–40, 201–05.

130 *Both Burroughs and Layten:* Smith, *Notable Black American Women, Book II*, 403–06; Higginbotham, *Righteous Discontent*, 159–60. From the beginning Burroughs and Layten clashed. While they agreed on essential issues relevant to the need to improve the status and fight for the rights of women and blacks, they perceived the world through different lenses related to their individual experiences. It is for these and other reasons that they maintained a contentious relationship for more than forty years. Because of their superb intellects and immense organizational and leadership skills, the WC succeeded in many of its ventures. But there were also instances where the organization suffered and its resources were dissipated because of the constant warfare between Burroughs and Layten, and their followers.

130 *She also refused:* NBC, *Journal of the Twenty-first Annual Session of the National Baptist Convention, Held in Cincinnati, Ohio, September 11–16, 1901* (Nashville: National Baptist Publishing Board, 1901), 29; NBC, *Journal of the Twenty-second Annual Session of the National Baptist Convention, Held in Birmingham, Alabama, September 17–22, 1902* (Nashville: National Baptist Publishing Board, 1902), 59; NBC, *Journal of the Third Annual Assembly of the Woman's Convention, Held in Birmingham, Alabama, September 17–22, 1903* (Nashville: National Baptist Publishing Board, 1903), 20, 38. For public discussions about the WC's status, see Nannie Helen Burroughs, "Woman's Department," *National Baptist Union*, June 21, 1902; Elias Camp Morris, "Great Meeting of the Baptists in Birmingham," ibid., September 27, 1902; E. W. D. Isaac, "Women Agreeing to Have a Board," ibid., March 7, 1903; S. Willie Layten, "President Layten Favors a Woman's Board," ibid., March 14, 1903; see also Higginbotham, *Righteous Discontent*, 159–60.

130 *Within three years:* E. W. D. Isaac, "The Women Fulfilling Prophecy!" *National Baptist Union Review*, March 14, 1903.

130 *The most immediate concern:* "The World Black and White Looks on in Disgust," *National Baptist Union Review*, March 3, 1915; "Shall We Have Two Conventions?" ibid., September 11, 1915; "Drs. Morris, Griggs, Parish, Rodgers and Their Followers Have Split the Convention," ibid., September 18, 1915.

131 *Questions of ownership:* "Baptists Squabble," *Washington Bee*, September 16, 1916. The Educational Board "practically smothered" the other NBC boards, and business and education overshadowed missionary interests—the primary reason for founding the convention. For an excellent discussion of the reasons for the breakup of the National Baptist Convention into two separate conventions, see Cassius Kent Jones, "The Fight in the Baptist Church," *Half Century Magazine* 7:1 (July 1919); Evelyn Brooks Barnett, "Burroughs and the Education of Black Women," in *The Afro-American Women: Struggles and Images*, ed. Sharon Harley and Rosalyn Terborg-Penn (Port Washington, NY: Kennikat Press, 1978), 98.

131 *The more visible:* This discussion focuses exclusively on the activities of the NBC-USA's Woman's Convention, the largest and most dominant black Baptist women's group.

133 *"Many Negroes have colorphobia":* Nannie Burroughs, "Not Color, but Character," *Voice of the Negro* 1:7 (July 1904): 277–79; "Negroes Discriminate Against Negroes," *Washington Tribune*, March 19, 1926; "Nannie Burroughs Raps Race Leaders," *New York Age*, May 30, 1953; "Nannie Helen Burroughs Lists National Goals," *Chicago Defender*, July 18, 1953; see also Sharon Harley, "Nannie H. Burroughs: The Black Goddess of Liberty," in V. P. Franklin and Bettye Collier-Thomas, ed., *Journal of Negro History* 81 (1997): 62–71.

133 *"Stop making laws":* Nannie H. Burroughs, "Twelve Things the Negro Must Do for Himself, and Twelve Things the White People Must Stop Doing to the Negro," undated pamphlet.

133 *With a solid base:* Burroughs was supported by the most prominent editors of the national black press in her long struggle with the NBC. It was widely asserted that "[t]he people of the country, backed by the press and the level-headed members of the National Baptist Convention, were a unit for Miss Burroughs," and "[o]ur solid citizens, regardless of denomination or faction, are a unit in Miss Burroughs's favor." For quotes, see "Miss Burroughs Wins Her Case," *Indianapolis Freeman*, December 2, 1916; "News of the Nation's Capital!" ibid., October 14, 1916; Prominent Baptists, including clergy, such as Walter Brooks, W. H. Jernigin, Rev. William Alexander, and other national leaders, including Dr. Carter G. Woodson and William Pickens, supported Burroughs; "The Baptist Convention," *Washington Tribune*, September 16, 1916; *Washington Bee*, September 23, 1916; "Miss Nannie H. Burroughs," ibid., September 30, 1916; "Your Job," *Mission Herald* 23:7 (September 1919): 3; "Miss Burroughs's School," *New York Age*, June 12, 1926; "Convention Ownership," *National Baptist Union Review*, January 7, 1928; "Dean Pickens Praises Nannie H. Burroughs," *Pittsburgh Courier*, October 22, 1938.

133 *However, the opposition:* In *Righteous Discontent*, historian Evelyn Brooks Higginbotham notes the importance of the National Training School and its ability to attract a large percentage of the donations to the Woman's Convention. Though Higginbotham identifies differences between Burroughs, Layten, and Virginia Broughton during the first three years of the WC's existence, she suggests a level of solidarity and cooperation between Burroughs and Layten, and the WC and the NBC, as well as unanimity among the members of the WC Executive Board, that did not exist between 1903 and 1920. The NBC and Woman's Convention minutes, national press reports, and Baptist correspondence tell a different story.

133 *"uplift our sex":* Nannie Burroughs, "The Auditor's Report," *Washington Bee*, September 30, 1916. From the beginning of the Woman's Convention, Burroughs and Layten were engaged in an ongoing struggle for power. Between 1915 and 1950 the WC was torn apart by internal power struggles. Beginning with the failed efforts to establish the NBC as the owner of the National Training School in Washington, D.C., WC President S. Willie Layten and her NBC cohorts did everything in their power to destroy Burroughs's reputation and influence. But rank-and-file Baptist church women were proud of the institution, and continued to sponsor dinners, bake sales, and a variety of fund-raising activities to support it. Between 1900 and 1920, the majority of the donations to the Woman's Convention's were for the school. The school was the first site of the NBC Executive Board's long-term struggle to gain total control of the Woman's Convention finances.

134 *There were widespread:* "Crucify the Women Too," *National Baptist Union Review*, December 25, 1915, reprinted from the *Atlanta Independent*.

134 *Under the new charter:* Burroughs, "Auditor's Report."

134 *Moreover, disposition:* Ibid.; the NBC-USA was incorporated on May 17, 1915. See "Miss Burroughs on the Job," *Washington Bee*, September 23, 1916.

134 *Confronted with mounting:* "Miss Burroughs Wins Her Case"; "Miss Burroughs Vindicated," *Washington Bee*, June 9, 1917; "Miss Burroughs on the Job."

135 *"must be both in name":* NBC, *Journal of the Forty-fourth Annual Session of the National Baptist Convention, Held with the Baptist Churches, Nashville, Tennessee, September 10–15, 1924* (Nashville: National Baptist Publishing Board, 1924), 47.

135 *Fearing that the public:* "Miss Burroughs Denies Baptists Aided School," *Chicago Defender*, April 11, 1925.

135 *Refusing to be subordinated:* Nannie H. Burroughs, "Nannie H. Burroughs Discusses the Training School Situation," *New York Age*, January 14, 1928; "Baptist Convention Can't Have Her School Says Nannie Burroughs," *Baltimore Afro-American*, January 7, 1928.

136 *Following the dictates:* "Miss Burroughs Terms Charges Falsehoods," *Washington Afro-American*, August 20, 1938; "Baptists Purchase School Grounds," *Pittsburgh Courier*, January 11, 1936. Roger Williams University was established in the late nineteenth century by the American Baptist Home Mission Society as a school for black youth. In 1938, S. Willie Layten announced that the WC would assume financial responsibility for the National Missionary Training School. In 1950, following her election as WC president, Burroughs disputed claims that the Woman's Convention had ever accepted responsibility for the Nashville school. See Letter to A.M. Townsend from Nannie Helen Burroughs, April 28, 1956, Box 43, NHB-LC.

136 *"pass upon the resolution":* "Baptists May Not Re-Open National Training School," *Pittsburgh Courier*, August 6, 1938; "Baptists Fail to Restore Support to National Training School in D.C.," ibid., September 24, 1938; "Miss Burroughs Says School Will Open in October," ibid., October 1, 1938; "National Baptist Convention Accused of Double-Crossing Training School in Washington," *New York Age*, October 1, 1938; "My Hands Are Clean—My Soul Unsullied—My Chin Up!—Nannie Helen Burroughs Defends Action," *Pittsburgh Courier*, October 8, 1938. In 1947, in anticipation of Burroughs's election as WC president, the NBC-USA rescinded the 1938 motion to withdraw support from Burroughs's school. See NBC, *Proceedings of the Forty-sixth Annual Session of the Woman's Convention, Auxiliary to the National Baptist Convention, U.S.A., Inc., Held in Kansas City, Missouri, September 10–14, 1947* (Nashville: Sunday School Publishing Board, 1947), 356–60.

137 *At the behest:* NBC, *Proceedings of the Fortieth Annual Session of the Woman's Convention, Auxiliary to the National Baptist Convention, U.S.A., Inc., Held in Cleveland, Ohio, September 10–14, 1941* (Nashville: Sunday School Publishing Board, 1941), 278–79, 286, 291–92, 274; NBC, *Proceedings of the Forty-first Annual Session of the Woman's Convention, Auxiliary to the National Baptist Convention, U.S.A., Inc., Held in Memphis, Tennessee, September 9–13, 1942* (Nashville: Sunday School Publishing Board, 1942), 245–47, 254–55, 285–86, 279–82, 297; NBC, *Proceedings of the Forty-second Annual Session of the Woman's Convention, Auxiliary to the National Baptist Convention, U.S.A., Inc., Held in Chicago, Illinois, September 8–12, 1943* (Nashville: Sunday School Publishing Board, 1943), 285; NBC, *Proceedings of the Forty-third Annual Session of the Woman's Convention, Auxiliary to the National Baptist Convention, U.S.A., Inc., Held in Chicago, Illinois, September 6–10, 1944* (Nashville: Sunday School Publishing Board, 1944), 220, 223.

137 *Though it had sponsored:* NBC, *Proceedings of the Forty-fourth Annual Session of the Woman's Convention, Auxiliary to the National Baptist Convention, U.S.A., Inc., Held*

in Detroit, Michigan, September 5–9, 1945 (Nashville: Sunday School Publishing Board, 1945), 336.

137 *All challenges:* NBC, *Proceedings of the Forty-second Annual Session of the Woman's Convention, 1943,* 315.

138 *Burroughs concluded that:* For discussion of issues relevant to the WC's status under Burroughs's presidency, see the following correspondence: Letters to D. V. Jemison from Nannie Helen Burroughs, April 21, 1950, and October 1, 10, 25, 1951, Box 38, NHB-LC,; Letters from D. V. Jemison to Nannie Helen Burroughs, September 19, 1951, October 28, 1951, Box 15, ibid. For reiteration of Burroughs's position regarding the WC turning over money to the NBC-USA without "becoming part of the policy-making body for it," see NBC, *Proceedings of the Seventy-first Annual Session of the National Baptist Convention, U.S.A., and Minutes of the Woman's Convention, Held in Oklahoma City, Oklahoma, September 5– 9, 1951* (Nashville: National Baptist Publishing Board, 1951), 360–61.

138 *"[W]e are living":* NBC, *The Record of the 92nd Annual Session of the National Baptist Convention U.S.A., Inc., and the 72nd Annual Session of the Woman's Convention, Held in Fort Worth, Texas, September 5–10, 1972* (Nashville: National Baptist Publishing Board, 1972), 182. Mary O. Ross of Detroit, Michigan, began her rise to power in the WC during the 1940s as the chairman of the ministers' wives committee. She served as WC president from 1961 to 1995. As the wife of a minister, Ross was willing to accommodate the WC to the demands of the NBC-USA; under her administration the WC was an auxiliary in every sense of the word. For biographical information regarding Ross, see Margaret Taylor Goss, "Baptist Women's Auxiliary Brings Leaders Together," *Chicago Defender,* September 18, 1943; National Baptist Convention, USA, Inc., "History of the Woman's Auxiliary," http://www.nationalbaptist.com. Since 1995 the WC, now known as the "Woman's Auxiliary," has had three presidents: Cynthia Perry Ray (1995–2000), Rosa Burrell Cooper (2001–2004), and Hugh Dell Gatewood (2005–present).

138 *Thus, at the beginning:* Aldon D. Morris and Shayne Lee, "The National Baptist Convention: Traditions and Contemporary Challenges," undated paper, 28–29.

139 *As a witness:* Please note that Smith did not claim that this was the first national convention of black women, just the "first large convention." Mrs. W. T. Anderson, "Women's Mite Missionary Convention," *Christian Recorder,* July 20, 1893; Richard R. Wright Jr., ed. *The Centennial Encyclopaedia of the African Methodist Episcopal Church* (Philadelphia: AME Book Concern, 1916), 324; Christine S. Smith, "The Woman's Parent Mite Missionary Society of the AME Church," ca. 1943, National Archives for Black Women's History, NCNW Collection, Ser. 18, Box 1, Mary McLeod Bethune National Historic Site, Washington, DC.

139 *Black Methodist Episcopal:* Among the many black Episcopal women's organizations were the Acolytes' Guild, Women's Auxiliary, Helping Hand Society, Altar Guild, and Church Aid Society. See "St. Phillip's Is Happy over Age, Growth," *Amsterdam News,* May 8, 1937; "Mrs. Pettiford Is Accorded Service," ibid., April 4, 1936.

139 *However, in the early:* For the plight of Methodist Episcopal women, see "The Memorial of the Women," *Baltimore Afro-American,* September 13, 1913; "St. Clement's Send Delegation to N.Y.," ibid., May 15, 1937; "Episcopal Women Confine Efforts to Works of Mercy," *Baltimore Afro-American,* October 26, 1935. The National Council of Catholic Women was founded in 1920 as part of the Lay Organization Department of the National Catholic Welfare Conference. It is a federation of Catholic women's organizations. It is not clear when black

women's organizations were accepted in the federation, or the extent to which they participated in the national organization. Black Catholic women typically belonged to the Ladies Sodality, and a number of clubs with diverse names, which performed functions similar to those of the Baptist and Methodist ladies aid and women's missionary societies. For examples of the activities engaged in by the Ladies Sodality, see "Young Ladies Sodality Breakfast," *St. Elizabeth's Chronicle* 1:2 (April 1928): 28; Charles H. Anderson, "The Carnival," ibid., 13; Rev. William M. Markoe, "The New School Campaign," ibid., 6; "Parish Items," ibid., 1:10 (December 1928): 21–22.

140 *The MECS attempted:* Theressa Hoover and Mary Lou Van Buren, *To a Higher Glory: The Growth and Development of Black Women Organized for Mission in the Methodist Church, 1940–1968* (New York: Methodist Episcopal Church, 1980), 28; John Patrick McDowell, *The Social Gospel in the South: The Woman's Home Mission Movement in the Methodist Episcopal Church, South, 1886–1939* (Baton Rouge: Louisiana State University Press, 1982), 84–115. For definition and discussion of the biracial work of white Methodist and other women, see chapter 7.

141 *With the exception:* William Jacob Walls, *The African Methodist Episcopal Zion Church: Reality of the Black Church* (Charlotte, NC: AME Zion Publishing House, 1974), 376; Idonia Elizabeth Rogerson, *Historical Synopsis of the Woman's Home and Foreign Missionary Society, African Methodist Episcopal Zion Church* (Charlotte: AME Zion Publishing House, n.d.), 32. The majority of CME women leaders were wives of ministers, not bishops and elders.

142 *A hegemonic masculinity:* As Patricia Hill Collins explains, "Hegemony is a mode of social organization that relies on ideology to make oppressive power relations seem natural and normal. One goal of hegemonic ideologies is to absorb the dissent of oppressed groups, thereby dissipating its political effects. . . . Hegemonic ideologies may seem invincible. But ideologies of all sorts are never static but instead are always internally inconsistent and are resisted." See Patricia Hill Collins, *Black Sexual Politics: African Americans, Gender, and the New Racism* (New York: Routledge, 2004), 332n12.

143 *Thus, during the first:* For quote and analysis of the CME Church's status during the late nineteenth century, see Randall Albert Carter, "Southern Methodism's Oldest Daughter," *Christian Index*, May 25, 1939; see also chapter 2, "Colored Methodism and the New Paternalism," in Reginald F. Hildebrand, *The Times Were Strange and Stirring: Methodist Preachers and the Crisis of Emancipation* (Durham: Duke University Press, 1995), 15–27.

144 *Caroline W. Poe:* Othal Hawthorne Lakey, *The History of the C.M.E. Church* (Memphis, Tenn.: C.M.E. Publishing House, 1985), 270. Sources were not found for documenting the history of the CME Women's Missionary Society in the state conferences prior to the forming of a national organization.

144 *This eliminated the need:* "Constitution of the Woman's Missionary Society," *Christian Index*, February 18, 1888; F. M. Hamilton, "The Woman's Missionary Society," ibid., June 9, 1888.

144 *The remaining funds:* "Constitution of the Woman's Missionary Society"; whereas the original constitution had required that 20 percent of all funds collected be set aside for the General Mission Board, the 1890 constitution required twenty-five percent. "The Woman's Missionary Society," ibid., June 9, 1888; CME, "Journal of General Conference," 1890, 424, handwritten journal, CME Archives, Memphis, Tennessee. General Conference minutes for the years 1870 to the beginning of 1906, and from 1906 to 1914 are handwritten in two volumes. Volume I

is held by the CME Archives, and Volume II is in the private collection of Rev. Clyde Williams in Atlanta, Georgia. After 1914, General Conference minutes were published and distributed to the membership.

145 *"preachers, possessing evil hearts"*: Christianna E. Lloyd, "Alabama Letter," *Christian Index*, August 27, 1887; Jennie E. Lane, "The Woman's Missionary Society," ibid., March 24, 1888; Alice Parham, "To the Ladies of the Woman's Missionary Society of Missouri and Kansas," ibid., October 27, 1888.

145 *Rev. F. M. Hamilton:* F. M. Hamilton, "The Woman's Missionary Society," *Christian Index*, June 9, 1888.

145 *Hamilton later admitted:* F. M. Hamilton, Editorial, *Christian Index*, December 8, 1888.

145 *"a strong indication":* F. M. Hamilton, Editorial, *Christian Index*, September 13, 1890.

145 *Of great importance:* F. M. Hamilton, Editorial, *Christian Index*, February 6, 1892.

146 *Blocked from performing:* Lillie B. Morris, "Shelby (N.C.) District Women's Missionary Society," *Christian Index*, July 5, 1902.

147 *Spearman felt that:* Rev. G. W. Spearman, "General Conference Nuts," *Christian Index*, January 11, 1902.

147 *With the aid:* According to Sara J. McAfee, the bishops were adamantly "against the bill" to grant the women national status, and it was only because of the direct involvement and intervention of white Methodist women that CME women were able to progress. Beginning with the founding meeting and for many years afterward, Mrs. Hume Steele, secretary of the Educational Department of the MECS Woman's Council, served as a key adviser to Mattie Coleman and the CME women. See Sara J. McAfee, *History of the Woman's Missionary Society in the Colored Methodist Episcopal Church* (Phenix City, Ala.: Phenix City Herald, 1945), 127–29; Lawrence L. Reddick III, ed., "Minutes of the First Session of the Connectional Woman's Missionary Society of the C.M.E. Church, Held in Nashville, Tennessee, September 3–8, 1918, and the Second Session, Held at Thirgood C.M.E. Church, September 10–14, 1919, Birmingham, Alabama," sixty-page typed booklet, February 1998, 3, 40, 51, 57.

147 *Helena Cobb and a small cadre:* In 1902, Helena Cobb and a cadre of CME women leaders, including Sara J. McAfee and Mamie Dinkins, decided that it was time to confront denominational leaders on the issue of women's rights in general, and the need for a national women's missionary department in particular. Cobb and McAfee met with the Council of Bishops and General Conference and pleaded with them to allow women the privilege of working on behalf of the church. Described as the "most influential" woman in the church, Cobb was a graduate of Atlanta University, and became the principal of several public schools in Georgia. She was representative of the new CME women leaders in the twentieth century—an educated and confidant feminist. See McAfee, *History of the Woman's Missionary Society*, 60–63.

147 *"I beg the General Conference":* Ida E. Roberts, "A Plea to the General Conference for the Woman's Mission," *Christian Index*, April 25, 1918. At this date Rev. Roberts was pastoring a church and serving as the president of the North Carolina Woman's Missionary Society.

148 *"when the women have tried":* Mattie E. Coleman, "From Nashville, Tenn.[essee]," *Christian Index*, August 29, 1918; George C. Parker, "Colored Methodist Women," ibid., September 13, 1918; Othal Hawthorne Lakey and Betty Beene Stephens, *God in My Mama's House: The Women's Movement in the CME Church*

(Memphis, Tenn.: CME Publishing House, 1994), 140–41; Lena Jones Rice, "Woman's Connectional Work," *Christian Index*, February 3, 1938.

148 *Coleman's speech targeted:* Coleman also criticized church leaders for poor business methods and alluded to "the short comings and sins of the ministers and laymen of the Church." See Reddick, "Minutes of the First Session," 16, 53, 56.

148 *At that meeting:* W. A. Bell, ed., *Minutes of the Sixteenth General Conference and the Fifteenth Quadrennial Session of the Colored Methodist Episcopal Church, Held in Kansas City, Missouri, May 5–18, 1926* (Jackson, Tenn.: C.M.E. Publishing House, 1926), 34, 89, 130. "C.M.E. Conference in Louisville Ends," *Chicago Defender*, May 31, 1930.

148 *It managed to raise:* McAfee, *History of the Woman's Missionary Society*, 127–28; Lakey and Stephens, *God in My Mama's House*, 140.

148 *Their plight is:* W. A. Bell, ed., *Journal of the Eighteenth General Conference and the Seventeenth Quadrennial Session of the Colored Methodist Episcopal Church, Held in St. Louis, Missouri, May 2–14, 1934* (Jackson, Tenn.: C.M.E. Publishing House, 1934), 51.

150 *The MECS provided:* This fund was designated for support of salaries for the WCMC president and missionary secretary, partial payment of the salary of a religion professor at the CME school—Lane College, a scholarship for a student majoring in religion, rural work, Collins Chapel CME Hospital, missionary publications, and mission churches. Though small at first, by 1965 the WCMC realized at least $40,000 or more from a 15 percent per capita membership tax. The WCMC purchased a church building in California for $6,000 and paid $4,000 for an obstetric ward in the CME hospital and nursing home established by Collins Chapel Church in Memphis, Tennessee, in 1912. It provided thousands of dollars in scholarships for young women attending church-related colleges, including Drew University, and various theological seminaries. See McAfee, *History of the Woman's Missionary Society*, 300–01; Eula Wallace Harris and Maxie Craig Harris, *Christian Methodist Episcopal Church Through the Years* (Jackson, Tenn.: C.M.E. Publishing House, 1965), 81–83; Lakey, *The History of the CME Church*, 375.

150 *This was extremely important:* Pauline Grant was succeeded by Thelma Dudley, who was even more accommodating to the bishops and other male church leaders. Ironically, some of the male leaders initially felt that "Thelma might not be manageable." The election of Sylvia Faulk and Judith Grant as WMC presidents in the 1980s and '90s coincided with the rise of a new and younger generation of bishops. See Harris and Harris, *Christian Methodist Episcopal Church*, 82–83; Lakey and Stephens, *God in My Mama's House*, 186–94.

151 *CME women leaders:* See discussion of the "Persistence of Patriarchy," in Lakey and Stephens, *God in My Mama's House*, 195–97.

151 *Rather, it was the result:* Richard R. Wright Jr., ed., *The Centennial Encyclopaedia of the African Methodist Episcopal Church* (Philadelphia: AME Book Concern, 1916), 324; "The Women's Missionary Society of the AME Church: Over a Century of Commitment and Service," *National Black Monitor* (June 1989): 4–5, 8–9, 10, 12–13.

151 *Following four decades:* Georgia Teal Ransom, "Greetings from the Missionary Women of America," *Voice of Missions* (June 1951): 4; "The Women's Missionary Society of the AME Church," 2.

152 *To ensure that:* Tanner reprinted articles published in the white religious press, and wrote editorials illustrating the fund-raising prowess of Christian white

women. See Mary S. Sargeant, "Women and Missions," *Christian Recorder*, December 18, 1873 (reprint from *Zion's Herald*, October 29, 1873); Benjamin T. Tanner, "The Mite Missionary Society," ibid., May 28, 1874; Benjamin T. Tanner, "Woman's Foreign Missionary Society of the M.E. Church," ibid., July 2, 1874. Long after AME women had organized a national society, Tanner continued to publish articles, write editorials, and suggest books for AME women to read about the work of white women's organizations. See Benjamin T. Tanner, "The Work of Women," ibid., June 24, 1880; "Our Book Table," ibid., June 9, 1881.

152 *He admitted that:* The editorial page of the February 19, 1874, issue of the *Christian Recorder*, containing Tanner's letter to the bishops' wives, is missing. Excerpts from the letter are quoted in Wright, *The Centennial Encyclopaedia*, 324–25. Tanner wielded a great deal of influence as editor of the *Christian Recorder* (1868–84) and the *AME Church Review* (1884–88). Please note that Tanner was not a bishop when this letter was written. Tanner's elevation to the episcopacy came in 1888, at the end of his editorial career. His views about women's role in the church and community were complex and in some ways contradictory. He separated women's secular functions from their religious ones. He believed that black women needed political enfranchisement to protect their gender and race interests, but not in the male-dominated AME Church. By 1870 he concluded that women could function in the church and community, but in supportive roles. He was not against women preaching as long as they were not ordained and accepted as equals with men. Like Bishop Daniel A. Payne and numerous clergy, Tanner adhered to Victorian notions about domesticity, but supported women's involvement in "acceptable social activities in the community or church." For Tanner's promotion of foreign mission work and views on women, see William Seraile, *Fire in His Heart: Bishop Benjamin Tucker Tanner and the AME Church* (Knoxville: University of Tennessee Press, 1998), 30, 35, 47–48, 51–52, 103–4. On Payne's attitude toward women, see David W. Wills, "Womanhood and Domesticity in the AME Tradition: The Influence of Daniel Alexander Payne," in *Black Apostles at Home and Abroad: Afro-Americans and the Christian Mission from the Revolution to Reconstruction*, ed. David W. Wills and Richard Newman (Boston: G. K. Hall, 1982), 139–43.

152 *Tanner urged the:* "Our Letter," *Christian Recorder*, February 26, 1874 (italics by Tanner).

152 *"ridiculed and trampled":* Mary E. Davis, "The Work of Women," *Christian Recorder*, March 26, 1874.

154 *"[T]hey are waiting":* Mattie V. Holmes, "A Woman's Letter," *Christian Recorder*, April 9, 1874.

154 *He envisioned AME:* B. G. Mortimor, "That Letter," *Christian Recorder*, March 12, 1874 (italics by Mortimor).

154 *"if woman was first":* Thomas S. Malcom, "Women's Missionary Societies," *Christian Recorder*, March 18, 1875.

154 *Clergy wives were:* Wright, *The Centennial Encyclopaedia*, 324–25; Mrs. Mary Quinn, Eliza Payne, Harriet A. E. Wayman, Mary Campbell, Maria Shorter, Mary L. Brown, and Mrs. Bishop Ward, "An Open Letter," *Christian Recorder*, May 14, 1874.

154 *"our missionary coffers":* Benjamin T. Tanner, "The Mite Missionary Society," *Christian Recorder*, May 28, 1874.

154 *In August 1874:* "The Women's Mite Missionary Society of the AME Church," *Christian Recorder*, June 24, 1874; "The Convention on Organization," *Christian Recorder*, August 20, 1874.

155 *At the same time:* "An Urgent Appeal!—Come Over and Help Us," *Christian Recorder,* August 18, 1898.

155 *The exclusion of:* "The Women's Mite Missionary Society," *Christian Recorder,* August 13, 1874. There was no published call or written appeal for the organizing convention. Thus, few people outside of the closed circle of bishops and prominent clergy network concentrated in the Philadelphia, Washington, D.C., New Jersey, New York, and Delaware areas were aware of the event. The denomination was informed in the above-cited article that a convention had been held in Philadelphia at the Mother Bethel AME Church and that "[t]he Woman's Parent Mite Missionary Society is a fixed institution of our Church." See also Howard D. Gregg, *History of the African Methodist Episcopal Church* (Nashville, Tenn.: AME Sunday School Union, 1980), 198.

155 *At the beginning:* W. E. B. Du Bois, ed., *The Negro Church: Report of a Social Study Made Under the Direction of Atlanta University; Together with the Proceedings of the Eighth Conference for the Study of the Negro Problems Held at Atlanta University, May 26th, 1903* (Atlanta: Atlanta University Press, 1903), 40–43. After 1865, AME Conferences were organized in California (1864), Louisiana (1865), Texas (1865), western Florida (1865), North Carolina (1867), Virginia (1867), Georgia (1867), Kentucky (1868), Alabama (1868), Mississippi (1868), Arkansas (1868), Tennessee (1868), and West Virginia (1908). Gregg, *History of the African Methodist Episcopal Church,* 110–21.

155 *The organization of:* Lucy Laney, "General Conditions of Mortality," in W. E. B. Du Bois, ed., *The Atlanta University Publications, No. 1: Mortality Among Negroes in Cities* (Atlanta: Atlanta University Press, 1896), 35–37.

156 *However, in expressing:* Harriet Wayman, "The Work of Women," *Christian Recorder,* May 21, 1874.

156 *In light of the scandal:* Brown contended that southern preachers were not "Quakers" and that historically Methodist preachers believed in "praying and fighting." For details of the debacle and overall confusion, see "Letter from Bishop Campbell," *Christian Recorder,* January 7, 1875; "Reply to Bishop Campbell's letter on Missionary Laws, Addressed to J. M. Brown," ibid., January 28, 1875, and February 4, 1975; J. W. Randolph, "From Helena Arkansas," ibid., October 1, 1874; Benjamin T. Tanner, "Our Haytian Mission—Again," ibid., October 29, 1874; Theophilus G. Steward, "Hayti," ibid., October 29, 1874. Jualynne Dodson, in an undocumented account, suggests that the WPMMS had raised funds for the Haitian mission, "but refused to release it to a messenger who was sent to collect it for the Council of Bishops." The published record does not support Dodson's assertion. Rather, it indicates that the local Women's Mite Missionary Societies rejected the candidate and refused to submit any funds to the WPMMS. Moreover, Bishops Jabez P. Campbell, James A. Shorter, and others rejected Brown's choice and reminded him that only the bishops had the power to appoint foreign missionaries. See Jualynne Dodson, *Engendering Church: Women, Power, and the AME Church* (Lanham, Md.: Rowman and Littlefield Publishers, Inc., 2002), 89.

156 *"rally not only":* Benjamin T. Tanner, "The Mite Society," *Christian Recorder,* March 4, 1875.

156 *"qualified brother":* Malcom, "Women's Missionary Societies"; Mary A. Campbell, "Word from the President of the Mite Society," *Christian Recorder,* April 1, 1875; Benjamin T. Tanner, "A Word to the Mite Society," ibid., July 13, 1876.

156 *Mossell's departure:* Benjamin T. Tanner, "Our Missionary Off," *Christian Recorder,* April 18, 1877.

157 *Admitting that support:* Mary A. Campbell, "Address of Mrs. Bishop Campbell," *Christian Recorder*, November 28, 1878.

157 *"apparently ceased":* Sarah E. Tanner, "To the Parent and Auxiliary Mite Missionary Societies," *Christian Recorder*, December 12, 1878; Sarah E. Tanner, "Mite Society," ibid., August 26, 1880; Sarah E. Tanner, "To the Mite Societies," ibid., December 23, 1880; "Annual Meeting," ibid., December 7, 1882.

158 *"It was really amusing":* Rev. J. W. Gazaway, "Women's Mite Missionary Convention," *Christian Recorder*, February 2, 1893; Mrs. W. T. Anderson, "Women's Mite Missionary Convention," ibid., July 20, 1893; Mrs. W. T. Anderson, "Notice," ibid., September 14, 1893.

158 *"waxed warm over":* Henry M. Turner, "Convention of the Women's Mite Missionary Society of the Third Episcopal District, Held in Cleveland, Ohio," *Voice of Missions* 2:8 (August 1894): 1.

158 *"Christian duty":* Susie A. Shorter, "Ohio Women in Convention," *Voice of Missions* 6:9 (September 1898): 1.

158 *The council ruled:* Edward W. Lampton, comp., *Digest of Rulings and Decisions of the Bishops of the African Methodist Episcopal Church from 1847 to 1907* (Washington, DC: Record Publishing Company, 1907), 63.

159 *Though Thurman succeeded:* Like her AME and AME Zion counterparts, in the early 1890s, Lillian Thurman was appointed to conference committees such as temperance, and served as the conference reporter to the *Christian Recorder*, activities designated as appropriate for the service of female evangelists. Wright, *The Centennial Encyclopaedia*, 320; Sara J. Duncan, *Progressive Missions in the South* (Atlanta: Franklin Printing and Publishing Co., 1906), 101. For information regarding Lillian Thurman's participation in the Michigan Annual Conference, see Dennis C. Dickerson, "Michigan Minister and Missionary Leader: Lillian Thurman in the 1890's," *AME Church Review* 121:398 (April–June 2005): 49–52.

160 *The meeting emphasized:* News clippings titled "A National Conference," "That Woman's Convention," "Woman's Convention," and miscellaneous undocumented materials are included in the Winfield Henry Mixon Papers, Special Collections Library, Duke University, Durham, North Carolina. "Their National Convention," *Christian Recorder*, May 2, 1895; "The Woman's National Convention Called by Rev. W. H. Mixon," *Indianapolis Freeman*, May 18, 1895; W. H. Mixon, "Against Women Preaching," *Christian Recorder*, March 18, 1886; Mixon was a founder of Payne University in Selma, Alabama, editor in chief of *The Southern Christian Age*, deputy grand master of the Alabama Masons, and held prominent offices in numerous other fraternal orders. For biographical information on Mixon, see "Many Sided Life of Presiding Elder Mixon," *Baltimore Afro-American*, November 16, 1912. Duncan, *Progressive Missions*, 63, 70. See also Dennis C. Dickerson, "Winfield Henri Mixon: A Pioneer Presiding Elder in Alabama," *AME Church Review* 106:338 (April–June, 1990): 18–22.

160 *In an effort:* "First Episcopal District," *Voice of Missions* 3:9 (September 1895): 4.

160 *Women such as:* Jennie E. Johnson, "The Mite Missionary Society's Call—What Is Lacking," *Christian Recorder*, September 12, 1895.

160 *Following Thurman's resignation:* In November 1897, Rev. Lillian F. Thurman resigned to accept an appointment as pastor of the Brown Chapel AME Church. Henry M. Turner, Editorial, *Voice of Missions* 4:6 (June 1896): 2; Wright, *The Centennial Encyclopaedia*, 320; Duncan, *Progressive Missions*, 2; Henry M. Turner, Editorial, *Voice of Missions* 4:3 (March 1896): 2; Mrs. H. E. Carolina, "Africa for Christ," ibid., 4:7 (July 1896): 2; Henry M. Turner, Editorial, ibid., 5:12 (December 1, 1897): 2; David M. Katzman, *Before the Ghetto: Black Detroit in the Nine-*

teenth Century (Chicago: University of Illinois Press, 1973), 143. Please note that Rev. Lillian F. Thurman (Mrs. G. T. Thurman) is sometimes confused with Lucy Smith Thurman, a noted leader in the National Association of Colored Women and the WCTU. For example, see Dennis C. Dickerson, "Gender and the Gospel: Bishop Henry M. Turner and the Rise of Female Clergy in Georgia, 1896–1908," *AME Church Review* 116:378 (summer 2000): 36–37.

160 *It is for these:* Duncan, *Progressive Missions*, 7–8, 15–20, 164. As a member of the executive board of the Interdenominational, International State Sunday School, Duncan's credentials were impressive. During Reconstruction, Jordan Hatcher, Duncan's grandfather, served as the postmaster of Cahaba, Alabama, and was a member of the 1868 Alabama Constitutional Convention.

160 *For most black:* Duncan, *Progressive Missions*, 40.

161 *"The American people":* Many scholars have embraced Evelyn Higginbotham's "Politics of Respectability," which suggests that black leaders overemphasized morality, cleanliness, standard speech, and comportment as ways in which blacks might gain the acceptance of white Americans. See Higginbotham, *Righteous Discontent*, 185–229. Anthea D. Butler takes issue with Higginbotham's thesis, arguing, "Their notion of respectability . . . found its locus and meaning in their belief in scripture and in putting its lessons into practice in their daily lives, rather than in imitating the demeanor and styles of the black middle class or seeking recognition from white people." See Anthea D. Butler, " 'Only a Woman Would Do': Bible Reading and African American Women's Organizing Work," in *Women and Religion in the African Diaspora*, ed. R. Marie Griffith and Barbara Dianne Savage (Baltimore: Johns Hopkins University Press, 2006), 157.

161 *"gone through every":* Duncan, *Progressive Missions*, 40.

161 *She implored AME:* Ibid., 45.

161 *Duncan predicted that:* Ibid., 48.

162 *"thought it was unladylike":* Ibid., 52.

162 *"Mrs. So and So":* Ibid., 53–55.

162 *"heretofore woman has":* Ibid., 102–03.

162 *With a membership:* Ibid., 85–88, 91–93.

163 *Some bishops perceived:* S. P. Hood, "Report of Philadelphia Conference," *Voice of Missions* 6:6 (June 1898): 4; "Celebrated Women at Work for Missions," ibid., 6:10 (October 1898): 6.

163 *It would take:* "Mission Board's Annual Report: Large Sums Raised by Auxiliaries of AME Denomination," *Pittsburgh Courier*, June 10, 1911.

164 *For those waiting:* This discussion, including the reference to the *Christian Recorder*, is included in Sara J. Duncan, "In Vindication of Vital Questions–Our Missionary Department," *Voice of People* (March 1904), reprinted in Duncan, *Progressive Missions*, 140–45.

164 *"We mean to be":* Prior to her marriage to AME Bishop Henry M. Turner in 1907, Lemon, a young, educated, and self-possessed feminist in the "New Woman" tradition, had established a reputation for her dedication to the women of the South, in particular to the WHFMS. In 1903, at the age of twenty-three, Lemon was elected president of the Atlanta Annual Conference WHFMS. Wright, *Encyclopaedia of African Methodism*, 425; Duncan, *Progressive Missions*, 135–36; for a brief biography of Lemon, see ibid., 137–38. Stephen Ward Angell, *Bishop Henry McNeal Turner and African-American Religion in the South* (Knoxville, Tenn.: University of Tennessee Press, 1992), 246.

164 *"wearing sleeveless dresses":* "Bobbed Hair and Bare Arms Banned at Conference," *Pittsburgh Courier*, May 17, 1924; "Bobbed Hair Scored," *Philadelphia Tribune*,

May 17, 1924. In 1924 the only formal offices available to AME women were those of deaconess, stewardess, and class leader.

165 *Women preachers, such as:* Ibid.; "Women's Mite Missionary Society Meets," *Baltimore Afro-American*, September 19, 1908; "The General Conference of 1912," ibid., December 23, 1911; Margaret Black, "Woman's Column," ibid., March 18, 1916; Clara E. Harris, "The Twenty-Ninth Annual Convention of the Baltimore Conference Branch," *Christian Recorder*, November 5, 1925; "Our Women," ibid., July 16, 1925. Legislation was enacted at the 1928 AME General Conference meeting in Chicago granting the presidents of the WPMMS and the WHFMS the right to participate as delegates at the General Conference. See AME, *Journal of the Twenty-eighth Quadrennial Session, General Conference of the AME Church, May 7–23, 1928* (Philadelphia: AME Book Concern, 1928), 98.

166 *Similarly, at the 1935:* Julia B. Jones, "Hectic Scenes Mark First Effort of Lay Members to Obtain Equal Representation at AME Confab," *Pittsburgh Courier*, May 7, 1932; "Women Leaders Demand Scalps of 11 Bishops," *Washington Tribune*, August 12, 1932; "Women Will Ask for Change in AME Discipline, *Pittsburgh Courier*, April 25, 1936.

166 *"When I think of":* Christine S. Smith, "Mrs. Christine Smith," *AME Church Review* 53:2 (April–June, 1937): 215–16. Smith was one of several leaders invited by Rev. J. G. Robinson, editor of the *AME Church Review*, to address questions regarding the future of the denomination, and what was "most necessary for the advancement" of the church. Smith argued that if "evils" such as the treatment of delegates were corrected then the denomination had "a fine contribution to make to future generations."

166 *However, the delegates:* "AME's Oust Bryant as S[unday] S[chool] Union Head" and "AME's Close Conference in Rush to Go," *Baltimore Afro-American*, May 23, 1936.

167 *At the 1940:* In 1932 Hughes was defeated in her first run for the position. She was reluctant to announce her candidacy too early for fear that clergy would organize against her. Though laity rights was a major issue, the episcopacy was more threatened by the women's bid for power in the polity. The concern for containing and controlling women's influence was of paramount importance, for they were "the bedrock of the denomination's financial structure. See "Think Bishops Will Recommend 10 Per Cent Cut," *Baltimore Afro-American*, March 5, 1932; in 1939 Claude Barnett informed Lucy Hughes, "You are ambitious to attain a place high in the council of a great organization. Therefore, as we have previously agreed, we must find a way to impress your ability, your personality and your general ability to fit into a position previously not held by women." Recognizing the importance of having powerful allies and supporters outside of the denomination, Barnett advised Hughes to affiliate with the National Association of Colored Women and "Mrs. Bethune's Council of Negro Women." For correspondence between Barnett and Hughes, see Claude A. Barnett Papers, American Negro Press, General Correspondence, Series J, "Churches, Information About," May 17, 22 and August 16, 1939, microfilm edition, Reel 1; for biographical information on Hughes, see "Mrs. L. M. Hughes Dies in Cameron," *Houston Informer*, April 14, 1945.

168 *Unification would reduce:* "Mrs. Handy Makes Denial," *Indianapolis Recorder*, May 6, 1911; J. T. Jennifer, "What Next AME General Conference Is Likely to Do," *Chicago Defender*, December 28, 1918; "AME Church General Officers Turn in Their Reports," ibid., May 14, 1932; "Women Missionaries to Merge and Settle Difficulties Later," *Pittsburgh Courier*, May 28, 1932; "No Progress in Merger of

AME Mission Bodies," *New York Age*, January 20, 1934; "Merger of AME Missionary Societies Delayed," *Norfolk Journal and Guide*, February 17, 1934; "AME Missionary Bodies Defy 1932 Conference Edict," *Baltimore Afro-American*, October 19, 1935; "Fireworks Predicted as AME's Arrive," ibid., May 9, 1936; "Do the AME's Own Anything?" ibid., June 27, 1936.

168 *"You had better stick"*: "No Progress in Merger of AME Mission Bodies," *New York Age*, January 20, 1934.

168 *The Women's Home:* "AME Women Sure of Mission Merger," *Philadelphia Afro-American*, July 3, 1943.

169 *It eliminated the:* Ruth E. Dinkins, "New Dimensions of Missions," *Christian Recorder*, July 9, 1963.

169 *As editor:* Wilda Robinson-Smith, "The Woman's Column," *Christian Recorder*, June 30, 1955; Artisha W. Jordan, "What Is Your Missionary 'I.Q.'?" Ibid., June 6, 1967; Robert Leslie Morgan, "Sister A. B. Williams Smiles Again," ibid., May 24, 1966; Robert Leslie Morgan, "She Walks the Earth with Dignity," ibid., June 25, 1959; Robert L. Morgan, "Mrs. A. B. Williams—A Remarkable Woman," ibid., February 25, 1964. The *Women's Missionary Recorder*, established in 1912, was "merged" with the *Voice of Missions*. Though some women, such as Robinson-Smith, were not opposed to the move, they favored combining the publications "into one excellent magazine with the [male] Secretary of Missions and a Woman's Editor as co-editors" to produce "a creditable missionary journal." In effect, AME women lost their publication, editorial position, and the ability to broadly articulate their views. After 1951 the "Women's Missionary Magazine" was limited to one page. It later became a separate publication funded by subscriptions.

169 *Lucy Hughes was:* "AME Church Merges 2 Missionary Societies," *Chicago Defender*, May 27, 1944; "Women Church Groups Unite," ibid., December 30, 1944.

169 *At Hughes's death:* "Mrs. Heath Heads AME Missions," *Pittsburgh Courier*, May 4, 1945.

169 *"Christian social concerns":* Mary E. Frizzell, "Great Days Ahead for Missions," *Christian Recorder*, September 5, 1967. In 1947 the WMS invited Thomasina Johnson, the director of the Minority Group Section of the United States Employment Service, to discuss employment issues at the women's meeting in New Orleans. Johnson stated that in the postwar period thousands of blacks were losing their jobs. Johnson emphasized that the USES was intimately involved in efforts to persuade employers not to fire employees for "non-performance factors such as race, creed, [and] color." Christine Smith asserted WMS's interest in "all phases of life" that impacted Christian citizens, including employment conditions. "AME Women Hear Labor Expert on Jobs," *Pittsburgh Courier*, August 16, 1947.

170 *They also garnered:* "Bishops Name Mrs. Alexander Their Lawyer," *Philadelphia Tribune*, June 3, 1944; Albert Dunmore, "Laymen of AME Church Check Power Long Held by Bishops," *Pittsburgh Courier*, May 29, 1948. For biographical data on Alexander, see Theresa Snyder, "Sadie Alexander (1898–1989)," in Smith, *Notable Black American Women, Book I*, 5–8.

170 *Recognizing that they:* For biography on Robinson-Smith and Polk, see Helen B. Suber, "The Obsequies of Alma A. Polk," *Christian Recorder*, October 21, 1969; Thelma Anderson Wills, "Periscoping with a General Conference Delegate," ibid., June 23, 1964; "Church's Public Relations, Headed by Brilliant Faithful Woman," ibid., May 6, 1969.

171 *"The laity must"*: "The Role of Women in the Church," *Voice of Missions* 53:4 (April 1952): 9; J. S. Benn Jr., "Shall We 'Re-Think' the AME System or Continue as We Are?" *Christian Recorder*, January 19, 1950; Jesse L. Glover, "Straight from the Shoulder," Ibid., June 8, 1950; A. Wayman Ward, "Wit, Wisdom, and Wisecracks," ibid., June 9, 1955. At the local level, the general practice was to elect at least one, and no more than two women as lay delegates to the General Conference.

172 *Others thought that:* In 1928, 1936, 1940, and 1944, the General Conference enacted legislation granting laymen equal representation in the General Conference, the right to serve on the Episcopal Committee, and equal representation on all denominational boards. Between 1912 and 1946, male laity seeking a greater, if not equal, voice in the polity with male clergy, organized the Laymen's Missionary League (1912), the Connectional Lay College (1916), and finally the Connectional Laymen's Organization (1946). As laymen advanced in the polity and were elected to key denominational offices, they became more closely allied with the male clergy. After the 1920s, by dint of the fact that they had gained suffrage, women were eligible for election as "laymen." After 1940, though women mostly held the offices of secretary, treasurer, and lay adviser, in the Connectional Laymen's Organization, few served as president, or district director. In the upper echelons of the church, men dominated as connectional lay leaders. For a brief history of laymen's organizations, the Brotherhood Movement, and budget issues, see Howard D. Gregg, *History of the African Methodist Episcopal Church* (Nashville, Tenn.: AME Church Sunday School Union, 1980), 302–07, 312–13, 361–92, 522; "The State of the Church," *Christian Recorder*, February 2, 1950; "Proposed Legislation to be Enacted at the 35th Session of the General Conference," ibid., March 24, 1955; Rev. T. S. Clements, "Objective Reflections," ibid., June 12, 1958; A. Beatrice Williams, "The Missionary Women Look toward Miami," Ibid., May 10, 1956. For a discussion of how the Brotherhood exerted power over the bishops, see "Makes Decision After Conference," *Chicago Defender*, October 5, 1957.

173 *WMS women:* "AME Bishops Play Distinguished Role in N.C.C. Confabs," *Christian Recorder*, November 7, 1957; Vera G. Powe, "Impressions—An Open Letter," Ibid., April 9, 1959.

173 *"We [women] can raise"*: Loretta C. Spencer, "It's Time to Speak Up," *Christian Recorder*, April 18, 1957. As a veteran public schoolteacher, delegate to three General Conferences (1948, 1952, 1956), and trustee and member of St. John AME Church in Frankfort, Kentucky, Spencer was a highly respected community and church leader. For biographical details, see C. C. Richardson, "Makes Marquis' Who's Who Among American Women, '58," ibid., February 12, 1959.

173 *Wayman was referring:* A. Wayman Ward, "Wit, Wisdom, and Wisecracks," *Christian Recorder*, June 9, 1955.

174 *"Let us not"*: Loretta C. Spencer, "It's Time to Speak Up," *Christian Recorder*, April 18, 1957.

174 *"Let the women"*: Ward, "Wit, Wisdom, and Wisecracks."

174 *Williams stressed that:* A. Beatrice Williams, "Present Activities Under Difficulties—Why?" *Christian Recorder*, April 23, 1959.

175 *"We the women"*: Alma A. Polk, "Our Fathers' Church . . . Our Mothers' Church," *Christian Recorder*, December 5, 1957; Pennie Esther Gibbs, "Says Women of Church Should Have Fair Chance to Speak in Defense of their Cause," Ibid., March 26, 1959.

175 *Rev. Roberts added:* J. E. Roberts, "The Bitter Cry," *Christian Recorder*, June 18, 1959.

176 *Passage of the WMS:* Jesse L. Glover, "Straight from the Shoulder," *Christian Recorder*, April 30, 1959; Jessie L. Glover, "Straight from the Shoulder," ibid., July 30, 1959; "The Unheralded Hero," *Voice of Missions* 61:7 (July 1959): 4; A. Lewis Williams and Emory G. Davis, "Women's Missionary Quadrennial," ibid.

176 *The address emphasized:* "The Council of Bishops Meet," *Voice of Missions* 61:7 (July 1959).

176 *At the 1960:* AME Church, *The Official Minutes of the Thirty-sixth Session of the General Conference of the African Methodist Episcopal Church, Held in Los Angeles, California, May, 1960, at the Shrine Auditorium* (Nashville: AME Sunday School Union, 1960), 247–48.

176 *Davis indicted the:* Sam Davis, "Straight to the Target," *Christian Recorder*, January 22, 1963.

177 *Henry urged AME:* Myrtle Battiste Henry, "A Reply to an Insult," *Christian Recorder*, February 12, 1963. Cheryl Townsend Gilkes, sociologist and Baptist minister, accurately asserts that generations of black women of different religious persuasions have "responded to [male] criticism and challenges" with "if it wasn't for the women," an assertion of the importance of their roles and functions in the church. See Cheryl Townsend Gilkes, *"If It Wasn't for the Women . . . : Black Women's Experience and Womanist Culture in Church and Community* (Maryknoll, NY: Orbis Books, 2001), 5.

177 *Suggesting that perhaps:* Mrs. P. W. Rogers, "Missionary 'Hustlers'?" *Christian Recorder*, April 9, 1963.

177 *Davis assured the:* Sam Davis, "Straight to the Target," *Christian Recorder*, April 16, 1963. Between 1950 and 1963, Rachel W. Valentine was the first vice president and president of the Washington Conference Branch Women's Missionary Society. See Josephine S. Grant, "Washington Conf[erence] Branch Reports Successful Session," ibid., April 29, 1954; Melvina Offutt, "Washington Conf[erence] Branch Holds Annual Session," ibid., October 2, 1962. Male clergy sometimes invoked the image of Jezebel, the biblical character, to rebuke strong, assertive women who challenged male authority. "Jezebel" conjured up images of an immodest and impudent woman who did not know "her place."

178 *"dissatisfaction and grief":* Administrative Committee of the Women's Missionary Society, AME Church, "Resolution," *Christian Recorder*, July 9, 1963.

178 *Missionary training:* Esther B. Hill Isaacs, "Let's Stop and Think," *Christian Recorder*, May 30, 1967.

178 *"unhindered and unmolested":* For Heath's comments, see J. W. Yancy, "Mrs. Sherman's Missionary Meeting Shatters Texas Records, *Christian Recorder*, September 7, 1965.

179 *All legal barriers:* Bettye Collier-Thomas, *Daughters of Thunder: Black Women Preachers and Their Sermons, 1850–1979* (San Francisco: 1997), 22–23. In 2008, Mildred Hines became the first female ever to be elected a bishop in the AME Zion Church. See Margena A. Christian, "AME Zion Church Elects First Female Bishop," *JET*, August 18, 2008.

180 *The male general secretary:* The titles of these organizations suggest domestic and foreign programs, but the initial focus of their work was outside the United States. Walls, *The African Methodist Episcopal Zion Church*, 374–76, 380–81, 388–90; "African Missions of American Methodists, *Voice of Missions* 1:12 (December 1893): 1; Rogerson, *Historical Synopsis*, 32; Aurora Evans, "Origin and Work of

the Daughters of Conference and Kindred Societies," *AME Zion Quarterly Review* 8:1 (January 1898): 66–67; W. E. B. Du Bois, ed., *The Atlanta University Publications, No. 14: Efforts for Social Betterment Among Negro Americans* (Atlanta: Atlanta University Press, 1909), 27; W. E. B. Du Bois, ed., *The Atlanta University Publications, No. 1*, 35–37.

180 *"If I would go"*: Walls, *The African Methodist Episcopal Zion Church*, 389–93.

181 *In part, their:* Collier-Thomas, *Daughters of Thunder*, 23. For an understanding of how issues of respect and religious masculinity contributed to the drive to develop foreign missionary programs in the 1880s and '90s, see L. G. Jordan, "Why They Are Influential," *Mission Herald* 13:4 (June 1908): 2.

181 *Regardless of the reasons:* AME Zion Church, *Report of the Ladies' Gen'l Conference Home and Foreign Missionary Society of the AME Zion Church* (York, Pa.: Teachers' Journal Office, 1884), 12–13; Rogerson, *Historical Synopsis*, 42.

182 *Bishops' wives and widows:* Rogerson, *Historical Synopsis*, 45, 49.

182 *The funds collected:* J. W. Hood, "Our Mission Work," *Star of Zion*, May 9, 1901. The article opens with a letter from Bishop Hood to Mr. F. P. Turner, and concludes with a summary of AME Zion mission work, 1866–1901.

182 *Clarifying the subordinate:* J. W. Hood, "WH and FM Society: Collects but Does Not Disburse Mission Money," *Star of Zion*, January 3, 1901.

182 *"be distinctly understood":* G. L. Blackwell, comp., *Official Journal of the Twenty-second Quadrennial Session of the General Conference of the African Methodist Episcopal Zion Church, Held in Washington Metropolitan AME Zion Church, St. Louis, Missouri, May 4–19, 1904* (no pub., 1904), 145.

182 *However, the AMEZ-WHFMS:* Rogerson, *Historical Synopsis*, 45.

183 *To circumvent the:* David Henry Bradley Sr., *A History of the A.M.E. Zion Church*, part 2: *1872–1968* (Nashville: Parthenon Press, 1970), 233–34; "Report of the Sixth Quadrennial Session of the Woman's Home and Foreign Missionary Society," *Star of Zion*, July 5, 1928; Lynwood Westinghouse Kyles, comp., *Official Journal of the Twenty-eighth Quadrennial Session of the General Conference of the African Methodist Episcopal Zion Church, Held in St. Louis, Missouri, May 2–21, 1928* (no pub., 1928).

183 *In 1931 women:* "Women to Advocate Radical Changes in Mission Department," *Pittsburgh Courier*, April 23, 1932.

183 *The new constitution:* Rogerson, *Historical Synopsis*, 39–40.

183 *However, they were:* Please note that the location of the city is not identified in any extant source. Walter R. Lovell, "Who Will 'Call the Tune,' " *Star of Zion*, March 16, 1944.

183 *Having their wives:* Rogerson, *Historical Synopsis*, 394–96.

184 *The Board of Bishops:* Mrs. C. C. Pettey, "The Proceedings of the Woman's H[ome] and F[oreign] Missionary Convention," *Star of Zion*, August 29, 1901. Bishop Small, the first bishop appointed by the denomination to oversee African missions, is considered "the real founder" of the AME Zion African mission work. For a brief history of the denomination's mission work, see W. H. Davenport, "The AME Zion Denomination," ibid., June 9, 1932.

184 *the General Conference:* J. W. Hood, "Facts Versus Fiction," *Star of Zion*, January 29, 1903.

185 *From Hood's perspective:* Ibid.

185 *The discussion was:* G. L. Blackwell, comp., *Official Journal of the Twenty-second Quadrennial Session of the General Conference of the African Methodist Episcopal Zion Church, Held in Washington AME Zion Church, St. Louis, Missouri, May 19, 1904* (pub. unknown, 1904), 80–81, 319–20.

185 *"a forward few women"*: "A Woman for General Secretary of Missions, the candidacy of the Rev. Florence Randolph Advocated by W.H.F.M. Society of N.J.," unsigned handwritten document, March 6, 1924.

186 *Building on the:* Ibid.

186 *"Weep, if necessary"*: Ibid.

CHAPTER 4 *"The Relief Corps of Heaven"*

188 *Donohoo claimed that:* Bettye Collier-Thomas, " 'The Relief Corps of Heaven': Black Women as Philanthropists," *ARNOVA* 1:1 (2001): 25.

190 *Most children worked:* Individuals ten years of age and over were classified as literate or illiterate on the basis of their ability "to write in some language, irrespective of the ability to read." For statistics and discussion of the status of African Americans in the nineteenth and early twentieth centuries, see U.S. Department of Commerce, *Negro Population 1790–1915* (Washington, DC: Government Printing Office, 1918), 88–89, 91, 388, 403, 409, 414–16, 572–78.

190 *Several years later:* For quote, see Evelyn Brooks Higginbotham, *Righteous Discontent: The Women's Movement in the Black Baptist Church 1880–1920* (Cambridge, Mass.: Harvard University Press, 1993), 101; "Sister Joanna Moore Passes Away in Selma, Ala[bama]," *National Baptist Union-Review*, April 22, 1916; "Miss Joanna P. Moore Laid to Rest," ibid., April 29, 1916.

191 *The work of black women:* Hope, December 3, 1885. For examples of how Moore utilized scripture to teach reading, and as a defense for women's work in the church, see issues of *Hope* 1885–1910. For discussion of the role of Joanna Moore and *Hope* in the development of the National Women's Convention of the Church of God in Christ, see Anthea Butler, "A Peculiar Synergy" (PhD diss., Vanderbilt University, 2001), 36–40.

191 *Proponents of domesticity:* "Woman's Missionary Work with the Colored Populations of the South," *Indianapolis Freeman*, December 17, 1907.

192 *"racial disagreements"*: Josephine E. Holmes, "The Negro Woman and Religion in Problem Solutions," in "Woman's Part in the Uplift of the Negro Race," *Colored American Magazine* 12:1 (January 1907) 53–61.

192 *"[I]t seems that"*: For an example of how Baptist women defined missionary work, see the "Official Program" of the Woman's Convention for 1920 in NBC, *Journal of the Fortieth Annual Session of the National Baptist Convention and the Twentieth Annual Session of the Woman's Convention Auxiliary, Held in Indianapolis, Indiana, September 8–13, 1920* (Nashville: Sunday School Publishing Board, 1920), 296–300. In the 1940s, the WC constitution specified that the program must be placed under home missions, foreign missions, and education. See NBC, *Proceedings of the Forty-fourth Annual Session of the Woman's Convention, Auxiliary to the National Baptist Convention, U.S.A., Inc., Held in Detroit, Michigan, September 5–9, 1945* (Nashville: Sunday School Publishing Board, 1945), 336.

192 *"life depends upon"*: "Nannie H. Burroughs Discusses the Training School Situation," *New York Age*, January 14, 1928.

193 *"helping the poor"*: Mrs. H. L. Shelton, "An Open Letter to the Women's Home and Foreign Missionary Societies of Georgia, by the President," *Voice of Missions* 6:12 (December 1898). For Baptist comments on the purpose of home missions, see "Report of Committee on Home Missions," in NBC, *Journal of the Twenty-third Annual Session of the Woman's Convention, Auxiliary to the National Baptist Convention, U.S.A., Inc., Held in Los Angeles, California, September 5–10, 1923* (Nashville: Sunday School Publishing Board, 1923), 371.

193   *In December 1940:* Ruth Esther Meeker, *Six Decades of Service: A History of the
      Woman's Home Missionary Society of the Methodist Episcopal Church, 1880–1940*
      (New York: Continuing Corporation of the Woman's Home Missionary Society
      of the Methodist Episcopal Church, 1969), 111–78, 314; Mason and Bowen were
      the wives of two of the most prominent black leaders in the Methodist Episcopal
      Church. By 1895, Rev. M. C. B. Mason, the assistant corresponding secretary for
      the Freedmen's Aid and Southern Education Society, and Rev. Dr. J. W. E.
      Bowen, professor of historical theology at Atlanta, Georgia's Gammon Theolog-
      ical Seminary and former field agent of the MECS Missionary Society, were
      among the foremost black spokesmen in the Methodist Episcopal Church. See
      J. W. E. Bowen, ed., *Africa and the American Negro: Addresses and Proceedings of
      the Congress on Africa* (Atlanta: Gammon Theological Seminary, 1896), 143, 161;
      Theressa Hoover and Mary Lou Van Buren, *To a Higher Glory: The Growth and
      Development of Black Women Organized for Mission in the Methodist Church, 1940–
      1968* (New York: Methodist Episcopal Church, 1980), 14–18, 28.

194   *Though the home:* For definitions and evaluations of AME women's missionary
      work, see Anita Boyer, "Missionary Work," *Christian Recorder*, January 3, 1878;
      Martha J. Bryant, "Home Missionary Work," *Baltimore Afro-American*, August
      26, 1916. For quote, see Rebecca Stiles Taylor, "Home and Foreign Mission Is
      Prime Duty of a Church," *Chicago Defender*, December 16, 1939.

194   *In the ongoing:* Mary S. Crawford, "The Missionary Work," *Christian Recorder*,
      December 18, 1884; Willa Thomas, "Church Events of the City," *Indianapolis
      Recorder*, August 15, 1959. According to Thomas, a Baptist woman, some reli-
      gionists thought that "all you have to do to be a missionary group is to meet, eat,
      discuss the Bible and raise money."

194   *"use the money only":* Shelton, "An Open Letter."

195   *The New Jersey AME:* Ibid.; Richard R. Wright Jr., ed., *The Centennial Encyclopae-
      dia of the African Methodist Episcopal Church* (Philadelphia: AME Book Concern,
      1916), 323–24, 330.

196   *Since each church:* Editorial, *Missionary Messenger* 3:17 (January 1953): 1.

196   *The WC Executive Committee:* NBC, *Journal of the Thirty-fourth Session of the
      National Baptist Convention and the Fourteenth Annual Assembly of the Woman's Con-
      vention Auxiliary, Held in Philadelphia, Pa., September 9–14, 1914* (Nashville: Sun-
      day School Publishing Board, 1915), 165.

196   *The Baptist Woman's:* For Catholic women's organizations, see "C.Y.W.C.A.,"
      Miscellaneous Negro Newspapers, *The Afro-American*, May 9 and June 27, 1896,
      March 27 and April 17, 1897; for identification of the first black YWCAs, see
      Juliet O. Bell and Helen J. Wilkins, *Interracial Practices in Community Y.W.C.A.'s*
      (New York: National Board, Y.W.C.A., 1944), 2–3; "Woman's Department,"
      Missionary Seer 13:8 (December 1913): 5.

197   *While some female:* NBC, *Journal of the Thirty-[ninth] Session of the National Baptist
      Convention and the Nineteenth Annual Session of the Woman's Convention Auxiliary,
      Held in Newark, New Jersey, September 10–15, 1919* (Nashville: Sunday School
      Publishing Board, 1920), 213; During World War I, the War Camp Community
      Service work of black women was extensive. Throughout the U.S. black women's
      organizations engaged in patriotic war activities in support of black soldiers.
      Organized in groups known as "circles" and "units," women sewed and "knitted
      sweaters, helmets, wristlets, and socks for colored soldiers," and raised money to
      support their efforts. Ministers' wives and leading church women recruited
      members of their denomination and organized numerous groups for the work.
      For an example of this type activity among Baptist women, see "Washington

Woman Achieves Great Success," *Washington Bee*, August 31, 1918; Belle Davis, "The Circle for Negro Relief," *Opportunity* 3:27 (March 1925): 86–87.

198 *"stage a stay away"*: Leadership training institutes for domestic missionaries offered courses in missionary education, organization, administration, family life, and the use of audio-visual aids. NBC, *Journal of the Fifty-[ninth] Annual Session of the National Baptist Convention, USA, Inc., and the Thirty-ninth Annual Session of the Woman's Convention Auxiliary, Held in Philadelphia, Pennsylvania, September 6–10, 1939* (Nashville: Sunday School Publishing Board, 1940), 351; NBC, *Journal of the Sixtieth Annual Session of the National Baptist Convention, USA, Inc., and the Fortieth Annual Session of the Woman's Convention Auxiliary, Held in Birmingham, Alabama, September 4–9, 1940* (Nashville: Sunday School Publishing Board, 1941), 239; "Women's Bureau Studies Problems of Negro Woman Worker," *Opportunity* 17:2 (February 1939): 56.

198 *This was the traditional:* See Noel Ignatiev, *How the Irish Became White* (New York: Routledge, 1996).

198 *"the relations between"*: NBC, *Thirty-[ninth] Session*, 210–33.

198 *"community work among"*: NBC, *Twenty-third Session*, 371.

199 *In cities such as:* "AME Church in D.C. Feeds White and Colored," *Baltimore Afro-American*, February 6, 1932; "South Carolinians Hold NRA Meetings," *Norfolk Journal and Guide*, September 23, 1933.

200 *Thus, black workers:* "WPA Study Shows Conditions of Rural Negro," *Star of Zion*, August 4, 1938.

200 *At Clinton College:* "Samaritan AME Zion Church in Erie," *Star of Zion*, August 20, 1936; Geraldine Byard, "News from Worcester, Massachusetts," ibid., January 18, 1940; "New Britain, Connecticut AME Zion Church," ibid., February 23, 1939; Helen Williams, "St. James, San Mateo, Marches Ahead with Rev. R. A. Cooper," ibid., September 7, 1939; "Mrs. Esther C. Bingham Passes," ibid., June 4, 1936; "Many Negroes Employed in West Virginia WPA Projects," ibid., February 17, 1938; "N.Y.A. Aided 4,178 Colored Students in South Carolina," ibid., June 24, 1937; "Clinton College News," ibid., January 27, 1938.

200 *They became more:* For discussion of the WMU's Seven-Point Home Missions Program, developed in cooperation with Nannie Burroughs and the WC, see *The Worker* 3:10 (April–June 1936): 3; ibid., 8:35 (July–September 1942): 78–79; ibid., 17:82 (October–December 1954): 88–89; ibid., 21:95 (January–March 1958): 129; see Vonnie E. Lance to Una Roberts Lawrence, June 29, 1936, Box 5, Folder 28, "Black Missions," Una Roberts Lawrence Resource Files, Home Mission Board Records, Southern Baptist Historical Library, Nashville, Tennessee. For a detailed analysis of the intricacies of the WMU's program with the black Baptist women and its political import, see chapter 7. For evaluation of the Woman's Missionary Council of the MECS's biracial missionary work with CME women, see Mary Frederickson, " 'Each One Is Dependent on the Other': Southern Churchwomen, Racial Reform, and the Process of Transformation, 1880–1940," in *Visible Women: New Essays on American Activism*, ed. Nancy A. Hewitt and Suzanne Lebsock (Urbana: University of Illinois Press, 1993).

201 *Local societies were:* NBC, *Proceedings of the Fortieth Annual Session of the Woman's Convention, Auxiliary to the National Baptist Convention, U.S.A., Inc., Held in Cleveland, Ohio, September 10–14, 1941* (Nashville: Sunday School Publishing Board, 1941), 273, 279.

201 *Evaluating the change:* Rebecca Stiles Taylor, "Federated Clubs," *Chicago Defender*, March 3, 1945.

202 *She realized that:* Ibid.

202 *Most denominations had:* Patricia R. Hill, *The World Their Household: The American Woman's Foreign Mission Movement and Cultural Transformation, 1870–1920* (Ann Arbor: University of Michigan Press, 1985), 8. There is no general study of African American missionaries. Likewise, there is no history of black women's missionary societies, or of their role in the foreign mission enterprises of black denominations. Histories of foreign mission boards and their missions are important sources for understanding the mission work undertaken by black denominations. However, these works include very little discussion of either women missionaries or women's missionary societies and conventions. See Lewellyn L. Berry, *A Century of Missions of the African Methodist Episcopal Church, 1840–1940* (New York: Gutenberg Printing Co., 1942); George A. Singleton, *The Romance of African Methodism: A Study of the African Methodist Episcopal Church* (Hicksville, NY: Exposition Press, 1952); David Henry Bradley, *A History of the African Methodist Episcopal Zion Church* (Nashville: Parthenon Press, 1970); Lewis Garnett Jordan, *Up the Ladder in Foreign Missions* (Nashville: National Baptist Publishing Board, 1901); C. C. Adams and Marshall A. Talley, *Negro Baptists and Foreign Missions* (Philadelphia: Foreign Mission Board of the National Baptist Convention, U.S.A., 1944); Edward A. Freeman, *The Epoch of Negro Baptists and the Foreign Mission Board, National Baptist Convention, U.S.A., Inc.* (Kansas City, Ks.: Central Seminary Press, 1953); Leroy Fitts, *Lott Carey: First Black Missionary to Africa* (Valley Forge, Pa.: Judson Press, 1978). The best source for discussion of black Baptist missionary work in Africa is Sandy D. Martin, *Black Baptists and African Missions: The Origins of a Movement 1880–1915* (Macon, Ga: Mercer University Press, 1989). In this study, Martin cites the annual journals, which include the minutes of the National Baptist Convention's annual meetings for 1898–1912, 1914, and 1915. However, he did not use the corresponding reports of the NBC Woman's Convention.

202 *Aggregate membership numbers:* As for Baptist women—in particular the Woman's Convention—the editor of the *National Baptist Union-Review* stated, "[O]nly the fringe of the organization garment of women has been touched. Perhaps not 800 have at any time or place been enrolled." This estimate does not include the several thousand Baptist women who affiliated with their local church-based missionary societies. "Baptist Women," *National Baptist Union-Review*, April 22, 1916. Figures for black Methodists and other Christian missionary societies are not available. Estimates are based on aggregate membership numbers for the latter groups.

202 *The National Baptist:* NBC, *Proceedings of the Forty-third Annual Session of the Woman's Convention, Auxiliary to the National Baptist Convention, U.S.A., Inc., Held in Dallas, Texas, September 6–10, 1944* (Nashville: Sunday School Publishing Board, 1944), 110. Though women might hold membership in both groups, the Women's Missionary Society was separate from the Woman's Convention.

203 *At the same:* For example, in the first twenty-five years of its existence (1869–1895) the Methodist Episcopal Church Woman's Foreign Missionary Society raised almost $3.5 million for foreign missions alone. See Rosemary Skinner Keller, "Creating a Sphere for Women: The Methodist Episcopal Church, 1869–1906," in *Perspectives on American Methodism: Interpretive Essays*, ed. Russell E. Richey, Kenneth E. Rowe, and Jean Miller Schmidt (Nashville: Kingswood Books, 1993), 342.

204 *"once Africa is filled":* Mrs. E. J. Dodson, "The Relation of the American Negro to the Evangelization of Africa," *Star of Zion*, June 11, 1908.

204 *Most missionaries saw:* The "Theory of Providential Design" began in the nine-

teenth century with white colonizationists as a justification for expansionism. See Walter L. Williams, *Black Americans and the Evangelization of Africa, 1877–1900* (Madison, Wisc.: University of Wisconsin Press, 1982), 4–7; Sylvia M. Jacobs, "African Missions and the African American Christian Churches," in Larry G. Murphy, J. Gordon Melton, and Gary L. Ward, *Encyclopedia of African American Religions* (New York: Garland Publishing, Inc., 1993), 10–23; Sylvia M. Jacobs, "Their 'Special Mission': Afro-American Women as Missionaries to the Congo, 1894–1937," in *Black Americans and the Missionary Movement in Africa*, ed. Sylvia M. Jacobs (Westport, Conn.: Greenwood Press, 1982), 172; Dodson, "The Relation of the American Negro to the Evangelization of Africa"; Ibrahim Sundiata, *Brothers and Strangers: Black Zion, Black Slavery, 1914–1940* (Durham, NC: Duke University Press, 2003), 7.

204　*"the Divine Permission"*: Mary Mason, "The World of Women," *Star of Zion*, May 7, 1925.

204　*"There is no manhood"*: Henry McNeal Turner, "Essay: The American Negro and the Fatherland," in *Africa and the American Negro: Addresses and Proceedings of the Congress on Africa*, ed. J. W. E. Bowen (Atlanta: Gammon Theological Seminary, 1896), 195–98.

204　*There was a concern:* For diverse black views of Africa during the 1880s, see John B. Reeve, Rufus L. Perry, Solomon Porter Hood, and C. H. Thompson, "Symposium—What Should Be the Attitude of Colored Americans Towards Africa?" *AME Church Review* 2:1 (July 1885): 68–75.

205　*"He is too valuable"*: John Mitchell Jr., *Richmond Planet*, February 18, 1899.

205　*As editor of:* For quote, see Turner, "Essay: The American Negro and the Fatherland," 195–98. For examples of letters and articles addressing these topics in the 1890s, see Henry M. Turner, "Anti-African Emigrationists as Lynchers," *Voice of Missions* 3:10 (October 1895); Mary R. Burkett, "Celebrated Women at Work for Missions," ibid., 6:10 (October 1898); H. A. Grant, "What Is the Outlook for the Success of Our Mission Work on the Continent of Africa?" ibid. 4:11 (November 1896); E. L. Coffey, "Africa the Hope of the Negro," ibid., 4:2 (February 1896); John M. Henderson, "The Redemption of Africa, and Her Future Civilization and Grandeur," ibid. 7:3 (March 1, 1899); "What a White Lady Has to Say," ibid. 2:6 (June 1894); see also Stephen Ward Angell, *Bishop Henry McNeal Turner and African American Religion in the South* (Knoxville, Tenn.: University of Tennessee Press, 1992), 5, 119–22, 219; V. P. Franklin, *Black Self-Determination: A Cultural History of African American Resistance* (Westport, Conn.: Lawrence Hill and Company, 1984).

205　*Many black Baptists:* For a discussion of how the black church associated black "manhood with mission to Africa," see William H. Becker, "The Black Church: Manhood and Mission," in *African American Religion: Interpretive Essays in History and Culture*, ed. Timothy E. Fulop and Albert J. Raboteau (New York: Routledge, 1997), 179–95. In 1853 Bishop Nazrey asserted that it was "the duty of the AME Church to assist in sending the gospel to the heathen, who are out of the limits of civilization and [C]hristianity. We have, as an Episcopal Church as much right to look after perishing Africa, the West Indian Islands, St. Domingo and all those who are not [C]hristianized as any other Christian Church upon the face of the globe." For Nazrey quote, see Daniel A. Payne, *History of the African Methodist Episcopal Church* (Nashville, Tenn.: Publishing House of the AME Sunday-School Union, 1891), 293; S[olomon] P[orter] Hood, "Report of Philadelphia Conference," *Christian Recorder*, June 1, 1898.

206　*In 1890, with:* The signing of the Treaty of Berlin in 1885 gave formal sanction to dividing up Africa among European nations. Informal colonial empires date back to the eighteenth century. European rule in Africa began to crumble after World War I and the establishment of the United Nations. Beginning with Ghana in 1957, one by one African nations gained their independence. This process continued to the 1980s. Lillie M. Johnson, "Missionary-Government Relations: Black Americans in British and Portuguese Colonies," in Jacobs, *Black Americans*, 196–215.

206 *"The Department of Missions":* Reflecting upon the growing influence of the AME Church, the National Baptist Convention was concerned that the AME Church's African missionary program was much more advanced than theirs. Thus, the competition was between black and white denominations, as well as black denominations. For the quotation from the AME Council of Bishops Quadrennial Address to the General Conference of 1892, see L. G. Jordan, "Why They Are Influential," *Mission Herald* 13:4 (June 1908): 2. For examples of the use of this argument by other black denominations, see Editorials, *Missionary Seer* 14:3 (July 1914): 2. For an examination of the ambivalence, dilemmas, and conflicts inherent in the debates and decisions of black Methodist and Baptist denominations to undertake foreign missionary work in Africa, Haiti, Cuba, the Caribbean, and other areas inhabited by peoples of color, see Lawrence S. Little, *Disciples of Liberty: The African Methodist Episcopal Church in the Age of Imperialism, 1884–1916* (Knoxville: University of Tennessee Press, 2000); James T. Campbell, *Songs of Zion: The African Methodist Episcopal Church in the United States and South Africa* (New York: Oxford University Press, 1995); and Martin, *Black Baptist and African Missions*.

206 *"progress and development":* Alexander Crummell, "Civilization as a Collateral and Indispensable Instrumentality in Planting the Christian Church in Africa," in Bowen, ed., *Africa and the American Negro*, 119–24; Williams, *Black Americans*, 134–40. For the position taken by most black denominations see L. G. Jordan, "Rev. John Chilembwe Is No More Among the Living—'In the Midst of Life We Are in Death,' " *Mission Herald* 19:5 (May 1915): 2.

206 *"African Methodist Imperialism":* Williams, *Black Americans*, 37.

207 *"[T]he American Negroes":* For quote, see *Official Journal of the Twenty-ninth General Conference of the African Methodist Episcopal Zion Church, America (East and West Gold Coast Africa, and Demerara, South America), Held in the Wesley Center AME Zion Church, Pittsburgh, Pennsylvania, May 4th–17th, 1932* (Charlotte, NC: AME Zion Publishing House, 1932), 109–10. For an excellent discussion of black Americans' engagement with notions of imperialism and the relationship of colonization to notions of black manhood, see Michele Mitchell, *Righteous Propagation: African Americans and the Politics of Racial Destiny After Reconstruction* (Chapel Hill: University of North Carolina Press, 2003), 50–75.

207 *This statement might:* After 1920, Africans educated in the United States returned to their native lands and occupied positions as AME and AME Zion ministers and missionaries. They were anxious to assume leadership of the denominational affairs, schools, and mission stations in Africa. However, like the European churches, black denominational preference for black Americans as administrators of the episcopal districts and other church entities caused dissatisfaction and protest among the native Africans.

207 *The Liberian constitution:* M. H. Garnet Barboza, "Independence Day in Liberia," *Southern Workman* 13:11 (November 1884): 118; Tom Shick, *Behold the Promise Land: A History of Afro-American Settler Society in Nineteenth Century Liberia* (Baltimore: Johns Hopkins University Press, 1980).

207 *By 1880 the:* Ibid.; White denominations such as the Southern Baptist (1822), Methodist Episcopal (1833), Presbyterian (1834), Episcopalian (1836), and Catholic (1842) established mission stations in Liberia before the Civil War. See Miles Mark Fisher, "The Negro Churches," *Crisis* 45:7 (July 1938): 220, 239, 245–46.

208 *European Protestant:* Robert Needham Cust, "Alphabetical List of Missions," in Bowen, ed., *Africa and the American Negro*, 240–42. The NBC's South African mission station was not included in Cust's list. For details regarding the NBC mission work in South Africa between 1894 and 1900, see NBC *Journal of the Twentieth Annual Session of the National Baptist Convention, Held in the Fifth Street Baptist Church, Richmond, Virginia, September 12–17, 1900* (Nashville: National Baptist Publishing Board, 1900), 43.

208 *AME and NBC mission:* J. E. Roy, "Africa and America illustrated: Their Mutual Relation of History and of Service," in Bowen, ed., *Africa and the American Negro*, 223–25; Eugene Smith, "African Missions of American Methodists," *Voice of Missions* 1:12 (December 1893): 1. For discussion of the beginnings of AME Zion and AME African mission work, see Bishop E. D. W. Jones, *Comprehensive Catechism of the AME Zion Church* (Washington, DC: n.d.), 69–71; Alfred Lee Ridgel, *Africa and African Methodism* (Atlanta: Franklin Printing and Publishing Co., 1896); Campbell, *Songs of Zion*; NBC, *Journal of the Twentieth Annual Session*, 43; Frances B. Watson, "Stark Color Fear Prevails in the British Empire," *Baltimore Afro-American*, February 13, 1932.

208 *As European nations:* The 1896 *Plessy v. Ferguson* Supreme Court decision fueled the growth and spread of segregation and discrimination in the United States and influenced the decision of many mainstream denominations to either limit the number of black missionaries or eliminate blacks from their mission programs. For the concerns of European colonial powers such as France regarding the influence of black missionaries on Africans, see "Presbyterians Fear Fascism in Roosevelt's New Deal," *Baltimore Afro-American*, October 19, 1935. For discussion of racism within the missionary movement, see Wilber Christian Harr, "The Negro as an American Protestant Missionary in Africa" (PhD diss., University of Chicago, 1946), 65–67. See also Robert Vann, " 'Sedition' in Africa," *Pittsburgh Courier*, September 26, 1936.

209 *"problems of relations":* James E. East, "Missionary Work in Africa Compared with Missionary Work in Other Lands," *Mission Herald*, 28:3 (April 1925): 4; "Mixed Tongues Aid Prejudice in Africa," *Baltimore Afro-American*, November 1, 1930; Williams, *Black Americans and the Evangelization of Africa*, 20–22.

210 *However, Marcus Garvey's:* "The Le Zoute Conference," in NBC, *Journal of the Forty-seventh Annual Session of the National Baptist Convention, Lighthouse Guard Armory, Detroit, Michigan, September 7–12, 1927* (Nashville: Sunday School Publishing Board, 1927), 214; "Missionaries," *Star of Zion*, May 9, 1929, reprint of a *Crisis* editorial by W. E. B. Du Bois. See also "Prejudice Only Matter of Color," *Washington Tribune*, December 1, 1923; after 1880, the Southern Baptist Church ceased its recruitment of black missionaries, and by 1882 called for "white missionaries only" and refused to accept black volunteers. Williams, *Black Americans and the Evangelization of Africa*, 41; Letter from Sallie Olou MacKinnon to Claude A. Barnett, February 10, 1950, Claude Barnett Papers, "Foreign Missions of AME and Other Churches, Correspondence 1950–63," Series J, Microfilm Reel 1.

210 *Some white and black:* "Americans Succeed in African Missions," *Pittsburgh Courier*, January 28, 1933; "New Englander Sails as African Missionary: Will Work in Monrovia for Methodists," ibid., March 2, 1940; Cleveland G. Allen,

"Methodist Missionary Sends Message Home," ibid., August 31, 1940; "Methodists Map Plans for Africa," ibid., December 18, 1943; Jacobs, "African Missions," 22. For MacKinnon quote, see Minutes of Meeting of Africa, "Committee of the Foreign Missions Conference of North America," September 26, 1950, Claude Barnett Papers, "Foreign Missions of AME and Other Churches, Correspondence 1950–63"; Margaret Smith, "Peace Corps Versus Christian Missions," *Mission Herald* 63:6 (May–June 1961): 4–5.

211 *"Christianity stood forth":* Mary L. Mason, "A Bird's Eye View of the World's Womanhood," *Star of Zion*, October 9, 1924. As editor of the "World of Women" column, Mason had access to a broad spectrum of AME Zion readers as well as many others who avidly read the newspaper throughout the U.S., Africa, and the Caribbean. This article appeared in the inaugural column. In the Foreword, Mason defined the scope of the column and stated her intent to "present a synopsis of the condition of woman throughout the world." The word "pagan" was frequently used by missionaries and other Christians to refer to those individuals or groups who worshipped idols, animals, and other objects.

211 *This belief became:* "Women in the Church," *Christian Century*, December 11, 1940, 1542–43. Commenting on the findings of a Federal Council of Churches' study of "Women's Status in Protestant Churches," the editor of the *Christian Century* asserted that this argument flew in the face of actual facts. The report demonstrated that rather than being progressive, the church was in fact "one of the most backward of all institutions in the place it accords women and the attitude it exhibits toward them."

211 *Leading black intellectuals:* For biographical information on Crummell, see V. P. Franklin, *Living Our Stories, Telling Our Truths: Autobiography and the Making of the African-American Intellectual Tradition* (New York: Oxford University Press, 1995), 19–58; Gregory U. Rigby, *Alexander Crummell: Pioneer in Nineteenth Century Pan-African Thought* (Westport, Conn.: Greenwood Press, 1988); Wilson J. Moses, *Alexander Crummell: A Study of Civilization and Discontent* (New York: Oxford University Press, 1989); Alfred Moss Jr., "Alexander Crummell: Black Nationalist and Apostle of Western Civilization," in *Black Leaders of the Nineteenth Century*, ed. Leon Litwack and August Meier (Urbana: University of Illinois Press, 1988), 237–51.

211 *Crummell's views were:* In 1822 the American Colonization Society established a colony on the west African coast comprised of disaffected black Americans who willingly emigrated to Africa to escape racial oppression in the United States. At least half of the emigrants were females, including freeborn and emancipated blacks. As a group that was predominantly Christian, the settlers viewed traditional African religions and Islam as paganistic and concentrated on educating and converting native Africans to Christianity. As forerunners of black women missionaries, female settlers raised money to build churches and introduced cultural patterns related more to the United States than to Africa. Alexander Crummell was well aware of the success of early settlers in educating and Christianizing Liberian women. Debra L. Newman, "Liberian Women's Cultural Assimilation in the Nineteenth Century," *Negro History Bulletin* 63:1–4 (January-December 2000): 55–61.

212 *He warned AME:* Rev. Alexander Crummell, "Letter from Rev. A[lexander] Crummell, B.A.," *Christian Recorder*, November 19, 1870. For discussion of the "civilizing" influences of Christianity, see L. G. Jordan, "Making Christians of Non-Christian Peoples," *Mission Herald* 16:2 (March 1912): 3.

213 *Between 1900 and 1930:* Carole Summers, " 'If You Can Educate the Native

Woman . . . ': Debates over the Schooling and Education of Girls and Women in Southern Rhodesia, 1900–1934," *History of Education Quarterly* 36:4 (winter 1996): 449–50.

213 *"Mohammedanism encourages polygamy"*: For quotations by Walters, see William Jacob Walls, *The African Methodist Episcopal Zion Church: Reality of the Black Church* (Charlotte, NC: AME Zion Publishing House, 1974), 238. Prior to the mid-twentieth century, the Islamic religion was referred to as "Mohammedanism." Founded by the prophet Mohammed in the year 622, in a series of religious wars, the Mohammedans succeeded in subverting Christianity along the coast of northern Africa. It was only in Egypt that the Coptic Christians survived. African American missionaries frequently contrasted Mohammedanism with Christianity, illustrating what they believed were the detrimental effects of the religion on Africans. Rev. Alfred Lee Ridgel, presiding elder of the AME Liberian Annual Conference wrote about his experiences in Africa. For an excellent and detailed perception of black Christians' views on Mohammedanism, see Ridgel, *Africa and African Methodism*, 65–74.

214 *Crummell recommended that:* Crummell, "Letter from Rev. A[lexander] Crummell."

214 *"Who among our young"*: For biographical information on Cain, see Rayford W. Logan and Michael R. Winston, *Dictionary of American Negro Biography* (New York: W. W. Norton and Co., 1982), 84; R. H. Cain, "Africa," *Christian Recorder*, July 2, 1885.

214 *Highly publicized reports:* For letters and other reports of Amanda Berry Smith's missionary work, see *Christian Recorder*, September 23, 1880, March 26, 1885, January 17, 1885, October 1, 1885, February 21, 1895, and *Indianapolis Freeman*, April 6, 1889; Amanda Berry Smith, *An Autobiography: The Story of the Lord's Dealing with Mrs. Amanda Smith* (Chicago: Christian Witness, 1893).

214 *Struck by the plight:* Pinkey Davis, "Woman the True Missionary for Africa," *Voice of Missions* 4:4 (April 1896): 2.

215 *In the nineteenth:* Missionaries such as Emma DeLaney, Frances Watson, and others, often commented about the impact of traditional African beliefs and customs on females. DeLaney said, "According to heathen customs the worst of everything must be put on the women." See Emma B. DeLaney, "From Miss DeLany (sic)," *Spelman Messenger* 20:4 (January 1904): 7; Frances B. Watson, "Black Man's Land," Box 1, Folder 27, "Black Missions," unpublished manuscript, Una Roberts Lawrence Resource Files, Home Mission Board Records, Southern Baptist Historical Library, Nashville, Tennessee. For nineteenth-century attitudes and practices regarding the appointment of women as missionaries, see Eddie Stepp, "Interpreting a Forgotten Mission: African American Missionaries of the Southern Baptist Convention in Liberia, West Africa, 1846–1860" (PhD diss., 1999, Baylor University), 111.

216 *Education was proposed:* "Fitness for Missionary Service," *Mission Herald* 23:5 (July 1919): 3; Jordan, "Making Christians of Non-Christian Peoples."

216 *"practiced without restraint"*: Mrs. H[ilda] M. Nasmyth, "Africa As It Was and As It Is, from Sacred and Profane Sources," *AME Zion Quarterly Review* 9:1 (October–December 1899): 32; "Some of Our Noble Women," *Star of Zion*, November 12, 1896.

217 *Thus, the missionary:* "Difficulties of Missionary Work in Africa," *AME Church Review* 17:31 (January 1901): 257.

217 *Affectionately referred to:* "Breaking Work," *Spelman Messenger* 30:1 (October 1913): 2–3.

217 *It was their duty:* Jacobs, "Their 'Special Mission'," 155–72; Sylvia M. Jacobs, " 'Say Africa When You Pray': The Activities of Early Black Baptist Women Missionaries among Liberian Women and Children," *SAGE* 3:2 (fall 1986): 16.

218 *Spelman was a key:* "Spelman Seminary: Atlanta, Georgia," *Home Mission Monthly* 13:5 (May 1891): 128–29; "Spelman Seminary," ibid., 13:8 (August 1891): 225; "Vacation Work of Students," ibid., 13:2 (February 1891): 73–76.

218 *Most denominational missionary:* "Our Foreign Missions," *Christian Recorder*, February 8, 1901. Howard Gregg, *History of the African Methodist Episcopal Church* (Nashville: AME Church Sunday School Union, 1980), 194; home and foreign mission boards were organized in several AME Zion conferences, but it was not until 1880 that the General Conference approved the establishment of a denominational Home and Foreign Missions Board. See William J. Walls, *The African Methodist Episcopal Zion Church: Reality of the Black Church* (Charlotte, NC: AME Zion Publishing House, 1974), 374–77.

218 *This organization:* The Baptist Foreign Mission Convention was founded in 1880 as a regional association limited to the South. In 1895 the BFMC's program was merged into the Foreign Mission Board of the newly formed National Baptist Convention. For discussion of the BFMC, the NBC, and Lott Carey Foreign Mission Convention, see Martin, *Black Baptists*, 3, 43–106.

219 *Though her career:* Though numerous articles have been written about Betsey Stockton, the most authoritative source is Albert J. Raboteau and David W. Wills, eds., *African-American Religion: A Historical Interpretation with Representative Documents* (Chicago: University of Chicago Press, 2000).

219 *In keeping with:* Stepp, "Interpreting a Forgotten Mission," 111.

219 *By the 1880s:* Prior to 1910 the U.S. Census does not include numerical breakdowns for black women missionaries or clergy. All black female church workers are listed as religious workers.

220 *Rather, they are:* There were many married missionary women who worked alongside their husbands in the field in the nineteenth and twentieth centuries. In most cases, the husbands held prominent positions at the mission stations, and wives were either not mentioned or were called assistants. The religious press, most notably the Baptist *Mission Herald*, frequently published letters written by husbands describing the mission station's activities, but rarely included letters of wives. A married woman's status was usually defined by her husband's accomplishments. Therefore, obituaries for women whose husbands had been deceased for years focused mostly on the achievements of the dead husband. When a man died, however, even if the wife's accomplishments outranked his, she was described in terms of her role as a wife, mother, and "helpmate" to her husband.

220 *As the children:* Lawson A. Scruggs, *Women of Distinction: Remarkable of Works and Invincible of Character* (Raleigh, NC: L. A. Scruggs, Publisher, 1893), 187–89.

221 *These included the:* In the late nineteenth century the majority of black missionaries were sent to Africa by white mission boards for two reasons. First, because foreign mission work was not an established feature in most black denominations. Second, because of the relatively high death rate of white missionaries from tropical disease by the 1880s West Africa was considered "the white man's grave." See Harr, "The Negro as an American Protestant Missionary," 11–12; J. Shirley Shadrach, "Mrs. Jane E. Sharp's School for African Girls," *Colored American Magazine* 17:3 (March 1904): 181–84; Scruggs, *Women of Distinction*, 61–64, 158–61, 187–89, 197, 203, 217–22, 256–59, 300–02; Julia L. Smith, "Off for Liberia," *Southern Workman* 17:6 (June 1888): 74; Sylvia M. Jacobs, "The Sons and Daughters of Africa: Nancy Jones, Missionary in Mozambique and Southern Rhodesia,

1888–1897," *SAGE* 9:2 (summer 1995): 88–89; "Francis A. Davis, Evangelist for Africa," *Christian Recorder*, May 18, 1893; "Grad of 1892 Cited for Her Contributions," *New York Age*, June 21, 1952; "Educational Items," *Christian Index*, December 4, 1897.

222 *What was lacking:* Shadrach, "Mrs. Jane E. Sharp's School."

222 *The Mount Coffee Association:* Ibid.

224 *Morris also felt:* "The Negro Church Has Reached a Most Critical Point in Its Missionary History," in NBC, *Journal of the Forty-seventh Annual Session*, 243; for the report by Rev. Charles S. Morris, see NBC, *Journal of the Twentieth Annual Session*, 53, 55–56, 57.

224 *Black American women:* In November 1922, Rev. Nora Taylor, a highly influential and nationally known AME evangelist and organizer, the founder and president of the Chicago District Missionary Society, an active member of the Women's Parent Mite Missionary Society, and the grand daughter ruler of the Daughter Elks, went to Africa as an unpaid missionary teacher at the AME Industrial School for Girls in Freetown, Sierra Leone, in west Africa. For biographical data on Taylor, see Wright, *The Centennial Encyclopaedia*, 222–23; "Quinn Chapel AME Church," *Chicago Defender*, November 18, 1922; Nora F. Taylor, "An Address to the Chicago Union Mite Missionary Society," *AME Church Review* 38:3 (January 1922): 109–12; AME Zion pastor Rev. Florence Spearing Randolph was among the most noted black women leaders of the early twentieth century. As a minister, missionary, suffragist, organizer, politician, and temperance worker, Randolph was one of the most influential women of her time. Among other things, she was the founder of the New Jersey Federation of Colored Women and a leading figure in the interracial movement. She served as president of the AME Zion's New Jersey Women's Home and Foreign Missionary Society for twenty-five years. In January 1922, Randolph ostensibly went on a fact-finding tour, but also as an unpaid missionary, to west Africa. Over a period of sixteen months, she traveled throughout Liberia and the Gold Coast lecturing and preaching. However, her missionary work was most concentrated in Quittah, where she spent seven months pastoring a church and assisting with the AME Zion school, teaching a domestic science class. For general biography and discussion of Randolph's African work, see Collier-Thomas, *Daughters of Thunder*, 103–06; "Jerseyites to Honor Woman Worker Who Goes to Africa," *New York Age*, November 12, 1921; "Rev. Florence Randolph Now in Monrovia, Liberia, Africa," ibid., June 2, 1923.

225 *Hailed as the first:* J. R. Frederick, "In Memoriam of Sarah E. Gorham, Who Departed This Life August 10th, 1894," *Voice of Missions* 11:10 (October 1894): 4; J. T. Jennifer, "A Tribute to the Memory of Sarah E. Gorham," ibid., 11:11 (November 1894): 4.

226 *Thus, she stressed:* "Mrs. Fanny Coppin," *Christian Recorder*, March 27, 1902; *Southern Workman* 32:3 (March 1903): 188; Fanny Jackson-Coppin, *Hints on Teaching: Reminiscences of School Life* (Philadelphia: AME Book Concern, 1913), 125–26; John Cromwell, *The Negro in American History* (Washington, DC: American Negro Academy, 1914), 218; Benjamin Brawley, *Negro Builders and Heroes* (Chapel Hill: University of North Carolina Press, 1937), 276; Mrs. Louise B. Gow, "Fifteenth Episcopal District Supervisor," *Voice of Missions* 61:7 (July 1959): 6; Campbell, *Songs of Zion*, 228.

226 *The work of Williamson:* For a brief discussion of black Baptist women missionaries, see Leroy Fitts, *A History of Black Baptists* (Nashville, Tenn.: Boardman Press, 1985), 126–34.

227 *Between 1893 and 1919:* "Lucy Houghton Upton," *Spelman Messenger* 35:3 (February 1919): 5.

228 *Flora Zeto graduated:* Flora E. G. Zeto, "Spelman in Africa and Africa in Spelman," *Spelman Messenger*, 32:2 (November, 1915): 1, 2; "Spelman in Africa," editorial, ibid., 29:8 (May 1913): 5, 6; L. Alice Turner Blowe, "Spelman in Africa," ibid. 42:8 (May 1926): 4.

228 *During the early 1920s:* Flora Z. Malekebu, "A Letter from Liberia," *Spelman Messenger* 39:3 (December 1922): 7; "Persons of Mark in Missions," *Mission Herald* 55:5 (March–April 1952): 4; "Origin of the Work," ibid. 65: 4 (January–February 1963): 13.

228 *Employing labor to:* NBC, *Journal of the Twentieth Annual Session*, 45, 50; NBC, *Journal of the Twenty-first Annual Session of the National Baptist Convention, Held in the AME Zion Baptist Church, Cincinnati, Ohio, September 11–16, 1901* (Nashville: National Baptist Publishing Board, 1901), 28.

229 *They erected laws:* The indictment of white missionaries by African American political and social activists grew louder as the twentieth century progressed. In 1936, *Pittsburgh Courier* editor Robert Vann wrote a scathing editorial in which he blamed Europeans for three centuries of exploitation of Africa and the devastating oppression of Africans. Vann claimed, "The [white] Christian missionaries who swarm over the land are in open cahoots with the exploiters." Vann, " 'Sedition' in Africa." For Fanny Jackson-Coppin quote, see Jackson-Coppin, *Hints on Teaching*, 127; R. A. Jackson, "A Voice from Africa: Prejudice in the Dark Continent," *Richmond Planet*, March 18, 1899; Emma B. DeLaney, "From Our Letter File," *Spelman Messenger* 19:6 (March 1903): 5; Harr, "The Negro as an American Protestant Missionary," 60.

229 *"inhuman treatment":* "From Miss DeLaney," *Spelman Messenger* 19:2 (November 1902): 4; Harr, "The Negro as an American Protestant Missionary."

230 *After all, she:* Emma B. DeLaney, "Why I Go as a Foreign Missionary," *Spelman Messenger* 18:5 (February 1902): 5.

230 *"the horrid condition":* Emma B. DeLaney, "News from Miss DeLaney," *Spelman Messenger* 19:1 (October 1902): 6. This letter was published four months after it was written on June 20, 1902; DeLaney, "From Miss DeLaney," ibid. (November 1902); DeLaney, "From Our Letter File," ibid. 19:6 (March 1903): 5.

230 *Acclimation to the lack:* DeLaney, "News from Miss DeLaney"; DeLaney, "From Miss DeLaney."

230 *Standing in the door:* Ibid.

231 *The most immediate:* Ibid.; Emma B. DeLaney, "From the Zambesi," *Spelman Messenger* 19:4 (January 1903): 7.

231 *"not a single school":* DeLaney, "From the Zambesi."

232 *DeLaney had plenty:* Ibid.

232 *In November 1903:* Ibid.; Willie Mae Hardy Ashley, *Far From Home* (Fernandina Beach, Fla.: Willie Mae Hardy Ashley, n.d.), 12.

233 *"heathenism and barbarism":* DeLaney, "From Our Letter File."

233 *"including all white":* Ram Desai, ed., *Christianity in Africa as Seen by the Africans* (Denver: Alan Swallow, 1962), 18; Wilson S. Naylor, *Daybreak in the Dark Continent* (New York: Eaton and Mains, 1908), 45–47.

234 *"I like to talk":* Emma B. DeLaney, "From Africa," *Spelman Messenger* 20:1 (October 1903): 5–6.

234 *Having spent almost:* Emma B. DeLaney, "Missionary Department," *National Baptist Union*, November 18, 1903; Emma B. DeLaney, "News from Africa," *Spelman Messenger* 21:8 (May 1905): 6.

234 *Moreover, to obscure:* For an excellent discussion of King Leopold's use of forced labor, mutilation, killing, and general brutalization of Africans in the Congo, and the Belgian government's policy regarding exclusion of black American missions and missionaries, see chapter 5, "Atrocities Protest," in William E. Phipps, *William Sheppard: Congo's African American Livingstone* (Louisville, Ky.: Geneva Press, 2002), 132–75.

235 *It was there:* "They Sailed for Africa," *Washington Bee,* June 15, 1912; Fitts, *A History of Black Baptists,* 126.

235 *And there was:* Emma B. DeLaney, "From the Field," *Mission Herald* 16:4 (August 1912): 1; Emma B. Delaney, "From the Field," ibid. 16:5 (September 1912): 1.

235 *Her first task:* DeLaney, "From the Field," ibid. (September 1912).

235 *It appears that:* Emma B. DeLaney, "From the Field," ibid. 16:9 (January 1913): 4.

236 *An additional private:* Ashley, *Far from Home,* 14–15.

236 *The new laws:* Watson, "Black Man's Land," 20; Jeanine DeLombard, "Sisters, Servants, or Saviors? National Baptist Women Missionaries in Liberia in the 1920s," *International Journal of African Historical Studies* 24:2 (1991): 339–40.

236 *"[W]ithout 'Breaking Word' ":* "Breaking Word," *Spelman Messenger* 30:1 (October 1913): 2–3.

237 *She could see soldiers:* Ibid.

237 *"I forfeit my life":* Ibid.

238 *Poro had the power:* J. Gus Liebenow, *Liberia: The Quest for Democracy* (Bloomington, Ind.: Indiana University Press, 1987), 43–45; Frances B. Watson, "Standards of African Life," *Mission Herald* 41:5 (November–December, 1937): 12, 34; George W. Ellis, *Negro Culture in West Africa* (New York: Neale Publishing Co., 1914), 49–56; Naylor, *The Dark Continent,* 54–55.

238 *It was generally:* Watson, "Black Man's Land," 60.

238 *"Some of them":* Emma B. DeLaney, "From Liberia," *Spelman Messenger* 31:1 (October 1914): 7.

238 *"A woman and her children":* Emma B. DeLaney, "Miss DeLaney's Report," *Mission Herald* 18:10 (October 1914): 3.

239 *Since Suehn was not:* Ashley, *Far From Home,* 62. Iron wood was preferred to other types of lumber because of its durability. DeLaney's "iron" house was covered with corrugated aluminum.

239 *After struggling so hard:* Emma B. DeLaney, *Spelman Messenger* 31:4 (January 1915): 8; Emma B. DeLaney, ibid. 32:2 (November 1915): 3.

240 *She repeated her vow:* Emma B. DeLaney, "A Letter from Miss DeLaney," *Spelman Messenger* 32:7 (April 1916): 7. For Liberian population statistics, see Marmax Wilmore, "The Catholic Church in Liberia," *Chronicle* 3:4 (April 1930): 88.

240 *As the war progressed:* Emma B. DeLaney, *Spelman Messenger* 33:2 (November 1916): 8.

240 *Suffering from sheer exhaustion:* Emma B. DeLaney, *Mission Herald* 21:8 (September 1917): 3–4.

241 *"Humanly speaking":* Emma B. DeLaney, *Spelman Messenger* 35:4 (January 1919): 5.

241 *The government informed:* Letter to Mr. Kpingbar Karnley, Paramount Chief, Suehn, from B. Mars, Secretary of the Interior, Liberia, West Africa, October 11, 1918. Reprinted in *Mission Herald* 22:10 (October 1918).

241 *"that no one can":* "Two Stories Retold," *Mission Herald* 24:7 (November 1920): 2–3.

241 *"her African heritage":* "Miss Emma B. DeLaney," *Spelman Messenger* 39:1 (October 1922): 4.

242 *Viewing themselves as:* Lombard, "Sisters, Servants, or Saviors?" 331.

242 *The need was:* Sarah C. Williamson, "This Is My Call," *Mission Herald* 27:6 (July 1924): 33; "Two Missionary Services at First Baptist Church," *Norfolk Journal and Guide*, October 11, 1924; "Norfolk Woman Sent to Africa as Missionary," ibid., October 18, 1924. For quotes, see Sarah Williamson Coleman, "Suehn Industrial Mission," *Mission Herald* 43:11 (December 1931): 9–12, 30.

243 *In 1932, Williamson:* Sarah Williamson received extensive support from Rev. Adam Clayton Powell and the Abysinnia Baptist Church. Instead of badgering the Foreign Mission Board to pay her passage home, Williamson persuaded the white captain of the ship to allow her to travel to New York City C.O.D. The following Sunday after her arrival she agreed to speak at Abysinnia, in exchange for payment of her travel and expenses. White philanthropists such as Hattie M. Strong and Harper Sibley provided substantial funding for building projects at Suehn. Individual black leaders, such as the Rev. Charles Morris, personally contributed thousands of dollars to Suehn. For information regarding financial support, the tenor and tone of Williamson's letters, her relationship with the Africans, references to Williamson as "God Sister," and her first marriage to Matthew Shields and subsequent African missionary appointments, see James East, "Miss Sarah C. Williamson's Furlough Coming to a Close," *Mission Herald* 31:8 (September 1928): 4; Sarah Williamson Coleman, "The Heart of Gold," ibid. 73:8 (September–October 1970): 13–15; Sarah C. Williamson, "A Day from My Diary," ibid. 27:11 (December 1924): 32–33; "Letters from the Foreign Field," ibid. 34:10 (November 1931): 31–33; "Letters from the Field," ibid. 30:8 (September 1927): 31–32; Mrs. Henry A. Strong, "The Philanthropist Remembers Africa," ibid. 31:2 (March 1928): 10–11; "The Return Home of Miss S. C. Williamson and Miss M. Louise Reid," ibid. 34:8 (September 1931): 4; James East, "What the Foreign Mission Board Is Doing to Save the Day for Africa," ibid.; "Miss Sarah C. Williamson to Wed During the Month of June," ibid. 35:5 (June 1932): 2; "Additional Missionaries," ibid. 41:4 (September–October 1937): 9; Sarah Williamson Shields, "In His Vineyard," ibid. 43:6 (January–February 1940): 36; "My Second Missionary Journey," Sarah Williamson Coleman, ibid. 58:5 (March–April 1955): 13–16.

244 *He was well aware:* H. Laurence McNeil, "Dayton Minister Thinks Austin Not Suited for Secretary of Missions," *Pittsburgh Courier*, November 10, 1934; Sarah Williamson Shields, "True Evangelism Will Bring the World to Christ," *Worker* 7:30 (April–June 1941): 76–79.

244 *Moreover, East proclaimed:* "Are the Christian Forces at Home Refusing to be Ropeholders?" *Mission Herald* 32:5 (June 1929): 5–6.

245 *In the nineteenth:* Barbara Welter, "She Hath Done What She Could: Protestant Women's Missionary Careers in Nineteenth-Century America," *American Quarterly* 30:5 (1978): 624–38. Welter focuses on white women missionaries and their denominational organizations. However, this source is useful for providing a context for understanding many of the attitudes and patterns of development that influenced the growth of female missionaries among Protestant denominations.

245 *At stations such as:* DeLombard, "Sisters, Servants, or Saviors?" 332.

245 *In accordance with:* R. W. Thompson, "Church Politics," *Indianapolis Freeman*, February 6, 1904.

246 *They were enrolled:* L. G. Jordan, "Five to Go to Africa," *Mission Herald* 23:5 (July 1919): 1; "Miss Adelaide Tantsi," *Voice of Missions* 6:8 (August 1898): 2; Edwin W. Smith, "James Emman Kwegyir Aggrey, *Star of Zion*, November 20, 1930; "Persons of Mark in Missions," *Mission Herald* 55:5 (March–April 1952): 4; "The

Story of Anna Ruth Malekebu," *Spelman Messenger* 22:6 (March 1906): 1–2; "A Letter from Liberia," ibid. 39:3 (December 1922): 7; Jesse Jai McNeil, "A Long Awaited Deed," *Mission Herald* 65:4 (January, February 1963): 7–11. For a discussion of South African students such as Charlotte Manye, Charles Dube, Adelaide Tantsi, and Amanda Smith who studied at Wilberforce University, see Campbell, *Songs of Zion,* 249–94.

247 *For example, Charity Zomelo:* Isaac Sackey, "The Burden of the African Missions of the AME Zion Church," *Star of Zion,* February 5, 1920; W. W. Jones, "The African Bishopric," ibid., February 19, 1920; "Africa to Have Missionary Superintendent with Ordaining Powers," ibid., June 17, 1920; "The Needs of the AME Zion Church in Africa," ibid., April 2, 1936; T. W. B. Amissah, "Women's Night at West Ghana Annual Conference," ibid., April 23, 1959; "Debate over African Work Stirs AMEZ's," *Baltimore Afro-American,* May 16, 1936. In 1892, black Methodists in Pretoria, South Africa, withdrew from the Wesleyan Methodist Missionary Society and established an independent African Methodist Church. They designated their movement the Ethiopian Church. Leaders of the South African Ethiopian Church later merged with the AME Church. Similarly, in the twentieth century, in Liberia and other African nations, black Methodists left the AME and AME Zion denominations to join the Wesleyan Methodists and establish independent African churches that adhered to the Methodist creed. For a discussion of Ethiopianism in South Africa, see Carl J. Murphy, "The Ethiopian Church," *AME Church Review* 34:3 (January 1918): 133–38; Juanita C. Byrd, "The Ethiopian Church," ibid. 34:4 (April 1918): 252–53; Campbell, *Songs of Zion,* 103–38.

247 *"far more costly":* "Bishop Jones Warns the Church That If It Continues Its Present Ways, It Will be a Millstone Around the Neck of the Race Rather Than a Means of Progress," *Norfolk Journal and Guide,* September 23, 1933.

248 *Walter White:* Lidia T. Brown, "NAACP Head Speaks," *Missionary Seer* 42:6 (June 1945): 6.

248 *Widespread unrest:* Minutes of meeting of Africa Committee of the Foreign Missions Conference of North America, September 26, 1950.

249 *He questioned the lack:* Dr. J. W. DeGraft Johnson, "A Voice from Africa," *Star of Zion,* July 14, 1955.

249 *Bishop Larte presided:* Walls, *The African Methodist Episcopal Zion Church,* 241–43, 386, 423.

249 *In 1947, in a speech:* Letter from Claude A. Barnett to Margaret Wrong, August 12, 1947, Claude Barnett Collection, Series J, Microfilm Reel 1. For biographical information on Etta Moten Barnett, see Ruth Edmonds Hill, "Etta Moten Barnett," in Smith, *Notable Black American Women, Book I,* 51–55.

250 *Barnett made reference:* Letter from Claude A. Barnett to Christine S. Smith, September 6, 1947, Claude Barnett Collection, Series J, Microfilm Reel 1.

250 *In 1950 Annie Heath:* Letter from Annie E. Heath to Claude A. Barnett, August 29, 1950, Claude Barnett Collection, Series J, Microfilm Reel 1.

250 *"right on the job":* Letter from Claude A. Barnett to Helen A. Williams, August 25, 1950, Claude Barnett Collection, Series J, Microfilm Reel 1.

252 *Education and preaching:* G. N. Collins, "How Much Do We Really Know About Our Missionary Investments Abroad?" *Christian Recorder,* January 15, April 2, 1963. The Eighteenth Episcopal District encompassed Swaziland and Basutoland.

252 *To this long:* Gregg, *History of the African Methodist Episcopal Church,* 199–200.

253 *Symbolic of the times:* William J. Harvey, "Where There's a Will There's a Way," *Mission Herald* 66:3 (November–December 1963): 25.

253 *"faced with Islam's confidence":* E. H. Robertson, "The Bible in Young African Churches," *Mission Herald* 64:3 (November–December 1961): 1, 21.

254 *The addition of:* William J. Harvey, "Men and World Missions," *Mission Herald* 65:5 (May–June 1963): 24; Margaret Smith, "Peace Corps Versus Christian Missions," ibid. 63:6 (May–June 1961): 4–5. Mattie Mae Davis, "Suehn Industrial Mission," ibid. 66:1 (July–August 1963): 9.

254 *For the AME-WHFMS:* Edra Mae Hilliard, as the wife of AME Zion Bishop William A. Hilliard, the presiding bishop over the Nigerian Annual Conference (1960–64), served as the WHFMS foreign mission supervisor. Idonia Elizabeth Rogerson, *Historical Synopsis of the Woman's Home and Foreign Missionary Society, African Methodist Episcopal Zion Church* (Charlotte: AME Zion Publishing House, n.d.), 57–58, 75–79, 87. For discussion of the AME Women's Missionary Program, see Alma A. Polk, "Many of 42 Foreign Students Here on Scholarships Granted by W. M. Society," *Christian Recorder*, February 5, 1959.

255 *However, these denominations:* Walls, *The African Methodist Episcopal Zion Church*, 387.

255 *"personal symbolism of love":* Ibid.

CHAPTER 5 *"Righteous Guidance"*

258 *Anxious to add:* The lack of a national protest against discrimination in the women's suffrage movement and congressional antagonism toward black women voters did not preclude African American women's speaking in favor of the Susan B. Anthony amendment—the platform of the National Woman's Party—and otherwise organizing and agitating for the franchise at the local level. In 1916, in her annual address to the WC, Layten proclaimed that the Anthony amendment "is to secure suffrage for every [woman] in the United States regardless of race or color. Colored men must see their chance and vote for the amendment, which means our political freedom, our industrial advancement, our restoration to Citizenship." Following the ratification of the Nineteenth Amendment in 1920 black women became actively involved in partisan politics. For Layten quote, see NBC, *Journal of the Thirty-sixth Session of the National Baptist Convention and the Sixteenth Annual Session of the Woman's Convention Auxiliary, Held in Savannah, Georgia, September 6–11, 1916* (Nashville: Sunday School Publishing Board, 1916), 183; NBC, *Journal of the Forty-first Annual Session of the National Baptist Convention and the Twentieth Annual Session of the Woman's Convention Auxiliary, Held in Chicago, Illinois, September 7–12, 1921* (Nashville: Sunday School Publishing Board, 1921), 305.

258 *As a theoretical concept:* Nancie Caraway, *Segregated Sisterhood: Racism and the Politics of American Feminism* (Knoxville: University of Tennessee Press, 1991), 158–59.

258 *For example, forty-three:* For an examination of the role of black women in the American Equal Rights Association, American Woman Suffrage Association, and the National Woman Suffrage Association; and an analysis of Harper's role in the abolitionist, suffrage, and other major reform movements of the nineteenth century, see Bettye Collier-Thomas, "Frances Ellen Watkins Harper: Abolitionist and Feminist Reformer, 1825–1911," in *African American Women and the Vote, 1837–1965,* ed. Ann D. Gordon et al. (Amherst: University of Massachusetts Press, 1997), 41–65. For the Harper quotation, see Rosalyn Terborg-Penn, *African American Women in the Struggle for the Vote, 1850–1920* (Bloomington: Indiana University Press, 1998), 26, 47. For black women participants in the suffrage parade, see "Suffrage Paraders," *Crisis* 4:6 (April 1913): 297; *Woman's Jour-*

nal 64:2 (March 15, 1913): 7; "Marches in Parade Despite Protests," *Chicago Defender*, March 8, 1913; "Suffragette Movement," ibid.

259 *She advised:* Fannie Barrier Williams, "Illinois," *Woman's Era* 1:8 (November 1894): 12–14.

259 *Williams's assessment:* For example, in an analysis of the ideology and politics of white women, Burroughs noted that during World War I "[o]nly a few of the millions of white women who pleaded for Belgium, wept over Armenia, [and donated] to the relief of Korea, have said one word against the atrocities in their own land. The very people who will give thousands of dollars to educate and evangelize the Negro in America will not give a dollar to an anti-lynching fund, nor will they lift their voices in protest." Burroughs told the WC members that they must "seek the co-operation of organizations composed of white women. Urge the leaders in these organizations to speak out." In other words, black women had no illusions about the nature of white racism. But, at the same time, Burroughs and her cohorts knew that change could not occur without engaging and converting white leaders to their cause, especially white women. See NBC, *Journal of the Thirty-[ninth] Session of the National Baptist Convention and the Nineteenth Annual Session of the Woman's Convention Auxiliary, Held in Newark, New Jersey, September 10–15, 1919* (Nashville: Sunday School Publishing Board, 1919), 233; see Burroughs's comments on white women's role after World War II. NBC, *Proceedings of the Forty-third Annual Session of the Woman's Convention, Auxiliary to the National Baptist Convention, U.S.A., Held in Dallas, Texas, September 6–10, 1944* (Nashville: Sunday School Publishing Board, 1944), 268–69. For discussion of the American response to the Armenian atrocities, see Merrill D. Peterson, *Starving Armenians: America and the Armenian Genocide, 1915–1930 and After* (Charlottesville: University of Virginia Press, 2004).

259 *African American women:* Glenda Gilmore is among the few historians who have theorized the church as a political force. Discussing the relationship of the black church to politics in North Carolina during the Progressive Era, she concludes that "the church was a political structure, and politics was a practical means to a religious end. To fail one was to fail the other." See Glenda Elizabeth Gilmore, *Gender and Jim Crow: Women and the Politics of White Supremacy in North Carolina, 1896–1920* (Chapel Hill: University of North Carolina Press, 1996), 116. For an analysis of how African American Christianity promotes the political activism of black people, and the relationship of religion and gender in black American political life, see Frederick C. Harris, *Something Within: Religion in African-American Political Activism* (New York: Oxford University Press, 1999).

259 *"[P]olitics is one form":* Gertrude Rush, described by S. Willie Layten as "a lawyer of no mean ability," was also a leader in the Iowa Federation of Colored Women. See NBC, *Journal of the Forty-second Annual Session of the National Convention and the Twenty-[second] Annual Session of the Woman's Convention Auxiliary, Held in St. Louis, Missouri, December 6–11, 1922* (Nashville: Sunday School Publishing Board, 1922), 368–70. In 1925, Rush joined eleven black male lawyers in founding the National Bar Association, which became the major organization for the African American legal profession. S. Joe Brown, "Our Origin," *National Bar Journal* 2 (September 1944): 161–64.

259 *"joined [the] law":* NBC, *Journal*, 1919, 233.

259 *"The Ballot when used":* Ibid.

260 *Years before women's:* Evelyn Brooks Higginbotham, *Righteous Discontent: The Women's Movement in the Black Baptist Church 1880–1920* (Cambridge, Mass.: Harvard University Press, 1993), 226–27.

260 *"What could they do"*: For quote, see Burroughs, "Divide Vote or Go to Socialists," *Baltimore Afro-American*, August 22, 1919; Nannie H. Burroughs, "Black Women and Reform," *Crisis* 10:4 (August 1915): 187.

260 *Similarly, WC President:* "Prominent Woman to Be Asked to Serve on Republican Women's Committee of Philadelphia," *Philadelphia Tribune*, March 27, 1920.

260 *"The Afro-American woman"*: M[ary] Mossell Griffin, "Early History of Afro-American Woman," *National Notes* 47 (March–April 1947): 7; Griffin was very active in the Congregational Church. In 1914 she was one of three women elected as delegates to the National Convention of Congregational Workers; see "Congregational Workers," *Washington Bee*, April 18, 1914.

261 *"The time for resistance"*: "Dr. Donald As a Sign of the Times," *Woman's Era* 2:4 (July 1895): 13. For well into the twentieth century the NACW promoted anti-lynching and anti–poll tax bills, and employment and health legislation, through its Legislative and Public Affairs Committee. See "Mrs. Smith Announces NACW Plans," *Pittsburgh Courier*, September 6, 1947; "Women Leaders Take Part in NACW 24th Biennial Convention," ibid., July 3, 1948; "Expansion Program Part of NACW Plans," ibid., September 7, 1949.

262 *As NACW historian:* There is no full-length history of the NACW. With the exception of a brief article written in the 1950s by a member of the organization, most scholarly studies are limited to the first three decades of the organization's existence. See Ruby M. Kendricks, " 'They Also Serve': The National Association of Colored Women, Inc.," *Negro History Bulletin* 42 (March 1954): 171–75; Tullia Hamilton, "The National Association of Colored Women, 1896–1920" (PhD diss., Emory University, 1978); Stephanie F. Shaw, "Black Club Women and the Creation of the National Association of Colored Women," *Journal of Women's History* 3:2 (fall 1991): 10–25; Dorothy C. Salem, "To Better Our World: Black Women in Organized Reform, 1890–1920" (PhD diss., Kent State University, 1986).

262 *"Negroes were still"*: W. E. B. Du Bois, "Slavery," *Crisis* 22:1 (May 1921): 86.

262 *Few whites were:* Archibald H. Grimke, "Frenzied Prejudice: Southern Social Evil," *New York Age*, April 27, 1905. In this article, Grimke castigates the National Council of Women for speaking out against the practice of polygamy among Mormons, and ignoring the "deep rooted" and "widespread" practice of black "concubinage" among white men in the South.

263 *The NACW developed:* Because of the unflagging anti-lynching efforts of Ida Wells-Barnett, the subject of lynching became a national and international concern. Wells-Barnett toured Great Britain speaking about the evils of lynching. In defense of the white South, John W. Jacks, president of the Missouri Press Association, responded to Wells-Barnett's charge that the majority of African Americans who were lynched were not rapists, and that black men were often accused of rape when they were found engaging in consensual relationships with white women. Wells-Barnett also related the practice of lynching to an effort on the part of whites to counter the progress and suppress the development of the black middle class. For a discussion of the Jacks letter and the response of black women leaders, which led to the calling of the Boston meeting and the founding of the National Federation of Afro-American Women, see Josephine St. Pierre Ruffin, "Be Bold, But Not Too Bold," *Woman's Era* 2:4 (July 1895): 2–3; "Some Information Concerning Jacks, the Letter Writer," ibid. 2:9 (January 1896): 12–13; Florida Ridley, "Club Notes," ibid. 3:3 (August and September, 1896): 14; see also Wilson Jeremiah Moses, *The Golden Age of Black Nationalism, 1850–1925* (New York: Oxford University Press, 1988), 104, 114–16.

263 *Methodist and Baptist:* The convention was held in Boston July 29–31, 1895. Letters were sent by Sada J. Woodson Anderson, corresponding secretary of the Ohio AME Women's Mite Missionary Society; the Cleave Circle of King's Daughters of Antioch Baptist Church, and the women of the Bethel AME Church in New York City. See *Woman's Era* 2:5 (August 1895): 8, 9.

263 *Gardner was also:* "Eliza A. Gardner, Mother of AME Zion Missionary Society," *Star of Zion*, September 15, 1955; "Boston Wakes the Echoes," *New York Age*, August 20, 1887; "Letters and Resolutions," *Woman's Era* 2:5 (August 1895): 4; Susan J. Sierra and Adrienne Lash Jones, "Eliza Ann Gardner (1831–1922)," in *Notable Black American Women, Book II*, ed. Jessie Carney Smith (New York: Gale Research, 1996), 239.

263 *Alice Felts was a prominent:* For an example of Felts's political activism in the AME Church, see "Women's Rights," *Christian Recorder*, December 10, 1891; "Conference Notes," *Woman's Era* 2:4 (July 1895): 1–2; ibid. 2:5 (August 1895): 20.

263 *"were actively at work":* "Letter of One Thousand Women of Bethel Church, New York," July 24, 1895, in *Woman's Era* 2:4 (August 1895): 8.

264 *Women's clubs began:* See Gerda Lerner, "Community Work of Black Club Women," *Journal of Negro History* 59:2 (April 1974): 158–67; Anne Firor Scott, "Most Invisible of All: Black Women's Voluntary Associations," *Journal of Southern History* 56 (February 1990): 3–22.

264 *These groups formed:* Bettye Collier-Thomas, "Black Women in Maryland History, 1700–1920," July 18, 1978, 50, unpublished paper in possession of author. For identification of women's clubs that were represented at the Boston conference, see "List of Delegates to National Conference," *Woman's Era* 2:5 (August 1895): 13; see also Shaw, "Black Club Women," 433–36. Following the organization of the NACW in 1896, and the establishment of state federations, the Federation of Christian Women was recognized as the NACW state federation for Maryland. Maintaining its original name, by 1916 the organization included fifty-five clubs, with a total membership of 2,024. In August 1916, with Mary F. Handy serving as president, the Maryland Federation hosted the NACW's annual convention in Baltimore. This meeting featured a symposium on suffrage that included presentations by Hallie Quinn Brown (Ohio), Alice Dunbar Nelson (Delaware), Mary E. Jackson (Delaware), and Henrietta Harper (Kansas)— delegates from states where women could vote. For discussion of this event, see "Plans for Meeting of National Association of Women's Clubs," *Baltimore Afro-American*, January 15, 1916; "Baltimore Preparing to Entertain Women's Clubs," ibid., July 22, 1916; "Many Delegates Already Here," ibid., August 5, 1916; "Four Hundred Delegates Attend National Asso[ciation] of Colored Women," ibid., August 12, 1916.

264 *"among the masses":* "Letter of One Thousand Women."

265 *"Our woman's movement":* "Address of Josephine St. Pierre Ruffin, President of Conference," *Woman's Era* 2:5 (August 1895): 13–15.

265 *"women's clubs were tabooed":* Florida Ruffin Ridley, "Tells of 42 Years Ago in Her Address," *Chicago Defender*, May 22, 1937. Emphasizing the NACW's uniqueness, in 1911 President Josephine Silone Yates asserted that, unlike the "National Association of Colored Women, an organization founded and controlled entirely by women, . . . most black women's organizations are auxiliary societies founded and controlled by men, or by the combined efforts of men and women; also that usually they are secret orders, or connected with various church denominations." See Mrs. John E. Milholland, "Talks About Women," *Crisis* 1:4 (February 1911): 28.

266 *As Washington explained:* "List of Delegates to National Conference"; "Call to the National Federation of Afro-American Women," *Woman's Era,* 2:6 (October 1895): 1–2. In 1895 a national association, called the National Federation of Colored Women, was formed at the Boston conference. In 1896 the National Federation united with the National League of Colored Women under the name National Association of Colored Women. See Josephine Bruce, "Colored Women's Clubs," *Crisis* 10:4 (August 1915): 190.

266 *The point was stressed:* "The National Colored Woman's Congress," *Woman's Era* 3:1 (January 1896): 2–8; "The Women's Wonderful Convention," *Christian Recorder,* November 14, 1895; "A Religious Congress of the Colored Methodist Episcopal Church in America, to be Held in Atlanta, Ga, Nov. 14th, 1895," *Voice of Missions* 3:10 (October 1895): 3; Lottie Wilson Jackson, "Two Weeks in Atlanta, Georgia," ibid. 4:5 (May 1896): 1. The AME Church proudly announced that the wives of bishops Levi Coppin, Jabez P. Campbell, Benjamin Tucker Tanner, Henry McNeal Turner, A. W. Wayman, Charles Smith, and W. B. Derrick attended the Atlanta First National Congress of Colored Women; see "The Women's Wonderful Convention," *Christian Recorder,* November 14, 1895.

267 *"Owing to conditions":* For Terrell quotation, see Rebecca [Stiles] Taylor, "National [Association of] Colored Women at Half Century Mile Post July 22, 1946," *Chicago Defender,* June 23, 1945. In a manner similar to that of the AME women in Boston, the National Virginia Baptist Sunday School Union sent delegates to the NFAAW's 1896 meeting to represent "over a thousand members"; see *Woman's Era* 3:2 (July 1896): 7.

268 *"The women who attended":* Mary Taylor Blauvelt, "The Race Problem as Discussed by Negro Women," *American Journal of Sociology* 6 (1901): 663.

268 *These included:* Albreta (sic) M. Smith, "Chicago Notes," *Colored American Magazine* 2:2 (December 1900): 147–48; *Star of Zion,* January 28, 1897. In 1900, Booker T. Washington organized the National Negro Business League in Boston. Among the elected officers were Alberta Moore-Smith, the second vice president and only female. See "Miscellaneous," *AME Church Review* 17:2 (October 1900): 183.

269 *The members of:* Ibid., Ida Wells-Barnett and Alberta Moore-Smith, as members of the Institutional AME Church, were instrumental in the founding of the Institutional Church Woman's Club, the Civic League, and the South End Women's Political Club. Historian Wanda A. Hendricks notes that the first meeting, to explore the "feasibility" of affiliating with the NACW, was held in 1899 at the Institutional AME Church in Chicago. Please note that the Institutional Church was African Methodist Episcopal, not Baptist. Hendricks explains, "Almost all were well educated . . . [and] were also quite religious. With few exceptions, they had ties with and maintained membership in various churches throughout the state." See Wanda A. Hendricks, *Gender, Race, and Politics in the Midwest: Black Club Women in Illinois* (Bloomington: Indiana University Press, 1998), 23, 31. For discussion of the Colored Women's Business Club, the educational needs of women, and the quotation regarding women's equality, see Alberta Moore-Smith, "Women's Development in Business," in *Proceedings of the National Negro Business League: Its First Meeting, Held in Boston, Massachusetts, August 23 and 24, 1900"* (Boston: J. R. Ham, 1901), 131–41.

270 *Taylor said:* Rebecca Stiles Taylor, "CNDA Holds 2nd Quarterly Meeting at Quinn Chapel," *Chicago Defender,* December 9, 1950; Taylor's observations of the tensions between the "church elders" and the NACW are supported by the claims of *Southern Workman* editors, who called for "the unification of social

movements and the promotion of a religious spirit in all organizations." They observed that the Virginia Federation of Colored Women did not always "receive the complete support of the churches. Often the churches and women's clubs have not pulled together." See H. B. Frissell, W. A. Aery, and J. E. Davis, "Federation of Colored Women," *Southern Workman* 40:8 (August 1911): 453.

270 *Taylor concluded that:* Rebecca Stiles Taylor, "Illinois Association [of] Colored Women Opens 54th Year," *Chicago Defender*, December 13, 1952. Taylor was born and raised in Savannah, Georgia. She was a founder and president of the NACW's Georgia Federation, and an officer in the Southeastern Federation. During the early 1920s Taylor was active in the Savannah Suffrage Club, which was founded in 1919. See "Women's Meeting Strikes a Snag," *Savannah Tribune*, April 17, 1920.

270 *As a leading:* Elizabeth Lindsay Davis, *Lifting as They Climb* (Chicago: National Association of Colored Women, 1933), 246.

270 *The internal struggle:* Higginbotham, *Righteous Discontent*, 159–60; "Nannie Burroughs Answers Back," *Baltimore Afro-American*, July 15, 1916; "Miss Burroughs Vindicated," *Washington Bee*, June 9, 1917; "N. Burroughs Keeps Control of Her School," *New York Age*, December 10, 1927; "National Baptist Convention Accused of Double-Crossing Training School in Washington," ibid., October 1, 1938; "My Hands Are Clean—My Soul Unsullied—My Chin Up!—Nannie Burroughs Defends Action," *Pittsburgh Courier*, October 8, 1938.

270 *After that date:* Harris, *Something Within*, 156.

270 *However, some interjected:* For examples of the diverse views of ministers regarding women voting and engaging in other political activities, see NBC, *Journal*, 1919, 259; NBC, *Journal of the Thirty-eighth Session of the National Baptist Convention and the [Eighteenth] Annual Session of the Woman's Convention Auxiliary, Held in St. Louis, Missouri, September 4–9, 1918* (Nashville: Sunday School Publishing Board, 1918), 202.

270 *"for their victory":* NBC, *Journal of the Thirty-first Annual Session of the National Baptist Convention and the Eleventh Annual Session of the Woman's Convention Auxiliary, Held in Chicago, Illinois, September 13–18, 1911* (Nashville: Sunday School Publishing Board, 1911), 74.

270 *Black church women:* Rev. Nicholas B. Stewart, pastor of an AME church in Wesson, Mississippi, in defending the religious rights of AME women asserted that there was a great deal of male prejudice against women assuming leadership roles in the church. Stewart felt that it was the same prejudice that argued against women gaining political suffrage. See Nicholas B. Stewart, "On the Defense and Rights of Women Workers in the AME Church," *Voice of Missions* 6:12 (December 1898): 4.

271 *"If women cannot vote":* NBC, *Journal of the Thirty-second Annual Session of the National Baptist Convention and the Twelfth Annual Session of the Woman's Convention Auxiliary, Held in Chicago, Illinois, September 11–15, 1912* (Nashville: Sunday School Publishing Board, 1912), 39.

271 *Burroughs contended that:* For NACW quote see "The National Association of Colored Women," *Voice of the Negro* 1:7 (July 1904): 310–11; Burroughs, "Black Women and Reform."

271 *In less than:* For example, Alice W. Seay, president of the Dorcas Home and Foreign Missionary Society of the Concord Baptist Church (1877–1913), also served as president of the NACW's Northeast Federation. See "Dorcas Society in Uplift Work," *Indianapolis Freeman*, January 11, 1913.

272 *For many male:* For definitions of the "new woman," see Sarah Dudley Pettey, "The Up-To-Date Woman," *Star of Zion*, August 13, 1896; Mrs. M. W. Reddick, "The Awakened Woman," *Spelman Messenger* 31:6 (March 1915): 7–8; Margaret Black, "The New Girl," *Baltimore Afro-American*, December 9, 1916; "The New Woman," *Iowa Baptist Standard*, May 21, 1897. For a journalistic impression of the impact of the new woman ideology on AME women, see "The New Woman," *Indianapolis Freeman*, June 11, 1898. Focusing on white women's experiences, Carroll Smith-Rosenberg discusses the ways in which women engaged the discourse and practice of the new woman ideology during the Progressive Era. See Carroll Smith-Rosenberg, *Disorderly Conduct: Visions of Gender in Victorian America* (New York: Oxford University Press, 1985), 173–78. For a discussion of the shift from Victorian ideals of true womanhood, see Sara M. Evans, *Born for Liberty: A History of Women in America* (New York: Free Press, 1997), 147–52.

272 *"the same old woman":* Dora J. Cole, "Pennsylvania," *Woman's Era* 2:3 (June 1895): 7.

272 *"in the light":* Dora J. Cole, "Pennsylvania," ibid. 2:7 (October 1895): 9. Alberta Moore-Smith argued that though many theories were promulgated suggesting that woman was new, "the only satisfactory evidence of conclusion agreed upon is that she is simply progressing; her natural tendencies having not changed one iota." See Moore-Smith, "Women's Development in Business."

273 *"Now, we do not mean":* Belle B. Dorce, "The American Girl," *Christian Recorder*, December 15, 1887. For other writings by Dorce see "The Voices of Power," ibid., December 9, 1886; "Our Boys and Girls," ibid., March 3, 1887; "Bacon and Essex," ibid., June 16, 1887; and "The New Education," *AME Church Review* 4:1 (July 1887): 509–11.

273 *Like Fannie Williams:* Sarah Dudley Pettey, "Woman's Column," *Star of Zion*, October 15, 1916.

273 *Well known among:* "A Chicago Episode," *Indianapolis Freeman*, November 24, 1894. Williams and her husband were active in the All Souls Unitarian Church of Chicago. Williams's membership in a white church was in part related to her belief that the theology preached in most black churches was passe and not in keeping with the rational religious doctrines represented in the Protestant Episcopal, Unitarian, Presbyterian, and other predominantly white churches. For a discussion of Williams's membership in mainstream organizations and "her peculiar faculty to reach and interest influential men and women of the dominant race" to interpret the needs of blacks, see Mrs. N. F. [Gertrude] Mossell, *The Work of the Afro-American Woman*, 2nd ed. (Philadelphia: George S. Ferguson Co., 1908), 111–12; Fannie Barrier Williams, "What Can Religion Further Do to Advance the Condition of the American Negro?" in *The World's Parliament of Religions*, vol. 2, ed. John Henry Barrows (Chicago: Parliament Publishing Co., 1893), 1114–15; Fannie Barrier Williams, "The Intellectual Progress of the Colored Women of the United States Since the Emancipation Proclamation," in *The World's Congress of Representative Women*, ed. May Wright Sewall (Chicago: Rand, McNally and Co., 1894), 698–729.

273 *The tension surrounding:* "Fannie Barrier Williams," Cleveland, Ohio, *Gazette*, November 17, 1894.

274 *Simply put:* Fannie Barrier Williams, "The New Colored Woman," *Indianapolis Freeman*, December 19, 1896.

274 *Commenting on the congress's:* S. Willie Layten, "California," *Woman's Era* 2:4 (July 1895): 8.

274 *"I am certain"*: S. Willie Layten, "California," ibid. 2:7 (November 1895): 5–6.

274 *Responding to the plea:* Layten, "California," ibid. (July 1895): 8; "Mrs. Layten Paid Highest Tribute at Funeral Services," *Philadelphia Afro-American*, January 28, 1950; Theodore Sylvester Boone, *Negro Baptist Chief Executives in National Places* (Detroit: A. P. Publishing Co., 1948), 287–33.

274 *One thing was clear:* For an excellent analysis of the "new" or "modern woman," see Margaret Black, "Woman's Column," *Baltimore Afro-American*, August 12, 1916. When the NACW held its national convention in Baltimore in 1916, Black commented on the changes that had occurred in African American women's perceptions of themselves and their roles, i.e., their views about domesticity, dress, and deportment. For example, Black asserted that "the modern woman or modern girl simply refuses to stay in the background. . . . A spectacle like Baltimore presents this week, of hundreds of women . . . meeting together . . . with thoughts of bettering the race and planning for the good of the coming generation of children, was unheard of in olden times."

274 *Layten, Burroughs:* For a brief discussion of the National League of Colored Republican Women between 1924 and 1932, see Evelyn Brooks Higginbotham, "In Politics to Stay: Black Women Leaders and Party Politics in the 1920s," in *Women, Politics, and Change,* ed. Louise Tilly and Patricia Gurin (New York: Russell Sage Foundation, 1990), 208–12.

275 *"demand absolute respect"*: Eunice Lewis, "The Black Woman's Part in Race Leadership," Letter to the Editor of the Women's Department, *Negro World*, April 19, 1924.

275 *Most of the women:* Saydee E. Parham, "The New Woman," *Negro World*, February 2, 1924. Most of these "new" women lived well into the 1940s and '50s. For example, S. Willie Layten, Rev. Florence Spearing Randolph, Mary McLeod Bethune, and Mary Church Terrell's deaths occurred in the 1950s, and Nannie Helen Burroughs died in 1961. All of these women remained politically active until death.

275 *"missionary work"*: Gilmore, *Gender and Jim Crow*, 155–56.

277 *Lucy Craft Laney:* Monroe Work, *Negro Year Book: The Negro in 1917–1918* (Tuskegee, Ala.: Tuskegee Institute, 1919), 57–58; "Women's Meeting Strikes a Snag," *Savannah Tribune*, April 17, 1920; "Woman Suffrage News," ibid., January 10, 1920.

277 *Answering the critics:* Lawson A. Scruggs, *Women of Distinction: Remarkable in Works and Invincible in Character* (Raleigh, N.C.: L. A. Scruggs, 1893), 169.

277 *Others prodded:* Glenda Gilmore, in her examination of black women in North Carolina, presents an excellent example of how some southern black women achieved their political goals. For a case study of how black Baptist and Methodist women utilized their denominational and interdenominational networks in one state to engage in political reform, see Glenda Gilmore, *Gender and Jim Crow*.

277 *For a number:* For biographical information on Adella Hunt Logan, see Adele Logan Alexander, "Logan, Adella Hunt (1863–1915), in *Black Women in America: An Historical Encyclopedia,* vol. 1, ed. Darlene Clark Hine (Brooklyn: Carlson Publishing, 1993), 729–30.

277 *In 1912 it:* Adella Hunt Logan, "Colored Women as Voters," *Crisis* 4:5 (September 1912): 242–43; "States in Which Women May Vote," *Baltimore Afro-American*, November 9, 1912. In 1886 Kansas was the first state to grant women the franchise. Five hundred and forty-three black women voted in Leavenworth, Kansas. Florencia Grier, a member of the AME Church, who served as church

organist, was "in command of the line of colored women" and cast the first vote. See "Odds and Ends," *New York Age*, May 7, 1887; and "Florencia A. T. Powella Grier," in Frank Lincoln Mather, *Who's Who of the Colored Race* (Chicago: Frank Lincoln Mather, 1915).

278 *Prior to 1920:* "Mrs. Mary Handy Voted 25 Years Ago," *Baltimore Afro-American*, October 29, 1920; "Registrar Hides When Women Seek to Vote," *Chicago Defender*, February 22, 1919; "Race Women Elected Delegates," ibid., May 29, 1920; "Women Boost Republican Vote in N.Y.," *New York Age*, July 20, 1918; Fannie Barrier Williams, "Suffrage in Illinois," *AME Church Review* 30:2 (October 1913): 122–24.

279 *"This contest showed":* The Voting Rights Act of 1965 called on the U.S. attorney general to challenge the constitutionality of state poll taxes as a requirement to vote. In 1966 the Supreme Court held that the poll tax was unconstitutional. See Bettye Collier-Thomas and V. P. Franklin, eds., *My Soul Is a Witness: A Chronology of the Civil Rights Era, 1954–1965* (New York: Henry Holt and Company, 1999), 229. For specific references to Richmond, Virginia, and a broad discussion of women's participation in southern black political life after the Civil War, see Elsa Barkley Brown, "Negotiating and Transforming the Public Sphere: African American Political Life in the Transition from Slavery to Freedom," in *The Black Public Sphere: A Public Culture Book* (Chicago: University of Chicago Press, 1995). For discussion of women's political activism in Birmingham, Alabama, see "The Importance of Afro-Americans Paying Their Poll Tax," *New York Age*, November 7, 1907.

279 *In 1920:* "Mrs. Mary Handy Voted 25 Years Ago"; untitled, *Woman's Era* 2:2 (May 1895): 7 (note error in pagination, see second page numbered as 7); "National League of Colored Women," *Indianapolis Freeman*, May 9, 1896; "Temporary Rules Issued by the Executive Committee of the [NACW]," *Woman's Era* 3:4 (October–November, 1896): 3–4; James A. Handy, *Scraps of AME Church History* (Philadelphia: AME Book Concern, n.d.), 10.

279 *During the early:* "Pastor's Wife Is Dead," *Washington Bee*, May 9, 1914; "Work of Mrs. Dr. F[loyd] G. Snelson Since Her Husband Left for Africa in 1897," *Voice of Missions* 7:11 (November 1899): 1. By 1895 Waterloo Bullock Snelson, a psychologist, teacher, and lecturer, was well known for her work in the AME Church and for organizing a Woman's Club in Athens, Georgia. At the 1899 NACW convention, she was appointed to committees on ways and means and resolutions. The Snelsons were also well known in Republican Party politics. During the 1880s, Floyd Snelson attended several national conventions. He was a member of the Georgia delegation to the 1888 Republican Convention and a candidate for a congressional seat. During the late 1880s he was elected county commissioner in Liberty County, Georgia. Following the election of President Benjamin Harrison, Snelson lost his bid for an appointment as U.S. minister to Liberia. See "The Liberian Mission," *Savannah Tribune*, February 16, 1889. For biographical sketch of Rev. Floyd Grant Snelson, see "Hold Last Rites for Dr. Snelson, Friday," *Baltimore Afro-American*, March 5, 1932.

280 *"advocated woman suffrage":* "Haven M. E. Church," *Philadelphia Tribune*, February 17, 1912.

280 *"We seldom go":* May M. Brown, "A Woman's Views on Current Topics," *AME Zion Church Quarterly*, title page missing (1891): 199, 201.

281 *Some, like Callie House:* Mary Frances Berry, *My Face Is Black Is True: Callie House and the Struggle for Ex-Slave Reparations* (New York: Alfred A. Knopf, 2005).

281 *Women employed as:* For an excellent discussion and analysis of the class base of

black women's religious and benevolent societies in Memphis, Tennessee, see Kathleen C. Berkeley, " 'Colored Ladies Also Contributed': Black Women's Activities from Benevolence to Social Welfare, 1866–1896," in *The Web of Southern Social Relations: Women, Family, and Education*, ed. Walter J. Fraser Jr., Frank Saunders Jr., and Jon L. Wakelyn (Athens, Ga.: University of Georgia Press, 1985), 181–203. By 1915 black women in northeastern and midwestern cities were finding employment in factories. In cities like Baltimore the NACW recruited factory workers and organized new branches. See "Federation Organizer Here," *Baltimore Afro-American*, April 30, 1920; and "Wise Brothers Entertain Their Employees," ibid., October 11, 1918. In 1943, Jennie L. Moton, president of the NACW, explained that for forty-three years the organization had worked "For the Race in General and Black Women in Particular." For a discussion of the civil rights activities of the New Jersey Federation of Colored Women, and the role of working-class women in the NACW, the WC, and other organizations, see Bettye Collier-Thomas and V. P. Franklin, eds., *Sisters in the Struggle: African American Women in the Civil Rights–Black Power Movement* (New York: New York University Press, 2001), 21, 23–25. For Nannie Burroughs's commentary on working-class women in the WC, see NBC, *Journal*, 1919, 213, 220.

281 *Between 1910 and 1940:* In an excellent study of black women domestic servants in the District of Columbia, Elizabeth Clark-Lewis illustrates how black women migrants to urban areas rejected live-in employment because it restricted their church attendance and participation in church activities. Women such as Costella Harris explained that in the South, "[e]ven working-out . . . you'd go to church." Eula Montgomery emphasized that women who had "their Sundays free" could serve "on the church's special committees." See Elizabeth Clark-Lewis, " 'This Work Had a End': African-American Domestic Workers in Washington, D.C., 1910–1940," in *"To Toil the Livelong Day": America's Women at Work, 1780–1980*, ed. Carol Groneman and Mary Beth Norton (Ithaca: Cornell University Press, 1987), 203–11; G. J. Barker-Benfield and Catherine Clinton, *Portraits of American Women: From Settlement to the Present* (New York: St. Martin's Press, 1991), 476–77.

281 *Recognizing that:* In discussing the impact of the Great Migration, Burroughs noted that the "new opportunities to serve in shops and stores [have] been grasped by our girls." However, she stressed that "[f]ifty-seven percent of our women [are] wage workers and work as domestics, and we should see that they [are] organized to increase their efficiency and give them needed protection." See NBC, *Journal*, 1919, 213, 220.

281 *In addition to:* For example, Elizabeth Ross Haynes, in a detailed history and analysis of African Americans in domestic service, found that "[t]he social life of the older domestic Negro workers centers largely in their church and secret order society connections. From 1916 to 1920 seven out of every eleven Negroes were enrolled in churches." See Elizabeth R. Haynes, "Negroes in Domestic Service in the United States," *Journal of Negro History* 8 (October 1923): 433–34; NBC, *Journal*, 1918, 165; "Baptist Women Break Their Record," *New York Age*, September 27, 1919; "Women Form Great Labor Organization," *Washington Tribune*, November 5, 1921; see also Evelyn Brooks Barnett, "Nannie Burroughs and the Education of Black Women," in *The Afro-American Woman: Struggles and Images*, ed. Sharon Harley and Rosalyn Terborg-Penn (Port Washington, N.Y.: Kennikat Press, 1978), 97–108. For biographical data on Sallie Stewart, see "Nationally Known Clubwoman and Ex-Teacher Dies at Evansville," *Indianapo-*

lis Recorder, August 4, 1951. The National Race Congress was founded in 1915. Its purpose was to provide a forum to address national and international issues pertaining to the social, economic, and political status of persons of African descent. For information pertaining to the organization see "Race Congress Closes Seventh Convention Here," *Washington Tribune*, May 6, 1922; "Racial Progress and Opinion," *Christian Recorder*, April 14, 1921.

282 *Like Burroughs:* For biographical data on Violet A. Johnson and Maggie Lena Walker, see "New Honor for Miss Johnson," *Indianapolis Freeman*, July 31, 1909; Bettye Collier-Thomas and V. P. Franklin, "For the Race in General and Black Women in Particular: The Civil Rights Activities of African American Women's Organizations, 1915–50," in Collier-Thomas and Franklin, eds., *Sisters in the Struggle*, 24–25; and Gertrude W. Marlowe, "Walker, Maggie Lena (1867–1934), in Hine, *Black Women in America, Book II*, 1214.

282 *"by the help":* Charles Harris Wesley, *The History of the National Association of Colored Women's Clubs: A Legacy of Service* (Washington, D.C.: National Association of Colored Women's Clubs, Inc., 1984), 42, 64.

282 *During Thurman's:* "Michigan State Federation of Colored Women," *Colored American Magazine* 1:4 (September 1900): 257; "Michigan Club Women Foremost in Race's Progress," *Chicago Defender*, January 7, 1939.

282 *On numerous occasions:* Wesley, *The History of the National Association*, 357; " 'A Remedy' for Lynching," *Indianapolis Freeman*, September 1, 1900; "Resolutions Passed by Women's National Convention," ibid., July 21, 1906.

282 *The petition included:* Blauvelt, "The Race Problem," 669. For information about the lynching of Frazier J. Baker, see "A Great Baptist Gathering Here," *Richmond Planet*, September 15, 1900.

283 *These women delivered:* Wesley, *The History of the National Association*, 66, 67.

283 *"We want representation":* "Detroit Women Plan for 1939," *Chicago Defender*, January 7, 1939.

283 *In the twentieth:* As the guest speaker on the first program presented by the NACW's Chicago Northern District Association Finance Committee's male associate members, Dr. Metz Lochard, editor of foreign news for the *Chicago Defender*, stressed the importance of the work of the NACW in the United States and the national recognition it had achieved. See "Men Form Auxiliary to Aid Club Women," *Chicago Defender*, October 2, 1937. After 1920, there are literally hundreds of examples of black women serving on local, state, and federal boards. Mary McLeod Bethune and Irene McCoy Gaines are examples of NACW leaders who were "tapped" by the federal government for special service. In 1931, President Herbert Hoover appointed Gaines to the Committee on Negro Housing at the president's Conference on Home Building and Home Ownership. Between 1930 and 1954, Mary McLeod Bethune received appointments to several federal and state commissions and boards. In 1935, President Franklin Delano Roosevelt appointed Bethune director of the Office of Minority Affairs in the National Youth Administration, the first federal office created especially for a black woman. For discussion of these women and examples of their political appointments, see "Appointed," *Chicago Defender*, April 25, 1931; Rackham Holt, *Mary McLeod Bethune* (Garden City, N.Y.: Doubleday, 1964), 148; Joyce B. Ross, "Mary McLeod Bethune and the National Youth Administration: A Case Study of Power Relationships in the Black Cabinet of FDR," *Journal of Negro History* 60:1 (January 1975): 1–28.

283 *Similar to the interlocking:* The Chicago City Federation was founded in 1906 and incorporated in 1921 under a new name, the Chicago and Northern District

Federation of Colored Women's Clubs, with a membership of more than two thousand women. It included clubs in Chicago and the suburban Illinois towns of Elgin, Aurora, Batavia, Hinsdale, La Grange, Maywood, Evanston, and Joliet. For information on the history of the Illinois Federation, see Elizabeth Lindsay Davis, *Lifting As They Climb* (Washington, D.C.: National Association of Colored Women, 1933), 132–45.

283 *In 1937:* By 1926 the Illinois State Federation comprised ninety-two clubs, with 2,074 members. "Illinois Federation of Colored Women's Clubs," *National Notes* 28 (July 1926): 24; "Illinois to Celebrate Silver Anniversary," *National Notes* 26 (July 1924): 16; "A Scrapbook for Women in Public Life," *Chicago Defender*, October 1, 1932; "Mrs. Fannie Turner Gives 37 Years to Women's Clubs," ibid., October 23, 1937.

284 *Its Civics Department:* "An Extensive Program Is Planned for the New Year," *Chicago Defender*, September 25, 1937.

284 *Wells-Barnett stated that:* "Playing Their Parts Well in Upbuilding," *Chicago Defender*, May 3, 1930; Ida Wells-Barnett was referring to Nellie D. Calloway, a candidate for the Illinois General Assembly in 1922. However, in 1918, Mrs. W. L. Presto of Seattle, Washington, was a candidate for state senator from the Thirty-seventh District. See "Shall Women Make Laws to Rule the Men?" *Chicago Defender*, January 21, 1922; "Club Woman Dies After Long Illness," ibid., December 5, 1925; and Work, *Negro Year Book, 1917–1918*, 56–58.

285 *Davis insisted that:* Nettie George Speedy, "My Scrap Book of Doers," *Chicago Defender*, November 28, 1923; "Playing Their Parts Well in Upbuilding" *Chicago Defender,* May 3, 1930; "Elizabeth Lindsey (sic) Davis, Pioneer Club Leader, Lies Dangerously Ill," *Chicago Defender*, July 22, 1944.

285 *While serving as:* For a discussion of Henry McNeal Turner's life, see Stephen Ward Angell, *Bishop Henry McNeal Turner and African-American Religion in the South* (Knoxville: University of Tennessee Press, 1992). AME Zion minister William Hooper Councill was the founder of Huntsville Normal Institute (later known as Alabama Agricultural and Mechanical College), in Normal, Alabama. Councill read the law and was admitted to the Alabama Supreme Court in 1883. He had a national reputation as a leader in religious, temperance, and charitable organizations. For biographical data on Councill, see "Slave Who Rose to Prominence," *Indianapolis Recorder*, May 2, 1904; Debi Broome, "Councill, William Hooper," in *Encyclopedia of African-American Culture and History*, vol. 2, ed. Jack Salzman, David Lionel Smith, and Cornell West (New York: Simon and Schuster Macmillan, 1996), 667–68; and Earl E. Thorpe, "William Hooper Councill," *Negro History Bulletin* 19:1 (January 1956): 12.

285 *As the director:* Elizabeth Lindsay Davis and Mrs. S. Joe Brown, *The Story of the Illinois Federation of Colored Women's Clubs* (Chicago: 1922), 20; "A Scrap Book for Women in Public Life," *Chicago Defender*, January 25, 1930; "Mrs. Carrie Lee Hamilton, Civic and Club Worker, Dies," ibid., June 21, 1930.

286 *Unlike any of:* For a discussion of the American Baptist Home Mission Society and the WABHMS support for black education and home mission work, see Higginbotham, *Righteous Discontent*, 25–28, 35–36, 42, 90–95. Northern Baptist support for the education of freedmen was initiated during Reconstruction. For an interpretation of black Baptist women's racial self-determination, see ibid., 166.

287 *However, with the exception:* At the local level, some branches of the Woman's Mite Missionary Society and individual AME, AME Zion, CME, and Methodist Episcopal women were outspoken and active in the women's suffrage, anti-lynching, and Civil Rights Movements. However, unlike the WC, the Methodist

women's missionary societies did not consistently agitate on behalf of these issues, or develop programs to address them. For example, in 1898 Mary R. Burkett, a *Baltimore Afro-American* journalist and outspoken AME political activist, at the third Annual Convention of the AME Women's Mite Missionary Society of the Baltimore Conference, implored the women "to endeavor to do something to arouse public sentiment against lynching even to the point of an appeal to the president and congress." Though few members disagreed with Burkett's suggestion, there was no action taken on this issue. Rather, the group focused on how to maximize its own power within the church, and raised the question, "Should Woman's Work Be Controlled by Women?" Other issues discussed at the meeting included temperance and fund-raising to support the AME Church's missionary activities. For the Burkett quotation and details of the 1898 AME WMMS meeting, see "Celebrated Women at Work for Missions," *Voice of Missions* 5:10 (October 1898): 6. Similarly, in 1917 at the WMMS's Baltimore Branch's quarterly conference, the importance of organizing black women for women's suffrage was emphasized. See "Mite Missionary Society," *Washington Bee*, March 24, 1917.

287　*Florence Randolph:* Bettye Collier-Thomas, "Florence Spearing Randolph (1866–1951)," *Notable Black American Women, Book II,* 537–40.

287　*S. Willie Layten's:* At the national level, Layten served as the head of the NACW's Department of Domestic Work (1908); see "Departments of NACW," *National Notes* 10 (October 1908): 3; "Prominent Woman to Be Asked to Serve on Republican Women's Committee"; Jessie Carney Smith, "S. Willie Layten (1863–1950)," *Notable Black American Women, Book II,* 403–06.

288　*In 1920 Lawton:* For biographical data on Maria C. Lawton, see "Women Surround Legislators," *Baltimore Afro-American,* March 19, 1910; "New Monthly Magazine," ibid., August 17, 1912; "Testimonial Tendered to Women Workers," *New York Age,* April 4, 1912; Walter R. Lofton, "A Digest of Brooklyn Happenings," *Chicago Defender,* May 15, 1920; "Mrs. M. C. Lawton Now Member of Ashland Place Y.W.C.A. Board," ibid., June 22, 1929; "Republican Women in Plea for Representation," ibid., June 6, 1925; "New York Woman in Race for State Legislature," ibid., August 6, 1932; "Mrs. Maria Lawton Opens Office as Chairman of New Organization Set Up by GOP State Committee," *New York Age,* October 1, 1938.

288　*These women were:* NBC, *Journal of the Fortieth Annual Session of the National Baptist Convention and the Twentieth Annual Session of the Woman's Convention Auxiliary, Held in Indianapolis, Indiana, September 8–13, 1920* (Nashville: Sunday School Publishing Board, 1920), 391. Mary Talbert of Buffalo, New York, was elected president of the NACW at its tenth biennial session. Nominated by Nannie Helen Burroughs, and opposed by prominent AME leader Hallie Quinn Brown, Talbert won by a two-thirds majority on the second ballot. For details of the election, see "Four Hundred Delegates Attend National Asso[ciation] of Colored Women, *Baltimore Afro-American,* August 12, 1916.

288　*"arena for discussion":* For quote and examples of how the WC "endorsed the work of secular organizations whose objectives complemented their own," see Higginbotham, *Righteous Discontent,* 148, 181–83.

289　*"matter of principle":* NBC, *Journal,* 1920, 339, 340.

289　*A suffrage committee:* NBC, *Journal,* 1920, 391.

290　*Morris was:* "Hutchinson, Kansas," *Negro Star,* October 29, 1920.

290　*Urging black men:* Founded in 1901, by 1904 the Socialist Party had taken hold in Chicago and Milwaukee and was rapidly spreading to a number of the large cities in the Northwest. By 1910 it was recognized as a force in many northeastern cities as well. Though there were objections to some of its tenets, for blacks concerned with the growing discrimination in the Republican Party and the virulent racism of the Democratic Party it represented a "splendid field for negotiations." See "The Spread of Socialism," *Voice of the Negro* 1:6 (June 1904): 259; Nannie Helen Burroughs, "Divide Vote or Go to Socialists," *Baltimore Afro-American*, August 22, 1919.

290 *Though they were:* Historian Rosalyn Terborg-Penn asserts that white female suffragists abandoned black women and did not defend their right to vote. As a result, by the mid-1920s black women became "discontented" and "disillusioned," and turned away from mainstream electoral politics, choosing instead to focus their attention on "race issues within black organizations." To the contrary, Evelyn Brooks Higginbotham posits that black women continued to be involved in the electoral process. My findings support Higginbotham's thesis, and suggest that black women became more involved in politics, organized, and engaged in electoral politics than ever before. See Rosalyn Terborg-Penn, "Discontented Black Feminists: Prelude and Postscript to the Passage of the Nineteenth Amendment," in *Decades of Discontent: The Women's Movement, 1920–1940*, ed. Lois Scarf and Joan M. Jensen (Westport, Conn.: Greenwood Press, 1983), 487–501; Higginbotham, "In Politics to Stay," 200–03; "Women's Party Honor Terrells," *Baltimore Afro-American*, February 25, 1921.

290 *Instead they faced:* By 1900 it was clear to African American women leaders that white women would not support them in either their bid for the ballot or their struggle for equality. Frances Willard and the WCTU were taken to task by the NACW for failing to condemn the practice of lynching. To appease the white South, the WCTU and the NAWSA chose not to support the anti-lynching and suffrage efforts of black women. For details regarding Willard and the WCTU controversy, see Josephine St. Pierre Ruffin, "Miss Willard and the Colored People," *Woman's Era* 2:4 (July 1895): 12–13. The records of the 1899 and 1903 NAWSA conventions reveal the willingness of white suffragists to cooperate with southern racist practices and abandon support for enfranchising black women. At the 1899 convention, Lottie Wilson [Jackson], a suffragist, member of the Michigan NAWSA chapter, and leading figure in the Michigan Federation of Colored Women, implored white suffragists to protest lynching and the South's Jim Crow policies. Elizabeth Cady Stanton and Susan B. Anthony rejected Wilson's plea, arguing that "women are a helpless disfranchised class," and that it was not prudent to argue the dual issues of gender and race. See ibid. 7:9 (September 1, 1899); Nancie Caraway, *Segregated Sisterhood: Racism and the Politics of American Feminism* (Knoxville: University of Tennessee Press, 1991), 150.

291 *If the church:* R. R. Wright, "Women, Politics, and the Church," *Christian Recorder*, September 16, 1920.

291 *"In many of the states":* Mamie E. Steward, "Afro-American Woman and the Church," in "Woman's Part in the Uplift of the Negro Race," *Colored American Magazine* 14:1 (January 1907): 53–61.

291 *Similarly, in 1924:* Sadie Tanner Alexander, "A Demand for Women as Executive Officers of the Church," undated typescript address delivered on Women's Day at the Union AME Church, Philadelphia, Pennsylvania, Sadie Tanner Mossell Alexander Collection, Box 1, Folder 28, University of Pennsylvania Library.

291 *In 1920, while:* "The League of Republican Women," *Washington Bee*, October 2, 1920.

292 *Using the WC's:* Ibid.; "Letters to Women," *Washington Bee*, August 20, 1921.

292 *During the 1920s:* In 1897 Julia Mason Layton was a member of the Colored Woman's League Rescue Committee, and in 1898 she was elected to the organization's board of directors. See: *Fourth Annual Report of the Colored Woman's League of Washington, D.C., for the Year Ending January 1, 1897* (Washington, D.C.: F. D. Smith Printing Company, 1897), 4; and *Fifth Annual Report of the Colored Woman's League of Washington, D.C., for the Year Ending June 30, 1898* (Washington, D.C.: Smith Brothers, 1898), 3. For biographical data on Julia Mason Layton, see "A Woman Highly Honored," *Washington Bee*, August 7, 1909; ibid., June 12, 1915; "Blaine Invincible and State Republican Clubs," ibid., July 2, 1921; ibid., October 29, 1921; "An Active Worker for the Republican Party," ibid., September 10, 1921.

292 *In the late 1920s:* The Bethel Literary and Historical Society was the oldest black literary society in the United States. For discussion of the society and the political and social activism of Marie Madre-Marshall, see Mary Church Terrell, "Society Among the Colored People of Washington," *Voice of the Negro* 1:4 (April 1904): 156; "Bethel Sets High Standard," *Indianapolis Recorder*, April 17, 1909; Richard R. Wright, *Centennial Encyclopaedia of the AME Church* (Philadelphia: AME Book Concern, 1916), 367–68; "Women's Federation," *Washington Bee*, May 22, 1915; "This Week in Society," ibid., April 28, 1917; "Madre-Marshall," ibid., October 5, 1918; "Washington Letter," *New York Age*, July 26, 1917; "Negro Bishops Assigned," *Washington Bee*, June 3, 1916; "An Organizing Genius," *The Negro Woman's World* (January 1935); "Their Work Concluded," *Baltimore Afro-American*, September 19, 1908.

293 *During the early 1930s:* Geraldine Chaney was first vice president of the Colored Welfare Organization and director of the South Side Settlement House in Jamaica, New York. See Charles E. Shaw Jr., "Jamaica, L. I.," *Amsterdam News*, November 29, 1933; "Jamaica Vice Drive Opened," ibid., August 11, 1934; "N.Y. Church Woman for Aldermanic Post," *Baltimore Afro-American*, August 24, 1935; " 'Mayor' to Help Chaney Crusade," *Amsterdam News*, September 28, 1935.

293 *Chaney's comments resulted:* "Queens Ministers Flayed for Civic Inactivity," *Amsterdam News*, August 10, 1935.

294 *For a number:* " 'Mother' Warfield Funeral Rites Held Mon[day], June 11," *Indianapolis Recorder*, June 16, 1951.

294 *"is a distinct honor":* "Mayme L. Copeland," *Christian Index*, September 13, 1928. Copeland, a founding member of the Woman's Connectional Council, served as corresponding secretary. Employed as a teacher in the Hopkinsville, Kentucky, public school system, she was also a leader in local civic affairs.

294 *She was widely known:* Jessie Carney Smith, "Mattie E. Coleman (1870–1942)," *Notable Black American Women, Book II*, 125–28.

295 *In 1932 she:* "Woman at Head of Cal[ifornia] Dem[ocrat]s," *Pittsburgh Courier*, July 9, 1932; Various Groups Active," ibid., May 7, 1932; "Trend of Negro in Politics Discussed," *Washington Tribune*," April 1, 1927. In the 1924 presidential election, blacks voted a split ticket. This election marked the beginning of a shift in allegiance from the Republican to the Democratic Party. In 1932, three-fifths of the black electorate voted for the Republican Party. A major shift to the Democratic Party began with the congressional elections of 1934. See Bishop R[everdy] C. Ransom, "Why Vote for Roosevelt?" *Crisis* 39:11 (November 1932): 343; and Nancy J. Weiss, *Farewell to the Party of Lincoln: Black Politics in the Age of FDR* (Princeton: Princeton University Press, 1983), 21–26. For discussion of why blacks abandoned the Republican Party see "Republicans Prepare for Comeback," *AME Church Review* 53:3 (July–September, 1937): 235. "Service"

was the term used to differentiate between women employed as day workers and live-in domestics. Many black women dreaded being "in service" because of the extreme demands their white employers frequently made on their time. A woman "in service" was literally on call twenty-four hours a day, and could be exposed to emotional and sometimes physical abuse. Young women like Jones were aware of the problems inherent in the work and sought other employment. However, black women of all classes, especially the uneducated, had very few employment opportunities. For a discussion of the plight of black women domestic servants, see Haynes, "Negroes in Domestic Service in the United States."

295 *When Jones protested:* "Refused Admittance to Exclusive Club Because of Color," *Pittsburgh Courier*, October 24, 1930.

296 *In an assessment:* Little scholarly attention has been given to the importance of black women's political study clubs as grassroots organizations that educated black women about the nature and function of politics, and mobilized them for political action. "Los Angeles Sorors Name Mrs. Hill As 'The Outstanding Woman of 1940,' " *Chicago Defender*, January 18, 1941.

296 *As the first:* Ibid., "California Women Denounce Mitchell's Stand on Lynching," *Pittsburgh Courier*, April 20, 1935. For a discussion of Arthur Mitchell's political career, see Karen E. Reardon and Durahn Taylor, "Mitchell, Arthur Wergs," in Salzman et al., eds., *Encyclopedia of African-American Culture and History*, vol. 4, 1831–32. See also Dennis S. Nordin, *The New Deal's Black Congressman: A Life of Arthur Wergs Mitchell* (Columbia, Mo.: University of Missouri Press, 1997).

296 *Arguing that foreign:* "Women Rap Bias in Capital City," *Chicago Defender*, March 2, 1946.

296 *Taken as a whole:* "Head of [California] GOP Women Visits Chicago," *Chicago Defender*, June 4, 1955.

297 *Horne was a member:* "Noted Clubwoman Dies," *Chicago Defender*, September 24, 1932.

297 *"[w]hen one becomes":* Horace Holley, "The World Issue of Race," *Crisis* 43:7 (July 1936): 204.

297 *For many years:* Terrell was appointed to the District of Columbia School Board in 1895. See Debra Newman Ham, "Mary Church Terrell (1863–1954)," in Smith, ed., *Notable Black American Women, Book I,* 1118; "Cleveland Elects Woman to Board of Education," *Pittsburgh Courier*, November 16, 1929; "Cleveland Names Race Woman on Education Board," *New York Age*, November 16, 1929; "Mrs. Martin, Named to School Board, Dies," *Chicago Defender*, November 25, 1939.

298 *Explaining how:* "The First Colored Woman," *Indianapolis Freeman*, April 19, 1890.

299 *She continued to be:* Cleveland Courier, March 1, 1950, news clipping, Lethia Cousins Fleming Collection (3525), Box 1, Folders 2 and 3, Western Reserve Historical Society, Cleveland, Ohio (hereafter cited as LCFC-WRHS); Davis, *Lifting As They Climb*, 372–73.

299 *Like the Masons:* In 1946, Grace Witherspoon, a religious and fraternal leader, informed members of the Order of Eastern Star that "51 percent of the national voting power is vested in women." She urged them to use the vote as a weapon against discrimination. For Witherspoon's speech see "Mrs. Witherspoon Cites Voting Power of Women at OES Fete," *Washington Afro-American*, March 23, 1946.

300 *During the late 1940s:* Ibid.; Lethia Cousins Fleming, "The Call to All Lodges and Temples of Elks," pamphlet, 1949, LCFC-WRHS, Box 1, Folder 3. In 1948

Rosa Lee Ingram and her two teenage sons were sentenced to life imprisonment for killing John Stratford, a white farmer, who attempted to rape her. Enraged by Ingram's resistance to his advances, Stratford began beating her with a gun. Ingram's thirteen-year-old son took the gun and killed Stratford. The Elks were among the many secular and religious organizations that contributed money to aid the NAACP's defense of the Ingrams. Following ten years of incarceration, Rosa Ingram was paroled in 1959. For discussion of the Ingram case, see "Ingram Story Featured at NAACP Conference," *Negro Star*, June 25, 1948; "High Georgia Court to Hear Ingram Plea," ibid., June 4, 1948; "Contributions to Ingram Fund," ibid., October 8, 1948. For an excellent overview of the Daughter Elks' varied activities, see "Women Seen as Important Force in National Elkdom," *Indianapolis Recorder*, September 11, 1954. For further details regarding the Ingram case, see Virginia Shadron, "Popular Protest and Legal Authority in Post World War II Georgia: Race, Class, and Gender Politics in the Rosa Lee Ingram Case" (PhD diss., Emory University, 1991).

300 *She was a member:* For biographical data on Florence Spearing Randolph see Bettye Collier-Thomas, *Daughters of Thunder: Black Women Preachers and Their Sermons, 1850–1979* (San Francisco: Jossey-Bass Publishers, 1997), 101–6; Bettye Collier-Thomas, "Florence Spearing Randolph (1866–1951)," in Smith, ed., *Notable Black American Women, Book II*, 537–40. For a discussion of Lillian Feickert, see Felice D. Gordon, "Lillian Ford Feickert, 1877–1945," in *Past and Promise: Lives of New Jersey Women*, ed. Joan N. Burstyn et al. (Metuchen, N.J.: Scarecrow Press, Inc., 1990), 136–37.

300 *She viewed the federation:* Ibid.

301 *"We are 70,000":* Florence Spearing Randolph, "Our Big American Responsibility, or the Challenge of the Hour," typescript speech delivered at the Republican Women's Jubilee Luncheon at the Robert Treat Hotel in Newark, New Jersey, ca. January 1921, Florence Spearing Randolph Collection (hereafter cited as FSRC). For details regarding the luncheon, see "Rev. Mrs. Florence Randolph Leads New Jersey Republican Women—Makes Notable Speech," *Star of Zion*, January 27, 1921.

301 *She disputed claims:* "Dr. Florence Randolph Writes Race Relations Editorial for *Summit Herald*," *Star of Zion*, March 4, 1943. The occasion for this comment was the observance of Race Relations Sunday in Summit, New Jersey, when Randolph was selected by the interracial Ministerial Association to write an editorial focused on race relations. The editorial, entitled "If I Were White," was based on a sermon she delivered on Race Relations Sunday. The editor of the *Summit Herald* refused the editorial on the grounds that the topic of race relations was "not a religious question." The editor later relented and published part of the editorial.

302 *"As church women":* Florence Randolph, untitled, handwritten speech delivered on the "9th anniversary of the Eighteenth Amendment," ca. 1928, FSRC. For discussion of the theological importance of the theme "that power demands responsibility," see Jeffrey Weiss, "Ethics According to Spidey," *Philadelphia Inquirer*, July 18, 2004.

303 *Indignant over:* "An unholy, unchristian attitude," undated typescript letter addressed as "Dear Editor," ca. 1930s, FSRC. It is possible that this letter appeared in the *Summit Herald*, which published several letters written by Randolph to the editor.

303 *An important but often:* Gary Jerome Hunter, "'Don't Buy Where You Can't Work': Black Urban Boycott Movements during the Depression, 1929–1941" (PhD diss., University of Michigan, 1977), 156–62.

304 *Peck served as:* "First Ladies of Colored America—No. 8," *Crisis* 50:4 (April 1943): 113; "Housewives Get Down to Work," *Negro World*, October 10, 1931; *Baltimore Afro-American*, December 19, 1931; "Housewives League of Detroit," *Detroit Tribune*, February 27, 1943. For brief overviews of the organization, see Richard W. Thomas, *Life for Us Is What We Make It: Building Black Community in Detroit, 1915–1945* (Bloomington: Indiana University Press, 1992), 214–21; and Darlene Clark Hine, "Housewives' League of Detroit," in Hine, *Black Women in America*, vol. 1, 584–86.

304 *To establish and maintain:* "Housewives' League News," *Detroit Tribune*, March 6 and 20, 1943; John T. Wood, "Detroit's Leadership Is Changing Hands as Result of Riot," *Kansas Plaindealer*, August 13, 1943; see also Davis, *Lifting As They Climb*, 327–29.

305 *Other activities included:* In a sweeping generalization, Richard W. Thomas asserts that the Booker T. Washington Trade Association represented a "cross section" of black professionals, but included few working-class members. He assumed that "[s]ince the Housewives League was the sister organization, its composition was similar." Thomas presents no evidence to sustain this claim. See Thomas, *Life for Us Is What We Make It*, 216. For a discussion of the organization's leaders and members, see "Housewives' League of Detroit," "Housewives League News," and "Housewives' Program," *Detroit Tribune*, February 27, 1943.

305 *Reflecting on the struggle:* "Women's Club Heads Address Crowd of 300," *Chicago Defender*, October 17, 1942.

305 *As one who:* Lawson A. Scruggs, *Women of Distinction: Remarkable in Works and Invincible in Character* (Raleigh, N.C.: L. A. Scruggs, 1893), 251–55.

305 *Her religious work:* For biographical information on Christine Smith see Cary B. Lewis, "AME Church Ends 44th Michigan Confab," *Chicago Defender*, September 13, 1930; "35th Annual Session of Pittsburgh Conference Branch Missionary Meet in Canonsburg," *Pittsburgh Courier*, August 8, 1931; "Mrs. Christine S. Smith Passes," *Christian Recorder*, November 18, 1954; R. R. Wright Jr., comp., *Encyclopaedia of African Methodism* (Philadelphia: AME Book Concern, 1947), 255–56.

306 *Smith also made:* "Women Must Help Develop Enterprises," *Baltimore Afro-American*, December 9, 1931.

307 *The delegation:* "Detroit Women Quiz Sec[retary] Wallace on Meat Prices," *Baltimore Afro-American*, August 24, 1935.

307 *Similar to Randolph:* "Mrs. Mary Talbert," *Star of Zion*, October 25, 1923.

307 *In 1912 the federation:* "Women Deplore Lynching," *Baltimore Afro-American*, August 10, 1912. For a general overview of black women in the anti-lynching movement see Rosalyn Terborg-Penn, "African-American Women's Networks in the Anti-Lynching Crusade," in *Gender, Class, Race and Reform in the Progressive Era*, ed. Noralee Frankel and Nancy S. Dye (Lexington: University Press of Kentucky, 1991), 148–61.

307 *Wells-Barnett revealed:* "Self-Help the Negro's First Duty," *Washington Bee*, October 13, 1917.

307 *At the NACW's convention:* "Second Official Call of National Association of Colored Women," *Washington Bee*, March 23, 1918.

307 *During that year:* "New York Women Protest to Congress Against Lynching," *New York Age*, July 19, 1919; Bettye Collier-Thomas, "Minister and Feminist Reformer: The Life of Florence Spearing Randolph," in *This Far by Faith: Readings in African-American Women's Religious Biography*, ed. Judith Weisenfeld and Richard Newman (New York: Routledge, 1996), 183.

308 *Sixteen black women:* "A Million Women United to Suppress Lynching," *Negro Star*, October 13, 1922.

308 *In his first message:* Jessie Fauset, "The 13th Biennial of the N.A.C.W.," *Crisis* 24:6 (October 1922): 260. The women appointed to represent the pivotal states were: Ida Brown, New Jersey; Mary B. Jackson, Rhode Island; Ida Wells-Barnett, Illinois; Mary Parrish, Kentucky; Hallie Q. Brown, Minnie Scott, Estelle Davis, and Lethia Fleming, Ohio; Cora Horne, New York; E. G. Rose, Delaware; Ida Postles, Michigan; Pearl Winters, California; Myrtle F. Cook, Missouri; C. Chiles, Kansas; Ruth Bennett, Pennsylvania.

308 *The need was:* NBC, *Journal*, 1922, 368; "Mrs. Mary Talbert," *Star of Zion*, October 25, 1923.

308 *Burroughs suggested:* NBC, *Journal*, 1922, 350.

308 *Stressing the need:* For Helen Curtis quotation see "Women's Anti-Lynching Drive Arouses Interest at Buffalo," *New York Age*, October 7, 1922. For a discussion of the activities of the Anti-Lynching Crusaders in New York, see Helen Curtis, "Anti-Lynching Crusaders' Weekly Letter," ibid., November 11, 1922. Helen Curtis, a member of the Empire State Federation of Women's Clubs and a social worker in New York City, in 1922 was elected historian for the organization; see "Women's Federation in Annual Meeting," ibid., July 22, 1922. Curtis is incorrectly identified as president of the New Jersey Federation in 1922; see Rosalyn Terborg-Penn, "African American Women in the Anti-Lynching Crusade," 157. This position was held by Rev. Florence Spearing Randolph.

309 *Bethune announced:* Mary McLeod Bethune, "Women Will Keep Fighting," *New York Age*, December 16, 1922.

309 *As the national president:* John Hope Franklin, *From Slavery to Freedom: A History of African Americans*, 8th ed. (New York: Alfred A. Knopf, 2000), 392; Mary McLeod Bethune, "Closed Doors," in Collier-Thomas and Franklin, eds., *Sisters in the Struggle*, 14–20; Audrey Thomas McCluskey and Elaine M. Smith, eds., *Mary Mcleod Bethune: Building a Better World* (Bloomington: Indiana University Press, 2000).

310 *Like the YWCA:* "International Organization of Colored Women Is Formed," *New York Age*, August 26, 1922; International Council of Women of the Darker Races of the World, "Constitution," undated typescript, Papers of Mary Church Terrell, Library of Congress (hereafter cited as MCT-LC), Washington, D.C.; Herbert Aptheker, ed., *A Documentary History of the Negro People in the United States, 1910–1932*, vol. 3 (Seacaucus, N.J.: Citadel Press, 1973), 616–18; "Colored Women's International Council," *Southern Workman* 52 (January 1923): 7–10; "Women's International Council of Darker Races Holds Meet," *Indianapolis Recorder*, August 2, 1930; see also Michelle M. Rief, " 'Banded Close Together': An Afrocentric Study of African American Women's International Activism, 1850–1940, and the International Council of Women of the Darker Races" (PhD diss., Temple University, 2003); Cynthia Neverdon-Morton, *Afro-American Women of the South and the Advancement of the Race, 1895–1925* (Knoxville, Tenn.: University of Tennessee Press, 1989), 197–201.

310 *All black women:* The NACW took every opportunity to solicit the support of white women. In 1901, at the annual meeting of the National Council of Women, the NACW stressed "the importance of [NCW] . . . rendering aid to the support of kindergartens and day nurseries in the South." These institutions were critical to black working women who could not afford child care. See May Wright Sewall, ed., *National Council of Women of the United States Report of Its Twelfth Annual Executive and Its Fourth Triennial Sessions* (Boston: E. B. Stillings

Co., 1902), 106. For a discussion of white women and southern progressivism see Anne Firor Scott, *The Southern Lady: From Pedestal to Politics 1830–1930* (Chicago: University of Chicago Press, 1970), and "The 'New Woman' in the New South," *South Atlantic Quarterly* 61 (August 1962): 473–83; Gilmore, *Gender and Jim Crow*, 149; For quote regarding domestic servants, see NBC, *Journal*, 1916, 195.

CHAPTER 6 *"Across the Divide"*

314 *The interracial movement:* In addition to riots in Chicago, Washington, D.C., Springfield, Illinois, and several other cities, there was tension bordering on open conflict in at least twenty-one cities.

314 *To offset what:* George Edmund Haynes, *Toward Interracial Peace* (New York: Carnegie Corporation, 1940), I–1.

315 *In simple language:* Ibid., I–3.

316 *The DRR would:* In 1928 the name of the Commission on the Church and Race Relations was changed to the Commission on Race Relations of the FCC in America. However, the commission became known and was referred to as the Department of Race Relations. FCC, "Minutes of a Meeting of the Commission on the Church and Race Relations," December 6–7, 1928, Federal Council of the Churches of Christ Collection, Commission on the Church and Race Relations Papers, Presbyterian Historical Society, Philadelphia, Pa. (hereafter cited as FCC-DRR:PHS). Haynes, *Toward Interracial Peace*, II–1; throughout its history the DRR was poorly funded by the FCC. Many of the white organizers viewed the DRR as a necessity; however, it was given low priority. FCC leaders emphasized that the purpose of the DRR was to create a dialogue between black and white Christians that would help to alleviate racial tension and maintain racial harmony. They had little interest in contending for equality of the races. The lives of many social reformers, politicians, philanthropists, and educators were heavily invested in systems of segregation. Similar to white abolitionists whose primary concern was the eradication of slavery, the initial concern of the interracialists was to eliminate the practice of lynching and improve the living conditions of black Americans. Equality and integration were not the stated goals of the movement during the early years. As the movement evolved, civil rights became a major objective.

316 *George Haynes:* George Edmund Haynes, a sociologist and labor expert, the first African American to receive a PhD from Columbia University (1912), was a pioneer in the interracial movement. An original member of the NAACP, Haynes served as chairman of Fisk University's Social Science Department (1910–21) and director of the U.S. Department of Labor's Division of Negro Economics (1918–21) prior to his appointment as executive secretary of the Department of Race Relations (1921–47). For biographical information on Haynes, see Daniel Perlman, "Stirring the White Conscience: The Life of George Edmund Haynes" (PhD diss., New York University, 1972). For an excellent examination of Haynes's career as a pioneering labor historian and social scientist, see Francille Rusan Wilson, *The Segregated Scholars: Black Social Scientists and the Creation of Black Labor Studies, 1890–1950* (Charlottesville: University of Virginia Press, 2006).

316 *Although the DRR:* Samuel Cavert McCrea, ed., *United in Service—Quadrennial Report of the Federal Council of the Churches of Christ in America, 1920–1924* (New York: Federal Council of Churches of Christ in America, 1925), 128; FCC, *Annual Report 1921* (New York: Federal Council of the Churches of Christ,

1922), 80–81; "Excerpts from the Minutes of the Meeting of the Committee on Women's Work, June 8–9, 1939, at Swarthmore College—Friday Morning Session," Box 1, Church Women United Collection, General Commission on Archives and History—United Methodist Church, Drew University (hereafter cited as CWU:GCAH).

317 *In effect, the WCTU:* For information regarding Carrie Parks Johnson, see Jacquelyn Dowd Hall, *Revolt Against Chivalry: Jessie Daniel Ames and the Women's Campaign Against Lynching*, rev. ed. (New York: Columbia University Press, 1993); For a discussion of black women and the WCTU, see Bettye Collier-Thomas, "Frances Ellen Watkins Harper: Abolitionist and Feminist Reformer, 1825–1911," in *African American Women and the Vote, 1837–1965*, ed. Ann D. Gordon et al. (Amherst: University of Massachusetts Press, 1992), 55–60; and Bettye Collier-Thomas, *Black Women Organized for Social Change, 1800–1920* (Washington, D.C.: Bethune Museum-Archives, Inc., National Historic Site, 1984), 20–21. Roslyn V. Cheagle, "The Colored Temperance Movement: 1830–1860" (MA thesis, Howard University, 1969), 10–18, 63–71; Ruth Bordin, *Frances Willard: A Biography* (Chapel Hill, N.C.: University of North Carolina Press, 1986).

318 *Methodist and CIC:* Hall, *Revolt Against Chivalry*, 102–03. For a discussion of black women in the YWCA, see Adrienne Lash Jones, "Young Women's Christian Association," in *Black Women in America: An Historical Encyclopedia*, vol. 2, ed. Darlene Clark Hine (Brooklyn: Carlson Publishing, 1993), 1299–1303; and Judith Weisenfeld, *African American Women and Christian Activism: New York's Black YWCA, 1905–1945* (Cambridge, Mass.: Harvard University Press, 1998), 1–12.

319 *The establishment of:* The Department of Evangelistic Work was later known as Religious Welfare (1908), and Church Relations (1928). "Departments of N.A.C.W.," *National Notes* (October 1908); "Heads of Departments," ibid. (April 1923); "Major and Minor Departments," ibid. (September and October 1928); for a discussion of the National Association of Colored Women, see Stephanie J. Shaw, "Black Club Women and the Creation of the National Association of Colored Women," *Journal of Women's History* 1:3 (1990): 13–44; Tullia Kay Brown Hamilton, "The National Association of Colored Women, 1896–1920" (PhD diss., Emory University, 1978); Ruby Moyse Kendricks, " 'They Also Serve': The National Association of Colored Women, Inc.," *Negro History Bulletin* 42 (March 1954): 171–75. Activities of women in church and civic groups are included in Dorothy C. Salem, *To Better Our World: Black Women in Organized Reform, 1890–1920*, vol. 14 in *Black Women in United States History: From Colonial Times to the Present*, ed. Darlene Clark Hine (Brooklyn: Carlson Publishing, 1990); and Gerda Lerner's "Early Community Work of Black Club Women," *Journal of Negro History* 59 (April 1974): 158–62. Other works that treat the organized self-help efforts of black women include Anne Firor Scott, "Most Invisible of All: Black Women's Voluntary Associations," *Journal of Southern History* 56 (February 1990): 3–22.

319 *Most of these women:* For Layten quote, see NBC, *Journal of the Twenty-fourth Annual Session of the National Baptist Convention and the Fifth Annual Assembly of the Woman's Convention Auxiliary, Held in Austin, Texas, September 14–19, 1904* (Nashville: Sunday School Publishing Board, 1904), 328.

320 *Casting an eye:* Alice G. Knotts, *Fellowship of Love: Methodist Women Changing American Racial Attitudes, 1920–1968* (Nashville: Kingswood Books, 1996), 50–52; for an excellent discussion of the YWCA's racial policies regarding the estab-

lishment and operation of "Colored" branches of the YWCA, and how black women worked within that structure, see Weisenfeld, *African American Women and Christian Activism*, 9–14.

321 *A product of its time:* Ibid., 51.

321 *This was the beginning:* Hall, *Revolt Against Chivalry* , 86–88, 90; Rouse, *Lugenia Burns Hope*, 107–09; Ruth Wysor Atkinson, "Inter-Racial Co-Operation," *Opportunity* (September 1923): 276; Taylor, "How Southern Black Women Met"; see also Cynthia Neverdon-Morton, *Afro-American Women of the South and the Advancement of the Race, 1895–1925* (Knoxville: University of Tennessee Press, 1989), 226–31.

321 *For the members:* Knotts, *Fellowship of Love*, 52; Rebecca Stiles Taylor, "How Southern Black Women Met Southern White Women," *Chicago Defender*, January 22, 1938; Jacqueline Anne Rouse, *Lugenia Burns Hope: Black Southern Reformer* (Athens, Ga.: University of Georgia Press, 1989), 107–08.

323 *Four black women:* Lily H. Hammond, "Southern Women and Racial Adjustment," occasional paper published by the Trustees of the John H. Slater Fund, 2nd ed., 1920; Monroe Work, *The Negro Year Book, 1921–22* (Tuskegee, Ala.: Tuskegee Institute, 1922), 6; Taylor, "How Southern Black Women Met." See also John Patrick McDowell, *The Social Gospel in the South: The Woman's Home Mission Movement in the Methodist Episcopal Church, South, 1886–1939* (Baton Rouge: Louisiana State University Press, 1982), 88–90.

323 *Though the statement:* Rebecca Stiles Taylor, "Southern Black Women and Race Cooperation," *Chicago Defender*, January 22, 1938.

324 *"all the privileges":* Hall, *Revolt Against Chivalry*, 95–97; Taylor, "How Southern Black Women Met"; Taylor, "Race Cooperation."

325 *the Memphis conference:* Ibid.; Southeastern Federation of Negro Women's Clubs, "Southern Negro Women and Race Co-Operation," pamphlet, ca. 1921; "Inter-Racial Co-Operation: Constructive Measures Recommended by Southern White Women," *Southern Workman* (January 1921): 31–37; Bettye Collier-Thomas, "Across the Divide: The Interracial and Interdenominational Efforts of Black and White Church Women: An Historical Reconnaissance," in *Black Women's History at the Intersection of Knowledge and Power: ABWH's Twentieth Anniversary Anthology*, ed. Rosalyn Terborg-Penn and Janice Sumler-Edmond (Acton, Mass.: Tapestry Press, 2000), 32.

325 *"the strongest force":* Ibid.; Knotts, *Fellowship of Love*, 53; Monroe Work, the director of the Department of Records and Research at Tuskegee Institute, published the CIC and MECS statement, and the Southeastern Federation's pamphlet "Southern Negro Women and Race Co-Operation." See Monroe Work, *The Negro in 1919–1921: The Negro Yearbook* (Tuskegee, Ala.: Tuskegee Institute, 1922), 6–10.

325 *This attitude undoubtedly:* For articles proclaiming the Southeastern Federation as the progenitor of the southern interracial movement, see "Southeastern Federation's Triple-Plank Platform," *Chicago Defender*, April 9, 1938; "Southeastern Federation Colored Women's Clubs Meet at Tuskegee Inst[itute]," ibid., February 3, 1940; "Southeastern Federation Colored Women's Clubs Will Meet in Richmond, Va.," ibid., June 18, 1946; "Southeastern Federation of Colored Women Meets at Alabama State College," ibid., July 5, 1947.

326 *Among the eight:* Knotts, *Fellowship of Love*, 53; Hall, *Revolt Against Chivalry*, 94–95; H. L. McCrorey, "One Road to Interracial Peace," *Home Mission Monthly* 37:6 (April 1923); "Black and White Seek a Means to Exile Prejudice," *Negro World*, May 14, 1927; In 1927 Bethune was a member of the CIC's Executive

Committee. This appointment followed her election as NACW president. Maggie Lena Walker and Eva Bowles were elected to membership on the commission in 1926. See "Colored Members Added to Race Relations Body," *Star of Zion*, April 29, 1926. For biographical data on Bowles, see Adrienne Lash Jones, "Bowles, Eva Del Vakia," in Hine, ed., *Black Women in America*, vol. 1, 152–53.

326 *White and black members:* Rouse, *Lugenia Burns Hope*, 114; local committees were organized throughout Georgia. For example, in Augusta, Georgia, an all-white local race relations committee was formed by whites in 1925. A "cooperating colored committee," headed by Lucy Laney, was also organized. See "Form Race [Relations] Committee," *Savannah Tribune*, February 26, 1925. Segregated committees were also formed in other cities.

327 *Selena Butler:* "Interracial Committee of Georgia Meets," *Negro World*, April 4, 1925.

327 *As the women's:* For example, Selena Butler, a native of Thomasville, Georgia, and a graduate of Spelman College (1888), was a founder of the Atlanta Woman's Club, an organizer of the Atlanta Colored YWCA, and the first president of the Georgia State Federation of Colored Women. In the late 1920s she served as chair of the Georgia State Committee on Race Relations. In January 1930, as president of the National Congress of Colored Parents and Teachers, Butler was a participant in the White House Conference on Child Health and Protection. Founded in 1926, by 1930 the black Parent-Teachers Association represented twenty thousand members in sixteen states. For biographical details on Selena Butler, see " 'Speaking Up' for the Negro Parent and Teacher," *Pittsburgh Courier*, January 18, 1930.

327 *Known for her work:* "Know Something About Club Life: Mrs. Helen Sayre Stands Out as Woman of Prominence," *Chicago Defender*, May 4, 1929.

327 *With the support:* Hall, *Revolt Against Chivalry*, 59–60.

328 *Ames believed that:* Continuation Committee of the Interracial Conference of Church Women, *Church Women in Interracial Cooperation* (New York: FCC, 1926), 3, 4, 7, 8; Hall, *Revolt Against Chivalry*, 249–50.

328 *Burroughs agreed that:* W. C. Jackson to Nannie Helen Burroughs, March 24, 1931, NHB-LC; Elizabeth Head to Nannie Helen Burroughs, November 9, 1931, ibid.; Jessie Daniel Ames to Nannie Helen Burroughs, January 31, 1934, ibid.; Nannie Helen Burroughs to Jessie Daniel Ames, February 2, 1934, ibid.

328 *"felt no obligation":* Hall, *Revolt Against Chivalry*, 250–51.

328 *Most studies of women:* Jacquelyn Dowd Hall's *Revolt Against Chivalry* is one of the few studies to discuss the roots of women's activism in the interracial movement. She identifies the cooperative efforts between black and white church women, which began in the late nineteenth century, as laying the groundwork for the twentieth-century southern movement of interracial cooperation. Scholars are beginning to document the activism of white southern women who were active in the early twentieth-century movements such as Church Women United and in the Civil Rights Movement of the 1950s and '60s. See Gail S. Murray, ed., *Throwing Off the Cloak of Privilege: White Southern Women Activists in the Civil Rights Era* (Gainesville, Fla.: University Press of Florida, 2004); Susan M. Hartmann, *The Other Feminists: Activists in the Liberal Establishment* (New Haven: Yale University Press, 1998).

329 *"not mere paper bodies":* "Annual Survey," by the Associated Negro Press, *Washington Tribune*, January 3, 1925; Neverdon-Morton, *Afro-American Women of the South*, 234.

329 *Randolph was also:* For examples of black women, such as Rev. Florence Spearing Randolph, who successfully utilized their religious and secular organizations as networks for social reform, see Bettye Collier-Thomas and V. P. Franklin, eds., *Sisters in the Struggle: African American Women in the Civil Rights–Black Power Movement* (New York: New York University Press, 2001), 23–27; Bettye Collier-Thomas, *Daughters of Thunder: Black Women Preachers and Their Sermons, 1850–1979* (San Francisco: Jossey-Bass, 1997), 105–06; CWCRR, "Minutes," March 28, 1938, *Church Women's Committee of the Commission on the Church and Race Relations Papers* (FCC-CWCRR:PHS); Mary Jackson McCrorey, an educator and political activist, was the founder of one of the first YWCAs in the South. In North Carolina, McCrorey was a member of the North Carolina NACW and the regional and state commissions on interracial cooperation. She served on the boards of numerous organizations, including the NCNW and the Presbyterian Church, and was the corresponding secretary for the International Council of Women of the Darker Races. For biographical information on McCrorey see Glenda Elizabeth Gilmore, "McCrorey, Mary Jackson," in Hine, ed., *Black Women in America*, vol. 2, 767–68; for a discussion of similar white women, such as Carrie Parks Johnson—director of woman's work for the CIC—and Jessie Daniel Ames—CIC and the Association of Southern Women for the Prevention of Lynching leader—see Hall, *Revolt Against Chivalry*, 58, 94–95.

330 *The FCC was concerned:* FCC, *Annual Report, 1921*, 52; "Notes Taken at Discussion Called by Mrs. Olmstead and Mrs. Pulcifer," New York, N.Y., March 6, 1941, Women's Cooperating Commission Papers, Federal Council of the Churches of Christ Collection, Presbyterian Historical Society, Philadelphia (hereafter cited as FCC-WCC).

330 *However, members:* FCC, *Annual Report, 1925*, 193; FCC, *Biennial Report, 1936*, 154; CWCRR, "Minutes," November 25, 1940, FCC-CWCRR:PHS. For example, in 1944, of the forty-four NBC-USA FCC representatives, there was only one woman—Nannie Burroughs. See "List of Members of the Federal Council of the Churches of Christ in America from the National Baptist Convention, U.S.A., Incorporated," in NBC, *Proceedings of the Sixty-fifth Annual Session of the National Baptist Convention, U.S.A., Inc., Held with the Baptist Churches of Dallas, Texas, September 6–10, 1944* (Nashville: Sunday School Publishing Board, 1944), 57–58.

331 *In 1921, in response:* In 1901 four prominent AME women leaders attended the fourth conference of the Woman's Board of Foreign Missions. Josephine Heard read a paper on "Missions in Africa." See "Personals," *Christian Recorder,* January 24, 1901; FCC, *Annual Report, 1921;* "The Council of Women for Home Missions," 157.

331 *The CWHM suggested:* George Edmund Haynes, "The Work of the Commission on Race Relations, Federal Council of Churches," typescript, ca. 1932, chapter 5, "The Church Women's Committee," 1 (hereafter cited as chapter 5). Please note that the chapters in this report are numbered separately.

332 *"feeling of suspicion":* George Edmund Haynes, *Toward Interracial Peace* (New York: Carnegie Corporation, 1940), chapter 8–1; George Edmund Haynes, "The Work of the Commission," chapter 5, 1–2.

332 *Focusing its attention:* "Women's Missionary Council of M.E. Church Hear Mrs. Janie Barrett," *New York Age,* March 27, 1926.

332 *Ignoring segregation:* McDowell, *The Social Gospel,* 99.

333 *"interracial meeting":* Haynes, "The Work of the Commission," chapter 5, 2;

Collier-Thomas, "Across the Divide," 31–32; "The Churches and Race Relations," *Star of Zion*, May 13, 1926; for a description of the CIC and MECS's plans for interracial cooperation, in particular how the state interracial committees were organized and operated at the local level, see "Women Plan Inter-Racial Cooperation," *Washington Bee*, March 26, 1921.

333 *He criticized:* For Du Bois's quote and commentary on the relationship between the Catholic Church and blacks, see W. E. B. Du Bois, "The Catholic Church and Negroes," *Crisis* 32:7 (July 1925): 120–21.

334 *Similar to the YWCA:* Regarding discussion of the work and patterns of interaction between southern white Methodist women and black women leaders in the Colored Methodist Episcopal Church, see Mary E. Frederickson, " 'Each One Is Dependent on the Other': Southern Churchwomen, Racial Reform, and the Process of Transformation, 1880–1940," in *Visible Women: New Essays on American Activism*, ed. Nancy A. Hewitt and Suzanne Lebsock, (Urbana, Ill.: University of Illinois Press, 1993), 296–324; "Writer Depicts the Work and Problems of Y.W.C.A.," *Norfolk Journal and Guide*, September 23, 1933. For an excellent discussion of the patterns of interaction that occurred between the CIC Women's Committee and NACW black women leaders, see Hall, *Revolt Against Chivalry*, 95–106.

335 *The widespread publicity:* Hall, *Revolt Against Chivalry*, 95–98.

335 *What the FCC:* Haynes, "The Work of the Commission," chapter 5; FCC, *Annual Report, 1926*, 107–08.

336 *A number of:* Ibid.; Nettie George Speedy, "National Interracial Conference in Session," *Chicago Defender*, April 4, 1925.

336 *Mary van Kleeck:* Ibid.; the National Interracial Conference called for a comprehensive examination of black economic and social life. A grant of $5,000 from the Social Science Research Council underwrote the 1928 publication of *The Negro in American Civilization: A Study of Negro Life and Race Relations in the Light of Social Research*, which discussed the role of black labor in the creation of the United States. See Wilson, *The Segregated Scholars*, 160–61.

336 *At a meeting:* Haynes, "The Work of the Commission," chapter 5; "The Church Women's Committee," chapters 1–2.

337 *In this manner:* "Church Women to Hold Interracial Parley," *Norfolk Journal and Guide*, July 7, 1928; "Church Women Make Effort to Solve Problem," *Philadelphia Tribune*, September 25, 1926; "Women of Both Races in Meet," *Chicago Defender*, December 4, 1926. During the early twentieth century Miles Mark Fisher, a noted scholar of African American religion, charted the growth of influential laymen who became leaders in the churches and threatened the leadership of pastors. Fisher asserted, "Laymen were in complete control of the Y.M.C.A. and Y.W.C.A. and other religious organizations. It was found to be good business and also good religion to ignore denominational bounds." See Miles Mark Fisher, "The Negro Churches," *Crisis* 45:7 (July 1938): 245.

338 *Discussions on these:* For a list of organizational representatives and the conference program, see Continuation Committee, *Church Women in Interracial Cooperation*, 3, 4, 7, 8; the other CIC delegates were Madge Headley and Maud Henderson. Although Jesse Daniel Ames became the director of woman's work in 1929, and founder of the Association of Southern Women for the Prevention of Lynching in 1930, at this time she was a member of the CIC General Woman's Committee. Estelle Haskin, an influential member of the CIC General Woman's Committee, attended the conference as the official representative of the Woman's Missionary Council of the Methodist Episcopal Church, South;

"Race Relations to Occupy Time of the Women," *Philadelphia Tribune*, September 18, 1926.

339 *To ensure a black:* "Minutes of an Informal Conference of Women Members of the Commission on the Church and Race Relations," February 18, 1926, FCC-CWCRR:PHS; "Minutes of a Meeting of the Women's Continuation Committee," November 22, 1926, ibid.; "Minutes of a Meeting of the Church Women's Committee on Race Relations," December 27, 1926, February 28, 1927, ibid.; and "Minutes of a Meeting of the Personnel Committee," February 4, 1927, ibid.; CWCRR, "Minutes," October 29, 1928, ibid.; Continuation Committee, *Church Women in Interracial Cooperation.*

340 *AKA's political activities:* Haynes, *Toward Interracial Peace*, chapter 7, pp. 2, 6; Elizabeth Ross Haynes served as the YWCA student secretary for work among black women from 1908–1910, and was the first African American to serve on the YWCA National Board (1924–34). Haynes represented both the YWCA and the NBC-USA on the CWCRR. For biographical information on Haynes and Mabel Keaton Staupers, see Hine, ed., *Black Women in America*, vol. 1, 548–49, and vol. 2, 1106–08. Ida Louise Jackson served as national basileus of AKA, 1934–36. For biographical information on Jackson, see Marjorie H. Parker, *Past Is Prologue: The History of Alpha Kappa Alpha, 1908–1999* (Washington, D.C.: Alpha Kappa Alpha Sorority, Inc., 1999), 83–86; FCC, "Summary of Church Women's Committee Work on Hospitalization," undated typescript, ca. 1938, FCC-CWCRR:PHS. For a discussion of AKA's Non-Partisan Council on Human Rights, see Collier-Thomas and Franklin, eds., *Sisters in the Struggle*, 28–32.

340 *Between 1927 and 1942:* For information regarding participation of black women on the CWCRR, and issues discussed, see CWCRR, "Minutes," February 4, February 28, June 6, 1927; January 28, 1929; November 30, 1931; March 28, 1932; November 26, 1934; November 25, 1935; November 30, 1936; November 25, 1940, FCC-CWCRR:PHS; for Ella Barksdale Brown, see "The 6th Annual N. J. Youth Conference," *Star of Zion*, May 30, 1940; also see list of CWCRR members, untitled and undated typescript, FCC-CWCRR:PHS.

340 *"integration of members":* "Excerpts from the Minutes of the National Committee of Church Women, October 3 and 4, 1939," Box 1, CWU: GCAH.

341 *Black Methodist:* For election of CWCRR chairmen and vice chairmen, see CWCRR, "Minutes," November 24, 1930; November 28, 1932; November 17, 1933; December 14, 1934; November 25, 1935; November 30, 1936; November 28, 1938; November 27, 1939; November 24, 1941, FCC-CWCRR:PHS. Women serving in these positions 1931–41 were as follows: 1931, Caroline Chapin (white) and Helen Curtis (black); 1932–34, Chapin and Susan Payton Wortham (black); 1935, Mrs. Douglass Falconer (white) and Mrs. H. H. Proctor (black); 1936, Falconer and Eva Del Vakia Bowles (black); 1937, Falconer and Creola Cowan (black); and 1939–41, Josephine Humbles Kyles (black) and Mrs. Emory Ross (white). Helen Sayre, a black Episcopal woman from Chicago, served as the first black vice chairman. For information regarding Sayre's work in the Illinois and national interracial movement, see "Know Something About Club Life," *Chicago Defender*, May 4, 1929.

341 *And, in 1941:* CWCRR, "Minutes," May 17, 1937; March 28, 1938; January 30, 1939; and January 27, 1941, FCC-CWCRR:PHS. In 1922, the Federal Council of the Churches designated the Sunday before Abraham Lincoln's birthday as Race Relations Sunday. In an effort to make Christianity "really effective," the FCC felt that at least one sermon a year should be devoted to race relations, and

that one program in every Sunday school, church organization, and other religious groups should emphasize this theme. Black and white ministers exchanged pulpits, and religious leaders crossed "the divide" and visited other churches. For a brief history of Race Relations Sunday, see James F. Findlay Jr., *Church People in the Struggle: The National Council of Churches and the Black Freedom Struggle, 1950–1970* (New York: Oxford University Press, 1993), 18–19.

341 *The CWCRR recommended:* CWCRR, "Minutes," May 15, 1939, FCC-CWCRR:PHS.

342 *In a few instances:* For discussions of the need to raise money for women's work see CWCRR, "Minutes," February 28, June 6, 1927; October 8, November 26, 1928; February 25, 1929; March 28, 1932; May 15, 1939, FCC-CWCRR:PHS. Haynes unilaterally extended an invitation to Annie Malone to accept membership on the CWCRR and in the FCC. A member of the AME denomination, Malone was a black beauty culture pioneer, whose worth in the 1920s was estimated at $1 million. Malone deferred her membership until the fall of 1927. She attended a CWCRR meeting in February 1929. However, there is no evidence that she was an active participant in the organization. CWCRR, "Minutes," February 25, 1929, ibid. For biographical information on Malone, see Bettye Collier-Thomas, "Annie Turnbo Malone," in *Notable Black American Women, Book I*, ed. Jessie Carney Smith (Detroit: Gale Research, 1992), 724–26.

342 *Interracial committees worked:* Haynes, *Toward Interracial Peace*, 2–9.

342 *By 1928:* "Church Women Hold Second General Interracial Conference," *Star of Zion*, October 4, 1928; "New Leadership in Race Relations: Miss Gardner Becomes Secretary of Church Women's Committee," *Federal Council Bulletin*, September [n.d.], 1928, 20. Katherine Gardner, a social worker, was a member of the CWCRR. Following her graduation from the New York School of Social Work in 1910, Gardner was employed as director of the New York Charity Organization Society's investigation bureau. She later served as the executive secretary of the Civic Association of Englewood, New Jersey. In Englewood, Gardner was involved with issues related to the growing black population. Under her administration a League for Social Service was launched and developed. As the secretary of the Board of National Missions of the Presbyterian Church, USA, she was responsible for the promotional work of the Division of Schools and Hospitals, and of the Work Among Colored People.

343 *Among the black women:* Ibid.; Dr. Sarah W. Brown, a physician and lecturer on social hygiene, was employed by the Women's Division of the Council of National Defense. See "Advancement of Colored Women," *Christian Recorder*, January 20, 1921.

344 *The conference admitted:* "Church Women Hold Second General International Conference."

344 *After four years:* "Oberlin College Host to Interracial Church Women," *Chicago Defender*, June 21, 1930; "Interracial Conference Closes Session," *Chicago Defender*, July 5, 1930. Lucy D. Slowe, dean of women at Howard University and the president of the National Association of College Women, and Leslie Pinckney Hill, president of the Cheyney Training School for Teachers, delivered keynote addresses. Discussion groups were led by Rhoda McCulloch, editor of the *Woman's Press* and a member of the National Board of the YWCA, and Margaret Forsyth of the Department of Religious Education, Teachers College, Columbia University.

345 *Local groups were:* Ibid.

346 *Examining her appearance:* "White Men and a Colored Woman," *Crisis* 37:12 (December 1930): 416. Revelations of rape and sexual harassment may be found

in slave memoirs and testimony, autobiographies of ex-slaves, speeches, newspaper articles, organizational minutes, and any number of other sources. The majority of disclosures were made long after the occurrence of the abuse. Sexual violations that took place between a servant and her employer frequently remained hidden for many years. Reports of sexual harassment in the interracial movement were rare. They were difficult to prove, and many middle-class women realized their vulnerability and that they might be blamed for possibly encouraging the unwanted attention. The white community would most likely believe and defend a prominent white man, and black community leaders were fearful of bringing charges against "liberal" whites and risking the loss of much-needed resources and material support from the white community. In cases such as this, black women dissembled and avoided conflict. For the "culture of dissemblance," see Darlene Clark Hine, "Rape and the Inner Lives of Black Women in the Middle West: Preliminary Thoughts on a Culture of Dissemblance," *Signs* 14 (summer 1989): 912–20.

346 *She is offended:* "White Men and a Colored Woman."

347 *"What would he think":* Ibid.

347 *During the 1930s:* Haynes, *Toward Interracial Peace*, chapter 4, pp. 18–20.

348 *Jews, in turn:* Haynes, *Toward Interracial Peace*, chapter 4, p. 11; CWCRR, "Minutes," November 26, 1934; May 15, 1939, FCC-CWCRR:PHS; for discussion of black-Jewish relationships, see V. P. Franklin et al., eds., *African Americans and Jews in the Twentieth Century: Studies in Convergence and Conflict* (Columbia, Mo.: University of Missouri Press, 1998).

348 *The question of placing:* National Council of Churches, Department of Racial and Cultural Relations, 1950–65, and Commission on Religion and Race, 1963–1967, Presbyterian Historical Society, Philadelphia, RG 6, Series 5; Samuel Kelton Roberts, "Crucible for a Vision: The Work of George Edmund Haynes and the Commission on Race Relations, 1922–1947" (PhD diss., Columbia University, 1974), 123.

349 *In March 1940:* CWCRR, "Minutes," November 26, 1934; May 15, 1939; January 29, March 26, 1940, FCC-CWCRR:PHS; Eva Hills Eastman to CWCRR, May 26, 1939, ibid.; for CWCRR's efforts to promote "study and action" on the anti-Semitism among FCC affiliate women's organizations, see "Excerpts from the Minutes of the National Committee of Church Women, October 3 and 4, 1939," Box 1, CWU:GCAH.

350 *Their goal was:* The first piece of race interpretation was begun in 1926 by the American Friends Service Committee, which had established an interracial committee. Crystal Bird, a member of the YWCA National Board, was willing to take on the role of race interpretation. She began in fall 1927 speaking to audiences in Philadelphia at public and private schools, colleges, church organizations, and community meetings. She delivered 210 talks during the first year. See Alice Dunbar Nelson, "Quakers Experiment in Racial Understanding," *Star of Zion*, January 31, 1929.

350 *The DRR and the CWCRR:* Crystal Bird Fauset was the first YWCA secretary for Negro girls. In this position, she traveled throughout the U.S., Mexico, and Cuba studying the living conditions of people of African descent. By 1927 she was considered an expert on the "problems of the Negro," and was an accomplished speaker. In 1927, the American Friends Service Committee, a Quaker organization, hired Fauset as an interracial secretary, whose role was to educate white Americans about the concerns of black Americans. Fauset was the initiator of the Institute of Race Relations at Swarthmore College, sponsored by the

AFSC during the summers of 1933, 1934, and 1935. During World War II she served as race relations advisor in the National Civil Defense set up under Fiorella H. La Guardia, Eleanor Roosevelt, and Dean James Landis of Harvard University. Fauset's election to the Pennsylvania State Legislature in 1938 distinguished her as the first black woman in the U.S. to serve in such a capacity. For Fauset's role as a race interpreter, see "Friends Conference Discusses Race Relations," *Star of Zion*, August 9, 1928. For biographical information on Fauset, see "Crystal Byrd (sic) Fauset," *Philadelphia Tribune*, August 3, 1963; Ruth Bogin, "Fauset, Crystal Dreda Bird," in *Notable American Women: The Modern Period: A Biographical Dictionary*, ed. Ilene Kantrov et al. (Cambridge, Mass.: Harvard University Press, 1980), 224–25; Marie Garrett, "Crystal Dreda Bird Fauset (1893–1965)," in Smith, ed., *Notable Black American Women, Book I*, 333–35; V. P. Franklin, "Fauset, Crystal Bird (1894–1965)," in Hine, ed., *Black Women in America*, vol. 1, 410–11.

350 *"I go often"*: Florence L. Dyett, "Church Worker Emphasizes 'Good Will' and the Spirit of Missions," *Pittsburgh Courier*, February 24, 1940.

350 *The CWCRR decided:* CWCRR, "Minutes," September 26, 1932, FCC-CWCRR:PHS.

351 *Race Relations Sunday:* Haynes, *Toward Interracial Peace*, chapter 6, p. 6.

351 *To address this:* CWCRR, "Minutes," September 23, 1929, FCC-CWCRR:PHS; Haynes, *Toward Interracial Peace*, chapter 6, p. 6.

352 *The CWCRR brought:* CWCRR, "Minutes," January 30, 1928, FCC-CWCRR:PHS. Between 1890 and 1930 hotels maintained exclusively for African Americans could be found in many cities. By 1923 there were at least one hundred first-rate black hotels in the United States. However, most black hotels were small and lacked the services associated with first-rate white establishments. Among the most celebrated during the 1920s were the Whitelaw, in Washington, D.C.; the Dale, in Cape May, New Jersey; the Vincennes, in Chicago; the Royal Palace, in Baltimore, and the Golden West, in Portland, Oregon. Hotels for African Americans were located in major urban areas in states such as Georgia, Ohio, Nebraska, Pennsylvania, Tennessee, South Carolina, Connecticut, Missouri, California, New York, Massachusetts, Michigan, and Indiana. For discussion of black hotels, see J. A. Jackson, "Some Hotel Thoughts," *Billboard*, September 1, 1923; "Negro Hotel Men Organize," ibid., February 21, 1925.

352 *Discovering that the CWHM:* Roberts, "Crucible for a Vision," 122; CWCRR, "Minutes," January 27, May 26, July 21, November 24, 1930; January 26, May 20, 1931; January 27, September 28, 1936; January 29, March 29, 1940; September 29, 1941, FCC-CWCRR:PHS.

353 *"urged denominations"*: CWCRR, "Minutes," September 29, 1930, FCC-CWCRR:PHS. For discussion of the brutal lynching that took place in Sherman, Texas, and the criticism of Governor Daniel Moody, CIC leader Will Alexander, and other southern white interracial leaders for their failure to condemn the practice of lynching see "23 Texas Lynchers Indicted: Citizens Flee, Troops Guard," *Pittsburgh Courier*, May 17, 1930; Floyd J. Calvin, "Calvin Criticizes Interracial 'Comish' in Mob Murders," ibid., July 12, 1930.

353 *In 1933 the women:* CWCRR, "Minutes," March 28, 1932; November 27, 1933, FCC-CWCRR:PHS.

353 *In 1938 the CWCRR:* CWCRR, "Minutes," January 29, March 26, 1934; January 26, May 13, September 30, 1935; March 28, May 9, 1938; January 29, 1940, FCC-CWCRR:PHS; "Question Attitude on Lynch Measure," *Pittsburgh Courier*, October 18, 1937. Though the CWCRR minutes list the ASWPL as one

of the organizations that participated in the distribution of the flyers, it is more likely that flyers were sent to organizational leaders but not widely distributed to the members. Jessie Daniel Ames and the ASWPL did not support the national anti-lynching campaign for congressional legislation.

354 *She became more:* CWCRR, "Minutes," October 8, November 26, 1928, FCC-CWCRR:PHS.

355 *During the late 1930s:* CWCRR "Minutes," February 25, 1929; April 28, 1930; January 30, 1933, FCC-CWCRR:PHS; CWCRR, "Draft," undated typescript statement in support of the ASWPL, ibid. To avoid working with the CWCRR—especially northern women in the FCC—Southern Baptist church women developed a cooperative arrangement with Nannie Helen Burroughs and the NBC-USA's Woman's Convention. Haynes, *Toward Interracial Peace*, chapter 6, p. 6. In 1939, the CWCRR, working cooperatively with southern Methodist women, surveyed black health facilities and health conditions throughout the South. The collaboration opened up an opportunity for Katherine Gardner to speak to groups of interested women in Arkansas, Mississippi, and Tennessee who became advocates of better health care for African Americans. For information related to the Scottsboro case, see Dan Carter, *Scottsboro: A Tragedy of the American South* (Baton Rouge, La.: Louisiana State University Press, 1969). In 1931 nine young black men were arrested, jailed, and sentenced to death in Scottsboro, Alabama, on charges of raping two white women on a freight train. The case received international attention. Numerous organizations, such as the CIC Women's Committee, the NACW, and the YWCA, supported the efforts of the International Labor Defense, the NAACP, and the Communist Party in protesting and overturning the court's verdict.

355 *Few southern churches:* "Excerpts from the Minutes of the Meeting of the Committee on Women's Work, June 8–9, 1939, at Swarthmore College," Box 1, CWU:GCAH.

356 *However, it was also:* The Commission on the Church and Race Relations, *Church Women at Work on the Race Problem* (New York: Federal Council of Churches of Christ, 1928), 5–8; CWCRR, "Minutes," February 28, 1927; September 25, 1928; September 25, 1933, FCC-CWCRR:PHS; CWCRR, "Report of the Special Committee on Techniques," undated typescript, ibid.

356 *At the same time:* Haynes, *Toward Interracial Peace*, chapter 6, p. 2.

356 *As a tactical move:* Because of its relationship to the FCC, the CWCRR was able to persuade the National Commission of Protestant Church Women to table its plans to establish interracial committees throughout the U.S. and to organize its activities under the aegis of the CWCRR. For discussion related to this, see CWCRR, "Minutes," April 29, June 24, 1929, FCC-CWCRR:PHS; for other examples of efforts to coordinate the CWCRR's race relations program with other women's organizations see CWCRR, "Minutes," April 28, 1930; May 25, 1931; March 28, 1932, ibid.

358 *Haynes also thought:* Haynes, *Toward Interracial Peace*, chapter 6, p. 5; CWCRR, "Minutes," May 23, 1932; May 7, 1934; September 28, 1936; March 28, September 26, 1938; May 13, November 15, November 25, 1940; March 31, May 12, 1941, FCC-CWCRR:PHS; Collier-Thomas and Franklin, eds., *Sisters in the Struggle*, 26–27.

358 *To some extent:* Haynes, *Toward Interracial Peace*, chapter 6, p. 8.

358 *The CWCRR could:* CWCRR, "Minutes," September 29, 1930; January 26, 1931, FCC-CWCRR:PHS.

359 *In spite of all:* In 1936 the FCC created the Woman's Co-operating Commission

solely for the purpose of building support among women for the FCC budget and defending its program. While women endorsed the WCC, its program did not appear to include their thinking. See Gladys Gilkey Calkins, *Follow Those Women: Church Women in the Ecumenical Movement: A History of the Development of United Work Among Women of the Protestant Churches in the United States* (New York: National Council of the Churches of Christ, 1961), 56.

359 *In many ways:* Katherine Gardner to Mrs. Josephine Humbles Kyles, January 26, 1942, FCC-CWCRR:PHS. In her letter of resignation from the CWCRR, Gardner states that "perhaps the most important thing our committee has done is to increase the number of churchwomen who realize the need for interracial work and who are trying to do something about it."

359 *The CWCRR voted:* CWCRR, "Minutes," January 26, 1942, FCC-CWCRR:PHS.

360 *He also said:* FCC, "Administrative Committee, Department of Race Relations Meeting on February 4, 1942," FCC-DRR:PHS; CWCRR, "Minutes," March 23, 1942, FCC-CWCRR:PHS.

360 *In October 1942:* CWCRR, "Minutes," March 23, May 22, October 6, 1942, FCC-CWCRR:PHS.

360 *Cavert also informed:* Louise Young to Dr. Samuel McCrea Cavert, November 11, 1943, FCC:PHS; Dr. Samuel McCrea Cavert to Miss Louise Young, November 18, 1943, ibid.

360 *In that year:* Federal Council of the Churches of Christ, *Annual Report* (New York: Federal Council of the Churches of Christ, 1948), 342.

361 *"American Christianity is brutal":* "Negro's Path a Thorny One," *Indianapolis Freeman*, December 19, 1896. See also David Wills, "Reverdy C. Ransom: The Making of an A.M.E. Bishop," in *Black Apostles: Afro-American Clergy Confront the Twentieth Century* (Boston: G. K. Hall, 1978); Calvin Sylvester Morris, "Reverdy C. Ransom: A Pioneer Black Social Gospeler" (PhD dissertation, Boston University, 1982).

361 *"What bearing has":* Richard H. Bowling, "The Guide Post," *Norfolk Journal and Guide*, February 3, 1934.

362 *The organization rapidly:* "Negroes to Form Federal Council of Churches," *Pittsburgh Courier*, January 20, 1934; "Henderson Says Clergy Should Study Federation Plans," ibid., February 3, 1934; "Church Federation Is Organized in Chicago," ibid., September 1, 1934; "6,000,000 in 5 Church Bodies Under One Head—Denominations Form World's Largest Negro Denomination," *Norfolk Journal and Guide*, September 4, 1934. Similarly, frustration with the conservatism of the Foreign Missions Council of North America led to the founding of an all-black organization by the black Baptists and Methodists' denominational secretaries of missions. See "Mission Heads Elect Officers," *Pittsburgh Courier*, February 5, 1944. The CME, the Central Jurisdiction of the Methodist Church, and the African Orthodox, Freewill Baptist, COGIC, and Apostolic churches later affiliated with the organization. During its heyday, the council represented seven million members. See William J. Walls, *The African Methodist Episcopal Zion Church* (Charlotte: AME Zion Publishing House, 1974), 490–91.

362 *Weighing in on:* For discussion of the Fraternal Council of Negro Churches, the first black ecumenical organization, see "Has Negro Church the Vision to Speak with a United Voice?" *Pittsburgh Courier*, January 26, 1935; "Bishop Ransom Makes Plea to Organized Denominations in the United States," ibid., July 13, 1935; Reverdy C. Ransom, *The Pilgrimage of Harriet Ransom's Son* (Nashville:

AME Sunday School Union, 1949), 269, 296–300. For basic details on its founding and history, see Larry G. Murphy, J. Gordon Melton, and Gary L. Ward, eds., *Encyclopedia of African American Religions* (New York: Garland Publishing, Inc., 1993), 543; David W. Wills, "An Enduring Distance: Black Americans and the Establishment," in *Between the Times: The Travail of the Protestant Establishment in America, 1900–1960*, ed. William R. Hutchison (New York: Cambridge University Press, 1989), 186–88; Spurgeon E. Crayton, "The History and Theology of the National Fraternal Council of Negro Churches" (M.Div. thesis, Union Theological Seminary, New York, 1979); for a brief history of the FCNC, see Mary R. Sawyer, *Black Ecumenism: Implementing the Demands of Justice* (Valley Forge, Pa.: Trinity Press, 1994), 15–34. See also Barbara Dianne Savage, "Biblical and Historical Imperatives: Toward a History of Ideas About the Political Role of Black Churches," in *African Americans and the Bible: Sacred Texts and Social Textures*, ed. Vincent L. Wimbush (New York: Continuum, 2000), 378–79.

362 *Having observed that:* "Council of Negro Church Women Meet," *Pittsburgh Courier*, April 25, 1931.

362 *The organization, open:* "The Fraternal Council of Negro Churches Holds Annual Meeting," *Star of Zion*, September 3, 1936. By 1936, the FCNC numbers had swelled with the addition of the Union AME Church, the Central Jurisdiction of the Methodist Episcopal Church, and the Congregational churches.

363 *For example, in addition:* "Chicago Churches Form Interdenominational Council," *Kansas Plaindealer*, April 4, 1941. The diversity of organizations represented in the Chicago Council reflected the ways in which African American religion had changed in Chicago as a result of the Great Migration. An excellent source for examining these changes is Wallace D. Best, *Passionately Human: No Less Divine* (Princeton: Princeton University Press, 2005).

363 *Women were highly:* "The Fraternal Council of Negro Churches Holds Annual Meeting"; "Church Federation Is Organized"; "Church Council Plans Militant Program," *Pittsburgh Courier*, September 21, 1946; "Church Council Launches Drive," ibid., April 9, 1949; Bishop Reverdy C. Ransom, "Bishop Ransom Makes Plea to Organized Negro Denominations in the United States," ibid., July 13, 1935; "Religious Co-operation to Claim Attention of Leaders at Washington Gathering," ibid., April 30, 1938; for reference to women serving on the original "executive committee," attempts to organize a women's auxiliary, and the role of women in the late 1940s and '50s, see B. H. Logan, "Around the World with the White Churches," ibid., June 4, 1949; and Mary R. Sawyer, "Black Religion and Social Change: Women in Leadership Roles," in Larry G. Murphy, ed., *Down by the Riverside: Readings in African American Religion* (New York: New York University Press, 2000), 307–08. For biographical data on Dr. Dorothy Boulding Ferebee and Jane Spaulding, see Margaret Bernice Smith Bristow, "Dorothy Boulding Ferebee," in *Notable Black American Women, Book II*, ed. Jessie Carney Smith (New York: Gale Research, 1996), 340–42; Patsy B. Perry, "Jane Morrow Spaulding," ibid., 609–12.

364 *The FCC's reluctance:* Sawyer, *Black Ecumenism*, 4, 16; Walls, *The African Methodist Episcopal Zion Church*, 486–87.

364 *Frazier argued that:* Quoted in Roberts, "Crucible for a Vision," 221.

365 *"sectarian feuding":* "Confusion in Fraternal Council of Negro Churches," *Christian Index*, May 22, 1947. For an excellent discussion of the issues surrounding the demise of the FCNC, see Sawyer, *Black Ecumenism*, 30–31.

365 *During the late 1940s:* "AME Bishops Back Lobby Plan," *Kansas Plaindealer*, March 7, 1941; "Church Council Votes to Continue D.C. Bureau," *Chicago Defender*, February 3, 1945.

365 *Though the FCNC:* Murphy, Melton, and Ward, eds., *Encyclopedia of African American Religions*, 543.

CHAPTER 7 *"Womanpower"—Religion, Race, Gender*

367 *In doing so:* At its founding, Church Women United was known as the United Council of Church Women. In 1950, the UCCW became the General Department of United Church Women of the National Council of Churches. In 1966 the UCW withdrew from the NCC to resume its autonomous national existence, and became Church Women United. For the purpose of this discussion and to avoid confusion, Church Women United or CWU is used throughout this book. For histories of the organization, see Gladys Gilkey Calkins, *Follow Those Women: Church Women in the Ecumenical Movement: A History of the Development of United Work Among Women of the Protestant Churches in the United States* (New York: National Council of the Churches of Christ, 1961); Margaret Shannon, *Just Because: The Story of the National Movement of Church Women United in the U.S.A., 1941 through 1975* (Corte Madera, Calif.: Omega Books, 1977); 1950 figures for CWU as cited in "A Call to Daily Prayer Issued," *Star of Zion*, December 14, 1950; also see Susan Hill Lindley, *"You Have Stept Out of Your Place": A History of Women and Religion in America* (Louisville, Ky.: Westminister John Knox, 1996), 307; Virginia Lieson Brereton, "United and Slighted: Women as Subordinated Insiders," in *The Travail of the Protestant Establishment in America, 1900–1960*, ed. William R. Hutchison (New York: Cambridge University Press, 1989), 151–64; Susan M. Hartmann, *The Other Feminists: Activists in the Liberal Establishment* (New Haven: Yale University Press, 1998), 92–131.

367 *"movement is destined":* NBC, *Proceedings of the Sixty-sixth Annual Session of the National Baptist Convention, U.S.A., Held in Atlanta, Georgia, September 4–8, 1946* (Nashville: Sunday School Publishing Board, 1947), 332.

368 *Women were not afforded:* The ratification of the Nineteenth Amendment in 1920 enfranchised all women. However, in the South, legal segregation and racial intimidation restricted black women's access to the ballot.

368 *"had a larger potential":* Calkins, *Follow Those Women*, 55.

368 *"Women are ready":* Ibid.

368 *"even in so liberal":* Calkins, *Follow Those Women*, 56.

369 *"I have always contended":* Nannie Helen Burroughs, "The Dawn of a New Day in Dixie," *The Worker* 8:39 (July–September, 1943): 6–8.

369 *Most immediately:* Calkins, *Follow Those Women*, 52–53; the National Council of Federated Church Women was also known as the National Committee of Church Women.

370 *This included Jewish:* For example, in 1934 the National Council of Federated Church Women reported that its Race Relations Committee had sent letters to all state presidents urging them to appoint committees on race relations and had received initial replies from New England and Southern California. The California chapters sent telegrams to Governor Rolph of California and President Franklin D. Roosevelt regarding the impact of the Laundry Code on black women. The NCFCW also sent telegrams to Indiana senators urging their support for the Costigan-Wagner Anti-Lynching Bill. All NCFCW state leaders were asked to have their members send letters to their congressmen urging their

support for the bill. Mrs. William F. Rothenburger, "Report of Race Relations Committee," National Council of Federated Church Women, Sixth Annual Conference, May 17, 1934, Kansas City, Mo., Box 1, Church Women United Collection, General Commission on Archives and History, United Methodist Church (hereafter cited as CWU-GCAH); "Excerpts from the Minutes of the National Committee of Church Women," October 3 and 4, 1939, Box 1, CWU-GCAH. At this time Jewish persons were not considered white, but were referenced as a racial minority along with African Americans, Asians, Native Americans, and other nonwhite groups.

370 *Some of these women:* There were interracial city and state women's councils and federations throughout the North and Midwest that worked closely with the CWCRR. For example, in 1934 the Oakland, California, Council of Church Women voted unanimously to support the Costigan-Wagner Anti-Lynching Bill. This council represented two thousand white and one hundred black church women. Noted black journalist Delilah L. Beasley served as the head of the council's Department of International and Race Relations for a number of years. "California Church Women Back the Anti-Lynch Bill," *Pittsburgh Courier*, March 31, 1934.

370 *For example, the NACW:* In 1940 the YWCA Interracial Committee, in conjunction with the Phyllis Wheatley YWCA (black), conducted a study of women domestic workers in the District of Columbia to determine the characteristics of the employees, pay scales, and the conditions under which they worked. Studies like this were used to define social and political actions for improving the economic and social conditions confronting women workers. See Grace Fox, "Women Domestic Workers in Washington, D.C., 1940," *Monthly Labor Review* 54:2 (February 1942): 338–59; The NACW Department of Inter-Racial Relations was established in 1927 during the presidency of Mary McLeod Bethune. "Our Seven-Plank Platform," *National Notes* 28:5 (January 1927): frontispiece.

370 *It was as if:* Letter to Miss Louise Young from Dr. Samuel McCrea Cavert, November 18, 1943, FCC:PHS.

370 *From the outset:* "A Proposed Plan for a National Organization of Church Women," September 11, 1940, Box 1, CWU:GCAH.

371 *Beginning with her:* The Paine College summer Leadership Training School was sponsored by the MECS in cooperation with CME women. For discussion of Tilly and the Leadership Training School, see Mrs. L. D. McAfee, *History of the Woman's Missionary Society in the Colored Methodist Episcopal Church* (Phoenix City, Ala.: Phoenix City Herald, 1945), 158–68; for information regarding the impact of the school conducted by the Methodist women at Paine College, see M. E. Tilly, "Unity in Action in the Southland," *Church Woman* 5:12 (October 1939): 19–20.

371 *In 1949, Tilly:* For a brief sketch of Dorothy Tilly (also known as Mrs. M. E. Tilly), see Brereton, "United and Slighted," 152; also, see Barbara Sicherman et al., *Notable American Women: The Modern Period: A Biographical Dictionary*, vol. 4 (Cambridge, Mass.: Harvard University Press, 1980), 691–93; Edith Holbrook Riehm, "Dorothy Tilly and the Fellowship of the Concerned," in *Throwing Off the Cloak of Privilege: White Southern Women Activists in the Civil Rights Era*, ed. Gail S. Murray (Gainesville, Fla.: University Press of Florida, 2004), 23–43.

371 *Discussions of this:* Anna Arnold Hedgeman, *The Trumpet Sounds: A Memoir of Negro Leadership* (New York: Holt, Rinehart and Winston, 1964), 52. Representative Abraham J. Multer of New York explained to Congress that "the use of the word integration in connection with our schools and other areas of life has been

unfortunate, since to many that term has become synonymous with amalgamation of the races." Quoted in *Congressional Record*, January 30, 1958, Claude A. Barnett Papers, Series J, Religion 1924–1966, Reel 1 (hereafter cited as CAB-J).

372 *"Fears of personal"*: "Eliminate Fear of Racial Intermarriage," *Christian Index*, September 12, 1946. In *An American Dilemma*, Gunnar Myrdal found that the "chief fear" of whites in America was intermarriage of blacks and whites. See Gunnar Myrdal, *An American Dilemma: The Negro Problem and American Democracy* (New York: Harper and Bros., 1944).

372 *"[T]he white man"*: Myrdal, *An American Dilemma*.

372 *Schuyler asserted that:* George S. Schuyler, "Views and Reviews," *Pittsburgh Courier*, January 23, 1943.

373 *Most of these:* The most vocal black critics were members of the Fraternal Council of Negro Churches, which included Bishop Reverdy C. Ransom and other male leaders of mostly the black Methodist and Baptist denominations.

373 *However, in deference:* For a discussion of discrimination in the women's suffrage movement, see Rosalyn Terborg-Penn, *African American Women in the Struggle for the Vote, 1850–1920* (Bloomington: Indiana University Press, 1998).

374 *"Protestant expression"*: In 1932 Marion Cuthbert, a graduate of the University of Minnesota, former dean of women at Talladega College, and a PhD student at Columbia University, was appointed to a newly created position in the YWCA leadership division. As the head of the "Colored Leadership Division," Cuthbert had direct responsibility for national training and development of volunteer and professional leadership, including local associations and branches. In consultation with National Board staff members, Cuthbert was charged with the selection of staff for placement in local associations and the recommendation of branch secretaries. This required evaluation of branch leadership needs through the organization of conferences, seminars, and training courses. For biographical information on Cuthbert, see "New Y.W.C.A. Worker," *Washington Tribune*, June 10, 1932; "New Leader of Y.W.C.A. Named," *Pittsburgh Courier*, May 28, 1932; "Miss M. Cuthbert to Head New 'Y' Work," *New York Age*, May 21, 1932. As a member of the YWCA National Board for twelve years (1932–1944), Cuthbert gained national visibility. During the 1940s, having earned a PhD in sociology, Cuthbert became the first black scholar hired to teach at Brooklyn College, New York. She was a member of the NAACP National Board, the National Council of Religion and Higher Education, and the Assembly Committee of the Federal Council of the Churches of Christ. See J. A. Rogers, "Your History," *Pittsburgh Courier*, April 7, 1945.

374 *The willingness of many:* Marion Cuthbert, "The Role of the Young Women's Christian Association," in *The Christian Way in Race Relations*, ed. William Stuart Nelson (New York: Harper and Brothers, 1948), 166, 177.

374 *"We just kept talking"*: Sharlene Voogd Cochrane, " 'And the Pressure Never Let Up': Black Women, White Women, and the Boston YWCA, 1918–1948," in *Women in the Civil Rights Movement: Trailblazers and Torchbearers, 1941–1965*, ed. Vicki L. Crawford, Jacqueline Anne Rouse, and Barbara Woods (Brooklyn: Carlson Publishing, 1990), 266–68.

375 *And, given the YWCA's:* In a historical overview of the first four years of the growth and development of the YWCA among black women, Addie Hunton observed, "It is not strange, therefore, that many of the intelligent colored women have been quick to discern the magnificent opportunity offered by this movement for the solution to their problems." See Mrs. W. A. Hunton, "Women's Clubs," *Crisis* 1:10 (October 1911): 121.

375 *Philosophically speaking:* Juliet O. Bell and Helen J. Wilkins, *Interracial Practices in Community Y.W.C.A.'s* (New York: National Board, Y.W.C.A., 1944), 2.

375 *Following the 1906:* Ibid., 2–3. In 1906 the YWCA National Board was established under the leadership of Grace Dodge.

376 *Also, in addition:* "Reception to Mrs. Hunton," *New York Age*, June 13, 1907; "Y.W.C.A. Growing," ibid., August 20, 1908; Elizabeth Wilson, *Fifty Years of Association Work Among Young Women* (New York: YWCA National Board, 1916), 271. Addie Hunton attended the Boston Latin Grammar School and the Spencerian Business College in Philadelphia, and received degrees from Heidelberg and Kaiser-Wilhelm universities in Germany. For biographical information on Hunton, see "Mrs. Addie Hunton Is Taken by Death," *Amsterdam News*," June 26, 1943, and "Mrs. Addie W. Hunton, Noted Civic Leader of Brooklyn, Succumbs," *New York Age*, June 19, 1943. For the quote regarding the NACW/ YWCA relationship, see Jane Olcott, comp., *The Work of Colored Women* (New York: National Board YWCA, 1919), 11–12. For a discussion of Hunton's initial work with the YWCA, the Ross report, and the question of why black women affiliated and worked with the YWCA in spite of its racism, see Judith Weisenfeld, *African American Women and Christian Activism: New York's Black YWCA, 1905–1945* (Cambridge, Mass.: Harvard University Press, 1997), 55, 9–14. For an assessment of how black women leaders viewed the YWCA, its relationship to the varied organizational work of black women, and its significance as an interdenominational association that could attract women from all religions and sections of a city, see Betty G. Francis, "The Colored Young Women's Christian Association of Washington," *Colored American Magazine* 10:2 (February 1906): 126–29.

377 *Some of the YWCA's:* W. E. B. Du Bois, "Intermarriage," *Crisis* 5:4 (February 1913): 180. Du Bois explained that although black Americans were forced by their circumstances into a "cruel dilemma . . . [n]evertheless they must not allow anger or personal resentment to dim their clear vision." While white people "profess to see but one problem: 'Do you want your sister to marry a Nigger!,' " black problems were defined by disenfranchisement, segregation and discrimination in public accommodations, lynching, and other threats to their "public security." Cochrane, " 'And the Pressure Never Let Up,' " 266–68.

377 *Summing up the philosophy:* Victoria Graham, "Negro Women to the Front," *Indianapolis Freeman*, April 6, 1907.

378 *She asserted:* " 'Over Here' with the Y.W.C.A.," *Washington Bee*, May 25, 1918.

378 *"highest development":* For an understanding of Hope's role in transforming the YWCA, see the following petitions and letters: Petition to "The National Board of the Young Women's Christian Association New York City," on behalf of "300,000 Negro women of the South," ca. 1915, submitted by Mrs. John Hope, Chairman, n.d., the Neighborhood Union Collection, Atlanta University, Woodruff Library (hereafter cited as NUCAU), Mrs. John Hope to Eva D. Bowles, March 15, 1922, NUC; "Minutes of the Conference," April 6, 1920, ibid.

378 *Between 1915:* Hope to Bowles, March 15, 1922, ibid.; Jacqueline A. Rouse, "Hope, Lugenia Burns (1871–1947)," in *Black Women in America: An Historical Encyclopedia*, vol. 1, ed. Darlene Clark Hine (Brooklyn: Carlson Publishing, 1993), 574.

379 *Black branch secretaries:* Hope, Petition to "The National Board of the Young Women's Christian Association New York City," on behalf of "300,000 Negro women of the South"; "Minutes of the Conference, April 6, 1920," NUCAU; "Minutes of the Meeting of the South Atlantic Field Committee, Richmond, Virginia, July 5, 1920," ibid.; Bell and Wilkins, *Interracial Practices*, 4.

379 *By 1920 black women:* Handwritten note attached to the 1915 "Petition to the National Board," submitted by Lugenia Hope, NUCAU; "Elect Mrs. Haynes to Nat[ional] Y.W.C.A. Board," *Chicago Defender*, May 17, 1924.

379 *During World War I:* "War Work Among Colored Girls and Women," *Women's International Quarterly* 8:1 (October 1918): 61. The YWCA set aside $200,000 of the National War Work Council's $5 million budget for the expansion of its work with black women during World War I. This money was used to provide staff for Hostess Houses frequented by the families of black troops, emergency housing for African American women in war industrial centers, and employment of field-workers to recruit and prepare women for the numerous industrial job openings.

379 *Southern white delegates objected:* "Women Workers Jim Crowed in Cleveland," *Baltimore Afro-American*, April 30, 1920.

380 *Specifically, the YWCA:* Bell and Wilkins, *Interracial Practices*, 5–9; for discussion of the Council of Colored Work, see also " 'Y' Work Among Women," *New York Age*, December 26, 1926; Ruth Logan Roberts, Howard University Dean of Women Lucy Slowe, and AME leader Emma S. Ransom were among the black women appointed to important committees and who served on the Council of Colored Work. The purpose of the council was to study the history of African Americans; to discuss race problems "frankly and with unbiased minds"; to use their influence to cooperate with all agencies and individuals to implement their agenda; and to launch a nationwide anti-lynching educational campaign for passage and enforcement of legislation and the creation of public opinion supportive of the eradication of mob violence and lynching in the United States.

380 *Instead, they formed:* The Fraternal Council of Negro Churches was founded in 1934 by AME Bishop Reverdy C. Ransom, a long-standing critic of the interracial movement. The organization declined in the 1960s as the Civil Rights Movement and other African American Christian organizations such as the National Conference of Black Churchmen and the Southern Christian Leadership Conference came into existence.

381 *Also, the NACW:* Bethune's correspondence to Eleanor Roosevelt after President Roosevelt's death reveals the nature of the friendship. See Bethune correspondence in the National Archives for Black Women's History, Mary McLeod Bethune Council House National Historic Site.

382 *"In the life":* Bell and Wilkins, *Interracial Practices*, 9–10; "YWCA Report Advocates Segregation Elimination," *Pittsburgh Courier*, May 6, 1944.

382 *By unanimous vote:* "Women's Parley Votes for Full Integration," *Chicago Defender*, March 16, 1946; George Edmund Haynes, "Along the Interracial Front," *Messenger*, July 1946, 4; Cuthbert, "The Role of the Young Women's Christian Association," 164.

382 *This would be:* For a discussion of the opposition the YWCA confronted in getting the Interracial Charter adopted and its efforts to implement the recommendations in the document, see Dorothy Height, *Open Wide the Freedom Gates* (New York: PublicAffairs, 2003), 117–20.

383 *Given that many:* Ibid., 112–29; see also Dorothy I. Height, *Step by Step with Interracial Groups* (New York: Woman's Press, 1946).

383 *The competition for:* Charles [S.] Johnson, "Fifty Years of Progress in Social Development," *Pittsburgh Courier*, September 30, 1950.

384 *In the midst:* "Troops Bring Truce to Riot-Torn Detroit," *Amsterdam News*, June 26, 1943; " 'Race Riot' Hits Atlantic City," and "Plain Talk," ibid., July 10, 1943; "Push Couple off 'Bama Bus Then Shoot One," ibid., July 19, 1943; "Detroit Fact Finding Board Probing Riots Hits Negro Leaders and Press, Declare Disor-

ders Were Not Premeditated," *Kansas Plaindealer*, August 20, 1943; see also John Hope Franklin, *From Slavery to Freedom: A History of Negro Americans*, 5th ed. (New York: Alfred A. Knopf, 1980), 397, 442–43.

384 *The demand for:* For a discussion and analysis of the effects of World War II on American women's lives during and after the 1940s, see Susan M. Hartmann, *The Home Front and Beyond: American Women in the 1940s* (Boston, Mass.: Twayne Publishers, 1982).

384 *Employed in a variety:* NBC, *Proceedings of the Forty-fourth Annual Session of the Woman's Convention, Auxiliary to the National Baptist Convention, Held in Detroit, Michigan, September 5–9, 1945* (Nashville: Sunday School Publishing Board, 1945), 341; and L. Baynard Whitney, "Calvin's Digest," *Kansas Plaindealer*, October 8, 1943.

385 *Blanche Williams Anderson:* "First Ladies of Colored America," *Crisis* 49:9 (September 1942): 321, 143, 290.

386 *However, Alpha Kappa Alpha:* For discussion of AKA's political activities, see Bettye Collier-Thomas and V. P. Franklin, eds., *Sisters in the Struggle: African American Women in the Civil Rights–Black Power Movement* (New York: New York University, 2001), 28–34; see also Susan M. Hartmann, *The Home Front and Beyond*, 147–48.

386 *Claiming its religious:* For quotation regarding AKA and Christianity, see Brenda Ray Moryck, "Just a Message to My Sisters," *Ivy Leaf* 2:1 (1922–1923): 47.

386 *From the beginning:* For quotation, see Lorraine Richardson Green, "Message of the Supreme Basileus," *Ivy Leaf* 1:1 (December 1921): 3–4.

386 *Green worked closely:* Ibid.; "Alpha Kappa Alpha Sorority Will Live Forever!" *Ivy Leaf* 74:1 (spring 1996): 57.

387 *Thomasina Johnson Norford:* Collier-Thomas and Franklin, eds., *Sisters in the Struggle*, 28–34. In 1947, Thomasina Johnson Norford, the chief of the minority group section of the United States Employment Service (USES), was invited by Christine Smith, president of the AME Woman's Missionary Society, to speak about postwar employment conditions and the role of USES in resolving issues of employment discrimination faced by blacks and women; see "AME Women Hear Labor Expert on Jobs," *Pittsburgh Courier*, August 6, 1947.

387 *During the 1940s:* "Justifies Greek Letter Societies," *Norfolk Journal and Guide*, February 17, 1934; "Our Skirts Not Always Clean, Says Sorority," *People's Voice*, November 3, 1945.

387 *Spelman, Hartshorn, and other:* Evelyn Brooks Higginbotham, *Righteous Discontent: The Women's Movement in the Black Baptist Church, 1880–1920* (Cambridge, Mass.: Harvard University Press, 1993), 22, 24.

387 *The missionaries worked:* Ibid., 197–98; For a discussion of the Woman's Missionary Union of the Southern Baptist Convention, especially its relationship to the Woman's Convention of the National Baptist Convention, see Paul Harvey, "Saints but Not Subordinates: The Woman's Missionary Union of the Southern Baptist Convention," in *Women and Twentieth-Century Protestantism*, ed. Margaret Lamberts Bendroth and Virginia Lieson Brereton (Urbana, Ill.: University of Illinois Press, 2002), 4–21. Though WMU leaders initiated the contact with the WC and brokered an agreement, the work was carried on under the auspices of the male-dominated Home Mission Board of the Southern Baptist Convention. Like the WC, the WMU was an auxiliary to the board. For a discussion of the history of the Home Mission Board's work with African Americans between 1900 and 1934 see Una Roberts Lawrence, *The Negro Woman and Her Needs* (Birmingham, Ala.: Woman's Missionary Union, ca. 1938), 12; Nannie H. Bur-

roughs to Una Roberts Lawrence, May 24, 1932, Box 1, Folder 27, "Black Missions," Una Roberts Lawrence Resource Files, Home Mission Board Records, Southern Baptist Historical Library, Nashville, Tennessee (hereafter cited as URL-SBHL).

388 *For example:* For a definition and discussion of biracial work, see chapter 6, "Interracial vs. Biracial Work: Tensions Between Southern and Northern Women." Lily H. Hammond, *Southern Women and Racial Adjustment* (Lynchburg, Va.: J. P. Bell, 1917), 14–15. For evaluation and quotation regarding the WMU's work with CWU, see Harvey, "Saints but Not Subordinates," 17.

390 *In 1933 the WC:* In response to the burgeoning interracial movement, especially the women's meetings and conferences initiated by the CWCRR, in 1933 the WMU invited the WC to join them in a program of "Christian Interracial Cooperation." The WC accepted the WMU's Seven-Point Home Missions Program, which included WMU financial support and sponsorship of leadership training institutes, Sunday School training classes, and missionary study classes; a study of black contributions; sponsorship of joint lecture programs in black and white churches; and preparation and publication of *The Worker*, a missionary and educational quarterly established in 1912 by Nannie Helen Burroughs, president of the National Training School for Women and Girls. For discussion of the program, see *The Worker* 3:10 (April–June, 1936): 3; ibid. 8:35 (July–September 1942): 78–79; ibid. 17:82 (October–December 1954): 88–89; ibid. 21:95 (January—March, 1958): 129.

390 *In the morning:* Mrs. F. H. Bancroft to Una Roberts Lawrence, July 10, 1936, Box 5, Folder 28, "Black Missions," URL-SBHL; Olivia Davis to Una Roberts Lawrence, June 20, 1936, ibid. To improve the skills of their servants and other women who were planning to enter "service," WMU state leaders donated funds to black colleges to support domestic science departments. In 1918 and 1919 the South Carolina WMU gave Morris College a total of $700 to support the salary of a domestic science teacher. See Vonnie E. Lance to Una Roberts Lawrence, June 29, 1936, Box 5, Folder 28, "Black Missions," URL-SBHL.

391 *"It would mean everything":* Una Roberts Lawrence to Nannie H. Burroughs, June 23, 1934, Box 5, Folder 28, "Black Missions," URL-SBHL. A copy of the July–September 1934 issue of *The Worker* could not be located.

391 *"underprivileged people":* Nannie H. Burroughs to Una Roberts Lawrence, July 2, 1934, Box 1, Folder 27, URL-SBHL.

392 *"God has been too good":* Nannie H. Burroughs, "Editorials," *The Worker* 2:6 (April–June 1935): 4–9.

392 *Lawrence stated that:* Una Roberts Lawrence to Nannie H. Burroughs, June 19, 1935, Box 18, NHB-LC.

392 *"I love your race":* Nannie H. Burroughs to Una Roberts Lawrence, June 29, 1935, Box 31, Folder 27, "Black Missions," URL-SBHL.

392 *However, Burroughs's scathing:* A survey of *The Worker* between 1935 and 1942 reveals that Nannie Burroughs allowed Una Roberts Lawrence and the WMU to take control of the publication and use it for their purposes. Lawrence's name is no longer listed as a contributor after 1942. See *The Worker* 8:37 (January–March 1943). Burroughs's editorial in the next issue signals her new freedom. See Nannie Helen Burroughs, "Editorial," ibid., 6–8. For examples of Burroughs's commentary on American racism, see "Nannie Warns National Against 5th Column J.[im] C.[row]," *Baltimore Afro-American*, September 21, 1940; "Eating in Public Places Is Not Social Equality, Insists Nannie Burroughs," ibid., May 12, 1934; "You Ask, 'How Does It Feel?' Well, Here Is Your Answer,"

Chicago Defender, August 6, 1938; "The High Cost of Being a Negro," ibid., November 12, 1938.

393 *Unfortunately, the WMU:* See NBC, *Journal of the Fifty-fourth Session of the National Baptist Convention and the Thirty-fourth Annual Session of the Woman's Convention Auxiliary, Held in Oklahoma City, Oklahoma, September 5–9, 1934* (Nashville: Sunday School Publishing Board, 1934), 257, 262. See also Una Roberts Lawrence, "A Greeting to the Woman's Auxiliary of the National Baptist Convention," *The Worker* 1:4 (October–December 1934): 10–13. Historian Nancy Hewitt describes a similar relational pattern that existed between white and black women in Tampa, Florida. Hewitt asserts, "Well-to-do Black women maligned the abilities of their working-class counterparts in order to garner white support for an educational endeavor to train domestics." See Nancy Hewitt, *Southern Discomfort: Women's Activism in Tampa Florida, 1880s-1920s* (Urbana, Ill.: University of Illinois Press, 2001), 168. In May 1935, on a CBS nationally syndicated program, the Rev. John M. Cooper, a white professor of anthropology at the Catholic University, described in stark detail the major factors responsible for what he termed the "interracial wolfishness" of white religionists whose assumption of physical and mental superiority undergirded the interracial movement of the 1920s and '30s. Cooper explained that blacks were no longer interested in "interracial charity. . . . The American Negro is increasingly asking, not for charity and philanthropy, but for justice." See John M. Cooper, "Religion and the Race Problem," *Crisis* 42:6 (June 1935): 170, 178.

393 *Burroughs indicated that:* The Worker 4:14 (April–June, 1937): 3.

393 *The Department of Leadership:* Fletcher Mae Howell, "In Missionary Perspective," *Mission Herald* 47:5 (March–April, 1944): 18; "Baptist White Women Join Black Women in Christian Cooperation," *Chicago Defender*, April 18, 1942.

393 *As a result:* "Baptists Open Fellowship Center Here," *Pittsburgh Courier*, January 27, 1945; Sadie T. M. Alexander, "Fellowship," *The Church Woman* 9:3 (March 1943): 15.

393 *The Philadelphia Race:* Alexander, "Fellowship."

395 *Sara Estelle Haskin:* In 1920, as a member of the MECS Executive Committee, Haskin put forward the motion to create the commission that initiated the meeting at Tuskegee with NACW leaders and led to the establishment of the CIC Woman's Committee, which included black women. McAfee, *History of the Woman's Missionary Society*, 175–78. For a discussion of the role of Haskin, the MECS, and the CIC in the interracial movement, see chapter 6; "Race Pool Efforts to Establish Center," *Pittsburgh Courier*, January 11, 1936; "Bethlehem House in Augusta," *Christian Index*, January 6, 1938. For discussion of the settlement movement see chapter 2.

395 *White women who:* McAfee, *History of the Woman's Missionary Society*, 175–77.

395 *Frederickson argues that:* Mary Frederickson, " 'Each One Is Dependent on the Other': Southern Churchwomen, Racial Reform, and the Process of Transformation, 1880–1940," in *Visible Women: New Essays on American Activism*, ed. Nancy A. Hewitt and Suzanne Lebsock (Urbana, Ill.: University of Illinois Press, 1993), 297.

395 *The relational pattern:* In 1957, in the wake of the Civil Rights Movement, Burroughs, as president of the WC, announced that the time had come for the WC to rethink the traditional program and relationship it had with the ABHMS and the WMU and develop a plan of "Understanding and Cooperation." She stressed the need for white women to unite and work with black women "on the kind of program that will teach both races how to work—together—jointly, in America

and in other lands." Burroughs suggested that the time had come for white women to stop working for black women and begin working with black women as equals. See: NBC, *The Record of the 77th Annual Session of the National Baptist Convention and the Woman's Convention Auxiliary, Held in Louisville, Kentucky, September 3–8, 1957* (Nashville: Sunday School Publishing Board, 1957), 309.

396 *In supporting educational:* Higginbotham, *Righteous Discontent*, 197. Since white women had access to white male leaders at all levels of the society, black Baptist women perceived them as essential conduits for achieving their civil rights agenda. At its annual meeting in 1916, the NBC Woman's Convention recommended that each delegate "pledge herself to secure one white woman who is honest and true and willing to acknowledge the injustice accorded Negroes in Jim Crow car laws, and [who] will pledge herself to win one white man who will use his ballot and influence toward securing justice for Negroes in the courts, endeavor to suppress mob violence and give fair trial and justice in the courts, give equal accommodations in travel and simply give justice to Negroes." For quote see NBC, *Journal of the Thirty-sixth Session of the National Baptist Convention and the Sixteenth Annual Session of the Woman's Convention Auxiliary, Held in Savannah, Georgia, September 6–11, 1916* (Nashville: Sunday School Publishing Board, 1916), 211.

396 *For almost half:* For examples of Burroughs's commentary on these issues, see "Only God, Negroes Can Understand Negro Philosophy," *Baltimore Afro-American*, September 27, 1930; "Educated Parasites and Satisfied Mendicants," *Pittsburgh Courier*, February 20, 1932; "Nannie Out of Jim Crow Mission Plan," *Washington Afro-American*, February 1, 1941; "Miss Burroughs Pleads for Baptists to Get Together," *Washington Tribune*, September 9, 1922; "The High Cost of Jim Crow Civilization," *Chicago Defender*, February 22, 1930.

396 *Much later:* "Baptist Woman Prexy Comments on Subjects," *Indianapolis Recorder*, May 23, 1964.

397 *As a member:* For biographical information on Dorothy Boulding Ferebee and Vivian Carter Mason, and discussion of the NCNW's civil rights and interracial programs during the 1940s, see Bettye Collier-Thomas, *NCNW, 1935–1980* (Washington, D.C.: Mary McLeod Bethune Museum, 1981).

398 *In 1944, following:* Jessie Daniel Ames, "Church Women and Color," *The Church Woman* 10:1 (January 1944): 10.

399 *Following this event:* Ella Barksdale Brown, "Erasing the Color Line," *The Church Woman* 7:2 (February 1941): 7.

399 *Brown also emphasized:* Ibid., 7, 8.

399 *Addressing the question:* "The Place of the Women of the Thirteenth Episcopal District in the United Church Women," *Christian Recorder*, May 24, 1966.

400 *Between 1945 and 1966:* "Catching Up with the News for and About Women," *The Church Woman* 16:10 (December 1950): 3; "United Church Women Elect Mrs. Lynem," *Christian Recorder*, August 27, 1959; "The Place of the Women of the Thirteenth Episcopal District," ibid. Lynem, a writer and columnist for numerous secular and religious journals, a public school teacher and member of Zeta Phi Beta, was religious editor and fourth vice president of the AME Women's Missionary Society. Among the few black women elected officers in local and state CWU councils prior to the 1960s were Mrs. Edwin Smith (Baptist) of Hackensack, New Jersey (1950); Abbie Clement Jackson, who was a leader in the AME Zion Church and the first black and first woman elected as vice president of Louisville's Council of Churches (1950); and Mabel M. Hayden, who was elected fourth vice president and was the first black woman elected to office

in the Missouri State Council (1951). Hayden was president of the AME Missouri Conference Branch Missionary Society. See "News and Notes," *The Church Woman* 16:5 (May 1950): 39; "Catching," ibid. 16:7 (August–September 1950): 3; "Minister's Wife Elected Vice President of Missouri Church Women," April 25, 1951, CAB-J, Reel 1.

400 *Smith, a CWU:* Christine Smith, elected third vice president of CWU, was the only black woman on CWU's board at its founding. See "Church Women United," press release, December 13, 1941, Box 1, CWU-GCAH. For names of officers and members of the first CWU Board of Managers, see: "United Council of Church Women," untitled typescript, December 23, 1942, Box 1, Folder 35, ibid.

400 *Her recommendation was:* See Minutes, "The First Assembly of the United Council of Church Women," December 7, 1942, Box 4, Folder 46, CWU-GCAH.

401 *In 1943 CWU:* Shannon, *Just Because*, 30; "Minutes of the Executive Committee," September 10–11, 1942, Box 1, Folder 35, CWU-GCAH; "Minutes of the Executive Committee," March 9–10, 1944, Box 2, Folder 2, ibid.; Committee on Social, Industrial and Race Relations, "Recommendations Presented to the Executive Committee," Appendix IV, March 9–10, 1944, Box 2, Folder 2, ibid.; "For Immediate Release," June 22, 1944, ibid.; Hartmann, *The Home Front and Beyond*, 4. In 1944 the CWU reversed itself and decided that the term "Race Relations" came closest to defining the focus of their work on behalf of African Americans, Japanese, and other nonwhite Americans.

401 *In 1945:* Committee on Social, Industrial and Race Relations, "Recommendations Presented to the Executive Committee."

401 *The creation of this:* Calkins, *Follow Those Women*, 67; Will W. Alexander, "What Next in Race Relations," *The Church Woman* 13:1 (January 1947): 13. Funding from the Rosenwald Fund enabled CWU to hire a full-time director of race relations—Louise Young, a professor at Scarritt College—and to initiate several race relations projects. Will Alexander was vice president of the Julius Rosenwald Fund.

402 *"Why do we feel":* "A High Point in the Assembly," *The Church Woman* 9:2 (February 1943): 29. Christine Smith was a member of the organizing committee for the formation of CWU.

402 *"In a certain city":* Jessie Daniel Ames, "Church Women and Color," *The Church Woman* 10:1 (January 1944): 10.

403 *Durr said that:* Hollinger F. Barnard, Studs Terkel, Virginia Foster Durr, eds., *Outside the Magic Circle: The Autobiography of Virginia Foster Durr* (Tuscaloosa, Ala.: University of Alabama Press, 1990), 243–45; In 1951, following years of living in the Washington, D.C., metropolitan area, Virginia Foster Durr and her husband, attorney Clifford Durr, returned to Alabama, where she became active in civil rights. Her letters reveal a great deal about her political activism. See Virginia Foster Durr and Patricia Sullivan, eds., *Freedom Writer: Virginia Foster Durr, Letters from the Civil Rights Years* (New York: Routledge, 2003).

403 *The discussion:* M. M. Dozier, "Growth Marks on the Wall," *Church Woman* 15:6 (June–July 1949): 18–20.

404 *In 1949 the Texas:* "News and Notes: Activities," ibid. 15:2 (February 1949): 29.

404 *More than one hundred members:* "White Georgia Churches Take Lead in Demanding Legal Action Against Monroe, Ga., Lynchers," *Christian Index*, October 31, 1946; "News and Notes," *Church Woman* 14:6 (June–July, 1948): 30; ibid. 15:4 (April 1949): 34; ibid. 17:3 (March 1951): 33. In 1951 the Georgia Council petitioned the state assembly urging defeat of a proposed anti-mask bill

that sanctioned the use of masked parades and assemblies, and asked for legislation outlawing the wearing of masks in public.

404 *Hamilton's efforts paved:* Delores P. Aldridge, "Hamilton, Grace Towns (1907–1992)," in Hine, ed., *Black Women in America*, vol. 1, 520–21.

405 *"many of the evil":* Mrs. M. E. Tilly, "Overcoming Prejudice," *Church Woman* 16:1 (January 1950): 5–6.

405 *By the late 1950s:* Ibid.; "Human Relations Most Needed, Says Mrs. [Tilly]," *Star of Zion*, May 1, 1958.

405 *Tilly believed that:* Tilly, "Overcoming Prejudice," 8; "News and Notes: Civil Rights," *The Church Woman* 15:9 (November 1949): 37; "Play Leading Role in Fight to 'Free Ten Million Voters,' " *Pittsburgh Courier*, November 14, 1942; Rebecca Stiles Taylor, "10,000,000 Church Women Say: 'Abolish Poll Tax,' " *Chicago Defender*, December 1, 1945; see also Riehm, "Dorothy Tilly and the Fellowship of the Concerned."

406 *The Lincoln Journal:* "News and Notes: Accomplishments," *The Church Woman* 16:1 (January 1950): 35.

406 *They noted that:* "Catching up with the News for and About Women: Opportunities," *The Church Woman* 15:3 (March 1949): 3.

406 *The Rhode Island Council:* "News and Notes: Cooperation," *The Church Woman* 15:4 (April 1949): 35.

406 *"equality of educational":* "News and Notes," *The Church Woman* 14:10 (December 1948): 22; ibid. 16:10 (December 1950): 36.

407 *In 1941 the Georgia:* "There's a Way," *The Church Woman* 7:3 (March 1941): 24. Few states made provisions for delinquent black girls and boys. Rather, young offenders were placed in jail with hardened adult criminals. To address this issue, NACW state federations raised the funds and built institutions that were eventually turned over to the states to operate. For discussion of the reasons for delinquency among African American girls see Gertrude E. Rush, "Forces Contributing to the Delinquency of Our Girls," *National Notes* 26 (July 1924): 11. For examples of this pattern in Virginia, North Carolina, South Carolina, and Mississippi state federations, see William Anthony Aery, "Helping Wayward Girls: Virginia's Pioneer Work," *Southern Workman* 44:10 (November 1915): 598–604; "Women in Club Meet Launch Girl's Home," *Chicago Defender*, May 1, 1926; "S.S. Club Women to Hold Big Meet," ibid., June 11, 1927; "To Aid Backward Carolina Girls," ibid., June 25, 1927; "Celebration by Women in Mississippi," ibid., April 26, 1930; "Boys Home Hope of Club Women," ibid., July 30, 1927.

407 *The council opened:* "There's a Way: Community Issues and Major Social Problems," *The Church Woman* 7:4 (April 1941): 35–37.

407 *The center's success:* "News and Notes," *The Church Woman* 14:7 (September 1948): 34–35.

408 *Included in the project:* "News from the Field," *The Church Woman* 9:1 (March 1943): 31–35; "Hands That Feed Us," ibid. 11:9 (November 1945): 24–25.

408 *Many organizations:* "There's a Way: Interracial Tea," *The Church Woman* 7:5 (May 1941): 37–38.

408 *"justice and fair play":* "A Year with Albion, Michigan," *The Church Woman* 10:8 (October 1944): 32.

409 *In 1944 and 1946:* Calkins, *Follow Those Women*, 94–95.

410 *The NCC united:* Ibid., 88. The NCC was established by representatives from twenty-nine Protestant, Anglican, and Orthodox denominations in Cleveland, Ohio. The eight interdenominational organizations that came together were

Church Women United, the Federal Council of the Churches of Christ, the Foreign Mission Conference of North America, the Home Missions Council of North America, the International Council of Religious Education, the Missionary Education Movement of the USA and Canada, the National Protestant Council of Higher Education, and the United Stewardship Council.

410 *"If men from outer space":* "AME Church Women at Assembly," *Christian Recorder*, May 12, 1970.

411 *In 1959 there were:* "AME Church Delegates to Nat'l Council of Churches," *Christian Recorder*, October 28, 1954; Mrs. Sherman L. Greene (Zadie) and Mrs. D. Ward Nichols (Kay Bailey) were the wives of bishops; Anne E. Heath served as president of the Women's Missionary Society and Nora W. Link was a licensed evangelist and former teacher. Geraldine Bradford, "Quadrennial Missionary Convention Meets in Detroit," *Christian Recorder*, May 7, 1959.

411 *However, as a general:* Calkins, *Follow Those Women*, 90, 91.

411 *The Brown decision:* Bettye Collier-Thomas and V. P. Franklin, eds., *My Soul Is a Witness: A Chronology of the Civil Rights Era, 1954–1965* (New York: Henry Holt, 2000), xiv.

411 *Anticipating the Brown:* "Southern Leaders Confer," Church Woman 20:7 *(August–September 1954): 30–31.*

412 *In southern and midwestern:* "Recommendations and Resolutions of the Sixth National Assembly Atlantic City, New Jersey, October 5–8, 1953," *The Church Woman* 19:9 (November 1953): 40–42; CWU, "This Is How We Did It," October 1955, Box 62, Folder 2, 4–13, CWU-GCAH; Ida Milner, "Coming to Grips with Segregation," *The Church Woman* 21:8 (October 1955), 19, 37.

412 *Fearing that others:* CWU, "This Is How We Did It," 7–9.

412 *It was published:* Ibid., 12–13.

413 *They succeeded in:* Ibid., 4–6, 11.

413 *CWU used:* Calkins, *Follow Those Women*, 96.

414 *Project committees were:* "Church Women United Toward the Achievement of Racial Justice," *United Church Herald*, November 16, 1961; "Report on Assignment: RACE," November 1963, Box 62, Folder 12, 1–5, CWU-GCAH.

414 *Instead of embracing:* The importance of CWU's program "Assignment: RACE," as well as the organization's contributions to the civil rights struggle, have been dismissed in the writings of some historians who have chronicled the role of ecumenical organizations and mainline denominations in the Civil Rights Movement. For examples of this, see James F. Findlay Jr., *Church People in the Struggle: The National Council of Churches and the Black Freedom Movement, 1950–1970* (New York: Oxford University Press, 1993), 49–50. Findlay admits that CWU's "rank and file leadership, symbolized an important constituency within the churches, too often overlooked"—however, he sees the role of CWU as "provi[ding] strong support for the new programs of the [NCC] Commission on Religion and Race." Findlay inaccurately states that "the project disappeared shortly after the money funding the first three years was not renewed." In 1964 CWU launched Assignment: RACE 2.

414 *"racial justice":* "Report on Assignment: RACE," November 1963.

414 *Between the spring:* For detailed information on the sit-ins, Freedom Rides, voting rights campaigns, and identification of the locales, patterns, and dates of specific direct-action protest events, see Collier-Thomas and Franklin, ed., *My Soul Is a Witness.*

414 *More than one thousand:* Rhetta M. Arter, "United Church Women Assignment: RACE: Report of Inventory," 1965, 4, Box 63, Folder 1, CWU-GCAH. In cases

where respondents did not follow directions and provided data that was not applicable to the questions asked, the returns were eliminated.

415 *Reports from councils:* For a report on the accomplishments of phases 1 and 2 of the project, see "Assignment: RACE 1961–1964," Box 62, Folder 12, CWU-GCAH.

415 *Some clergy feared:* Arter, "Report of Inventory," 29, 34–39.

416 *"subtle web of conformity":* Elizabeth Lee Haselden, "How Free Is This Church?" *The Church Woman* 27:4 (April 1961): 3–6. Haselden's work with CWU began in the 1940s in Minneapolis. A southerner by birth, Haselden was married to a minister. The couple lived in a number of cities, where she invariably participated in the activities of CWU councils. In Minneapolis, Rochester, and Charleston, West Virginia, Haselden contributed to the organizing and was active on the human relations commissions. See Janine Marie Denomme, "To End This Day of Strife: Churchwomen and the Campaign for Integration, 1920–1970" (PhD diss., University of Pennsylvania, 2001), 206.

417 *Like the white church women:* "It Happened in Shippensburg," *The Church Woman* 28:7 (August–September 1962): 22–23, 34.

417 *"Christian urgency":* "Report on Assignment: RACE," November 1963, 4–5.

417 *Though there were:* For example, South Carolina councils focused on anti-poverty work. See Cherisse R. Jones, " 'How Shall I Sing the Lord's Song?': United Church Women Confront Racial Issues in South Carolina, 1940s–1960s," in Murray, ed., *Throwing Off the Cloak of Privilege*, 131–48.

418 *"a channel for concerted":* "Assignment: RACE 2: In Partnership for Equal Opportunity Now for All in Church and Community," Box 62, Folder 12, CWU-GCAH.

418 *Councils were asked:* Ibid.

419 *The WIMS experience:* Polly Cowan, "Wednesdays in Mississippi," *The Church Woman* 31:5 (May 1965): 14, 18; "Wednesdays in Mississippi, 1964–1965," and "Racism Program," Box 62, Folder 15, CWU-GCAH; Height, *Open Wide the Freedom Gates*, 168–69, 184–85, 189, 193–94. Serving in various capacities, between 1946 and her retirement in 1971 Dorothy Height played a key role in the desegregation of southern YWCAs. As the associate director of YWCA leadership services, Height was a paid employee. However, until 1971, as president of the NCNW, Height was an unpaid volunteer. The NCNW offered an additional network through which she could achieve her YWCA goals and expand the considerable social and political capital she had amassed during three decades of YWCA employment and as president of Delta Sigma Theta.

419 *The total membership:* "Conclusions—in—Brief from the Inventory, Assignment: RACE, United Church Women 1966," Box 62, Folder 16, CWU-GCAH.

420 *"the needs of nonwhite":* Ibid.

420 *In contrast:* Findlay, *Church People in the Struggle*, 222–23.

420 *Like the ubiquitous:* Louis Cassels, "Historic Race-Religion Parley to Open," *Chicago Defender*, January 12–19, 1963; "Confab to Study Church's Interracial Role," ibid.

421 *"Negroes felt they":* Benjamin E. Mays, *Born to Rebel: An Autobiography* (Athens, Ga.: University of Georgia Press, 2003), 261–63; "Rev. King Sees Church 'Eclipse' Without Bold Stand on Race Issue," *Chicago Defender*, January 19–25, 1963; "Race, Religion Meet Hit for 'Snubbing' of Negro," ibid.

421 *Hedgeman criticized Mays:* Hedgeman, *The Trumpet Sounds*, 175–76; for biographical data on Hedgeman, see Jessie Carney Smith, *Notable Black American Women, Book I* (Detroit: Gale Research Inc., 1992), 483–85; Mark L. Chapman, *Christian-*

ity on Trial: African American Religious Thought Before and After Black Power (Eugene, Ore.: Wipf and Stock Publishers, 2006), 140–41.

421 *Like the earlier:* "Church Parley Issues Appeal to U.S. Conscience," *Chicago Defender*, January 19–25, 1963; "Church Meet Ends with Plea to Halt Racism," ibid.

421 *"too little and too late":* "Rev. King Sees Church 'Eclipse' Without Bold Stand on Race Issue"; Mays, *Born to Rebel*, 262–63; "Confab to Study Church's Interracial Role."

421 *The NCC and mainline:* Findlay, *Church People in the Struggle*, 222–23.

CHAPTER 8 *"Jesus, Jobs, and Justice"*

425 *This is resistance:* Phyl Garland, "Builders of a New South," *Ebony* (August 1966): 27–30, 34, 36–37.

425 *These single acts:* Jacqueline Jones, *Labor of Love, Labor of Sorrow: Black Women, Work and the Family, from Slavery to the Present* (New York: Basic Books, 1985), 279; John Dittmer, *Local People: The Struggle for Civil Rights in Mississippi* (Urbana: University of Illinois Press, 1995).

426 *According to Burks:* Mary Fair Burks, "Trailblazers: Women in the Montgomery Bus Boycott," in *Trailblazers and Torchbearers, 1941–1965*, ed. Vicki L. Crawford, Jacqueline A. Rouse, and Barbara Woods (Brooklyn: Carlson Publishing, 1990), 78; For a detailed history of the Women's Political Council and the Montgomery bus boycott, see David J. Garrow, ed., *The Montgomery Bus Boycott and the Women Who Started It: The Memoir of Jo Ann Gibson Robinson* (Knoxville, Tenn.: University of Tennessee, 1987).

426 *Acknowledging that class:* Burks, "Trailblazers," 77–79.

427 *This action was:* Ibid., 80.

427 *The students registered:* Ibid., 81.

427 *Black women were:* Lamont H. Yeakey, "Black Women and the Civil Rights Movement: The Montgomery Bus Boycott as a Case Study," unpublished paper presented at the October 1979 annual meeting of the Association for the Study of Afro-American Life and History, 9, 10.

428 *Though Colvin and Smith:* For details regarding the arrests of Claudette Colvin and Mary Louise Smith, and the NAACP's reasons for rejecting them as possible candidates for launching a test case, see Richard Willing, "Civil Rights' Untold Story," *USA Today*, November 28, 1995; Bettye Collier-Thomas and V. P. Franklin, eds., *My Soul Is a Witness: A Chronology of the Civil Rights Era, 1954–1964* (New York: Henry Holt, 1999), 23.

428 *Colvin later commented:* Willing, "Civil Rights' Untold Story"; Larry Copeland, "Parks not Seated Alone in History," *USA Today*, November 29, 2005.

428 *Garrow asserted that:* For a discussion of Rosa Parks and the launching of the Montgomery bus boycott, see Bettye Collier-Thomas and V. P. Franklin, eds., *Sisters in the Struggle: African American Women in the Civil Rights–Black Power Movement* (New York: New York University Press, 2001), 61–74; Willing, "Civil Rights' Untold Story."

429 *She was highly:* Willing, "Civil Rights' Untold Story"; Alma Polk, "Pokin' Around," *Christian Recorder*, November 2, 1965. For a discussion of Rosa Parks's work in the AME Church, see Barbara A. Robinson, "A Continuous Faith: Rosa Parks in the AME Church," *AME Church Review* 117:383 (July–September 2001): 49–50.

429 *However, it was:* Burks, "Trailblazers," 82–83.

429 *"nameless cooks and maids"*: Ibid.

429 *Eighty-five percent:* Yeakey, "Black Women and the Civil Rights Movement," 5.

430 *Stories about this:* "Negro Progress," *Star of Zion*, August 21, 1902.

430 *She articulated what:* Ann M. Owens, "Women in the News," *Christian Recorder*, August 18, 1964. For a discussion of SNCC workers and voter registration campaigns in the South, and a listing of cities where protests occurred, see Collier-Thomas and Franklin, *My Soul Is a Witness*, 165, 195. In 1956 Mrs. Johnnie A. Carr, a businesswoman and member of the WPC, traveled throughout the United States speaking about the "threats, the reprisals, the mass arrests," and raising funds to help support many persons who lost their jobs because they participated in the Montgomery bus boycott. See "Woman Leader in Ala[bama] Bus Boycott to Speak Here," *Indianapolis Recorder*, March 31, 1956.

431 *Their protests were:* Burks, "Trailblazers," 82–83.

431 *"This must be":* Mary McLeod Bethune, "Mrs. Bethune Sees School Ruling as a Milestone in U.S. History," *Chicago Defender*, May 29, 1954; Pierre J. Muss, "Africa Has Balance of Power in World Affairs," *Norfolk Journal and Guide*, July 28, 1956.

432 *Throughout her career:* As a public intellectual, Burroughs represented the voice of the NBC-USA Woman's Convention in calling for an end to Jim Crow laws and demanding justice for black Americans.

432 *For many years:* For example, in 1905, at the Fifth Triennial Meeting of the National Council of Women of the U.S., held in Washington, D.C., Mary Church Terrell explained what citizenship meant to black women, and its relationship to labor discrimination. See excerpt from Terrell's speech in National Council of Women of the United States, Inc., "Background Papers for Platform Proposals to the Democratic and Republican Parties, Summer 1964," eight-page typescript, National Council of Negro Women Papers, Series 10, Box 2, Bethune Council House, National Historical Site, Washington, D.C. (hereafter cite as BCH-NHS).

432 *In her usual:* Nannie Helen Burroughs, "Editorial," *The Worker* 17:81 (July–September 1954): 3.

432 *"the grossest insult":* Ibid.

432 *"[W]e are facing":* NBC, *Journal of the Seventy-fifth Annual Session of the National Baptist Convention, U.S.A., Inc., and the Woman's Auxiliary, Held with the Baptist Churches of Memphis, Tennessee, September 7–11, 1955* (Nashville: Sunday School Publishing Board, 1955), 363 (italics by Burroughs).

432 *"[w]e can beat":* Ibid.

433 *"God's Army":* See Nannie Burroughs, "Fighting a Condition," in NBC, *Journal of the Thirty-[ninth] Session of the National Baptist Convention and the Nineteenth Annual Session of the Woman's Convention Auxiliary, Held in Newark, New Jersey, September 10–15, 1919* (Nashville: Sunday School Publishing Board, 1919), 231.

433 *"discourse of resistance":* For quote, see Evelyn Brooks Higginbotham, *Righteous Discontent: The Women's Movement in the Black Baptist Church, 1880–1920* (Cambridge, Mass.: Harvard University Press, 1993), 222.

433 *If laws are unjust:* Josephine St. Pierre Ruffin, "Editorial," *Woman's Era* 3:2 (June 1896): 4; "Our Exchanges," *Christian Index*, October 16, 1897; "The National Association," *Indianapolis Freeman*, October 2, 1897; "The Awakening of Woman," *National Notes* 19 (January 1917): 3–4; "National Convention of Colored Women," *Washington Bee*, July 21, 1906.

433 *In challenging:* For an excellent discussion of lawsuits initiated by African American women who encountered racial discrimination in seating arrangements and

poor treatment aboard trains and boats during the latter part of the nineteenth century, see Janice Sumler-Edmond, "The Quest for Justice: African American Women Litigants, 1867–1890," in *African American Women and the Vote, 1837–1965*, ed. Ann D. Gordon et al. (Amherst, Mass.: University of Massachusetts Press, 1997), 100–19.

433 *She was revered:* Sharon Harley, "Nannie Helen Burroughs: 'The Black Goddess of Liberty,' " *Journal of Negro History* 76:1/4 (winter 1991): 63–71.

434 *"quite three million":* "The President's Annual Address," *The Worker* 21:95 (January–March, 1958): 12. For a discussion of the concerns of black and white women at the beginning of the interracial movement in the South, and Burroughs assessment of the importance of the work that ensued, see "Interracial Advance," ibid. 17:82 (October, November, December, 1954): 88–89.

434 *"The Negroes must":* NBC, *Journal of the Seventy-fifth Annual Session,* 368; "Mrs. Layten Paid Highest Tribute at Funeral Services," *Philadelphia Afro-American,* January 28, 1950.

434 *In September 1960:* I was unable to locate a copy of the July–September 1960 special issue of *The Worker,* which focused on the sit-in movement. See "The President's Annual Message," *The Worker* 24:107 (January–March, 1961): 16. In this issue, Burroughs also stressed that *The Worker,* which distributed 100,000 copies quarterly (or 400,000 annually), was "the most widely read magazine by Negro women," ibid.

435 *These were the:* Nannie H. Burroughs, "Have the Churches and Government 'Ganged Up' on the American Negro?" *The Worker* 23:106 (October–December, 1960): 3–4. At the beginning of 1961, Burroughs predicted that there would be more sit-in demonstrations and additional boycotts; see "Predictions," *Baltimore Afro-American,* January 7, 1961.

435 *In other words:* The 1956 convention gave considerable attention to the question of civil rights—in particular, the role that the NBC-USA should play in areas where the NAACP was outlawed by state legislatures. See "Four Vital Problems on Program," *Norfolk Journal and Guide,* August 25, 1956; for Joseph H. Jackson's quote and specific discussion of his position on the role of the church in civil rights, see "Jackson Snubs Historic Race and Religion Conference: Negro Baptists Only Religious Group Not Cooperating," December 24, 1964, Claude A. Barnett Papers, "Dr. J. H. Jackson news clippings," Reel 3, CAB-J; William J. Harvey, "A Message from the President," *Mission Herald* 66:4 (January–February 1964): 3; for a brief analysis of Jackson's reaction to the rise of Martin Luther King Jr., see Nick Salvatore, *Singing in a Strange Land: C. L. Franklin, the Black Church, and the Transformation of America* (Urbana, Ill.: University of Illinois Press, 2006), 194–96.

437 *Lewis and Forman:* For the NBC-USA's position on the Civil Rights–Black Power Movement as articulated by its president, Joseph H. Jackson, and sanctioned by its all-male Board of Directors and the leaders of the Woman's Convention, see NBC-USA, *The Record of the Eighty-ninth Annual Session of the National Baptist Convention, U.S.A., Inc., and the Woman's Auxiliary, Held with the Baptist Churches of Kansas City, Missouri, September 9–14, 1969* (Nashville: Sunday School Publishing Board, 1970), 44, 70, 85, 242–56, 442, 445, 447; and "President Jackson's Address," in NBC-USA, *The Record of the Ninetieth Annual Session of the National Baptist Convention, U.S.A., Inc., and the Woman's Auxiliary, Held with the Baptist Churches of New Orleans, Louisiana, September 8–13, 1970* (Nashville: Sunday School Publishing Board, 1971), 254–81; *New York Times,* June 18, 1963; *JET,* August 5, 1963; ibid., February 6, 1964.

437   *"race haters":* Pat L. Williams, "Indianapolis Women Play Active Role in Civil Rights," *Indianapolis Recorder,* January 27, 1962.

437   *In 1956:* "Woman Leader Attends Civil Rights Meeting," *Indianapolis Recorder,* March 10, 1956.

437   *"new integrated relationships":* Nannie Burroughs, "To Make Integration Stick," *The Worker* 17:82 (October–December, 1954): 11–12.

437   *In programs sponsored:* "Mission Work Among the Negroes," *Home Mission Monthly* 16:7 (July 1894): 291–93; "Training Girls for Home Life," ibid. 4:8 (August 1882): 28–30. Mrs. William Scott, a black woman employed by the American Baptist Home Mission Society as a lecturer, argued that the society's work had paid off. Noting that through evangelization the numbers of black Baptists had increased almost fivefold, she credited the society with training a "safe class of citizens," decreasing crime, and teaching women to keep better homes. See Mrs. William Scott, "Has It Paid?" ibid. 23:4 (April 1901): 115–17.

438   *"standard of living":* St. Clair Drake and Horace R. Cayton, *Black Metropolis: A Study of Negro Life in a Northern City* (Chicago: University of Chicago Press, 1993, 4th ed., rev. and enl.), 661–62; utilizing Drake and Cayton's theory, historian Evelyn Higginbotham illustrates the ways in which black Baptists practiced "the Politics of Respectability." See Higginbotham, *Righteous Discontent,* 14–15.

439   *Hollis was responding:* Rossie T. Hollis, "Editorials," *Missionary Messenger* 8:9 (September 1958): 3–4.

439   *She advised young:* Ibid.

440   *Moreover, white supremacy:* Collier-Thomas and Franklin, eds., *My Soul Is a Witness,* 65, 69, 70, 87, 117, 118, 132.

440   *King, Abernathy:* I agree with Frederick C. Harris's argument that there is a relationship between the gendered practices in black churches and men's resistance to women's political leadership outside the church. Harris argues, "[I]t is not surprising that women activists such as Baker and Clark met resistance from this all-male black clergy." See Frederick C. Harris, *Something Within: Religion in African-American Political Activism* (New York: Oxford University Press, 1999), 163.

440   *Leaders and organizers:* For the single best source for discussion of Ella Baker's life and career in the "black freedom movement" and role in the NAACP, the SCLC, and other male-dominated organizations, as well as the impact of her upbringing in a Baptist church in North Carolina and her mother's work in the North Carolina Baptist Woman's Convention, see Barbara Ransby, *Ella Baker and the Black Freedom Movement: A Radical Democratic Vision* (Chapel Hill: University of North Carolina Press, 2003); for additional discussion of the roles and treatment of women in the Civil Rights Movement, see John Dittmer, *Local People: The Struggle for Civil Rights in Mississippi* (Urbana, Ill.: University of Illinois Press, 1995), 30–31; Charles M. Payne, *I've Got the Light of Freedom: The Organizing Tradition and the Mississippi Freedom Struggle* (Berkeley, Calif.: University of California Press, 1995), 76–77, 92.

441   *Wedel noted that:* Cynthia Wedel, "United Church Women's President Writes on the Supreme Court Decision," *The Church Woman* 22:4 (April 1956): 8–10.

441   *However, Harvey stressed:* Clarie Harvey, "The Black Woman: Keeper of the Faith," *Christian Recorder,* June 2, 1970.

442   *Still, few CWU:* "Board of Managers to Meet," *The Church Woman* 22:4 (April 1956): 38–39.

442   *They also urged:* "Missionaries Okay President's Policy in War-time Crisis," *New York Age,* January 24, 1942.

442 *The group identified:* "Church Women Promote Integrated Christian Society," *Star of Zion*, July 8, 1954.

443 *Frizzell concluded that:* Mary E. Frizzell, "Missions," *Christian Recorder*, January 7, February 4, April 7, 1964.

443 *"remedial methods employed":* Robert L. Morgan, "Sister A. B. Williams Poses Answer," *Christian Recorder*, October 11, 1966.

444 *"in the vanguard":* Howard D. Gregg, *History of the African Methodist Episcopal Church* (Nashville: AME Church Sunday School Union, 1980), 393.

444 *"Black Nationalists":* *JET*, June 6, 1961; *New York Times*, June 18, 1963; *The Official Minutes of the Thirty-Seventh Session of the General Conference of the African Methodist Episcopal Church, Held in the Cincinnati Gardens, Cincinnati, Ohio, May 1964* (Nashville: AME Sunday School Union, 1964), 168–69.

445 *Pained by what:* "An Address by Mrs. Daisy Bates at the AME Connectional Laymen's Convention," *Christian Recorder*, October 29, 1959.

445 *"reverted to violence":* Morgan, "Sister A. B. Williams Poses Answer."

445 *In 1950 the national:* "Brown Memorial AME Church," *Christian Recorder*, June 22, 1950.

446 *The Conference Branch:* Thelma Anderson Wills, "West Tennessee Conference Branch Elects Delegates to Quadrennial Convention, St. Louis, July 1963," *Christian Recorder*, October 30, 1962. The West Tennessee Conference Branch was the largest of the five women's societies in the Thirteenth District. See also Collier-Thomas and Franklin, eds., *My Soul Is a Witness*, 122.

446 *In response to:* "Echoes from the East Tennessee Missionary Conference Branch," *Christian Recorder*, October 23, 1962. For details regarding Septima Clark's role in the launching of SCLC's Citizenship Schools, grassroots literacy program, and voter registration campaign, see Jacqueline A. Rouse, " 'We Seek to Know . . . in Order to Speak the Truth': Nurturing the Seeds of Discontent—Septima P. Clark and Participatory Leadership," in Collier-Thomas and Franklin, eds., *Sisters in the Struggle*, 106–17.

446 *"[I]t is our purpose":* Octavia Dandridge, "Missions to Serve the Present Age," *Christian Recorder*, October 2, 1962.

446 *Dandridge also stressed:* Ibid.

446 *In 1963 the WMS:* "W.M.S. of the Northeast South Carolina Conference Holds Epoch-Making Meeting," *Christian Recorder*, October 1, 1963.

446 *Protesting the bombing:* "Tennessee Conference Branch Sends Telegram to President Kennedy Urging Protection for All Americans," *Christian Recorder*, October 22, 1963.

447 *"fighting for Civil Rights":* Alma Polk, "Pokin' Around," *Christian Recorder*, March 1, 1966.

447 *During the 1960s:* "Mary Lou Henderson, an Institution," *Christian Recorder*, February 16, 1965. Born in 1891, Henderson began her career as a child evangelist. She was licensed to preach at the age of sixteen, held a local preacher's license by the age of twenty-five, and pastored twelve churches between 1920 and 1960. As a social reformer, during the early twentieth century Henderson was a speaker for the Ohio Temperance Union and served on the Red Cross Board of Belmont County, Ohio. In Barnesville and the surrounding towns in Ohio, she was highly respected by both whites and blacks. She received numerous citations for her interracial and interfaith work. Henderson was married and had two children.

447 *Crawford was well:* Minna Smith Dezon, "Minister's Wife Puts New Rights Law to Test," *Christian Recorder*, August 4, 1964.

447 *"No longer is"*: Loretta C. Randolph, "Report of Mid-South Area Migrant Planning Committee Meets in Memphis," *Christian Recorder*, March 2, 1965.

448 *"total civil rights"*: A. B. Lynem, "Woman's Word," *Christian Recorder*, January 28, 1964.

448 *"We must be"*: Mary E. Williams, "Illinois Conference Branch W.M.S. Holds Sixty-fifth Annual Convention," *Christian Recorder*, September 20, 1966; Mary E. Frizzell, "Great Days Ahead for Missions," ibid., September 5, 1967; "Fourth Episcopal District Executive Missionary Board Meets in Chicago," ibid., May 20, 1969.

448 *At the National Council:* "Poverty Seen as Main Target in Drive Against Racial Bias," *Baltimore Afro-American*," November 21, 1964. These comments were made by Dunnigan in a speech she delivered at the NCNW's Twenty-ninth Annual Convention.

448 *Dunnigan also noted:* Ibid.

450 *Participants on the program:* "Women Plan Nationwide Poverty Attack Program," *Amsterdam News*, October 10, 1964.

450 *In 1966:* The Alpha Kappa Alpha Sorority established a Women's Residential Training Center in Cleveland, Ohio, where women in the Job Corps were taught bookkeeping, typing, cosmetology, data processing, and basic office skills. For a discussion of the AKA Job Corps grant and program, see "Women in the News," *Christian Recorder*, June 1, 1965; "Sorority Gets $4,000,000 Poverty Program Package," *Amsterdam News*, March 6, 1965; "AKA to Open Job Corps Center with OEO Contract, *Pittsburgh Courier*, March 13, 1965. For information related to the NCNW's job training program, see *New York Times*, August 22, 1966.

451 *"Women must act"*: On July 9, 1963, three hundred leaders of women's organizations in attendance at a White House meeting were asked by President John F. Kennedy to consider how their associations could contribute to the advancement of minority groups in their communities. Following that meeting, a number of organizations adopted resolutions urging support of civil rights legislation and devised plans for local community action. For discussion of the programs and support provided by women's organizations, see Sue Cronk, "Civil Rights Supported by Thousands of Women," *Washington Post*, January 1, 1964. For details of the meetings held in Atlanta in 1963 and 1964, the launching of Wednesdays in Mississippi during the summer of 1964, and the names of the participants, see "Secret Visits of 48 Prominent Women to Mississippi Revealed," *Washington Afro-American*, September 5, 1964.

451 *"the injustices inflicted"*: Josephine Weiner, *The Story of WICS* (Washington, D.C.: Women in Community Service, Inc., 1979), 2, 7, 20–22. The organization was initially known as "WIC"—the Women's Inter-Organizational Committee. Contrary to Dorothy Height's assertion that "seldom before had southern middle-class women come together across racial lines as they did in Atlanta," the record shows that interracial meetings of this sort had been held in the South, in particular in Atlanta, since the 1920s. Black and white women active in CWU and on the CIC and Southern Regional Council's women's committees had participated in many meetings in Atlanta and in other cities as well. For quote, see Height, *Open Wide the Freedom Gates*, 164.

451 *At the conclusion:* Weiner, *The Story of WICS*, 10.

452 *However, though a small:* Ibid., 2, 7, 20–22.

452 *Womanpower Unlimited:* Womanpower Unlimited was organized by Clarie Collins Harvey on May 29, 1961, in Jackson, Mississippi. "Secret Visits of 48

Prominent Women"; Justine Randers-Pehrson, "Wednesdays in Mississippi," *Radcliffe Quarterly* 65:1 (March 1979): 43–45; see also Dittmer, *Local People*, 98.

452 *This project, launched:* Weiner, *The Story of WICS*, 2–3; Polly Cowan, "Wednesdays in Mississippi," *Church Woman* 31:5 (May 1965): 14–15, 18; Randers-Pehrson, "Wednesdays in Mississippi," 43–45. Also, see discussion of the Wednesdays in Mississippi program and CWU in chapter 7. For a discussion of the Mississippi Freedom Summer Project, see Collier-Thomas and Franklin, eds., *My Soul Is a Witness*, 213.

452 *"it broke down barriers":* Weiner, *The Story of WICS*, 4.

453 *In 1965 the group:* Louise Pfuetze, "WICS—Women in Community Service," *Church Woman* 31:3 (March 1965): 15–16; Weiner, *The Story of WICS*, 2, 7, 20–22. Jeanne Noble, the director of Women's Job Corp, encouraged the group to incorporate and become recruiters and screeners for the Women's Job Corp. As an incorporated nonprofit group, WICS received a government contract to launch the Women's Job Corp centers. Thus WICS was formed as an organization to facilitate a government program to train and aid poor women in finding employment. Though the YWCA did not join the coalition, it was represented on the WICS Board of Directors, provided services and space for WICS projects, and worked closely with the organization in the recruitment of young women for participation in the program.

454 *"women's liberation movement":* For information related to NOW and the use of the terms and phrases "liberation" and "women's liberation movement," see Judith Hole, "National Organization for Women (NOW)," in *The Reader's Companion to U.S. Women's History*, ed. Wilma Mankiller et al. (New York: Houghton Mifflin, 1998), 396–97; Jo Freeman, "Women's Liberation," ibid., 650–51.

454 *Initially it was:* For an excellent analysis of the relationship of the women's liberation movement to the black movement and the difference between white and black women's "oppression," see Linda La Rue, "The Black Movement and Women's Liberation," *Black Scholar* 1 (May 1970): 36–42.

454 *As the press:* For articles on NOW and women's liberation, see Hole, "National Organization for Women (NOW)," 396–97; Jo Freeman, "Women's Liberation," ibid., 650–51.

455 *Many of the issues:* For a discussion of black feminist organizing between 1960 and 1980, in particular the National Black Feminist Organization and the Combahee Collective, see Duchess Harris, "From the Kennedy Commission to the Combahee Collective," in Collier-Thomas and Franklin, eds., *Sisters in the Struggle*, 280–305.

455 *Though some leaders:* "BLACK POWER, Statement by National Committee of Negro Churchmen, July 31, 1966," in *Black Theology: A Documentary History*, vol. 1: *1966–1979*, ed., James H. Cone and Gayraud S. Wilmore (Maryknoll, N.Y.: Orbis Books, 1993), 20. For discussion of the views of Roy Wilkins and Dorothy Height, see *New York Times*, July 6, 1966, and *JET*, January 5, 1967; see also Height, *Open Wide the Freedom Gates*, 150–52. These leaders were fearful that the term "black power" would drive away white supporters, in particular philanthropists, foundations, government agencies, and other influential leaders. Height "suggested that the young militants find a more constructive rallying call."

456 *Moreover, it was:* James Cone, *For My People: Black Theology and the Black Church* (Maryknoll, N.Y.: Orbis Books, 1990), 14–15; "The Black Manifesto," in Cone and Wilmore, eds., *Black Theology*, vol. 1, 27–36; John L. Kater, "Experiment in Freedom: The Episcopal Church and the Black Power Movement," *Historical Magazine of the Protestant Episcopal Church* 48:1 (March 1979): 72.

457 *What was needed:* "The Black Manifesto," in Cone and Wilmore, eds., *Black Theology*, vol. 1.

457 *She was the sole:* In response to the criticism of Hedgeman, Pauli Murray, and Theressa Hoover, and the sensitivity of many black women to the exclusivity of the term "Churchmen," in 1982 the National Conference of Negro Churchmen was renamed the National Conference of Black Christians. See Cone, *For My People*, 133–34. By 1965 Hedgeman was nationally known for her civil rights work. In 1944, as the executive director of the National Council for a Permanent Fair Employment Practices Commission, she initiated national legislation and educational programs. In 1949 she was appointed assistant to the administrator of the Federal Security Agency (later known as the United States Department of Health, Education and Welfare). Between 1954 and 1958, Hedgeman worked as an assistant to New York City Mayor Robert Wagner Jr. During the early 1960s she served as the National Council of Churches' director of Ecumenical Action. In this position she "became a major architect" of the 1963 March on Washington. She was instrumental in recruiting thousands of white Protestants to participate in the march and instrumental in the efforts to gain passage of the 1964 civil rights bill. For biographical data on Hedgeman, see "Woman in the News," *Church Woman* 31 (October 1965): 35; Jessie Carney Smith, *Notable Black American Women, Book I* (Detroit: Gale Research Inc., 1992), 483–85.

457 *Although most of:* For an excellent summary and critique of the key issues in the ongoing debate among the Christian theologians responding to the global liberation movements occurring among oppressed peoples, see Pauli Murray, "Black Theology and Feminist Theology: A Comparative View," *Anglican Theological Review* 60:1 (January 1978).

457 *Thus, black power:* James H. Cone, *Black Theology and Black Power,* (New York: Seabury Press, 1969), reprint (New York: Harper and Row, 1989), 6–8, 11–14, 23, 54, 71, 84–85, 124.

457 *Cone's highly:* In the highly politicized environment of the late 1960s black women became increasingly concerned about their marginalization in the debates taking place among black men and white women. To address the sexism and racism evident in the black power and feminist movements, activists, religious leaders, and scholars such as Toni Cade, Frances Beale, Theressa Hoover, and Pauli Murray published books and articles that analyzed and clarified the plight of black women and suggested strategies for dealing with their situation. See Toni Cade, ed., *The Black Woman* (New York: Signet, 1970); Frances Beale, "Double Jeopardy: To Be Black and Female," in Cone and Wilmore, eds., *Black Theology*, vol. 1, 284–92; Theressa Hoover, "Black Women and the Churches: Triple Jeopardy," ibid., 293–303; Pauli Murray, "Black Theology and Feminist Theology: A Comparative View," ibid., 304–22.

458 *"the relation between":* Bettye Collier-Thomas, *Daughters of Thunder: Black Women Preachers and Their Sermons, 1850–1979* (San Francisco, Calif.: Jossey-Bass Publishers, 1997), 230.

458 *In the fall:* Pauli Murray, "The Negro Woman in the Quest for Equality," typescript address delivered at the Leadership Conference of the National Council of Negro Women, held at the Statler Hilton Hotel, November 14, 1963, BCH-NHS; see also Beale, "Double Jeopardy." Murray's speech was heard by leaders and many representatives of the twenty-seven organizations affiliated with the NCNW who attended the 1963 conference.

458 *Her request:* Anna Arnold Hedgeman, *The Trumpet Sounds: A Memoir of Negro Leadership* (New York: Holt, Rinehart and Winston, 1964), 176–80.

459 *However, she advised:* Pauli Murray, "The Negro Woman in the Quest for Equality." In 1970, in "A New Dilemma for Black Women," Jeanne Noble asserted, "Slowly and painfully we realized that black men wanted to determine the policy and progress of black people without female participation in decision-making and leadership positions." Noble argued that middle-class black women had retreated from their "history of activism including leadership in at least two revolutions: emancipation of Negroes and the women's suffrage movement," and had become "passive observers" rather than "movers and shakers of institutions." See "A New Dilemma for Black Women," *Christian Recorder*, April 21, 1970.

459 *"[j]ust a bunch":* Helen J. King, "The Black Woman and Women's Lib," *Ebony* (March 1971): 69.

459 *Speaking for CME:* Mrs. Nathaniel [Phyllis] Bedford to Dorothy I. Height, September 1, 1970, AME Church Women's Missionary Society, Series 18, Box 1, National Council of Negro Women Papers, BCH-NHS.

459 *In the 1960s:* Deborah Gray White, *Too Heavy a Load: Black Women in Defense of Themselves, 1894–1994* (New York: W. W. Norton, 1999), 180–81.

460 *She argued that:* Myrtice H. Goree, "An Open Letter to Black Women," *Christian Recorder*, April 29, 1969.

461 *"However, time and exposure":* Saundra Willingham, "Why I Quit the Convent," *Ebony* (December 1968): 64–70.

461 *"there are no Negroes":* "Negro Nun: Black Power Response to White Racism," *Christian Recorder*, January 14, 1969; for quote, see John J. O'Connor, "Washington Reporter," *Interracial Review* (September 1963): 170–72.

462 *The NBSC incorporated:* "Negro Nun: Black Power"; "An Awakening of Black Nun Power," *Ebony* (October 1968): 44–46, 48–50. In the aftermath of Selma, black Catholic priests and nuns began to assess the status and treatment of African Americans in the church at all levels. Following King's assassination, in April 1968 sixty of the 150 members of the recently organized all-male Black Catholic Clergy Caucus met in Detroit to define an agenda for black Catholics. See Daniel J. Mallette, "Black Priests Denounce the Church," *Liberator* 8:5 (May 1968): 8–10. For discussion of the Selma to Montgomery March, see Collier-Thomas and Franklin, eds., *My Soul Is a Witness*, 229; M. Shawn Copeland, "A Cadre of Women Religious Committed to Black Liberation: The National Black Sisters' Conference," in *U.S. Catholic Historian* 14:1 (winter 1996): 123–44.

462 *Sister Martin de Porres:* M. Shawn Copeland, "African American Catholics and Black Theology: An Interpretation," in Cone and Wilmore, eds., *Black Theology*, vol. 2, 102; Mallette, "Black Priests Denounce the Church."

463 *Determined not to:* Few black priests were in leadership positions as pastors or religious superiors in the early 1960s. For discussion of the status of black priests and religious communities as well as the nine demands made by the Black Catholic Clergy Caucus, see Cyprian Davis, *The History of Black Catholics in the United States* (New York: Crossroad Publishing Company, 1996), 256, 258; "An Awakening of Black Nun Power." Father George Clements, an activist black Catholic priest in Chicago, was among the first to speak out about discrimination in the Catholic Church, see " 'Militant' Black Chicago Priest Demands More Black Control," *JET*, August 29, 1968.

464 *She recognized sexism:* "An Awakening of Black Nun Power." Sister Mary Roger Thibodeaux, *A Black Nun Looks at Black Power* (New York: Sheed and Ward, 1972), 71.

464 *Like black Presbyterians:* Copeland, "African American Catholics and Black Theology," 127–28.

465 *"end the oppression"*: "Women's Liberation Theme of Methodist Executive," *Christian Recorder*, June 23, 1970. Prior to this appointment, Theressa Hoover was employed as a field-worker for the MECS.

465 *"take clearly defined"*: "Southern Methodist Women Denounce Bilbo, Eastland," *Philadelphia Afro-American*, August 25, 1945; "Methodist Women Call for End to Segregation," *Indianapolis Recorder*, February 20, 1960; Alice G. Knotts, "Bound by the Spirit, Found on the Journey: The Methodist Women's Campaign for Southern Civil Rights, 1940–1968" (PhD diss., Iliff School of Theology and University of Denver, 1989).

465 *Hoover emphasized that:* "Strong Support for Women's 'Lib' Expressed at Methodist Meeting," *Christian Recorder*, December 1, 1970.

465 *A national officer:* "Presbyterian Women Act on Several Major Issues," *Christian Recorder*, August 18, 1970; "American Baptists Debate Woman's Role in the Church," *Christian Recorder*, September 8, 1970.

466 *"go forth and accomplish"*: "What Is It Women Really Want . . . Ask Men," *Christian Recorder*, September 22, 1970; "Women's Liberation Amendment Passed," ibid.; For a sample of the articles that appeared on the AME "Woman's Page," see "More 'Woman Power' Is Urged for United Church of Canada," ibid., September 29, 1970; "British Women Seek More Church 'Power,' " ibid.; "Women's Role in World Issues Cited at Indonesia Parley," ibid., October 27, 1970; "Asian Church Women Name Indian as Executive Secretary," ibid., November 3, 1970; "Mormon Women Urged to Oppose Views on Motherhood," ibid., November 17, 1970; " 'National Womanhood Day' Urged by Mormon Housewife," ibid.; "Woman's Lib Held Creating 'Crisis' in Radical Left," ibid.

466 *This traditional view:* For example, Edythe M. Primm, the wife of Bishop H. Thomas Primm, as the supervisor of the Fourth Episcopal District WMS frequently spoke to large groups of women in the states represented in that conference. She talked about the "role" of women in "modern times," emphasizing that women must exert their influence and continue to "shape" the world "by getting out of the house more." In doing so, Primm advised them that they "must never forget that they are women." See "Mrs. Edythe M. Primm Speaks to Women of Coppin," *Christian Recorder*, August 5, 1969. See also "A Woman as an Individual," ibid., December 15, 1970; "Graham: Traditional Woman's Role 'Is Essential to God's Plan,' " ibid., December 29, 1970.

466 *At least three-fifths:* Murray, "The Negro Woman"; in April 1965, the Labor Department published a special report that revealed that there were 3.4 million nonwhite women workers in the United States, representing 45 percent of nonwhite women and 13 percent of all women workers. These women were employed in all major occupational groups, with the largest number working in private household and industrial work. See "Women in the News," *Christian Recorder*, August 31, 1965.

466 *Comparing her life:* King, "The Black Woman and Women's Lib."

467 *"theological repudiation"*: Cone and Wilmore, ed., *Black Theology*, vol. 1, 6.

467 *By 1980 the voices:* For a listing and short biographical sketches of women ministers and religious scholars who came of age during the 1970s and early '80s, see Payne, *Directory*, 183–97; Randall Frost, "Vashti M. McKenzie (1947–)," in *Notable Black American Women, Book III*, ed. Jessie Carney Smith, (Detroit: Gale, 2003), 422–23.

468 *She questioned the:* Jacquelyn Grant, "Black Theology and the Black Woman," in Cone and Wilmore, eds., *Black Theology*, vol. 1 , 325, 331, 334. For Cone's admis-

sion of using sexist language in the first edition of *A Black Theology of Liberation*, see Cone, *Black Theology and Black Power* (San Francisco, Calif.: Harper Collins, 1969), x, xi.

468 *Harvey's rise to:* Susan M. Hartmann was one of the first scholars to recognize the importance of Church Women United as a feminist organization. For a discussion of CWU's struggle during the 1950s and '60s as a general department of the National Council of Churches, and how it sowed the seeds of feminism, see Susan M. Hartmann, *The Other Feminists: Activists in the Liberal Establishment* (New Haven: Yale University Press, 1998), 93–98.

469 *"Never once did":* "An Address to the Closing Session of the Church Women United Ecumenical Assembly," Wichita, Kansas, April 25, 1971, Box 46, Folder 50, CWU-GCAH.

469 *However, some of:* In 1965, the United Church of Christ named Mrs. Robert Johnson assistant moderator of the General Synod. She was the first black woman in the history of the church to hold a leadership position. See "United Church Names First Negro Woman to National Honor Post," *Chicago Defender*, June 19, 1965; in 1968 at the formation of the United Methodist Church, the Woman's Division reorganized and became the Women's Division. Methodist women selected Theressa Hoover to head the newly formed Women's Division, the largest and most powerful women's organization in the United States. See Knotts, "Bound by the Spirit," 279–80.

469 *Having engaged in:* Clarie Harvey, "The Black Woman," *Christian Recorder*, June 2, 1970.

469 *However, those who:* Clarie Harvey, "The Black Woman: Keeper of the Faith," *Christian Recorder*, June 2, 1970.

470 *The leadership consisted:* Hoover, "Black Women and the Churches," 299–302.

471 *Referencing the political:* Barbara Harris, "A Cloud of Witnesses: Black Women in the Anglican Communion," paper presented at Afro-Anglicanism Conference, Barbados, BWI, June 1985, typescript in the collection of Marjorie Farmer.

472 *In hindsight, Pierce:* Janette Pierce, "Black Women's Agenda," *Witness* 65:2 (February 1982): 4.

472 *She said black women:* Deborah Harmon Hines, "Part 1: Black Women's Agenda," *Witness* 65:2 (February 1982): 5–8.

472 *In four separate:* Deborah Harmon Hines, "Racism Breeds Stereotypes," *Witness* 65:2 (February 1982): 5–8; Myrtle Gordon, "Bigotry 'fashionable' Again," ibid.; Mattie Hopkins, "Other Struggles Seducing Blacks," ibid. 65:3 (March 1982): 14–16; Barbara Harris, "You Don't See Most of Us," ibid. 16–18.

473 *Pierce reported that:* Pierce, "Black Women's Agenda," 4; Marjorie Nichols Farmer, "Different Voices: African American Women in the Episcopal Church," in *Episcopal Women: Gender, Spirituality and Commitment in an American Mainline Denomination*, ed. Catherine M. Prelinger (New York: Oxford University Press, 1992), 224–26. There is a discrepancy in the reports of Pierce and Farmer. Farmer refers to a "Black Women's Task Force" and Pierce identifies a "three person conference subcommittee" as the central planning group for the session on racism and sexism. It appears that the group began as a subcommittee and was continued in an advisory capacity to the national Episcopal Church Women's Committee as the "Black Women's Task Force."

473 *Murray and Hoover:* Cone, *For My People*, 135.

473 *The publication of:* For a comprehensive definition of the term "womanist," see Alice Walker, *In Search of Our Mothers' Gardens: Womanist Prose* (New York: Harcourt Brace Jovanovich, 1983), xi, xii.

473 *Among the first:* Stacey M. Floyd-Thomas, ed., *Deeper Shades of Purple: Womanism in Religion and Society* (New York: New York University Press, 2006), 4. See Floyd-Thomas for a listing of the first, second, and third generation of womanist scholars.

474 *Though it is difficult:* Most of these women are ordained ministers. For a sampling of the early womanist scholarship, see Katie Geneva Canon, *Katie's Canon: Womanism and the Soul of the Black Community* (New York: Continuum Publishing Company, 1995); Jacquelyn Grant, "Womanist Theology: Black Women's Experience as a Source for Doing Theology, with Special Reference to Christology," *Journal of the Interdenominational Theological Center* 13 (spring 1986): 195–212; Delores Williams, "Womanist Theology: Black Women's Voices," *Christianity and Crisis*, March 2, 1987, 66–70; Toinette Eugene, "Moral Values and Black Womanists," *Journal of Religious Thought* 44 (winter–spring 1988): 23–34; Cheryl J. Sanders, et al., "Roundtable Discussion: Christian Ethics and Theology in Womanist Perspective," *Journal of Feminist Studies in Religion* 5:2 (fall 1989): 82–112; Emilie M. Townes, ed., *A Troubling in My Soul: Womanist Perspectives on Evil and Suffering* (Maryknoll, N.Y.: Orbis, 1993; Renita Weems, "Womanist Reflections on Biblical Hermeneutics," in Cone and Wilmore, eds., *Black Theology*, vol. 2; Clarice J. Martin, "Womanist Interpretations of the New Testament: The Quest for Holistic and Inclusive Translation and Interpretation," ibid.; Cheryl Townsend Gilkes, "Womanist Ideals and the Sociological Imagination," *Journal of Feminist Studies in Religion* 8 (fall 1992): 147–51; Shawn M. Copeland, "The Interaction of Racism, Sexism and Classism in Women's Exploitation," in *Women, Work and Poverty*, ed. Anne Carr (Edinburgh: T and T Clark, 1987).

474 *"accountable to the survival":* Cone and Wilmore, eds., *Black Theology*, vol. 2, 257.

474 *A womanist is also:* Walker, *In Search of Our Mothers' Gardens*, xi, xii.

475 *Womanist theologians:* Cone and Wilmore, eds., *Black Theology*, vol. 2, 258; Historian Elsa Barkley Brown argues, "It is the need to overcome the limitations of terminology that has led many black women to adopt the term 'womanist.' " For examples of the ways in which historians, literary critics, and others have defined and used the term, see Elsa Barkley Brown, "Womanist Consciousness: Maggie Lena Walker and the Independent Order of Saint Luke," *Signs* 14:3 (spring 1989); Chikwenye Okonjo Ogunyemi, "Womanism: The Dynamics of the Contemporary Black Female Novel in English," *Signs* 11:1 (autumn 1985): 63–80; Cone and Wilmore, *Black Theology*, vol. 2, 258.

475 *"most illustrative":* Delores S. Williams, *Sisters in the Wilderness: The Challenge of Womanist God-Talk* (Maryknoll, N.Y.: Orbis Books, 1993). For a discussion of how black women have used the text of the Bible through their own experiences and have developed their own canonical understandings of the text, particularly as relates to the biblical characters Hagar and Sarai (Genesis 16:1–16; 21:1–21), see Delores S. Williams, "Hagar in African American Biblical Appropriation," in *Hagar, Sarah, and Their Children: Jewish, Christian and Muslim Perspectives*, ed. Phyllis Trible and Letty M. Russell (Louisville, Ky.: Westminster John Knox Press, 2006), 171–84; Renita J. Weems, "A Mistress, a Maid, and No Mercy," in *Just a Sister Away: A Womanist Vision of Women's Relationships in the Bible* (Philadelphia, Pa.: Innisfree Press, Inc., 1988), 1–19. For examples of the diverse African American cultural contexts in which Hagar appears, including naming, art, literature, poetry, and religion, see the following: Sylvia R. Frey and Betty Wood, *Come Shouting to Zion: African American Protestantism in the American South and British Caribbean to 1830* (Chapel Hill, N.C.: University of North Carolina Press, 1998), 173; Diana L. Hayes, *Hagar's Daughters: Womanist Ways of Being in the*

World (Mahwah, N.J.: Paulist Press, 1995); Collier-Thomas, *Daughters of Thunder*, 126, 274; Katherine Davis Tillman, "Afro-American Women and Their Work," *AME Church Review* 11:4 (April 1895): 477–99; Frances Ellen Watkins Harper, *Iola Leroy: Or Shadows Uplifted* (Boston: Beacon Press, 1987), 239; E. Franklin Frazier, "Hagar and Her Children," in *The Negro Family in the United States* (Chicago: University of Chicago Press, 1939); Toni Morrison, *Song of Solomon* (New York: Alfred A. Knopf, 1977); Maya Angelou, "The Mothering of Blackness," in *Poems* (New York: Bantam Books, 1981), 19; "Farewell! We're Good an' Gone," *Chicago Defender*, December 30, 1922. In this narrative poem dedicated to the thousands of migrants who left the South seeking better opportunities in the North, Hagar is referenced in the last stanza as the mother of the migrants, who were literally children in the wilderness.

Coda

478 *Among Baptist denominations:* Lori Sharn, "Policies on Female Clergy," *USA Today*, July 9, 1997.

478 *Elder Crouch was:* "Special Ordination," *JET*, August 24, 1998.

478 *At the opening:* Beginning with a small group of adherents in the late nineteenth century, by 2000 the numbers of black Pentecostal/Holiness groups had grown substantially, and are now acknowledged to be the fastest-growing segment among black religious groups today. The Church of God in Christ is the largest of the black Pentecostal groups. There are a number of Pentecostal bodies, but COGIC, followed by the Apostolic, Overcoming Holy Church of God, Triumph the Church and Kingdom of God in Christ, Pentecostal Assemblies of the World, Bible Way Churches of Our Lord Jesus Christ, World Wide, and the United House of Prayer for All People are the largest. There are also numerous independent Pentecostal churches bearing a variety of names, and several denominations and mega-churches founded by women and headed by women. These include the Mount Sinai Holy Church of America, Inc., the Sanctuary Church of God, the Christ Universal Temple in Chicago, and the Hillside International Truth Center in Atlanta. Labeled as a poor people's movement, during most of the twentieth century it was ignored by mainstream institutions and scholars of religion. For discussion of the growth of mega-churches, the impact of the neo-Pentecostal movement in urban areas, and citation of statistics regarding black women clergy, see Renita J. Weems, "Black America and Religion," *Ebony* 61:1 (November 2005): 122–24.

478 *In 2009 the:* Faye Flam, "Baptist Church Gets First Female Pastor," *Philadelphia Inquirer,* June 1, 2009; Christopher Maag, "Spiritual Journey Leads to a Historic First," *New York Times*, June 6, 2009.

480 *"her campaign was an expression":* For biographical data on Carrie Hooper's life and career, see F. B. Livingstone, "First Female Candidate to Aspire to the Office of Bishop," *Christian Recorder*, July 14, 1964; Carrie T. Hooper, "A Vision," ibid., November 12, 1963; Funeral Program, "A Service of Praise and Thanksgiving 'Obsequies' for the late Rev. Dr. Carrie T. Hooper, 1894–1996," December 20, 1996, AME Church Records, Department of Research and Scholarship, AME Sunday School Union, Nashville, Tennessee. For information pertaining to Octavia Douglass see Thelma Anderson Wills, "Periscoping with a General Conference Delegate," ibid., June 23, 1964.

480 *In the 1980s:* In 1964 Alma A. Polk was elected AME director of public relations, a position she held until her death in 1969. In 1984 and 1988 Jayme Coleman

Williams was elected editor of the AME *Church Review*. Elected in 1992, Williams's successor, Paulette Coleman, served as editor until 1996. For a biography of Polk, see Helen B. Suber, "The Obsequies of Alma A. Polk," *Christian Recorder*, October 21, 1969; "Church's Public Relations, Headed by Brilliant Faithful Woman," ibid., May 6, 1969. For Octavia Douglass, see Wills, "Periscoping with a General Conference Delegate"; for details regarding the elections of Williams and Coleman, see Dennis C. Dickerson, *A Liberated Past: Explorations in AME Church History* (Nashville: AMEC Sunday School Union, 2003), 75–84.

480 *The elections:* Laurie Goodstein, "After 213 Years, AME Church Chooses a Woman as a Bishop," *New York Times*, July 12, 2000; Dennis C. Dickerson, "General Conference 2000: The Making of a Female Bishop: From Jarena Lee to Vashti Murphy McKenzie," *AME Church Review*, 116:378 (summer 2000): 14–16; "A Crack, a Break, a Shattering of the Glass: A Theological Interpretation of the Election of Bishop Vashti Murphy McKenzie," ibid., 17–19; Dennis C. Dickerson, "New Bishops for a Global Church," ibid. 120:395 (July–September 2004): 17–18, 20.

480 *More recently, in 2008:* Margena A. Christian, "AME Zion Church Elects First Female Bishop," *JET*, August 18, 2008.

481 *In 1988 the Episcopal:* Bishop McKenzie is a member of the Baltimore *Afro-American* newspaper clan. Gustav Niebuhr, "Women Smash Yet Another Barrier," *New York Times*, August 15, 1998; Laurie Goodstein, "After 213 Years, AME Church Chooses a Woman as a Bishop," ibid., July 12, 2000; Dennis C. Dickerson, "General Conference 2000: The Making of a Female Bishop: From Jarena Lee to Vashti Murphy McKenzie," *AME Church Review*, 116:378 (summer 2000): 14–16; "A Crack, a Break," 17–19; Bettye Collier-Thomas, *Daughters of Thunder: Black Women Preachers and Their Sermons, 1850–1979* (San Francisco, Calif.: Jossey-Bass Publishers, 1997), 279.

481 *Fitchue became the first:* Leah Gaskin Fitchue, "So High a Mission, So Holy a Calling," *AME Church Review* 121:397 (January–March 2005): 19.

481 *Established in 1989:* African Methodist Episcopal Church, "Annual Report of the Connectional Women in Ministry to the General Board Commission on Women in Ministry," June 22–23, 1998, Sheraton Birmingham Hotel, Birmingham, Alabama, program booklet in possession of the author.

481 *She also acknowledges:* Fitchue, "So High a Mission," 23, 24.

481 *AME men such as:* Ibid., 24.

482 *Black Presbyterian:* Gayraud S. Wilmore, *Black and Presbyterian: The Heritage and the Hope* (Louisville, Ky.: Witherspoon Press, 1998), 73; Arthur Jones, "Unearthing Black Catholic History," *National Catholic Reporter*, February 12, 1999.

482 *"It ain't likely":* Wilmore, *Black and Presbyterian*, 54–55.

483 *There was a growing:* Ibid., 59; Jones, "Unearthing Black Catholic History"; V. P. Franklin, " 'A Way Out of No Way': The Bible and Catholic Evangelization Among African Americans in the United States," in *African Americans and the Bible: Sacred Texts and Social Textures*, ed. Vincent L. Wimbush (New York: Continuum, 2000), 653–57.

483 *"We don't like":* Arthur Jones, "Black Catholics: Life in a 'Chilly Church,' " *National Catholic Reporter*, August 14, 1998.

483 *"still view the church":* Robert McClory, "Black and Catholic: Many Say They Are Faithful Despite Church's Inattention," *National Catholic Reporter*, March 13, 1998.

483 *"Implicitly, racism":* Jones, "Black Catholics: Life in a 'Chilly Church.'"

483 *As a leader:* For Dexter Watson quote, see Robert McClory, "Black Men Ponder Their Place in the Church," *National Catholic Reporter*, December 18, 1998. Similar to the Men and Religious Forward Movement of 1911–12, the Promise Keepers focus on the masculinization of middle-class Protestantism. Founded in 1990 by Bill McCartney, a former Catholic who joined the charismatic Protestant Vineyard Fellowship, the organization is known for large Christian rallies in urban centers that attract thousands of men. See Al Janssen and Larry K. Weeden, eds., *Seven Promises of a Promise Keeper* (Colorado Springs, Colo.: Focus on the Family, 1994); Pamela Schaeffer, "10 Years Later, Thea Bowman Still Inspires," *National Catholic Reporter*, March 24, 2000.

484 *Father Stallings also:* Wilmore, *Black and Presbyterian*, 65; Franklin, "'A Way Out of No Way,'" 657.

484 *During the 1970s:* Jones, "Black Catholics: Life in A 'Chilly Church.'"

485 *These scholars have:* Diana L. Hayes, "Standing in the Shoes My Mother Made: The Making of a Catholic Womanist Theologian," in *Deeper Shades of Purple: Womanism in Religion and Society*, ed. Stacey M. Floyd-Thomas (New York: New York University Press, 2006), 54–79, 315; M. Shawn Copeland, "A Thinking Margin: The Womanist Movement as Critical Cognitive Praxis," ibid., 226–35, 313; Diana L. Hayes, *Hagar's Daughters: Womanist Ways of Being in the World* (New York: Paulist Press, 1995); Diana L. Hayes, *And Still We Rise: An Introduction to Black Liberation Theology* (New York: Paulist Press, 1996); Diana L. Hayes, "Strong, Faith-Filled Black Women Enrich U.S. Catholic Church," *National Catholic Reporter*, February 21, 2003; Jamie T. Phelps, ed., *Black and Catholic* (Milwaukee: Marquette University Press, 1997); Diane Batts Morrow, *Persons of Color and Religious at the Same Time* (Chapel Hill: University of North Carolina Press, 2002).

485 *She also accused:* Constance Holloway, "Black Catholic Women Seek Renewal," *National Catholic Reporter*, August 10, 2001. For an excellent example of the early treatment of black women who attended white Catholic churches, see "Jim Crow Balks Woman's Prayer in Capital: Ordered from Her Knees in Immaculate Conception Church," *Baltimore Afro-American*, March 26, 1932; "Sacred Heart Jim Crows a Worshipper: Usher Tells Praying Woman to Get on Colored Side," ibid., April 2, 1932; "Catholics Urged to Stay Out of J[im] C[row] Churches," ibid., April 9, 1932; Carl Murphy, "Pulled from Their Knees," ibid., April 16, 1932.

486 *She asserted that:* Robert J. McClory, "Family Gathering: At National Congress, Black Catholics Tackle Racism, Call for Stronger Ties with Africa," *National Catholic Reporter*, September 13, 2002.

486 *By 2003 black Catholic:* Washington Post, October 18, 2003.

486 *However, between 1965:* Cheryl Townsend Gilkes, "Plenty Good Room: Adaptation in a Changing Black Church," *Annals of the American Academy of Political and Social Science* 558 (July 1998): 116.

487 *Most agreed that:* "Black Men Converge on Washington for Rally," *USA Today*, October 16, 1995. For black women's views about the Million Man March, see Andrea L. Mays, "Women's Reactions Run from Elation to Disdain," ibid., October 17, 1995.

488 *She stressed that:* Michael Janofsky, "Million Woman March Is Set with High Hopes," *New York Times*, October 23, 1997; CNN, "Million Woman March Fills Philadelphia Streets," October 25, 1997; Michael Janofsky, "At Million Woman March, Focus Is on Family," *New York Times*, October 26, 1997; Kelly Starling, "The Million Woman March," *Ebony* (December 1997).

488 *His Man Power:* Greg Garrison, "Jakes' Novel Targets Spiritual Secrets," *Birmingham Post Herald*, October 3, 2003; "Bishop T. D. Jakes: 'The Hearts of Men' Speaking Tour for Men and Women," *African American Diversity Newswire @ Unity First.com*, July 26, 2004.

488 *"The black church currently":* Gilkes, "Plenty Good Room," 116.

489 *They prefer to handle:* For discussion of contemporary sexual-gender relations in the African American church, see Marcia Y. Riggs, *Plenty Good Room: Women Versus Male Power in the Black Church* (Cleveland, Oh.: Pilgrim Press, 2002); for diverse views on what constitutes clergy misconduct and malfeasance, see Anson Shupe, William A. Stacey, and Susan E. Darnell, eds., *Bad Pastors: Clergy Misconduct in Modern America* (New York: New York University Press, 2000), 1–3; David O'Reilly, "Study Finds Embezzlement to Be Common in Dioceses," *Philadelphia Inquirer*, January 5, 2007.

489 *Christian moral teaching:* James V. Spickard, "Guide to Enlightenment of Strayed Shepherds? The Problems of Claimed Clergy Malfeasance in Interreligious Perspective," in Shupe, Stacey, and Darnell, eds. *Bad Pastors*, 94, 95.

490 *"drunkenness and other immoral":* William H. Hillery was licensed to preach in 1860 and ordained a deacon and an elder in 1864 and 1866 respectively. He was elected bishop in 1876 and after trial was formally removed from office at the 1884 General Conference. For biographical details, see David Henry Bradley Sr., *A History of the A.M.E. Zion Church, Part II: 1872–1968* (Nashville: Parthenon Press, 1970), 52; William J. Walls, *The African Methodist Episcopal Zion Church: Reality of the Black Church* (Charlotte, N.C.: A.M.E. Zion Publishing House, 1974), 579. For details regarding his history of misconduct between the late 1860s and 1884, the numerous charges brought against Hillery, and the events that transpired at the 1884 General Conference see C.R. Harris, comp., *Daily Proceedings of the Seventeenth Quadrennial Session of the General Conference of the A.M.E. Zion Church of America, Held in New York City, May 1884* (New York: A.M.E. Zion Book Concern, 1884), 35–43, 58–81.

491 *The bishops selected:* Bradley, *A History of the A.M.E. Zion Church*, 139, 398–99; Harris, comp., *Daily Proceedings of the Seventeenth Quadrennial Session*, 36, 37, 62.

491 *"It was hinted":* Harris, comp., *Daily Proceedings of the Seventeenth Quadrennial Session*, 39, 41–43.

491 *Though Hood was:* The most accurate source for understanding and analyzing the charges brought against Hillery and the events that transpired at the 1884 General Conference are the conference proceedings. See Harris, comp., *Daily Proceedings of the Seventeenth Quadrennial Session*, 35–43, 58–81; Bradley, *A History of the A.M.E. Zion Church*, 52, 139, 399. For an analysis of Bishop Hood's religious and political leadership and a recapitulation of David Henry Bradley's findings relevant to the 1884 trial see Sandy Dwayne Martin, *For God and Race: The Religious and Political Leadership of AMEZ Bishop James Walker Hood* (Columbia, S.C.: University of South Carolina, 1999), 98–104.

491 *Moreover, at the:* Bradley, *A History of the A.M.E. Zion Church*, 150.

492 *Rather, similar patterns:* For examples of clergy malfeasance, as well as the arrogance of some bishops regarding their right to use church funds as they saw fit, see "Bishop Heard Says 2nd Trial Freed Pastor: The Rev. J. A. Simmons Transferred to Cincinnati Charge," *Baltimore Afro-American*, February 13, 1932; "AME Ministers Shy at Bishop's Mystery Fund," ibid.; "Bishop Flays Defaulters in Mystery Fund," ibid., February 27, 1932; "Claim Bishop Heard Minutes in Ohio Church," ibid.; "Church Racketeers Rapped by Speaker," ibid., March 5,

1932; "Say Pastor Loved Church Secretary," ibid., March 12, 1932. For contemporary examples and commentary about the sexual exploitation of black female church members by male clergy, see Johnnetta Betsch Cole and Beverly Guy-Sheftall, *Gender Talk: The Struggle for Women's Equality in African American Communities* (New York: Ballantine Books, 2003), 114–27.

493 *Others optimistically:* Ralph Matthews, "Watching the Big Parade," *Baltimore Afro-American*, February 6, 1932. Between 1920 and 1932 the AME Church lost 100,000 members. For a discussion and analysis of the reasons for the loss of members, see "100,000 Left AME Church Says Beard," ibid., March 26, 1932. Rev. Jesse Beard, chairman of the South Carolina delegation to the 1932 AME General Conference, "gave a scathing indictment of the bishops of the AME Church. " See also "Schuyler Notes Definite Swing from the Pulpit," ibid.

493 *"reduced to a feudal":* Ibid.; Ralph Matthews, "Sifting the News," *Baltimore Afro-American*, March 5, 1932.

494 *He was jailed:* Ollie Glass was seventeen years of age at the time of the sexual incident. "Hangs Head When She Talks," *Atlanta World*, December 13, 1931.

494 *The Council of Bishops:* "AME Bishops Condemned Reds and Ira Bryant," *Baltimore Afro-American*, April 16, 1932.

495 *"colored folk's business":* "Ala[bama] Jury Frees AME Bishop in Baby Case," *Baltimore Afro-American*, April 23, 1932; Carl Murphy, "Bishop Grant's 489 Chances," ibid.; for basic biographical details relevant to Bishop Robert Alexander Grant, see Howard D. Gregg, *History of the African Methodist Episcopal Church* (Nashville: AME Church Sunday School Union, 1980), 435. Gregg fails to mention or discuss anything about the Ollie Glass affair.

495 *"accuser of Bishop Grant":* Carl Murphy, "The Church Should Try Bishop Grant," *Baltimore Afro-American*, April 30, 1932. Other black newspapers, such as the *Newport News Star,* weighed in on the Grant case and suggested that Bishop Grant resign. See "Bishop Grant Vindicated?" ibid., May 7, 1932.

495 *Prior to the court:* Ibid.; "Mrs. R. A. Grant Would Stick by the Bishop Even Though He Were Guilty," *Baltimore Afro-American*, May 21, 1932.

495 *AME ministers in different:* "Pastor Says Court Action Vindicates Bishop Grant," *Baltimore Afro-American*, April 23, 1932.

496 *"Nobody wants me":* "AME's Suspend Dr. Vernon for Four Years: Committee Also Votes to Suspend Bishop Jones," *Baltimore Afro-American*, May 14, 1932; "Charges Filed Against Three AME Bishops in Cleveland," ibid.; Bishop Reverdy C. Ransom, "Confessions of a Bishop," *Ebony* (March 1950): 80; Bishop William Tecumseh Vernon at one time was the registrar of the United States Treasury, one of the highest offices held by an African American at that date. For biographical data on bishops Vernon and Jones, see Gregg, *History of the African Methodist Episcopal Church*, 437, 447. Jones died shortly after the 1932 General Conference. According to Gregg, following his death he was exonerated of the charges. In the case of Vernon, Gregg states that "many believed that his suspension was undeserved and more political than valid."

496 *Since subsequent:* Ransom, "Confessions of a Bishop," 80; Gregg, *History of the African Methodist Episcopal Church*, 322, 447.

496 *Mrs. Grant stated:* "Mrs. R. A. Grant Would Stick by the Bishop."

496 *As for the suspensions:* Ibid.

497 *Typical of clergy:* Ibid.

497 *The subject of his:* "Dr. Jemison Heads Baptists," *Kansas Plaindealer*, September 17, 1943. As a young Baptist minister at the New Salem Baptist Church in Memphis,

Tennessee, Rev. C. L. Franklin seduced and impregnated Mildred Jennings, a teenage girl. Though there was widespread public knowledge about Franklin's misdeeds with Jennings and "other affairs as well," no action was taken by the trustees. See Nick Salvatore, *Singing in a Strange Land: C. L. Franklin, the Black Church, and the Transformation of America* (Urbana, Ill.: University of Illinois Press, 2006), 61–63.

497 *Although Martin Luther King's:* For discussion of Martin Luther King's extramarital affairs and the FBI wiretaps of King's conversations discussing his sexual encounters, see Taylor Branch, *Parting the Waters: America in the King Years, 1954–63* (New York: Simon and Schuster, 1988), 239, 242, 860–62; David J. Garrow, *Bearing the Cross: Martin Luther King, Jr., and the Southern Christian Leadership Conference* (New York: William Morrow 1986), 310, 312, 313, 318–19, 323, 340, 360–66, 373–74, 376–77, 422.

498 *"[W]omen stand in":* Riggs, *Plenty Good Room*, 83.

498 *"preachers that prey":* Marcia L. Dyson, "When Preachers Prey," *Essence* (May 1998).

498 *McFadden-Weaver's complaints:* Ruth E. Igoe, "$6 Million Award in Harassment Case: Former Pastor Said Problems Had Gone On for Years," *Kansas City Star*, December 4, 1999; Dan Margolies, "Court Throws Out Harassment Award Against AME Church," ibid., March 30, 2001.

499 *In December 1999:* Igoe, "$6 Million Award."

499 *As for Elder Williams:* Margolies, "Court Throws Out Harassment Award."

500 *Following his 1994:* Donald P. Baker and Laurie Goodstein, "Leader of Largest Black Church Is in Apparent Domestic Woe," *Washington Post*, July 9, 1997.

500 *Upon his release:* Vickie Chachere, *Philadelphia Inquirer*, November 30, 2003.

501 *Jackson not only:* Tracy Connor, "Jesse Admits He's Love Child's Dad," *New York Post*, January 18, 2001; "Disappointing Behavior: A Lesson for All in Jackson Affair," *Philadelphia Inquirer*, January 20, 2001; "Jesse Jackson's Love Child," *National Enquirer*, January 30, 2001.

501 *The Jackson scandal:* Annette John-Hall, "In Phila., Blacks' Reaction Varies on Jackson Story," *Philadelphia Inquirer*, January 19, 2001; David O'Reilly, "Opinions Divided on Jackson Disclosure," ibid., January 20, 2001; William Raspberry, "Mea Culpa (Sort of)," *Washington Post*, January 22, 2001.

502 *"less forgiving":* John-Hall, "In Phila., Blacks' Reaction."

502 *Referencing the Bible:* O'Reilly, "Opinions Divided."

502 *"spiritual hypocrisy":* DeWayne Wickham, "Jesse Jackson Forges Ahead Despite Personal Error," *USA Today*, January 23, 2001.

502 *Making the connection:* "Reverend Wyatt Tee Walker's Letter to Jesse Jackson," in Peter Noel I, "The 'Wrongs' of 'Mr. Civil Rights,' " *Village Voice*, February 1, 2001.

503 *Ironically, many white:* Vern L. Bullough, "Homosexuality and Catholic Priests," historynewsnetwork.org/articles, May 13, 2002; Anthony DePalma, "Tough Policies on Priests Stir Some Dissension in the Pews," *New York Times*, May 21, 2002; "The Boston Priest Scandal," *Philadelphia Inquirer*, May 15, 2002; "Mass[achusetts] Priest Indicted in Sex Case," ibid., May 16, 2002; John Salveson, "Call Hearings on Abuse, Senator," ibid., July 22, 2005; Rachel Zoll, "Bishops Extend Ban on Abusive Priests," ibid., June 18, 2005; "Philadelphia Archdiocese Avoids Charges," *USA Today*, September 22, 2005; Cathy Lynn Grossman, "Vatican to Spell Out Policy on Seminary Admissions," ibid., November 23, 2005; John Holl, "Speaking Out, but for Whom? Opinion of

Church's Ruling on Gays Leads to Firing," *New York Times*, December 11, 2005; Sister Maureen Paul Turlish, "In Effect, Archdiocese Gives Sexual Predators a Pass," *Philadelphia Inquirer*, November 26, 2007.

503 *Of course, there is:* Kelly Brown Douglas, *Sexuality and the Black Church: A Womanist Perspective* (Maryknoll, N.Y.: Orbis Books, 1999), 81, 87, 97–99.

503 *Homosexuality is considered:* Douglas, *Sexuality and the Black Church*, 99–103.

504 *The announcement stated:* "From a Contemporary Perspective," AME *Church Review*, 119:391 (July–September 2003): 13.

504 *Speaking before a:* Mark Niesse, "Ga. Black Pastors Rally Against Gay Marriage," *Philadelphia Inquirer*, March 23, 2004.

505 *"Girl, please!":* Rev. Irene Monroe, "I Really Felt Called to Be Who I Am; and I Didn't Want to Leave My Identity at the Threshold of the Church," in *A Whosoever Church: Welcoming Lesbians and Gay Men into African American Congregations*, ed. Gary David Comstock (Louisville, Ky.: Westminster John Knox Press, 2001), 65.

506 *"struggling, dying Presbyterian":* Ibid., 59–61.

506 *In recent years:* Ibid., 2–3. David Comstock, *A Whosoever Church*, is a collection of twenty interviews of ten black religious leaders, women and men, who have publicly voiced their support for lesbians and gay men and are actively working to break down the discrimination against these people in their institutions. This is an excellent source for gaining an understanding of the issues and problems confronting those who wish to participate as homosexuals in black religious institutions.

506 *The stakes are:* Herb Lusk, "Black Churches Boosted by Bush," *Philadelphia Inquirer*, October 31, 2004.

507 *Rev. A. Cecil Williams:* Comstock, *A Whosoever Church*.

507 *Although relatively few:* For an excellent history of black gay congregations, see chapter 7, "The Emergence of African American Lesbian/Gay Christian Congregations in the United States," in Horace L. Griffin, *Their Own Receive Them Not: African American Lesbians and Gays in Black Churches* (Cleveland, Oh.: Pilgrim Press, 2006), 185–206.

507 *He felt that:* "Black Churches Urged to Open Dialogue with Parishioners," *Washington Post*, July 22, 2000; "New Attitude of Openness Found in Poll of Pastors," ibid.

507 *Nine out of ten:* "Across the USA: News from Every State: D.C.," *USA Today*, November 27, 2007.

507 *Approaching the end:* CNN, " 'CNN Presents': Black in America: The Black Woman and Family," July 23, 2008.

508 *"In spite of the problems":* Marla F. Frederick, *Between Sundays: Black Women and Everyday Struggles of Faith* (Berkeley: University of California Press, 2003), 4.

508 *The growth of:* Weems, "Black America and Religion;" Gilkes, "Plenty Good Room"; Harvey Cox, *Fire from Heaven: The Rise of Pentecostal Spirituality and the Reshaping of Religion in the 21st Century* (Cambridge, Mass.: Da Capo Press, 2001); Rose-Marie Armstrong, "Turning to Islam: African American Conversion Stories," *Christian Century*, July 12, 2003; Amiri YaSin Al-Hadid, Lewis V. Baldwin, and Anthony P. Pinn, *Between Cross and Crescent: Christian and Muslim Perspectives on Malcolm and Martin* (Gainesville, Fla.: University Press of Florida, 2002). The New Age movement is not a formal religion. It has no formal clergy, membership, central organization, dogma, creed, or holy text. Rather, it is a spiritual movement of believers who share beliefs and practices that they simply add

to whatever formal religion they follow, in the absence of sermons and religious services. The movement began in England in the 1960s and was popularized during the 1970s. Its roots lie in Spiritualism, Hinduism, Gnostic traditions, and other Neo-pagan traditions. At this point there is a lot of confusion about the movement. See J. Gordon Melton, "Whither the New Age?" in *America's Alternative Religions*, ed. T. Miller (Albany, N.Y.: SUNY Press, 1995).

508 *"Hope is something"*: Carrie M. Green, "Hope," *Christian Index*, February 25, 1888.

508 *"I've watched changes"*: Schaeffer, "10 Years Later."

Index

Page numbers in *italics* refer to illustrations.

A NOTE ON THE TYPE

THIS BOOK was set in Janson, a typeface long thought to have been made by the Dutchman Anton Janson, who was a practicing type-founder in Leipzig during the years 1668–1687. However, it has been conclusively demonstrated that these types are actually the work of Nicholas Kis (1650–1702), a Hungarian, who most probably learned his trade from the master Dutch typefounder Dirk Voskens. The type is an excellent example of the influential and sturdy Dutch types that prevailed in England up to the time William Caslon (1692–1766) developed his own incomparable designs from them.

Composed by North Market Street Graphics
Printed and bound by Berryville Graphics
Designed by Virginia Tan